STRATIFICATION IN HIGHER EDUCATION

A Comparative Study

*Edited by Yossi Shavit, Richard Arum,
and Adam Gamoran, with Gila Menahem*

STANFORD UNIVERSITY PRESS
STANFORD, CALIFORNIA
2007

Stanford University Press
Stanford, California
© 2007 by the Board of Trustees of the Leland Stanford Junior University. All rights reserved.

No part of this book may be reproduced or transmitted in any form or by any means, electronic or mechanical, including photocopying and recording, or in any information storage or retrieval system without the prior written permission of Stanford University Press.

Printed in the United States of America on acid-free, archival-quality paper

Library of Congress Cataloging-in-Publication Data
Stratification in higher education : a comparative study / edited by Yossi Shavit . . . [et al.].
p. cm.
Includes bibliographical references and index.
ISBN 978-0-8047-5462-0 (cloth : alk. paper)
1. Educational equalization—Cross-cultural studies.
2. Educational change—Cross-cultural studies.   3. Educational attainment—Cross-cultural studies.   4. Education, Higher—Social aspects—Cross-cultural studies.   I. Shavit, Yossi.
LC213.S77 2007
379.2'6—dc22

2007007758

Typeset by Newgen in 10/14 Sabon

STRATIFICATION IN HIGHER EDUCATION

STUDIES IN SOCIAL INEQUALITY

EDITORS

David B. Grusky STANFORD UNIVERSITY
Paula England STANFORD UNIVERSITY

EDITORIAL BOARD

Hans-Peter Blossfeld
Mary C. Brinton
Thomas DiPrete
Michael Hout
Andrew Walder
Mary Waters

CONTENTS

Preface xi
Contributors xiii

CHAPTER ONE
More Inclusion Than Diversion: Expansion, Differentiation, and Market Structure in Higher Education 1
Richard Arum, Adam Gamoran, and Yossi Shavit

PART I: DIVERSIFIED SYSTEMS

CHAPTER TWO
Israel: Diversification, Expansion, and Inequality in Higher Education 39
Yossi Shavit, Hanna Ayalon, Svetlana Chachashvili-Bolotin, and Gila Menahem

CHAPTER THREE
Japan: Educational Expansion and Inequality in Access to Higher Education 63
Hiroshi Ishida

CHAPTER FOUR
South Korea: Educational Expansion and Inequality of Opportunity for Higher Education 87
Hyunjoon Park

CHAPTER FIVE

Sweden: Why Educational Expansion Is Not Such a Great Strategy for Equality—Theory and Evidence   113
Jan O. Jonsson and Robert Erikson

CHAPTER SIX

Taiwan: Higher Education—Expansion and Equality of Educational Opportunity   140
Shu-Ling Tsai and Yossi Shavit

CHAPTER SEVEN

United States: Changes in Higher Education and Social Stratification   165
Josipa Roksa, Eric Grodsky, Richard Arum, and Adam Gamoran

PART II: BINARY SYSTEMS

CHAPTER EIGHT

Great Britain: Higher Education Expansion and Reform—Changing Educational Inequalities   195
Sin Yi Cheung and Muriel Egerton

CHAPTER NINE

France: Mass and Class—Persisting Inequalities in Postsecondary Education   220
Pauline Givord and Dominique Goux

CHAPTER TEN

Germany: Institutional Change and Inequalities of Access in Higher Education   240
Karl Ulrich Mayer, Walter Müller, and Reinhard Pollak

CHAPTER ELEVEN

The Netherlands: Access to Higher Education—Institutional Arrangements and Inequality of Opportunity   266
Susanne Rijken, Ineke Maas, and Harry B. G. Ganzeboom

CHAPTER TWELVE

Russia: Stratification in Postsecondary Education Since the Second World War   294
Theodore P. Gerber

CHAPTER THIRTEEN

Switzerland: Tertiary Education Expansion and Social Inequality   321
Marlis Buchmann, Stefan Sacchi, Markus Lamprecht, and Hanspeter Stamm

PART III: UNITARY AND OTHER SYSTEMS

CHAPTER FOURTEEN

Australia: Changes in Socioeconomic Inequalities in University Participation   351
Gary N. Marks and Julie McMillan

CHAPTER FIFTEEN

The Czech Republic: Structural Growth of Inequality in Access to Higher Education   374
Petr Matějů, Blanka Řeháková, and Natalie Simonová

CHAPTER SIXTEEN

Italy: Expansion, Reform, and Social Inequality in Higher Education   400
Ettore Recchi

Appendix: Supplemental Tables   421
Notes   425
Bibliography   443
Index   473

PREFACE

Research on social stratification, and particularly on the relation between education and stratification, has for decades recognized the importance of cross-national comparisons. A book edited by Shavit and Blossfeld in 1993 and published in the Social Inequality Series (then at Westview Press) has served as a classic in the field and as a manual for subsequent cross-national comparative research (e.g., Shavit and Müller 1998; Arum and Müller 2004; Breen 2004; Heath and Cheung forthcoming). Much of this past work was carried out by members of the Research Committee on Social Stratification (RC28) of the International Sociological Association, an important intellectual forum for the exposition and discussion of ideas and findings contained in this scholarship.

This book pursues the tradition of the earlier studies. Although Shavit and Blossfeld examined educational stratification in general, the distinctive focus of this book is on higher education. Also, whereas Shavit and Blossfeld reported trends through the 1980s, most of the chapters in our volume examine changes in stratification and higher education through the 1990s. In addition, the meanings of stratification and inequality are re-examined in light of conceptual developments in the last decade. Thus, the present volume both reconceptualizes and updates the cross-national comparative analysis of educational stratification, with particular reference to inequality in higher education.

The project began in late 2000; that is when we selected the countries, invited the teams to participate, and issued initial guidelines for the country chapters. In the spring of 2002, the teams met in New York University's international site in Prague for a three-day conference during which we presented and discussed early drafts of our papers. We also discussed and revised the guidelines to accommodate suggestions made by project members. Papers were revised by December 2002 and were anonymously reviewed by two or three project members. The leaders of the project acted as an editorial board in the review process. The papers (including the introductory chapter) were then presented and discussed in several meetings of RC28: in New York in August 2003, in Neuchâtel in May 2004, and in Rio de Janeiro in August 2004. At each of these meetings project members, as well as other conference participants, provided additional feedback that led to further revisions of the chapters. The editors and reviewers of the Social Inequality Series at Stanford University Press provided additional valuable comments, which resulted in final revisions of the manuscript as a whole.

The editors express their deep and sincere appreciation to the collaborators in the project, whose names are listed in the table of contents; to the many participants at RC28 sessions and a host of other seminars around the world at which earlier drafts of the chapters in this book were presented; to Kate Wahl and staff at Stanford University Press, and to Claudia Buchmann for excellent comments and suggestions on an earlier draft of the volume. In addition, we are grateful for administrative assistance from Lois Opalewski and critical editorial assistance on the project from Andrew Sieverman, Becky Holmes, and Gaby Lanyi. We also thank several agencies that provided support for the project, including the David Horowitz Research Institute on Society and Economy at Tel Aviv University, the School of Education and Global Initiative Office at New York University, and the Wisconsin Center for Education Research at the University of Wisconsin, Madison. Yossi Shavit also thanks Nuffield College in Oxford for its gracious hospitality during the final stages of work on the project.

CONTRIBUTORS

Yossi Shavit is professor of sociology at Tel Aviv University and head of the B.I. and Lucille Cohen Institute for Public Opinion Research. His main areas of interest are social stratification and sociology of education. With Hans-Peter Blossfeld, he led an international comparative project on educational stratification that was published as *Persistent Inequality* (Westview Press, 1993). With Walter Müller, he led a comparative project on the school-to-work transition that appeared as *From School to Work* (Clarendon Press, 1998). His current work focuses on stratification in Israeli education.

Richard Arum is professor of sociology and education at New York University. His research focuses on education, law, and stratification. He is author of *Judging School Discipline: The Crisis of Moral Authority in American Schools* (Harvard University Press, 2003) and editor with Walter Müller of *The Reemergence of Self-Employment: Comparative Study of Self-Employment Dynamics and Social Inequality* (Princeton University Press, 2004).

Adam Gamoran is professor of sociology and educational policy studies and director of the Wisconsin Center for Education Research at the University of Wisconsin, Madison. His research focuses on inequality in education and school reform, and current studies include work on the causal effects of school segregation and school resources on black–white inequality in achievement and labor market outcomes. A member of the U.S. National Academy of Education, he has co-authored or co-edited three recent books, including (with Andrew C. Porter) *Methodological Advances in Cross-National Surveys of Educational Achievement* (National Academy Press, 2002).

Gila Menahem is a senior lecturer in the Department of Public Policy and the Department of Sociology and Anthropology at Tel Aviv University, Israel. Her main research interests are policy processes and public policy formation. She has published articles on public policy formation in the urban context, water policy, and educational policy. She is co-editor of the volume *Public Policy in Israel* (Frank Cass, 2002).

Hanna Ayalon is professor and chair of the Department of Sociology and Anthropology at Tel Aviv University, Israel. Her main research field is sociology of education. Her recent publications are on the curriculum as a source of educational inequality, and the expansion of higher education. She has published in journals such as *Sociology of Education, Educational Evaluation and Policy Analysis, Teachers College Record,* and *European Sociological Review.*

Marlis Buchmann is professor of sociology at the University of Zurich and managing director of the Jacobs Center for Productive Youth Development, University of Zurich. Her areas of specialization are life-course analysis; work, occupations, and labor markets; social stratification and mobility; and cultural change. She has published widely in these fields with, among others, the University of Chicago Press, *European Sociological Review, Work and Occupations,* and *Kölner Zeitschrift für Soziologie und Sozialpsychologie.*

Svetlana Chachashvili-Bolotin is a PhD student in the Department of Sociology and Anthropology at Tel Aviv University, Israel. Her main research interest is the impact of immigration on inequality in education.

Sin Yi Cheung is a principal lecturer in the Department of International Relations, Politics and Sociology, Oxford Brookes University, Oxford. Her main research interests are in social stratification and the sociology of education. She is currently co-editing a volume (with Anthony Heath) on ethnic minority disadvantage in the labor market of thirteen countries. She has recently completed a research project commissioned by the Department for Work and Pensions in Britain (with A. Heath), investigating the extent to which ethnic penalties in the labor market vary by such employer characteristics as industry, size of establishment, and sector. Her work also includes studies on women's occupations in Hong Kong and socially disadvantaged groups in Britain, such as lone parents and children in care.

Muriel Egerton studied at Queens University, Belfast, and Oxford University. She has worked at Oxford, Manchester, London, and Essex Universities, returning to Oxford in October 2006. Her main research interests are in the relationship between education and social stratification and in time use research, particularly the valuation of unpaid work. She has published widely on these topics.

Robert Erikson is professor of sociology at the Swedish Institute for Social Research, Stockholm University. His research interests concern social stratification, education, family, and health, especially the study of individual change over the life course and how it can be understood with regard to individual and structural conditions. He has published articles in these areas and is co-author (with John Goldthorpe) of *The Constant Flux* as well as co-editor (with Jan Jonsson) of *Can Education be Equalized?*

Harry B. G. Ganzeboom is professor of sociology and social research methodology at the Department of Social Research Methodology of the Free University Amsterdam. His main research interest is the analysis of social stratification and social mobility in a cross-nationally and historically comparative perspective.

Theodore P. Gerber is professor of sociology at the University of Wisconsin, Madison. His research examines socioeconomic stratification, demographic processes, public opinion, institutional change, and science in contemporary Russia. His articles have appeared in the *American Sociological Review, American Journal of Sociology, Social Forces, International Security, Social Science Research, Sociology of Education, Contexts, International Migration Review,* other sociology and area studies journals, and several edited volumes. He has developed (in whole or in part) thirteen large-sample surveys in Russia since 1998 and has also conducted numerous focus groups and in-depth interviews.

Pauline Givord is a researcher at CREST (Research Center for Economics and Statistics), Institut National de la Statistique et des Études Économique (INSEE) in Paris.

Dominique Goux is head of the mission of research animation at the Department of research animation, studies and statistics (DARES) of the French ministry of Labor in Paris. She is also associate professor of applied econometrics at the Ecole Normale Supérieure de la rue d'Ulm, Paris.

Eric Grodsky is assistant professor of sociology at the University of California, Davis. His work involves race/ethnicity and social stratification with a focus on inequality in higher education, and his research includes projects on race-based and class-based affirmative action and inequality in parents' knowledge of college costs. Grodsky's work has been published in the *American Sociological Review, Social Science Research,* and *School Effectiveness and School Improvement.*

Hiroshi Ishida is a professor of sociology at the Institute of Social Sciences, University of Tokyo. His research interests include social mobility, school-to-work transition, and social inequality in health. He is the editor of *Social Science Japan Journal* published by Oxford University Press and directs a panel survey of Japanese youth. He is the author of *Social Mobility in Contemporary Japan* (Macmillan and Stanford University Press, 1993) and is currently co-editing a volume entitled *Researching Social Class in Japan*.

Jan O. Jonsson is professor of sociology at the Swedish Institute for Social Research, Stockholm University and director of the Swedish Level of Living Surveys. His research interests are: social stratification, especially educational inequality and social mobility; sociology of the family; and life-course studies. His publications include *Can Education be Equalized?* (edited with Robert Erikson, Westview, 1996), *Cradle to Grave: Life Course Change in Modern Sweden* (edited with Colin Mills, Sociologypress, 2001), and "Inequality of Opportunity in Comparative Perspective: Recent Research on Educational Attainment and Social Mobility" (with Richard Breen, *Annual Review of Sociology*, 2005).

Markus Lamprecht is a senior lecturer at the Swiss Federal Institute of Technology, Zurich. He has published a range of sociological articles and books in the field of social inqualities, education, and health as well as sport and leisure. Together with Hanspeter Stamm he founded the L&S Sozialforschung und Beratung AG, a privately owned research company based in Zurich.

Ineke Maas is associate professor in the Department of Sociology/ICS, Utrecht University, the Netherlands. Her main research interests are international and historical comparisons of career, intergenerational, and marital mobility. In addition, she has published on cultural participation, the economic integration of immigrants, and inequality of educational opportunities.

Gary N. Marks is a principal research fellow at the Australian Council for Educational Research and a research associate in the Melbourne Institute at the University of Melbourne. His main interest is "modernization" in all its forms, so he is particularly interested in changes over time and cross-national differences in the importance of social structural factors on social, economic, and political outcomes. His other interests include the school-to-work transition, social and educational policies, and the dynamics of poverty, income, and wealth. Since 2003 he has authored 19 published or accepted journal articles, including articles in the *British Journal of Sociology*, the *Journal of Sociology*, *Ethnic and Racial Studies*, *International Sociology*, *Educational Research and Evaluation*, *Journal of Comparative Family Studies*, and *Educational Research*.

Petr Matějů is chair of the Department of Sociology of Education and Stratification at the Institute of Sociology of Academy of Sciences of the Czech Republic. Currently he serves as Deputy Minister for Science and Higher Education.

His major research interests are social stratification and mobility as well as inequality and equity in education. He has published a number of articles on social transformation in East Central Europe and has co-edited three books: *Ten Years of Rebuilding Capitalism. Czech Society after 1989* (English translation published in 1998), *Inequality—Justice—Politics* (2000, in Czech), and *Unequal Chances for Education* (2006, in Czech).

Karl Ulrich Mayer is chair and professor in the Department of Sociology at Yale University. He also serves as director of its Center for Research on Inequalities and the Life Course (CIQLE). His research interests lie in the areas of stratification and mobility, life course and aging, and comparative welfare states. Recent publications include: *After the Fall of the Wall: Life Courses in the Transformation of East Germany* (edited with M. Diewald and A. Goedicke, 2006); *Geboren 1964 und 1971* (edited with Steffen Hillmert, Wiesbaden, 2004); *Life Courses and Life Chances in Comparative Perspective* (2005); *The De-Standardization of the Life Course. What It Might Mean and If It Means Anything Whether It Actually Took Place* (with Hannah Brueckner, 2005); *Whose Lives? How History, Societies and Institutions Define and Shape Life Courses* (2004); *Abschied von den Eliten* (2006); and *The Berlin Aging Study. Aging from 70 to 100* (edited with P. B. Baltes, 1999).

Julie McMillan is a senior research fellow at the Australian Council for Educational Research and an associate of the Research School of Social Sciences at the Australian National University. She currently works on the Longitudinal Surveys of Australian Youth, and she has published on a broad range of topics including early school leaving, higher education participation and attrition, and career satisfaction. Other research interests include the measurement of social class and stratification.

Walter Müller is professor emeritus of sociology at Mannheim University and was a cofounder, department head, and director of the Mannheim Centre for European Social Research. From 1997 to 2003 he also was the president of the European Consortium for Sociological Research (ECSR). His research focuses on the comparative study of social structures of European societies and their change in the process of European integration. He has published extensively on the role of education for social inequality and patterns of social mobility in modern societies, in particular on social inequalities in educational opportunities and on the impact of education on individuals work careers. Recent publications include *Transitions from Education to Work in Europe*, edited with Markus Gangl (Oxford University Press, 2003), and *The Reemergence of Self-Employment: A Comparative Study of Self-Employment Dynamics and Social Inequality*, edited with Richard Arum (Princeton University Press, 2004).

Hyunjoon Park is a Korea Foundation Assistant Professor of Sociology at the University of Pennsylvania. His research interests include sociology of education, social stratification, health inequality, and transition to adulthood in cross-national comparative perspective, focusing on Korea and other East Asian countries. Recent publications include "Age and Self-Rated Health in Korea" (*Social Forces*, 2005) and "Intergenerational Social Mobility among Korean Men in Comparative Perspective" (*Research in Social Stratification and Mobility*, 2004).

Reinhard Pollak is a research associate for Methods of Empirical Social Research and Applied Sociology in the Department of Social Sciences at the University of Mannheim and involved in various research projects at the Mannheim Centre for European Social Research (MZES). His main research interests include educational inequality, social mobility, social inequality, and measures of social stratification. In his dissertation project, he analyzes the effects of declining educational inequality on social mobility in Europe.

Ettore Recchi is an associate professor of sociology at the University of Florence, Italy. He is co-director of the Euro-Mediterranean School on Migration and Development at the European University Institute and is director of the Social Work program at the University of Florence. His current research interests revolve around social and territorial mobility in Europe. Since 2003, he has coordinated a comparative research project on mobile European citizens (the PIONEUR project) funded by the European Commission. Recently he has co-edited the volume *Comparing European Societies: Towards a Sociology of the EU* (Monduzzi, Bologna, 2005).

Blanka Řeháková is a senior research worker in the department of value orientations in society at the Institute of Sociology of the Academy of Sciences of the Czech Republic. Her main research interests are value orientations in the broad sense.

Susanne Rijken is an inspector at the Netherlands Inspectorate of Education. Previously, she wrote her PhD thesis at the department of sociology, Utrecht University, and worked as a postdoctoral researcher at Utrecht University and the University of Amsterdam. Her main research topic was inequality of educational opportunity in a comparative perspective: over time and between countries.

Josipa Roksa is assistant professor of sociology and education at the University of Virginia. Her research encompasses a wide range of issues concerning social inequality, with a specific focus on stratification in higher education. She is currently engaged in two lines of inquiry. The first includes a set of projects examining transfer from community colleges to four-year institutions. The second line of inquiry involves a collaborative project on inequality in learning outcomes in higher education, funded by Ford and Lumina Foundations.

Stefan Sacchi is senior researcher at the Professorship of Sociology at the Swiss Federal Institute of Technology. His research and publications focus upon education, labor markets, and social stratification as well as political value change and social movements. Most recently he published "Long Term Dynamics of Skill Demand in Switzerland, 1950–2000" in *Contemporary Switzerland: Revisiting the Special Case* (Palgrave Macmillan, 2005).

Natalie Simonová is a senior researcher at the Department of Sociology of Education and Stratification, Institute of Sociology, Academy of Sciences of the Czech Republic. She focuses on the development of educational mobility during socialism and after its demise. She has published a number of articles on inequality of educational opportunities and recently edited a book entitled *Czech Higher Education at the Crossroads* (in Czech, 2005).

Hanspeter Stamm is a partner with L&S Sozialforschung und Beratung AG in Zurich. His research interests—on which he has published extensively—include social inequality and quality of life as well as health, sport, and leisure issues.

Shu-Ling Tsai is a research fellow in the institute of sociology at Academia Sinica, Taipei, Taiwan. Her main research interests are social stratification and social mobility. She has published articles on Taiwan's educational attainment, occupational stratification, earnings determination, and assortative mating.

CHAPTER ONE

More Inclusion Than Diversion: Expansion, Differentiation, and Market Structure in Higher Education

Richard Arum, New York University

Adam Gamoran, University of Wisconsin, Madison

Yossi Shavit, Tel Aviv University

INTRODUCTION

For scholars of social stratification, the key question about educational expansion is whether it reduces inequality by providing more opportunities for persons from disadvantaged strata, or magnifies inequality by expanding opportunities disproportionately for those who are already privileged. The expansion of higher education and its relation to social stratification deserves special scrutiny. First, whereas primary and secondary education have now become nearly universal in most economically advanced societies, we are witnessing rapid expansion and change at the tertiary level. In addition, higher education is the gatekeeper of managerial and professional positions in the labor market. Finally, and from a theoretical point of view most important, the structure of higher education has been transformed as it has expanded. Particularly in economically advanced countries, expansion has been accompanied by differentiation. Systems that had consisted almost exclusively of research universities developed second-tier and less selective colleges, and much of the growth in enrollment was absorbed by these second-tier institutions. Thus, at the same time that members of the working class found new opportunities to enroll in higher education, the system was being hierarchically differentiated so that these new opportunities may have had diminished value.

Differences between systems of higher education provide us with the opportunity to revisit theories about the role of expansion and differentiation in shaping stratification regimes in education. These theories were developed through research on secondary education at the time when it was being transformed from elite to mass education (e.g., Heyns 1974; Rosenbaum 1976; Shavit 1984; Gamoran 1987; Raftery and Hout 1993). Now the educational frontier has shifted and similar debates arise concerning higher education. Some scholars suggest that higher education expansion, especially when it occurs through hierarchical differentiation, is a process of *diversion,* whereby members of the working class are diverted from elite opportunities and are channeled to positions of lower status (Brint and Karabel 1989). Others have noted, however, that even lower-tier postsecondary schooling represents enhanced opportunity, so that the important effect of expansion may be one of *inclusion* (Dougherty 1994).

Another important dimension along which systems of higher education vary is the extent to which expansion is supported through market-based private financing or more exclusively through public sources. American research on expansion tends to ignore this distinction, taking expansion entirely for granted as a historically inevitable response to consumer demand (Walters 2000). In many other countries, however, higher education is centrally regulated and expansion is tightly controlled. While market-based systems likely result in greater expansion overall, they charge tuition fees that may hinder attendance by the working class. Thus, market-based systems may not promote equality of opportunity any more or less than state-centered systems.

This chapter synthesizes the findings reported by the 15 country chapters that comprise the bulk of this volume. The countries were drawn mainly from Western Europe (France, Italy, Germany, the Netherlands, Sweden, Switzerland, Great Britain), Eastern Europe (Russia, Czech Republic), and East Asia (Japan, Korea, Taiwan) and also include Israel, the United States, and Australia. Across countries and over time, these systems of higher education varied in the rate of expansion, the extent of differentiation, and market structure. These differences allow us to assess several propositions about the relation between forms of higher education expansion and social stratification. We examine how class inequalities in access to higher education vary across systems with different levels of expansion, institutional differentiation, and private versus public allocation logics. At the conclusion of this chapter we introduce the main findings of each of the country-specific analyses, which are laid out in full in the remainder of the book.

Expansion and Stratification

Following Mare (1980, 1981), many sociologists of education view the educational attainment process as a sequence of transition points at which students either continue to the next level or drop out. Some transition points involve multiple options such as whether, after high school, to attend a first-tier college or a second-tier college or to enter the labor force. At each transition point, students differ greatly in their transition probabilities. For example, those raised in middle-class homes are less likely to drop out, and are more likely to attend first-tier than they are to attend second-tier institutions, compared with students from disadvantaged social origins.

While educational expansion is associated with many advantages, including enhancement of peoples general well-being and of societies' macroeconomic development, scholars have observed that, in and of itself, expansion does not reduce class inequalities in education. Raftery and Hout (1993) have argued that inequality between any two social strata in the odds of attaining a given level of education persists until the advantaged class reaches the point of saturation. Saturation is defined as the point at which nearly all sons and daughters of advantaged origins attain the educational level under consideration. Until that point, the advantaged group is typically better equipped to take advantage of any new and attractive educational opportunities, and class inequalities will persist or even increase as opportunities are expanded. Only when the privileged class reaches saturation at a given level of education, would further expansion of that level contribute to the reduction of inequality in the odds of its attendance because the privileged cannot increase their attendance rates past the 100% mark.

This hypothesis, known as "Maximally Maintained Inequality" (MMI), is consistent with results reported by Shavit and Blossfeld (1993) who found that in most countries educational expansion did not reduce educational inequality. More recent studies (e.g., Jonsson, Mills, and Müller 1996; Shavit and Westerbeek 1998) found that as primary and secondary education expanded, class inequalities in their attainment declined. This result is consistent with Raftery and Hout's argument because the middle classes have reached saturation with respect to attainment of lower educational levels. In a recent paper, Hout (forthcoming b) analyzed data for 25 nations and found that among market economies, socioeconomic inequality in overall educational attainment is inversely related to the prevalence of higher education. This is also consistent with MMI because in societies with market economies, lower levels of education tend to be saturated in the privileged strata.

Although there are also empirical exceptions to MMI (e.g., in some former state socialist societies, inequality is not related to the degree of saturation (Hout forthcoming a)), it is consistent with most cases and is considered a useful working hypothesis for studies of educational expansion and stratification (Hout and DiPrete 2006).

Institutional Differentiation and Stratification

An important critique of the MMI hypothesis and of the Mare model is that they both ignore tracking and other forms of qualitative differentiation within education (e.g., Breen and Jonsson 2000; Lucas 2001; Ayalon and Shavit 2004). Educational choices involve more than just the two options—to continue or to drop out. Most education systems are tracked, in one form or another, and students must choose among various tracks within the system. Several scholars have argued that concurrent with expansion, qualitative differentiation replaces inequalities in the quantity of education attained (e.g., Shavit 1984; Gamoran and Mare 1989). Lucas (2001) recently argued that once saturation has been reached with regard to a given level of education, inequalities in the odds of this level's attainment may be replaced by inequalities in the odds of placement in the more selective track.

A well-known tenet of organization theory is that organizational growth tends to be accompanied by differentiation (Blau 1970). Differentiation is viewed as a means to operate more efficiently by dividing "raw materials" or "clients" into more homogeneous units. Educational expansion often follows this pattern, with systems becoming more complex as greater numbers of students enroll. While differentiation is commonly regarded as a consequence of expansion, it may also *contribute* to expansion, as new places become available in new segments of the education system. Whereas a functionalist view suggests that differentiation allows greater efficiency

(Thompson 1967), social control theorists point out that a differentiated system of higher education preserves the elite status of those born into privilege (Trow 1972; Brint and Karabel 1989).

The mode of differentiation in higher education varies between countries. In some countries, tertiary education is offered primarily by a single type of institution—usually, a research university. Meek and his associates refer to this type of system as *unified* (Goedegebuure et al. 1996). Unified systems tend to be quite rigid. They are controlled by professorial elites who are not inclined to encourage expansion, either of their own universities or through the formation of new ones. Very few systems still belong to this type. In our comparative project, only the Italian and Czech higher education systems are strictly unified. Other systems consist of a mix of institutions that are stratified by prestige, resources, and selectivity of both faculty and students. A well-known example is the American system, which consists of prestigious research universities, a second tier of private and public four-year colleges, as well as many two-year colleges (Karabel 1972; Brown 1995; Grodsky 2003). Meek and his associates refer to this type as *diversified* higher education (Goedegebuure et al. 1996).

Often, the second tier of tertiary education takes the form of vocational or semiprofessional training (e.g., the German *Fachhochschulen*). This system is labeled as *binary* because it consists of two main types of institutions: academic and vocational. Some diversified systems are also binary in the sense that second-tier colleges primarily provide vocational training. In other cases, vocational institutions were upgraded to university status in an attempt to transform the system from a binary to a formally unified one (e.g., Britain and Australia).

The co-occurrence of expansion and differentiation is the basis for claims that higher education expansion is primarily a process of *diversion*, channeling members of the working class to lower-status postsecondary opportunities in order to reserve higher-status opportunities for the elite (Brint and Karabel 1989). According to this view, as tertiary education expands and as differences between social strata in the odds of attaining tertiary education decline, between-strata differences widen with respect to the *kind* of tertiary education attended. Swirski and Swirski (1997) argued that as the second-tier system expands, first-tier institutions become more selective and class inequalities in access to first-tier institutions increase. An alternative view, however, is that expansion of lower-tier postsecondary education enhances opportunity by bringing into higher education students who would otherwise not have continued past secondary school (Dougherty 1994). Furthermore, one could argue that as higher education expands, first-tier institutions must compete for students and may lower admission thresholds. According to this logic, education expansion that leads to higher overall rates of tertiary enrollments is a process of *inclusion,* even if expansion is accompanied by differentiation.

TERTIARY MARKET STRUCTURE AND EDUCATIONAL INEQUALITY

Many studies of the relation between educational expansion and educational stratification suffer from an important theoretical inconsistency. On the one hand, they assume that expansion is *exogenous* to the stratification process, and that it affects the educational opportunities available to individuals (e.g., Raftery and Hout 1993). At the same time, these studies assume that educational expansion reflects rising individual incentives to attend school for longer periods of their life course. Some argue that incentives rise in response to changes in the occupational structure (e.g., Blau and Duncan 1967; Treiman 1970b). Others believe that incentives rise because groups and individuals compete for access to the best jobs (Collins 1979) or because parental expectations are such that children's education is likely to equal or exceed that found in the prior generation (Erikson and Jonsson 1996a). Regardless of the specific mechanism, these theoretical orientations share the assumption that expansion is *demand-driven,* namely, that schools expand in response to growing aggregate demand by individuals for education.

Garnier, Hage, and Fuller (1989) and Walters (2000) argue convincingly that this assumption is applicable to the American case, where education is decentralized and deregulated and where private and local educational institutions expand to meet consumer demand. As Walters writes:

> The literature on American school expansion has largely treated the growth of enrollments as a demand-driven process, determined almost exclusively by the decisions of students and their families about whether to send their children to school. *The availability of schooling is taken for granted....* (p. 242, emphasis added)

In many other countries, education is centrally regulated and numerous constraints are imposed on its expansion. As Garnier et al. (1989) argue, where states are strong, they can ration elite education (e.g., in first-tier institutions) while expanding mass education (e.g., through second-tier colleges). In some countries, there are formal quotas on admissions (e.g., Sweden; see Jonsson and Erikson in Chapter 5 of this volume). In addition, states can simply constrain funding for education, enact rigorous curricular prerequisites or institute restrictive accreditation requirements that effectively limit expansion.

Systems of higher education vary greatly in the degree to which they rely on public or private provision to support tertiary education. Furthermore, the responsiveness of education systems to consumer demand changes over time. Since the 1980s, some systems have undergone deregulation and privatization that facilitates rapid expansion in response to growing demand. In some systems private institutions aggressively stimulate and generate demand for their services through the use of promotional and marketing strategies (witness the increase in "nontraditional" students, the spread of the concept of "life-long learning," or the "College for All" campaigns implemented in the United States).

We anticipate that where higher education is largely funded from private sources, enrollment rates exceed those found in publicly funded systems. Privately funded colleges and universities rely on enrollment for revenue and are thus client-seekers. Furthermore, private institutions may engage in demand-generating activities, such as advertising, and the development of specialized programs that cater to well-defined groups of potential clients. Expanded funding from private sources can also potentially increase the overall level of support for higher education by supplementing—as opposed to substituting for—sustained public sector resource commitments (Arum 1996). At the same time, however, some institutions of higher education are also status-seekers. That is, they engage in various activities intended to enhance their prestige in terms of attracting "high quality" faculty and students relative to competing institutions. Most important in this regard is social exclusion in the process of student selection through the elevation of admissions criteria.

Clearly, the imperatives of client-seeking and status-seeking behaviors conflict with one another. Client-seeking implies low admissions criteria while status-seeking implies fewer clients than could otherwise be admitted. The conflict is often resolved through the differentiation of a status-seeking first tier of institutions and a client-seeking second tier, which is less selective and enjoys lower prestige. Thus, we expect to find greater enrollment rates and more institutional differentiation in market systems than in state-funded systems.

Class inequalities in the odds of progression to tertiary education may also differ between the two regimes, but we are unable to hypothesize a priori what direction these differences might take. Class inequalities in the odds of educational progression are due primarily to class differences in ability (including cultural capital), financial resources, and motivation. It is likely that in regimes that have expanded tertiary education through reliance on private sector funding there is less stringent educational selection on ability and there could thus be lower class inequalities than in more rigid government funded systems. At the same time, in highly privatized systems class inequalities may be mediated more directly by family differences in the ability to pay tuition fees.

SUMMARY OF PROPOSITIONS

The discussion of educational expansion, differentiation, and market structure suggests six propositions as follows.

Expansion and Educational Stratification
1. Expansion is not associated with inequality at the level where expansion occurs, unless saturation is approached (i.e., inequality is maximally maintained).

Institutional Differentiation and Selection
2. Tertiary expansion and differentiation are related, with causal effects operating in both directions: diversified systems are more likely to have higher overall enrollments rates, and vice versa.
3. The differentiation of higher education (both the diversified and binary modes) diverts students away from first-tier enrollment.

Market Structure, Differentiation, and Access
4. On average, enrollment rates are higher in systems with more funding from private sources.
5. Systems with higher levels of funding from private sources are likely to be more diversified than state-centered systems.

6. The degree of reliance on private funding is associated with inequality in access to higher education, but the direction of the association cannot be determined a priori.

METHODOLOGY: A COLLABORATIVE COMPARATIVE STUDY

This research project reflects what has been termed the "fourth generation" of comparative stratification research that has focused on the extent to which organizational variation across countries affects both intergenerational mobility and associations between social class and educational attainment (Treiman and Ganzeboom 2000; see also Ganzeboom, Treiman, and Ultee 1991). We employ a collaborative comparative methodology of the kind previously used by Shavit and Blossfeld (1993), Shavit and Müller (1998), Arum and Müller (2004), and others. Research teams in a sample of countries were asked to conduct similar studies of higher educational attainment using nationally representative data. The country studies each applied a common theoretical and methodological framework that had been agreed upon by the teams and was capable of generating findings comparable across countries. Once the country studies were completed, we as the project coordinators analyzed the findings comparatively and report the results in this chapter.

Our sample of countries is not a probability sample. Rather, we selected countries that represent variation in the main macrolevel variables of interest (extent of expansion, differentiation, degree of privatization), and where researchers were available who were familiar with our paradigmatic framework and had access to the necessary data (see Appendix Table A, pages 421–422, for a description of the data sets utilized for this project). The project includes 15 national teams consisting of 34 researchers and focuses on higher education systems in advanced economies, where expansion of secondary and tertiary education is further along than elsewhere (for a review of the strengths and limitations of applying such a framework to countries at earlier stages of development, see Buchmann and Hannum 2001).

Each country chapter contains a detailed description of tertiary education in the country, including organizational arrangement, size, regulation, administration, funding, and a description of changes and reforms that the system may have undergone in recent decades. In addition, the chapters report the results of logit regressions of several educational transitions including:

i. eligibility for higher education;
ii. entry into higher education; and
iii. entry into first-tier higher education.

Most regressions are estimated for roughly 10- to 15-year cohorts born since World War II and include the following independent variables: parental education, father's occupational class when respondent was in secondary school, and gender. Additional regressions also include track placement at the secondary level and ethnicity (where appropriate).

To sort out changes that reflect secondary expansion from those that reflect variation in postsecondary education, chapters report analyses that are both conditional and not conditional on eligibility for higher education. In addition to these compulsory components, teams could include "free style" information in supplementary analyses that they considered important for an understanding of tertiary educational attainment and stratification in their specific countries.

VARIABLES AND CLASSIFICATIONS

Higher Education Eligibility and Attendance

The main objective of this research project is to reveal systematic inequalities in access to higher education across social strata. We define higher education as tertiary programs that are either academic or occupationally oriented. We operationalize the former as all programs leading to academic degrees such as a BA or BsC (undergraduate degrees), Laurea, Diplom, MA or MsC (lower-level graduate degrees), or their equivalents. The second tier includes all two-year college programs, whether vocational or academic, as well as polytechnics (e.g., in the U.K.), *Fachhochschulen* (Germany), *Srednee Spetsial'noe Uchebnoe Zavedenie* (SSUZy in Russia), or *instituts universitaires technologiques* (IUT in France). We exclude programs that are typically shorter than two years or those attended predominantly by students of upper secondary school ages (e.g., vocational and technical programs in Australia and Israel).[1] Students who attended either academic or second-tier programs are defined as having attended higher education. Those who attended academic programs are defined as having attended first-tier programs, except in the United States and Israel. In the former, the first tier was defined as having attended four-year programs in selective institutions, while in the latter it was defined as having attended a university rather than a college.

Eligibility for higher education is defined as a certificate, or completed course of study at the secondary level, that formally allows continuation into some form of academic higher education. Higher education systems differ in their eligibility requirements. In some cases (France, Germany, Israel, Italy, Russia, and Switzerland) admission into higher education requires a secondary school matriculation certificate. In the Czech Republic, Japan, Korea, Taiwan, and the United States, completion of secondary education is required. In Australia, it entails completion of Year 12—the preparatory year for university study. In Britain, eligibility for upper tertiary education requires two or more A-level examinations (i.e., advanced secondary qualification examinations). In the Netherlands, there are multiple routes into higher education, but the most common are via the completion of academic five-year secondary education (VWO) or via four-year vocational postsecondary education (HBO). In Sweden, the eligibility rules have changed several times during the period of observation. Until the mid-1960s, eligibility for university studies was defined as having passed the examination at the upper secondary level (studentexamen). Since then, it was defined as having completed a three- or four-year program of study at the upper secondary level. In all countries, there are both main and alternative routes into higher education. The operationalization of eligibility in this chapter proxies the main routes into higher education in the various countries and tends to ignore the secondary ones. A related limitation is that in some countries different tiers of higher education have different eligibility requirements. In the country-specific chapters, this issue when relevant is addressed at length (see in particular Chapter 5 on Sweden and Chapter 11 on the Netherlands). For the comparative analysis presented here, however, a uniform definition was required. These compromises are necessary, since modelling such a large number of alternative routes into higher education would not be empirically feasible.

Modes of Differentiation

As noted, we capitalize on the existence of marked differences between countries in the organizational form of higher education. However, these

TABLE 1.1
Classification of countries by mode of differentiation in higher education

Country	Mode of differentiation
Britain	Binary
France	Binary
Germany	Binary
Netherlands	Binary
Russia	Binary
Switzerland	Binary
Israel	Diversified
Japan	Diversified
Korea	Diversified
Sweden	Diversified
Taiwan	Diversified
United States	Diversified
Australia	Other/mixed
Czech Republic	Unified
Italy	Unified

differences also thwart a strictly comparable definition of higher education across cases. National postsecondary educational programs vary in eligibility requirements, content, duration, form of accreditation and certification, and in the settings in which they are offered (university, college, private institute, etc.). While educational systems typically exhibit some mix of organizational forms, we follow Meek et al. (1996) who classify them into three ideal typical modes of differentiation. Column 2 in Table 1.1 classifies countries by these organizational categories. The classification pertains to the most recent decades covered by the data in each country and is based on information provided in the respective chapters. Six of the cases are binary, six are diversified, and two are unitary. Australia does not fall comfortably into any of the three categories, but whether we include it as a unified case or exclude it from the analysis does not substantially affect the results we report in findings that pertain to mode of differentiation.[2]

In *unified systems,* the bulk of postsecondary education is held in universities, is predominantly academic and theory-oriented, and is designed to train students for entry into research or high-skill professions. *Binary systems* combine academic higher education with second-tier programs that are occupationally oriented. However, occupationally oriented programs vary greatly in length and prestige across countries. In Germany, for example, *Fachhochschule* programs typically last four years, whereas in France the *diplôme universitaire technologique* (DUT) requires only two years. And yet, the French *instituts universitaires technologiques* (IUT), in which the DUT programs are offered, are more selective than regular universities, whereas in Germany the *Fachhochschulen* are often less selective than universities. In most *diversified systems,* second-tier education includes both occupationally oriented programs and programs that may lead to academic education. The prime examples are the American, Japanese, and Taiwanese junior colleges that offer both vocational and academic two-year preparation for entry into four-year programs.

Market Structure

Private/public distinctions in education can be proxied in many ways, such as the degree of state institutional control, student enrollments in the private sector, the number of private institutions, and the private/public mix of funding. We conceptualize the market structure of higher education by focusing on the extent to which the system is driven by a consumer logic, that is, the extent to which colleges and universities are dependent on resources provided by private sources. We operationalize this variable as the percent of national expenditures on higher education that come from private as opposed to public sources as reported by the OECD (OECD 1985–92, table II.1.9, p. 50; OECD 1996, table F1.1c, p. 61).[3] We rely on OECD data here because they report reliable and comparable data on privatization for most countries in our sample. Our focus on examining the implications of private compared to public financial support for higher education systems is consistent with resource dependency theoretical orientations from the sociology of organi-zations literature; this approach suggests that institutional dependence on particular resource flows has consequences for the form, structure, and practices of organizations (Pfeffer and Salancik 1978).

Measures of Inequality

As noted above, logit regressions (i)–(iii) include measures of father's class and parental education. Father's class was measured on an EGP or a very similar class schema (Erikson and Goldthorpe 1992), and parental education was measured on the CASMIN educational schema (Müller et al. 1989). Both schema are shown in Appendix Table B. From each equation we extracted the log-odds of attaining a particular educational outcome contrasting respondents whose fathers were in classes I or II (the so-called service classes that include professionals, managers, and owners of large firms) against those whose fathers were in classes V and VI (the skilled working class). We also extracted the log-odds of achieving an educational outcome contrasting parents with higher education against those with only secondary education. The average of these two log-odds statistics provides a composite summary measure of the relative effects of social background on educational transitions and thus serves as our measure of inequality between social strata, for each educational outcome (i)–(iii).[4]

COMPARATIVE CASE-STUDY RESEARCH

There is a long-standing debate about the merits of variable-oriented and case-oriented comparative research (e.g., Abbott 1992; Ragin 1997; Goldthorpe 2000a). The former aims to test hypotheses about relationships between variables and to generalize from samples to populations of cases. This genre assumes probabilistic models of causation. Change in X (e.g., educational expansion) can increase or decrease the probability of an outcome (e.g., equalization of educational opportunities between social classes) but does not determine the outcome fully. Therefore, probabilities can only be computed in relatively large samples of cases. However, with a large number of cases, it is difficult for the researcher to gain an intimate understanding of the idiosyncratic narratives and causal processes operating within cases. Variable-oriented studies have been criticized for tracking cases as mere carriers of variables and categories and ignoring their other characteristics. Causality is attributed to statistical associations between variables by the degree of statistical fit between a theoretical model and data rather than sought in narrative and process (Abbott 1992). By contrast, case-oriented research treats cases holistically and seeks to achieve a deep and full understanding of each. Causality, if sought, is to be found in the historical development of the case, the narrative prevalent within it, or its cultural or structural context. Case-oriented studies are usually limited to one or a few cases and no formal attempt is made to generalize beyond them. Thus, variable-oriented researchers are frustrated by their inability to fully understand their cases while case-oriented researchers are limited by their narrow, if deep gaze, and weak capacity to generalize from sample to population.

The collaborative comparative method aims to bridge these extremes. On the one hand, in this chapter we study a sufficient number of cases to attempt to formulate some tentative generalizations about the relationships between variables.[5] On the other hand, the individual country chapters provide detailed contextual, historical, institutional, and statistical information on each of the cases.

ANALYSIS AND FINDINGS

Expansion and Educational Stratification

In Figure 1.1 we describe change across cohorts in the rates of eligibility and attendance of higher education and of the first tier. The horizontal axis of the figure is labeled by the decade during which the birth cohort would have made the transition from secondary to higher education.[6] We see a marked expansion, across the four decades, in all three educational levels. On average, the eligibility rate for higher education increased from about 35% to about 80%, and attendance of higher education increased from under 20% to over 40% on average. Attendance rates in the first tier also increased about twofold during the four decades.

Following Raftery and Hout's MMI hypothesis, our Proposition 1 suggests that inequality between social strata in the odds of attaining an educational level is stable over time and is unaffected by educational expansion unless the proportion attaining it nears saturation. We begin to assess this hypothesis in Figure 1.2, which depicts the association across countries between eligibility rates and change in inequality of eligibility. The data points in the plot are labeled by the country acronym and the decade during which the youngest cohort attended higher education. We measured change in inequality as the percent difference between the two youngest cohorts in the mean effects of father's class and parental education on the log-odds of eligibility.

Figure 1.2 reveals that inequality in eligibility declined in five countries, was about stable in nine, and increased significantly in one (Italy). The observed pattern is largely consistent with the saturation hypothesis. For this project, we operationalize saturation as educational attainment rates exceeding 80%.[7] In four of the five countries in which inequality declined, eligibility was greater than 80%, and in all but one or two of the countries (Australia is borderline) in which eligibility rates were lower than 80%, inequality was stable or increased over time.

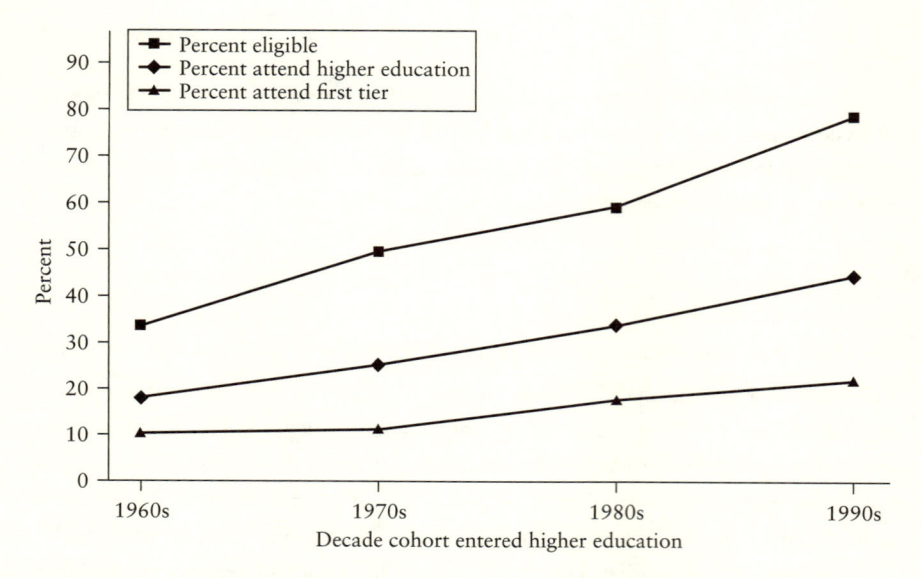

Figure 1.1. Average Trends in Higher Education Eligibility and Attendance in 15 Countries

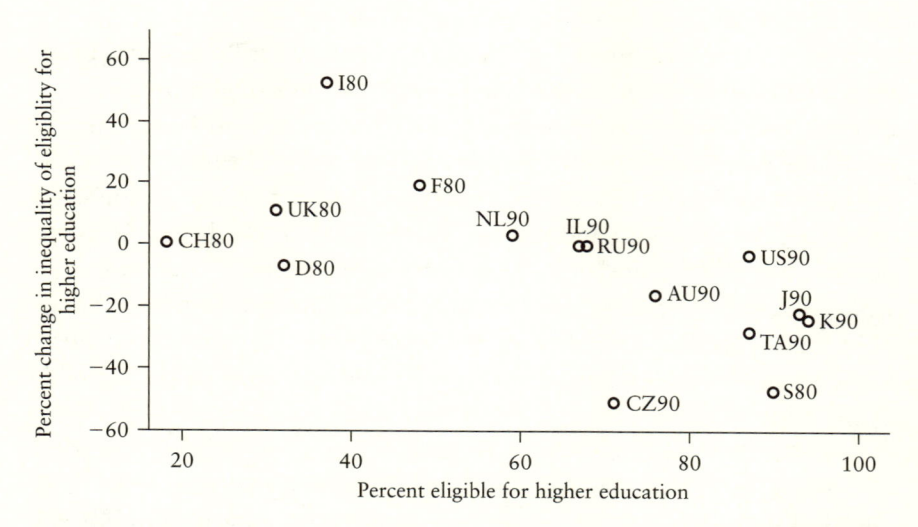

Figure 1.2. Association between Percent Eligible for Higher Education and Percent Change in Inequality of Eligibility

NOTE: In this and subsequent scatterplots, the countries are labeled by their acronym and the decade during which the last cohort attended higher education. The acronyms are: AU, Australia; CH, Switzerland; CZ, Czech Republic; D, Germany; F, France; I, Italy; IL, Israel; J, Japan; K, Korea; NL, Netherlands; RU, Russia; S, Sweden; TA, Taiwan; UK, Britain; US, United States.

The limitation of Figure 1.2 is that it depicts the relation between changing inequality and saturation, but does not represent expansion. We address this limitation by examining the partial correlations between saturation and expansion on the one hand, and changing inequality on the other hand. We measure expansion as percent *change* between the two youngest cohorts in eligibility rates. The bivariate correlation of expansion with change in inequality of eligibility is weak (0.13). To take account of expansion and saturation simultaneously, we define a dummy variable, which is coded 1 for the five cases in which 80% or more of the youngest cohort were eligible for higher education (i.e., U.S., Japan, Korea, Taiwan, and Sweden) and estimate a linear regression of change in inequality of eligibility on both expansion of eligibility and the saturation dummy ($R^2 = 0.24$). The standardized effect of expansion is virtually null ($r = -0.04$) but the effect of saturation is sizeable and negative as expected ($r = -0.50$). This is precisely the pattern of results predicted by MMI and Proposition 1.

Next we repeat the analysis for the transition from eligibility to the actual attendance of higher education. First, we relate change in inequality in the log-odds of making the transition to higher education to the percent of eligibles who attended higher education. We hypothesize that, in the presence of expansion, as the proportion of eligibles who attend higher education exceeds 80%, inequality at that transition point would decline. Figure 1.3 displays the bivariate relation between the percent of eligibles who attended higher education and change in inequality in the transition from secondary to higher education attendance ($r = -0.36$).[8] A detailed inspection of the figure shows that inequality in the transition from eligibility to higher education was relatively stable in six of the thirteen cases shown (Korea, U.S., France, Britain, Czech Republic, and the Netherlands), increased in three, and declined in four. Of these four cases, the proportion of eligibles who continued to higher education exceeded 80% in two (Israel and Italy). The exceptions are Taiwan and Japan, where inequality declined without saturation. In both cases, colleges were allowed to expand rapidly in the 1990s, after a period of retrenchment and consolidation (for details, see Chapters 3 and 6). In both, but especially in Taiwan, college enrollments expanded at a much faster pace than the rate of eligibility, and inequality in the transition to higher education declined. Figure 1.3 also reveals one case in which inequality in the parameters examined did not decline despite saturation: in the United Kingdom, rates of higher education enrollment

18   Arum, Gamoran, and Shavit

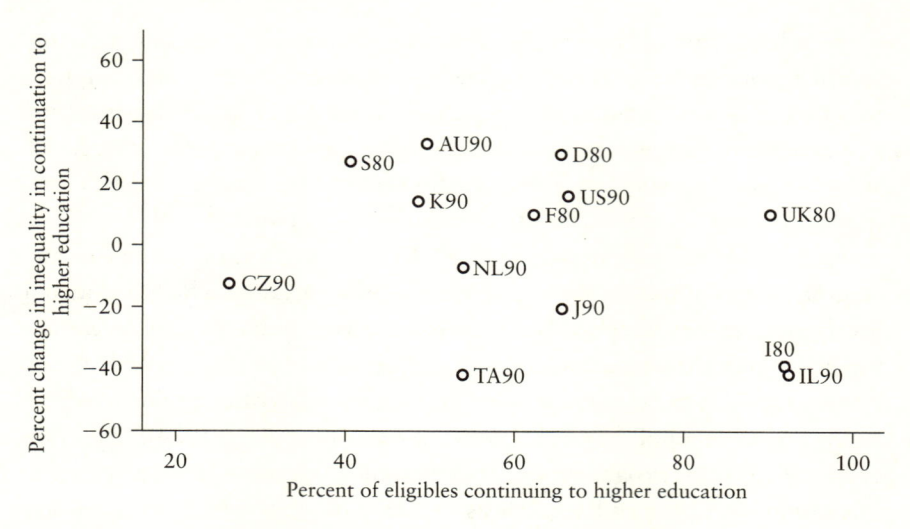

Figure 1.3. Association between Percent of Eligibles Who Continued to Higher Education and Change in Inequality in the Log-odds of Continuation

NOTE: Switzerland and Russia are excluded (see note 8).

among those eligible were very high, but little expansion occurred over the period covered by the data (see Chapter 8).

Next, we estimate a regression similar to the one reported earlier, in which we study the combined effects of saturation and expansion on change in inequality of higher education attendance. The dependent variable is inequality in the transition from eligibility to higher education, and the independent variables are two: a dummy variable representing saturation (coded 1 for countries in which 80–100% of eligibles attended higher education, i.e., Italy, Israel, and the U.K.), and expansion in the transition rate from eligibility to higher education (measured as the percent increase between the two youngest cohorts in the proportion of eligibles who attend higher education). The bivariate correlations between expansion and saturation on the one hand, and the dependent variable on the other hand, are −0.36 and −0.45 respectively. However, when both variables are included in the regression equation ($R^2 = 0.21$) their standardized effects are 0.06 and −0.50. Thus, on average, across the thirteen countries that are included in this analysis, saturation would seem to reduce inequality while expansion alone does not.

In sum, MMI is supported by our data: expansion can attenuate educational inequality but its effect is not a linear one. Rather, educational expansion tends to attenuate inequality when it reaches the point at which educational attainment at a particular level is nearly universal.

DIFFERENTIATION AND INCLUSION

Our next empirical question concerns the extent to which institutional differentiation stratifies opportunities in higher education. Specifically, we address two hypotheses: first, that differentiation and expansion are related (Proposition 2); and second, that the differentiation of higher education diverts students from first-tier education (Proposition 3). To this end, we compare attendance rates in higher and first-tier education in unified, diversified, and binary systems. In addition, we compare inequalities of access to higher and first-tier education between diversified and binary systems.

Table 1.2 examines the relations between expansion, differentiation, and inequality. Although we do not have sufficiently detailed measurement of differentiation nor adequate variation within country over time to model formally the relationship between change in differentiation and change in enrollment, we nevertheless find substantial differences in eligibility rates between diversified systems as well as between binary and unified systems. In the diversified systems eligibility is nearly universal (86%) on average, compared with 42% and 54% in the other two categories. Moreover, diversified systems have the highest tertiary attendance rates. Thus, we find general support for Proposition 2: both eligibility and attendance rates tend to be higher in diversified systems. Table 1.2 does not reveal the mechanisms that link differentiation and higher rates of tertiary enrollments, but the country-specific chapters suggest that more diversified systems tend to have more lenient requirements for eligibility for higher education. In most diversified systems (U.S., Japan, Korea, Taiwan, and Sweden in recent decades) eligibility is conferred upon graduation from secondary school, whereas in most binary systems (Britain, Germany, France, Russia, and Switzerland) students must pass a series of matriculation examinations to be eligible. Matriculation examinations are generally more selective than graduation. Therefore, where matriculation examinations determine eligibility, fewer students are eligible than in systems that require only graduation. In addition, in most

TABLE 1.2
Means and standard deviations (in parentheses) of eligibility, attendance, and inequality by mode of differentiation

Mode of differentiation	n	(1) Percentage eligible for higher education	(2) Percentage attend higher education	(3) Percentage attend first-tier higher education	(4) Inequality in eligibility	(5) Inequality in higher education	(6) Inequality in first-tier higher education
Binary	6	42.3 (18.2)	30.7 (7.6)	12.2 (5.0)	1.00 (.49)	0.99 (.30)	.85 (.33)
Diversified	6	86.3 (9.9)	51.8 (10.0)	24.2 (2.2)	.77 (.29)	.80 (.26)	1.30 (.99)
Unified	2	54.0 (24.0)	26.5 (10.6)	26.5 (10.6)	.92 (.71)	.85 (.33)	1.60 (1.21)
Total	14	62.8 (26.0)	39.1 (14.2)	19.0 (8.1)	.90 (.43)	.88 (.28)	1.40 (1.01)

NOTE: Australia is excluded (see footnote 2). The figures in columns 4–6 are average logit coefficients of fathers' class effects (the effect of the service class versus the skilled manual working class) and parental education (higher versus secondary education).

binary systems the distinction between vocational and academic education begins at the secondary level, where many students are already diverted from tertiary education (Kerckhoff 1993).

Proposition 3 suggested that the differentiation of higher education may divert students from first-tier higher education. Column 3 of Table 1.2 contradicts this claim as it pertains to diversified systems: the cohort proportions attending the first tier in diversified and unified systems are similar. By contrast, in binary systems first-tier attendance rates are very low.

Whereas columns 1–3 of Table 1.2 respond to questions about differentiation and overall rates of eligibility and higher education attendance, columns 4–6 address questions about inequality, as represented by average logit coefficients for effects of parents' educational and occupational backgrounds on eligibility for and attendance in higher education and its first tier. In column 4 we compare the three modes of differentiation with respect to inequality of eligibility. We find that inequality of eligibility is similar in unified and binary systems (0.92 and 1.00) and is somewhat lower in diversified ones (0.77), consistent with our interpretation that diversified systems have more lenient eligibility requirements. Thus, we conclude that diversified systems are more inclusive than both binary and unified systems: a larger proportion of the population is eligible for and attends higher education, and inequality occurs at a lower rate. The contrast between diversified and binary systems is particularly compelling, favoring diversified systems, which exhibit both more expansion and less inequality.

The greater inclusiveness of diversified systems could be illusory, if students from disadvantaged backgrounds lacked access to first-tier higher education. Column 6 suggests this is not the case. Inequality of access to the first tier appears slightly lower in diversified than in binary systems (1.30 versus 1.60 in the logit metric). This contrast is robust to controls for expansion: in a regression on first-tier inequality controlling for percent of first-tier enrollment, diversified systems exhibited lower inequality by the same margin as reflected in column 6.

In both diversified and binary systems, inequality is greater for first-tier enrollment than for enrollment in higher education overall (compare columns 5 and 6). Unified systems have only one tier, so that comparison is not relevant, but it is noteworthy that while diversified systems exhibit lower inequality in higher education enrollment than unified systems, the latter exhibits lower rates of first-tier enrollment inequality. Thus, the differentiation of higher education may come at some cost to inequality of first-tier enrollment, although this conclusion is necessarily tentative since it is based on only two unified cases. The more robust conclusion is that diversified systems exhibit both greater enrollment levels and less inequality than binary systems at all levels of higher education. Thus, we find strong support for Proposition 2 (differentiation and expansion are related), but Proposition 3 (differentiation leads to diversion) is largely refuted. Diversified systems exhibit more first-tier enrollment at lower rates of inequality than binary systems. The relative class-based odds of first-tier enrollment still appear lowest in the unified systems (which have only one tier), but diversified systems offer more access to higher education overall at little cost to enrollment in the first tier.

MARKET STRUCTURE, DIFFERENTIATION, AND ACCESS

Finally our analysis turns to a set of questions that focus on the role of market structure on higher education differentiation, expansion, and inequality (Propositions 4–6). As noted above, we operationalize market structure as the percent of higher education funding that is provided through private sector sources. As was the case in our analysis of differentiation, data limitations prevent formal modeling of changes in funding from private sources within country over time. Nevertheless, we are able to explore the extent to which private sector involvement is related to the scale, scope, and allocation of higher education (i.e., the extent to which it is associated with expansion, differentiation, and inequality).

Figure 1.4 displays the relation between market structure and the size of the higher education sector. There is a strong positive association between these variables ($R^2 = 0.44$), consistent with Proposition 4. However, in supplementary analysis (results not shown), we found no significant relation between private funding and attendance in higher education when the latter was considered only for the subset of the cohort that was eligible. This finding suggests that where higher education is largely funded by private sources, it expands through the adoption of lenient eligibility criteria. Similar results were found when we examined attendance rates solely for first-tier higher education.[9]

Table 1.3 examines the relation between private funding and mode of institutional differentiation (classified as unified, binary, or diversified).

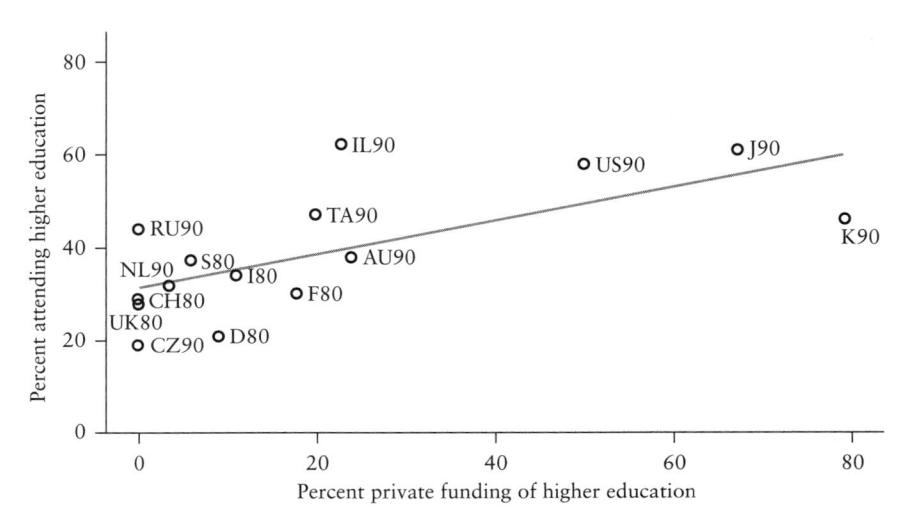

Figure 1.4. Association Between Percent Private Funding and Percent Attending Higher Education

TABLE 1.3
Private sector funding and mode of differentiation in higher education

Mode of differentiation	TERTIARY EDUCATION RELIANCE ON PRIVATE-SECTOR FUNDING		
	Low	Moderate	High
Unified	Italy		
	Czech Republic		
Binary	Germany	France	
	Russia		
	Switzerland		
	Britain		
	Netherlands		
Diversified	Sweden	Israel	Japan
		Taiwan	Korea
			United States

Both unified systems exist in settings where tertiary education is funded primarily through public sources. When variation and delineation in organizational type occur in systems with low levels of private funding, it is usually binary rather than the less structured and weakly demarcated diversified form (Sweden is the one exception). Diversified higher education systems appear primarily in countries where higher education relies on private funds to a larger degree. Thus, we find support for Proposition 5: reliance on private sources of funding is conducive to greater differentiation. More important however, in systems with a high degree of private funding, the mode of differentiation is more likely to be diversified than binary.

Given that greater reliance on private funding of higher education is associated with institutional differentiation, one would also expect increased rates of tertiary attendance in these settings. We find this indeed to be the case. The partial correlation coefficient between private funding and higher education expansion (i.e., change over time), net of the overall original size of the higher education system is 0.29. Countries with lower rates of expansion tend to have lower rates of private funding and to have either unified or binary institutional forms. This pattern is also consistent with Proposition 5.

Finally, we address Proposition 6 by exploring the relation between the degree of reliance on private funding and inequality in attendance at higher education. When exploring zero-order correlations between our measures of inequality in higher education attendance and the extent to which the system was supported by private sector funding, we found no evidence of any significant association (correlation coefficient = 0.03). We found similar patterns when we examined the association of private funding with change over time in social background effects and when considering attendance solely in first-tier institutions. However, the absence of a direct correlation between private sector funding and inequality in higher education masks the presence of two contradictory patterns of association underlying this phenomenon of null overall (or "total") effects.

In Figure 1.5, we present a path diagram that captures the extent to which private sector funding is associated with variation in both higher education attendance and higher education inequality. Specifically, private sector funding exhibits a positive direct association with inequality in higher education, as identified by the partial correlation coefficient of 0.31 in the diagram. However, the extent to which private sector funding contributes to increased inequality is mitigated by the indirect link between private sector funding and inequality via higher overall rates of tertiary enrollments. In path diagrams, such an indirect effect can be calculated as the multiplicative product of the two partial correlation coefficients (0.67 × −0.43 = −0.29).

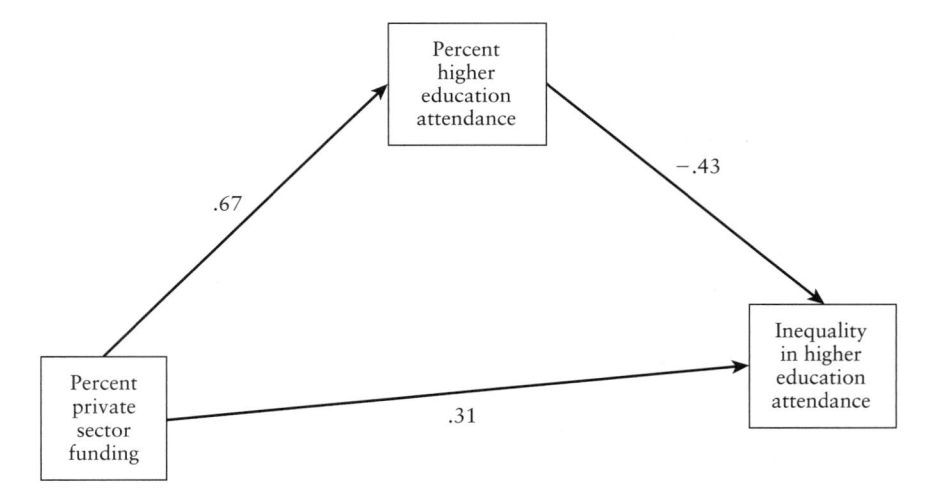

Figure 1.5. Path Diagram of Associations Between Private-sector Funding, Higher Education Attendance, and Inequality in Higher Education

These results indicate that the beneficial effect of private funding is due to its positive effect on increased levels of educational attendance, which in turn reduces inequality of access. Net of this indirect connection, increased reliance on private sources of funding tends to magnify inequality. We suspect that in highly privatized systems, class inequalities may reflect family differences in the ability to pay tuition fees.

In sum, our findings suggest that privatization of financial sources of support for higher education can be beneficial up to a point. In so far as it contributes to the expansion of higher education, it reduces inequality. Controlling for expansion, privatization enhances inequality of access; taken as a whole, however, privatization is associated with larger higher education systems and similar aggregate levels of inequality overall.

A NOTE ON GENDER INEQUALITY

Although it was not the main focus of our inquiry, we would be remiss if we did not mention the findings related to variation in gender inequality, which also appear in each of the country-specific chapters. Consistent with what other researchers have observed (e.g., Bradley 2000), our findings indicate that men's advantages in educational attainment declined dramatically during the second half of the twentieth century. The erosion of the male advantage is especially pronounced for participation in postsecondary education. In all countries for which data are available, and in both the conditional and unconditional models, men's relative advantage declined. Only among German, Korean, and Taiwanese high-school graduates do men still hold a small advantage relative to women in the odds of entering postsecondary education. In late-Soviet Russia, where women already held a substantial advantage in the odds of postsecondary enrollment given secondary completion, men reduced the gaps but still enroll at lower rates than women. A similar picture is seen with regard to gender differences in the odds of attending first-tier institutions of higher education.

How did gender inequality in higher education change between the two most recent cohorts in our data? Already in the next-to-last cohort, men and women reached parity, on average, in the odds of attending higher education. The mean effect of gender in that cohort was negligible. By the last cohort, the gender gap increased in favor of women who, on average, were 1.14 times as likely as men to attain higher education. On average, women's advantage (or men's disadvantage) increased by 20% between the two most recent cohorts. We also find that the decline in the male advantage is related to its magnitude in the next-to-last cohort: it declined most in countries where men initially enjoyed a large advantage (Taiwan, Korea, Japan, Israel, and Czech Republic). The correlation between the magnitude of the decline and the prior male advantage is 0.57. In addition, women's advantage in access to higher education increased (or their disadvantage declined) more rapidly in countries where higher education expanded fastest. The partial correlation between female's advantage and the expansion of higher education between the two recent cohorts (controlling for female advantage in the next to last cohort) is 0.29 suggesting that women took somewhat better advantage of expansion than men. The correlation between women's advantage and reliance on private sector funding is -0.22, reflecting the fact that in two of the countries with very high proportion of private funding (Korea and Japan) gender inequality in higher education was large until recently. Among other countries there is no systematic relationship between private funding and gender inequality. Similarly, we do not find notable differences when comparing gender inequality of access to higher education between binary, diversified, and unitary systems.

In sum, our data show an average widening of the gender gap in higher education favoring women, and indicate that the gap expanded fastest in systems where attendance rates expanded most. While there are differences across systems in the rate of change, overall there is a fairly uniform pattern of women's increasing participation in higher education, closing the gap, and then often coming to outperform men in higher education enrollment.

DISCUSSION AND CONCLUSIONS

Findings from this project provide evidence of the relations among institutional expansion, differentiation and privatization, and the stratification of individual educational opportunity. We briefly review the findings in these three areas, before discussing their theoretical and policy implications. We conclude with an outline of the chapters found in the rest of this book.

Our synthesis of country-specific findings indicated that expansion is pervasive, and that under certain conditions, it may lead to declining inequality. In particular, expansion to the point of saturation was associated with declining inequality in eligibility for higher education in four countries (Japan, Korea, Taiwan, and Sweden), and with a decline in inequality in the transition from secondary to tertiary education in two countries (Italy and Israel). With a few exceptions, inequality rates were stable or increased in other cases. These findings supported Proposition 1, that inequality is maximally maintained. Among the exceptions, we took particular note of declining inequality in the transition to higher education in two other countries that underwent sharp expansion after a period of consolidation (Japan and Taiwan). These cases suggest that rapid expansion in a diversified and deregulated system of higher education can broaden involvement in higher education across the social strata, apparently without any greater tendency to divert those of disadvantaged origins to lower-tier institutions.

We also found that expansion and institutional differentiation are related; in particular, diversified systems of higher education exhibit higher rates of eligibility and correspondingly higher rates of enrollment than unified and binary systems (consistent with Proposition 2). Moreover, we found that binary systems divert students away from higher education as a whole and from its first tier. In diversified systems, the proportions attending higher education are much larger than in other systems and, contrary to our expectations (see Proposition 3), the proportions attending first-tier institutions are more comparable to those of unified ones.

Finally, we examined the extent to which variation in private support for higher education was associated with institutional expansion and differentiation as well as stratification of educational opportunities. Our synthesis of country-specific findings suggests that systems with more private sector involvement tend to expand more rapidly and are more diversified (consistent with Propositions 4 and 5). In approaching this project, we hypothesized that while privatization is associated with inequality of access to higher education, we could not specify a priori the shape of the association (Proposition 6). On the one hand we assumed that the client-seeking behavior of private institutions would be associated with expansion, a weakening of social selection, and thus greater inclusion of the lower strata. On the other hand we expected that reliance on private funding could potentially lead to higher tuition fees on average and would increase inequality of access. Our analysis suggests that both mechanisms are likely operative and that these countervailing trends in combination largely balance each other out in their effects. Specifically, privatization is associated with expansion of opportunity and a corresponding lessening of social inequality, but privatization net of expansion is associated with increased inequality of access. Thus, whereas privatization through the indirect effect of expansion tends to draw persons into higher education, it also has direct effects that are exclusive; overall, the total effect of privatization on educational stratification is neutral.

How do these findings stand with respect to claims about inclusion and diversion? Overall, we found much stronger evidence of inclusion than of diversion. Whereas privatization was associated with inclusion and diversion in about equal amounts, expansion and diversification tended to be largely inclusive. First, overall expansion was inclusive in the sense that even when social selection is stable, expansion means that more students from all strata, including those from disadvantaged backgrounds, are carried further into the education system, and for the cohort as a whole inequality is reduced. Second, expansion in a context of saturation often results in declining inequality, clearly a case in which expansion stimulates inclusion. We observed this pattern for both eligibility and attendance of higher education. Third, whereas binary systems tended to exhibit both more inequality and lower rates of tertiary enrollment, diversified systems offered much higher rates of enrollment with no greater inequality overall, and just moderately greater inequality of first-tier enrollment compared to our two unified cases. Diversified systems are thus more inclusive overall than either binary or unitary systems.

Our first claim, that expansion is inclusive even without declining inequality, gives a new interpretation to a familiar set of findings. Previous work characterized cases of rising enrollment and stable odds ratios for educational transitions as "persistent inequality" (Shavit and Blossfeld 1993). In our view, this conclusion misses an important point: When a given level of education expands, we should expect increasing inequality of enrollment at the *next* level due to the increased heterogeneity of the eligible population (see Rijken, Maas, and Ganzeboom, Chapter 11 of this volume). Consequently, when inequality in an expanding system is stable rather than on the rise, the system should be regarded as increasingly inclusive because it allows larger proportions of all social strata to attend. By this notion, not only should most of our cases be regarded as increasingly inclusive, but so should those reported by Shavit and Blossfeld (1993) despite the stability that they find in the parameters of the educational stratification process. Looking within countries over time, our findings generally mirror those in *Persistent Inequality*: stable odds ratios, conditional on eligibility (Figure 1.3). Only post-Soviet Russia exhibited increasing inequality.[10] Of the four cases of downward changes in odds ratios, two may be explained by saturation (Israel and Italy) and two by rapid expansion following consolidation (Japan and Taiwan).[11]

Our findings and conclusions have policy implications. *Persistent Inequality* emphasized that expansion enables the privileged classes to retain their relative edge in the process of educational stratification. Our interpretation is different. Of course, we recognize that class inequalities in the *relative* shares of education persist over time and are difficult to change. Much research has shown that in most instances the privileged classes manage to maintain their advantages over time. Given the stability of *relative* inequalities, the most that policy can achieve under ordinary (i.e., nonrevolutionary) political circumstances is change in the absolute size of the educational pie (i.e., expansion). Yet we reach a slightly more optimistic conclusion here: namely that the expanding pie is increasingly inclusive even when relative advantages are preserved, because it extends a valued good to a broader spectrum of the population. Moreover, we found that diversified systems tend to be more inclusive than binary systems—without diverting students from the first tier—and we noted four cases of expansion in which relative inequalities actually diminished somewhat. Our findings thus imply that educational expansion is an equalizing force and that diversification is not inconsistent with inclusion.

Critics of our position may argue that education is a positional good (Hirsch 1976). That is, the value of an educational credential is not absolute but rather is determined by relative ordering on the hierarchy of credentials. To the extent that education *is* a positional good, change in the size of the educational pie is not likely to affect the opportunity structure that individuals and classes face in the labor market, which can only be affected by change in *relative* educational inequalities between classes. But is education a strictly positional good? The value of education also lies in the human capital it instills in students (e.g., Kerckhoff, Raudenbush, and Glennie 2001). This seems particularly clear for specific vocational and professional training (Boesel et al. 1994, 137), as well as for basic and advanced literacy and numeracy, but it is arguably more generally applicable (Kerckhoff, Raudenbush, and Glennie 2001). To the extent that attainments in the labor market reflect the human capital component of education, it makes sense to enhance the latter through the expansion of higher education. Moreover, even if education were strictly a positional good, it would still make sense for individual countries to expand their systems of higher education. Workers now compete in a global labor market and education is positional in relation to its global distribution. Therefore, countries that enhance the absolute educational distribution of their youths give them an edge in the competition against youths in other countries.

The fifteen country specific case studies in the book are organized into three broad categories: (1) diversified systems, (2) binary systems, and (3) unified and other systems. Here we offer an outline of the presentation with key findings from the country-specific chapters highlighted to aid the reader in approaching this volume.

Diversified Systems

Chapter 2 examines recent changes in higher education in Israel. During the 1980s there was a growing imbalance between increasing demand for higher education and the restricted capacity of the few universities that existed at the time. As demand mounted, the universities raised their admissions criteria resulting in growing social inequality of access through the late 1980s. The expansion of higher education through the creation and accreditation of colleges and foreign extensions reversed this trend during the 1990s. These less selective institutions provided students from less privileged social origins with an alternative to the university; as a result, inequalities between strata in the odds of attending higher education declined. Social inequality in access to the veteran universities remained high but stable.

Chapter 3 describes a highly diversified Japanese higher education system that expanded dramatically in both the 1960–75 and the post-1985 periods due to newly established private universities, but stagnated in the intervening decade due to state regulatory policies. There was little change in the effects of social background on higher educational attainment over the period of observation. While parental education effects were constant over time: parental occupation had weakening effects on higher education attendance but increasing effects on the sorting of students between four-year and two-year institutions.

Distinctive features of South Korean higher education identified in Chapter 4 include its high degree of centralization, high level of privatization, and its rapid expansion, particularly during the 1990s and especially in the junior college sector. Inequality of eligibility, overall higher education enrollment, and four-year university enrollment were largely stable throughout the second half of the twentieth century, with one important exception: the impact of father's education on university enrollment increased substantially. In the oldest cohort, respondents whose fathers completed tertiary education were about twice as likely as those whose fathers completed only secondary education to enroll in university; by the youngest cohorts, these rates differed by a factor of five.

Chapter 5 reports that during the twentieth century, higher education expanded dramatically in Sweden, and class inequality in the odds of enrollment declined. However, the two processes may not be causally related. The authors propose that expansion and the lowering of admissions criteria may have had a small beneficial effect leading to a slight decrease in social inequality. They suggest that the reason for the limited effect is that new educational opportunities are to a large extent used by middle-class students with mediocre grades but high educational aspirations.

Chapter 6 demonstrates that Taiwanese higher education since the 1940s has been expanding quickly, but the expansion was not linear. During the 1970s, in an attempt to meet the economy's demand for skilled labor, national constraints were imposed on the relative share of academic secondary education and on the expansion of academic tertiary institutions. During this decade, inequalities between social strata increased and then declined after restrictions were lifted and the expansion of academic education resumed. In addition, social inequality in the odds of attending the more selective four-year institutions increased by comparison to two-year colleges.

The volume's final chapter on diversified higher education systems (Chapter 7) presents an examination of changes in higher education in the United States. Unfettered by strong governmental regulation, U.S. higher education has expanded dramatically and in multiple directions. This expansion has solidified the diversified character of the higher education system and established a strong vocational component. Social-class differences have remained stable across cohorts. Students from more privileged families continue to have an advantage in all educational transitions, from eligibility to higher education to entry into elite colleges and universities. Although the disparities between social strata are reduced after controlling for academic achievement, they are still substantial and persist over time. In contrast to the stability of social-class differences, women and African Americans have made substantial inroads in access to higher education.

Binary Systems

The volume begins its examination of binary higher education systems with Chapter 8 on Britain, where increasing enrollment in higher education has increased opportunities for all individuals since the late 1980s. A comparison of two cohorts immediately prior to this period (from the late 1970s and the late 1980s) shows some lessening of inequality in eligibility for lower tertiary levels but no change in inequality of upper tertiary eligibility or of postsecondary qualifications attained. For the cohort entering higher education in the late 1980s, although service-class children maintained their advantage, children from unskilled or semiskilled manual origins made some gains relative to children from skilled manual origins. Perhaps the most dramatic change between these two cohorts was the complete disappearance of the male advantage in eligibility for upper tertiary education and in postsecondary attainment conditional on eligibility.

In France (Chapter 9), the decrease in social inequality in attending tertiary education, characteristic of the first half of the twentieth century, stopped since WWII and was followed by an increase in social inequality for the cohorts born in the late 1960s. Although the rise in the rate of tertiary education was impressive, it did not lead to a reduction in social inequalities. One explanation for persistent inequality of access to higher education in France is that the rise in the completion rate of secondary education was partly achieved through the creation of vocational *baccalauréat*, which may have diverted many working-class students from higher education to direct entry into the labor force. In addition, inequality of access to the *grandes écoles* has increased because these elite institutions expanded at a much slower pace than the university system.

The authors of Chapter 10 identify a pattern of declining effects of social background on attainment within German's segmented higher education system over time. These effects occurred prior to 1980 and have leveled off subsequently. These changes reflect declining effects of social background on secondary education (*Arbitur*) and completion occurring at rates greater than the increasing effects of social background on those making successful post-*Arbitur* transitions into higher education.

Contradictory pressures in the Netherlands (Chapter 11) were found to lead to stability in inequality of higher education attainment: an expanding risk set may contribute to increased social selectivity, even as education policies aim to reduce inequality of access. While the authors expected these pressures to operate differently at different levels of the Netherlands's binary system of postsecondary education, this was not the case. In general, patterns of inequality were stable over the last two decades of the twentieth century. These findings were reconciled with previous research on the Netherlands through presentation of unconditional models in which inequality *did* decline significantly. Most of the change has occurred at the transition between lower secondary and senior vocational education, so the conditional inequality parameters for higher education attendance were not affected.

Chapter 12 reveals increasing effects of social background on Russian higher education in the post-Soviet era. The growing significance of parental education and occupation on all higher education outcomes modeled occurred as the baseline odds of completing secondary education decreased. Prior to this change, however, the Soviet system was characterized by a bottleneck limiting access at the postsecondary transition point.

Chapter 13 provides findings on the binary higher education system in Switzerland, which experienced a gradual expansion of both levels from the late 1960s to the late 1980s. While this expansion was associated with the gradual differentiation of the institutions of tertiary vocational education, the changes were not related to variation in the effects of social background on either higher education enrollment or completion. The effects of parental education were particularly strong determinants of higher education access. Not only were social background effects stable across cohorts in Switzerland, but the effects of gender and the underrepresentation of women in higher education also remained relatively constant.

Unified and Other Systems

The final three chapters of the book focus on unified and other systems of higher education. Chapter 14 focuses on changes in the higher education system in Australia involving reorganization of institutions into a comprehensive national system, changes in financing, and increasing enrollments. These changes have been associated with declining class-based inequality in attendance. Specifically, the effect of parental occupation on higher education participation has decreased for the latest cohorts.

Chapter 15 shows that despite substantial reform efforts, higher education in the Czech Republic has been slow to change. Higher education expansion has not kept pace with rising educational aspirations, nor with substantial increases in the number of secondary graduates. Tertiary education remains a unified system with essentially no lower tier. As a result, the transition from secondary to tertiary education has become extremely competitive, and the offspring of semiskilled and unskilled workers have been the big losers in this competition: inequality between this group and all other class categories has increased significantly during the postcommunist period.

Chapter 16, the book's concluding chapter, examines Italy, a country with one of the lowest levels of higher education attainment in the industrialized world. While higher education has expanded, such growth has not occurred as spectacularly as in other countries. Furthermore, university enrollments have grown faster than the number of degrees conferred. Many more Italians start tertiary-level programs than complete them. The exclusively academic nature of postsecondary education (modified only in the late 1990s) accounts for this discrepancy. Italian universities do not cater to weaker students and thereby tend to reduce the opportunities for higher education of individuals originating from lower socioeconomic strata. Class inequalities in the odds of attaining a university degree decrease progressively, but the effects of parental education, which are stronger than those of class, have been stable and have even increased.

Overall, the chapters provide a detailed description of how variation in expansion, differentiation, and privatization shape access to higher education in advanced countries. It is only through understanding these institutional effects that effective education policy and social theory can be developed.

PART I: DIVERSIFIED SYSTEMS

CHAPTER TWO

Israel: Diversification, Expansion, and Inequality in Higher Education

Yossi Shavit, Tel Aviv University

Hanna Ayalon, Tel Aviv University

Svetlana Chachashvili-Bolotin, Tel Aviv University

Gila Menahem, Tel Aviv University

INTRODUCTION

During the 1980s and 1990s, the Israeli system of higher education underwent a radical change. The number of degree-granting institutions increased from about 10 to over 80, and the number of undergraduate students increased from about 50,000 to over 120,000. Until the late 1990s, the vast majority of students attended one of six research universities. The expansion was achieved primarily through the establishment of less selective, nonresearch colleges that specialized in undergraduate education. New types of colleges—public, private, and extensions of foreign universities—changed higher education from a unified system to a diversified one. The purpose of the paper is to evaluate the consequences of the transformation for the stratification of admissions to different institutions of higher education and the odds of obtaining an academic degree (BA or equivalent). Specifically, we ask the following empirical questions:

1. Did the reform increase individuals' odds of attending institutions of higher education, or did it simply enable the system to meet the growing demand caused by immigration and endogenous demographic growth?

2. Did the reform reduce social selection in access to higher education in general and to the universities in particular?

3. How did the expansion of higher education affect the social stratification of graduation?

We begin by describing the education system in Israel and the reform of higher education during the late 1980s and the 1990s. We then draw on theory and previous research to formulate hypotheses concerning the consequences of the reform for stratification in higher education. Next, we describe the data and variables, present the findings, and conclude with a brief discussion of the results.

THE ISRAELI EDUCATION SYSTEM

At the age of 12, after a year in preschool and six years in primary school, Israeli children proceed to middle schools (grades 7 through 9) and secondary schools (grades 10 through 12). Students in secondary school can choose between the academic track, which prepares them for the matriculation ("bagrut") exams and certificate required for admission by most institutions of higher education, and the technical track, which combines academic and vocational training—with only a proportion of students taking the matriculation exams. In recent years this portion has been rising, and now about 20% of students obtain the certificate.

THE UNIVERSITIES

During the late 1980s and the 1990s, Israeli higher education went through a radical transformation. Until the late 1980s, the system consisted primarily of six universities regulated by the national Council for Higher Education (CHE). The CHE, chaired by the Minister of Education, accredits the programs of all institutions of higher education, and its operational body, the Planning and Budgeting Committee, regulates the government's financial allocations to these institutions. Yogev (2000) described the universities as catering to different segments of the population and offering different clusters of academic programs. The main distinctions were between core institutions (the Technion, the Hebrew University, and Tel Aviv University) and the peripheral ones (the University of Haifa, Ben Gurion University, and Bar-Ilan University) serving specific populations: residents of the northern and southern peripheries and religious Jews. For all their differences, the six universities share several important similarities. First, they are subject to CHE regulations and funded largely from the same national budget. Second, their institutional structure is similar in that their management is primarily academic rather than administrative or political. Third, with some small differences, their processes of selection and admission into the various fields of study are similar across institutions. Finally, their degrees are about equally valued in the labor market and by the general public.

Two universities differ from the six. The Open University offers BA and BSc programs in numerous fields of study; since 1996, it has also offered graduate training. However, only 10% of its students, compared with 70% in the other universities, complete the course of studies and obtain a degree (Israel Central Bureau of Statistics 2001). The Weizmann Institute of Science offers graduate and postgraduate training in the physical and life sciences, and it enrolls under 1,000 students per year. Several teacher training institutions and a handful of smaller colleges have been operating in addition to the universities, but until the reform did not offer academic degrees.

Admission to the six universities hinges on the matriculation certificate, and applicants are required to take a national psychometric test. Admission to specific departments and faculties is determined by a weighted average of scores of the matriculation certificate and the psychometric test. The Open University admits everyone.

THE TRANSFORMATION

In less than a decade, Israeli higher education in the 1990s was transformed from a centralized, compact, and organizationally homogenous system into a diverse one in which numerous forms of institutions compete for students. The transformation began in the late 1970s with the academization of the teacher training institutions and gained momentum in the early 1990s. The decision to expand the colleges and give academic accreditation to their undergraduate programs was made by the CHE during the early 1990s, in anticipation of a growing demand for higher education owing to massive immigration from the former Soviet Union, a significant increase in the number of high-school graduates, and rising demand for university graduates in the labor market (Guri-Rosenblit 1993).

The growing demand for higher education was already apparent in the 1970s, but the expansion of higher education did not start until the mid-1980s. Wishing to avoid the formation and accreditation of colleges that might compete with the universities over resources, the CHE opted initially for the expansion of undergraduate studies in smaller universities (Yogev 2000). When this did not meet the growing demand and public pressures for further expansion mounted, the CHE decided to expand the "second tier" of higher education. This was the early 1990s, and by then the universities, which had previously opposed the formation of new institutions, supported the expansion of the colleges hoping that they would admit students of lower scholastic achievements thereby enabling the veteran institutions to maintain higher standards and social selection.

The expansion of higher education was implemented through a three-pronged set of reforms introduced during the early 1990s. First, the CHE voted to expand public colleges (Israel CHE 1993). Second, it encouraged the formation of private colleges (Volansky 1996). Third, foreign universities were authorized to establish extensions in Israel (Rubinstein 1993). Between 1994 and 1998, the number of colleges and universities operating in Israel quadrupled from about 21 to 84. Of these, 49 were local and 35 were extensions of overseas universities.

Like the veteran universities, the public and private colleges require applicants to hold a matriculation certificate, and some also demand the psychometric test, but their admission criteria are lower than those of the universities. Extensions of foreign universities are even less strict, and some require neither a matriculation certificate nor psychometric test scores. The private colleges and some of the extensions offer programs in fields of study that are in high demand, such as law and business administration. They cater mainly to students who cannot meet the admissions requirements of the universities but can afford to pay much higher tuition.

The 1990s were years of massive immigration, especially from the former Soviet Union. Nearly 400,000 immigrants arrived in 1990–91, and about 70,000 in each of the following years. Overall, nearly a million immigrants arrived during the 1990s, representing about 20% of Israel's population. The educational attainments of Russian immigrants who had arrived in earlier decades were higher than the Israeli average, and a large proportion of their children sought higher education. When mass immigration began in 1989, policy makers assumed that the new Russian immigrants would also demand higher education in large numbers. The expansion of higher education was driven, in part, by anticipatory policies intended to accommodate the pending demand by new Russian immigrants. As it turned out, their demand was much lighter than expected.

Between the mid-1980s and 2000, the number of undergraduates rose from about 50,000 to 126,900. The expansion was due in part to rapid demographic growth, but even when adjusted for demography the growth was impressive. Between 1985 and 2002, age-adjusted enrollment rates in all types of institutions doubled from just over 20% to over 40%, while the cohort proportion attending universities increased only slightly from about 20% to 22%. Thus, universities expanded just enough to accommodate demographic growth, and it was the expansion of colleges that enabled the overall increase in attendance rates. Whereas in 1986 about 90% of all undergraduate students attended universities, in 2000 about 50% attended other types of higher education.

To summarize, during the late 1980s and the 1990s, Israeli higher education expanded dramatically through the creation and accreditation of regional and private colleges, the academization of teacher training colleges, and the proliferation of foreign extensions. The added capacity of these new institutions more than doubled student enrollment within a decade. The universities expanded just enough to accommodate demographic growth, but the system did more than accommodate the large demographic expansion and increased the opportunity for higher education by 50%.

THEORY AND HYPOTHESES

What were the consequences of these changes for the stratification of tertiary education by gender, class, and ethnicity? We know from previous research that broadening educational opportunities can raise educational attainment rates among working-class and minority students without necessarily reducing inequalities. When education systems expand, opportunities are created not just for the less privileged social classes but for everyone. Students of privileged social origins do better in school on the average, and are better prepared than those less privileged to take advantage of new educational opportunities. As argued by Raftery and Hout in their "Maximally Maintained Inequality" (MMI) hypothesis (Raftery and Hout 1993), educational expansion does not reduce educational inequalities between classes. The MMI hypothesis received support from several studies (e.g., Mare 1981; Smith and Cheung 1986; Shavit and Blossfeld 1993) showing that educational inequalities persist despite the expansion of education systems.

The MMI hypothesis may be particularly poignant with regard to higher education where students and parents of different classes vary considerably in their familiarity with the system (McDonough 1997). Members of privileged groups have a better understanding of the availability and stratification of the alternatives provided in higher education and a better capacity to manipulate the system to meet their goals. This provides them with an advantage in the competition over emerging educational opportunities. In the case at hand, the MMI hypothesis predicts that the expansion of higher education would raise enrollment rates among all ethnic and social groups while retaining the pattern of inequality between them. The findings of Bolotin-Chachashvili, Shavit, and Ayalon (2002), who examined the effects of the recent expansion of Israeli higher education on ethnic inequalities in attendance rates and found that as the system expanded all ethnic groups increased their enrollment rates, provide some support for the MMI hypothesis in this context. However, increases were most pronounced among the more privileged. Because of data limitations, Bolotin-Chachashvili, Shavit, and Ayalon were not able to distinguish between universities and colleges.

The MMI hypothesis has also been criticized recently for disregarding qualitative differences within education systems. Following this criticism, Breen and Jonsson (2000) and Lucas (2001) developed educational transition models that deal with both quantitative and qualitative educational stratification. Lucas argued that when quantitative equality is reached at some level of education, attention should be paid to qualitative inequalities within that level. Ayalon and Shavit (2004) further argued that qualitative differentiation enables education systems to reduce inequalities along the quantitative dimension because qualitative differences replace quantitative ones as the basis for educational selection. Analysis of reforms in Israeli matriculation examinations showed that when a given level of education is tracked, socioeconomic inequalities in the odds of its attainment may decline while qualitative inequalities persist or even increase.

Qualitative differentiation is of special value in analyzing expansion in higher education systems, particularly in a comparative framework, because expansion can be implemented in different ways. It is reasonable to assume that the effect of the expansion of higher education on inequality in enrollment depends on the characteristics of the new institutions. As noted, the expansion in Israel was accomplished largely through the establishment of degree-granting colleges and the upgrading of colleges to degree-granting status. Being academically less demanding and less prestigious than the veteran universities, the colleges can be defined as a second tier of higher education. Still, these colleges provide an opportunity to obtain an academic degree, and as such they probably attract less able members of privileged groups who are unable to meet the scholastic demands of the veteran universities.

Hypotheses
1. Inequalities between social strata in the odds of obtaining postsecondary and higher education declined during the 1990s.
2. At the same time, the odds of attending universities did not change over time.
3. Inequalities between social strata in these odds were also stable.
4. Finally, the privileged classes are more likely than less privileged ones to attend universities rather than colleges.

DATA

We obtained survey data from two random samples of men and women aged 25–45. The samples were interviewed by telephone during the summer of 2001 and during the winter of 2002.[1] Each survey yielded approximately 1,500 complete questionnaires for a total of 2,952 respondents. The samples were restricted to native Israelis and to immigrants who arrived by the age of 14. The 25–45 age group was chosen because its members include the vast majority of men and women who attended and graduated from Israeli colleges and universities during the 1980s and 1990s, just before and since the reforms of the 1990s. The questionnaires in the two surveys were similar: respondents were questioned about their educational histories with special focus on postsecondary education, current employment status, and social background.

VARIABLES

Our analysis adheres closely to the guidelines agreed upon by the team of the comparative project at the Prague meeting. We studied change in higher educational attainment across three birth cohorts: 1956–63, 1964–70, and 1971–77. These cohorts would have completed secondary school in

1974–81, 1982–88, and 1989–95, and entered postsecondary education during the late 1970s through the early 1980s, in the 1980s through the early 1990s, and during the 1990s.

The dependent variables of the study were as follows.

- *Eligibility for higher education.* In Israel eligibility is determined by the matriculation certificate. This variable was coded 1 for respondents who reported that they were eligible for the matriculation diploma and 0 otherwise. As seen in Table 2.1, the proportion of those eligible is nearly 60%. This figure is higher than other estimates of eligibility in comparable cohorts. Shavit, Ayalon, and Kurleander (2002) analyzed matriculation rates for cohorts born in the 1960s. They employed data drawn from the merged file of the 1983 and 1995 censuses and estimated this proportion for men and women born between 1974 and 1978 at about 50%. Because we do not find large upward biases in other measures of education, we suspect that this one results from exaggerated self-reported matriculation rates.
- *Postsecondary education.* This dummy variable was coded 1 for respondents who attended any form of postsecondary education. Table 2.1 shows that nearly 53.6% of the sample did so.
- *Attending a BA-granting institution.* This variable was coded 1 for respondents who attended a tertiary educational program in a university, a public or private academic college, including an extension of a foreign university or college, or the Open University.
- *Attending a university.* This dummy variable was coded 1 for respondents who attended higher education in one of the six universities (excluding the Open University).[2]
- *Obtaining a BA.* This variable was coded 1 for all respondents who obtained a BA, BSc, BEd (Bachelor of Education), or equivalent degree.

The independent variables were as follows.

- *Male.* A dummy variable was coded 1 for men. As seen in Table 2.1, women were overrepresented in the sample, comprising about 56% of respondents.
- *Father's class.* This variable was coded on a six-category version of the EGP classification (Erikson and Goldthorpe 1992; Yaish 2000). Where we tested for the effects of interaction between father's class and cohort class, it was coded as a dummy variable representing classes I and II.
- *Parental education.* This variable measured the attainment of the parent with the highest education. The variable was coded on a four-category version of the CASMIN Educational Schema (Müller et al. 1989). In tests for interactions between parental education and the cohort, parental education was coded as a dummy variable representing tertiary parental education.

TABLE 2.1
Percent distributions of dependent and independent variables by cohort

Variables	BIRTH COHORTS 1956–63	1964–70	1971–77	Total
Matriculation diploma	48.1	61.5	67.4	59.9
Any postsecondary education	43.4	51.7	61.7	53.6
Any BA-granting institution[a]	39.2	44.1	55.7	47.6
University	21.5	24.1	26.0	24.2
Private college	3.3	6.3	7.7	6.0
Public college	12.6	12.8	20.0	15.7
Males	44.2	42.4	45.0	43.9
Father's class (EGP class designations in parents)				
Higher-grade professionals & administrators (I)	7.9	10.3	12.5	10.4
Lower-grade professionals & administrators (II)	4.7	6.8	10.1	7.5
Routine nonmanual workers (III)	11.2	11.9	12.9	12.1
Employers & self-employed (IV)	28.1	34.2	28.5	30.1
Skilled blue-collar workers and supervisors (V, VI)	33.6	25.4	27.0	28.4
Unskilled manual workers (VII)	14.6	11.4	8.9	11.4
Parental Education				
Primary	53.7	34.8	20.9	34.4
Secondary	27.9	37.3	42.8	36.9
Nonacademic tertiary	4.9	9.2	10.2	8.4
Academic tertiary	13.5	18.7	26.1	20.3
Ethnicity				
2nd-generation native Jews	8.3	14.9	23.1	16.5
Middle Eastern Jews	21.1	18.4	14.6	17.7
North African Jews	21.0	19.3	15.4	18.1
Arab	25.3	21.9	20.1	22.1
Ashkenazim	24.3	25.5	26.7	25.6
Secondary school academic track	52.5	62.1	66.3	61.0
n of cases	866	900	1185	2951

[a] Including the Open University, which was attended by about 2% of the sample. The category "University" does not include the Open University.

- *Ethnicity* distinguished by five ethnic categories: Ashkenazim (Jews of European origins), second-generation native Jews, Jews of Middle Eastern origins, Jews originating from North Africa, and Palestinian Arabs.[3]
- *Secondary School Track*. A dummy variable was coded 1 for respondents who attended secondary education in an academic track. It was coded 0 for those who attended nonacademic tracks and for those who did not report a track. The latter constitute 8.7% of the sample and, ceteris paribus, do not differ significantly from technical track students with regard to any of the dependent variables in the model.

RESULTS

Table 2.1, where we present cohort differences in the variables, shows that matriculation rate increased sharply, as did the proportion of students attending an academic track at the secondary school level. The proportion attending a BA program also increased, especially during the 1990s (between the second and third cohorts), reflecting the expansion of higher education. The proportion attending university increased slightly during the 1990s while the proportion attending public and private colleges increased sharply.

In Israel, as in other economically advanced countries, there has been an expansion of the professional, managerial, and technical classes and a decline in the number of manual workers as a percentage of the population. This change is reflected in the distributions of the father's class across the three cohorts. Similarly, we see an improvement in the educational distribution of parents. From the point of view of ethnicity there is an increase in the proportion of second-generation native Jewish parents and a decline in the share of most other categories. The share of Ashkenazim also increased somewhat, reflecting the immigration from the former Soviet Union in recent decades.

MATRICULATION—ELIGIBILITY
FOR HIGHER EDUCATION

Table 2.2 presents the analysis of eligibility for higher education. In this and all subsequent tables we present three models: Model 1 includes cohort, gender, father's class, and parental education; Model 2 adds secondary school track to these variables; Model 3 adds ethnicity and any statistically significant interactions of cohort with other independent variables.

In Model 1 of Table 2.2, the significant positive effect of the youngest cohort reflects the increase in matriculation eligibility during the 1990s. The inclusion of secondary school track reduced the cohort effects, implying that the increase in matriculation eligibility was due, at least partly, to changes in tracking and its effect on matriculation rates. As seen in Table 2.1, cohort proportions attending academic rather than technological tracks increased during the 1990s. The effect of gender, which is negative and significant in the first model, declines and loses its statistical significance after the inclusion of track. This indicates that the advantage of women in

TABLE 2.2
Logit regressions of obtaining the matriculation certificate (eligibility for higher education)

Independent variables	1 B	1 exp(B)	2 B	2 exp(B)	3 B	3 exp(B)
Cohort (Reference: 1956–63)						
1971–77	0.34*	1.40	0.24	1.27	0.73*	2.07
1964–70	0.18	1.20	0.13	1.14	0.39*	1.48
Male	−0.37*	0.69	−0.12	0.89	−0.07	0.93
Father's class (Reference: skilled manual)						
Higher-grade professionals & administrators	0.21	1.24	0.01	1.01	−0.01	0.99
Lower-grade professionals & administrators	0.40	1.49	0.26	1.30	0.30	1.36
Routine nonmanual workers	−0.06	0.94	−0.01	0.99	−0.08	0.92
Employers & self-employed	−0.21	0.81	−0.12	0.88	−0.18	0.83
Unskilled manual workers	−0.66*	0.51	−0.72*	0.49	−0.67*	0.51
Parental education (Reference: secondary)						
Primary	−0.84*	0.43	−0.86*	0.42	−0.53*	0.59
Nonacademic tertiary	0.56*	1.75	0.44*	1.55	0.35	1.42
Academic tertiary	1.36*	3.89	1.22*	3.39	1.08*	2.95
Academic track at secondary school			1.51*	4.52	1.99*	7.34
Ethnicity (Reference: Ashkenazim)						
2nd-generation native Jews					−0.41*	0.66
Middle Eastern Jews					0.09	1.10
North African Jews					−0.53*	0.59
Arab					−1.11*	0.33
Interactions						
Academic Track × Cohort 1971–77					−0.62*	0.54
Academic Track × Cohort 1964–70					−0.37	0.69
Constant	0.64*	1.90	−0.27	0.76	−0.29	0.75
−2 log likelihood	2,626		2,402		2,330	
n of cases			2,290			

NOTE: None of the following interactions was significant at any conventional level: cohort × father's class, cohort × parental education, cohort × ethnicity, cohort × male.

*Significant at $p < 0.05$.

matriculation eligibility stems mainly from their overrepresentation in the academic track. The effect of father's class is limited to the contrast between the unskilled and skilled manual classes. Members of the latter are about twice as likely as those of the former to obtain the certificate. As expected, parental education increases the odds of matriculation. In the third model, where ethnicity and the interaction between track and cohort are added to the equation, we can see the marked advantage of Ashkenazim over all other groups except those of Middle Eastern origins whose matriculation rates, ceteris paribus, do not differ significantly from those of Ashkenazim. The main effects of the two younger cohorts and the negative interactions with track indicate that there was stability in the odds of matriculation among academic track students and an increase among technical track students. This increase was due to the academization of technical secondary education during the 1990s (Ayalon and Shavit 2004). We tested all two-way interactions between cohort and the other independent variables and found none to be significant.

POSTSECONDARY EDUCATION

Tables 2.3a and 2.3b present unconditional and conditional logit regressions of attending any postsecondary education program. As seen, the effect of the youngest cohort is significant and positive in both unconditional and conditional models. This pattern reflects both the increase in matriculation rates and the expansion of postsecondary education during the 1990s.

The effects of gender and its interactions with cohort indicate that in the oldest cohort, men had higher odds for postsecondary education, but their advantage declined and was eliminated by the youngest cohort. Father's class affected postsecondary attendance but its effect was limited to the difference between the class of professionals and administrators vis-à-vis all other classes. Adding track to the model does not substantially change the effects of either father's class or parental education.

Tables 2.3a and 2.3b show a positive interaction between parental tertiary education and cohort. In the oldest cohort, the effect of parental education was weak and irregular in both the conditional and unconditional analyses. However, the effects of parental tertiary education show a significant and substantial increase by the second cohort, followed by a slight decline by the third. These results suggest that the expansion of higher

TABLE 2.3A
Logit regressions of entering postsecondary education (unconditional)

Independent variables	1 B	1 exp(B)	2 B	2 exp(B)	3 B	3 exp(B)
Cohort (Reference: 1956–63)						
1971–77	0.37*	1.45	0.26*	1.29	0.47*	1.60
1964–70	0.10	1.10	0.00	1.00	−0.05	0.96
Male	−0.08	0.92	0.20*	1.22	0.57*	1.78
Father's class (Reference: Skilled manual)						
Higher-grade professionals & administrators	0.62*	1.86	0.58*	1.78	0.52*	1.68
Lower-grade professionals & administrators	0.39*	1.48	0.25	1.28	0.27	1.31
Routine nonmanual workers	−0.11	0.89	−0.09	0.91	−0.15	0.86
Employers & self-employed	−0.19	0.82	−0.10	0.90	−0.17	0.84
Unskilled manual workers	−0.31*	0.73	−0.04	0.96	0.00	1.00
Parental education (Reference: Secondary)						
Primary	−0.95*	0.39	−0.73*	0.48	−0.37*	0.69
Nonacademic tertiary	0.78*	2.18	0.63*	1.88	−0.17	0.84
Academic tertiary	0.88*	2.40	0.43*	1.53	−0.40	0.67
Academic track at secondary school			0.56*	1.74	0.69*	1.99
Matriculation			2.00*	7.39	1.96*	7.11
Ethnicity (Reference: Ashkenazim)						
2nd-generation native Jews			−0.02	0.98	−0.04	0.96
Middle Eastern Jews			−0.36*	0.70	−0.39*	0.67
North African Jews			−0.25	0.78	−0.25	0.78
Arab			−1.34*	0.26	−1.37*	0.26
Interactions:						
Male × Cohort 1971–77					−0.59*	0.56
Male × Cohort 1964–70					−0.23	0.79
Parents' tertiary ed × 1971–77					0.74*	2.09
Parents' tertiary ed × 1964–70					0.94*	2.55
Constant	0.14	1.16	−1.54*	0.21	−1.33*	0.26
−2 log likelihood	2,753		2,302		2,218	
n of cases			2,290			

NOTE: None of the following interactions was significant: cohort × father's class, cohort × ethnicity, cohort × academic track.
*Significant at $p < 0.05$.

TABLE 2.3B
Logit regressions of entering postsecondary education (conditional on matriculation certificate)

Independent variables	1 B	1 exp(B)	2 B	2 exp(B)	3 B	3 exp(B)
Cohort (Reference: 1956–63)						
1971–77	0.41*	0.66	0.42*	0.65	0.58*	1.79
1964–70	0.01	0.66	0.00	0.65	−0.06	0.94
Male	0.02	1.02	0.15	1.16	0.64*	1.90
Father's class (Reference: Skilled manual)						
Higher-grade professionals & administrators	0.58*	1.78	0.51	1.67	0.53*	1.69
Lower-grade professionals & administrators	0.30	1.35	0.22	1.24	0.22	1.24
Routine nonmanual workers	−0.14	0.87	−0.15	0.86	−0.19	0.83
Employers & self-employed	−0.12	0.88	−0.10	0.91	−0.15	0.86
Unskilled manual workers	0.05	1.05	−0.03	0.97	0.02	1.02
Parental education (Reference: Secondary)						
Primary	−0.50*	0.61	−0.56*	0.57	−0.25	0.78
Nonacademic tertiary	0.66*	1.93	0.62*	1.85	0.60*	1.83
Academic tertiary	0.44*	1.55	0.38*	1.47	0.31	1.37
Academic track at secondary school			0.73*	2.07	0.86*	2.35
Ethnicity (Reference: Ashkenazim)						
2nd-generation native Jews					−0.09	0.91
Middle Eastern Jews					−0.52*	0.59
North African Jews					−0.22	0.80
Arab					−1.31*	0.27
Interactions						
Male × Cohort 1971–77					−0.71*	0.49
Male × Cohort 1964–70					−0.43	0.65
Parents' tertiary ed × 1971–77					0.87*	2.39
Parents' tertiary ed × 1964–70					1.05*	2.85
Constant	0.81*	2.25	0.26	1.29	0.49	1.63
−2 log likelihood	1,526		1,502		1,449	
n of cases			1,423			

NOTE: None of the following interactions was significant: cohort × father's class, cohort × ethnicity, cohort × academic track.
*Significant at $p < 0.05$.

education during the 1990s may have halted, and possibly reversed, a trend toward growing inequalities in tertiary education between strata.

HIGHER EDUCATION (BA-GRANTING INSTITUTIONS)

Tables 2.4a and 2.4b (on pages 54–55) present logit regressions of attending any BA-granting institution. As seen in the first column of Table 2.4a, the odds of attending such an institution are largest in the youngest cohort. After controlling for matriculation and track and after conditioning the analysis on matriculation, cohort differences are no longer significant though still quite large: the youngest cohort is 31% more likely than the oldest to attend higher education.

Among holders of matriculation certificates (Table 2.4b), men were at an advantage in the oldest cohort (column 3) but the gender gap declined in the second cohort and was reversed slightly by the third. This change could reflect stages in the expansion of the colleges. The veteran colleges offered fields of study that catered mainly to males (e.g., engineering), while the new colleges added many programs that usually attract women (e.g., social sciences).

The effects of father's class are similar to those seen in Tables 2.3a and 2.3b: class differences are limited to the contrast between the two service classes (higher- and lower-grade professionals and administrators) vis-à-vis all other classes. The effects of parental tertiary education are also similar to the pattern seen earlier: weak in the oldest cohort, largest in the middle cohort, and showing decline, this time more dramatically, in the youngest cohort.

As seen in Column 3, the conditional odds of higher education are significantly larger for the youngest cohort. Net of the other variables and interaction terms in the model, this cohort is 70% (the exponent of its effect is 1.70) more likely than the oldest one to attend BA-granting institutions.

UNIVERSITIES

Tables 2.5a and 2.5b (on pages 56–57) present logit regressions of attending a university. Focusing on the third model in each of the two tables, we find no change in the main effects of cohort on the odds of attending university. Among holders of matriculation certificates (Table 2.5b) men of the

TABLE 2.4A
Logit regressions of attending any BA-granting institution (unconditional)

Independent variables	1 B	1 exp(B)	2 B	2 exp(B)	3 B	3 exp(B)
Cohort (Reference: 1956–63)						
1971–77	0.31*	1.37	0.19	1.20	0.21	1.23
1964–70	−0.03	0.97	−0.16	0.86	−0.32*	0.73
Male	−0.17	0.85	0.08	1.08*	0.14	1.15
Father's class (Reference: Skilled manual)						
Higher-grade professionals & administrators	0.55*	1.74	0.53*	1.69	0.50*	1.64
Lower-grade professionals & administrators	0.57*	1.77	0.48*	1.62	0.52*	1.69
Routine nonmanual workers	−0.06	0.94	−0.03	0.98	−0.07	0.93
Employers & self-employed	−0.19	0.83	−0.09	0.91	−0.14	0.87
Unskilled manual workers	−0.34*	0.71	−0.06	0.94	0.00	1.00
Parental education (Reference: Secondary)						
Primary	−0.77*	0.46	−0.49*	0.62	−0.12	0.89
Nonacademic tertiary	0.65*	1.92	0.49*	1.64	−0.14	0.87
Academic Tertiary	0.90*	2.47	0.49*	1.63	−0.18	0.84
Academic track at secondary school			0.54*	1.71	0.64*	1.90
Matriculation			2.08*	8.01	2.04*	7.65
Ethnicity (Reference: Ashkenazim)						
2nd-generation native Jews					−0.13	0.88
Middle Eastern Jews					−0.39*	0.68
North African Jews					−0.34*	0.72
Arab					−1.31*	0.27
Interactions						
Parents' tertiary ed × 1971–77					0.42	1.52
Parents' tertiary ed × 1964–70					0.85*	2.35
Constant	−0.10	0.90	−1.91*	0.15	−1.57*	0.21
−2 log likelihood	2,807		2,353		2,285	
n of cases			2,290			

NOTE: None of the following interactions was significant: cohort × father's class, cohort × sex, cohort × ethnicity, cohort × academic track.
*Significant at p < 0.05.

TABLE 2.4B
Logit regressions of attending any BA-granting institution (conditional)

Independent variables	1 B	1 exp(B)	2 B	2 exp(B)	3 B	3 exp(B)
Cohort (Reference: 1956–63)						
1971–77	0.26	1.30	0.27	1.31	0.53*	1.70
1964–70	−0.13	0.87	−0.15	0.86	−0.21	0.81
Male	−0.01	0.99	0.10	1.10	0.56*	1.74
Father's class (Reference: Skilled manual)						
Higher-grade professionals & administrators	0.52*	1.68	0.47*	1.60	0.48*	1.61
Lower-grade professionals & administrators	0.42	1.52	0.36	1.43	0.38	1.47
Routine nonmanual workers	−0.08	0.93	−0.08	0.92	−0.11	0.89
Employers & self-employed	−0.14	0.87	−0.12	0.88	−0.17	0.84
Unskilled manual workers	−0.02	0.98	−0.09	0.92	−0.04	0.96
Parental Education (Reference: Secondary)						
Primary	−0.30*	0.74	−0.34*	0.71	−0.04	0.96
Nonacademic tertiary	0.46*	1.58	0.42*	1.53	−0.23	0.79
Academic tertiary	0.50*	1.64	0.45*	1.56	−0.24	0.78
Academic track at secondary school			0.62*	1.87	0.73*	2.08
Ethnicity (Reference: Ashkenazim)						
2nd-generation native Jews					−0.23	0.79
Middle Eastern Jews					−0.51*	0.60
North African Jews					−0.31	0.73
Arab					−1.27*	0.28
Interactions						
Male × Cohort 1971–77					−0.65*	0.52
Male × Cohort 1964–70					−0.37	0.69
Parents' tertiary ed × 1971–77					0.43	1.54
Parents' tertiary ed × 1964–70					0.89*	2.43
Constant	0.55*	1.73	0.07	1.07	0.28	1.33
−2 log likelihood	1,699		1,679		1,631	
n of cases			1,423			

NOTE: None of the following interactions was significant: cohort × father's class, cohort × ethnicity, cohort × academic track, cohort × gender.
*Significant at $p < 0.05$.

TABLE 2.5A
Logit regressions of attending a university (unconditional)

Independent variables	1 B	1 exp(B)	2 B	2 exp(B)	3 B	3 exp(B)
Cohort (Reference: 1956–63)						
1971–77	−0.14	0.87	−0.31*	0.73	−0.06	0.95
1964–70	−0.07	0.93	−0.18	0.83	−0.19	0.83
Male	−0.09	0.92	0.22	1.25	0.92*	2.50
Father's class (Reference: Skilled manual)						
Higher-grade professionals & administrators	0.67*	1.96	0.63*	1.88	0.62*	1.86
Lower-grade professionals & administrators	0.56*	1.74	0.45*	1.57	0.50*	1.64
Routine nonmanual workers	0.00	1.00	0.01	1.01	−0.01	0.99
Employers & self-employed	−0.01	0.99	0.12	1.12	0.08	1.09
Unskilled manual workers	−0.39	0.68	−0.17	0.85	−0.15	0.86
Parental education (Reference: Secondary)						
Primary	−0.68*	0.51	−0.36*	0.70	−0.07	0.94
Nonacademic tertiary	0.79*	2.20	0.64*	1.90	−0.11	0.90
Academic tertiary	1.02*	2.78	0.67*	1.96	−0.10	0.90
Academic track at secondary school			1.06*	2.89	1.17*	3.21
Matriculation			2.40*	10.98	2.37*	10.66
Ethnicity (Reference: Ashkenazim)						
2nd-generation native Jews					−0.30	0.74
Middle Eastern Jews					−0.52*	0.60
North African Jews					−0.56*	0.57
Arab					−1.33*	0.26
Interactions						
Male × 1971–77					−0.93*	0.39
Male × 1964–70					−0.74*	0.48
Parents' tertiary ed × 1971–77					0.59*	1.81
Parents' tertiary ed × 1964–70					0.96*	2.60
Constant	−1.27*	0.28	−4.02*	0.02	−3.78*	0.02
−2 log likelihood	2,278		1,945		1,887	
n of cases			2,290			

NOTE: None of the following interactions was significant: cohort × father's class, cohort × ethnicity, cohort × academic track.
*Significant at $p < 0.05$.

TABLE 2.5B
Logit regressions of attending a university (conditional)

Independent variables	1 B	1 exp(B)	2 B	2 exp(B)	3 B	3 exp(B)
Cohort (Reference: 1956–63)						
1971–77	−0.29*	0.75	−0.30*	0.74	−0.07	0.93
1964–70	−0.12	0.88	−0.14	0.87	−0.13	0.88
Male	0.07	1.07	0.23*	1.26	0.98*	2.66
Father's class (Reference: Skilled manual)						
Higher-grade professionals & administrators	0.71*	2.03	0.65*	1.91	0.65*	1.92
Lower-grade professionals & administrators	0.55*	1.73	0.47*	1.60	0.50*	1.65
Routine nonmanual workers	−0.03	0.97	−0.05	0.95	−0.06	0.94
Employers & self-employed	0.07	1.07	0.11	1.11	0.08	1.09
Unskilled manual workers	−0.11	0.90	−0.20	0.82	−0.20	0.82
Parental Education (Reference: Secondary)						
Primary	−0.21	0.81	−0.28	0.76	−0.02	0.98
Nonacademict tertiary	0.65*	1.91	0.61*	1.84	−0.14	0.87
Academic tertiary	0.68*	1.97	0.62*	1.86	−0.16	0.85
Academic track at secondary school			1.09*	2.97	1.19*	3.30
Ethnicity (Reference: Ashkenazim)						
2nd-generation native Jews					−0.24	0.78
Middle Eastern Jews					−0.50*	0.61
North African Jews					−0.59*	0.55
Arab					−1.23*	0.29
Interactions						
Male × 1971–77					−1.01*	0.36
Male × 1964–70					−0.78*	0.46
Parents' tertiary ed × 1971–77					0.63*	1.87
Parents' tertiary ed × 1964–70					0.89*	2.45
Constant	−0.77*	0.46	−1.65*	0.19	−1.46*	0.23
−2 log likelihood	1,784		1,733		1,683	
n of cases			1,423			

NOTE: None of the following interactions was significant: cohort × father's class, cohort × ethnicity, cohort × academic track.
*Significant at $p < 0.05$.

oldest cohort were 2.66 times as likely as women to attend a university. The interactions of cohort with gender and parental tertiary education again reveal the familiar pattern: the male advantage disappeared and inequalities between social strata (indicated by parental education) increased between the first and second cohorts and then declined slightly.

OBTAINING AN UNDERGRADUATE DEGREE

In Tables 2.6a and 2.6b, we model the odds of obtaining a BA. Column 3 in Table 2.6a shows that in the oldest cohort men were nearly 60% more likely than women to obtain a degree, but women's odds of obtaining a BA increased across cohorts while the odds of the men declined. Eventually, the male advantage was reversed: in the youngest cohort, women were significantly more likely to obtain the degree than men. In addition, we find the familiar advantages associated with academic secondary education and of Ashkenazim over other ethnic groups as well as a positive (but nonlinear) effect of parental education.

In Table 2.6b we condition the analysis on a matriculation certificate (columns 1–3) and on attending higher education (column 4). The reversal of gender inequality appears here as well. We also see an increase in the odds of obtaining a BA between the oldest and second cohort, followed by an apparent decline. The latter is probably due to data censoring: among the youngest cohort, some respondents were still working on their degrees at the time of the survey.

SUMMARY AND DISCUSSION

During the 1980s and 1990s, Israeli higher education was transformed from a small, centralized, and homogenous system centered mostly around six research universities into a large and diverse system consisting of scores of institutions. These institutions form two main strata: veteran research universities that are more selective of students, and a multiplicity of public and private colleges and extensions of foreign universities whose scholastic admission requirements are lower. In the course of the transformation, the number of students more than doubled and the odds of attending higher education grew by 50%.

TABLE 2.6A
Logit regressions of obtaining a BA (unconditional)

Independent variables	1 B	1 exp(B)	2 B	2 exp(B)	3 B	3 exp(B)
Cohort (Reference: 1956–63)						
1971–77	−0.15	0.86	−0.30*	0.74	0.26	1.30
1964–70	0.15	1.17	0.10	1.10	0.37*	1.45
Male	−0.50*	0.60	−0.33*	0.72	0.46*	1.59
Father's class (Reference: Skilled manual)						
Higher-grade professionals & administrators	0.31	1.36	0.24	1.27	0.18	1.20
Lower-grade professionals & administrators	−0.19	0.83	−0.35	0.71	−0.36	0.70
Routine nonmanual workers	−0.08	0.92	−0.07	0.94	−0.10	0.90
Employers & self-employed	−0.21	0.81	−0.14	0.87	−0.18	0.84
Unskilled manual workers	−0.41*	0.67	−0.16	0.85	−0.15	0.86
Parental education (Reference: Secondary)						
Primary	−0.62*	0.54	−0.30*	0.74	−0.16	0.86
Nonacademic tertiary	0.78*	2.17	0.64*	1.90	0.54*	1.71
Academic tertiary	0.69*	1.99	0.34*	1.40	0.21	1.24
Academic track at secondary school			0.66*	1.94	0.69*	2.00
Matriculation			1.92*	6.84	1.90*	6.71
Ethnicity (Reference: Ashkenazim)						
2nd-generation native Jews					−0.10	0.91
Middle Eastern Jews					−0.45*	0.64
North African Jews					−0.38*	0.69
Arab					−0.62*	0.54
Interactions						
Male × 1971–77					−1.36*	0.26
Male × 1964–70					−0.64*	0.53
Constant	−0.52*	0.60	−2.42*	0.09	−2.47*	0.08
−2 log likelihood	2,678		2,357		2,280	
n of cases			2,731			

*Significant at $p < 0.05$.

TABLE 2.6B
Logit regressions of obtaining a BA (conditional)

<table>
<tr><th rowspan="3">Independent variables</th><th colspan="8">CONDITIONAL ON</th></tr>
<tr><th colspan="4">OBTAINING A MATRICULATION</th><th colspan="4">ATTENDING COLLEGE OR UNIVERSITY</th></tr>
<tr><th colspan="2">1</th><th colspan="2">2</th><th colspan="2">3</th><th colspan="2">4</th></tr>
<tr><td></td><td>B</td><td>exp(B)</td><td>B</td><td>exp(B)</td><td>B</td><td>exp(B)</td><td>B</td><td>exp(B)</td></tr>
<tr><td>Cohort (Reference: 1956–63)</td><td></td><td></td><td></td><td></td><td></td><td></td><td></td><td></td></tr>
<tr><td>1971–77</td><td>−0.25</td><td>0.78</td><td>−0.25</td><td>0.78</td><td>0.35</td><td>1.42</td><td>0.04</td><td>1.04</td></tr>
<tr><td>1964–70</td><td>0.19</td><td>1.20</td><td>0.19</td><td>1.20</td><td>0.50*</td><td>1.64</td><td>0.63*</td><td>1.88</td></tr>
<tr><td>Male</td><td>−0.31*</td><td>0.73</td><td>−0.31*</td><td>0.73</td><td>0.62*</td><td>1.86</td><td>0.44</td><td>1.56</td></tr>
<tr><td>Father's Class (Reference: Skilled manual)</td><td></td><td></td><td></td><td></td><td></td><td></td><td></td><td></td></tr>
<tr><td>Higher-grade professionals & administrators</td><td>0.11</td><td>1.12</td><td>0.11</td><td>1.12</td><td>0.04</td><td>1.04</td><td>−0.06</td><td>0.94</td></tr>
<tr><td>Lower-grade professionals & administrators</td><td>−0.39</td><td>0.68</td><td>−0.39</td><td>0.68</td><td>−0.42*</td><td>0.66</td><td>−0.65*</td><td>0.52</td></tr>
<tr><td>Routine nonmanual workers</td><td>−0.09</td><td>0.91</td><td>−0.09</td><td>0.91</td><td>−0.14</td><td>0.87</td><td>−0.08</td><td>0.92</td></tr>
<tr><td>Employers & self-employed</td><td>−0.16</td><td>0.85</td><td>−0.16</td><td>0.85</td><td>−0.19</td><td>0.83</td><td>−0.02</td><td>0.98</td></tr>
<tr><td>Unskilled manual workers</td><td>−0.22</td><td>0.80</td><td>−0.22</td><td>0.80</td><td>−0.25</td><td>0.78</td><td>−0.37</td><td>0.69</td></tr>
<tr><td>Parental education (Reference: Secondary)</td><td></td><td></td><td></td><td></td><td></td><td></td><td></td><td></td></tr>
<tr><td>Primary</td><td>−0.09</td><td>0.91</td><td>−0.09</td><td>0.91</td><td>−0.04</td><td>0.96</td><td>−0.03</td><td>0.97</td></tr>
<tr><td>Nonacademic tertiary</td><td>0.62*</td><td>1.86</td><td>0.62*</td><td>1.86</td><td>0.53*</td><td>1.71</td><td>0.30</td><td>1.35</td></tr>
<tr><td>Academic tertiary</td><td>0.40*</td><td>1.50</td><td>0.40*</td><td>1.50</td><td>0.29</td><td>1.34</td><td>0.19</td><td>1.21</td></tr>
<tr><td>Academic track at secondary school</td><td>0.68*</td><td>1.97</td><td>0.68*</td><td>1.97</td><td>0.71*</td><td>2.03</td><td>0.52*</td><td>1.68</td></tr>
<tr><td>Matriculation</td><td></td><td></td><td></td><td></td><td></td><td></td><td></td><td></td></tr>
<tr><td>Ethnicity (Reference: Ashkenazim)</td><td></td><td></td><td></td><td></td><td></td><td></td><td></td><td></td></tr>
<tr><td>2nd-generation native Jews</td><td></td><td></td><td></td><td></td><td>−0.16</td><td>0.85</td><td>−0.18</td><td>0.84</td></tr>
<tr><td>Middle Eastern Jews</td><td></td><td></td><td></td><td></td><td>−0.51*</td><td>0.60</td><td>−0.39*</td><td>0.67</td></tr>
<tr><td>North African Jews</td><td></td><td></td><td></td><td></td><td>−0.35*</td><td>0.71</td><td>−0.35</td><td>0.70</td></tr>
<tr><td>Arab</td><td></td><td></td><td></td><td></td><td>−0.42*</td><td>0.66</td><td>0.04</td><td>1.04</td></tr>
<tr><td>Interactions</td><td></td><td></td><td></td><td></td><td></td><td></td><td></td><td></td></tr>
<tr><td>Male × 1971–77</td><td></td><td></td><td></td><td></td><td>−1.52*</td><td>0.22</td><td>−1.41*</td><td>0.24</td></tr>
<tr><td>Male × 1964–70</td><td></td><td></td><td></td><td></td><td>−0.79*</td><td>0.45</td><td>−0.92*</td><td>0.40</td></tr>
<tr><td>Constant</td><td>−0.60*</td><td>0.55</td><td>−0.60*</td><td>0.55</td><td>−0.68*</td><td>0.50</td><td>0.23</td><td>1.26</td></tr>
<tr><td>−2 log likelihood</td><td colspan="2">1,910</td><td colspan="2">1,883</td><td colspan="2">1,845</td><td colspan="2">1,376</td></tr>
<tr><td>n of cases</td><td colspan="2">1,423</td><td colspan="2"></td><td colspan="2"></td><td colspan="2">1,100</td></tr>
</table>

NOTE: None of the following interactions was significant: cohort × father's class, cohort × ethnicity, cohort × academic track.
*Significant at $p < 0.05$.

As our findings show, during the 1980s, just before the transformation, inequality between categories of parental education in access to higher education was on the rise. This resulted from the growing imbalance between increasing demand for higher education and the restricted capacity of the universities. As demand mounted the universities, rather than expand, raised their admissions criteria; the result was growing social inequality of access through the late 1980s. The expansion of higher education through the creation and accreditation of colleges and foreign extensions reversed this trend. These less selective institutions provided students from less privileged social origins with an alternative to the university, as a result of which inequalities between strata in the odds of attending higher education declined. Social selection in access to the veteran universities remained much higher than it had been before the 1980s, although it did decline slightly and its upward trend may have been halted by the expansion of second-tier higher education. Clearly, these developments are not consistent with the MMI hypothesis, which predicted persistent inequalities in higher education so long as it is not universally attended (Raftery and Hout 1993).

Compared to universities, second-tier institutions were disproportionately attended by students of less privileged social and ethnic origins. Thus, inequalities in access to higher education were replaced by inequalities in the odds of attending elite institutions. It seems that expansion of higher education through stratification enables the system simultaneously to accommodate less privileged social strata that had previously been excluded and allow the universities to maintain exclusivity. These results are consistent with Lucas's Effectively Maintained Inequality hypothesis (2001), and with Ayalon and Shavit's echoing argument (2004) that the differentiation of a given educational level can substitute qualitative inequalities for quantitative ones.

Gender inequalities follow a different but familiar pattern: marked decline and even reversal. During the 1970s men were at a clear advantage, but by the 1990s women were as likely to attend all forms of higher education and even more likely than men to obtain undergraduate degrees. This pattern appears in most economically developed Western countries, as other chapters in this volume bear witness. In these societies, women are no longer educationally disadvantaged relative to men. These days, gender differences are confined to the type, rather than the quantity, of education. Studies of gender inequality in education now focus less on access and more on choice of field of study and type of institution. With regard to the latter, we have found marked gender differences in the relative odds of attending universities rather than colleges. We speculate that these differences stem from gender differences in fields of study. Within the universities, women constitute 56% of entering students and have reached, and even surpassed, parity with men in all fields of study except engineering and the hard sciences. However, women are more likely than men to turn to teaching as a profession, and because most teacher preparation in Israel is done by teachers' colleges, their overrepresentation in colleges is even greater than in the universities.

CHAPTER THREE

Japan: Educational Expansion and Inequality in Access to Higher Education

Hiroshi Ishida, Institute of Social Sciences, University of Tokyo

INTRODUCTION

Japan experienced an expansion of its postsecondary educational system during the latter half of the twentieth century. As in many other industrial nations, enrollment rates in postsecondary institutions jumped dramatically, from less than 10% in the early 1950s to over 50% at the end of the century. The expansion of higher education is one of the major social transformations that took place in postwar Japan, with access to universities and junior colleges growing substantially during the high economic growth period.

However, this postsecondary expansion did not occur in a linear fashion. The development of the postsecondary educational system went through four stages: preparation for take-off, a first stage of expansion, stagnation, and a second stage of expansion. Different types of postsecondary institutions expanded in different periods. And it is an open question whether access to different types of postsecondary education by people from different social backgrounds has changed or not. To fully understand the development of the Japanese educational system and both the changes and the stability of educational opportunities in the country, it is important to consider the different historical stages of this development and the various institutional forms of postsecondary education in Japan.

JAPANESE POSTSECONDARY EDUCATIONAL SYSTEM

One of the most important features in understanding the development of postsecondary education in Japan is the diversity of institutions. The postsecondary educational system in Japan consists of four types of institutions: four-year universities, two-year junior colleges, two-year colleges of technology, and special vocational schools. Four-year universities and colleges form the core of postsecondary education. There are more than seven hundred universities with 2.8 million students, including graduate students. About two-thirds of the institutions offer graduate courses, but the graduate student body comprises only about 230,000 students. Female students account for 39% of all students. Universities offer a wide range of studies, most of which require four-year programs, except medicine and dentistry, which require six years.

Admission to universities is usually determined by an entrance examination administered by each individual school. Public universities and some private universities require that the applicants take subject examinations administered by the National Center for University Entrance Examination, and the results of the examinations are often used as a first screening device. Recently, as a result of a shortage of applicants, the number of students admitted based on the recommendations from their high school and without an examination has been on the rise, especially among lower-ranking universities.

In 2004, 508 junior colleges enrolled 234,000 students, almost 90% of them female. These colleges offer nontechnical courses in home economics, education, and the humanities. Unlike two-year schools in other countries, which provide opportunities for transfer to four-year institutions, Japanese junior colleges offer terminal degrees, and very few students transfer to four-year schools. In 2004, only 11% of junior college graduates continued their education in four-year universities Students are admitted to junior colleges by taking an entrance examination administered by the individual school or based on a recommendation from their high school.

Colleges of technology specialize in technical training of engineering subjects. There are 63 of these schools, most of them public, enrolling 58,000 students. Women account for 18% of the student body. These schools admit junior high–school graduates and offer a five-year educational program, the last two years of which, attended by approximately 20,000 students, are considered higher education. Although these schools play an important role in producing engineers in Japan (Honda 1997), they constitute a very small proportion of students in higher education. About 40% of the graduates of technical colleges enroll in engineering departments in universities.

Special vocational schools that offered courses to high-school graduates were incorporated into the system of higher education after the amendment of the School Education Law in 1975. These special vocational schools, often called "special training schools," are recognized as a part of the higher educational system, but they are comparable to postsecondary schools in many other nations (Kaneko 1993). Most of these schools offer various types of vocational training, including bookkeeping, data processing, typing, English language, and dressmaking. Some train lower-level professional workers, such as nurses and nursery school teachers.

It is worth noting that distinctive institutional features characterize Japanese postsecondary education. First, Japanese postsecondary education is heavily dependent on private institutions. Over 70% of all four-year institutions are private, and over 70% of the student body attends private schools. About 90% of junior colleges are private, and over 90% of all students study in private schools. Although colleges of technology are predominantly public, over 90% of special vocational schools are private. The private sector plays an important role in providing access to higher education in Japan. Private schools receive much less support from the government than public schools and must rely heavily on tuition and donations from students and their parents. The average tuition and fees for private universities amounted to about US$12,000 in 1998, slightly more than twice the amount charged by national universities (Kondo 2001).

Second, Japanese higher education is gender segregated to a great extent (Matsui 1997). Although female students increasingly attend universities, they remain a minority and constituted 39% of all students in 2004. In contrast, junior colleges are attended disproportionately by female students. A small number of male students are enrolled in specialized junior colleges, but most junior colleges are attended exclusively by women. Two-year colleges of technology are attended mostly by men, although the proportion of female students increased slightly in the 1990s and reached 18% in 2003. Special vocational schools are attended almost equally by both male and female students. Even among university students, gender segregation is apparent in the field of specialization. Science and engineering subjects are dominated by men, while women are overrepresented in the humanities.

Third, there is a hierarchy of types of postsecondary institutions. Four-year universities that offer BA degrees administer the most competitive entrance examinations and occupy the top position in the hierarchy in postsecondary education. Two-year junior colleges and colleges of technology, which offer associate degrees, occupy the second tier, and special vocational training schools are at the bottom of the hierarchy. Given that students rarely transfer between the types of institutions, they are placed into a rigid hierarchical structure when they complete their high-school education. Universities are further differentiated by quality, which is reflected in the difficulty of their entrance examinations. Top-quality institutions are usually national universities, although some private schools are also ranked near the top.

Fourth, the institutions of higher education are under the strict control of the Ministry of Education.[1] New institutions must be approved by the Ministry, and any significant changes to existing institutions are also subject to its approval. To integrate the various rules governing higher education, the Ministry in 1956 issued an ordinance called "The Standards for Founding Universities and Colleges," which laid out detailed rules regarding the organizational structure of the institutions, faculty and student composition, curriculum, and methods of student selection. For example, the Ministry must approve the total number and composition of the faculty, the number of students admitted, and the curriculum whenever a university proposes to create a new department. Even the name of the department requires approval. Since the 1980s, the Ministry of Education allowed universities more flexibility in student selection and more independence and creativity in curriculum design, but the basic control mechanism has not changed until the present time.

Fifth and last, the transition from secondary to postsecondary schools is sequential, and there is usually no break between the time students graduate from secondary school and the time they begin their higher education. In 2003, 77% of new entrants to four-year universities had graduated from high school the previous month. The rest had graduated the previous year, or two or more years before, spending the intervening time preparing for the entrance examination. Similarly, over 90% of new entrants to junior colleges are fresh high-school graduates, and all entrants to colleges of technology, which offer five-year programs, are recent junior high–school graduates. The special vocational schools attract some students who have already graduated from high school and have some work experience, but over 70% of new entrants are high-school students who graduated from high school the previous month.

These figures highlight the distinctive institutional arrangement in Japan: the segregation between the educational system and the labor market (Ishida 1993). It is difficult for those who entered the labor market to return to the formal and full-time educational system. Entrance examinations to competitive universities are too demanding for those who have full-time work. Moreover, Japanese companies do not hire university and junior college graduates who are older than the normal age of graduating students. In other words, students and parents must attend to obtaining the best possible education while students are going through the system once and for all. There is virtually no chance of entering higher education for those who take a job immediately after graduating from high school. And because it is not possible to delay higher education by working for several years, high-school graduates are heavily constrained by labor market conditions and the state of higher education at the time of their graduation from high school.

HISTORICAL DEVELOPMENT OF JAPANESE POSTSECONDARY EDUCATION

The origin of Japanese postsecondary education can be traced back to the late nineteenth century. The first Japanese university was created in 1877, the University of Tokyo, a comprehensive institution of higher learning consisting of four departments: law, science, humanities, and medicine. Eventually seven national universities were established by the beginning of the twentieth century. The Japanese government created the national universities to produce national elites, especially bureaucrats (Kaneko 1993). Graduates of the national universities enjoyed a special advantage competing for positions in the bureaucracies of the national government (Amano 1990).

In the late nineteenth century, in addition to universities that offered comprehensive subjects, postsecondary technical schools (*senmon gakko*) were established, which offered advanced training in certain areas such as law, commerce, foreign languages, and engineering. These schools were ranked below universities because they concentrated on a single subject and used Japanese as the language of instruction, requiring no foreign languages for admission. Private technical schools did not enjoy the privileges bestowed upon national universities by the government, and the employment opportunities of their graduates (e.g., middle school teachers and

TABLE 3.1
Trends in the number of institutions of higher education, the number of students in higher education, and the number of entrants to higher education

	NUMBER OF INSTITUTIONS				NUMBER OF STUDENTS				NUMBER OF ENTRANTS			
	UNIVERSITY		JUNIOR COLLEGE		UNIVERSITY		JUNIOR COLLEGE		UNIVERSITY		JUNIOR COLLEGE	
	Total	% private	Total	% private	Total	% private	Total	% private	Total	% private	Total	% private
1955	228	53.5	264	77.3	523355	59.7	77885	81.1	132296	61.0	37544	81.9
1960	245	57.1	280	76.4	626421	64.4	83457	78.7	162922	68.2	42318	81.6
1965	317	65.9	369	81.6	937556	70.5	147563	85.3	249917	74.5	80563	88.8
1970	382	71.7	479	86.4	1406521	74.4	263219	90.1	333037	77.6	126659	91.8
1975	420	72.6	513	84.6	1734082	76.4	353782	91.2	423942	79.7	174930	92.8
1980	446	71.5	517	83.6	1835312	75.0	371124	90.9	412437	76.8	178215	92.5
1985	460	72.0	543	83.8	1848698	72.7	371095	89.7	411933	75.9	173503	91.4
1990	507	73.4	593	84.0	2133362	72.7	479389	91.4	492340	76.6	235195	93.3
1995	565	73.5	596	83.9	2546649	73.2	498516	92.4	441142	77.6	232741	93.8
2000	649	73.7	572	86.9	2740023	73.3	327680	91.2	473023	78.9	141491	92.5
2001	669	74.1	559	87.5	2765705	73.4	289198	90.8	476815	78.9	130246	92.4
2002	686	74.6	541	87.8	2786032	73.5	267086	90.8	609337	79.1	121441	92.3
2003	702	74.9	525	88.2	2803980	73.5	250062	91.0	604785	78.7	113029	92.7

technicians in private firms) were less prestigious than those reserved for university graduates (Amano 1986, 1990).

In 1895, 47 technical schools, mostly private, enrolled 8,700 students, while the University of Tokyo, the only university at the time, enrolled 1,300 students (Amano 1986). Therefore, from the very beginning of its development, two trends appear in Japanese higher education: (1) two stratified sectors of universities and technical schools, as well as the distinction between national and private schools; and (2) heavy dependence on the private sector. Following the enactment of the University Legislation in 1917, some of the technical schools were upgraded to universities. In 1935, there were 45 universities, 25 of them private, and 183 technical schools, 114 of them private. Together these institutions enrolled about 3% of 17–21-year-olds (Amano 1986).

The end of World War II and the introduction of American-type education marked the beginning of major changes in Japanese education (Amano 1996; Hata 1999). Starting in 1948, various prewar institutions of postsecondary education, including universities, technical schools, and teacher training colleges, began to be integrated into the single category of four-year universities. In the course of establishing new universities, technical schools that usually offered courses on a single subject were merged. Some prewar technical schools judged to have inadequate physical facilities and faculty organization to become universities, were instead upgraded to two-year junior colleges (Muta 1997). In 1950, there were 201 four-year universities (70 national, 26 local public, and 105 private) and 149 junior colleges (17 local public and 132 private). Four-year universities enrolled about 225,000 students and junior colleges 15,000 students. Altogether these students represented about 6% of 18–21-year-olds (Ichikawa 1995).

Despite the postwar reorganization of Japanese higher education, the number of new entrants to higher education fluctuated around 170,000 in the 1950s, an enrollment rate of about 10%. A major expansion of higher education took place during the 1960s and early 1970s, marking what Trow (1961) called the transformation from elite to mass higher education. As shown in Table 3.1, the number of new entrants to universities and junior colleges jumped about threefold, from 205,000 in 1960 to 599,000 in 1975. The enrollment rate (the proportion of 18-year-olds entering universities and junior colleges) increased almost fourfold from 10% to 38% during the 15-year period between 1960 and 1975.

The rapid expansion of higher education was due in large part to the increased share of private institutions. As shown in Table 3.1, the number of universities increased from 245 in 1960 to 420 in 1975, and during the same period the proportion of private universities increased from 57% to 73%. Similarly, from 1960 to 1975, the number of junior colleges increased from 280 to 513 with the corresponding increase in the proportion of private schools from 76% to 85%. The proportion of students enrolled in private institutions also increased by more than 10%.

Demographic and economic circumstances were conducive to the rapid expansion of higher education in the 1960s and early 1970s. First, the enrollment rate in high school increased rapidly from 58% of all middle school graduates in 1960 to 92% in 1975, thereby increasing the number of high-school graduates who wanted to attend institutions of higher learning. Second, with the first wave of the baby-boom generation reaching college age, the size of the 18-year-old population increased in the late 1960s, which increased the competition for entry into higher education. Third, following the rapid economic growth of the 1960s, the private sector required young trained manpower adaptable to new technology (Aramaki 2000).

This demographic and economic environment forced the Ministry of Education to relax the requirements for founding new universities and junior colleges (Pempel 1973; Kuroha 1993). For private institutions, which were heavily dependent on tuition fees for their business, it was an ideal opportunity to increase revenues. Newly established schools usually occupied the bottom of the ranking system, so the expansion of higher education took place by adding institutions of lower status. In addition to the creation of new private schools, those already in operation increased the number of students they admitted every year. Private universities with a student body in excess of 10,000 grew from 9 in 1960 to 32 in 1975. Furthermore, private universities admitted more students than the Ministry of Education approved them to admit. Overadmission was allowed because students usually applied to more than one school and some renounced their admission, but the extent of overadmission escalated. In 1960, the average private university admitted 1.57 times more students than the number approved by the Ministry, and in 1975, 1.84 times more. Consequently, private schools were able to increase their revenue without additional investment in physical facilities and faculty because the number of faculty was set at the time of the approval by the Ministry of Education (Amano 1999).

Beginning in the mid-1970s, the expansion of higher education was put on hold by the Ministry of Education. Between 1976 and 1985, the number of 18-year-olds was stable around 160,000, so there was no demographic reason to continue the expansion. The Ministry was concerned with the quality of education, especially in the private schools that admitted almost twice the number of students they were supposed to. Following enactment in 1975 of the legislation for promoting subsidies for private schools, the Ministry decided to exercise stricter control over the number of admissions by private schools and in return offered special subsidies for private institutions to compensate them for the loss of revenue due to the decreased number of admissions (Amano 1999). The Ministry also acted to equalize the access of various regions to higher education and rejected proposals to increase the number of students in major cities, whether by establishing new schools and departments or by increasing the number of students in existing departments (Kuroha 1993).

The educational policies of the Ministry were successful. As shown in Table 3.1, between 1975 and 1985 the number of universities and junior colleges (mostly in nonmetropolitan areas) increased only slightly. The number of new entrants to higher education was stable at about 600,000, and the rate of enrollment to universities and junior colleges remained about the same at around 37%. In the major cities, the university enrollment rate was reduced although it continued to increase slightly in nonmetropolitan areas (Aramaki 2000; Tsuburai and Hayashi 2000). The rate of overadmission was reduced from 1.70 times the official allowance in 1975 to 1.22 times in 1985 (Muta 1994, 21).

Another important factor that contributed to stability in higher education enrollment in the late 1970s and early 1980s was the special vocational school. Following the legislative change in 1975, special vocational schools that satisfied conditions set forth by the Ministry of Education were called "special training schools" and incorporated into the system of higher education. Although this was intended to boost the prestige of special vocational schools and recognize them as legitimate alternatives to universities and junior colleges, these schools were still considered suitable for students whose academic records were not good enough for a four-year university.

Special vocational training schools were therefore ranked at the bottom of the hierarchy in higher education.

In 1976, about 1,000 special vocational training schools were recognized as part of higher education, and the number increased to 3,000 by 1985. Over 200,000 students were admitted to these schools, and about 11% of all high-school graduates chose this path in 1985. Only ten years after their introduction, these special vocational training schools provided a viable alternative to students, especially in major cities where the expansion of universities and junior colleges was limited between 1975 and 1985 (Amano 1999).

Social pressure to expand the higher education system built up again in the mid-1980s from the second baby-boom generation, which was reaching the college age around that time. The population of 18-year-olds reached bottom in 1985 at 1.6 million and increased rapidly in the late 1980s, peaking in 1992 at 2.1 million. To maintain an enrollment rate of about 37%, which was the level between 1975 and 1985, the Ministry of Education allowed the higher education system to expand again (Amano 1999; Hata 1999).

The second stage of expansion took place following the Ministry's announcement in 1984 of its plan to relax restrictions on founding new institutions and departments. Proposals for expansion flooded the Ministry, as schools had been waiting for ten years to take advantage of this opportunity (Kuroha 1993). The number of new entrants to universities and junior colleges increased from 585,000 in 1985 to 728,000 in 1990, as shown in Table 3.1. As in the first stage of expansion, newly-established schools occupied the lower segment of the hierarchy in higher education. Because of the strong drive to expand higher education, especially on the part of the private schools, and increased application to universities by high-school students, the Ministry of Education was not able to block proposals for the expansion of universities in the late 1990s, although the population of 18-year-olds decreased sharply from 1993.

Junior colleges, however, faced difficulty in recruiting students because of increased openings in four-year universities (Matsui 1997). The number of junior colleges decreased from 596 in 1995 to 572 in 2000, partly because some were upgraded to four-year universities, and the number of new entrants dropped from 232,000 in 1995 to 141,000 in 2000 (Table 3.1). While the enrollment rate in universities and junior colleges increased from 36% in 1990 to 49% in 2000, the enrollment rate in junior colleges alone decreased from 12% in 1990 to 9% in 2000. Similarly, the number of high-school graduates who applied to special vocational training schools decreased from 1990 to 2000. Therefore, the beneficiaries of the expansive educational policies of the 1990s were the four-year universities.

In sum, the development of Japanese postsecondary education was not linear. Postwar development can be divided into four stages: an initial period of preparation for take-off (before 1960), the first stage of expansion (1960–75), a period of stability and stagnation (1976–85), and the second stage of expansion (after 1986). The following empirical analysis distinguishes between these four periods in examining the relationship between social background and access to different types of postsecondary institutions. The respondents of the national surveys are grouped into four cohorts based on when they completed secondary education. We examine whether the effects of social background on educational attainment differ between the four cohorts, and assess the possible impacts of the expansion of postsecondary education.

DATA, VARIABLES, AND METHODS

The data sets used in this paper come from the 1985 and 1995 Social Stratification and Social Mobility (SSM) National Surveys and the 2000 and 2001 Japanese General Social Surveys (JGSS).[2] Four separate surveys were combined into one data set. The SSM surveys have been conducted every ten years since 1955, but only the 1985 and 1995 surveys included both male and female respondents. The 1985 survey consisted of three surveys (A, B, and F). Although each survey used different questionnaires, some questions overlapped and we were able to combine the surveys. The combined sample size was 3,947. The 1995 survey consisted of surveys A and B, using separate questionnaires, and a special survey, P, for the construction of occupational prestige scores. We combined surveys A and B, which contained 5,357 respondents. For details of the SSM surveys, see Naoi and Seiyama (1990) and Hara and Seiyama (1999). The 2000 and 2001 JGSS contain 2,893 and 2,790 respondents, respectively. For details of the JGSS, see the codebooks (Institute of Regional Studies, Osaka University of Commerce, and Institute of Social Science, University of Tokyo 2002, 2003). The original samples above were further restricted to respondents who completed their postsecondary education in postwar educational institutions because the focus of the analysis was on the development of the postsecondary education that took place in the postwar period.

The analyses were based on a series of binary and multinomial logit regressions conducted separately for respondents in different cohorts. The effects of social background variables on educational attainment were compared across cohorts to determine the trends and their effects. The dependent variables in the logit regression were (1) completion of high-school education, (2) attendance of any type of postsecondary education, (3) attendance of university and junior college,[3] (4) completion of four-year university or two-year junior college, and (5) attainment of a BA degree (university) relative to an AA degree (junior college).[4]

We used the following independent variables. First, a dummy variable representing males was entered into the regression equation to assess the gender gap in educational attainment. We also conducted separate analyses for males and females whenever sample size permitted. Second, a series of social background variables were considered. Parental education was determined by the highest level of education attained either by the father or the mother. The responses were coded by the CASMIN scheme (Ishida 1998; Shavit and Müller 1998): (1) the social minimum of education (compulsory education) (CASMIN category 1abc); (2) full secondary education, including both academic and vocational (2bc); and (3) tertiary education, including both junior colleges and universities (3ab). The second category was used as the reference group. The 1985 SSM survey did not ask about the mother's education, so parent's education was based on the father's education.

Father's occupation was coded using the six-category version of the EGP class schema (Ganzeboom et al. 1989; Erikson and Goldthorpe 1992). These categories include: (1) the service class (EGP categories I+II); (2) the routine nonmanual class (III); (3) the petite bourgeoisie (IVab); (4) the farming class (IVc+VIIb); (5) the skilled manual working class (V+VI); and (6) the nonskilled manual working class (VIIa). The last category was used as the reference group.

Four cohorts were constructed according to when the respondents completed their high-school education. Closely following the development of postsecondary education in Japan, the youngest cohort consists of respondents who were born between 1968 and 1980 and completed high school between 1986 and 1999, which corresponds to the second stage of expansion. The next cohort consists of those born between 1958 and 1967, who completed high school between 1976 and 1985, when the expansion of higher education stagnated. The third cohort consists of those born between 1942 and 1957, who completed high school between 1960 and 1975, which corresponds to the first stage of expansion. The oldest cohort members were born before 1942 and completed high school before 1960, when postsecondary education was still preparing for take-off.

EMPIRICAL FINDINGS

Table 3.2 shows the descriptive statistics of the variables. The table presents the changes in educational attainment among respondents: the proportions of those who finished high-school education, those who attended postsecondary education, those who attended higher education (four-year university and two-year junior college), those who completed junior college, those who completed university. The proportions are also shown conditional on high-school graduation. A substantial upgrading of educational level is apparent as we move from the oldest cohort (those born before 1942) to the next youngest cohort (those born in 1958–67). Change in the level of educational attainment between the two youngest cohorts is much attenuated, and the rate of high-school graduation reached a saturation point in the mid-1980s.

These changes correspond to trends in the rate of enrollment in higher education. Respondents who were born between 1942 and 1957 completed high school between 1960 and 1975, when the rapid expansion of higher education took place, and some respondents clearly benefited from the expansion. Respondents who were born between 1958 and 1967 completed high school between 1976 and 1985, when college enrollment reached the high plateau. Respondents in the youngest cohort (born between 1968 and 1980) completed high school between 1986 and 1999, when the second expansion took place. However, the substantial increase in the number of institutions of higher education began in 1993, so the increase in the rate of attendance in higher education among members of the youngest cohort was moderately greater than that of the previous cohort.[5] In sum, the trends of educational attainment across the four cohorts reflect the postwar development of Japanese higher education, which is characterized by multiple stages of expansion.

TABLE 3.2
Descriptive statistics for variables used in the analyses by cohort

	BIRTH COHORTS			
Independent variables	Before 1942	1942–57	1958–67	1968–80
Unconditional distribution				
Completion of high school education	58.4	80.3	94.2	92.9
Attendance of postsecondary education	27.0	39.3	54.6	61.0
Attendance of higher education	15.3	26.2	42.4	47.4
Completion of junior college	3.2	8.2	15.8	19.3
Completion of university	11.7	17.2	23.4	21.1
Conditional on high school graduation				
Attendance of postsecondary education	37.3	45.0	56.4	64.4
Attendance of higher education	26.1	32.6	45.0	51.0
Completion of junior college	5.4	10.2	16.8	21.0
Completion of university	19.9	21.4	24.9	22.9
Parent's education				
Less than high school (CASMIN 1abc)	76.3	57.2	37.3	20.3
High school graduation (CASMIN 2bc)	15.7	29.0	41.3	52.6
Higher education (CASMIN 3ab)	8.0	13.8	21.4	27.1
Father's class				
Service class (I+II)	14.8	19.9	26.0	32.6
Routine nonmanual class (III)	4.6	7.0	7.8	9.8
Petite bourgeoisie (IVab)	24.6	24.9	26.5	24.8
Farming class (IVc/VIIb)	44.9	28.6	15.3	4.9
Skilled manual class (V/VI)	6.2	11.7	14.0	16.5
Nonskilled manual class (VIIa)	5.0	8.0	10.4	11.5

Table 3.2 presents the changing distribution of parents' education across cohorts. Again, the changes are not linear and are influenced by the uneven development of Japanese education. The proportion of the CASMIN 2bc category, corresponding to high-school completion, increased substantially from the oldest cohort (born before 1942) to the 1942–57 cohort. The proportion of respondents whose father or mother attended higher education (CASMIN 3ab) increased most dramatically from the 1942–57 to the 1958–67 cohort. Table 3.2 also shows the changes in the distribution of father's class. These changes are consistent with earlier studies of class mobility (Ishida 1993, 2001), which reported significant trends in father's class: the rapid contraction of the farming class (IVc+VIIb), the corresponding increase in the manual working class (V+VI and VIIa) and the service class (I+II), and the stability in the urban self-employed sector (IVab).

Table 3.3 presents the results of the binary logistic regression model predicting the odds of high-school completion, that is, the eligibility for

TABLE 3.3
Logit regression of high school completion

	BIRTH COHORTS			
Independent variables	Before 1942	1942–57	1958–67	1968–80
Male	0.474**	0.105	−0.659**	−0.300
Parent's education (base 2bc)				
Less than high school (1abc)	−1.151**	−0.913**	−1.529**	−0.889**
Higher education (3ab)	0.873**	0.634*	0.396	0.657
Father's class (base VIIa)				
Service class (I+II)	1.777**	1.424**	0.915†	0.559
Routine nonmanual class (III)	1.352**	0.668**	1.312†	1.482†
Petite bourgeoisie (IVab)	0.886**	0.259	0.250	−0.107
Farming class (IVc/VIIb)	0.266	−0.214	0.085	0.792
Skilled manual class (V/VI)	0.388	0.199	0.036	0.224
Constant	1.249**	2.251**	3.345**	2.994**
−2 log likelihood	2549.554	3136.844	625.248	524.929
N	2235	3915	1729	1235

†$p < 0.10$; *$p < 0.05$; **$p < 0.01$.

attending higher education. The table shows some noticeable trends. Male advantage in completing high-school education is apparent in the oldest cohort, with men 1.6 times ($e^{0.4744} = 1.61$) more likely than women to finish high school, controlling for social background. This male advantage disappeared in later cohorts, and women were slightly more likely to complete high-school education than men, controlling for social background. As the rate of high-school enrollment increased rapidly from 58% in 1960 to 82% in 1975, many more women advanced to high-school education, and gender inequality in high-school completion quickly disappeared. The effect of father's class on the odds of high-school completion appears to have weakened for the two youngest cohorts.[6] Especially among female respondents, father's class does not seem to affect the likelihood of completing high-school education for the two youngest cohorts (table not shown). The effect of parental education, however, remains across cohorts; the disadvantage of coming from a family where parents had low educational attainment persists for both males and females.

Table 3.4 (upper half) shows the predictions of attending postsecondary education (any type of institutions of higher learning, including special vocational training schools) for the sample of respondents who completed their high-school education. Results are shown for the two youngest cohorts because the special vocational training schools, which offer vocational courses to high-school graduates, were formally recognized as a part

78 *Ishida*

TABLE 3.4
Logit regression of attendance of postsecondary education and of higher education conditional on high-school graduation

Independent variables	BIRTH COHORTS			
	Before 1942	1942–57	1958–67	1968–80
Attendance of postsecondary education				
Male			−0.121	−0.274
Parent's education (base 2bc)				
Less than high school (1abc)			−0.604**	−0.916**
Higher education (3ab)			1.256**	1.275**
Father's class (base VIIa)				
Service class (I+II)			0.960**	0.667*
Routine nonmanual class (III)			0.521	0.533
Petite bourgeoisie (IVab)			0.644*	0.231
Farming class (IVc/VIIb)			−0.087	−0.187
Skilled manual class (V/VI)			0.008	0.089
Constant			0.706**	0.688**
−2 log likelihood			1126.156	813.845
N			957	732
Attendance of higher education				
Male	1.496**	0.683**	0.276*	0.048
Parent's education (base 2bc)				
Less than high school (1abc)	−0.727**	−0.874**	−0.553**	−0.930**
Higher education (3ab)	0.729**	0.875**	0.926**	1.035**
Father's class (base VIIa)				
Service class (I+II)	1.885**	1.122**	1.285**	0.731**
Routine nonmanual class(III)	0.856	0.457*	0.686**	0.402
Petite bourgeoisie (IVab)	1.501**	0.475*	0.780**	0.072
Farming class (IVc/VIIb)	0.659	−0.039	0.188	−0.204
Skilled manual class (V/VI)	0.824	0.107	0.244	0.067
Constant	−1.282**	−0.461**	−0.019	−0.028
−2 log likelihood	1356.138	3664.016	2001.619	1415.718
N	1384	3287	1638	1159

*$p < 0.05$; **$p < 0.01$.

of higher education only in 1975. First, there was no gender difference in the odds of attending postsecondary education. Men and women were equally likely to continue education after high school, with or without controlling for social background. Second, parental education strongly affected the odds on attending postsecondary education, and its effect showed no sign of reduction across cohorts. Third, respondents whose fathers belonged to the service class were more likely to continue education after high school than those whose fathers were nonskilled manual workers. When we examined the table separately by gender, we observed that the impact of father's class was more apparent among men than women, although the effect of parental education was equally strong among men and women (table not shown). We estimated the same model using the entire sample, that is, without the condition of high-school graduation, and we obtained basically the same results.

Table 3.4 (bottom half) reports the predictions of attending higher education (university and junior college), conditional on high-school completion. The table shows a clear trend of reduction in the gender gap across cohorts. Among members of the oldest cohort, who completed high school before 1960, men were four times ($e^{1.4957} = 4.46$) more likely to attend institutions of higher learning than women, controlling for social background. This gap was substantially reduced among the members of the 1942–57 cohort who completed high school during the first expansion stage between 1960 and 1975. Men were two times ($e^{0.6827} = 1.97$) more likely to attain higher education than women, although the difference is still statistically significant. The shrinking of the gap is the result of women having benefited greatly from the expansion of higher education, especially of junior colleges, during this period. Among members of the 1958–67 cohort, men were 1.3 times ($e^{0.2764} = 1.32$) more likely to attend higher education, a difference that is barely significant. The gender gap was further reduced and became nonsignificant among members of the youngest cohort (born in 1968–80), who completed their high-school education at the time of the expansion of university education. This result reflects the increase of the proportion of women who enrolled in universities during this period. But even among members of the youngest cohort there remains a gender inequality in access to four-year universities as opposed to two-year junior colleges (see analyses that follow).

The effects of social background on the likelihood of attending higher education were examined separately by gender because there seems to be some gender difference in their effects. Table 3.5 presents predictions of the likelihood of attending higher education by gender. We can compare the trends in the effects of various social background variables between men and women. There is no cross-gender difference in the effect of parental education. When one of the parents attained higher education, men and women were at least two times more likely to attend institutions of higher education than men and women whose parents had only high-school educations. When both parents attained the lowest level of education, men and women were about two times less likely to attend institutions of higher

TABLE 3.5
Logit regression of attendance of higher education conditional on high-school graduation

Independent variables	Before 1942	1942–57	1958–67	1968–80
Male				
Parent's education (base 2bc)				
Less than high school (1abc)	−0.689**	−0.839**	−0.485**	−0.777**
Higher education (3ab)	0.913**	1.018**	1.104**	1.058**
Father's class (base VIIa)				
Service class (I+II)	1.774**	1.042**	1.262**	1.173**
Routine nonmanual class (III)	0.921	0.524†	1.090**	0.882†
Petite bourgeoisie (IVab)	1.344*	0.461†	0.572†	0.515
Farming class (IVc/VIIb)	0.417	−0.075	0.026	0.630
Skilled manual class (V/VI)	0.703	0.219	0.383	0.466
Constant	−0.422**	−0.047	0.249†	0.058
−2 log likelihood	896.389	2025.332	934.866	658.096
N	799	1733	773	539
Female				
Parent's education (base 2bc)				
Less than high school (1abc)	−0.775**	−0.915**	−0.580**	−1.118**
Higher education (3ab)	0.541†	0.755**	0.823**	1.009**
Father's class (base VIIa)				
Service class (I+II)	5.586	1.198**	1.316**	0.438
Routine nonmanual class (III)	4.046	0.377	0.383	0.098
Petite bourgeoisie (IVab)	5.303	0.489	0.982**	−0.210
Farming class (IVc/VIIb)	4.807	0.019	0.357	−1.083*
Skilled manual class (V/VI)	4.516	−0.088	0.120	−0.187
Constant	−2.749†	−0.879**	−0.244*	−0.186
−2 log likelihood	453.418	1634.991	1056.325	750.987
N	585	1554	865	620

†$p < 0.10$; *$p < 0.05$; **$p < 0.01$.

education than those whose parents had high school education. The effects of parental education were strong and persistent across the four cohorts for both genders.

The effects of the father's class on the odds of attending institutions of higher education seem to vary by gender. Among men, the sons of the service class (I+II) and of the routine nonmanual class (III) were at an advantage in attaining higher education compared with the sons of the nonskilled manual working class (VIIa).[7] Among men who were born before 1967, the sons of the urban petite bourgeoisie (IVab) also had a better chance of attending higher education than the sons of the nonskilled manual working class. Among women, the effect of the father's class was more limited. The daughters of the service class were more likely to attend higher education than those of the nonskilled manual working class for the 1942–57 and 1958–67 cohorts, as were the daughters of the petite bourgeoisie for the 1958–67 cohort. But for members of the oldest and the youngest cohorts, women's attainment of higher education was not affected by the father's class.[8] Nevertheless, this does not imply that women's advancement to higher education was not affected by the father's class in the oldest cohort, because the chances of completing high-school education were strongly affected by the father's class for both men and women in the oldest cohort. Because the proportion of women in high school who advanced to higher education was still small in the early period of postwar Japan (less than 15% in 1955), the effect of social background among women was most pronounced at the level of high-school completion. In contrast, among members of the youngest cohort, the absence of the effect of father's class on the women's attainment of higher education is coupled with the lack of effect of father's class on the women's chances of completing high school. In other words, the chances of attending higher education among women born after 1968 were not affected by the father's class.

The following analyses focus on stratification in higher education. Table 3.6 shows the results of a multinomial logit model comparing the chances of three outcomes: completion of university education (BA degree), completion of junior college (AA degree), and no higher education degree (the reference category). The sample was restricted to respondents who finished high-school education. The major findings are as follows. First, the extent of female advantage in the completion of junior college increased from the oldest to the next youngest cohort, and it continued to be substantial even among the members of the youngest cohort: women were more than three times more likely to obtain AA degrees than men, controlling for social background. In contrast, the extent of gender inequality in access to a university degree shows a clear trend of the reduction: among the respondents of the oldest cohort, men were eight times ($e^{2.126} = 8.38$) more likely to complete university education than women, controlling for social background, compared with two times ($e^{0.73} = 2.08$) more likely among respondents of the youngest cohort. Second, the attainment of both AA and BA degrees was affected by parental education. The impact of parental education was substantial and persistent across members of all cohorts, and there is no clear trend of an increasing or decreasing impact. Third, the effect of the father's class seems to be more prevalent on the chances of completing university than of completing junior college. Only among members

TABLE 3.6
Multinomial logit regression of completion of university or completion of junior college relative to no higher education degree

	BIRTH COHORTS			
Independent variables	Before 1942	1942–57	1958–67	1968–80
Completion of junior college				
Male	−0.152	−1.314**	−1.797**	−1.234**
Parent's education (base 2bc)				
Less than high school (1abc)	−0.452	−0.806**	−0.451*	−0.837**
Higher education (3ab)	1.038**	0.451*	0.421*	0.451*
Father's class (base VIIa)				
Service class (I+II)	1.281	1.061**	1.063**	0.423
Routine nonmanual class (III)	−1.022	0.570	0.468	0.001
Petite bourgeoisie (IVab)	0.936	0.354	0.731*	−0.133
Farming class (IVc/VIIb)	0.722	0.348	0.473	−0.737
Skilled manual class (V/VI)	1.041	0.225	0.377	−0.041
Constant	−3.402**	−1.599**	−1.221**	−0.464†
Completion of university				
Male	2.126**	1.569**	1.221*	0.730**
Parent's education (base 2bc)				
Less than high school (1abc)	−0.851**	−0.901**	−0.633**	−1.043**
Higher education (3ab)	0.596**	1.023**	1.115**	1.117**
Father's class (base VIIa)				
Service class (I+II)	1.934**	1.111**	1.582**	1.316**
Routine nonmanual class (III)	1.005	0.403	1.143**	1.066*
Petite bourgeoisie (IVab)	1.541*	0.467*	1.033**	0.558
Farming class (IVc/VIIb)	0.617	−0.294	0.197	0.479
Skilled manual class (V/VI)	0.698	0.072	0.374	0.341
Constant	−3.730**	−2.178**	−2.371**	−2.113**
−2 log likelihood	187.263	313.339	273.975	226.229
N	1384	3285	1568	1044

†$p < 0.10$; *$p < 0.05$; **$p < 0.01$.

of the 1942–57 and 1958–67 cohorts did father's class have a significant effect on attaining AA degrees. Respondents from the service class background (and for the 1958–67 cohort, those from the petite bourgeoisie) had a better chance of completing junior college than those from the nonskilled manual background, controlling for gender and parental education. At the same time, among the members of the youngest cohort, attainment of an AA degree was not affected by the father's class. These young respondents completed high school when the number of junior colleges reached the saturation point and the number of universities increased rapidly, so opportunities of attending four-year universities expanded and junior colleges were no longer considered a prestigious destination. In contrast, the attainment of a BA degree was affected by the father's class across all the cohorts.

In supplementary analysis (results available upon request), the chances of attaining a university degree (BA) and junior college degree (AA) were compared among respondents who earned a degree in higher education. Men had a clear advantage over women in attaining university rather than junior college degrees. The strong male advantage is persistent across cohorts. There was no sign of reduction in the gender gap during the first stage of expansion of higher education between 1960 and 1975. However, the gender gap was apparently reduced during the second expansion period in the late 1980s and the 1990s.[9] During this period, the number of junior colleges was reduced slightly while the number of universities expanded as some junior colleges were upgraded to the status of four-year institutions. Therefore, the increased number of women in the institutions of higher education was absorbed by the university sector. Nonetheless, even among the members of the youngest cohort, men remained more likely to complete BA degrees than women, controlling for social background.

We observe that the effects of social background have been increasing in recent cohorts. Among members of the three youngest cohorts, that is, those who entered institutions of higher education after 1960, respondents whose parents completed higher education were more likely to complete BA degrees than those whose parents had only high-school educations, controlling for other factors. Attainment of a university degree became dependent on parental education in recent cohorts. Similarly, father's class seems to exert significant impact only among the members of the youngest cohort, who were born between 1968 and 1980 and entered institutions of higher education after 1986. Sons and daughters of the service class and of the routine nonmanual class were more likely to complete BA degrees than those of the nonskilled manual class. Therefore, as the university sector expanded in the late 1980s and the 1990s, social background became increasingly more likely to affect the relative chances of attaining university rather than junior college education.

DISCUSSION

Japanese postsecondary education went through multiple stages of expansion. Universities and junior colleges expanded rapidly during the high-growth period of 1960 to 1975. The decade between 1975 and 1985 was a period of stagnation when the expansion of universities and junior colleges was put on hold by the policies of the Ministry of Education. However, during this period special vocational schools were incorporated into the system of higher education, and these schools offered an opportunity for postsecondary education for those whose academic records were not good enough to be admitted by the universities. The second stage of expansion started in 1985, following the Ministry of Education's plan to relax the restrictions on universities.

Postsecondary education in postwar Japan is characterized by a highly stratified system. Traditional national universities and a few prestigious private universities occupy the summit of the hierarchy, followed by the second-tier institutions. Private universities newly established during expansion periods usually occupy the bottom of the university hierarchy. Junior colleges are clearly ranked below four-year schools. The later addition of a vocational component to the higher education system did not lead to a binary character because the vocational schools were ranked at the bottom of the existing hierarchy.

In light of the structural changes in the Japanese educational system, we examined the trends in the relationship between gender and social background on the one hand and educational attainment on the other. Our analysis revealed that the gender gap in educational attainment has been reduced substantially in the postwar period. Gender inequality as a factor in the chances of completing high school almost disappeared by the early 1970s, when the rate of high-school enrollment reached 80%. Similarly, the extent of gender inequality in the attendance of higher education was substantially reduced, especially during the late 1980s and the 1990s when the university sector expanded rapidly. The exception to the decreasing trend of gender inequality was found among students of two-year junior colleges. The expansion of the junior college sector did not result in an influx of male students because most junior colleges were not coeducational; as a result, junior colleges continued to be dominated by women. Therefore, the reduction in gender inequality in the attendance of higher education follows primarily from the increased number of female students attending four-year universities in the younger cohorts. But men are still more likely to receive BA degrees than women, even among the members of the youngest cohort.

Analysis of the relationship between parental education and educational attainment showed no clear trend of diminishing the impact of parental education, despite the multiple stages of expansion in the institutions of higher education. The influence of parental education is substantial and persistent across cohorts. Sons and daughters of parents with low levels of education were disadvantaged at virtually all stages of educational advancement. This finding suggests that in addition to economic and social resources, parents' cultural resources are highly consequential to the educational achievement of their offspring.

The effect of father's class on educational attainment produced ambiguous trends. There was a weakening of the effect of father's class on completion of high school and attendance of higher education. In particular, for women born after 1967, the chances of finishing high school and advancing to institutions of higher education were not affected by father's class. However, the analysis focusing on the stratification in higher education revealed an increasing effect of social background on the chances of attending a university as opposed to a junior college. Father's class became a significant factor in distinguishing the chances of completing a university degree from completing a junior college degree only among respondents born after 1967; in the youngest cohort, the sons and daughters of the service class and of the routine nonmanual class had a distinct advantage over those of the nonskilled manual class. Parental education also had a significant impact among the members of the youngest cohorts. These findings are probably related to the fact that following the expansion of the university sector after 1985, junior colleges no longer led to prestigious employment. University education has become a critical factor in securing socioeconomic advancement, and social background appears to have increased in importance with regard to the chances of attending university in the last two decades.

In summary, gender inequality in access to higher education was reduced substantially in the postwar period, although gender inequality in access to university rather than junior college persisted. There was neither a clear correspondence between the pattern of the effects of social background and the stages of expansion, nor a linear pattern of diminishing or increasing effects of social background. The stability in the effect of parental education is remarkable given that Japanese higher education went through the series of changes previously described following the educational policies of the Ministry of Education. Although the educational policies of the Ministry did not explicitly attempt to reduce the impact of social background, the expansion of the higher educational system did not necessarily bring about equality of access to higher education. Rather, we observed an increasing impact of parental education and father's class on the attainment of a university degree relative to that of a junior college degree when the university sector expanded rapidly during the late 1980s and the 1990s.

This finding is consistent with recent empirical studies conducted in Japan. Kondo (2001) reports that the gap in university attendance by family income has widened in the 1990s. Ojima (2002) also reports that college plans of high-school students in the 1990s were more likely to be influenced by social origin than they were in the 1980s. Furthermore, if we were able to distinguish the quality or the rank of four-year universities, reported in previous studies (Ishida, Spilerman, and Su 1997; Ishida 1998; Aramaki 2000; Kondo 2000; Ono 2001, 2004), we may find that sons and daughters from advantaged families have better chances of attending high-quality institutions. The expansion of the higher educational system, therefore, does not necessarily lead to a reduction in inequality of access to higher education by social origin.

CHAPTER FOUR

South Korea: Educational Expansion and Inequality of Opportunity for Higher Education

Hyunjoon Park, Department of Sociology, University of Pennsylvania

INTRODUCTION

In the past few decades South Korea has experienced a remarkable expansion of its education system, as have many other industrial societies. The extent of Korea's educational expansion is so dramatic that few other countries have achieved a comparable increase in the last thirty years. Even more impressive is the fact that this educational expansion occurred not only at the primary level but also at the secondary and tertiary levels. Statistics complied by the Organization for Economic Cooperation and Development (OECD 2001), which show the percentage of the population that has attained given levels of education by age in 29 countries, reveal the magnitude of change in educational attainment in Korea over one generation. Within three decades, Korea has shifted from the lowest to the highest country in the proportion of the population that has completed at least high school. For the cohort aged 25–34, only Norway exceeds Korea in the proportion of people with a high-school degree. A comparison between the age groups of 25–34 and 55–64 shows the pace of educational expansion in Korea: the proportion of 25–34-year-olds who have attained a high-school diploma is more than three times higher than that of the 55–64 age group. Although the 25–34 age group in Japan or the Czech Republic has a proportion similar to the corresponding group in Korea, the difference between the 25–34 group and the 55–64 group is far less dramatic in Japan or in the Czech Republic than in Korea.

Educational expansion in Korea is manifest not only at the secondary but also at the tertiary level. Although in Korea only 8% of people aged 55–64 have completed a type A tertiary education, which corresponds to four-year university education, the proportion has grown to 23% for the 25–34 age group.[1] Korea has the third highest percentage of people aged 25–34 who have at least a type A tertiary qualification, following Norway and the United States.

The rapid expansion of higher education makes Korea an excellent case for examining the effect of educational expansion on equality of opportunity, especially for higher education. The Korean case displays great variation in educational attainment between older and younger cohorts, which is desirable for assessing the effects of expansion on the education system.

This study is part of an international comparative project investigating the consequences for educational stratification of different types of expansion in higher education system in various countries. Although a large number of empirical studies have addressed the effects of educational expansion on inequalities across several societies, their main focus was on the lower levels of the education system or on the overall tertiary education, without specific distinction between different types of tertiary education (Shavit and Blossfeld 1993; Erikson and Jonsson 1996a). There is relatively little research comparing the consequences of specific features of expansion in higher education for class and gender inequalities (Shavit 2001).

In addition to the massive expansion of higher education, Korea's distinctive change in the structural and organizational forms of its higher education system, described in detail to follow, provides a good cross-national comparison to help understand how the specific institutional and organizational transformation of higher education affects class and gender inequalities in attaining higher education, which is the main objective of the current international comparative project (Shavit 2001).

The following section describes the changes that took place in Korean higher education in the last few decades, with specific attention to institutional and organizational expansion. This description helps specify the type of transformation that occurred in the Korean higher education system. Next, we introduce the data and variables used in the study. After presenting the results, we conclude with a brief discussion of the empirical findings and their implications.

FEATURES OF THE KOREAN HIGHER EDUCATION SYSTEM

The structure of the education system in Korea is relatively simple compared with other countries.[2] It consists of six years of compulsory elementary school, three years of middle school, and three years of academic or vocational high school. There is no tracking in middle school. Vocational high school provides vocational skills or training to prepare students for the labor market, though the proportion of graduates of vocational high schools who attend higher education has increased over time. Academic secondary education prepares students for postsecondary education. Therefore, there are significant differences between the two types of schools in many aspects, including curriculum, academic pressure, and eventually access to opportunities for tertiary education.

After graduating from high school, students may proceed to higher education. The two main types of postsecondary educational institutions are junior colleges and universities; other types are teacher's colleges and industrial or technical colleges. Most junior colleges offer two-year programs aimed at practical and occupational skills. University programs typically last four years and lead to a bachelor's degree. Students must take the national entrance examination to apply for junior colleges or universities, and admission is determined primarily by their scores on these tests. Despite severe criticisms of the entrance examination system, test scores remain the most important criterion for college admission. Usually four-year universities require much higher test scores than do junior colleges. Given the substantial impact of educational qualifications, particularly college degrees, on life chances in Korea, high-school students suffer from intensive competition and pressure to study for higher test scores (Sorensen 1994).[3]

The Korean education system shows a high degree of standardization or centralization at all levels of education, with the same standards adopted nationwide (Allmendinger 1989; Shavit and Müller 1998). The government tightly regulates many aspects of higher education including teachers' training, school budgets, and curricula. It sets student quotas each year; administrates the national entrance examinations; and enforces government standards for academic programs, faculty, and facilities. Although recent reforms in higher education are moving in a direction that allows colleges and universities more autonomy in determining enrollment quotas and student selections, the government is still a major actor in higher education policy.

Overall, Korea has a very low level of public expenditure on tertiary education. According to international data on educational expenditure (OECD 1997), total expenditure on tertiary education (as a percentage of Gross Domestic Product) in Korea is comparatively high, exceeded only by Canada and the United Sates, and similar to that of Australia. At the same time, Korea shows the largest proportion of this expenditure funded by the private sector: households and other private entities. Private payments for tertiary education amount to 1.48% of GDP in Korea, while the public share of the expenditure represents only 0.3% of GDP, making the relative share of private funds for tertiary education 83%, the highest among the 19 OECD countries providing private expenditure data. Except for Korea, only in Japan (54%) and the U.S. (52%) is more than half the expenditure on tertiary education funded by the private sector. Moreover, in Korea most private expenditure comes from households, whereas in countries like Germany a large portion of the private expenditure for education is provided by businesses (OECD 1997).

CHANGES IN KOREAN HIGHER EDUCATION

Based on previous literature about the changes in educational policy, particularly for college admission and enrollment regulations, we can distinguish three periods in the development of the Korean higher education system: before 1980, the 1980s, and the 1990s (Kim et al. 1997; Kim 2000). During the 1960s, the government began to establish the higher education system. It strengthened its control over student quotas through the Presidential Decree on College and University Student Quotas (1965) and enforced the registration of bachelor's and master's degree holders in 1966 (Kim 2000). The government imposed student quotas until the mid-1970s, when it had to partially expand the number of students admitted, especially in the fields of engineering and business, reflecting economic demands for skilled workers associated with the industrialization of the country.

Although there are some disagreements about how to further subdivide the period before 1980, most researchers agree that the year of 1981 marked a critical point in Korean higher education. Responding to increasing social demands for higher education caused by the significant expansion of secondary education, the government in 1981 implemented a new way of regulating enrollment by setting up graduation quotas instead of admission quotas. The government allowed 30% excess admissions over graduation quotas. The larger number of entrants than the predetermined number of graduates was expected to encourage more competition among college students and thereby increase the quality of higher education. This policy resulted in a great expansion of higher education, although implementation problems forced its abolishment in 1987, when the government switched back to admission quotas. From 1981 to 1984, there was a yearly increase of over 14% in the number of college students. The expansion of higher education initiated by the graduation quota system continued during the 1990s. The gross enrollment rates for tertiary education increased from 39% in 1990 to 68% in 1997, compared with 15% in 1980 and 7% in 1970 (UNESCO 1999).[4]

In the 1990s, Korean higher education experienced not only continued expansion but also a new phase of education reform. Since the mid-1990s, facing increasing globalization, the government has begun to restructure the higher education system in the direction of diversification and specialization (OECD 1998; Park 2000). Strong government control and intervention have imposed on colleges and universities a similar structure with regard to educational programs and management despite differences in type, educational objectives, and size (OECD 1998). Believing this feature to be no longer useful in the era of globalization, the government began to encourage colleges and universities to make their own plans for diversification and specialization by allowing more autonomy in admissions and academic programs. The government provided financial incentives to institutions that have achieved successful reforms. Since the last cohort in our data was born in 1976, most of our samples were not affected by this set of reforms enacted in the mid-1990s, and as a result the current study cannot examine the consequences of reform on educational stratification.

RAPID INCREASE IN PARTICIPATION
IN HIGHER EDUCATION

We begin by examining the temporal changes in the rates of admission to higher education among high-school graduates, with attention to gender differences. Figure 4.1 presents the rates of admission to postsecondary

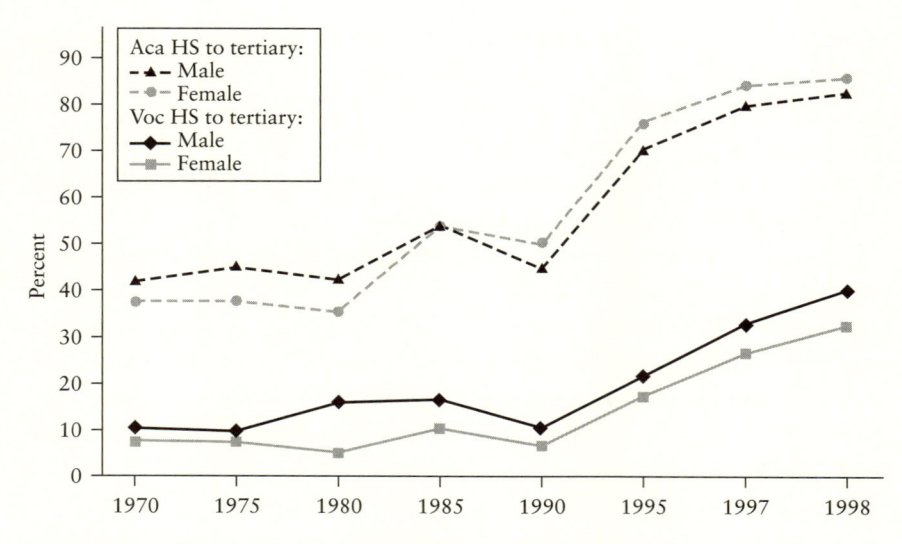

Figure 4.1. Changes in the Rates of Entering Higher Education
SOURCE: Korean Educational Development Institute (2000).

institutions among high-school graduates by gender, distinguishing between academic high schools and vocational high schools. Here tertiary education includes any type of postsecondary education, which consists mainly of junior colleges and universities. Most striking is the rapid rise after 1990 in advancement rates. For example, in 1990 only 45% of male and 50% of female academic high–school graduates made the transition to tertiary education, while in 1995 the corresponding figures were 70% and 76%. Advancement rates increased substantially since 1990 among vocational high–school graduates as well. The percentage of vocational high–school graduates attending any types of tertiary education increased from 10% in 1990 to 40% in 1998 among men, and from 6% to 32% among women.

The figure also shows parallel patterns of change over time in advancement rates between women and men. Since 1985, women have exceeded men in advancement rates from academic high schools to tertiary education. Although female graduates from vocational high schools were still less likely than male graduates to attend junior colleges or universities, advancement rates among female vocational high–school graduates also increased substantially since 1990.

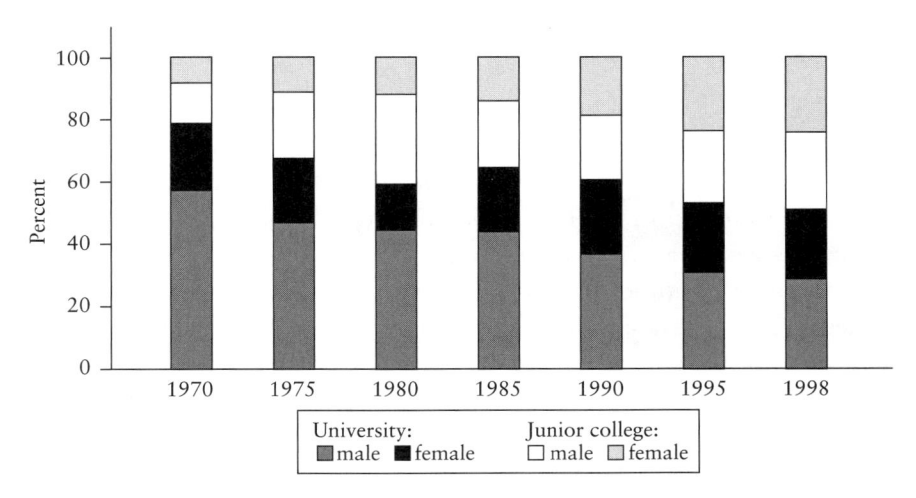

Figure 4.2. Distribution of Entrants by Type of Institution and Gender
SOURCE: Korean Educational Development Institute (2000).

Statistics on the change in the percentage of female students among total entrants to tertiary education each year confirm a significant increase of women's attendance in the past decades. For example, the proportion of female students among total entrants to universities increased from 27% in 1970 to 43% in 1998. The corresponding percentage among entrants to junior colleges increased from 36% in 1970 to 48% in 1998. Figure 4.2, showing the change over time in the distribution of entrants to higher education by types of institution and gender, illustrates the rise in the relative proportion of female over male entrants in both junior colleges and universities. The figure also indicates that the proportion of high-school graduates going to junior colleges relative to universities increased significantly during this period. The number of junior college entrants increased 30 times from 9,802 in 1970 to 304,637 in 1998, while the number of university entrants increased 9 times from 35,653 to 312,293 during the same period. Thus, in 1998 the ratio between the number of junior college and university entrants was about 1:1, pointing to one of the characteristics of the expansion in Korean higher education: the much faster rise of junior colleges than of universities as an alternative for higher education, notwithstanding the significant expansion of the universities.

THE GROWTH OF JUNIOR COLLEGES AND UNIVERSITIES

In Korea, junior colleges and universities are the two main types of institutions for tertiary education. Between 1965 and 1998, the number of universities offering BA or BS degrees rose from 70 to 156, while junior colleges increased from 48 to 158. In addition to these, the higher education system comprises some teacher's colleges, industrial universities, and a handful of other types of institutions. During the same period, the number of teacher's colleges remained stable: there were 11 colleges in 1998. Since 1985 a small number of institutions of a new type appeared: the industrial university.

Although both junior colleges and universities expanded between 1965 and 1998, their patterns of expansion seem to be somewhat different. Between 1980 and 1990, the number of junior colleges decreased from 128 to 117, while the number of universities increased from 85 to 131, after being stable in the 1970s. The different patterns in the expansion of junior colleges and universities are attributable in part to policy changes the Korean government adopted (Kim et al. 1997; Kim and Lee 2000). In the mid-1970s, the Korean government began to expand the number of students admitted yearly to both universities and junior colleges to meet social demands for higher education associated with rapid industrialization. In the 1980s, the number of students admitted to universities increased further as a result of the graduation quota system as described earlier. However, during the same period, the government adopted a different policy toward junior colleges, reducing the number of entrants and even closing some national and public junior colleges, because the quantitative increase in the number of junior colleges during the 1970s did not lead to a qualitative improvement in education and training. In addition, unemployment among junior college graduates became a serious issue the government needed to address. For example, the employment rate among junior college graduates in 1981 was only 28%. Therefore, in the 1980s the educational policy toward junior colleges was to prevent further quantitative expansion and improve academic capacities.

Since the early 1990s, however, social and economic demands for middle-level skills and technology increased further, reflecting industrial changes in the economy. This had a favorable effect on the chances of junior college graduates for better employment and therefore increased social demands for junior college education. The Korean government responded by changing its policy to one that bolstered junior colleges by increasing the quota of entrants and helping establish new institutions. Between 1990 and 1998, the number of junior colleges increased from 120 to 158. During the same period, university education continued its growth, which had begun in the 1980s, especially in the area of engineering and science (Kim et al. 1997).

PRIVATE AND PUBLIC INSTITUTIONS FOR HIGHER EDUCATION

A separate examination of the expansion of public and private institutions is needed to better understand implications of such expansion on educational inequality. Figure 4.3 presents the changes between 1965 and 1998 in the number of private and public junior colleges and universities. The figure shows clearly that private institutions are a main form of higher education in Korea. In 1998, private institutions made up 87% of junior colleges and universities. The expansion of higher education was driven mainly by the rapid increase in private junior colleges and universities. The number of private junior colleges increased from 36 in 1965 to 143 in 1998, although the change was relatively stable during the 1980s. After a stable period in the 1970s, the number of private universities doubled between 1980 and 1998 from 65 to 130. Although public junior colleges continued to grow until 1980, their number decreased rapidly since then, and only five remained by 1995. Although the number of public universities increased steadily, there were only 26 public universities in 1998.

The statistics on the number of students enrolled in higher education by institutional type also show the predominance of the private sector. In 1965, a total of 105,463 students were enrolled in four-year universities, 75% of them in private institutions. In 1996, the total number of university students increased to 1,266,876, and the proportion of students in private institutions remained 76%. During the same period, students enrolled in junior colleges increased from 23,159 in 1965 to 642,697 in 1996. In 1965, private institutions enrolled more than two-thirds of all junior college students, and by 1996 more than 95% (Weidman and Park 2000).

The rapid increase and predominance of private institutions for higher education may have some important implications for inequalities of opportunity for higher education, particularly because private institutions, with

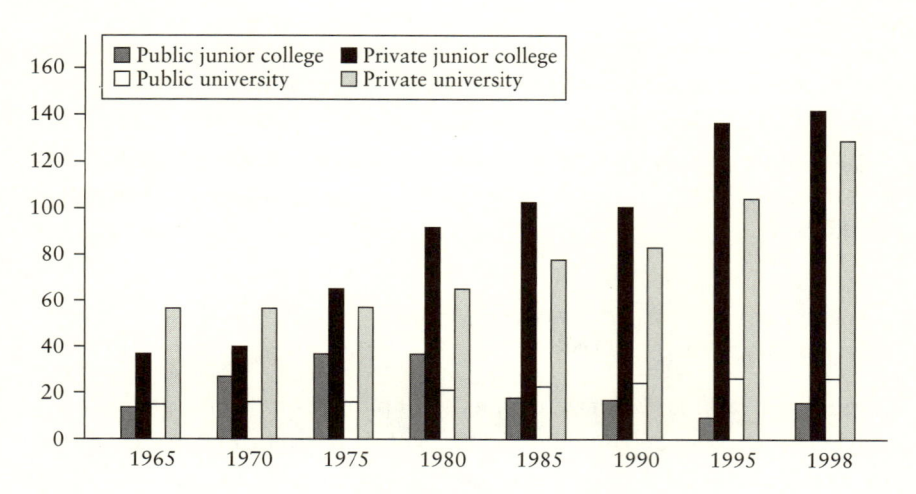

Figure 4.3. Public and Private Institutions for Higher Education: 1965–98
SOURCE: Korean Educational Development Institute (2000).

little financial support from the government, rely heavily on tuition as their main financial resource, and as a result usually charge substantially higher tuition fees than do public institutions. The predominance of private institutions is associated with the high share of private expenditure for higher education described earlier. This financial burden on households may affect educational opportunities, especially for students from poor families.

THE STRATIFIED SYSTEM OF KOREAN HIGHER EDUCATION

The change in Korean higher education during the past few decades can be summarized through its three main features: (1) greater expansion of junior colleges than of universities; (2) greater increase in attendance of tertiary education among women than men; (3) dominance of private over public institutions for higher education.

The greater expansion of junior colleges than of universities is a characteristic of the *stratified* model of expansion. In this model, expansion is driven primarily by creating a second-tier system of higher education, significantly lower in prestige than the first tier of universities—as in the case of community colleges in the U.S. This model is in clear contrast with the one in which expansion is accomplished by increasing the size of existing institutions or by creating additional universities similar to the existing ones, as it happened in Austria and Italy in the 1970s and 1980s (Shavit 2001). In Korea, admission to the lower-tier junior colleges requires much lower test scores on the national entrance examinations than admission to four-year universities. Associate degrees awarded by junior colleges to their graduates tend to have substantially lower labor market values than bachelor's degrees obtained by graduates of four-year universities.

The Korean higher education system closely resembles the stratified model not only because of the expansion of junior colleges but also because of a differentiation within four-year universities in prestige, test scores required for admission, and ultimately the social privileges of the graduates. Although the number of universities increased significantly during the last few decades, newly established universities are closer to junior colleges than to existing prestigious universities, and their degrees are valued far less in the labor market and in society at large than those of prestigious universities. In other words, although these institutions provide university degrees, their academically less demanding and less prestigious status can be defined as a second tier of higher education (Shavit et al. 2002). In short, the Korean higher education system can be best described as a stratified system in which expansion was facilitated by creating a second-tier system of higher education comprising junior colleges and universities of lower prestige.

CLASS AND GENDER INEQUALITIES

Has expansion of higher education in Korea, which we have characterized as conforming to the stratified model, contributed to reducing socioeconomic and gender inequalities in opportunities for higher education? Previous studies on the impact of educational expansion on educational opportunity have documented persistent inequalities in educational attainment despite significant expansion in various societies (Shavit and Blossfeld 1993). Unless the enrollment of advantaged groups at a certain level is saturated, expansion in participation is not accompanied by a decrease in inequality between social classes because the privileged groups are better able to take advantage of newly expanded opportunities, which they use to achieve much greater increase in educational attainment than do disadvantaged groups (Raftery and Hout 1993).

Based on this hypothesis of Maximally Maintained Inequality (MMI), we expect the effect of social origins on attending higher education not to have decreased in the last few decades despite the rapid expansion of the higher education system in Korea. Moreover, the fact that this expansion has been driven by an increase in private institutions enhances the expectation that the effect of social origins has persisted during this period.

Although the MMI hypothesis predicts an overall persistence in inequality despite educational expansion, it does not address potential variation in the patterns of the impact of social origin on educational transition between different tracks at a particular level of education. For instance, advocating a multinomial transition model that allows separate analysis of family background effects on different tracks at a given point in the educational career, Breen and Jonsson (2000) show that in Sweden class-origin effects are stronger for the comparison between those who attend academic paths and those who leave school, than for the comparison between those who attend vocational education and those who leave school. Similarly, Lucas (2001) emphasizes the implication of qualitative dimensions of education for educational inequality. Despite increasing enrollment, even approaching to be universal at a particular level of education from all social classes, social origin-based inequality is effectively maintained because advantaged groups are more likely to succeed in sending their children to qualitatively different and better placements within that level of education.

This line of research, which emphasizes the qualitative distinction within a level of education, indicates that it is necessary to examine the effects of social background separately for transitions to universities and to junior colleges in Korea. Given the rapid growth of junior colleges as an alternative path for higher education, we must examine the effect of this growth on the inequality of opportunity for higher education. It would also be useful to compare the effects of social origin on attending universities that occupy different positions in the prestige hierarchy, but data limitation prevents us from distinguishing between universities.

Although previous literature has consistently found persistent inequalities in educational attainment between social classes, there is evidence of reduced gender gap in educational opportunity. In the last few decades, gender differentials in the mean years of education completed have decreased significantly, and the association between gender and educational transitions has declined in the societies studied in a comparative analysis of

13 countries (Shavit and Blossfeld 1993). Summarizing the empirical findings in their international comparative analysis of educational inequality, Shavit and Blossfeld (1996), explain that class inequality in educational attainment has persisted, while the gender gap has been reduced significantly because the increase in the rate of educational participation among women tends to restrict the extent of participation among people from lower classes.

The separate consideration of access to universities and junior colleges is also useful for understanding gender inequality of opportunity in higher education. As discussed in the chapter about Japan in this volume, there is an apparent difference between the types of higher education institutions attended by Japanese men and women. Junior colleges are attended disproportionately by female students, while male students are overrepresented in universities. Higher education expansion for Japanese women has been driven mainly by their increase in attending junior colleges rather than universities. At the same time, the increase in university attendance has been the main path by which higher education has expanded for men.

This pattern of gender differences in higher education expansion in Japan is sharply distinct from that in Korea. Korean women advanced in relatively equal measure to junior colleges and universities (Brinton and Lee 2001). The similar increase in women's attendance at junior colleges and universities for Korean women leads us to expect that a decrease in gender gap in higher education attendance should manifest itself in both junior colleges and universities.

METHOD AND DATA

Models

The main objective of this analysis is to investigate changes in the effects of social background, such as father's education and occupation, on the respondents' educational attainment. As Mare elaborated in his influential papers (1980, 1981), the traditional linear regression model of the effect of family background on the highest completed years of education does not distinguish between the effect of social background and the impact of the expansion of the education system. Logit models, however, permit an analytical distinction between schooling distribution, which reflects marginal differences, and schooling allocation, which indicates the association between background and schooling-related decisions; they do so by examining the chances of continuing to a next level of schooling if the previous level has been completed. Stated differently, logit parameters for each transition in the education system are appropriate for detecting the genuine impact of social origin on school continuation and its temporal changes because these estimates are not contaminated by variation in schooling distribution across cohorts.

Using logit models, we examined temporal changes in the effect of social origin and gender on the odds of making the following three transitions: (1) completing high school to be eligible for higher education; (2) attending any type of postsecondary education given high-school completion; and (3) attending university rather than junior college given attendance at any types of tertiary education institution. The last one is in fact not a real sequential transition because high-school students go either to junior college or to university after graduation, but the analysis provides supplemental insight into differences between social classes in the type of tertiary education institutions attended.

To supplement the analysis of transition to university relative to junior college, two separate pathways were analyzed simultaneously using a multinomial logit model: from high-school completion to attending junior college, and from high-school completion to attending university (Breen and Jonsson 2000). The multinomial model of educational transitions showed specifically how each social background variable might have a different impact depending on the type of institution a student chooses, that is, junior college or university.

Data

The data for this analysis were taken from the Korean Labor and Income Panel Study (KLIPS), conducted in 1998 by the Korean Labor Institute. Starting in 1998, the KLIPS is a longitudinal survey of a representative sample of Korean households and individuals in the household residing in nonrural areas (see Phang et al. 1999). In the first year (1998), KLIPS succeeded in interviewing 13,317 persons in 5,000 households with a 76% response rate. The survey focuses on economic activity and contains detailed information on such occupation-relevant variables as employment status, wages, and working hours. In addition, the data set contains information on the highest levels of education respondents attended and whether they completed that level, with a detailed classification of education that clearly distinguishes between junior college and university degrees.

To obtain a sufficient number of cases for recent cohorts who attended higher education in the 1990s, we added to the 1998 sample those who were more recently interviewed in the second and fourth waves of KLIPS, conducted in 1999–2001. These include either respondents who were not interviewed in 1998 because of various reasons or who became newly eligible to the survey by becoming new household members. The analysis was limited to respondents who were aged 25 or over at the time of the survey and who were not in school. This age limitation was necessary to avoid a selection bias on educational attainment because the longest educational careers are not completed until around the age of 25.

VARIABLES

To analyze variation in the effect of social origin over time, four birth cohorts were constructed, reflecting historical change in Korean educational policy over the last few decades as described earlier. The oldest cohort in the samples was born before 1951, and therefore most people in this cohort attended junior colleges or universities before 1970 if at all. The Korean government did not begin to establish a systematic form of higher education until the mid-1960s. The next cohort consists of people born between 1951 and 1960 who attended tertiary education in the 1970s. During this period, Korean higher education began to grow in response to an increasing demand for educated people driven by industrialization. Most of the third cohort, born between 1961 and 1970, reached the age for entering higher education in the 1980s, a period of significant increase in the number of colleges and their students initiated by the policy shift from admission to graduate quota. During this period, the educational policy restricted somewhat the increase in the number of junior colleges. In the 1990s, when the youngest cohort, born after 1970, entered college, Korean higher education blossomed so that Korea became one of the countries with the highest proportion of college graduates among young people.

In addition to gender as a dummy variable (0 = male, 1 = female), the analysis included father's education and occupation as major independent variables to represent the effect of social origin. Father's occupation when the respondent was 14-years-old was measured by a six-category version of the EGP class schema (Erikson and Goldthorpe 1992): I+II (service class), III (routine nonmanual), Ivab (petite bourgeoisie), IVc (farmers), V+VI/VIIab (skilled and unskilled manual workers). To prevent unstable estimates due to the small number of cases, we combined skilled manual (V+VI) and unskilled manual (VIIab) workers.

Father's education was classified according to the CASMIN educational classification (Müller et al. 1989). Among the categories in the original schema, category 1c (primary education plus vocational training) and category 2c (full maturity certificate) do not exist in the Korean education system. In addition, our data did not distinguish between vocational (2a) and academic (2b) tracks at the secondary level for father's education. Furthermore, given the low levels of educational attainment among the Korean elderly, we do not have a sufficient number of cases with lower-level tertiary degrees (3a). Therefore, we classified father's education into three categories that correspond to important distinctions between educational levels in the Korean education system: primary education or less (1ab), secondary education (2a + 2b), and tertiary education (3a + 3b).

RESULTS

Educational Transition Rates Across Cohorts

Table 4.1 presents the proportion of each of the four cohorts completing each educational transition given completion of the previous transition by gender, and the distributions of the independent variables used in the analysis. With respect to the first transition (completing high school), both males and females show a linear trend of increasing rates across cohorts. For example, of the oldest 1,903 males and 2,178 females, only 44% and 16%, respectively, completed high school. By contrast, of those born after 1970, 93% of men and 96% of women obtained a high-school diploma. The difference in the proportion between younger and older people is striking, especially for women.

The overall proportion of high-school graduates entering postsecondary education also increased across the four birth cohorts for both men and women: from 38% and 22% in the oldest male and female cohorts to 51% and 46% in the youngest cohorts. The table also shows different patterns of transition to junior colleges and universities: the proportion of high-school

TABLE 4.1
Descriptive statistics by cohort

	Before 1951	1951–60	1961–70	1971 or later
A. Educational transition rates (%)				
Men				
High-school graduation	43.7	72.1	89.5	93.1
Postsecondary entry given HS graduation	38.4	37.2	48.7	50.5
Junior college	3.3	9.2	13.9	21.2
University	35.1	28.0	34.8	29.3
University graduation given university entry	86.6	90	95.7	88.3
Women				
High-school graduation	15.6	51.1	85.4	95.7
Postsecondary entry given HS graduation	22.3	22.9	32.4	46.1
Junior college	4.4	5.8	11.3	19.8
University	17.9	17.1	21.1	26.3
University graduation given university entry	86.9	89.6	93.0	96.3
B. Independent variables (%)				
Female	53.4	50.2	49.1	53.3
Father's class				
I+II (Service class)	3.2	5.4	6.4	7.0
III (Routine nonmanual workers)	5.9	9.6	11.0	14.0
IVa+b (Petite bourgeoisie)	6.1	9.5	11.5	13.6
IVc/VIIb (Farmers)	77.8	61.7	48.7	30.9
V+VI/VIIa (Manual workers)	7.1	13.8	22.4	34.6
Father's education				
1 (primary education or less)	86.1	70.2	53.9	36.7
2ab (secondary education)	10.7	22.0	35.9	52.8
3ab (tertiary education)	3.3	7.8	10.2	10.5

graduates going to junior colleges increased monotonically across cohorts for both men and women. Regarding the proportion of high-school graduates attending universities, we see a fluctuation only for men, while for women, the overall trend points to an increase, although not as substantial as the increase in the proportion of junior college attendance.

The fact that while the proportion of high-school graduates going to junior colleges increased, the corresponding percentage for university attendance did not show such a linear trend, resulted in the decline across male cohorts in the proportion of university students among respondents attending any type of tertiary education: from 91% (35.1%/38.4%) in the oldest cohort to 58% (29.3%/50.5%) in the youngest cohort. Despite the increasing proportion of female students attending universities, the proportion of university attendants among women attending any types of postsecondary education declined from 80% (17.9%/22.3%) in the oldest to 57% (26.3%/46.1%) in the youngest cohort because the percentage of women who chose junior colleges increased more rapidly. This pattern is in general consistent with our earlier description of the rapid increase in the number of junior colleges and their students, and it is a major feature of the changes that the Korean higher education system underwent during the past few decades.

Men and women, even in the oldest cohorts, made the transition from university entry to completing a first-degree such as BA or BS. In other words, most of the students who entered tertiary education completed a degree. There is a trend of slight increase across cohorts in the probabilities of making this transition among women, while among men the recent cohort does not show a greater proportion than the two previous cohorts.

Binary Logit Models of Attending
Any Type of Tertiary Education

Before examining the effects of gender and social background on college attendance, we first analyze the temporal changes in those effects on the likelihood of completing high school and thus being eligible for tertiary education. Since our data do not contain information on specific high-school tracks that respondents attended, the analysis estimates the impact of independent variables on the odds of completing any type of high school. Most of the youngest cohort, born after 1970, graduated from high school (94.5%). To obtain a reasonable sample size for those who have less than a high-school education, the two youngest cohorts were collapsed. Table 4.2 shows the results of logit models estimating the likelihood of completing high school across the four successive cohorts, with an additional column for the two youngest cohorts combined.

The table shows that gender inequality has been significantly reduced. In the oldest cohort, women's odds of completing high school were only one fifth of those for men ($e^{-1.683}$ = 0.19), controlling for social background. The gap has decreased across cohorts and the pattern has even reversed for the youngest cohort. Comparisons of the effects of father's education and class across cohorts, relying on the coefficients of the combined cohort, indicate that social-origin differentials in the odds of high-school graduation remained fairly constant. The only exception is that the advantage of

TABLE 4.2
Binary logit models of high school graduation

	Before 1951	1951–60	1961–70	1971 or later	1961 or later
Female	−1.683***	−0.979***	−0.416***	0.504*	−0.215*
	(0.086)	(0.085)	(0.115)	(0.242)	(0.102)
Father's education					
2ab (Secondary education): Reference					
1 (Primary education or less)	−1.591***	−0.981***	−0.994***	−0.740***	−1.004***
	(0.131)	(0.125)	(0.160)	(0.270)	(0.135)
3ab (Tertiary education)	1.045***	1.137***	0.642	1.557	0.820†
	(0.297)	(0.344)	(0.487)	(1.050)	(1.050)
Father's class					
I+II (Service class)	0.733**	0.670*	1.760*	0.273	1.168*
	(0.284)	(0.328)	(0.747)	(0.781)	(0.537)
III (Routine nonmanual workers)	0.732***	0.768***	1.278***	0.891	1.100***
	(0.218)	(0.224)	(0.412)	(0.627)	(0.344)
Iva+b (Petite bourgeoisie)	0.961***	0.748***	0.269	0.273	0.220
	(0.206)	(0.200)	(0.233)	(0.419)	(0.202)
IVc/VIIb (Farmers)	−0.407**	−0.403***	−0.257	−0.002	−0.310*
	(0.151)	(0.127)	(0.147)	(0.287)	(0.128)
V+VI/VIIa (Manual workers): Reference					
Constant	1.257***	1.792***	2.868***	2.860***	2.975***
	(0.183)	(0.161)	(0.181)	(0.267)	(0.150)
Number of cases	4081	2846	3059	1401	4460

†$p < 0.10$; *$p < 0.05$; **$p < 0.01$; ***$p < 0.001$.

TABLE 4.3
Binary logit models of attending any type of tertiary education

	Before 1951	1951–60	1961–70	1971 or later
Female	−1.104***	−0.889***	−0.885***	−0.208†
	(0.164)	(0.119)	(0.089)	(0.118)
Father's education				
2ab (Secondary education): Reference				
1 (Primary education or less)	−0.216	−0.648***	−0.731***	−0.825***
	(0.172)	(0.137)	(0.100)	(0.135)
3ab (Tertiary education)	0.764**	0.672***	1.086***	1.256***
	(0.265)	(0.196)	(0.169)	(0.252)
Father's class				
I+II (Service class)	0.631†	0.793**	0.588**	0.657*
	(0.345)	(0.271)	(0.214)	(0.295)
III (Routine nonmanual workers)	0.344	0.601**	0.571***	0.575**
	(0.300)	(0.217)	(0.160)	(0.200)
IVa+b (Petite bourgeoisie)	0.037	0.086	0.737***	0.112
	(0.303)	(0.224)	(0.155)	(0.192)
IVc (Farmers)	−0.239	−0.330†	−0.400***	−0.126
	(0.248)	(0.178)	(0.118)	(0.156)
V+VI/VIIab (Manual workers): Reference				
Constant	−0.304	−0.225	0.224*	0.087
	(0.258)	(0.179)	(0.109)	(0.128)
Number of cases	1172	1751	2676	1324

†$p < 0.10$; *$p < 0.05$; **$p < 0.01$; ***$p < 0.001$.

having self-employed fathers (IVab) rather than manual workers has been reduced significantly.

Table 4.3 presents the results of logit models predicting the odds of attending any type of tertiary education conditional on high-school completion. There is clear evidence that gender difference in the likelihood of continuing education beyond high school has substantially decreased, reflecting the significant rise in the number of Korean women participating in higher education in the past few decades.

There is no systematic decrease across cohorts in the effect of father's education, and the gap in the likelihood of attending colleges between those whose fathers had only primary education or less and those whose fathers completed secondary education seems to be increasing. The advantage of having a father with tertiary education relative to a father with secondary education for the chance of entering postsecondary education is substantial. For the youngest members, for instance, the odds of making the transition to colleges are 3.5 times greater for students whose fathers completed tertiary education than for those whose fathers completed secondary education ($e^{1.256} = 3.5$). The importance of the father's tertiary education impact on opportunities for higher education seems to increase for the two younger cohorts, although a statistical test indicated that differences among four coefficients of tertiary education across cohorts are not significant (not shown).

Students from higher socioeconomic backgrounds, particularly service class (I+II) or routine nonmanual class (III), are significantly more likely to continue their education beyond high school than those whose fathers were manual workers, even after taking the father's education into account. And we cannot find evidence that the importance of father's class impact on continuing education has declined for the two younger cohorts who entered colleges when higher education was dramatically expanded in the 1980s and 1990s.[5]

Multinomial Logit Models of Transitions to Tertiary Education

In the previous discussion on trends of transition probabilities, we observed a different pattern of temporal change in probabilities between entry into university and junior college. This was especially true for men, where we found a relatively linear trend of increasing proportion for entrance to junior colleges but a fluctuation for universities. We must therefore examine how the effects of social origins differ between the transitions to universities and to junior colleges. Table 4.4 reports the results of multinomial logit models of entering universities or junior colleges compared with no tertiary education, conditional on high-school completion. Because the number of respondents who attended junior colleges among the members of the oldest cohort is small, the two oldest cohorts were combined to obtain stable estimates.

Regarding the relative strength of the effects of independent variables between the two paths following high-school graduation, we see somewhat stronger impacts of family background on the path to university than to junior college. This finding is consistent with the expectation that social-origin differences in the likelihood of making transitions should be smaller for the transition to junior college than to university because the pathway to university is more difficult and therefore differences in socioeconomic resources are more consequential in determining success (Breen and Jonsson 2000).

TABLE 4.4
Multinomial logit models of attending university or junior college relative to no tertiary education

	BEFORE 1961		1961–70		1971 OR LATER	
	Junior college	University	Junior college	University	Junior college	University
Female	−0.621*** (0.172)	−1.089*** (0.104)	−0.625*** (0.126)	−1.020*** (0.101)	−0.177 (0.148)	−0.233 (0.139)
Father's education						
2ab (Secondary education): Reference						
1 (Primary education or less)	−0.131 (0.201)	−0.555*** (0.114)	−0.794*** (0.143)	−0.696*** (0.114)	−0.745*** (0.174)	−0.899*** (0.170)
3ab (Tertiary education)	0.586* (0.280)	0.726*** (0.165)	0.431† (0.240)	1.320*** (0.177)	0.658* (0.309)	1.578*** (0.265)
Father's class						
I+II (Service class)	0.257 (0.383)	0.886*** (0.225)	0.259 (0.187)	0.766*** (0.231)	0.760* (0.344)	0.598† (0.330)
III (Routine nonmanual workers)	0.465 (0.296)	0.551** (0.191)	0.261 (0.218)	0.745*** (0.179)	0.396 (0.248)	0.711** (0.227)
IVa+b (Petite bourgeoisie)	−0.288 (0.333)	0.204 (0.195)	0.568** (0.205)	0.839*** (0.176)†	−0.082 (0.251)	0.262 (0.225)
IVc (Farmers)	−0.592* (0.254)	−0.151 (0.158)	−0.627*** (0.169)	−0.267 (0.139)	−0.176 (0.199)	−0.081 (0.194)
V+VI/VIIab (Manual workers)						
Constant	−1.898*** (0.262)	−0.358 (0.267)	−0.719*** (0.148)	−0.286* (0.127)	−0.649*** (0.159)	−0.567*** (0.153)
Number of cases	2,923		2,676		1,324	

†$p < 0.10$; *$p < 0.05$; **$p < 0.01$; ***$p < 0.001$.

With regard to trends in the impact of independent variables, gender gaps have substantially decreased for transition to both university and junior college. For the older cohorts, born before 1961 and between 1961–70, women were significantly less likely to attend either universities or junior colleges than their male counterparts, whereas the youngest women, born after 1970, no longer experience significant disadvantages in the chances of going to either junior colleges or universities relative to men of the same age cohort.

Inequality of opportunities for higher education associated with the father's educational level has persisted over time. Indeed, father's tertiary education has become more important in determining the children's chances of attending universities. For the oldest members, the odds of attending universities were two times greater for those whose fathers completed tertiary education than for those whose fathers completed only secondary education ($e^{0.726} = 2.1$), while for the youngest cohort, the gap increases to almost five times ($e^{1.578} = 4.8$).

Respondents whose fathers belong to the service class (I+II) or the nonmanual class (III) enjoy substantial advantages in attending universities over those whose fathers belong to the manual working class (V+VI/VIIab). The significant gaps between social classes in the odds of entering universities did not change significantly over time.[6] But the advantages associated with the two highest classes for the transition to junior college were not substantial for the two older cohorts, while for the youngest cohort it is the effect of the service class that is significant.[7]

Binary Logit Models of Attending University Relative to Junior College

Finally, Table 4.5 shows the results of binary logit models of attending university relative to junior college, conditional on attending higher education.[8] Again, the two oldest cohorts were combined because of the small numbers of respondents attending junior colleges among the members of the oldest cohort, born before 1951. Overall, the father's class did not substantially affect the likelihood of attending universities rather than junior colleges. However, the effect of the father's tertiary education is significant and even stronger for the two recent cohorts, born after 1961, than for those born before 1961. The odds of entering universities rather than junior colleges were significantly lower for women than for men among the two

TABLE 4.5
Binary logit models of attending university rather than junior college

	Before 1961	1961–70	1971 or later
Female	−0.477*	−0.418**	−0.111
	(0.190)	(0.140)	(0.166)
Father's education			
2ab (Secondary education): Reference			
1 (Primary education or less)	−0.440*	0.083	−0.159
	(0.217)	(0.165)	(0.215)
3ab (Tertiary education)	0.138	0.913***	0.935***
	(0.282)	(0.224)	(0.259)
Father's class			
I+II (Service class)	0.628	0.470	−0.178
	(0.396)	(0.292)	(0.334)
III (Routine nonmanual workers)	0.100	0.489*	0.300
	(0.318)	(0.228)	(0.258)
IVa+b (Petite bourgeoisie)	0.545	0.292†	0.367
	(0.361)	(0.221)	(0.280)
IVc (Farmers)	0.424	0.332	0.079
	(0.283)	(0.198)	(0.241)
V+VI/VIIab (Manual workers)			
Constant	1.408	0.445***	0.119
	(0.256)	(0.145)	(0.179)
Number of cases	942	1095	637

†$p < 0.10$; *$p < 0.05$; **$p < 0.01$; ***$p < 0.001$.

cohorts born before 1961, whereas the difference is no longer significant among the members of the youngest cohort.

SUMMARY AND DISCUSSION

During the past few decades, higher education in Korea has expanded enormously, mainly through an increase in the second tier of higher education. Junior colleges have grown more rapidly than universities, and universities newly established during the period of expansion are much lower in prestige than the veteran ones. Korean higher education can therefore be characterized as a type of stratified system in which the first- and second-tier systems differ substantially in both prestige and the quality of education.

The study examined whether the expansion of the second-tier education system contributed to reducing inequalities of educational opportunity between social classes. Although the proportion of high-school graduates continuing to junior college showed significant increase across birth cohorts for men and women, no linear increase in the proportion entering university conditional on high-school graduation was observed, especially for men. This made it necessary to distinguish between university and junior college attendance and examine the effect of social background on the odds of attending each type of institution.

The basic pattern of temporal changes in the effects of social background and gender was similar between the university versus no postsecondary education contrast and the junior college versus no postsecondary education contrast, conditional on high-school completion. First, there was clear evidence of significant reduction in gender inequality in the likelihood of attending junior colleges or universities. Second, the effect of the father's education persisted across cohorts. In particular, the father's tertiary education became more important over time in determining the children's chances of attending universities. Finally, the father's class remained relatively constant in its influence on the likelihood of attending tertiary education.

In the models predicting university rather than junior college attendance among respondents who entered institutions of higher education, the father's class did not have significant impact. However, the impact of the father's tertiary education became stronger for the younger cohorts. Increasing female participation in education was also apparent at this transition.

In sum, we observed no evidence that the influences of the father's education or class on attending higher education decreased for the members of cohorts who entered college in the 1980s and 1990s, when higher education in Korea underwent a dramatic expansion. Consideration of the distinct characteristics of Korean higher education might help explain this persistent dependence of educational attainment on social origin. As described earlier, the private sector dominates Korean higher education, while government subsidies and support for higher education are minimal. Among its consequences, in addition to the prevalence of "shadow education" (private tutoring and cram schools), is the highest proportion of educational expenditure shouldered by the private sector among OECD countries. The financial burden on families to support the children's higher education may discourage students from disadvantaged backgrounds to proceed to the next stage of schooling.

However, the father's occupation used in this study as a major indicator of social background is not a complete measure of the family's socioeconomic status. Without specific measures of the family's financial situation, such as household income, it is difficult to assess with accuracy the extent to which the need for families to support the children's higher education is associated with educational inequalities between social classes.

Finally, as in other industrial societies, there has been a significant increase of women's participation in higher education in Korea, while social-origin differentials in educational opportunities have remained persistent. In addition to explaining this finding in cross-national comparative studies (Shavit and Blossfeld 1996), we must examine whether the reduction of the gender gap in college attendance may hide other persistent inequalities like gender segregation by field of study within higher education (Davies and Guppy 1997).

CHAPTER FIVE

Sweden: Why Educational Expansion Is Not Such a Great Strategy for Equality—Theory and Evidence

Jan O. Jonsson, Swedish Institute for Social Research, Stockholm University

Robert Erikson, Swedish Institute for Social Research, Stockholm University

INTRODUCTION

Democratization and expansion are two parallel and interrelated trends in the history of Swedish higher education. For more than a hundred years it has been a political aim to make higher education available to those who are capable and interested in pursuing it, irrespective of their ascribed characteristics. This chapter analyzes the dynamics of the educational expansion of the tertiary sector of education in Sweden and addresses the question of whether the expansion can explain changes in social inequality in educational attainment. The Swedish case is of interest for at least two reasons: first, Sweden has experienced not only strong growth in higher education, but unlike most other countries in the Western world, educational contraction as well; second, Sweden has pursued fairly radical reforms in order to equalize educational opportunities, ranging from comprehensive schooling to free tertiary education and a generous universal study loan system. Expansion policies have gone hand in hand with policies aimed at the reduction of inequalities in other spheres of life.

EDUCATIONAL POLICY IN THE PAST HUNDRED YEARS: EXPANSION AND DIVERSION

Two main currents describe the educational policies pursued in Sweden since the late nineteenth century: expansion and diversion. There is a prevalent conflict in the field of higher education policy between those who want to make higher education accessible to everyone and are thus willing to let a large proportion of a cohort enroll, and those who want to keep it the privilege of the brightest students. Like most nations, Sweden has an elitist past with an educational system that was fairly similar to the German one. Many politically influential people (such as clergymen and scientists) regarded academic excellence as an important goal and emphasized the need to divert students from the system who did not meet the high demands. Some also feared that a relatively deprived *Akademikerproletariat* could join "the masses" and become a threat to those in power.

The elitist groups dominated higher education policies for a long time, but the pressure from below was strong. Compulsory education was introduced in Sweden in 1842, and improved institutional links to higher education were created in 1904 and 1927. Still, few made it to the prestigious upper secondary school exam. During the 1930s and early 1940s, the universities led a quiet, secluded life, with enrollment rates fluctuating around 2,000 students per year, corresponding to less than 2% of a birth cohort.

In the late 1940s, population dynamics and a landslide postwar Social Democratic election victory created the basis for an expansive educational policy. The large birth cohorts of the 1940s began school at the same time as transition rates to lower secondary education continued to increase (Ohlsson 1986). The government proposed a school reform whereby the lower secondary school would be incorporated into the new comprehensive school, compulsory from grade 1 to 9 (age 7–16) and based on mixed ability classes. The reform was accomplished in the 1950s and 1960s, gradually as many new schools had to be built to accommodate the students.

The master plan was for a "rolling school reform" that followed the changes in cohort sizes and the rise in educational demand. Reforms in 1966 and 1971 aimed at accommodating the increasing numbers of students now eligible for upper secondary studies. This, in turn, exerted pressure for

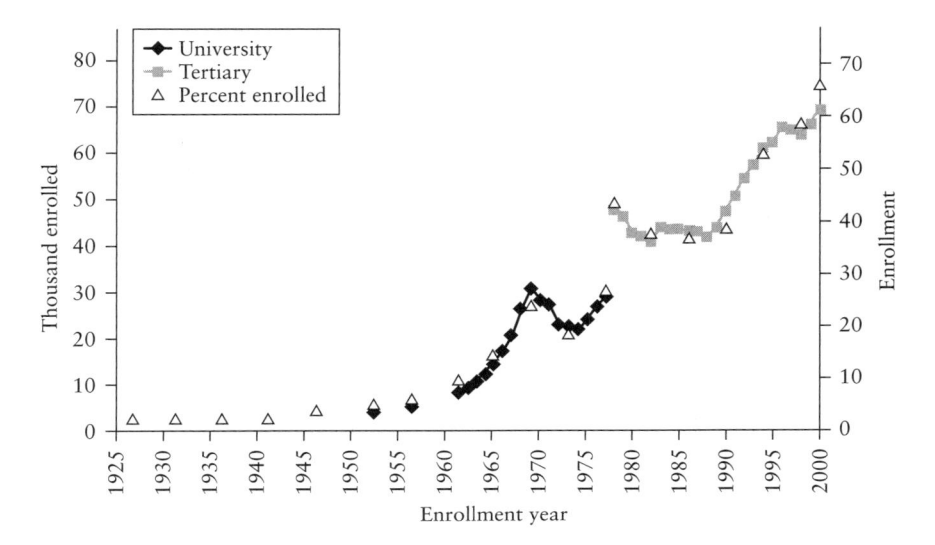

Figure 5.1. First-time Students Enrolled in University (1925–76) and in Tertiary-level Education (1977–99), in Thousands (left axis) and as the Percentage of an Average Cohort in the Ages 19–25 (right axis)

increasing the size of the tertiary level. From the mid-1940s through the 1950s and 1960s, there was continuous growth, although entrance to the Swedish university system was restricted for professional disciplines such as medicine and engineering. During the 1960s, the student population grew from less than 10,000 to around 30,000. The growth is depicted in Figure 5.1, which shows (1) the annual number of students who were enrolled for the first time in university (1925–76) and tertiary education (1977–99), respectively; and (2) the proportion of a cohort that enrolled in tertiary education (selected years; open triangles).[1]

The expansion of the universities in the 1950s and 1960s occurred in the "free faculty," that is, nonprofessional programs (mostly in the humanities and social sciences), for which there were no entry requirements at the time except for the standard requirement of eligibility (which also loosened). Increasing demand was thus met by segmented expansion.

The rapid expansion during the 1960s led the government to propose an all-encompassing *numerus clausus* system, but before it was enacted demand for university education dwindled. As can be seen in Figure 5.1, the number of first-time students enrolled decreased dramatically from 31,000 in 1968 to 22,000 in 1973. Like the growth some years before, the decrease in demand was in the area of the "free faculty."

EXPANSION AS DIVERSION: CREATING A BINARY SYSTEM

In 1977, the rolling school reform reached tertiary education. Traditional university education and the shorter vocational tracks were organizationally integrated into the new *Högskola*, creating a binary tertiary system. In Figure 5.1 this is reflected as a jump in enrollment figures. To a large extent, but not entirely, this is an artificial increase because it is the result of the inclusion of some short-cycle tertiary programs into educational statistics. During the 1980s, there was not much expansion in the combined tertiary sector, but unlike the stalling in the previous decade, this time the problem was not a lack of demand but political unwillingness to expand the system. A change toward the end of the 1980s resulted in renewed growth during the 1990s in an attempt to meet the government's ambitious goal that 50% of a birth cohort should enroll in tertiary education.

What was the background for the creation of the binary system? One of the goals of the expansion of the Swedish postcompulsory education was increased equality of access. At the same time, however, politicians were anxious to maintain academic standards. The compromise was to pursue "policies of diversion" (Murray 1988), whereby the expansion to a large extent was channeled into vocational or semivocational tracks. The expansion of secondary education between 1963 and 1971 consisted largely of the integration of such tracks into a reorganized upper secondary school. Only rarely did these tracks continue naturally to the tertiary level. Empirically, the transition probabilities to higher education differ vastly between tracks even when controlling for ability (Breen and Jonsson 2000). Diversion policy at the secondary level, fueled by demand for vocational studies, is an important reason why Sweden has been lagging behind many industrial societies in the proportion of students continuing to tertiary education from the time of the decreasing demand in the 1970s and until the late 1980s (OECD 2001, table C4.1).

The introduction of the binary tertiary system in Sweden in 1977 should be viewed in this light. Before the 1977 reform, the university sector comprised both traditional academic education (such as arts, law, and science), and part-academic/part-vocational training for the most prestigious professions (e.g., medicine, engineering, and business administration). Outside the university system, there were several organizationally different, short-cycle vocational tracks at the lower tertiary level aimed at semiprofessional occupations such as nursing and primary school teaching. By integrating the two into the new *Högskola*, the ostensive policy was to place the short-cycle vocational and the academic/professional study programs on par with each other. In practice, however, the old demarcation lines survived within the integrated system, just as they had previously done within upper secondary education. Differences in prestige and in labor market opportunities between the different tracks of the *Högskola* remained after the organizational reform.

Critics of the organizational integration of academic and vocational education feared that diversion policies may "entice" working-class students, who may prefer vocational skills to abstract knowledge, away from academic studies. Those of a more optimistic bent assumed that more working-class children than hitherto would study at a tertiary level when tracks with a vocational character became available. Although it is certainly true that the unified *Högskola* could not elevate the status of the short-cycle tracks to the level of the traditional academic tracks, as the intention was, the reforms succeeded in administratively uniting diverse vocational schools and facilitating the choice for students.

In a more recent development, regional colleges have expanded and their role in tertiary education has become numerically important and some have upgraded their status to universities. The early stages of this development may not have had any impact on social inequalities in the recruitment to tertiary education (Dryler 1998), but the consequences of the expansion during the 1990s remain to be studied.

THEORETICAL CONSIDERATIONS ON
EXPANSION AND EQUALITY

What is the expected consequence of expansion policies for the social inequality of educational opportunity?[2] Great hopes have been attached to educational expansion in the past (Halsey, Heath, and Ridge 1980), although skeptics have later maintained that equality of opportunity can come about only if the system expands after the most privileged groups have already reached saturation levels (Raftery and Hout 1993). In order to address the question whether expansion could lead to equality, we begin with devising a theoretical micromodel that attempts to predict how different social groups will react to increasing educational opportunities.

Our point of departure is that social differences in educational choice are a function of conscious considerations of the relative merits of different alternatives available within the individual's objective conditions and resources.[3] We propose a simple decision model in which individuals have several choices—in this case, educational routes—and want to maximize their "utility" (U). For each alternative, individuals estimate its benefits (B), associated costs (C), and the probability of success (P). Benefits are all types of rewards and advantages expected from a given alternative, both monetary and nonmonetary, immediate and long-term (although individuals are assumed to act on the present value of all benefits). Costs include that which must be forfeited for the sake of the given alternative, such as income foregone, and also the amount of time and effort one must exert to succeed in a given educational program. Benefits and costs must be measured with the same unit, which is psychological rather than economic, although economic considerations are crucial.

Probability of success reflects an estimate of how likely it is that an individual manages to complete the studies successfully; it relates primarily to "ability" (or grades, which can be seen as the school's estimate of P), but also to parental resources that improve educational performance. We assume that for individuals who fail to complete their studies the benefits become zero while the costs remain at C. Then, the expected utility of alternative i can be expressed as follows:

$U_i = P_i B_i - C_i$

In other words, an individual is assumed to compare the benefits from and costs of different educational alternatives, and thereby down-weight the benefits with the risk of not being able to complete the studies (in which case the individual will not reap any benefits, but will still have to cover the costs). The individual estimates the utility of all alternatives, including leaving school, and chooses the one that maximizes U. Obviously, no one can assess the exact values of P, B, and C, but it is sufficient to rank the various alternatives.[4]

The choice is restricted by two conditions. First, alternative i is considered only if it is part of an individual's feasible set of options (F) (cf. Elster 1979):

$i \in F$

Second, risk aversion should be taken into account. Let the risk r an individual takes by choosing alternative i be

$r_i = (1 - P_i)C_i$

and let R be the highest risk the individual is willing to accept. The choice is then restricted by

$R \geq r_i$

The restrictions take different forms. If, for instance, a student has poor grades or does not meet other requirements, some educational choices may be blocked, that is, not included in F. Additionally, there may be levels of $(1 - P)$ or of C at which an individual rules out an alternative i regardless of risk (i.e., of the value of their product). Furthermore, the *combination* of B, P, and C may be important. For any given U, someone who is risk averse may prefer a combination of a high P and low B or a low B and low C to an alternative with high B and high C.[5]

To what extent and in what way do probability of success, expected benefits and costs, and risk aversion vary with social origin? As measured by school grades and academic aptitude tests, the educational performance of children from higher social classes is better than that of their lower-class peers, which means that the probability of success (P) varies with social origin. Though this will to a large extent be because of preschool socialization, well-educated parents also help with school-work and provide accurate and accessible information about strategies to be followed in school. This effect on P appears at all branching points in the school system (Erikson and Jonsson 1996b). Costs (C) also vary because the cost of raising a given sum of money is higher for poorer families (Becker 1964/75). Because the highest risk one is willing to take depends among other things on parental wealth, R also contributes to the association between social origin and educational attainment. Finally, while actual benefits (B) do not vary much with social origin, there is probably a "direct effect" of social origin operating by way of educational aspirations (e.g., Boudon 1974). This is based on the assumption that an important objective of children (and their parents) is to achieve the credentials necessary for maintaining their social status across generations, that is, to avoid downward social mobility.[6] Benefits derived from higher education above this aspiration level have a lower marginal utility, and because those from more modest social origins reach this "breaking point" earlier in their educational career than those from higher origins, they will expect lower benefits than the latter in an absolute sense, although benefits for both groups increase at the same rate both below and above the aspiration level.

In what way would educational expansion (or contraction) at the tertiary level have an impact on the socially structured individual educational choices? We first consider expansion of the traditional university programs, that is, within the unified system. We are dealing with a tertiary system under a *numerus clausus* using academic ability as a criterion for restriction, which means that normally the demand for places at the university exceeds the supply. Costs to students are independent of the size of the system, unless expansion is based on fees or such. Benefits for any individual student may decrease, however, because competition for jobs increases if more people achieve as much education as the student, or more. If, however, benefits are weighed relative to other alternatives, the benefits of a particular education may decrease in absolute terms, but increase relative to not pursuing higher education because the value of a lesser education may decrease even more in absolute terms. Thus, it appears to be difficult to determine the total benefits. The probability of success of a single individual would not change unless academic standards decreased, but the average probability of success would decrease because expansion increases the number admitted with lower academic ability. Thus, expansion may have effects that are contrary to those of the diversion strategy in that it at least potentially leads to decreasing success in examinations. Predicting the net result of expansion is a complex issue that we treat separately.

The other development in Swedish tertiary education is the expansion of the lower vocational tertiary programs and their inclusion into the integrated *Högskola*. Predictions of the change in educational inequality following this expansion are similarly difficult to make. The introduction of the binary system has three corollaries: (1) costs at lower tertiary level are lower than at higher levels because study times are shorter, which should attract new groups to tertiary study; (2) probabilities of success (for someone at a given ability level) are probably greater at the lower level than in the traditional university sector, which should have the same result; and (3) those with high aspirations will avoid the lower tertiary program because the expected benefits in income and occupational status are smaller. Because all three consequences are related to social origin, there would be a lower association between social origin and transition probabilities to such short-cycle tertiary education than to traditional university studies.

Whether expansion of the lower tertiary sector would have an impact on the association between origin and education *at the traditional university level* is a moot point. Those who warn that the diversion strategy behind the expansion of short-cycle tertiary education leads to increasing social inequality assume that eligible students consider programs at both levels and that working-class children are more prone to switch from academic to vocational tracks when the latter expand. If this is true, the prediction is sound because the mechanisms described above suggest that educational tracks with higher P and lower r are more attractive to children from working-class backgrounds, and that the higher B at the university level is more attractive to children of the higher classes. We believe, however, that for many students who eventually end up at the lower tertiary level the alternative is not university studies but no tertiary studies at all.

Four questions, that we address in the following, emerge from our individual-level model of educational choice:

   1. In what way do the associations between social origin, on the one hand, and academic performance and educational choice, on the other, combine to produce different origin-education associations at different admission rates?
   2. To what extent do the expansion and contraction of the tertiary system coincide with changes in the association between origin and educational attainment?
   3. Is this association, as our model would predict, lower for the transition to lower tertiary education and higher for professional university programs?
   4. Did expansion at the lower tertiary level coincide with an increase in the origin-education association at university level?

DATA SOURCES

We use two data sources. The Swedish Governmental Commission on Educational Inequality (Erikson and Jonsson 1993, chap. 4; 1996a) collected data based on school record information on grade point averages, enrollment, and examination for people born between 1943 and 1974 and living in Sweden in 1990. The sample fraction was 25%, producing a total sample size of around 900,000. For each of these individuals we linked data on the characteristics of the parents and the household based on the censuses of 1960, 1970, and 1980 using the personal identification number assigned to every Swedish citizen.

We also use a set of combined data from the Swedish level-of-living surveys (LNU), which were started in 1968 and have been conducted five times since then (Erikson and Åberg 1987; Jonsson and Mills 2001) and from the annual surveys of living conditions (ULF) conducted by Statistics Sweden (Vogel et al. 1988). Both surveys are based on random samples of the adult Swedish population, using a sample fraction of around 1/1000, which results in sample sizes of about 5,000–7,000 people per wave. The surveys use the same coding standards for social origin and educational attainment.[7] The data on education are retrospective, and we include in the analyses birth cohorts born since the late nineteenth century. For one analysis we use a data set that combines several ULF surveys covering birth cohorts between 1902 and 1972.

VARIABLES

Social origin. We use a standard Swedish classification, SEI (Sweden SCB 1989) consisting of seven social classes (see Table A.2 in the Appendix).[8] If both parents were present and employed, we use the "dominant" class position, that is, the one that is assumed to be the most influential for household members' living conditions (Erikson 1984); in practice, most often this is the highest position.

Parents' highest level of education. We coded the standard Swedish classification, SUN (Sweden SCB 1988), into the CASMIN schema (Müller and Shavit 1998) (see Table A.1).

Grade point average (GPA) at upper secondary school. GPA (ranging from 1 (poor) to 5 (excellent)) is an average of the grades in about a dozen subjects. GPA is essential for admission to a university program, although it is not the only criterion for admission to the university.

Transitions to tertiary education. Enrollment is defined as the year in which a student begins tertiary studies, including part-time studies, for the first time (not available for the LNU/ULF samples). Tertiary education is divided into three levels:

- *Lower (or short-cycle) tertiary.* Mostly vocational programs for semi-professions, such as teacher training for grades 1–6, nursing and preschool teacher training, as well as some postsecondary technical and industrial programs of less than three years duration. This level is heavily dominated by women who seek jobs in the public sector (care, education).
- *University.* Traditional university education leading to a bachelor's degree (*Fil. kand.*) usually after three years of study.
- *Professional university programs.* Occupationally oriented programs with longer study times of 4–7 years, such as law, medicine, business administration, and civil engineering. Men dominate this level, mostly because of engineering.

Eligibility. It is practically impossible to construct a measure indicating who were eligible at any point in time for tertiary-level studies because the administrative rules have changed several times and because we would need information about respondents' qualifications that is not available. For example, an important change in enrollment regulations in the 1970s was the creation of a quota for those who had been gainfully employed for five years. A proxy for eligibility for university studies is to have (academic) upper secondary-level education (most of the above were eligible, although not for all university programs). One problem is that others could also enroll; for example, graduates of a two-year program at the *Gymnasium* could be admitted into teacher training colleges. Just as for university studies, it is difficult to identify a group that was eligible for lower tertiary studies. Here we include also those who completed a two-year vocational or semivocational program of study at the (upper) secondary level.

For the LNU/ULF data, where we rely on information on highest education completed for a wide range of birth cohorts, we must also assume that all those who have lower tertiary education were eligible for university studies. In most cases this was probably true, in particular for younger cohorts. But in the older cohorts many ended up at the lower tertiary level without having upper secondary-level qualifications, and it is likely that we overestimate the number of students who were eligible for university studies in this group. Eligibility for lower tertiary-level studies is even more difficult to assess. For younger cohorts we followed the principles outlined above, but for older ones we were not able to find a reasonable method for assessing eligibility, and therefore excluded cohorts born before 1940 from these analyses. Furthermore, the results for respondents born in the 1940s must be interpreted with caution.

EXPANSION AND INEQUALITY IN A *NUMERUS CLAUSUS* SYSTEM: THE ROLE OF EDUCATIONAL PERFORMANCE AND CHOICE

Consistent with the individual-level model presented above, the process of "educational inequality" is governed by two main overarching factors and an auxiliary one. The main factors are (1) differences in academic ability and educational performance between children from different social classes, and (2) differences in their propensity to continue to higher levels of education (or academic tracks) at given levels of performance. These two factors account about equally for the association between social origin and educational attainment in Sweden (Erikson and Jonsson 1993). The auxiliary factor (3) is the number of students admitted at each educational level. That number affects the association between class origin and educational outcome in conjunction with the two general factors. On the basis of empirical information on factors (1) and (2), we calculated the association between social origin and transition propensities at different grade limits to the university. It turns out that high grade limits (GPA = 4.5–5.0) lead to high class relativities, while grade requirements below that produces a rather stable pattern of educational inequality across a wide range of medium and low GPA (Erikson and Jonsson 1996c, fig. 1.3). The change is from an association of around Yule's Y = 0.4 to one of 0.3, which is a substantial equalization.[9] At the same time, only few educational programs have entry requirements as high as 4.5. The results suggest that expansion of the professional university programs, and a few other popular programs, would lead to a more socially equal distribution of their students (under the assumption that the relations between social class origin, on the one hand, and grade distribution and transition propensities, on the other, remain the same after the expansion).

Admission data are also useful for assessing the potentially equalizing effects of educational expansion when both GPA and transition propensities are considered. We collected register information on the choices of

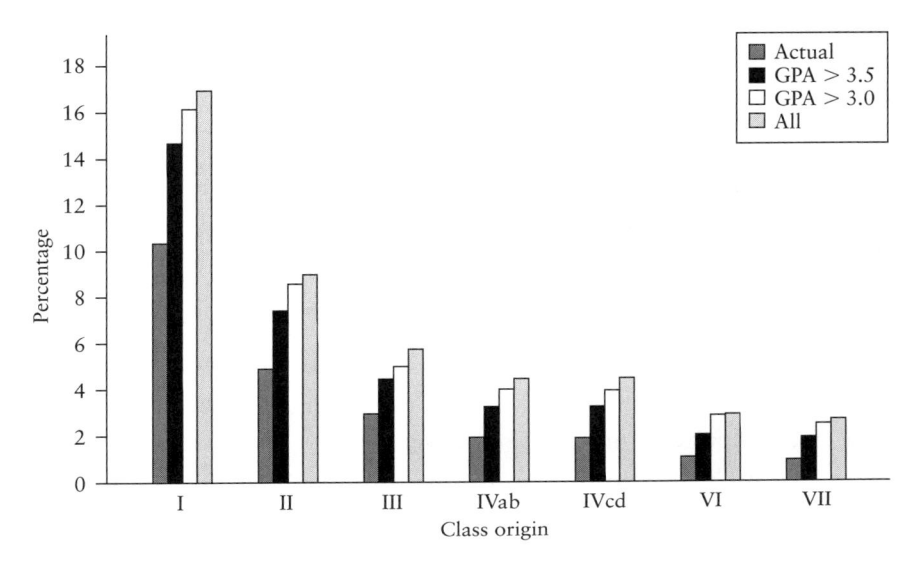

Figure 5.2. Proportion Admitted to University Education at Various Levels of Entrance Requirements, Men and Women Aged 18–24 in 1991

tertiary-level education programs made by eligible students who were 18–24-years-old in 1991. We used the first three choices in student applications and performed a simple comparison of the origin-education association as it was in reality and as it "would have been" if entrance requirements had been more liberal. The results show that expansion would, *ceteris paribus*, have increased university enrollment from all social origins, but that the absolute growth would have been largest for the highest social origin (Figure 5.2). Lowering entrance requirements to the approximate average grade at upper secondary level leads to the greatest system expansion. However, the effect on inequality would be small, leading to a slight decrease in class relativities.

Both the above analyses must make rather strong assumptions about the behavior of students from different origins and with different grades under changing admission rules. Given this caveat, the conclusion is that expansion may lead to some decrease in inequality, but probably not a large one. The reason for the limited effect is that new educational opportunities are to a large extent used by middle-class students with mediocre grades but high educational aspirations.

EDUCATIONAL EXPANSION AND LONG-TERM CHANGE IN EQUALITY OF EDUCATIONAL OUTCOMES

One way of assessing the impact of tertiary-level expansion on social inequality is to study long-term changes in such inequality, using a cohort approach, and relate it to system growth. This does not provide exact indication as to when individuals made their transitions, but because of data limitations it is the only feasible strategy.

Completion of Tertiary Education: Analysis of Broader Cohorts

We begin (Table 5.1) with a multinomial regression analysis of the completion of education at university and lower tertiary level—contrasted with any lower level—on class origin, parents' education, and country of birth (contrasting Sweden with other countries). For this analysis, we use the ULF data for those aged 27–74 in 1976–99. We identify five groups of *birth cohorts* according to approximate changes in enrollment in higher education. The first period (experienced by those born in 1902–18) is characterized by slow growth; the second (1919–40) by more rapid growth of upper secondary schooling but still only a slow growth of tertiary education; the third (1941–49) by very rapid increase in university enrollment; the fourth (1950–58) first by decreasing demand for higher education, then by some increase, but on the whole by stagnation; and the fifth (1959–72) by some resumption of the expansion. The last cohort also was the one that most fully experienced the introduction of the new integrated tertiary system (accomplished in 1977), although older cohorts benefited from it as well.

For degree level, the results reflect a weakening of the effect of parental education across cohorts and some weakening of the class effect between the second and third oldest cohorts. For lower tertiary education, there is a sharp decrease in the class origin effect between the two oldest cohorts, after which there is hardly any change. The estimated effect of parental education decreases between the 1919–40 and 1941–49 cohorts, and again between these cohorts and those born in the 1950s. The details of these patterns should be treated with caution because of possible problems of multicollinearity given that parents' class position and education are correlated. Furthermore, origin effects could be inflated in the oldest cohorts if there is an interaction between social mobility and mortality, that is, if downward mobility is associated with increased mortality rates. Likewise,

TABLE 5.1
Multinomial logistic regression of completion of lower and higher tertiary education (rather than any lower level) on social class origin, parental education, and country of birth

		1902–18 B	S.E.	1919–40 B	S.E.	1941–49 B	S.E.	1950–58 B	S.E.	1959–72 B	S.E.
Lower tertiary education vs. all nontertiary											
	Intercept	−3.12	0.62	−1.73	0.17	−1.55	0.16	−0.89	0.18	−1.27	0.17
Class of origin	I	1.43	0.46	0.62	0.17	0.70	0.16	0.87	0.18	0.88	0.16
	II	1.34	0.35	0.43	0.14	0.44	0.12	0.58	0.14	0.64	0.13
	III	0.96	0.39	0.31	0.14	0.42	0.12	0.27	0.14	0.49	0.14
	Ivab	0.52	0.33	0.32	0.11	0.38	0.10	0.35	0.12	0.19	0.13
	Ivcd	−0.09	0.32	−0.22	0.11	0.00	0.11	0.02	0.15	0.34	0.19
	VI	0.00		0.00		0.00		0.00		0.00	
	VII	−0.50	0.35	−0.43	0.11	−0.23	0.10	−0.03	0.12	−0.16	0.12
Parents' education	3ab	−0.36	0.53	0.45	0.18	0.61	0.17	0.00	0.19	0.37	0.15
	2c	−0.22	0.38	−0.05	0.16	0.26	0.14	0.06	0.16	0.26	0.14
	2ab	0.00		0.00		0.00		0.00		0.00	
	1c	−0.84	0.37	−0.60	0.14	−0.36	0.13	−0.57	0.14	−0.46	0.13
	1ab	−1.79	0.33	−1.35	0.13	−1.00	0.11	−1.08	0.13	−0.74	0.13
Born	Sweden	0.90	0.51	0.34	0.11	0.34	0.11	0.13	0.11	0.05	0.11

(continued)

TABLE 5.1 (continued)

	1902–18 B	S.E.	1919–40 B	S.E.	1941–49 B	S.E.	1950–58 B	S.E.	1959–72 B	S.E.
University degree vs. all nontertiary										
Intercept	−3.26	0.60	−2.09	0.19	−1.70	0.16	−1.05	0.20	−1.84	0.21
Class of origin										
I	2.00	0.51	1.27	0.16	1.22	0.15	1.22	0.19	1.58	0.18
II	1.74	0.45	0.94	0.14	0.81	0.12	0.73	0.16	0.94	0.16
III	1.07	0.54	0.75	0.15	0.73	0.13	0.64	0.16	0.79	0.17
Ivab	1.52	0.42	0.62	0.13	0.58	0.11	0.49	0.15	0.45	0.17
Ivcd	0.27	0.45	−0.18	0.13	0.11	0.13	0.22	0.18	0.48	0.25
VI	0.00		0.00		0.00		0.00		0.00	
VII	0.05	0.47	−0.44	0.14	−0.32	0.12	−0.30	0.16	−0.03	0.17
Parents' education										
3ab	1.39	0.47	1.05	0.17	1.10	0.16	0.85	0.19	0.88	0.17
2c	0.55	0.41	0.40	0.15	0.45	0.13	0.42	0.17	0.52	0.17
2ab	0.00		0.00		0.00		0.00		0.00	
1c	−0.44	0.42	−0.53	0.15	−0.41	0.13	−0.59	0.16	−0.40	0.17
1ab	−1.55	0.38	−1.40	0.14	−1.08	0.11	−1.19	0.15	−0.79	0.16
Born Sweden	−0.08	0.34	0.27	0.11	0.24	0.10	−0.28	0.11	−0.20	0.12
−2 LL	263		553.1		589.9		567		570.5	
R^2 Nag	0.225		0.191		0.185		0.193		0.188	
N (wt)	5,252		15,363		10,409		5,565		5,236	

SOURCES: ULF; Statistics Sweden.
NOTE: Men and women in different birth cohorts, aged 27–74 in 1976–99. Log odds (B) and standard errors (S.E.).

effects in the youngest cohort could be inflated if men and women of working-class background tend to enter and finish university education at higher ages. When the background variables are entered one by one, it is clear that their impact on attaining a university degree has weakened across cohorts, particularly between the 1902–18 and the 1919–40 cohorts, and again for the 1941–49 cohorts (results not shown). For lower tertiary education, the origin effects are weaker, and the trend toward equalization continues through the 1950–58 cohorts. It is difficult to evaluate how the pattern of equalization matches the expansion. Clearly, birth cohorts where tertiary-level education was most commonly achieved show the weakest origin effects, giving tentative support for the expansion hypothesis. However, broad cohorts do not offer opportunities for a more rigorous test.

The analyses in Table 5.1 show the cumulative impact of social origin across several educational stages and transitions. It is common knowledge that the influence of social origin emerges early in the school career and tends to appear at each subsequent transition. For Sweden, this was shown already by Boalt (1947). It could be argued that the importance of the expansion of the tertiary system would be better evaluated by considering only those who are eligible for tertiary-level studies. By restricting the group under study in this manner, we reduce the risk of confusing the effects of expansion at the tertiary level with changes at lower rungs of the educational hierarchy. For example, it is not unlikely that by equalizing access to upper secondary education the comprehensive school reform also contributed to the equalization. Ideally, we would like to relate tertiary-level expansion to changes in inequality for the group for which tertiary studies were an actual option. However, a study of eligible students is problematic. First, it is likely that the expansion of tertiary education also has repercussions for the lower educational levels: signals that higher education is becoming more accessible may inspire able children from disadvantaged social backgrounds to continue to secondary education. This would be the case if, for example, their risk (r) would decrease. Second, as described above, distinguishing a group of eligible students in the Swedish tertiary system is difficult in a longer perspective. In Table 5.2 we have attempted to restrict the risk set to those who could in theory be admitted to tertiary education, acknowledging that it cannot be done with any great precision.

Social origin effects are around half those in Table 5.1, confirming both that much of the inequality in the attainment of tertiary education has it

TABLE 5.2
Logistic regressions of completion of lower and higher tertiary education for eligible students on social class origin, parental education, and country of birth

		1902–18		1919–40		1941–49		1950–58		1959–72	
		B	S.E.	B	S.E.	B	S.E.	B	S.E.	B	S.E.

Lower tertiary education vs. all nontertiary for eligible students

		B	S.E.	B	S.E.	B	S.E.	B	S.E.	B	S.E.
	Intercept					−1.43	0.16	−1.08	0.17	−1.28	0.17
Class of origin	I					0.19	0.15	0.34	0.17	0.39	0.15
	II					0.20	0.12	0.35	0.14	0.44	0.13
	III					0.22	0.12	0.10	0.14	0.38	0.14
	Ivab					0.28	0.10	0.27	0.12	0.15	0.13
	Ivcd					0.02	0.12	0.04	0.15	0.29	0.19
	VI					0.00		0.00		0.00	
	VII					−0.13	0.10	0.03	0.12	−0.14	0.12
Parents' education	3ab					−0.04	0.15	−0.46	0.17	0.03	0.14
	2c					0.02	0.13	−0.12	0.15	0.12	0.14
	2ab					0.00		0.00		0.00	
	1c					−0.27	0.12	−0.37	0.14	−0.36	0.13
	1ab					−0.57	0.11	−0.68	0.13	−0.54	0.13
Born	Sweden					0.23	0.11	0.17	0.11	0.03	0.11
	−2 LL					6842.9		4845.7		4756.6	
	R^2 Nag					0.029		0.028		0.045	
	N (wt)					11,826		7,040		6,393	

University degree vs. all nontertiary for eligible students

		B	S.E.	B	S.E.	B	S.E.	B	S.E.	B	S.E.
	Intercept	−2.03	0.63	−1.42	0.20	−1.03	0.17	−0.84	0.21	−1.46	0.22
Class of origin	I	1.33	0.54	0.78	0.17	0.68	0.15	0.47	0.19	0.88	0.18
	II	1.11	0.48	0.62	0.16	0.42	0.13	0.18	0.17	0.42	0.17
	III	0.68	0.58	0.65	0.16	0.44	0.14	0.41	0.17	0.42	0.18
	Ivab	1.40	0.45	0.46	0.14	0.31	0.12	0.18	0.16	0.24	0.18
	Ivcd	1.05	0.48	0.28	0.15	0.27	0.14	0.20	0.20	0.30	0.27
	VI	0.00		0.00		0.00		0.00		0.00	
	VII	0.59	0.50	−0.07	0.15	−0.10	0.13	−0.34	0.17	0.06	0.18
Parents' education	3ab	1.50	0.53	0.71	0.18	0.65	0.16	0.90	0.19	0.64	0.17
	2c	0.54	0.45	0.32	0.16	0.28	0.14	0.43	0.17	0.41	0.17
	2ab	0.00		0.00		0.00		0.00		0.00	
	1c	0.23	0.47	−0.15	0.16	−0.15	0.14	−0.06	0.17	0.02	0.18
	1ab	−0.15	0.42	−0.41	0.15	−0.31	0.12	−0.29	0.16	−0.13	0.17
Born	Sweden	−0.24	0.37	0.38	0.12	0.19	0.11	−0.15	0.12	0.03	0.12
	−2 LL	610.1		4196.8		4887.2		3105.2		3017.2	
	R^2 Nag	0.152		0.107		0.081		0.104		0.085	
	N (wt)	1,004		5,936		6,388		3,915		3,474	

SOURCES: ULF; Statistics Sweden.

NOTE: Eligibility criteria are different in the two analyses. Eligibility cannot be ascertained with great precision (see text) and was not estimated for lower tertiary education for older cohorts. Men and women in different birth cohorts, aged 27–74 in 1976–99. Log odds (B) and standard errors (S.E.).

roots at lower levels of schooling, and also that much of it occurs at the transition to tertiary education. Concerning the university degree, equalization is evident between the oldest cohort and the younger ones, but there is no impressive change in the effects of the origin variables, a result in line with previous studies on other data (Jonsson and Mills 1993b).

For lower tertiary education, where we cannot analyze the change in the prewar cohorts, the picture is similar in that the origin effects are substantially weaker when we restrict the analysis to those we define as eligible. One difference, however, is that the origin effects at the lower tertiary-level increase in the youngest cohort. What seems to have happened is that secondary vocational education, which we consider sufficient for eligibility, grew in popularity, making many more children from less advantaged backgrounds eligible for tertiary-level studies (results not shown). These children, for some reason, could not match the transition rates of earlier cohorts, which resulted in increasing origin effects.

Detailed Cohort Analysis of Degree Attainment

In the next step, we keep the long-term perspective but use a more precise measurement of expansion. Combining the LNU and ULF data sets we define 15 birth cohorts, the oldest one born 1892–1900, the next oldest 1901–05, then 1906–10, and so on, using five birth-year groups up to 1966–70. We include only respondents who were 29–74 years old at the time of interview. We construct a single measure of educational inequality, taking as a point of departure the cross-tabulation of social origin by university exam (degree or not) by birth cohort. The risk set consists of all students, not only those eligible for university studies. We fit a log-linear model to each three-way table, where we assume that the pattern of interaction between social origin and educational attainment is the same across cohorts, but that the strength of the association could vary. This assumption is on the whole correct, as is evident from more detailed analyses (Erikson and Jonsson 1996c, fig. 1.7), and the model fits the data very well. The model can be expressed as:

$$\ln(F_{1ik}/F_{2ik}) = m + b_k X_i$$

where F_{1ik}/F_{2ik} is the expected odds that someone from social origin class i in cohort k has attained educational level 1 rather than 2; m is a constant; X is a vector where X_i represents a baseline effect of having an origin

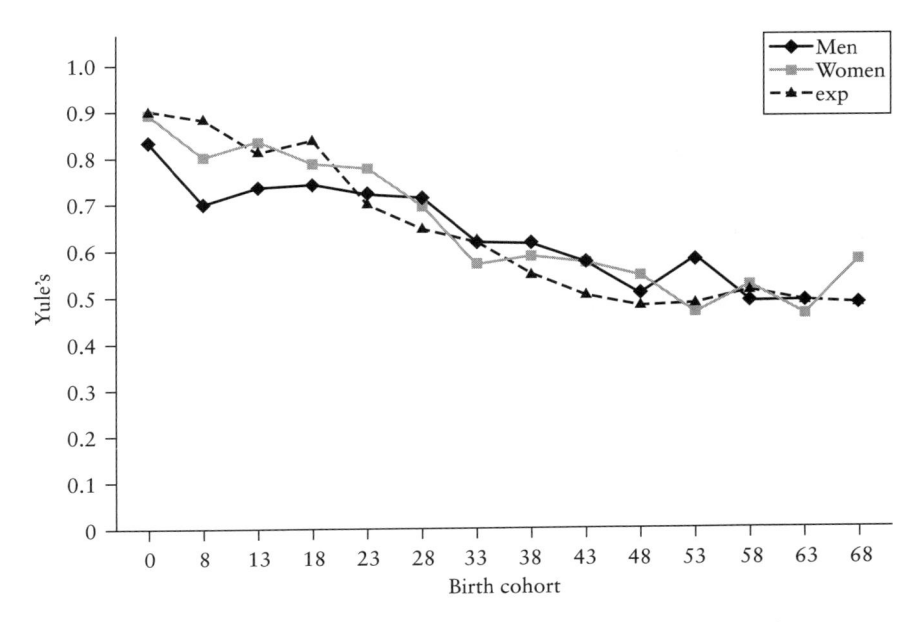

Figure 5.3. Association Between Social Origin and the Attainment of a University Degree for Men and Women in Cohorts Born 1892–1970 (five-year cohorts) and a Function of the Inverse of the Expansion in the Number of University Students

in class i; and b_k indicates the extent to which the odds for cohort k on average deviate from the baseline. From this so-called uniform difference model (Erikson and Goldthorpe 1992), the estimated parameter b_k is our measure of the relative educational inequality in a given birth cohort; as $b_k X_i$ is a measure of the association between social origin and educational attainment, variation in b_k can be interpreted as increases or decreases in educational inequality.

Figure 5.3 shows the changes in the association between social origin and the attainment of a university degree for birth cohorts 1892–1900 to 1966–70, where $b_k X_i$, applied to the contrast between class I and class VII, has been transformed into Yule's Y for ease of presentation and interpretation.

The curves slope downward indicating that the association weakens. Consistent with the results in Table 5.2, social origin has become less important for university studies. Although the first impression is that the entire period is characterized by educational equalization, the change between birth cohorts 1951–55 and 1966–70 is unimportant. Discounting the oldest birth cohorts (because the small number of observations makes estimates about them less reliable) a reasonable interpretation is that equalization at higher levels of education was most accentuated for the cohorts born between 1925 and 1950, with slightly different timing for men and women.

Superimposed on the curves for men and women is also a linear function of the inverse of the curve from Figure 5.1, describing the change in system growth over time. The estimates are based on the approximate number of people admitted when individuals were 20 years of age, and they are scaled to make the curve fall in the same area as the other two. At first glance, the trends appear to have a similar shape, with rapid change in the middle birth cohorts and slower at the ends. But despite some similarity, the changes are not simultaneous. For example, expansion accelerated before equalization, and the great expansion for cohorts born 1930–46 was not accompanied by rapid equalization but by a slow one. Thus, while the curves seem to coincide, the correlations of the differences between values for inequality and expansion in one period and those in the next are low: -0.06 for men and -0.05 for women. Thus, the analysis suggests that expansion has no effect on inequality. It may be that more precise measures of the timing of expansion and the change in inequality would show stronger correlations, but hardly of an impressive magnitude.

In a time-series analysis on the same data, Erikson (1996) studied the impact of different societal and educational trends on social inequality in educational attainment. He found that factors related to the inequality of living conditions in the parental generation were positively related to inequality of educational opportunity, and that the early introduction of a grant system and the establishment of the comprehensive school in the 1950s reduced inequality. Neither the expansion of the upper secondary school nor of the university (operationalized as the proportion of a cohort that enrolled) had any impact on inequality, however, supporting the results above.

EXPANSION AND TRANSITION TO TERTIARY EDUCATION BETWEEN 1967 AND 1988

For the period between 1967 and 1988, we have more detailed information on educational transitions. We know in which year every student made the first transition to tertiary-level studies, so we can address more precisely the question of expansion and contraction, and the simultaneous change, if any, of the origin-education association.

Our procedure follows that in our cohort analysis. First, for those aged 17–25, we calculate a yearly association between social origin and transition to traditional university programs and to professional programs, respectively.[10] Second, we relate the change in educational inequality, so measured, to the inverse of the educational expansion (as in Figure 5.3). As we expect the effect of educational expansion to be pronounced for those who are eligible, we limit the analysis to those who have completed academic upper secondary school. The results are shown in Figure 5.4a (professional education) and 5.4b (university).

First, there is some evidence of equalization during the period, particularly for the professional programs and for women to traditional university education. In part, but not entirely, this is due to the age limits we have chosen; had we included those between 26–30 years of age, changes would have been less striking. Second, tertiary-level reform in 1977 and the concomitant expansion of lower tertiary education did not coincide with an increase in origin-education association at the university level, giving no support to the pessimistic prediction that working-class students would be diverted from traditional university studies to the expanding shorter tertiary vocational tracks (this is also true when we include those who were not eligible into the analysis). Third, although Figures 5.4a and 5.4b do not represent a formal test, they suggest that there is no strong relation between the size of the tertiary-level system and social inequality in educational attainment. What speaks in favor of the hypothesis of a link between the two is that there was both expansion and equalization between the late 1970s and the 1980s. If we correlate first differences (i.e., between consecutive time periods) for equalization with those for educational expansion, the correlations for men are 0.35 for professional education and 0.32 for university, and for women 0.11 and −0.35, respectively. Thus, we find some support for the hypothesis that educational expansion leads to reduced inequality at the entrance to professional schools, which have been restricted during the entire period covered by our data.

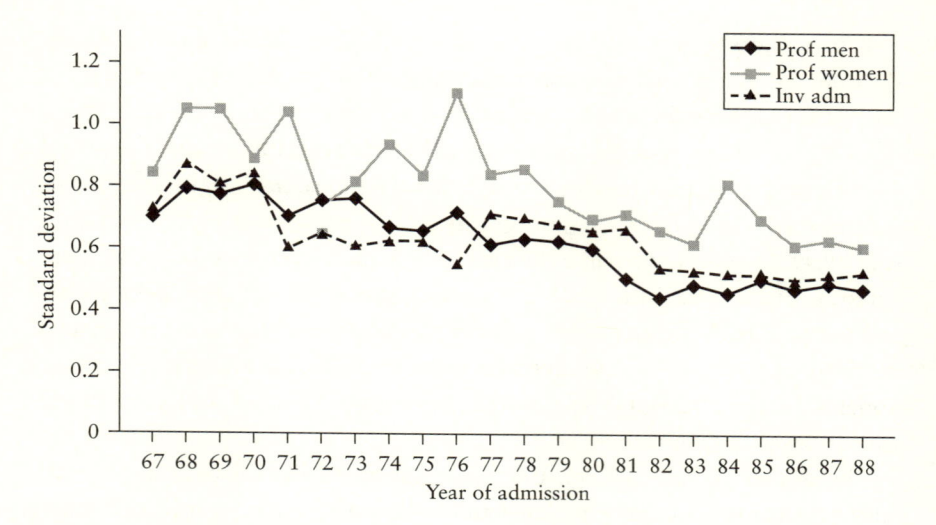

Figure 5.4a. Standard Deviation of Log Parameters for the Effect of Class Origin on Transition to Professional Education Among Eligible Men and Women Aged 17–25 in the years 1967–88 and a Function of the Inverse of Percentage Admitted

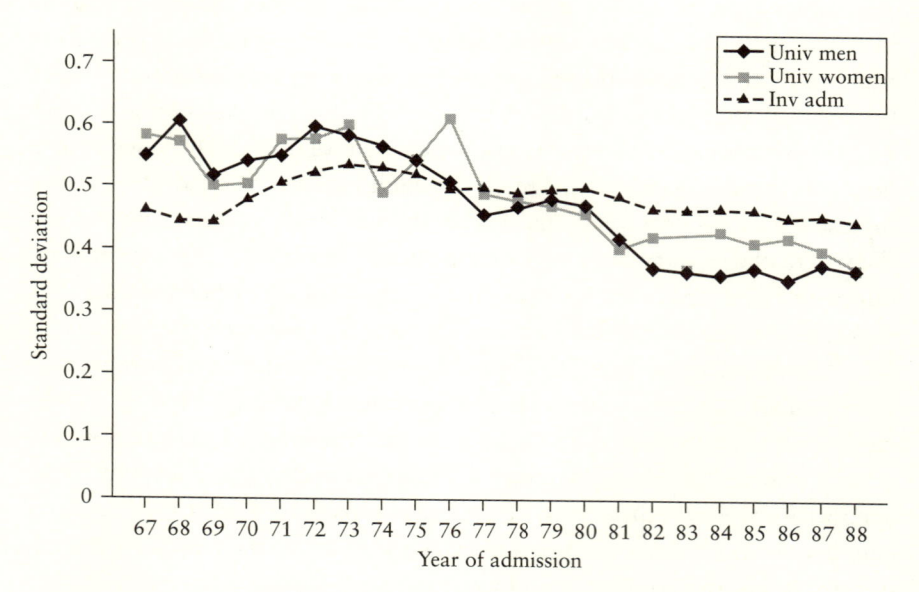

Figure 5.4b. Standard Deviation of Log Parameters for the Effect of Class Origin on Transition to University Education Among Eligible Men and Women Aged 17–25 in the Years 1967–88 and a Function of the Inverse of Percentage Admitted

CONCLUSIONS AND DISCUSSION

Based on an individual-level model of educational choice, we identified four questions related to the overarching issue of whether educational expansion at the tertiary level also may reduce educational inequality.

First, we ask how social differences in educational performance (as measured by GPA) and in educational choice (at given levels of GPA) combine in producing different levels of educational inequality at different enrollment levels—a crucial question in a tertiary system based largely on restricted intake. In our first analysis, it turns out that inequality decreases only if GPA requirements for entrance are lowered from very high to medium-high levels, which would be possible to do for some professional university programs, for example. At more moderate entrance requirements, the significance of expansion is limited. The conclusion of a weak effect of expansion is supported by our second analysis, where we studied university applications from students of different social origins and with different GPAs: lowering entry requirements would lead to equalization of a modest magnitude. It should be noted that the conclusions based on both these analyses hinge on the assumption that changes in entrance levels do not affect either social differences in GPA or in educational choice at given levels of GPA.

The second question concerns the extent to which actual educational expansion and contraction coincided with changes in educational inequality. The hypothesis that tertiary-level expansion is related to decreasing social differences in attainment receives only weak support in our analyses. Analyzing cohorts born 1892–1970 supplied little evidence of such a relation in a long-term perspective. Furthermore, there is little indication of it for women in the more detailed analyses of the 1967–88 period, although these analyses indicate a slight positive correlation between enrollment figures and equality for men. The latter support is based partly on the coincidence of increased inequality and system contraction in the 1970–73 period. However, because the contraction was due to decreasing demand and not to more severe limits on the supply of university places, we believe that the causal order is reversed: Owing to some exogenous factor, children from more disadvantaged origins found higher education less rewarding (relative to children of other origins), and, because of their decreasing propensity to enroll in tertiary education the system contracted.

While we cannot rule out that expansion has some limited positive effect on educational equality, our analyses suggest that other social forces are more efficient in reducing social inequalities in educational attainment. These include developments toward greater equality of condition and reforms that made the Swedish educational system less stratified (see further Jonsson and Erikson 2000). Our results also refute the pessimistic view that equalization is dependent on system growth because it is only possible when the transition rates of privileged groups already have reached saturation.

The third and fourth questions address the consequences of the introduction (or expansion) of a binary system of tertiary education in Sweden, particularly in relation to the tertiary school reform in 1977. As expected, transition to these lower-level programs show less association with social origin than do the longer, traditional university programs, which in turn are less correlated with origin than the even longer, professional programs. But the expansion of lower-level tertiary education did not coincide with any noteworthy change in social differences in transition to *other* university levels. Thus, the hypothesis that expansion at the lower level would divert working-class students to vocational rather than general academic studies at tertiary level finds no support. One explanation could be that the expansion was more illusory than real: most of the short-cycle programs that were included in the new *Högskola* existed already before the reform, although they were not part of the integrated system nor of the enrollment statistics available for analysis. Another possible explanation is that there is low substitutability between the vocational and academic tracks, and, therefore, the expansion of the former is not necessarily connected to the popularity of the latter.

In sum, our analyses provide little support for tertiary system expansion as an effective means of educational equalization. Under certain conditions, expansion may trigger equalization, especially when entrance requirements are very high to begin with. But it is hardly possible, on the basis of our analyses, to pass a general judgment on the ability of educational expansion to promote equality of educational outcomes; students face different constraints and opportunities within different education systems. It is likely that an expansion of the Swedish system, with its strong vocational tradition and restrictions on university admission, leads to different outcomes than a corresponding expansion in a demand-driven system. Similarly, expanding a system like the Swedish one, in which there are no fees for tertiary-level studies, may have different consequences than a similar growth in a system with fees. Again, expanding the tertiary sector by introducing new institutions with lower academic status may ostensibly lead to equalization, but it also creates stratification within the tertiary sector and may not lead to increased social mobility.

Finally, the fact that tertiary-level expansion appears to have little potential in equalizing educational opportunity does not mean that such expansion is futile. In fact, as the importance of social origin for occupational attainment tends to be less among those with higher education (Hout 1988; Erikson and Jonsson 1998), educational expansion may increase social mobility without equalizing educational opportunity. In addition, expansion may have other positive effects: for example, more people can realize their potentials, and more educated may mean positive "spill-over" effects for co-workers and children. These putative consequences must then be weighed against potential negative effects, such as overqualification and increased costs for educational provision.

CHAPTER SIX

Taiwan: Higher Education—Expansion and Equality of Educational Opportunity

Shu-Ling Tsai, Academia Sinica

Yossi Shavit, Tel Aviv University

INTRODUCTION

During the twentieth century there have been substantial increases in the enrollment, especially of girls, in education systems worldwide (LeVine, LeVine, and Schnell-Anzola 2001). Taiwan was no exception. In 1950, 80% of children aged 6 to 11 years were enrolled in school, and since the mid-1970s net enrollment rates for both boys and girls approached 100% (ROC Ministry of Education 2001a, 34). The proportion of the 12–17 age group enrolled in school increased from 65.7% in 1976 to 92.2% in 2000, and that of females (93.5%) exceeded that of males (91.0%). Similarly, in the 18–21 age group the net enrollment rate rose from 10.0% in 1976 to 38.7% in 2000, and again the increase was higher for females than for males. In 1976, the net enrollment rate of males aged 18–21 (11.2%) was higher than that of females (8.7%), but the opposite has been true since the mid-1980s. In 2000, the net enrollment rate for women aged 18–21 was 42.1%, as opposed to 35.5% for men of the same age (ROC Ministry of Education 2001a, 39).

The steady increase in educational attainment across cohorts has been paralleled by long-term growth in the number of higher education institutions. In Taiwan "higher education" refers to education provided by junior colleges, colleges, universities, and graduate schools. Junior colleges are designed to train skilled workers. The main task of colleges, universities, and graduate schools is to provide advanced study and educate professional personnel. In other words, Taiwan's tertiary education is both diversified and binary. It is binary because, as we shall see, there are clear distinctions between vocational and academic programs and institutions. It is diversified

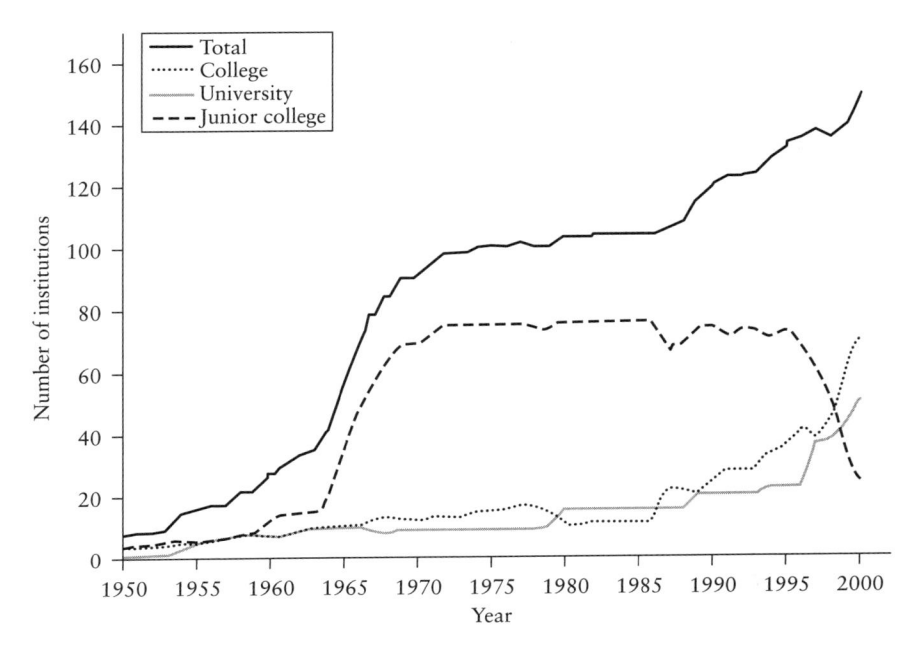

Figure 6.1. Trends in the Number of Institutions of Higher Education by Type and Year

in the sense in which academic institutions are different in organizational forms and clearly stratified by prestige. In 1950, there were 7 institutions of higher education with a total of 6,665 students; by the year 2000, the number of institutions was 150, serving 1,092,102 students (ROC Ministry of Education 2001a, 25, 27). The growth is depicted in Figure 6.1, which shows the number of institutions by type of higher education and year.

The Taiwanese system of higher education developed in a nonlinear manner. Since World War II we distinguish three phases in its development: a period of aggressive expansion until the early 1970s; a period of stagnation during which the state restricted the expansion of academic higher education and encouraged the proliferation of vocational colleges and programs; and since the late 1980s a period of resumed rapid growth of four-year colleges and universities through the formation of new institutions and the upgrading of older colleges to four-year institutions. The vast majority of Taiwanese colleges and universities now in operation were established since 1985, when deregulation took effect.

At the macro level, educational stratification in Taiwan is characterized by early social selection. Among cohorts born before 1956, severe limitations on the access of women to education occurred as early as the compulsory level (Tsai, Gates, and Chiu 1994). Nevertheless, in the better-educated postwar generations, parents desired and expected their children to attain more education than they themselves had achieved. In 2000, only 17.9% of the adult population aged 25 and over received tertiary education (ROC Ministry of Education 2001b, 65), but more than 80.0% of parents demanded a higher education for their children, irrespective of the child's sex (Tsai 2001). Because of excessive demand for higher education, access has been restricted through stringent eligibility examinations.

Using data derived from two social surveys conducted in 2000, this paper examines the possible effects of changes in the expansion of higher education on inequality between social strata, and between ethnic and gender groups in high-school graduation and in access to tertiary education. We describe the historical development of higher education in Taiwan and the competition in Taiwan's educational transitions. We then review the relevant theories of educational expansion on equality of educational opportunity. Finally, we describe the data, variables, and models used in the analysis and we show the empirical results. We conclude with a summary and a brief discussion of the results.

HISTORICAL DEVELOPMENT OF HIGHER EDUCATION IN TAIWAN

The global spread of schooling during the nineteenth and twentieth centuries was due largely to nation-building efforts by political leaders endeavoring to establish their peoples and geographic territories as modern nation-states (Bendix 1977; Craig 1984; LeVine, LeVine, and Schnell-Anzola 2001). In Taiwan, the Japanese imposed Western-style education systems during their colonial rule (1895–1945). A main objective of Japanese education in Taiwan was the assimilation of the island and its integration into Japan. This program was initially implemented at the level of basic compulsory schooling (*common school*) by educating the masses in literacy, economic usefulness, and political obedience (Lin 1929; Tsurumi 1977). Beyond the common school, schools were differentiated into academic and vocational tracks and segregated by gender and race (Japanese and Taiwanese, with the latter consisting of Hokkien, Hakka, and Aborigines). Four of Taiwan's first modern institutions of higher education—one university and three colleges (equivalent to junior colleges today)—were established during the first decades of the twentieth century. Taihoku (Taipei) Imperial University, which became National Taiwan University after WWII, was established in 1928. From its inception, Taihoku was defined mainly as a research center rather than a teaching institution, with a focus on studies of the subtropical regions of south China and the South Pacific, intended to serve the interests of the colonial government (Tsurumi 1977, 122–24). This highest of Taiwan's institutions of learning was attended primarily by Japanese from Taiwan and Japan. The few Taiwanese students who were admitted were allowed to earn degrees in the college of medicine (Epstein and Kuo 1991, 169). Young Taiwanese who aspired to a higher education but were not admitted to university either went to Japan to study or entered one of the three colleges specializing in commerce, agriculture, and technology. Given the role played by colonial education, it is not surprising that the Taiwanese were carefully channeled into two professions that the Japanese government was eager to promote among ambitious and able Taiwanese: teaching and medicine. Those who did not aspire to these two professions and who rejected the traditional Taiwanese occupations were channeled into skilled jobs in the new industries developed by the Japanese.

After the takeover of Taiwan by the Nationalist Chinese in 1945, education appeared to be the most direct way to bring the Japanized Taiwanese back to Chinese cultural orthodoxy and nationalist sympathies (Gates 1987). The Nationalist Chinese government (KMT) kept the basic pattern established by the Japanese, expanded education, and adopted the American system of 6-3-3-4 years of schooling (Smith 1991).[1] The three colleges established by the Japanese were upgraded and eventually transformed into national universities and new colleges were formed.

During the decades of National Party rule (1945–2000), Taiwanese higher education was transformed from elite into mass education through a nonlinear process (Figure 6.1). In the first period, between 1950–60, the number of tertiary institutions increased from 7 to 27 as a result of the establishment of new universities and colleges, both public and private. Five of these (three national universities, one private university, and one private college) were re-established institutions that were in existence on Mainland China before the war. Numerically, tertiary education expanded most rapidly in the 1960s through the explosive increase in the number of junior colleges (from 12 in 1960 to 76 in 1972).

Throughout the period discussed here, there have been three types of junior colleges in Taiwan: two-year junior colleges that admit graduates of vocational high schools; three-year junior colleges that admit graduates of both academic and vocational high schools;[2] and five-year junior colleges that admit graduates of junior high schools. The first three years in five-year junior colleges parallel upper secondary education, and students who complete this phase continue to fourth and fifth grades, which, although held in the same schools, are officially considered "tertiary education." These junior colleges constitute the lowest tier of Taiwan's tertiary education.

Taiwan's economic expansion began in the 1960s, with the transition from import-substitution (1953–60) to export-oriented industrialization (1961–72). As early as the 1960s, national manpower planning has been part of the economic development plans implemented by the state. The most profound influence exerted by the state was the enactment of compulsory education and the optional further education. In 1968, compulsory education was extended from six to nine years. Educational policies at almost all levels, especially those related to vocational education, were motivated by economic considerations (Yung and Welch 1991; Tien 1996). For instance, the Nationalist government encouraged the expansion of the vocational sector since 1966, while at the same time limiting the expansion of academic institutions, to meet the growing demand for skilled workers and technicians generated by industrialization. The state used two methods to achieve this goal: it increased the number of students enrolled in the vocational track, and it established new vocational schools and junior colleges. To speed the pace of industrialization, the educational policy encouraged the expansion of industry-oriented institutions and restricted the number of schools specializing in such fields as agriculture and nursing. In 1968, the Economic Construction Commission set as a policy goal to be achieved by 1977 a ratio of 30:70 between senior high-school students and senior vocational students. Since 1982, however, the demand for engineers has increased along with Taiwan's industrial upgrading. Consequently, the policy changed in the 1990s, leading to a recent growth in the number of senior high-school students. The ratio between academic and vocational students, which dropped rapidly from 61:39 in 1966 to 37:63 in 1977, increased gradually from 32:68 in 1990 to 46:54 in 2000 (ROC Ministry of Education 2001a, 25–27).

At the university level, the economic plan set a student ratio of 11:9 for natural science, engineering, agriculture, and medicine-related departments *versus* the social sciences and humanities (Tien 1996).

By 1972, there were 99 tertiary institutions: 9 universities, 14 colleges, and 76 junior colleges. Because of the rapid expansion in the previous period, the supply of qualified faculty members did not increase at the same rate as the number of students, and therefore the quality of higher education in general declined. Consequently, that year the state imposed restrictions on the formation of any new private institutions, and started limiting the rate of increase in enrollment to colleges and universities to 3% annually. This restrictive policy, reminiscent of developments in Japan at about the same time, was in effect until 1985. During the 1970s, demand for technicians with advanced professional knowledge and skills grew with the increasing sophistication of Taiwan's industries. To meet these needs, the National Taiwan Institute of Technology was established in 1974 with the explicit mission of training students in such fields as chemical engineering, electronic engineering, textiles, and construction. This four-year college was the first institution of higher education within the vocational education system, and it provided a channel for graduates of vocational schools to further their education, and thus vocational education was upgraded to the college and graduate levels. Since then, expansion through the parallel development of academic and vocational tertiary education has become policy.

Taiwan has changed rapidly since the 1980s. Most notably, politically it moved toward democracy. Before the lifting of martial law in 1987, education was highly centralized. In this state-managed system, the Ministry of Education tightly controlled both public and private schools. In addition to the structural barriers between vocational and academic tracks, which demarcated the educational pathway by deliberate government design, there were many other expressions of governmental influence—from obvious ones, such as the number and types of schools built or licensed, to more subtle mechanisms, such as the qualification of teachers hired or promoted, the timing of entrance examinations, the content of the subjects that were taught, and tuition levels.

Under the Nationalist regime's strategy based on Sun Yat-Sen's ideology, the low-tuition policy was designed with the explicit aim of reducing social inequality in educational attainment.[3] The extent to which the low-tuition policy achieved its goal remains controversial. There is no doubt, however, that without the freedom to raise tuition fees and with limited financial state support, private institutions have been caught in a vicious cycle and tended to rank lower than state institutions in prestige and quality.

During the 1980s and 1990s, the state exercised less and less control over educational policies, as criticism on the part of civil society mounted. To meet the growing social demand for higher education, tertiary education has expanded in two principal directions since the 1985 deregulation: the establishment or licensing of new institutions and, especially after 1997, the upgrading of existing institutions from the lower to the higher tier. Between 1997 and 1999, 55 institutions were upgraded (ROC Ministry of Education 2001a). For example, the National Taiwan Institute of Technology was upgraded and renamed the National Taiwan University of Science and Technology in 1997. More representative is the case of the National Taipei University of Technology, which was originally the School of Industrial Instruction established for Japanese students by the Japanese in 1912. In 1922, it was transformed into a five-year school named the Taipei First School of Industry, which admitted Japanese as well as Taiwanese students who had completed six years of compulsory education. In 1945, the school was renamed the Provincial Taipei Vocational School of Industry; in 1948 it was upgraded to the Provincial Taipei Institute of Technology; in 1981 it was further upgraded to the National Taipei Institute of Technology; and in 1997 it was finally transformed into a university.

In the present study, we focus on the possible consequences of change in secondary and higher education for educational stratification in Taiwan. Specifically, we study the association between educational attainment on the one hand and socioeconomic backgrounds and ascribed statuses, such as gender and ethnicity, on the other.

EDUCATIONAL TRANSITIONS IN TAIWAN

In Taiwan, as in most countries, the educational attainment process consists of a series of transitions between grade levels and of branching points where students choose or are assigned to one of several tracks or programs

(Mare 1981). Following the extension of compulsory education to nine years, students who complete elementary schools, usually at age 12, are assigned to a local junior high school based on their official place of residence. In 2000, 99.8% of all students, irrespective of sex, continued to junior high school (ROC Ministry of Education 2001a, 35). The transition from junior high school to senior high school is more difficult because schools are differentiated by function and stratified by prestige at the postcompulsory level. Students take competitive examinations and are assigned to tracked schools according to their results. Candidates whose grades are insufficient for acceptance into a "good" public senior high school often attend public vocational schools or private senior high schools. In 2000, 96.2% of the girls and 94.5% of the boys continued to senior high schools (ROC Ministry of Education 2001a, 35). The same year, the ratio of senior high school students to senior vocational students was 46:54 (ROC Ministry of Education 2001a, 27). The restriction on the proportion of academic students at the secondary level induces fierce competition among junior high students, and as a result school life is dominated by examinations.

Usually, students at age 18 take entrance examinations to enter tertiary education. Those who pass the national entrance examination are assigned to specific institutions and departments within these institutions, and those who fail are offered an opportunity to try again in subsequent years. Before 1995, the national entrance examination was the only mechanism of selection.[4] In 2000, 69.7% of female and 67.7% of male high-school students moved on to the tertiary level, while the corresponding figures for female and male vocational students were 42.8% and 33.8%, respectively (ROC Ministry of Education 2001a, 35).

In Taiwan, earlier studies found significant inequalities in educational opportunity among cohorts born before 1975 (e.g., Hsieh 1987, 1992; Tsai 1992; Tsai and Chiu 1993a, 1993b; Tsai, Gates, and Chiu 1994; Yang 1994; Broaded 1997; Luoh 2001). In addition to socioeconomic background, gender and ethnicity are two important factors associated with individuals' educational attainment. Tsai, Gates, and Chiu (1994), for example, showed that during the mid-twentieth century, severe limitations on the access of women to education occurred as early as the compulsory level, and that in the middle of the educational hierarchy significant ethnic differences and inequalities of educational opportunity due to the father's occupational class appeared. Although girls and boys in more recent cohorts enjoyed greater equality in educational opportunities than those in earlier cohorts, class and ethnic inequalities in education persist.

THEORY: EFFECTS OF EXPANSION ON THE EQUALITY OF EDUCATIONAL OPPORTUNITY

Socioeconomic background affects students' educational attainment, which, in turn, affects their performance in the labor market. One of the unresolved questions in the field of social stratification concerns the effects of educational expansion on socioeconomic inequality in education. It has been suggested that industrialization expands education and reduces the association between social origin and educational attainment (Treiman 1970a) because economic development produces a transition from an ascribed to an achieved allocation of roles. Industrialization leads to universalistic values within the economic sphere. Education systems become a rational mechanism for training workers, shifting the locus of human capital formation from the family to the school. School systems consequently expand to meet the increased need for a trained labor force, which, in turn, leads to a more meritocratic allocation of education.

Conflict theorists have challenged the common argument whereby advances in technology and the upgrading of the occupational structure have resulted in a need for a higher level of skill and training that education is said to supply. Collins (1979), for example, argues that the critical role played by education in industrialized societies is not to provide training but to preserve the status culture. Employers select the job candidates they believe will best fit into the status culture of the elite. Educational credentials represent a status "capital" that allows individuals to "buy" their way into occupational positions. Once the system is firmly in place, groups compete for education as they seek entry into the most lucrative jobs. The less advantaged groups attempt to improve their positions by increasing their levels of schooling, while the advantaged groups try to stay ahead and preserve their relative advantage by climbing ever higher on the educational ladder. As a consequence of status competition in society, education systems expand without increasing the equality of educational opportunity.

The idea of the education system as an ever-expanding pie whose slices are always cut in the same way prevails in the literature. For example, Boudon (1974) argues that once a minimum level of educational attainment has been established in a society, demand for education is created and becomes self-perpetuating as educated parents expect increasing amounts of education for their children.

In his landmark study, Mare (1981) found that in the United States the effects of parents' socioeconomic characteristics on the highest school grade completed were stable over cohorts born during the first half of the twentieth century. He explained the stability by describing a system characterized by a dynamic equilibrium, where the growing distribution of education across socioeconomic groups is counterbalanced by an increase in the importance of social background in the allocation of higher—and hence scarce—levels of education. Mare distinguished two aspects of formal educational stratification: the distribution of schooling and the extent to which some socio-demographic groups are allocated more schooling than others. It is important not to confuse changes in the distribution of formal schooling (i.e., the extent of educational expansion) with changes in the principles upon which schooling is allocated among groups. Therefore, Mare formulated a model of change in equality of educational opportunity whose parameters are not affected by the degree of educational expansion. Mare's educational transition model consists of a set of logistic response models corresponding to a sequence of transitions between grades that denote movement across the major institutional divisions of the education system.

During the 1980s and 1990s, Mare's transition model was the industry standard in the literature of the sociology of education. Through its repeated application, two empirical regularities were established. First, cross-national studies in a variety of countries at different stages of social, economic, and political development showed the persistence over decades in the effects on the log-odds of educational transitions (e.g., Shavit and Blossfeld 1993). Second, recent educational attainment research indicates that the estimated effects of family background on the odds of transition from one level to the next diminish at higher levels of education.

Raftery and Hout (1993) applied Mare's model to Irish data and formulated their influential thesis of "Maximally Maintained Inequality" (MMI): educational expansion does not weaken the association between social origin and education, unless demand for a given level of education is saturated for the upper class (that is, if some origin-specific transition rates approach 100%). In addition, MMI predicts that equalization can be reversed if, for example, public support for education is reduced.

In the criticism of Cameron and Heckman (1998), the schooling transition model assumes myopia on the part of agents, which is difficult to justify on choice-theoretic grounds. In addition, they showed that a pattern of declining logit coefficients for higher-grade transitions is critically dependent on choices of functional forms for the distribution of unobserved variables (e.g., ability). They formulated an alternative model based on rational economic decision making by agents, within which it is possible to take into account dynamic selection bias or educational selectivity. Lucas (2001) directly addressed the criticism of Cameron and Heckman (1998) by proposing a thesis of "effectively maintained inequality" (EMI), which frames educational transitions as students' movement through the stratified curriculum. He argued that tracking has become an important part of the educational transition process in the United States because students make decisions yearly about which structural path to follow: drop out; stay in school in college preparatory courses in academic subjects; stay in school in noncollege preparatory courses in academic subjects; or stay in school but avoid academic subjects. Using time-varying performance measures to predict students' track placement and school continuation, Lucas's analysis corroborates the validity of the educational transitions approach and suggests substantively important social background effects even for nearly universal transitions.

While MMI predicts that class inequality between families declines for levels of education that are saturated for the upper classes, EMI implies that for levels of education that are universal, competition takes place with regard to the type of education attained. In the case of Taiwan, secondary education is rationed by the structural barriers the government deliberately imposed between vocational and academic tracks. Earlier studies (e.g., Tsai and Chiu 1993b; Tsai, Gates, and Chiu 1994) have shown that after the extension of compulsory education, the transition from junior high to senior high school appeared to be most selective, upgrading to that level the most significant inequality in access to education: inequality by social origin. In the following analysis, we pay special attention to the role played by tracking in secondary education in determining access to different types of tertiary education. We also study the stratification of access to the different tracks at the higher level, specifically junior colleges versus four-year programs in colleges and universities. Following Lucas (see also Ayalon and Shavit 2004), we hypothesize that inequality of access to the more selective (four-year) programs persists even if it declines vis-à-vis higher education as a whole.

DATA, VARIABLES, AND METHOD

To explore recent trends in the inequality of educational opportunity, we used data from the Taiwan Social Change Survey (TSCS) conducted in 2000. TSCS is a series of island-wide surveys sponsored by the National Science Council and conducted by a large group of social scientists. It is an ongoing project designed to create data sets on the main themes of Taiwan's changing society. The data are collected annually on repeated cross-sectional representative samples. From the 2000 (I) and 2000 (II) samples, we selected 1,387 men and 1,330 women who were born between 1946 and 1979 and who provided complete information on all the variables considered in our models except the variable track placement in secondary education. Most of the analysis is based on the information derived from these 2,717 adults, although the conditional models and those that include secondary school track are based on fewer cases, as explained below.

In addition to gender (scored 1 if male; 0 if female), we considered five determinants of attainment of tertiary education: ethnicity, parental education, class origin, track placement at the secondary level, and cohort.

Ethnicity. Ethnicity refers to the contrast between the Hokkien (the numerical majority) and the other three groups (the Hakka, the Mainlanders, and the Aborigines). The Hokkien and Hakka (the minority) descended from early Chinese immigrants; they are differentiated primarily by their dialects and by the areas of Mainland China from which they originate. Together, the Hokkien and Hakka constitute the majority of "Taiwanese." By contrast, Mainlanders—post-WWII immigrants from the mainland and their Taiwan-born offspring—currently make up about 14% of the population. There is also an Aboriginal population of less than 2%.

Parental education. Parental education was indicated by the highest level of either the father's or the mother's educational attainment. If one of the two was missing, the variable measured the educational level of the parent for which data were available. The following educational levels were considered: (1a) did not complete elementary education, (1b) completed elementary education, (1c) completed junior high or vocational school, (2a) completed senior vocational school, (2b) completed senior high school, (3a) attended vocational education at postsecondary level (i.e., junior college), and (3b) attended university or college.[5]

Class origin. Class origin was measured by the father's occupational class when the respondent was 15 years old. We initially used the EGP five-class schema to sort the father's occupational titles: (1) white collar, (2) petite bourgeoisie, (3) farming class, (4) skilled worker, and (5) nonskilled manual worker. Later in the analysis we combined petite bourgeoisie with working classes to avoid small cells. We also included military as a category because the vast majority of Mainlander immigrants were affiliated with the military or the Nationalist regime, and therefore a significant portion of second-generation Mainlanders in Taiwan are children of military men.[6]

Tracking in secondary education. Tracking in secondary education is a dichotomous variable scored 0 for respondents placed in the academic track and 1 for those in the vocational track (attending either a vocational school or a vocational program in a high school).

Cohort. To detect trends in educational stratification in each of the three periods of educational expansion discussed earlier, we partitioned our sample into three broad birth cohorts: 1946–55, 1956–66, and 1967–79. The extension of compulsory education from six to nine years in 1968 affected cohorts born after 1955, and the 1985 deregulation of school expansion affected cohorts born after 1966. In contrast to the two younger cohorts, those born in 1946–55 had to pass an entrance examination to attend junior high or vocational school, but once they completed senior high or vocational school at age 18, their higher education took place most likely during the 1964–73 period, when the number of junior colleges increased rapidly (Figure 6.1). By contrast, cohorts born after 1955 had to compete for a good senior high school to obtain a university education. Among them, the 1956–66 cohort struggled through the period of restrictive expansion, while the 1967–79 cohort made the grade during the postderegulation period. Thus, comparisons across the three major cohorts reveal the potential impacts of educational expansion at the tertiary level on the equality of educational opportunity.

We used three dependent variables: a dummy variable representing the completion of secondary school; a dummy variable indicating whether or not respondent attended tertiary education; and a four-category variable distinguishing between the types of tertiary education as follows:

1. Junior college
2. Four-year college or university programs (hereafter, university)
3. Other (including military, police academy, etc.)
4. Did not attend tertiary education

This variable was used to test the hypothesis that as social selection in the odds of attending tertiary education declined, it increased with regards to the odds of attending a college or university rather than a junior college.[7]

Breen and Jonsson (2000) suggested the use of multinomial logit models of educational careers instead of the traditional binary logit model, because in most education systems students are often faced with several options rather than simply *continue* or *drop out*. Furthermore, the pathway a student has taken through the school system influences the probability of making subsequent educational transitions. Therefore, we employed both binary and multinomial logistic regressions predicting the two dependent variables, and we also paid special attention to the impact of track placement at the secondary level on tertiary education. Finally, as called for by the guidelines for the comparative project, we estimated both conditional and unconditional models of higher education. The former estimated the effects of the exogenous variables on the odds of attending tertiary education given the attainment of secondary education, and the latter estimated the effects of these variables for all respondents irrespective of prior educational histories.

RESULTS

Overall Patterns of Educational Disparity

Column 2 of Table 6.1 shows the average number of school years attended by men and women of the three cohorts. As seen, in the earlier cohort women were at a clear disadvantage, but by the youngest cohort they attained parity with men. Column 3 shows that secondary school graduation rates increased across cohorts from 45.8% to 86.9%, and that women, initially disadvantaged in this respect, now surpass men. What then are the overall effects of the educational expansion on women's and men's enrollment in tertiary education? Column 4 of Table 6.1 presents proportions of respondents attending higher education by gender and cohort. As seen, the proportion increased sharply. Column 5 presents the proportion of secondary school graduates who went

TABLE 6.1
Educational attainment by gender and cohort

Year of birth	(1) Sample size	(2) Mean years of schooling	(3) Percentage with 12+ years of schooling	(4) Percentage with tertiary education	(5) Percentage attaining tertiary education, given 12+ years of schooling
Men					
1946–55	348	10.47 (4.09)	54.9	28.4	51.8
1956–66	568	11.89 (3.02)	68.3	34.2	50.0
1967–79	471	12.93 (2.33)	85.8	45.6	53.2
Women					
1946–55	305	8.52 (4.40)	35.4	17.0	48.1
1956–66	577	10.93 (3.23)	60.5	23.0	38.1
1967–79	448	13.02 (2.30)	88.2	47.3	53.7
Total					
1946–55	653	9.56 (4.34)	45.8	23.1	50.5
1956–66	1,145	11.41 (3.16)	64.4	28.6	44.4
1967–79	919	12.97 (2.31)	86.9	46.5	53.4

NOTE: Parenthetical values are standard deviations.

on to tertiary education. The proportions stabilize at about 50% (except for a dip associated with the middle cohort for women). This means that most of the increase in the overall proportion attending tertiary education is due to the increase in the proportion completing secondary education. In other words, the expansion of tertiary education met the growing demand produced by the expansion of secondary education and did not exceed it greatly.

Trends in the Stratification of Upper Secondary School Completion

The project guidelines require that we estimate logit models of eligibility for higher education. In some countries, eligibility is determined by a matriculation certificate. In Taiwan, like in the United States, Japan, and other countries all high-school graduates are formally eligible even if their actual

TABLE 6.2
Unconditional logistic regressions predicting eligibility for tertiary education: secondary school completion by cohort

	COHORT		
Independent variables	1946–55	1956–66	1967–79
Male (Reference: Female)	**1.232***	.496*	−.264
	(.203)	(.145)	(.212)
Ethnicity (Reference: Hokkien)			
Aborigine	−2.237*	−1.494*	−1.175*
	(1.080)	(.472)	(.572)
Hakka	.184	.854*	.288
	(.310)	(.258)	(.408)
Mainlander	.746	.820*	.795
	(.460)	(.320)	(.509)
Parental education (Reference: Junior college and higher)			
Lower	−2.518*	−2.901*	−3.251*
	(.533)	(.630)	(.789)
Elementary	−1.089*	−1.373*	−2.030*
	(.523)	(.619)	(.760)
Junior high or vocational	−1.068	−.688	−1.142
	(.602)	(.666)	(.813)
Senior high or vocational	.483	−.402	−.142
	(.912)	(.718)	(.936)
Father's class (Reference: Farming class)			
White collar	1.264*	1.275*	.904*
	(.267)	(.216)	(.334)
Working class	−.010	.300	.549*
	(.237)	(.164)	(.239)
Military	2.451*	1.349*	**−.806**
	(1.151)	(.687)	(.768)
Intercept	.265	1.398*	3.353*
	(.547)	(.628)	(.788)
R^2	.424	.348	
N	653	1,145	919

NOTE: Parenthetical values are standard errors. For this and subsequent tables, we conducted significance tests for differences between the middle cohort and the youngest and oldest ones in the estimated intercepts and slopes. Boldface entries in the first and third columns of the table indicate significant differences.

*Significant at the level of α = 0.05.

chances of being admitted to the individual colleges and universities are determined by examination grades. Because we do not have information on grades and examinations, we define eligibility as having completed upper secondary education. Table 6.2 presents, for each of the three cohorts, the estimated effects of gender, ethnicity, parental education, and father's class on the log-odds of upper secondary school completion. For this and subsequent tables we conducted significance tests for differences between the middle cohort and the youngest and oldest ones in the estimated intercepts and slopes. Bold italics in the first and third columns of the table indicate significant differences.

The results are consistent with those in Table 6.1. First, across cohorts, the intercept increased dramatically from 0.265 to 3.353. This represents the marked increase in high-school completion since the 1960s. In the older cohort less than 50% graduated from secondary school as opposed to nearly 90% in the youngest cohort (Table 6.1). The second finding, concerning the effects of gender, reveals an elimination and slight reversal of the male advantage in the odds of graduation. Temporal changes in gender effects are statistically significant across the successive cohorts. In addition, there is a consistent decline in the relative disadvantage of Aborigines. The effects of Hakka, relative to Hokkien majority, seem to have increased between the first and second cohorts and then declined, but both inter-cohort differences are not statistically significant. Similarly, the effects of Mainlanders are quite stable. Nevertheless, as shown in Table 6.2, effects of ethnicity are most notable among the cohort of 1956–66.

Most interesting from the vantage point of the comparative project, inequality in the odds of secondary school completion between categories of parental education was enhanced across the three cohorts. This is reflected by the decline in the effects of both lower and elementary parental education relative to junior college and higher. By contrast, the advantages associated with military-class origins deteriorated markedly and significantly. This is consistent with the erosion of the social advantages of the Mainlander elite, of whom a disproportionate number came from highly educated families, especially those with fathers in the higher ranks of the military or the Nationalist regime/party. In sum, these results show an expansion of upper secondary school graduation rates coupled with declining gender, class, and even some ethnic stratification, coupled once again with growing inequality between categories of parental education.

Trends in Inequality of Attending Tertiary Education: Unconditional Logistic Regression

Table 6.3 presents results obtained from binary logistic regressions predicting the log-odds of attending higher education for the three cohorts. We note a significant male advantage in the two earlier cohorts, with estimated

TABLE 6.3
Unconditional logistic regressions predicting attendance of tertiary education by cohort

	COHORT		
Independent variables	1946–55	1956–66	1967–79
Male (Reference: Female)	0.942*	0.774*	−0.104
	(0.228)	(0.154)	(0.143)
Ethnicity (Reference: Hokkien)			
Aborigine	−0.667	−0.709	−2.145*
	(1.083)	(0.640)	(1.032)
Hakka	0.530	0.018	−0.057
	(0.335)	(0.241)	(0.253)
Mainlander	0.806*	0.460	−0.289
	(0.377)	(0.244)	(0.239)
Parental education (Reference: University and higher)			
Lower	−2.215*	−3.458*	−2.324*
	(0.505)	(0.541)	(0.458)
Elementary	−0.821	−2.265*	−1.304*
	(0.451)	(0.487)	(0.351)
Junior high or vocational	−0.944	−1.593*	−0.907*
	(0.535)	(0.511)	(0.368)
Senior vocational	−0.081	−0.690	−0.625
	(0.755)	(0.596)	(0.408)
Senior high	0.603	−1.301*	−0.339
	(0.666)	(0.536)	(0.429)
Junior college	−0.234	−0.114	0.384
	(0.642)	(0.633)	(0.460)
Father's class (Reference: Farming class)			
White collar	1.184*	0.942*	0.803*
	(0.285)	(0.205)	(0.226)
Working class	0.352	0.194	0.391
	(0.301)	(0.204)	(0.201)
Military	0.555	0.361	0.481
	(0.613)	(0.434)	(0.479)
Intercept	−1.330*	0.299	0.544
	(0.502)	(0.504)	(0.392)
R^2	0.324	0.310	0.173
N	653	1,145	919

NOTE: Parenthetical values are standard errors.
*Significant at the level of $\alpha = 0.05$.

log-odds of 0.942 for male advantage in the 1946–55 cohort and a corresponding coefficient of 0.774 in the 1956–66 cohort. The decline in male advantage across these two cohorts is not statistically significant at the level of $\alpha = 0.05$, but for the youngest cohort the gender coefficient switches from positive to negative (−0.104), and loses its significance. The change in the gender coefficient is statistically significant. This finding reflects dramatic improvement in women's educational attainment.

Similarly, when controlling for other variables in the model, the often-cited Mainlander advantage in educational attainment, which is evident for the cohort of 1946–55, disappears in the two more recent cohorts. Throughout the period under study there was a tendency toward equal opportunity of higher education between ethnic groups, except for the Aborigines whose disadvantage increased.[8]

As seen in Table 6.3, parental education has a significant and substantial effect on the log-odds of higher education. In the oldest cohort, the sons and daughters of the least educated parents were 11% ($e^{-2.215} = 0.11$) as likely to attend higher education as those born to college-educated parents. This inequality increased to 3% ($e^{-3.458} = 0.03$) in the second cohort, and then declined to its initial value in the youngest cohort. Although not formally significant, these changes across cohorts are sizeable. A similar curvilinear pattern is seen for the offspring of parents with elementary education only. By contrast to the large and partially significant changes in the effects of parental education, changes in the effects of father's class are small and insignificant. For example, the effect of white-collar fathers relative to farmers declined slightly from 1.184 to 0.942, and then to 0.803.

To sum up, cross-cohort comparisons of coefficients presented in Table 6.3 indicate that Taiwan moved toward greater equality in the odds of tertiary education. Inequalities between men and women and between ethnic groups (except the Aborigine disadvantage) declined significantly between the 1960s and the 1970s. Inequalities due to differences in parental education increased between the oldest and the middle cohort and then declined again. Although not formally significant, these changes are consistent with the stagnation of higher education during the late 1970s and most of the 1980s, and its subsequent expansion in the 1990s. These changes suggest that stagnation, which we know produced greater competition for higher education, led to greater inequality between social strata. After the administrative constraints were removed, inequality seems to have declined.

Effects of Earlier Tracking on Later Attainment: Conditional Logistic Regression

Table 6.1 showed that cohort proportions of secondary school graduates who attended tertiary education were stable among men and declined among women between the first and second cohorts, then returned to their original level. To evaluate the consequences of the restrictions on academic education in the 1970s and 1980s and the subsequent relaxation of restrictions on the stratification of tertiary education among secondary school graduates, we performed a multivariate conditional analysis of tertiary educational attainment.

Table 6.4 shows, for each cohort, two binary logit regressions estimated for respondents who completed 12 years of schooling. The two regressions are identical except that the second includes, among the independent variables, a dummy representing placement in vocational secondary education. As before, we tested for cohort differences relative to the 1956–66 cohort in the intercepts and slopes, and marked the significant ones with bold italics in the second, fifth, and sixth columns.[9]

We see an increase, although an insignificant one, in the gender gap between the first and second cohorts and a significant decline between the second and third cohorts. The advantage of the Mainlanders is not significant but positive in the first cohort and becomes negative by the third. The effects of parental education are large and significant. In the first cohort, the sons and daughters of highly educated parents were over three times as likely to attend tertiary education as those whose parents had the lowest level of education ($e^{1.238} = 3.4$). Their advantage increased substantially by the second cohort ($e^{2.6} = 14.0$) and then declined to 5.6. These changes are not statistically significant, but they are large and consistent with the expectation that constraint on the expansion of higher education increases inequalities while expansion reduces them. The sons and daughters of white-collar fathers are more likely than other classes to enter higher education, and this advantage does not change systematically across cohorts. Finally, the results reveal profound tracking effects. As expected, placement in the vocational track at the secondary level significantly retarded the students' log-odds of entering tertiary education. The effects of tracking declined over time as the relative disadvantage of vocational students over those in the academic sector diminished from -1.415 in the 1946–55 cohort to -0.881 in the 1956–66 cohort and to -0.804 in the 1967–79 cohort.

To sum up, the results of the conditional analysis are similar to those of the unconditional one. Secondary school graduates show a nonlinear pattern of change in the stratification of tertiary education: both gender and socioeconomic inequalities increased somewhat for cohorts who attended

TABLE 6.4
Conditional logistic regressions predicting attendance of tertiary education by cohort

	COHORT					
	1946–55		1956–66		1967–79	
Independent variables	(1)	(2)	(1)	(2)	(1)	(2)
Male (Reference: Female)	0.423	0.406	0.693*	0.609*	−0.035	−0.090
	(0.268)	(0.292)	(0.167)	(0.171)	(0.150)	(0.154)
Ethnicity (Reference: Hokkien)						
Hakka	0.559	0.497	−0.292	−0.260	−0.118	−0.083
	(0.398)	(0.439)	(0.250)	(0.254)	(0.262)	(0.269)
Mainlander	0.647	0.471	0.264	0.223	−0.383	−0.315
	(0.435)	(0.459)	(0.254)	(0.262)	(0.243)	(0.246)
Parental education (Reference: University and higher)						
Lower	−1.238*	−1.228	−2.643*	−2.356*	−1.727*	−1.428*
	(0.609)	(0.662)	(0.589)	(0.597)	(0.475)	(0.487)
Elementary	−0.689	−0.358	−2.119*	−1.816*	−1.056*	−0.732*
	(0.535)	(0.573)	(0.523)	(0.530)	(0.355)	(0.369)
Junior high or vocational	−0.878	−0.635	−1.594*	−1.255*	−0.791*	−0.520
	(0.619)	(0.659)	(0.546)	(0.554)	(0.373)	(0.388)
Senior vocational	−0.474	−0.714	−0.454	−0.221	−0.545	−0.396
	(0.794)	(0.906)	(0.661)	(0.677)	(0.415)	(0.430)
Senior high	0.455	0.630	−1.310*	−1.054	−0.434	−0.215
	(0.748)	(0.775)	(0.566)	(0.574)	(0.428)	(0.444)
Junior college	−0.674	−0.428	0.145	0.300	0.580	0.700
	(0.688)	(0.741)	(0.699)	(0.709)	(0.482)	(0.493)
Father's class (Reference: Farming class)						
White collar	0.697*	0.849*	0.532*	0.397	0.702*	0.642*
	(0.338)	(0.366)	(0.225)	(0.231)	(0.238)	(0.246)
Working class	0.477	0.742	0.063	0.049	0.316	0.334
	(0.364)	(0.390)	(0.224)	(0.230)	(0.214)	(0.220)
Military	−0.152	−0.224	−0.084	−0.097	0.525	0.457
	(0.664)	(0.694)	(0.451)	(0.460)	(0.511)	(0.520)
Tracking in secondary education	—	−1.415*	—	−0.881*	—	−0.804*
		(0.278)		(0.183)		(0.180)
Intercept	−0.122	0.337	0.950	1.336*	0.632	0.929*
	(0.612)	(0.664)	(0.547)	(0.563)	(0.401)	(0.419)
R^2	0.129	0.260	0.210	0.237	0.111	0.137
N	298	287	730	714	790	765

NOTE: Parenthetical values are standard errors. The Aboriginal sample is excluded from the analysis.
*Significant at the level of α = 0.05.

tertiary education during the period of stagnation, and declined for those who did so during the expansive policies of the 1990s. Ethnic inequalities seem to have declined throughout the period under observation. The negative effect of placement in the vocational track declined between the first and second cohorts, when vocational tertiary education expanded.

Trends in Inequality in the Type of Higher Education

We explored the potential impacts of the educational expansion on the type of tertiary education attained. Table 6.5 presents results obtained from conditional multinomial logistic regressions predicting the odds of attending a variety of institutions of higher education for secondary school graduates in the three cohorts. However, we present only the estimates for odds ratios contrasting the attendance of junior colleges with four-year institutions.

The results are summarized as follows: in the earlier two cohorts, when few people attended any tertiary education, junior colleges and four-year institutions were less socially distinct than they later became. This is indicated by the small and insignificant effects of gender, ethnicity, and father's class on the log-odds contrasting the two categories. Only parental education distinguished between those attending them, and, as expected, educationally privileged origins were associated with greater odds of attending a four-year institution. By the last cohort, both class and an ethnicity effects emerge. The white-collar class is now more likely to attend four-year institutions than the farming class, and the Hokkien are more likely to do so than the Hakka. As shown in Table 6.5, among the cohort of 1967–79, the sons and daughters of white-collar fathers were 0.28 times less likely to attend junior college as opposed to university than children of the farming class ($e^{-1.268} = 0.28$). The emergence of a class distinction between the two forms of tertiary education is consistent with Lucas's EMI hypothesis suggesting that as a level of education becomes more prevalent in the population, qualitative differences within it assume significance in the stratification process. In our case, as tertiary education expanded through an increase in the number of junior colleges, white-collar families lost interest in the education provided by junior colleges and preferred the universities.

Table 6.5 also demonstrates that placement in the vocational track at the secondary level channeled those who made it to the tertiary education into junior colleges rather than universities. The significant effects of tracking on students' log-odds of entering a junior college rather than a

TABLE 6.5
Conditional multinomial logistic regressions contrasting junior college with university, by cohort

	COHORT		
Independent variables	1946–55	1956–66	1967–79
Male (Reference: Female)	−0.450	−0.194	0.217
	(0.510)	(0.295)	(0.271)
Ethnicity (Reference: Hokkien)			
Hakka	0.686	−0.319	**1.040**
	(0.760)	(0.436)	**(0.535)**
Mainlander	−0.504	−0.355	0.107
	(0.732)	(0.410)	(0.420)
Parental education (Reference: University and higher)			
Lower	2.848*	0.853	0.594
	(1.233)	(0.854)	(0.864)
Elementary	1.021	0.912	0.408
	(1.000)	(0.660)	(0.593)
Junior high or vocational	2.092	0.834	0.498
	(1.147)	(0.711)	(0.626)
Senior high or vocational	0.438	1.388*	0.730
	(1.157)	(0.683)	(0.618)
Junior college	−1.756	1.062	−0.218
	(1.505)	(0.778)	(0.684)
Father's class (Reference: Farming class)			
White-collar	−0.268	0.469	**−1.268***
	(0.656)	(0.423)	**(0.490)**
Working class	0.569	0.453	**−0.801**
	(0.717)	(0.442)	**(0.460)**
Military	2.671*	0.429	−1.414
	(1.268)	(0.770)	(0.873)
Tracking in secondary education	4.142*	3.664*	4.342*
	(0.586)	(0.351)	(0.377)
Intercept	−3.151*	−2.715*	−2.180*
	(1.213)	(0.764)	(0.760)
R^2	0.512	0.423	0.442
N	279	697	755

NOTE: Parenthetical values are standard errors. The Aboriginal sample and respondents attending other types of schools (such as military or police academies) are excluded from the analysis. Regressions contrasting no tertiary education with university education are not shown in the table.

*Significant at the level of α = 0.05.

university varied over time—though insignificantly—as the relative disparity between vocational students and those in the academic sector diminished from 4.142 in the 1946–55 cohort to 3.664 in the 1956–66 cohort, then increased to 4.342 in the 1967–79 cohort. This changing pattern is a result of the three-stage development of Taiwan's diversified education system, where the expansion in higher education during the first and the third phases was due largely to the establishment of new junior colleges at the lower tier of tertiary education. During the period of stagnation, junior colleges represented an alternative of higher education for students in the academic sector, and the profound effect of tracking declined with the increased competition for attaining tertiary education.

SUMMARY AND CONCLUSIONS

During the decades of National Party rule (1945–2000) Taiwanese higher education was transformed from elite to mass education. However, the transformation was not linear. It consisted of three main phases. In the first period (through the early 1970s), the number of tertiary institutions increased rapidly. Tertiary education expanded most rapidly in the 1960s, through the explosive increase in the number of junior colleges (from 12 in 1960 to 76 in 1972). The second period (until the late 1980s) was sparked by the economic transition from import-substitution to export-oriented industrialization (1961–72). In an attempt to meet the economy's demand for skilled labor, national constraints were imposed on the relative share of academic (i.e., college-bound) secondary education and on the expansion of academic tertiary institutions. The third phase began in the late 1980s, after the democratization of Taiwan, during which restrictions were lifted and the expansion of higher education resumed.

In this paper we analyzed survey data collected in the year 2000 to assess the consequences of the expansion of higher education in Taiwan for inequalities between men and women, ethnic groups, and social strata in the odds of attending higher education and in the odds of attending four- and two-year institutions. In Taiwan, as in most other economically developed societies, gender inequalities in education generally, and in higher education specifically, have been completely eliminated and even seem to have reversed slightly. Inequalities between social strata seem to have increased during the restrictive phase of the 1970s and 1980s then declined during the 1990s after restrictions were lifted and expansion was encouraged. These changes appear in both the conditional (on secondary school completion) and unconditional analysis, and although not statistically significant, they appear to be systematic and consistent. We also found that compared with junior colleges, four-year institutions increased their social selectivity. This was indicated by the rise in the effects of father's class on the odds of attending a university rather than a junior college.

These results are consistent with those of several other studies in this volume and contradict much of the common wisdom concerning change in processes of educational stratification. First, they contradict Blossfeld and Shavit's (1993) attempt to generalize Mare's results whereby inequalities in the conditional log-odds of attaining successive educational levels tend to persist over time. This generalization was applied to Taiwan by Tsai and Chiu (1993b) in their analysis of data pertaining to cohorts born between 1919 and 1968. Taiwan has undergone far-reaching changes in the interim, including democratization and the deregulation of its education system, which might explain the demise of persistent inequalities between cohorts born in the 1960s and those born in the 1970s. Second, the results contradict Raftery and Hout's (1993) hypothesis that declines in these inequalities are likely only after the privileged classes have reached saturation. We have shown that all classes were quite far from the level of saturation. The results are reminiscent of those obtained by Lucas (2001) and Ayalon and Shavit (2004) who studied educational expansion in two different contexts (the U.S. and Israel) and found that it tended to be accompanied by a differentiation into distinct and unequal tracks. After it is in place, the social stratification of the type of education replaces some of the equalization achieved by overall expansion. The importance of qualitative differences in educational attainment increases while that of quantity decreases.

CHAPTER SEVEN

United States: Changes in Higher Education and Social Stratification

Josipa Roksa, University of Virginia

Eric Grodsky, University of California, Davis

Richard Arum, New York University

Adam Gamoran, University of Wisconsin, Madison

INTRODUCTION

Unfettered by much centralized government regulation, U.S. higher education has expanded dramatically and in multiple directions. This expansion can be described as stratified: characterized by increasing enrollments in lower-status institutions (nonselective four-year institutions and community colleges), and by the solidification of institutional hierarchies. The expansion also created a second tier of higher education focused on vocational and semiprofessional training through increased vocationalization of community colleges and establishment of exclusively vocational schools. These changes were accompanied by a range of policies, such as Title IV of the Higher Education Act, Title IX, and Affirmative Action, aimed at improving access of disadvantaged groups to postsecondary education.

This particular combination of expansion and government intervention may have contradictory consequences for stratification processes. The growth of public universities, the legislation against discrimination, the use of affirmative action, and development of student-aid policies may have reduced inequality in access to four-year institutions. However, most of the expansion has occurred at the level of community colleges, which may serve to increase inequality within higher education even as it improves equality in access to some type of postsecondary education. Many of the policies championed in the 1960s and 1970s, moreover, have been challenged or amended in recent decades. To address these opposing tendencies and understand whether and how equality of access to higher education has changed over time, we examine the likelihood of entering various types of postsecondary institutions for different gender, racial/ethnic, and socioeconomic groups. The results indicate persistent inequality with respect to socioeconomic background but notable improvements in access to postsecondary opportunities for women and African Americans.

CHARACTERISTICS OF THE U.S. HIGHER EDUCATION SYSTEM

Although dating back to the colonial colleges (see Collins 1979), U.S. higher education expanded dramatically following World War II. The GI Bill, which began the federal government's support for students' financial aid by financing the postsecondary education of war veterans, greatly assisted growth in enrollments (Geiger 1996; cf., Bound and Turner 1999). Total higher education enrollment rose from 20% of American youths ages 18–22 in 1945 to 77% in 1992 (Hout 1996). Today, over 4,000 institutions of higher education enroll approximately 15 million students (U.S. NCES 2002a), 63% of high-school graduates enter postsecondary education, and over one-quarter of the population has a college degree (U.S. Bureau of the Census 2002). Higher education has thus "transformed from a privilege into a right, and for an increasing number into an obligation" (Trow 1972, 2).

The size of the U.S. higher education system is accompanied by a remarkable variation among institutions. Students graduating from high school can enter postsecondary vocational schools, two-year institutions, or four-year colleges and universities. They can choose between private or public versions of those institutions, and they can attend more or less prestigious colleges and universities. However, the growth in enrollments has not been even across institutions. The expansion in the post–World War II period was led by the public sector, and particularly community colleges (see Figure 7.1). By the end of the twentieth century, three-quarters of students in degree-granting institutions were attending public colleges and universities. Moreover, half of the students in public institutions were enrolled in community colleges, up from 25% in 1965.

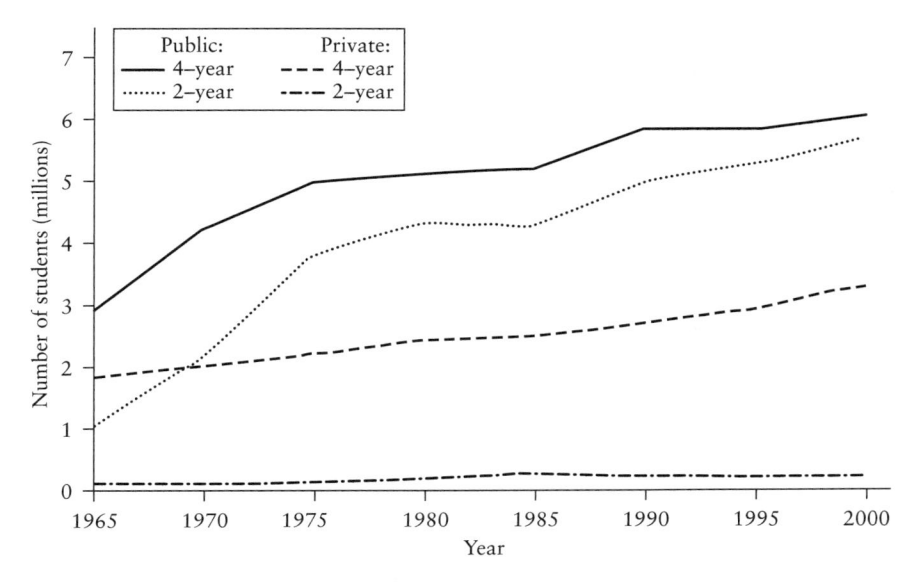

Figure 7.1. Postsecondary Enrollment in Degree-Granting Institutions
SOURCE: *Digest of Education Statistics*, 2002.

Increased provision of higher education in community colleges is remarkable for several reasons. Community colleges have an open-door admission policy, charge low tuition, are located within commuting distance of students' homes, and facilitate flexible attendance patterns. Consequently, they enroll a disproportionate number of working-class, minority, female, and older students. Moreover, community colleges have a strong vocational component: 40–60% of community college students are enrolled in vocational programs (Cohen and Brawer 1996; Dougherty 2001), and the majority of community college degrees are awarded in vocational fields (Townsend 2001; U.S. NCES 2002a). Finally, the benefits of attending community colleges remain contested. Only about one-third of traditional age community college students earn an associate or a bachelor's degree within eight years of completing high school (U.S. NCES 2003a). Although increasing access to higher education, community colleges have thus been criticized for hindering educational attainment, particularly the opportunities for earning bachelor's degrees (for an overview see Dougherty 1994, 2002; see also Brint and Karabel 1989). At the same time, community college education, especially the associate degree, provides substantial labor market rewards (Grubb 1996, 1999; Kane and Rouse 1995, 1999).

U.S. higher education includes another set of institutions not represented in Figure 7.1: public vocational schools and private proprietary schools that do not offer degrees but only short-term training ending in occupational certificates (often referred to as "less than two-year institutions").[1] These institutions are exclusively vocational and their certificates cannot be used as credentials for access to other higher education institutions. Minimal research on vocational and proprietary schools shows that they bestow at least some economic benefits on their graduates, but the size of these benefits compared to those of vocational training in community colleges is ambiguous (see Kerckhoff and Bell 1998; Dougherty 1994).

STRATIFICATION IN U.S. HIGHER EDUCATION

While postsecondary education became open to virtually all high-school graduates by the end of the twentieth century, solidification of an educational hierarchy and a split between elite and mass forms of education constrained student opportunities. The mass sector developed a diversified range of lower-status academic institutions and vocationally oriented programs, while the elite institutions maintained academic focus and selectivity, resulting in a highly stratified system of U.S. postsecondary education. Moreover, the U.S. system has a binary component: colleges and universities focus on awarding academic credentials while the lower tier of higher education (including two-year and less than two-year institutions) provides the majority of vocational training. How has this particular form of expansion, and the system resulting from it, affected socioeconomic, racial/ethnic, and gender stratification in U.S. higher education?

Socioeconomic Status

Since the seminal work of Blau and Duncan (1967), stratification researchers have examined how family background influences individuals' educational and occupational attainment, fostering a transfer of class advantage and disadvantage from parents to their children (see studies in Shavit and Blossfeld 1993; see also reviews in Ganzeboom, Treiman, and Ultee 1991; Kerckhoff 1995; Treiman and Ganzeboom 2000). The advantages of access to postsecondary education associated with high socioeconomic status appear stable over time. Among 1972 high-school graduates, 42% of those from the lowest SES quartile entered higher education within two years compared with 85% of their counterparts from the highest SES quartile. Twenty years later, high-school graduates from both groups were more likely to gain access to higher education, but the gap remained: 49% of students from the bottom quartile and 91% from the top quartile enrolled in higher education within two years of completing high school (U.S. NCES 1997). Thus, while students from all socioeconomic backgrounds have increased their entry into higher education over time, the disadvantage associated with less privileged family background has not declined (see also Baker and Velez 1996; Gamoran 2001).

While socioeconomic differences in access to postsecondary education have remained relatively stable over time, there is some indication that stratification within higher education is increasing. Several recent studies have suggested that advantages associated with high socioeconomic status in access to four-year institutions (Ellwood and Kane 2000) and elite colleges and universities (Karen 2002; Astin and Oseguera 2004) are greater for recent cohorts. In addition, differences in educational attainment have persisted or increased over time. Jencks and Riesman (1968) argued that educational expansion in the U.S. has disproportionately absorbed students from the upper class. Thus, while the overall educational level of the population has risen, the gap in educational attainment between the well educated and the poorly educated has also increased. More recently, Hout (1999) suggested that the influence of family background on educational opportunity decreased in the first half of the twentieth century, but that this trend has stopped and reversed since the late 1970s.

Studies of educational transitions, proliferating after Mare's (1980) pioneering work, provide further evidence of stratification in higher education. Much of this research has suggested that the influence of family background decreases over educational transitions, revealing a "waning coefficient pattern" (for a review see Lucas, Fucella, and Berends 2001). However, Lucas (1996) found that the waning coefficient pattern does not hold for 1980 sophomores: social background coefficients for college entry were not smaller but larger than those for high-school completion. He suggested that this pattern might be partly explained by rapidly increasing tuition and falling government support for financial aid following the Reagan reforms in the early 1980s. In addition, recent reanalysis of educational transitions

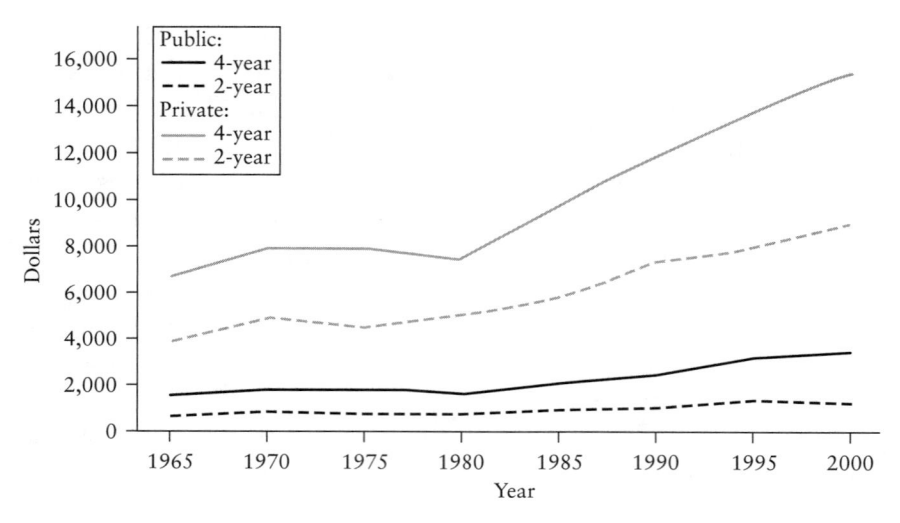

Figure 7.2. Postsecondary Tuition and Fees

SOURCE: *Digest of Education Statistics,* 2002.

NOTE: Tuition and fees for in-state full-time equivalent students, adjusted for inflation and expressed in 2000 dollars.

over three cohorts (1966, 1980, and 1990 sophomores) indicated no waning pattern for any of the cohorts studied (Lucas, Fucella, and Berends 2001). While requiring further investigation, these recent findings imply that the U.S. educational system is not becoming more egalitarian over educational transitions or over time.

Financing Higher Education

One of the prominent concerns in higher education, especially in discussions regarding the influence of socioeconomic background on educational attainment, is the high and rising cost of education. All postsecondary institutions in the U.S. charge tuition and/or fees, although the expenses are much higher at private than public institutions and at four-year than two-year schools (Figure 7.2). The tuition also generally increases with prestige: tuition and fees at a typical Ivy League institution in 1990 were approximately seven times the cost of in-state tuition and fees at an average public university.[2] Moreover, college expenses have escalated over time, especially at private four-year institutions.

The federal government has resisted shaping educational institutions directly, focusing instead on helping students meet rising educational costs (Gladieux 1995).[3] The landmark legislation in this area was Title IV of the Higher Education Act of 1965, which provided funds for several programs assisting students with exceptional financial need (e.g., Upward Bound, Talent Search, Work-Study). In the following years, Title IV was amended to allow students to use government money for community colleges and proprietary schools in addition to four-year institutions. The number of programs also increased. In 1972, the government adopted the Pell Grant Program offering direct grants to qualifying students. Today, the Pell Grant Program is the largest federal need-based grant program available to students in higher education, with awards made primarily to low-income students (U.S. NCES 2002b).

Since the 1970s, the federal assistance shifted in two ways: increasing the reliance on loans, and broadening programs to include middle-class students. As the cost of higher education increased and more students entered higher education, the government offered more support for students but largely in the form of loans: the percentage of full-time undergraduates receiving federal loans increased over time while the percentage of those receiving federal grants remained stable.[4] The amount of money students borrowed also began to increase. By the mid-1990s, the federal government spent over three times as much money on loans as on grants (U.S. NCES 1998). Today, loans are by far the largest source of financial aid, including aid for low-income students (Gladieux 1995; U.S. NCES 1998). Since the 1970s, the federal government also broadened its programs to assist middle-class students in meeting the financial demands of higher education (e.g., Middle Income Student Assistance Act in 1978). More recently, in the 1992 reauthorization of the Higher Education Act, the government expanded the Stafford Loan Program to include unsubsidized loans open to students regardless of financial need (U.S. NCES 1998, 2000).

Race/Ethnicity

In addition to class, U.S. higher education is stratified by race/ethnicity. Educational expansion following World War II and successes of the Civil Rights movement in the 1950s and 1960s increased the proportion of African Americans in higher education. In 1960, 3% of African Americans over

25 years of age earned a college degree, compared with 16.5% in 2000. Hispanics have also shown improvements in attainment of bachelor's degrees over time, from 4.5% of those 25 years or older in 1970 to 11% in 2000. Although these figures demonstrate progress, whites are still more likely to hold bachelor's degrees than either African Americans or Hispanics (U.S. Bureau of the Census 2002; see also a review in Kao and Thompson 2003).

Affirmative Action

Throughout the first half of the twentieth century, educational institutions in the U.S. were generally segregated by race. In 1954, the Supreme Court outlawed segregation in public education with the *Brown v. Board of Education* decision. A decade later, Title VI of the 1964 Civil Rights Act intended to enforce desegregation in higher education. However, as late as 1970, only 4.3% of students in predominantly white higher education institutions were African American, and the majority of African American students in higher education attended historically black colleges and universities (Wilson 1994; see also Weerts and Conrad 2002). The absence of African Americans was particularly pronounced in the elite colleges and universities. In 1967 African Americans represented only 2.3% of Ivy League undergraduate enrollments (Karen 1991b; see also Bowen and Bok 1998).

Responding to the changed legal/social climate and Civil Rights protests and riots, many of which occurred on college campuses, higher education leaders began diversifying their institutions in the 1960s and 1970s (Skrentny 2002; see also Skrentny 1996).[5] Bowen and Bok (1998) noted that "leading colleges and professional schools came to believe that they had a role to play in educating minority students (p. 6)." Selective higher education institutions developed various strategies to diversify their student bodies, ranging from summer enrichment camps and active recruitment of minority students to broadening of admission criteria to include nonacademic considerations and adopting affirmative action policies that favored minority applicants (Karen 1991a; Duffy and Goldberg 1998; Carroll, Tyson, and Lumas 2000). Over time, however, government commitment to affirmative action dissipated and political and public opposition to affirmative action grew. By the 1990s, affirmative action was under attack in the courts (e.g., *Hopwood v. Texas*) and the ballot box (California's Proposition 209; Washington's Initiative 200). However, a landmark U.S. Supreme court decision in 2003 (*Grutter v. Bollinger*) concluded that a narrow use of affirmative action is consistent with rights laid out in the U.S. Constitution: minority status could be used as one factor in admission decisions, though not the overriding factor.

While there is some discussion about how widespread race-based affirmative action programs are in higher education, most researchers agree that selective institutions are more likely than less selective ones to engage in the practice. Access to selective institutions, especially those in the top tier, although contested, is regarded as advantageous: elite institutions appear to enhance persistence, degree completion, enrollment in graduate schools, and income (e.g., Kingston and Smart 1990; Pascarella and Terenzini 1991; Eide, Brewer, and Ehrenberg 1998; Brewer, Eide, and Ehrenberg 1999). Research focused specifically on African Americans shows that access to highly selective institutions improves their educational and labor market outcomes (Bowen and Bok 1998; Kane 1998).

Gender

The changing status of women is perhaps one of the most notable social trends in twentieth-century America. Prompted by numerous factors, including the conscription of men during World War II, the feminist movement, equal employment laws, and an increasing need for two incomes in households, women's labor force participation, access to professional and managerial jobs, and income have increased over time (U.S. Bureau of the Census 2002). Additionally, specific legislation outlawing sex discrimination in education was passed in 1972. Title IX of the Educational Amendments of 1972 states that "No person in the United States shall, on the basis of sex, be excluded from participation in, be denied the benefits of, or be subject to discrimination under any educational programs or activity receiving federal financial assistance (U.S. Department of Education 1997)." On the 25th anniversary of Title IX, a report released by the U.S. Department of Education (1997) documented numerous gains women have made in education since 1972, accompanied by "change in our expectations of what women can achieve."

The improved position of women in the labor market, aided by increased competition for academically able students and a decline in the size of high-school graduation cohorts, increased women's presence in higher education. Women had reached parity in higher education enrollments by the mid-1970s and in attendance at four-year institutions by 1980 (U.S.

NCES 2002a). Since 1982, women have surpassed men in the number of bachelor's degrees earned (Jacobs 1996), and by 2000, women received approximately 60% of all associate, bachelor's, and master's degrees (U.S. NCES 2002a; see also U.S. NCES 2005).

However, although women earn over half of all baccalaureate credentials, they overwhelmingly receive degrees in particular fields of study, including education, health sciences, home economics, library and archival sciences, and public administration and services (U.S. NCES 2002a; for a review see also Jacobs 1996), which generally yield lower economic returns (e.g., Rumberger and Thomas 1993; Davies and Guppy 1997; Roksa 2005). Sex segregation across college majors decreased substantially during the 1970s and 1980s, but has stalled since. Approximately one-third of women would have to change their fields of study to ensure that women and men were evenly distributed across college majors (Jacobs 1995).

CHANGES IN SOCIAL STRATIFICATION: MMI AND TRENDLESS FLUCTUATION

Socioeconomic Status

Our predictions regarding socioeconomic status are drawn from the general theoretical framework of Maximally Maintained Inequality (MMI). According to MMI, privileged groups preserve their relative advantages in access to higher levels of education even as education undergoes a general expansion. This holds true until the privileged group reaches saturation at a given level, at which point disadvantaged groups may begin to catch up in relative terms (Raftery and Hout 1993). In the case of U.S. postsecondary education, no group has reached saturation, so we do not anticipate any reduction in relative inequality among individuals of different social backgrounds.[6]

Moreover, although some policy initiatives were implemented to improve access of students from lower socioeconomic status to higher education, we do not anticipate that they will affect the pattern of class stratification. Previous cross-national research has shown that neither educational expansion nor specific policy initiatives substantially alter the effects of socioeconomic background on educational attainment (Shavit and Blossfeld 1993). In addition, financial assistance provided by the government is neither limited to the lower socioeconomic strata nor sufficient to meet attendance costs at many four-year institutions. Consequently, inequality by socioeconomic background in access to higher education, particularly to more prestigious types of higher education, is likely to persist.

Race/Ethnicity and Gender

Although persistent inequality is likely to characterize the trend for class origins, this may not be the case for gender and racial/ethnic stratification. Both gender and racial/ethnic inequalities were affected by political and labor market changes that may have reduced the attainment gap between disadvantaged and advantaged groups over time (see Gamoran 2001). Sorokin's (1959) notion of "trendless fluctuations" implies that historically specific political and institutional characteristics determine the level of educational access for excluded groups. Mobilization of women and minorities in their quest for equity may thus be expected to produce changes in stratification patterns over time (Karen 1991a, 1991b). As a result of specific laws that were enacted to grant equal status in U.S. society to racial minorities and of actions taken by higher education institutions to diversify their campuses, coupled with improved economic status of minority groups and increasing high-school graduation rates, we expect that inequality in access to higher education and more prestigious types of institutions between minority and white students will decrease following the 1960s. However, these trends are likely to slow down or reverse in the last decade of the twentieth century under increasing financial strain of higher education institutions and challenges to affirmative action.

Improvement of the status of women in U.S. society is likely to be reflected in declining inequality between men and women in postsecondary enrollment in general, and in specific types of tertiary education in particular. Policies aimed at improving women's position in higher education have been based on the principle of nondiscrimination, and therefore have not encountered strong opposition or backlash as is the case with racial affirmative action. Therefore, the progress of women in higher education is expected to be steady throughout the century.

DATA AND METHODS

We used four nationally representative data sets to examine the stratification patterns in U.S. higher education: the General Social Survey (GSS), the

National Longitudinal Survey of the High School Class of 1972 (NLS-72), High School and Beyond (HS&B), and the National Education Longitudinal Study of 1988 (NELS). The General Social Survey (GSS) has been conducted semiannually since 1972, including a random sample of approximately 1,500–3,000 respondents per year.[7] The survey covers a broad range of topics, including socioeconomic background, educational attainment, and labor force participation. We utilized a sample of over 40,000 individuals surveyed cross-sectionally between 1972 and 2000.

In addition, we used three surveys conducted by the U.S. Department of Education based on nationally representative samples of high-school students.[8] The National Longitudinal Survey of the High School Class of 1972 (NLS-72) includes surveys and cognitive test scores from a probability sample of over 20,000 high-school seniors in 1972, as well as information from high-school and college transcripts. Respondents were reinterviewed up to five times between 1972 and 1986. The fifth wave, consisting of 12,917 respondents, serves as the analytic sample for our analyses (a response rate of 89%). High School and Beyond (HS&B) includes samples of sophomores and seniors, originally interviewed in 1980. HS&B sophomores were reinterviewed a total of four times, with the last follow-up administered as a phone survey between February 1992 and January 1993. Our sample includes 12,795 students who completed survey instruments in the fourth follow-up (a response rate of approximately 85%). Data include information from high-school transcripts and cognitive tests administered to students in their sophomore and senior years as well as parent surveys for a subsample of 2,534 students.

Lastly, the National Education Longitudinal Study of 1988 (NELS) is a representative sample of students who were in the 8th grade in 1988 and of the schools they attended. The baseline sample included 24,599 students, a random subsample of which has been reinterviewed up to four times, most recently in 2000. The analytic sample for our study includes 14,915 students included in the 1994 follow-up (94% response rate). We used the third follow-up since detailed 2000 data on the first postsecondary institution attended were not yet available at the time of writing this chapter.[9] NELS also includes parent surveys, and provides highly reliable and complete reports of origin characteristics and achievement scores from a sophisticated battery of cognitive tests.

Models

Instead of examining only the transition into higher education or completion of bachelor's degrees, which has been the focus of previous stratification research, we examined stratification processes for five educational outcomes, considering inequality of access to higher education in general and different types of tertiary institutions in particular. We estimate a series of logistic regression analyses separately by the period in which respondents were expected to complete high school. We then compare coefficients across birth cohorts using t-test to determine whether association between social origins and access to higher education has declined, increased, or remained stable. All findings discussed in the chapter refer to conditional models described below; unconditional models are available upon request from the authors.

We examined five educational transitions:

1. eligibility for higher education (i.e., completing high school);
2. attaining any postsecondary education, conditional on high-school graduation;
3. entering a baccalaureate-granting institution, conditional on entry into higher education;
4. attending highly selective relative to nonselective four-year institutions;
5. entering two-year institutions, conditional on high-school graduation.

GSS was used in the first model to examine the likelihood of high-school graduation, and educational data sets were used to estimate all other models. The educational data sets were omitted from the first model because of unique sampling characteristics described above (e.g., HS&B begins with a sample of students in their 10th grade, while NLS-72 begins with students in their last year of high school). GSS was excluded from models examining educational transitions subsequent to high-school graduation because it contains information only on degree completion and not entry into different types of postsecondary institutions.

In the fourth educational transition examined, we distinguished between the most selective and other four-year institutions using the average test scores of first-year college students.[10] Sorting schools in a descending order of test scores reported by colleges, we defined the top 10% of the distribution of institutions as selective.[11] We then predicted the probability that a student attended an elite postsecondary institution conditional on attending some baccalaureate-granting institution. We estimated three models for each dependent variable:

(i) The comparative model includes only individuals' social origins measured by parental education (the higher of the father's or mother's education; if information was available for only one parent, that education was considered the highest) and father's occupation (when absent, mother's occupation was used). Parental education was coded according to the CASMIN scheme, combining CASMIN 1a and 1b (those with less than 8th-grade and 8th–11th-grade education) because of the small number of observations in those categories in recent birth cohorts. Moreover, high-school graduates were not differentiated based on high-school curriculum (i.e., CASMIN categories of 2a, 2b, and 2c reflecting vocational, general, and academic high-school programs were combined into one category). The final scheme for parental education included: less than high school, high-school diploma (omitted), some postsecondary education, and four-year college and higher. Parents' occupation was coded in the seven-category EGP scheme, with EGP I/II combined (professional and managers) and unskilled workers (EGP VI) used as the reference category.

(ii) The baseline model includes the two measures of socioeconomic background described in (i) as well as gender, race, and single-parent indicators as reported by respondents. The single-parent family dummy variable indicates respondents who lived with only one parent or guardian. In HS&B and NELS, the parental status was recorded in the baseline survey, 10th grade for HS&B and 8th grade for NELS. In GSS, respondents were asked if they had lived with both parents at age 16. With respect to race, GSS contains only three racial categories: white (omitted), African American, and other racial minorities. Educational surveys contain larger sample sizes and thus allow more detailed racial breakdown, including dummy variables for African Americans, Hispanics, Asians, and other racial minorities.

(iii) The achievement model includes variables from the baseline model as well as several indicators of student achievement. Academic achievement (often measured by grades and test scores) plays a central role in educational and occupational attainment (Sewell and Shah 1967; Sewell, Haller, and Portes 1969) and is an important site of racial/ethnic inequality (Jencks and Phillips 1998). Likewise, the secondary school curriculum has been prominent in discussions of racial and socioeconomic disparities (Oakes

1985; Gamoran and Mare 1989; Gamoran 1992; Lucas 1999). Our achievement models thus include measures of test scores,[12] student grade point averages, and high-school track: academic (omitted), vocational, general, and other.

Missing data on background variables in all models were dealt with by using the dummy substitution method: substituting constants for the missing values and adding dummy variables to the model (coded 1 when a substitution was made). For clarity and simplicity of presentation, coefficients for missing dummies are not reported in the tables. In educational data sets, sampling weights were used to adjust for individuals' probability of being included in the sample and for nonresponse.

RESULTS

Tables 7.1, 7.2a, and 7.2b present logistic regression coefficients from baseline models for each of the educational transitions discussed. Following, Table 7.3 reports selected comparisons between baseline and achievement models. Results for high-school completion are based on GSS and include five cohorts. All other transitions are examined using educational surveys, spanning three cohorts. Cohort labels refer to the approximate time when respondents would have completed high school and been at risk to enter higher education. For brevity and coherence of the presentation, we describe the patterns of inequality across socioeconomic, racial, and gender groups by focusing on four sets of comparisons.

Socioeconomic Status

Parental Education (College Degree and Higher versus High-School Graduate). Parental education had a strong influence on access to higher education across cohorts. Students whose parents had earned college degrees or graduate credentials had greater access to higher education and more prestigious institutions within it than those whose parents ended their formal education after high school. Moreover, advantages associated with highly educated parents have persisted over time. As Table 7.1 shows, individuals with college-educated parents had significantly greater odds of graduating from high school across all cohorts than individuals whose parents only completed high school. This pattern of persistent inequality is also apparent in access to postsecondary education: conditional on high-school graduation and other covariates, students with college-educated parents were 5–6 times as likely to enter postsecondary education as students whose parents only graduated from high school (Table 7.2a on page 183).

Advantages associated with having highly educated parents are also evident in access to baccalaureate and elite baccalaureate institutions (Tables 7.2a and 7.2b). Conditional on entering higher education, students whose parents had a college degree or graduate credentials were significantly more likely to attend baccalaureate-granting institutions, including the most prestigious ones. In the 1990s, individuals whose parents graduated from college had approximately 5 times the odds of entering both baccalaureate and elite baccalaureate institutions as individuals whose parents graduated from high school, all else equal. Moreover, inequality in access to baccalaureate-granting institutions appears to have increased over time: the effect of highly educated parents on entry into baccalaureate-granting institutions was significantly higher for individuals entering higher education in the 1990s than in the 1980s ($t = 4.72$).

The second set of models in Table 7.2b (on page 184) consider entry into two-year institutions. In contrast to findings for entry into baccalaureate-granting institutions, and illuminating the stratified character of U.S. higher education, students whose parents ended their formal education after high school were slightly more likely to enter higher education through two-year institutions than children whose parents completed college. These effects have remained stable across the three cohorts examined.[13]

One of the factors that may help to explain the advantages associated with a privileged family background is academic achievement. Comparisons in Table 7.3 (on page 185) demonstrate that controlling for academic achievement reduces the effects of parental education on access to postsecondary opportunities. However, although smaller in magnitude, these effects remain strong and significant. In the 1990s, for example, students with college-educated parents were between 2.5 and 4 times as likely to gain access to higher education and more prestigious institutions within it as students whose parents were high-school graduates, even net of academic achievement. Thus, while affecting the absolute value of the coefficients, controlling for academic achievement does not alter the finding that students with highly educated parents are advantaged in access to postsecondary education, and that this advantage has persisted over time.

Father's Occupation (Professional/Managerial Relative to Unskilled). As would be expected, the effects of father's occupation on access to higher education are generally positive, but weaker than those of parental education. Although increasing proportions of students from all socioeconomic groups have graduated from high school over the course of the century, the advantage associated with having a father who is a professional or a manager relative to a father who is an unskilled laborer has not diminished. In the 1980s, students whose fathers were employed in professional/managerial occupations had 2.5 times the odds of graduating from high school as students whose fathers were unskilled workers—the same odds as in the period before WWII (Table 7.1).

Tables 7.2a and 7.2b report the association between father's occupation and access to higher education and different types of institutions within it, conditional on high-school graduation, parental education, family type, gender, and race/ethnicity. Individuals with fathers in professional/managerial occupations were significantly more likely to enter postsecondary education than individuals with fathers in unskilled occupations, and this effect has persisted over time.[14] Students entering higher education in the 1990s were approximately two times as likely to make this transition if their fathers were professionals/managers than if their fathers were unskilled laborers, all else equal.

In contrast, conditional on entry into higher education and other covariates, students whose fathers were unskilled workers were not disadvantaged in access to four-year institutions compared to students whose fathers were professionals/managers. Although the contrast between such students is statistically significant in the first cohort, the effect is modest (odds = 1.49). Moreover, the effects are not significant in the last two cohorts and t-tests indicate no significant change over time. Similarly, there are no significant differences associated with father's occupation in access to two-year institutions. Nor is there any change over time in the relation between father's occupation and that educational outcome. The most dramatic change over time occurred with respect to access to elite baccalaureate education: having a father in a professional/managerial occupation had no significant effect for students entering higher education in the 1980s, but it had a significant positive effect of similar magnitude for cohorts entering before and after. However, even in this case t-tests for change over time barely meet the significance criteria ($t = -2.00$ for decline between the

TABLE 7.1
Logistic regression models predicting eligibility for entry into higher education
(i.e., high-school completion)

Entering higher education	Cohort 1 Pre-WWII	Cohort 2 Post-WWII	Cohort 3 1960s	Cohort 4 1970s	Cohort 5 1980s
Parental education (high-school graduate omitted)					
College and higher	1.891**	1.184**	1.421**	1.795**	1.727**
	(0.427)	(0.262)	(0.286)	(0.296)	(0.312)
Some postsecondary	0.355	0.894**	0.513**	0.653**	0.795**
	(0.211)	(0.209)	(0.182)	(0.174)	(0.210)
Less than high school	−1.255**	−1.272**	−1.316**	−1.299**	−1.240**
	(0.105)	(0.084)	(0.090)	(0.095)	(0.140)
Father's occupation (unskilled labor omitted)					
Professional/managerial	0.984**	0.844**	0.764**	1.002**	0.893**
	(0.193)	(0.187)	(0.202)	(0.198)	(0.297)
Clerical/sales	1.085**	0.865**	1.115**	1.456**	1.013**
	(0.198)	(0.206)	(0.246)	(0.266)	(0.275)
Self-employed	0.604**	0.390**	0.414**	0.790**	0.604**
	(0.117)	(0.110)	(0.137)	(0.156)	(0.219)
Skilled	0.135	0.232*	0.165	0.424**	0.305
	(0.102)	(0.092)	(0.104)	(0.113)	(0.169)
Farmer	−0.471**	−0.407**	−0.291**	0.186	0.490
	(0.094)	(0.090)	(0.113)	(0.147)	(0.268)
Single parent	−0.199	−0.115	0.113	−0.303*	−0.186
	(0.114)	(0.100)	(0.128)	(0.120)	(0.151)
Female	0.022	0.078	−0.019	0.130	−0.097
	(0.063)	(0.058)	(0.071)	(0.079)	(0.116)
Race/ethnicity (white omitted)					
African American	−0.881**	−0.572**	−0.147	0.066	0.107
	(0.099)	(0.077)	(0.093)	(0.097)	(0.146)
Other nonwhite	−0.365	−0.737**	−0.415*	−0.347*	−0.184
	(0.334)	(0.199)	(0.175)	(0.167)	(0.198)
Constant	1.520**	1.994**	2.459**	2.093**	2.069**
	(0.125)	(0.105)	(0.111)	(0.113)	(0.176)
Observations	5,315	7,655	8,138	7,849	4,150

NOTE: Analyses based on the General Social Survey.
*$p < 0.05$; **$p < 0.01$.

first two cohorts and $t = 1.91$ for increase between the last two cohorts). Moreover, there is no significant difference in access to elite institutions between students whose fathers were unskilled workers and those whose fathers were professionals/managers after controlling for academic achievement (Table 7.3). Stability rather than change, thus, likely underlies the patterns of access to elite institutions.

Considering the effects of father's occupation and parental education jointly, we conclude that there are significant advantages in access to

TABLE 7.2A
Logistic regression models predicting entry into postsecondary and baccalaureate institutions (conditional models)

	ENTER ANY POSTSECONDARY			ENTER BACCALAUREATE		
Entering higher education Data set	Cohort 1 1970s NLS-72	Cohort 2 1980s HS&B	Cohort 3 1990s NELS	Cohort 1 1970s NLS-72	Cohort 2 1980s HS&B	Cohort 3 1990s NELS
Parental education (high-school graduate omitted)						
College and higher	1.605**	1.716**	1.835**	1.168**	1.050**	**1.664****
	(0.156)	(0.115)	(0.223)	(0.091)	(0.094)	(0.090)
Some postsecondary	0.766**	0.603**	0.501**	0.379**	0.247**	0.591**
	(0.101)	(0.074)	(0.121)	(0.083)	(0.081)	(0.074)
Less than high school	−0.374**	−0.450**	−0.885**	−0.208	−0.171	−0.381**
	(0.097)	(0.089)	(0.157)	(0.124)	(0.133)	(0.127)
Father's occupation (unskilled labor omitted)						
Professional/managerial	0.452**	0.298*	0.853**	0.399**	0.107	0.220
	(0.122)	(0.148)	(0.269)	(0.095)	(0.138)	(0.120)
Clerical/sales	0.642**	0.217	−0.244*	0.321**	0.074	−0.298**
	(0.146)	(0.125)	(0.114)	(0.114)	(0.111)	(0.075)
Self-employed	0.772	0.201	0.100	1.110	−0.009	0.274**
	(0.464)	(0.138)	(0.225)	(0.606)	(0.123)	(0.091)
Skilled	0.219*	−0.222**	0.097	0.199*	−0.292**	−0.268**
	(0.096)	(0.079)	(0.152)	(0.096)	(0.080)	(0.086)
Farmer	0.445**	0.015	0.050	0.210	0.067	−0.475
	(0.132)	(0.143)	(0.332)	(0.149)	(0.166)	(0.460)
Single parent		−0.012	−0.218		−0.044	−0.270**
		(0.088)	(0.115)		(0.094)	(0.099)
Female	−0.120	**0.422****	**0.141**	−0.133*	−0.159*	**0.299****
	(0.076)	(0.059)	(0.104)	(0.067)	(0.067)	(0.056)
Race/ethnicity (white omitted)						
African American	0.556**	**0.181**	−0.484**	0.299*	−0.011	−0.000
	(0.151)	(0.116)	(0.167)	(0.137)	(0.109)	(0.111)
Hispanic	0.478*	−0.400**	−0.142	−0.149	−0.317**	−0.186
	(0.204)	(0.090)	(0.145)	(0.275)	(0.102)	(0.098)
Asian	0.885*	1.449**	0.214	0.213	0.167	0.277*
	(0.383)	(0.258)	(0.342)	(0.258)	(0.171)	(0.135)
Other nonwhite	−0.493*	0.113	−0.724**	−0.513**	0.077	−0.806**
	(0.192)	(0.255)	(0.274)	(0.169)	(0.243)	(0.248)
Constant	0.314**	0.329**	1.741**	−0.627**	−0.296**	−1.202**
	(0.086)	(0.084)	(0.126)	(0.088)	(0.090)	(0.090)
Observations	12,732	10,533	13,121	9,824	7,901	11,876

NOTE: Bold coefficients indicate change over time for the four sets of comparisons discussed in the chapter. If a coefficient is bold then it is significantly different from the related coefficient in the previous cohort ($p < 0.05$). Additional differences significant at $p < 0.10$ are discussed in the text.
*$p < 0.05$; **$p < 0.01$ (robust standard errors in parentheses).

TABLE 7.2B
Logistic regression models predicting entry into elite baccalaureate and two-year institutions (conditional models) (continued)

	ENTER ELITE BACCALAUREATE			ENTER TWO-YEAR INSTITUTIONS		
Entering higher education Data set	Cohort 1 1970s NLS-72	Cohort 2 1980s HS&B	Cohort 3 1990s NELS	Cohort 1 1970s NLS-72	Cohort 2 1980s HS&B	Cohort 3 1990s NELS
Parental Education (high-school graduate omitted)						
College and higher	1.890**	1.340**	1.646**	−0.190	−0.334**	−0.370**
	(0.187)	(0.313)	(0.385)	(0.097)	(0.089)	(0.102)
Some postsecondary	0.880**	0.389	0.111	0.208**	0.143*	0.035
	(0.197)	(0.310)	(0.404)	(0.079)	(0.070)	(0.081)
Less than high school	−0.189	0.502	0.304	−0.157	−0.135	0.034
	(0.279)	(0.414)	(0.634)	(0.102)	(0.097)	(0.112)
Father's occupation (unskilled labor omitted)						
Professional/managerial	0.599**	−0.092	0.631*	0.038	−0.076	−0.138
	(0.228)	(0.259)	(0.275)	(0.097)	(0.123)	(0.137)
Clerical/sales	0.564	−0.231	−0.208	0.147	−0.000	0.020
	(0.292)	(0.273)	(0.200)	(0.114)	(0.104)	(0.081)
Self-employed	0.372	0.395	0.532*	−0.696	0.117	−0.203*
	(0.866)	(0.230)	(0.238)	(0.455)	(0.116)	(0.102)
Skilled	0.291	−0.366	−0.170	0.006	0.075	0.091
	(0.223)	(0.230)	(0.250)	(0.087)	(0.069)	(0.085)
Farmer	0.032	−1.995	0.952	−0.003	0.001	−0.210
	(0.519)	(1.025)	(0.936)	(0.123)	(0.145)	(0.385)
Single parent		−0.330	0.057		0.021	0.096
		(0.234)	(0.248)		(0.083)	(0.099)
Female	−0.504**	−0.330*	−0.290	−0.029	0.277**	0.078
	(0.161)	(0.140)	(0.158)	(0.067)	(0.057)	(0.060)
Race/ethnicity (white omitted)						
African American	0.218	−0.520*	−0.637	0.063	0.058	−0.194
	(0.239)	(0.235)	(0.346)	(0.139)	(0.098)	(0.117)
Hispanic	−1.242*	−0.298	0.327	0.497**	0.090	0.329**
	(0.543)	(0.240)	(0.326)	(0.181)	(0.086)	(0.097)
Asian	1.186**	0.195	0.666**	0.332	0.229	0.096
	(0.428)	(0.291)	(0.212)	(0.236)	(0.160)	(0.116)
Other nonwhite	−0.220	0.146	−1.050	−0.031	0.070	0.057
	(0.326)	(0.727)	(1.075)	(0.181)	(0.199)	(0.210)
Constant	−4.227**	−2.780**	−3.706**	−0.976**	−0.682**	−0.761**
	(0.230)	(0.333)	(0.405)	(0.083)	(0.079)	(0.092)
Observations	8,077	4,001	5,003	12,732	9,830	11,876

NOTE: See note to Table 7.2a.

TABLE 7.3
Comparisons of selected results across baseline and achievement models

Entering higher education	ENTER ANY POSTSECONDARY			ENTER BACCALAUREATE			ENTER ELITE BACCALAUREATE		
	Cohort 1 1970s	Cohort 2 1980s	Cohort 3 1990s	Cohort 1 1970s	Cohort 2 1980s	Cohort 3 1990s	Cohort 1 1970s	Cohort 2 1980s	Cohort 3 1990s
Data set	NLS-72	HS&B	NELS	NLS-72	HS&B	NELS	NLS-72	HS&B	NELS
Parental education (college and higher compared to high-school graduate)									
Baseline model	1.605**	1.716**	1.835**	1.168**	1.050**	1.664**	1.890**	1.340**	1.646**
	(0.156)	(0.115)	(0.223)	(0.091)	(0.094)	(0.090)	(0.187)	(0.313)	(0.385)
Achievement model	1.144**	1.150**	0.971**	0.842**	0.664**	1.062**	1.038**	0.793*	1.359**
	(0.162)	(0.116)	(0.232)	(0.103)	(0.097)	(0.102)	(0.198)	(0.343)	(0.410)
Father's occupation (professional/managerial compared to unskilled labor)									
Baseline model	0.452**	0.298**	0.853**	0.399**	0.107	0.220	0.599**	−0.092	0.631*
	(0.122)	(0.148)	(0.269)	(0.095)	(0.138)	(0.120)	(0.228)	(0.259)	(0.275)
Achievement model	0.336**	0.226	0.758**	0.354**	0.096	0.049	0.412	−0.023	0.406
	(0.128)	(0.155)	(0.291)	(0.107)	(0.143)	(0.128)	(0.240)	(0.285)	(0.304)
Female									
Baseline model	−0.120	**0.422****	0.141	−0.133*	−0.159**	**0.299****	−0.504**	−0.330*	−0.290
	(0.076)	(0.059)	(0.104)	(0.067)	(0.067)	(0.056)	(0.161)	(0.140)	(0.158)
Achievement model	−0.132	**0.372****	−0.036	−0.218**	−0.199**	**0.112**	−0.615**	0.005	−0.314
	(0.085)	(0.065)	(0.116)	(0.075)	(0.077)	(0.074)	(0.146)	(0.166)	(0.166)
African American (compared to white)									
Baseline model	0.556**	0.181	**−0.484****	0.299*	−0.011	−0.000	0.218	**−0.520***	−0.637
	(0.151)	(0.116)	(0.167)	(0.137)	(0.109)	(0.111)	(0.239)	(0.235)	(0.346)
Achievement model	0.998**	1.051**	0.228	0.855**	0.745**	0.815**	1.058**	0.495	0.313
	(0.161)	(0.121)	(0.159)	(0.163)	(0.125)	(0.128)	(0.274)	(0.317)	(0.38)

NOTE: Baseline models are those presented in Tables 7.2a and 7.2b; achievement models include additional controls for students' test scores, high-school grade point average, and high-school track. Bold coefficients indicate change over time. If a coefficient is bold then it is significantly different from the related coefficient in the previous cohort ($p < 0.05$).

*$p < 0.05$; ** $p < 0.01$ (robust standard errors in parentheses).

postsecondary education associated with high socioeconomic status, and that these advantages have not decreased over time. Moreover, controlling for students' academic achievement mediates but does not fundamentally alter these effects. Supporting our prediction based on MMI and previous stratification research, neither extensive educational expansion nor implementation of student-aid policies has altered the patterns of stratification in higher education based on socioeconomic status.

Race (African American Relative to White)

Although privileges associated with high socioeconomic status have remained stable over time, African Americans have made inroads in access to higher education. As Table 7.1 shows, African Americans were significantly less likely than whites to graduate from high school before WWII, all else equal. However, their likelihood of graduating has increased over time, and by the 1960s started to equal those of whites. Changes between the first three cohorts are significant, as measured by t-tests between coefficients ($t = 2.46$ between the first two cohorts and $t = 3.52$ between the second and third cohorts). Increasing parity in high-school completion made more African Americans eligible for higher education. However, as Table 7.2a reports, conditional on high-school graduation and other covariates, the likelihood of entering any type of higher education has decreased for African Americans across the three time periods examined ($t = -1.97$ for the decline between the first two cohorts and $t = -3.27$ for the decline between the second and third cohorts).

Conditional on entering higher education, African Americans were significantly more likely to attend baccalaureate-granting institutions than whites in the 1970s, although this advantage was small (odds = 1.35). In addition, there are no significant differences in coefficients over time, and the coefficients in the last two time periods are not significant. We therefore conclude that conditional on entering higher education, African Americans have had equal access to baccalaureate-granting institutions as whites across all three cohorts considered. Similarly, African Americans and whites had the same conditional likelihood of entering two-year institutions, an effect that has not changed over time.

Access to elite baccalaureate-granting institutions presents a different pattern (Table 7.2b). In the 1970s, African Americans were as likely to enter elite institutions as whites, conditional on entering any baccalaureate-granting institutions. However, there has been a significant decrease in the likelihood of African Americans attending elite institutions between the cohorts entering higher education in the 1970s and the 1980s ($t = -2.20$). Since the 1980s, African Americans have been significantly less likely to enter elite baccalaureate institutions than whites (coefficient for the 1990s is almost the same as for the 1980s and is significant at $p < 0.10$).

These patterns are consistent with trends in affirmative action policy. Affirmative action in higher education, affecting mostly selective institutions, has been pronounced in the 1960s and 1970s, but was substantially curtailed by the Reagan administration and by Supreme Court rulings in the 1980s and 1990s. Moreover, case studies of California have reported decreasing enrollments of minority students in selective institutions following the dismantling of affirmative action (Karabel 1999; Allen et al. 2000; Carroll, Tyson, and Lumas 2000). Although not conclusive, presented results underscore the importance of careful examination of the relation between affirmative action policies and access of minority students to elite baccalaureate institutions.

Another notable set of findings regarding race is seen in models controlling for academic achievement in Table 7.3. Net of academic achievement (test scores, GPA, and high-school track), African Americans fare much better in higher education than the baseline models suggest. Controlling for academic achievement, African Americans were significantly more likely to attend baccalaureate-granting institutions than whites across all three cohorts, conditional on entry into higher education. They were also significantly more likely to attend elite institutions in the 1970s, although the coefficient decreased and was not significantly different from that of whites in subsequent cohorts. These results imply that academic preparation of African Americans in high school is one of the key components in fostering racial equality in access to higher education.

These findings support our hypothesis based on Sorokin's notion of trendless fluctuation. African Americans reached parity with whites in high-school graduation in the 1960s, the era of the Civil Rights movement. By the 1970s, controlling for academic achievement, African Americans had higher likelihood of attending baccalaureate-granting institutions and equal likelihood of attending elite institutions. Therefore, it appears that the struggles of the Civil Rights movement, together with laws preventing discriminatory practices in postsecondary institutions, have facilitated greater equality between African Americans and whites in access to postsecondary opportunities.

Gender

Throughout the twentieth century, women were as likely to graduate from high school as men (Table 7.1), and by the 1990s they were faring equally well or better in access to higher education and specific types of postsecondary institutions (Tables 7.2a and 7.2b). The likelihood of women entering any higher education, conditional on high-school graduation and other covariates, has increased significantly between the first two cohorts ($t = 5.63$), but then decreased between the second and third cohorts ($t = -2.35$). The same pattern is evident for entry into two-year institutions. Thus, while women were significantly more likely than men to enter higher education as well as community colleges in the 1980s, they were equally likely to make these educational transitions in the other two cohorts.

Access to four-year institutions demonstrates a different pattern. Net of parental education, father's occupation, family type, and race/ethnicity, women were significantly less likely than men to enter baccalaureate-granting institutions in the 1970s and 1980s, but significantly more likely to make this educational transition in the 1990s (the change between the last two cohorts is statistically significant, $t = 5.25$). However, women have continued to lag slightly behind men in access to elite baccalaureate institutions across cohorts: they were significantly less likely to enter elite institutions than men in the 1970s, and that effect has persisted over time.[15] This may be partly a product of the institutional composition of the elite sector. Based on our definition, several schools with large engineering/science departments as well as military academies were designated as elite. Joint consideration of institutional type and field of study is needed in future research to provide a more comprehensive understanding of the position of women in elite higher education.

Results presented in Table 7.3 suggest that controlling for academic achievement does not substantially alter the effects of gender. The only exception is access to elite baccalaureate institutions. Controlling for academic achievement, women gained significantly in access to elite institutions between the first two cohorts ($t = 2.81$), and since then they have been as likely to enter elite baccalaureate institutions as men. Thus, net of academic achievement, women have either matched or surpassed men in attendance at every type of higher education institution by the end of the twentieth century.

Findings for women also support our predictions based on Sorokin's notion of trendless fluctuation. Over the course of the twentieth century, the position of women in U.S. society has been altered substantially. Propelled by numerous social, political, and economic forces, women have gained increased access to higher education and the labor market. By the 1990s, women have either equaled or exceeded men in access to higher education, although their access to elite institutions remains tenuous. Moreover, inequality has multiple dimensions. Women's access to different divisions, programs, and activities within postsecondary institutions remains to be considered before we can conclude that gender parity has been reached in postsecondary education.

CONCLUSION

U.S. higher education has expanded dramatically over the course of the twentieth century, but the growth has not been even. Increased enrollments in lower-status institutions (nonselective four-year institutions and community colleges) and solidification of institutional hierarchies has produced a highly stratified system. Moreover, development of a strong vocational component (through both increased vocationalization of community colleges and establishment of exclusively vocational schools) has added a binary element to U.S. higher education. Concurrently, policies such as Title IV of the Higher Education Act, Title IX, and Affirmative Action were implemented to improve access of disadvantaged groups to postsecondary education. This combination of expansion and policy intervention has allowed greater access to higher education and some changes in the landscape of inequality.

The benefits of access to higher education associated with privileged family background have remained stable over time. Consistent with the theoretical framework of Maximally Maintained Inequality (MMI) and with previous cross-national stratification research, extensive educational expansion and public policy interventions regarding financial aid have not reduced the advantages associated with high socioeconomic status.

The findings regarding race and gender are strikingly different and support Sorokin's emphasis on historically specific political and institutional characteristics. By the end of the twentieth century, women and African Americans had made important inroads in access to higher education, and in particular baccalaureate-granting institutions.

Research on educational stratification has consistently shown that expansion fails to reduce inequality of opportunity, as persons from privileged backgrounds tend to make the best use of expansion (Hout, Raftery, and Bell 1993; Hout and Dohan 1996). However, our results suggest that educational expansion, coupled with specific educational policies, can improve outcomes for some disadvantaged groups. African Americans and women, who have mobilized and gained recognition as "protected groups" in U.S. political discourse, have made substantial gains in access to higher education. In contrast, the poor and working class, who have not mobilized and gained legitimacy, remain disadvantaged in the current educational system (Karen 1991a, 1991b; see also Rubinson 1986). Stratification processes thus vary across groups, and the ability to mobilize appears to be one of the necessary (although not sufficient) conditions for altering patterns of inequality.

Although we have considered a range of educational outcomes across different time periods and for different demographic groups, there are at least two important considerations that require attention in future research. First, we examined entry into higher education, as opposed to completion. While most high-school students in the U.S. enter higher education, a much smaller number complete postsecondary degrees. For example, 42% of the 1992 high-school graduates who entered higher education attained no postsecondary degrees by 2000. Moreover, persistence and degree completion rates vary by gender, race, and socioeconomic status (U.S. NCES 2003b). Stratification patterns for degree attainment may therefore be distinct from those for entry, requiring future examination.

Second, we explored the relation between individual characteristics and educational transitions, without considering the final link in the traditional status attainment model: occupational destinations. Some researchers have proposed that educational expansion has decreased the association between origins and destinations, and that a college degree in particular cancels the effect of background status on occupational attainment (Hout 1988, 1996). At the same time, it is well documented that women's high educational attainment has not led to their equality in the labor market. Detailed analysis of the relation between attendance at particular types of postsecondary institutions and occupational destinations of different gender, racial/ethnic, and socioeconomic groups is needed to develop a more comprehensive understanding of the consequences of stratification in U.S. higher education.

PART II: BINARY SYSTEMS

CHAPTER EIGHT

Great Britain: Higher Education Expansion and Reform—Changing Educational Inequalities

Sin Yi Cheung, Department of International Relations, Politics and Sociology, Oxford Brookes University, United Kingdom

Muriel Egerton, Department of Sociology, Oxford University, United Kingdom

INTRODUCTION

Against the backdrop of major institutional reforms in higher education in the last four decades, we use the experiences of two birth cohorts to examine the changes of class and gender inequality of higher education. The advantages enjoyed by the sons and daughters of the service class persisted between the two cohorts, but that children from unskilled or semiskilled manual origins made some gains relative to children from skilled manual origins. Class inequalities were especially persistent in the more selective forms of higher education, but working-class children made gains in lower forms of higher education and more of them completed degrees. Generally, the combination of rising eligibility rates for higher education among the working class and rising participation in tertiary education, albeit in the less prestigious institutions, suggests some decrease in class inequality between the two cohorts. Similarly, the disadvantages of children with less educated parents decreased somewhat for the 1970 cohort. Finally, there is a clear decrease in gender inequality in eligibility for, and completion of upper tertiary education. Among those eligible for higher education, the probability of attaining postsecondary qualifications was actually higher for women than men for both birth cohorts.

POSTWAR REFORM: THE BINARY PERIOD

The British higher education system had undergone two phases of major reforms. First came the postwar expansion, followed by another period of rapid expansion in the late 1980s and early 1990s. Postwar policy-makers set about expanding and reforming a system that had recruited about 3% of the age group for full-time higher education: about 1.7% to universities, and 1.3% to teacher training and higher education in further education colleges (Halsey 1988, table 7.2).[1] The Robbins Committee Report of 1963 established the case that entrance to university should be open to all who could benefit from it, and its acceptance accelerated postwar expansion. Before the Robbins Report, there were 31 British universities, 10 colleges of advanced technology, 150 teacher training colleges, and sizeable numbers of further education colleges that offered advanced vocational training (Halsey 1988). Post-Robbins, the colleges of advanced technology were given university status and removed from local authority funding and control. Seven new universities were founded in England, some, such as Leicester University, based on the old London University Colleges. One new university was founded in Scotland, and another formed from the merger of technical institutes. All of these had autonomous governance and came under the generous funding regime of the University Grants Committee, a body that mediated between the universities and central government (for more detailed accounts see Archer 1979; Halsey 1992, chaps. 2 and 3). The Labour government of the time responded to the clear deficit in technical training in the United Kingdom and also set up 30 polytechnics intended to provide advanced vocational education and respond to local labor market and industrial research needs. These institutions were administered through local authorities. Unlike the universities, whose degrees were validated by external examiners from other universities, the qualifications of these institutions were certified by centralized external bodies such as the Council for National Academic Awards.

Ten Colleges of Advanced Technology (based on previous technical colleges) were designated as universities in 1957–62 (Halsey 1988, 280) and a systematic effort was made to improve technical training by establishing sectoral Industrial Training Boards, with authority to raise training levies from employers (Green and Lucas 1995). The Education Act of 1944 had established discretionary awards to cover student maintenance and tuition fees, and the Education Act of 1962 made awards to degree students mandatory on local authorities. Discretionary awards were also to be made available for courses in further education. However, it was expected that most higher education in further education colleges would be funded by employers through the Industrial Training Boards. These courses were advanced vocational training rather than degree-level courses and were mainly part-time, so the issue of student maintenance did not arise.

This dual or binary system set the scene for the next twenty years of expansion. Most of the teacher training colleges were soon incorporated within the polytechnics or within university departments of education. As teaching and social work became graduate occupations, polytechnics increasingly taught at degree level. The recession of the 1970s and industrial restructuring led to the demise of most of the sectoral Industry Training Boards and to a decline in apprenticeships, perhaps encouraging growth of first-degree teaching in polytechnics. In line with the general upgrading of qualifications, universities and particularly polytechnics energetically developed new vocational degrees, some based on prior subdegree courses. Therefore degree-level teaching in polytechnics expanded in the 1980s, and by 1990 more students were studying for first degrees in polytechnics and colleges than in universities. However, more than a quarter of polytechnic students were still enrolled in subdegree higher education courses, compared with less than 1% in the universities (UK DfE 1993). Although the colleges remained heterogeneous, much of their advanced teaching had migrated to the new technological universities (ex–Colleges of Advanced Technology) and polytechnics, and it became customary to combine colleges with polytechnics in official statistics for higher education. The university system that emerged from these reforms was selective but extremely efficient. With generous student funding, part-time study and dropout rates were low (estimated at about 6%) and well-trained graduates entered the labor market in their early twenties. The student population was dominated by middle-class boys, although the participation of girls and of adults grew gradually throughout the period (Egerton and Halsey 1993).

THE DISSOLUTION OF THE BINARY SYSTEM

The intake of higher education students more than trebled over the binary period, with full-time student numbers reaching 457,000 in 1970/71 and

717,900 in 1990/91 (Halsey 2000, tables 6.4 and 6.5). The higher education Age Participation Index[2] (API) grew from 7.2 in 1962 to 13.7 in 1984 and 23 in 1992. But demand remained strong. During the 1980s, the Department for Education and Science (DES) became convinced that the higher education system should expand more rapidly. The DES believed that employer demand for graduates would increase. In addition, they identified a demand for higher education at degree level among adults. The DES argued that rapid industrial change produced a need for adults to upgrade their qualifications as industries shrank and previous qualifications became obsolete (UK DES 1987). Reform bills in 1987 and 1988 laid the ground for the public sector institutions (polytechnics and colleges) to leave local authority control and financing. In 1992, polytechnics and some colleges were incorporated as universities, becoming responsible for their own budgets and for accreditation of degrees (Kogan and Hanney 2000, chap. 4). This marked the dissolution of the binary system and an attempt to create a comprehensive system, in which, vocational qualifications in particular would be held in greater esteem. The new university system teaches at both degree and subdegree level. While further education colleges offer some higher education teaching, the bulk of their teaching is either at further education or school level, awarding such certificates as General Certificate of Education Advanced level or General National Vocational Qualification, qualifications that are ranked below tertiary qualifications.

The traditional elitist model of restricted growth gave way to a model under which a larger proportion of the population could enroll in some kind of postsecondary education. There are now 169 higher education institutions in Britain, of which 67 offer mainly further education courses.[3] The population of full-time students in higher education reached 1,131,000 in 1997/98 in addition to 506,600 part-time students.[4] Growth was greatest between 1988 and 1994, when a cap was imposed on student numbers. After the 1997 election, growth resumed, together with an increasing number of 18-year-olds in the population. By 2001 the API in Britain was 34. There is a certain degree of transferability between different higher education institutions. For example, students can move to university degree courses after gaining matriculation or "access" qualifications in colleges of further education. Some universities have formed partnerships with colleges to offer "two plus two year" or "one plus three year" combinations of foundation study in the college and degree-level study in the university. However, no official figures are available for the extent of transfer.

While the dissolution of the binary divide was presented as an equalizing or "comprehensive" strategy, in practice a hierarchy of prestige can be found within the reformed system. Universities continue to compete for better (or easier to teach) students, using the A-level exams as the major criterion of academic ability. There is no universal admission system, although admissions are coordinated by the Universities and Colleges Admissions Service. Within this system, universities have very different entrance requirements. More prestigious universities require much better examination results at A-level. The ranking of universities is underpinned by the publication of mandatory performance assessments. The new assessment regime involves quality assessment of the teaching of individual university departments and assessment of the research output of individual departments via the Research Assessment Exercise (RAE), both of which produce fairly detailed scores and rankings. Both exercises have implications for the funding of universities, in particular, success in the RAE substantially affects the funding awarded to departments, and therefore affects the teaching unit of resource. While the ex-polytechnics have become legally autonomous, the universities as a whole have become more accountable to the state, a development that has been characterized as a combination of centralization and decentralization (Kogan and Hanney 2000). While the policy rhetoric is in favor of diversity, in practice quality assurance has brought about a decrease in diversity with departments adopting conservative strategies in order to conform to the perceived Quality Assurance Agency requirements (Fulton 1996).

Attempts at reforming the vocational qualifications system have also been largely unsuccessful. The National Vocational Qualifications in the late 1980s and the amended General National Vocational Qualifications in 1992–93 were not successful in standardizing various vocational qualifications into a national framework (Wolf 2002).

FUNDING THE EXPANDED SYSTEM

In the post-Robbins system the universities were funded by the University Grants Committee on a quinquennial grant system. Student fees were paid by local authorities and maintenance grants were also available, although means-tested for most of the period. The recent expansion saw the onset of financial stringency for both universities and students. From the early 1980s onward, student maintenance grants declined in value by about 20% over the decade (UK DfE 1993), and a student loan system was introduced in 1990/91. Maintenance grants were phased out at about this time. In 1988, funding for the universities was transferred to a new body, the Universities Funding Council, while funding for the polytechnics and colleges was administered by the Polytechnics and Colleges Funding Council. In 1992, three new funding councils were set up: the Higher Education Funding Councils for England, Scotland, and Wales. These provided core funding for the new university system, but as a proportion of overall funding, central government funding fell from over 70% in the late 1960s to just over 30% in the mid-1990s (Halsey 2000). Universities depended on other income (research contracts, short courses, conferences) and on student fees to make up the shortfall. Dependence on student fees, still funded by central government but administered through local authorities, introduced a market element to recruitment. As a result, a recruitment competition broke out, most strongly among the new universities (or ex-polytechnics) that gained little income from research. In 1998, the Labour government introduced tuition fees, initially set at £1,000 for all institutions and rising by 2.5% per year (approximately the inflation rate). Unit costs per student fell during the 1980s by about 15% for university students and by about 30% for Polytechnic and HE College students (UK DfE 1994). Unit costs declined further by about 30% during the 1990s from over £7,000 to less than £5,000.

Student participation rates in higher education trebled over the fifteen years following Robbins. It doubled again between the late 1980s and early 1990s (Figure 8.1). As Figure 8.1 illustrates, polytechnics expanded at a faster rate than universities and women caught up with men in access to postschool full-time courses of higher education. However, the rapid growth in the proportion of young people participating in higher education is also due to demographic changes in the early 1990s. The proportion of 18- and 19-year-olds has dropped by nearly 30% in the late 1980s and the early 1990s, making the rise in API appear to be steeper than the rise in the raw number of students.

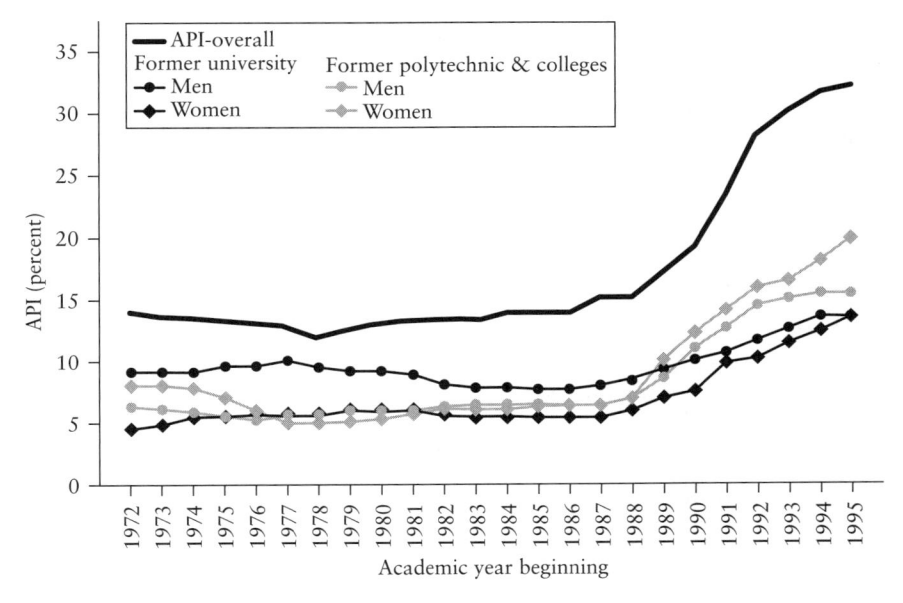

Figure 8.1. Higher Education Age Participation Index (API) in British Institutions, 1972–2001

SOURCE: Halsey (2000, fig. 6.1) and Department of Education and Skills.

CHANGES IN THE SECONDARY EDUCATION SYSTEM

Differentiation between and within schools is known to have major consequences in access to higher education (Halsey, Heath, and Ridge 1980; Kerckhoff 1993; Kerckhoff and Trott 1993; Ball 1994; Smith and Noble 1995). Prior to the 1970s, when comprehensive reorganization took place in Britain, state secondary education was organized as a tripartite system, comprised of three main types of schools: grammar, secondary modern, and technical. Selection to these schools was primarily based on the results of competitive examination at age 11 (the *11-plus*). Grammar schools offered an academic curriculum and were mainly for academically able pupils. They prepared pupils for either white-collar work or higher education. Technical schools, a relatively small sector, were more vocationally oriented and prepared pupils for various skilled industrial trades or vocational qualifications. Secondary modern schools provided a mixture of general and vocational education. A small independent school sector, focused on an academic curriculum, coexisted with the state sector. By the late 1960s the tripartite system was perceived as stunting the aspirations of children who had failed the *11-plus*. These children were disproportionately drawn from working-class homes, with middle-class children able to opt out into private education (either in private schools, or as fee-paying pupils in grammar schools). In the 1960s, the Labour government abolished the *11-plus* examination and the tripartite system, replacing it with a comprehensive system. However, the comprehensive reorganization, carried out by Local Education Authorities, took over a decade to complete. In other words, although the reform started in 1965, some schools went comprehensive as late as 1979. A significant proportion of the school population born in the late 1950s and early 1960s would have attended secondary education under the tripartite system. Compulsory education starts at age 5 and finishes at age 16 (15 until 1974). Many young people leave full-time education at this point, but the proportion continuing with education and training has increased steadily over time. While the state system currently schools over 90% of British children, it is possible to switch between private and state schooling at any age. However, the streaming of children into different school sectors has ended by the late 1970s, offering in theory a good general/academic education to all children.

The university system has always been stratified by prestige (Halsey 1992). However, the system that has emerged at the end of the twentieth century is more complex, both in partnership arrangements between different types of institutions, in stratification between different universities, and in regulation and management. The student body has become much more diverse in age, qualifications at entry, number of part-timers, and fields of study. In this chapter, we examine the extent to which expansion benefited those who traditionally have been disadvantaged, namely females and working-class students, taking into account the institutional framework of the expanded system.

DATA

Our analysis drew on data from two longitudinal studies in Britain, the National Child Development Study (NCDS) and the British Cohort Study (BCS70). The NCDS is a longitudinal study of respondents living in Great Britain who were born March 3–9, 1958. The origin of the NCDS is a birth survey conducted in 1958: the Perinatal Mortality Survey (PMS). There have been six follow-up surveys monitoring the physical, educational, social, and economic development of cohort members. These were carried out in 1965 (NCDS1), 1969 (NCDS2), 1974 (NCDS3), 1981 (NCDS4), 1991 (NCDS5), and in 2000 (NCDS6). In addition, in 1978, details of public examination entry and performance were obtained from schools and colleges. We used data from sweeps 3, 4, and 5, and from the 1978 qualifications survey. The sample of 11,441 at NCDS5 (in 1991, when respondents were aged 33) was representative of the original sample ($n = 17,414$). Children from poorer families and from ethnic minority origins were somewhat underrepresented (Shepherd 1993). However, biases are small (Nathan 1999). The 1970 Birth Cohort Study (BCS70) developed comparably to the NCDS, originating in the British Birth Survey of over 17,000 babies born in Britain in the week of April 5–11, 1970. Subsequently, five further major surveys have monitored the changing health, education, social, and economic circumstances of the surviving cohort members at ages 5, 10, 16, 26, and 30. The last wave of data was collected in 2000 and yielded a sample of 11,261. We used data from the age 5, 10, 16, and 30 sweeps. As with NCDS, children from disadvantaged origins are underrepresented. There is as yet no published detailed assessment of the extent of bias in the fifth sweep (at age 30), but it is believed that it is small. Both studies contain very detailed information on education and training, both during schooling and after the compulsory school leaving age (16 in both surveys), including the level of qualification attempted, length of course, mode of study (full-time or part-time), field of study, whether the courses were completed, and so on. We drew on these two studies to compare the experiences of the two cohorts at different stages of expansion of higher education in Britain. The NCDS cohort left school in the 1970s, when expansion was gradual and the binary system was still in force. The BCS70 cohort left school in the late 1980s, when expansion was more rapid and the binary division had begun to dissolve.

It could be argued that the 1970 birth cohort might not have profited from the expansion, being due to enter higher education in 1988, when the system had just begun to expand. However, this cohort was well placed to take advantage of the expansion as young adults, and many of them did. Many British young people do not enter higher education until ages 19 or 20, taking a gap year or years. Only 27% of the 1970 cohort graduates had gained their degrees by age 21, the age that is consistent with a 3-year honors degree course entered at age 18. Fifty percent had gained degrees by age 22 and 76% by age 23, with another 24% gaining degrees after this age. The percentage of very long degrees is small in the U.K. system, and the majority of later qualifiers will have entered at age 20-plus, when the expansion was well under way. Although the NCDS cohort also took advantage of the expansion of mature study, fewer had benefited by 1991, when the qualification data for this cohort were obtained.

DEFINITIONS AND VARIABLES

Data on eligibility for tertiary education are referenced at age 19 for both cohorts. For NCDS, we used the 1978 qualification data (qualifications attained by the previous year); for BCS70, we used the qualification histories collected at age 30. From these data we derived qualifications attained at age 19. For qualification in any postsecondary education, degree-granting institutions and universities we use data collected at age 33 and 30 for the two cohort studies.

UPPER AND LOWER TERTIARY EDUCATION

In Britain, upper tertiary education includes all first-degree programs at universities or the pre-1992 polytechnics. Lower tertiary education refers to all postsecondary, but lower than degree-level, courses, which lead to a wide range of qualifications, including higher education/national certificates, diplomas, and other professional qualifications.

ELIGIBILITY FOR TERTIARY EDUCATION

The issue of eligibility is a complex one within the British education system. First, there are slight variations between the English/Welsh and Scottish systems. The university matriculation qualification for the English/Welsh system during the period considered was two passes at the Advanced Level of the General Certificate of Education. This was usually taken at age 18. For the Scottish system, the main matriculation qualification was the Higher Level of the Scottish Certificate of Education.[5] This could be taken at age 17, and Scottish students often sat for examinations in more subjects (four or five examinations in two years). Although in the Scottish system entry could take place at a younger age, most degree courses were four years in duration, while in the English system three years was a more common duration. A further layer of complexity is introduced by the fact that universities traditionally have their own entrance examinations or access courses. Second, the meaning of eligibility has changed over time. With expansion, universities laid more emphasis on access courses or substitute qualifications, often technical qualifications such as Higher National Diplomas. Third, the entrance requirements differ between higher education institutions, with more prestigious institutions requiring higher grades in more subjects.

ELIGIBILITY FOR LOWER TERTIARY EDUCATION

We took as the definition of eligibility for lower tertiary education the attainment of Level 3 vocational qualifications (nominally equivalent to General Certificate of Education—Advanced-Level).

In view of these difficulties, we constructed the eligibility variable as follows:

1. eligible for upper tertiary education—respondents with two or more A-levels;
2. eligible for lower tertiary education—respondents with one A-level or Level 3 vocational qualifications;
3. not eligible for any form of tertiary education—General Certificate of Education Ordinary level, Certificate of Secondary Education, General Certificate of Secondary Education, National Vocational Qualification Level 2, or any qualification below these levels.

POSTSECONDARY EDUCATION

The proportion of students continuing their education beyond the minimum school-leaving age of 16 increased dramatically between the NCDS cohort (1974), when it was just over 10% (Fogelman 1985) and the BCS70 cohort (1986) when it was over 50%. We defined postsecondary education in Britain as any qualification or training courses after the age of 16, comprising all subdegree and degree courses in the higher education sector. This includes National Vocational Qualification Level 4 qualifications in further education colleges, colleges of education, technical institutes, (pre-1992) polytechnics, and universities. As our interest was focused on expansion within higher education institutions, we excluded any training courses offered by the government or employers in specialist training centers. The complexity of the British higher education system can be illustrated by the fact that one can be attending postsecondary (college) education at age 16 without being eligible for tertiary education (i.e., without having obtained Level 3 vocational qualifications or matriculation qualifications).

DEGREE-GRANTING INSTITUTIONS AND UNIVERSITIES

For the NCDS cohort, degree-granting institutions included universities, polytechnics, and colleges of higher education, with universities providing the main source of degree courses. For the BCS70 cohort, there may be some slippage of the definition between polytechnics and universities because the polytechnics were incorporated as universities in 1992 when the cohort was aged 22.[6]

To construct these tertiary education variables, we used completed qualifications from Sweep 5 (1991) data in the NCDS. For BCS70 we used the qualification histories collected in Sweep 5 (2000) because entry data are not available in the BCS70 data set. These covered all qualifications gained since age 16.[7] Thus we were able to compare directly the qualification variables over time. Although about 10% of the data for institutions of higher education were missing for the BCS70 cohort, checks suggest that this did not affect the overall findings.

PARENTAL EDUCATION

Information on parents' education in the NCDS was available only as the age at which the respondent's father and mother left full-time education. We have no information on whether they left school with any qualifications. As most parents left school at the age of 14 to 15, we coded them as having completed intermediate secondary qualifications. Those who left school at age 13 or below would have only had social minimum, low-level school qualifications or basic vocational qualifications. However, the number in this category is very low and was therefore combined with those who left school at age 14 to 15. We took the highest of the parents' education and recoded it into four categories following the CASMIN schema:

1. Upper tertiary—CASMIN 3b (left full-time education at age 21 or above)
2. Lower tertiary—CASMIN 3a (left at age 19 to 20)
3. Full secondary—CASMIN 2c (left at age 16 to 18)
4. Intermediate secondary or below—CASMIN 2ab, 1 (left at age 15 or below)

We added a further category to include the missing data.

To maintain comparability with the NCDS variable, the BCS70 variable (from the age 5 sweep), which recorded the parents' age at completion of full-time education, was used and coded as above.

SOCIAL CLASS ORIGIN

Both the NCDS and BCS70 contain information on father's occupation, collected at age 16, recorded with the Office of Population and Census Statistics 19-point Social and Economic Groups classification. We coded this information according to the Goldthorpe class schema to form a measure for class origin[8] (Erikson and Goldthorpe 1992), resulting in six categories suitable for cross-national comparison: (1) the upper service class, which includes higher-grade professionals and administrators; (2) the lower service class, which includes lower-grade professionals and administrators and higher-grade supervisors; (3) routine nonmanual workers; (4) nonprofessional own account workers (i.e., self-employed); (5) technicians, manual supervisors, and skilled manual workers; and (6) semiskilled and unskilled manual workers. As in the case of parents' education, we added a further category of missing data.

ANALYSES

We addressed four questions.

1. Who is eligible for upper and lower tertiary education by ascriptive characteristics such as social origin and gender?
2. To what extent is attaining any postsecondary education qualifications associated with social origin and gender?

TABLE 8.1
Descriptive statistics for key variables in the analysis

	NCDS (%)	BCS70 (%)
Gender		
Male	48.8	48.5
Female	51.2	51.5
Social class origin		
I	9.6	13.0
II	14.9	14.5
IIIab	8.4	4.5
Ivabc	4.1	11.0
V, VI	34.5	29.1
VII	18.6	11.3
Missing	9.9	16.7
Parental education		
Higher tertiary	3.5	7.2
Lower tertiary	4.6	4.7
Full secondary	15.4	28.8
Lower secondary or below	50.1	41.1
Missing	26.5	18.2
Eligibility to higher education—age 19		
Eligible for upper tertiary	14.2	17.1
Eligible for lower tertiary	15.1	14.0
Entry into any postsecondary education up to age 33/30	26.9	27.6
Entry into any degree-granting institutions up to age 33/30	20.9	21.1
Entry into universities up to 33/30	10.3	14.9
Higher education completion		
Upper tertiary	12.5	20.0
Lower tertiary	14.1	11.5
School (NCDS only)		
Grammar	9.3	
Secondary modern, technical	19.0	
Independent, direct grant	5.0	
Comprehensive	46.1	
No information	20.7	
Total number of observations included in the analysis[a]	11,135	11,225

[a] The sample included in the final analysis for the NCDS varies according to the response variable, ranging from 10,060 to 11,135.

3. How far is qualification in any degree-granting institution associated with gender and family background?

4. Is qualification in university degree programs stratified along the lines of class and gender?

Using the two cohort studies, NCDS and BCS70, we compared the answers to these questions and examined whether any changes took place over time. We carried out a series of multinomial logit models and logistic regressions to examine the above questions.

With the exception of the first model, for eligibility (measuring attainment at school), all models examined outcome variables both unconditionally and conditional on eligibility for tertiary education. The conditional models highlight the postschool effects of parental education or social class in tertiary education attainment. Next, by comparing the conditional and unconditional models, we evaluated the effect of the 1988 to 1992 reforms, which encouraged mature entry and weakened entry requirements enabling some recovery from poor school attainment. The effects of cohort were examined by fitting a term for cohort plus terms for cohort interactions with gender, parental education, and father's social class. The term for cohort indicates the degree of expansion between the two cohorts.[9] The main effects estimate the association between the explanatory variables and the response variables for the earlier cohort (NCDS). The interaction terms provide an estimate of the change in the effects of gender, parental education, and father's social class between the cohorts. Table 8.1 shows the distributions for the variables.

RESULTS

Eligibility for Higher Education

Ninety percent of the members of the 1958 cohort finished school in 1974 at the age of 16 and entered work, many of them obtaining qualifications through employment or part-time study. Conversely, only about half of the 1970 cohort left school at age 16. However, not all of these children gained Level 3 qualifications, which provide eligibility for first degree or advanced vocational education. We modeled eligibility for higher education for both birth cohorts using qualifications obtained in national examinations (either vocational or general academic) by age 19. The multinomial logit (unconditional) model has a three-category response variable: (1) eligible for upper tertiary education, (2) eligible for lower tertiary education, and (3) not eligible for any higher education. The third one is the reference category in the model. The results are presented in Table 8.2.

The results show a clear advantage in the NCDS cohort for male respondents, for those from a service-class background, and for those with

TABLE 8.2
Multinomial logit model of eligibility for higher education

Independent variables (reference categories in parentheses)	Upper tertiary	Lower tertiary
	Estimate (S.E.)	Estimate (S.E.)
Intercept	−2.69 (.08)	−2.17 (.07)
Gender (Female)		
Male	**.28 (.06)**	**1.10 (.06)**
Parents' education (Elementary/lower secondary)		
Missing	**.34 (.08)**	**−.25 (.07)**
Upper tertiary	**1.72 (.13)**	.09 (.19)
Lower tertiary	**1.23 (.12)**	−.07 (.15)
Full secondary	**.82 (.08)**	**.18 (.08)**
Social origin (Supervisor/skilled manual)		
Missing	.20 (.12)	**−.29 (.11)**
Upper service class	**1.38 (.10)**	**.26 (.11)**
Lower service class	**.92 (.09)**	**.29 (.08)**
Routine nonmanual	**.59 (.11)**	.10 (.10)
Petite bourgeoisie	−.04 (.18)	−.02 (.14)
Semi- and unskilled manual	**−.49 (.11)**	**−.44 (.08)**
Cohort (BCS70)		
NCDS	.14 (.11)	.06 (.09)
Cohort interactions		
Gender (Female × cohort)		
Male cohort	**−.31 (.08)**	**−.78 (.08)**
Parents' education (Elementary/lower secondary × cohort)		
Missing × cohort	**.44 (.12)**	**.47 (.11)**
Upper tertiary × cohort	.23 (.17)	**.62 (.23)**
Lower tertiary × cohort	.21 (.17)	**.75 (.20)**
Full secondary × cohort	.09 (.11)	**.25 (.11)**
Social origin (Supervisor/skilled manual × cohort)		
Missing × cohort	.01 (.15)	.21 (.15)
Upper service class × cohort	.19 (.13)	**.56 (.15)**
Lower service class × cohort	.19 (.13)	**.22 (.12)**
Routine non-manual × cohort	.11 (.17)	.04 (.18)
Petite bourgeoisie × cohort	**.46 (.21)**	.25 (.17)
Semi- and unskilled manual × cohort	**.39 (.17)**	.10 (.14)
Model chi-square (df)	3,169 (46)	
N	22,363	

NOTE: All estimates that are significant at the 5% confidence level are presented in bold.

better educated parents. Men were more likely to be eligible for both upper and lower tertiary education, although the gender gap was greater for lower tertiary education. In contrast, the effects of social origin and parental education were much more pronounced for eligibility for the more prestigious upper tertiary education than for lower tertiary education. Respondents from both service classes and routine nonmanual origins were more likely to be eligible. In contrast, respondents from semiskilled and unskilled manual class origins were disadvantaged compared with those whose fathers had technician or supervisory and skilled manual jobs. Parental education was also found to be important. Respondents whose parents had attained tertiary qualifications were more likely to be eligible.

The estimates suggest that there has been no expansion in the proportion of young people eligible for tertiary education. However, this disguises a change in composition, with 17% of the 1970 cohort being eligible for higher tertiary education at age 19, compared with 14% of the 1958 cohort. Conversely, more of the 1958 cohort had attained qualifications that provided eligibility for advanced vocational training. The cohort interactions for gender reflect the marked increase in girls' educational attainment over the 1980s. The male advantage in eligibility for upper tertiary education (0.28) disappeared for the later cohort (0.28 − 0.31 = −0.03) and has substantially decreased for lower tertiary education. The cohort interactions suggest that there has been little change in the effects of parental education on eligibility for higher education, although there are statistically significant effects on eligibility for lower tertiary education, with the children of better educated parents more likely to be eligible. Because eligibility for lower tertiary education includes respondents with one A-level GCE at age 19, this may simply reflect a failed attempt to gain university matriculation qualifications (two GCE A-levels). The cohort interactions for social class (adjusted for parental education) suggest that while the relative position of the children of the white-collar classes versus the skilled manual class has stayed much the same in eligibility for upper tertiary education, the position of the children of self-employed fathers and of semi- or unskilled manual workers has improved relative to children from Classes V and VII. Children of self-employed fathers are now more likely to be eligible (−0.04 + 0.46 = 0.42), while the children of semi- and unskilled manual fathers remain slightly disadvantaged (−0.49 + 0.39 = −0.10) compared with children from technician and skilled manual origins.

Postsecondary Educational Attainment

The results of both unconditional and conditional logistic regression models are presented together for comparison in the first two columns in Table 8.3. In the unconditional model, we compared respondents who completed

TABLE 8.3
Binary logistic regression for postsecondary education attainment and qualifications obtained from degree-granting institutions and universities

Independent variables (reference categories in parentheses)	POSTSECONDARY EDUCATION Unconditional Estimate (S.E.)	POSTSECONDARY EDUCATION Conditional Estimate (S.E.)	DEGREE-GRANTING INSTITUTIONS Unconditional Estimate (S.E.)	DEGREE-GRANTING INSTITUTIONS Conditional Estimate (S.E.)	UNIVERSITIES Unconditional Estimate (S.E.)	UNIVERSITIES Conditional Estimate (S.E.)
Intercept	−2.00 (.06)	−.37 (.10)	−2.43 (.07)	−.82 (.10)	−3.01 (.08)	−1.36 (.11)
Gender (Female)						
Male	.19 (.05)	−.73 (.08)	.23 (.05)	−.29 (.08)	.35 (.07)	−.01 (.09)
Parents' education (Elementary/lower secondary)						
Missing	.27 (.06)	.40 (.10)	.57 (.07)	.72 (.11)	.72 (.10)	.81 (.13)
Upper tertiary	1.57 (.12)	1.36 (.20)	1.62 (.12)	1.25 (.16)	1.54 (.14)	1.16 (.17)
Lower tertiary	1.08 (.10)	.86 (.17)	1.12 (.11)	1.03 (.16)	1.19 (.13)	1.06 (.17)
Full secondary	.65 (.07)	.63 (.11)	.67 (.07)	.70 (.11)	.76 (.10)	.71 (.13)
Social origin (Supervisor/skilled manual)						
Missing	.22 (.09)	.45 (.16)	.07 (.10)	.13 (.16)	.04 (.14)	.19 (.19)
Upper service class	1.09 (.08)	.80 (.13)	.98 (.09)	.66 (.12)	1.20 (.11)	.86 (.14)
Lower service class	.74 (.07)	.56 (.11)	.64 (.08)	.45 (.11)	.84 (.10)	.73 (.13)
Routine nonmanual	.47 (.08)	.31 (.14)	.59 (.09)	.47 (.14)	.51 (.13)	.56 (.17)
Petite bourgeoisie	−.07 (.13)	−.29 (.21)	−.07 (.15)	−.13 (.22)	.14 (.20)	.23 (.26)
Semi- and unskilled manual	−.42 (.08)	−.17 (.13)	−.37 (.09)	−.19 (.14)	−.27 (.13)	.03 (.18)

Cohort (BCS70)	.36 (.08)	.51 (.13)	.30 (.09)	−.09 (.14)	−.25 (.12)	−.77 (.17)
NCDS						
Cohort interactions						
Gender (Female × cohort)	−.07 (.06)	.76 (.11)	−.10 (.07)	.29 (.11)	−.12 (.09)	.14 (.11)
Male × cohort						
Parents education (Elementary/						
lower secondary × Cohort)						
Missing × cohort	.43 (.09)	.23 (.15)	.19 (.10)	−.07 (.15)	.10 (.13)	−.22 (.17)
Upper tertiary × cohort	.03 (.15)	.06 (.25)	.11 (.15)	.13 (.21)	.15 (.17)	.02 (.21)
Lower tertiary × cohort	.03 (.14)	−.09 (.23)	.03 (.15)	−.27 (.22)	−.06 (.18)	−.38 (.22)
Full secondary × cohort	.06 (.09)	−.18 (.14)	.08 (.10)	−.29 (.14)	−.04 (.13)	−.36 (.16)
Social origin (Supervisor/skilled						
manual × cohort)						
Missing × cohort	−.07 (.12)	−.24 (.20)	.11 (.13)	.13 (.20)	.22 (.18)	.09 (.23)
Upper service class × cohort	.07 (.11)	−.20 (.18)	.20 (.12)	.07 (.17)	.08 (.14)	−.16 (.19)
Lower service class × cohort	.01 (.10)	−.08 (.16)	.17 (.11)	.04 (.16)	.04 (.14)	−.27 (.18)
Routine nonmanual × cohort	−.07 (.14)	.02 (.23)	−.16 (.15)	−.04 (.23)	.07 (.19)	−.04 (.25)
Petite bourgeoisie × cohort	.32 (.15)	.28 (.25)	.35 (.17)	.28 (.26)	.20 (.23)	.00 (.30)
Semi- and unskilled						
manual × cohort	.34 (.12)	.20 (.20)	.33 (.14)	.42 (.22)	.31 (.18)	.15 (.25)
Model chi-square (df)	2248 (23)	651 (23)	2070 (23)	631 (23)	1732 (23)	616 (23)
n	22,147	6,709	21,340	6,599	21,285	6,590

NOTE: All estimates that are significant at the 5% confidence level are presented in bold.

any postsecondary education qualifications with all other respondents in the data set, whether or not they were eligible for higher education. In the conditional model, only respondents who were eligible for both lower and higher tertiary education were included in the analysis. The total numbers of cases included in the analyses are presented in the bottom row of the table.

The results of the unconditional model for the two cohorts are presented in Column 1. For the NCDS cohort, gender continued to affect postsecondary education, with boys having an advantage. Class origin continued to be an important factor, with the nonmanual classes having an advantage, as do the children of better-educated parents. The cohort interaction terms for more advantaged parents were not statistically significant. However, the children of Class VII fathers made gains relative to children of Class V+VI fathers, although remaining slightly disadvantaged, while the children of Class IV parents were slightly advantaged in the second cohort. As with eligibility, this signals a reduction of inequality in postsecondary education between the two cohorts.

In the conditional model (Column 2), several changes are visible. For the NCDS cohort, among the eligible respondents, female students were more likely than their male counterparts to complete any postsecondary education. Here the effects of social origin and parental education declined substantially. Turning to the cohort changes, none of the coefficients for higher parental education or father's social class were statistically significant. The decreased disadvantage found in the unconditional model for children from nonprofessional self-employed or semi- and unskilled manual families was reduced and was no longer statistically significant.

Qualifications Obtained from Degree-granting Institutions

The requirements for entry to degree-granting institutions are higher than for postsecondary education and training courses. Again, all respondents were included in the unconditional models regardless of their eligibility. For the conditional models, we selected only those who were eligible for lower and higher tertiary education. The results of the logistic regressions are presented in the third and fourth columns in Table 8.3.

In the unselected sample, there was a significant male advantage for the NCDS cohort in entering any degree-granting institutions, but the advantage was reversed in the selected sample. Eligible female respondents from the NCDS cohort were more likely to enter these institutions. The effects of parental education and class origin converge on a broadly similar pattern. They are statistically significant in the unconditional model in determining qualification in degree-granting institutions, and both sets of estimates decline somewhat in the conditional model, although they remain statistically significant. The effect of parental education appears to be stronger than that of social origins.

Turning to cohort effects,[10] the male advantage for the 1958 cohort was reproduced in the 1970 cohort for the unselected sample, while their disadvantage in the eligible subsample decreased. Little change is seen in the effects of parental education for the unselected sample, while there was a decrease in the effect of completed secondary education for the selected subsample. As in previous models, a gain for the children of self-employed and semi- and unskilled manual fathers is found in the unconditional model, though only the semi- and unskilled class gained in the conditional model. These models suggest again a small decrement of inequality for the later cohort.

Qualifications Obtained from Degree Programs in University

Entering a degree program at university is more selective than obtaining a place in a degree-granting institution, therefore qualification through a university is likely to be most stratified. We examined this using logistic regressions with unconditional and conditional models. The results are presented in the last two columns in Table 8.3.

For the NCDS cohort, there was a clear male advantage in the unconditional model in entering university degree programs. However, this advantage virtually disappeared in the conditional model. Women were still disadvantaged in university entry when the NCDS cohort was aged 18 (1976), but mature students were included in both samples and mature women students were more likely than mature men to enter through the traditional GCE A-level route.

Parental education and class origin had a strong effect. As before, the extent of the effect of these two variables was reduced in the conditional model. Previous British research (Halsey, Heath, and Ridge 1980) has shown that social class had a small effect at the university entrance level after entrance qualifications were taken into account. In our study, the criterion for eligibility was less strict, including eligibility for subdegree study, giving family origin variables some purchase.

The cohort term denotes the large increase in university study between the two cohorts, and the cohort interactions show that, with one exception, the effects of parental education and social class did not change at a statistically significant level between cohorts. The exception is that, as in previous models, the advantage of having a parent with full secondary education versus lower than full secondary education was reduced. The better school and early educational attainment of children from self-employed and manual origins in the 1970 cohort, as shown in the eligibility for upper tertiary model, translates into increased participation in the less prestigious tertiary institutions but not in the more prestigious ones. However, girls, who tended to follow a more academic route through education and training but received less training, became more successful in the more academically oriented institutions.

DISCUSSION AND CONCLUSION

Our research examined the extent to which class and gender inequalities have changed over time in Great Britain against a background of considerable expansion of higher education. We were particularly interested in internal stratification within higher education by programs and institutions. As was discussed earlier, changes in the effects of social origins and gender over time are probably related to different types of reform in Britain. The effects of reforms in secondary education were captured in the unconditional models and the effects of higher education reforms were seen in the conditional models. The results of the multinomial models and of logistic regression can be summarized in four points.

1. Class inequality persists in both eligibility for and completion of higher education qualifications.
2. Parental education is a predictor of success in higher education.
3. Attainment in postsecondary education, in degree-granting institutions, and in degree programs at universities is progressively stratified, suggesting stronger effects of class origin and parental education at the top of the educational system.
4. Gender equality in higher education improved significantly over time.

There are clear class differences in eligibility for, and completion of, higher education. Respondents from service-class backgrounds had a clear advantage over their peers from intermediate and manual backgrounds. For the NCDS cohort, who were born in 1958 and attended postsecondary education in the late 1970s and early 1980s, students from service-class backgrounds were likely to do better at public examinations and therefore be eligible for higher education. For the 1970 cohort, though service-class children maintained their advantage, children from unskilled or semiskilled manual origins made some gains relative to children from skilled manual origins. Where the institutional framework is concerned, there is a gradient for the class effect. It is strongest where selection is most pronounced, at the top of the educational system (i.e., degree programs at universities), where no statistically significant difference is found between the two cohorts. However, children from Class IV and Class VII families made gains in other forms of higher education and more of them completed degrees. An overall comparison of the unconditional with the conditional estimates for social class shows that decreased class disadvantage is greater in the unselected samples. This suggests that the reforms with their easing of entry criteria and encouragement of mature study were effective in reducing inequality. Generally, the combination of better school performance (in eligibility for upper tertiary education) and better participation in tertiary education, albeit in the less prestigious institutions, suggests some decrease in inequality for the 1970 cohort.

Our findings on parental education are consistent with previous research (Egerton 1997; Savage and Egerton 1997; Sullivan 2001; Van de Werfhorst, Sullivan, and Cheung 2003). However, the disadvantage of children with less educated parents decreased somewhat for the 1970 cohort in the conditional models. There is less change by cohort on the parental education variable than by social class, presumably underlining the continued importance of parental educational transmission.

Evidence from our analyses of the two birth cohorts suggests a clear decrease in gender inequality in eligibility to upper tertiary education. The male advantage shared by the NCDS cohort members was no longer visible for the 1970 cohort. While the unconditional models show that there was a significant gender change in obtaining postsecondary education qualifications for the second birth cohort, the conditional probability of attaining postsecondary qualifications was actually higher for women than men for both birth cohorts. For qualification in degree-granting institutions, the male advantage in the unconditional model is reversed in the conditional model for the NCDS cohort and has disappeared for the 1970 cohort in the conditional model. Similar patterns emerge in the analyses of qualifying through a university, suggesting that access to the higher education system in Britain has become to a large extent gender blind. Blossfeld and Shavit (1993) found the same decreasing gender inequality for a range of countries and attributed it to changing social and family attitudes that accompany broad industrial changes in Western economies. Nonetheless, although gender quotas for particular subjects are now illegal in the United Kingdom, there are still substantial differences in the subjects studied, with women being underrepresented particularly in the sciences (Van de Werfhorst, Sullivan, and Cheung 2003).

The experiences of two birth cohorts in higher education in Britain over the recent period of expansion and reform are largely consistent with evidence from previous research (Egerton and Halsey 1993; Halsey 1993; Shavit and Blossfeld 1993; Heath 2000), indicating that expansion in higher education had mixed impact in reducing inequalities. Our findings on school type also support previous research showing that school features strongly in shaping inequalities in access to higher education in Britain (Heath and Cheung 1998). Although the comprehensive reorganization in the 1970s, where grammar, secondary modern, and technical schools were renamed comprehensive schools, put an end to the tripartite system,[11] considerable differences between and within schools persisted. Comprehensive reorganization probably shifted the focus from access to school types to variations within school types, where competition for grammar school places has shifted to competition for more academically successful comprehensive schools (Heath 2000).

The gender gap in eligibility for and attainment in higher education has narrowed significantly, but class inequality persists. There are also significant variations by social class in types of higher education institution attended. In absolute terms, the overall enrollment in higher education in Britain has doubled in the last decade, with a third of the age group participating in some form of higher education. This growth has been accompanied by diversification in the higher education sector in the types of programs and institutions, often aligned with levels of prestige. Blossfeld and Shavit (1993, 20) have argued that expansion of vocational and non-college education has led to the opening up of the secondary education without disturbing the basically exclusive character of higher education. A similar argument can be made here, contending that the opening up of higher education in Britain has to some extent fulfilled rising aspirations of working-class students but has done relatively little to equalize access to the more exclusive programs and institutions.

CHAPTER NINE

France: Mass and Class—Persisting Inequalities in Postsecondary Education in France

Pauline Givord, INSEE

Dominique Goux, DARES

INTRODUCTION

The majority of French children now have the opportunity to obtain some postsecondary education. In this sense, the French system of postsecondary education has achieved its purpose of becoming a mass education system. At the same time, the inequalities within the system have widened, as the odds of obtaining a degree from the best institutions depend more and more on social background. Mass education has not prevented the persistence of significant class-based inequalities.

Specifically, to anticipate the remainder of the paper, the French data reveal three basic trends across cohorts born since World War II.

1. A significant increase in the probability of completing high school and obtaining a postsecondary degree
2. Conditional on high-school graduation, an increase of inequality in the probability of obtaining a degree from postsecondary education for students from different social backgrounds
3. Persisting cultural inequalities in the probability of obtaining a degree from the most selective French postsecondary institutions (*grandes écoles*)

The chapter is organized as follows. The first section presents the French system of postsecondary education, its place within the education system, and its main stratifications. This section also describes the main evolutions that took place in the French education system over the last century and their consequences for tertiary enrollment. The second section describes the data and method used. We make intensive use of the 1970 to 2003 Education, Training, and Occupations Survey (*enquêtes sur la formation et la qualification professionnelle*) carried out by the French National Institute of Statistics and Economic Surveys (INSEE). Finally, the last section explores the trends in inequality in enrollment in different types of postsecondary institutions, as well as, presents gender differences and their evolution.

THE FRENCH POSTSECONDARY EDUCATION SYSTEM

Since 1975, the French system of general education has consisted of five years of primary school, four years of lower secondary school (*collège*), and three years upper secondary education (*lycée*). The secondary course ends with a matriculation examination at the upper secondary level (*baccalauréat*), which entitles holders to enter university and other postsecondary institutions. The *baccalauréat* is an institution created by Napoleon in 1808. Next, there are three distinct types of institutions of postsecondary education: (1) universities; (2) vocational postsecondary institutions (technical institutes (*instituts universitaires technologiques* or IUT) and higher vocational training (*sections de techniciens supérieurs de lycées* or STS)); and (3) the system of *grandes écoles*. An important feature of the French postsecondary education system is that most of the institutions are public, and therefore school fees are very low. The three tracks differ in at least four aspects: selectivity, fields of study, size, and cost.

Various Degrees of Selectivity

Universities are open to all students who have a *baccalauréat*, without restriction, but access to the *grandes écoles* is highly selective. Access to IUTs and STSs is also selective, but competition is much weaker. To enter a *grande école* or an *école d'ingénieur*[1] students must first be accepted into specific preliminary classes (*classes préparatoires*). At the beginning of the 1990s, among those who have obtained the *baccalauréat* and kept studying in the postsecondary system, only 7–10% were admitted to these highly selective preliminary classes. In 2002 there were approximately 365 *lycées* with at least one *classe préparatoire*.[2] Students complete two to three years of intense preliminary training, but almost half of those admitted drop out and return to university. At the end of this preliminary course, pupils take entrance examinations at the *grandes écoles*. Most *grandes écoles* offer a three-year education. Graduates of the *grandes écoles* monopolize the highest management levels in French corporations, public administration, and universities. The chief executives and managing directors of about 60% of the 100 largest French firms are *grandes écoles* graduates. The *grandes écoles* include Ecole Nationale des Ponts et Chaussées (set up in 1747, it is the oldest engineering school in the world), Ecole Polytechnique (set up in 1794), Ecole des Hautes Etudes Commerciales (set up in 1881), Ecoles Normales Supérieures (the first one was founded in 1794), Ecole Nationale d'Administration (created in 1945), etc.

The vocational postsecondary education system consists mainly of two types of institutions, granting two different degrees. The first one is the *diplôme universitaire technologique (DUT)*, obtained in two years in universities called *instituts universitaires technologiques (IUT)*. There were about 110 IUTs in 2002. IUTs are allowed to select applicants based on their academic results in secondary education. The second one is the *brevet de technicien supérieur (BTS)*, also obtained in two years in the so called *sections de techniciens supérieurs (STS)* divisions of the *lycées*. In 2002, 146 types of BTS were conferred in more than 2,000 schools. Around 40% of BTS holders continue their studies after obtaining their diploma. The professional integration of the holders of a postsecondary vocational diploma is rather good. They usually find steady jobs and earn higher wages than university graduates. Most of them are lower-grade professionals or higher-grade technicians.

The coexistence of the *grandes écoles* and universities constitutes another basic stratification within the French system of education, and consequently within French society. Among young people who began their working life in the 1990s, around 3–4% were graduates of the *grandes écoles* versus 12% of graduates of three-year university programs. At the other end of the educational hierarchy, around 50% are either without a diploma or hold one of the (lower) secondary qualifications associated with early elimination from the general system.

Fields of Study

In regular university programs, teaching is oriented toward the acquisition of academic knowledge. Medicine is an exception, with teaching aimed at providing specific occupational skills. In principle, universities are charged with training teachers and researchers, although the number of students enrolled in universities today greatly exceeds the need for this kind of occupation. Universities are comprehensive educational institutions that cover various fields such as basic economics, humanities, law, and natural sciences. Vocational postsecondary education, created at the end of the 1950s in response to a shortage in qualified technical professionals, provides technical and professional training. Finally, the training of engineers, managers, and executives is the domain of scientific, technical, and business *grandes écoles* and engineering schools.

Size of the Institutions

Grandes écoles, vocational postsecondary institutions, and universities differ in their size. Each university enrolls on average more than 10,000 students. *Grandes écoles* are much smaller, usually of the size of a university department, with about 1,000 students, enrolling from 100 to 400 students per academic year. IUTs are also small institutions. Together the 144 IUTs enroll around 115,000 students, each one enrolling between 400 and 2,000.

Allocations for Postsecondary Students

The fourth difference between universities, *grandes écoles,* and short-course vocational postsecondary institutions is the money spent by the government in each institution. At the beginning of the 1990s, the annual budget allocated to each student enrolled in a *grande école* was about 11,000 euros, which is two and a half times more than the annual budget for a standard university student (4,500 euros). Expenditures for IUT and STS students were about 8,000 euros per student per year (France DEP 1993).

Since 1975, the annual public expenditures in education represent between 6.5 and 7.5% of GDP (Martinez, Moutin, and Ragoucy 2002). Only 13% of this amount was devoted to postsecondary education during the 1980s. In the 1990s, this amount reached about 15% of the total education budget (Blanc, Ildis, and Ragouzy 1995).

The Evolution of the French Education System During the Twentieth Century

Like other industrial countries, France has experienced a dramatic increase in the postsecondary education during the postwar period. The number of students rose from 310,000 in 1960 to 2,200,000 in 2002 (France DEP 1993, 2003). The schooling rate at age 19 rose from 28% at the beginning of the 1980s to 69% at the end of the 1990s (France INSEE 2001).

This expansion was induced partly by demand. The steady economic growth between the 1950s and the 1970s contributed to a rise in the standard of living. Other contributing factors were policies aimed at protecting workers (social security or *sécurité sociale,* a decree from October 4, 1945) and the extension of family subsidies (*allocations familiales,* a law from August 22, 1946). As families were using children less and less to contribute income through labor, they also demanded more education for the children. Demographic expansion has also contributed partly to this growth with the arrival of the baby boom cohorts in the 1960s.

However, the demographic effect alone cannot explain the sevenfold increase in the number of students in 40 years. The major expansion in tertiary educational enrollment was driven mostly by political decisions (Garnier, Hage, and Fuller 1989). We can distinguish at least two main developments in the French education system (for a comprehensive presentation see Prost, 1992): the standardization of high-school education, achieved gradually between the 1940s and the 1970s; and the development of vocational higher education since the 1960s. A strict social segregation prevailed in high schools until WWII, based on two types of secondary institutions: the *écoles primaires supérieures,* reserved for working-class children; and the *lycée,* for middle- and upper-class children. Only the latter were preparing for the *baccalauréat,* which opened the door to postsecondary education. The two systems were completely separate, with distinct educational programs. Consequently, the chances of a working-class child of completing high school and entering tertiary education were slim.

In the late 1930s and 1940s, a first series of reforms established links between the two systems, allowing the most academically talented working-class children to transfer to high school. In 1959, the government raised the age of compulsory schooling from 14 to 16 (*réforme Berthoin*). The objective of this reform, as stated in its preamble, was to expand the intermediate class of technicians. As a result, a growing number of students became eligible for postsecondary education, which led to the first stage of expansion in the number of students in the 1960s.

The second stage began in the mid-1980s with the enactment of policies designed to make at least 80% of a cohort complete secondary school in 1995 (as the Minister of the Education stated in 1985). Implementation of these policies became possible after the last step in the integration of the two secondary systems, achieved on July 11, 1975 (with the *réforme Haby*) with the final unification of the two systems and the creation of the present junior high school (grades 6 to 9). Another important change in the secondary education system has been the development of vocational education. Part of the increase in the rate of completion of secondary education was achieved by the development of vocational tracks. The *baccalauréat professionnel* was created in 1985, awarded by specific vocational high schools. It complemented the *baccalauréat technologique,* created in 1968. In 2003, graduates of these two vocational *baccalauréats, technologique* and *professionnel,* made up almost half of the number of the graduates with high-school diplomas against one-third in 1985 (France DEP 2003). The distribution between general and vocational tracks is highly related to social class, with working-class children being overrepresented in these vocational classes. The odds of vocational students attending preliminary classes that prepared for entrance to the *grandes écoles* were only 1%, as opposed to 12% for students in the general tracks.

The same evolution took place in postsecondary education. The Berthoin law (1959) led to the creation of postsecondary vocational classes (STS) and a corresponding diploma (BTS) in 1962. This vocational track was supplemented in 1966 by the creation of special vocational classes within universities (IUT), awarding a new diploma, the DUT. Ten years after their creation, at the beginning of the 1970s, vocational postsecondary institutions enrolled 50,000 students; they enrolled 120,000 in 1980 and 350,000 in 2002.

Finally, another important development in postsecondary education in France was the fast growth in the access of women to postsecondary education, consistent with the rise in women's participation in the labor force. Besides, a number of the selective *grandes écoles* were closed to women for a long time; they were finally opened to them in the 1970s.

Impact of the Developments in Postsecondary Education

The fast expansion of postsecondary education may be regarded as evidence of the reduction of social inequalities in access to education. But the reality of this "democratization" is questionable and leads to a recurrent debate in French sociology.[3]

Using long-term data, Thélot and Valet (2000) optimistically concluded that the link between social or cultural origins on the one hand and educational level on the other has weakened over the twentieth century. According to them, most of the changes took place just after WWII: the main reduction in social inequality occurred for cohorts born in the late 1930s and early 1940s.

However, the contingency table approach used by Thélot and Vallet did not make it possible to distinguish between a "quantitative" democratization, meaning an overall increase in the average education level, and a "qualitative" democratization of education, meaning a decrease in inequality for children from different backgrounds. A quantitative democratization—that is, a mass education—is consistent with the persistence in social inequality in educational attainment. A general increase in the duration of schooling can cause the overall population to reach the lowest educational levels: social inequalities mechanically decrease or disappear at these levels. But while declining at the lowest levels of educational attainment, inequalities may transfer to later stages (Maximally Maintained Inequality, according to Hout, Raftery, and Bell 1993). Examining transitions separately at several educational levels, Duru-Bellat and Kieffer (2000) found that social inequalities have shifted to higher levels of the education system. The decrease in the overall association between social origin and education obtained by the global contingency approach can be viewed as an artifact if all levels of education are equally weighted: it could reveal a rise only in the educational level of the least educated (Vallet 2004).

Moreover, as suggested by Merle (2002), differentiation by tracks may have replaced differentiation by levels. In other words, a horizontal stratification has supplanted the former vertical one. Note that the massification of the tertiary education in France was achieved mostly through an increase in vocational and professional education. Nonselective universities have also absorbed a large part of the increase in the number of the students. Looking at the social inequalities in the enrollment of French boys in the *grandes écoles*, Albouy and Wanecq (2002) concluded that the link between social origin and the access to this elite tertiary institution has increased for cohorts born in the 1960s compared with cohorts born in the postwar period. They attributed this result to the higher selectivity imposed by the *grandes écoles* in reaction against the massification of higher education. This higher selectivity was partly achieved through a strict control of the number of the students they enrolled. Attali (1998) reports that the number of the students enrolled in engineering schools represented only 3.7% of the total number of students at the end of the 1990s: this proportion was 14.3% at the beginning of the twentieth century.

We attempt to answer two main questions in this chapter: (1) did the expansion of education lead to a decrease in social and gender inequalities in enrollment rates in tertiary education? and (2) did differences in social inequalities manifest themselves by type of institution?

DATA AND METHOD

Data

We used the 1970, 1977, 1985, and 2003 samples of the Education, Training, and Occupations surveys (*enquêtes sur la formation et la qualification professionnelle*, or FQP). The surveys cover all conventional households in metropolitan France (mainland and Corsica). Around 39,000 persons aged 20–64 were interviewed in May 2003, and around 45,000 in May 1970, 1977, and 1985.[4] In these surveys, respondents describe their school career in great detail allowing us to code the information into the CASMIN educational schema. The surveys also contain detailed descriptions of the respondents' social background, including the socio-occupational categories of the respondents' fathers. Occupation is coded in the French national classification according to the 1982 PCS nomenclature (*code des professions et catégories socioprofessionnelles*), at the 2-digit level (29 *catégories socioprofessionnelles*). The French coding also allows us to measure the father's class with the Erikson-Goldthorpe-Portocarero (EGP) schema. The social background of respondents includes information on the educational attainment of the father.

The FQP surveys allow us to analyze cohorts born between 1915 and 1974. To ensure a higher degree of comparability, we selected from each survey the younger cohorts among those who have completed formal education at the time of the survey. Thus, the 2003 survey contains information on the 1965–74 and 1955–64 birth cohorts, the 1985 survey on the 1945–54 birth cohort, the 1977 survey on the 1935–44 birth cohort, and the 1970 survey on the 1915–24 and 1925–34 birth cohorts. Our concern was to use information collected in the same manner for all cohorts, that is, as soon as possible after leaving school.[5]

Method

We conducted separate logistic regressions for each cohort (for all persons, and by gender) for three indicators of educational attainment. We considered first the likelihood of completing high-school education (obtaining the *baccalauréat*). We then analyzed the likelihood of attending any type of postsecondary education (university, vocational education, or *grandes écoles*). Finally, we estimated the likelihood of obtaining a degree from the most selective postsecondary institutions, the *grandes écoles*. Two estimates were conducted: one for the full sample and one conditional on having obtained the *baccalauréat*.

The dependent variables were dummies, which received a value of 1 for persons who hold the degree under consideration, and a value of 0 for persons who do not. The set of independent variables included gender (for regressions conducted on all respondents) and two continuous variables indicating age in years and the age squared. Two social background variables were also included: father's occupation and father's education. Father's occupation was coded using the seven-class version of the EGP class schema (Erikson and Goldthorpe 1992): I (higher-grade professionals); II (lower-grade professionals and higher-grade technicians); IIIa (routine nonmanual employees in administration and commerce); IIIb (routine nonmanual workers in services); IVabc (small proprietors and artisans and self-employed farmers); V+VI (skilled workers and supervisors of manual workers); and VIIab (unskilled workers, including agricultural labourers).

Father's education was coded using the three-category version of the CASMIN schema (Müller et al. 1989): 1abc (level of compulsory school or basic vocational training); 2abc (advanced vocational training, secondary programs, or full maturity certificates); and 3ab (lower-level or high-level tertiary degrees). Information on mother's education and mother's occupation is available only in the 1985 and 2003 FQP surveys. For the sake of comparability with the oldest cohorts, we have chosen not to use this variable, and in any case, the small size of the sample does not allow us to make efficient use of them.

RESULTS

Table 9.1 describes the changes in educational attainment between cohorts born from 1915 to 1974 and shows that the proportion of high-school graduates has been multiplied by six across these cohorts. Among persons born during or just after WWI, only 8% obtained a high-school degree, as opposed to about half the children born between 1965 and 1974. The rate of increase has been fairly constant over the six cohorts considered, and it continues for the most recent ones. In 1985, the Minister of the Education decided that this trend must continue, and set as a reasonable objective that within ten years, 80% of a generation complete secondary education, formalized as article 3, chapter 1, of a law enacted on July 10, 1989 (*title 1 de la loi d'orientation sur l'éducation no. 89-486*). Official records show that this legal impetus has been followed by a massive increase in postsecondary attendance across the 1985–95 decade.

Table 9.1 also shows some important differences between males and females. For the oldest cohorts, born during or just after WWI, the odds of completing high school and of obtaining some postsecondary education were higher for males than for females. This is not the case anymore. For the youngest cohorts, the proportion of women who complete high school is six points higher than the proportion of men. These figures confirm official statistics from the Ministry of Education: since 1971, the majority of high-school graduates are females (Duru-Bellat, Kieffer, and Marry 2001). Men are much more exposed to early failure in primary or junior high school. About 50% of men aged 15 are late for school, about 12 points higher than women (Goux and Maurin 2000).

Several studies have shown that the relative success of women in secondary and tertiary education is mostly a "quantitative" one (see, for instance, Baudelot and Establet 1992). If we examine gender differences by field of education, the proportion of men who obtain "scientific" degrees (the most selective programs in France) remains much higher than that of

TABLE 9.1
The FQP surveys: Some basic statistics (%)

Birth cohort	1915–24	1925–34	1935–44	1945–54	1955–64	1965–74
Left school by the time of the survey						
Males	100.0	99.9	99.9	99.8	100.0	99.7
Females	100.0	100.0	99.9	99.9	100.0	99.8
Overall	100.0	99.9	99.9	99.9	100.0	99.7
Academic post-secondary degree						
Males	2.4	2.8	4.0	6.0	8.4	14.5
Females	2.1	2.2	3.2	6.4	9.0	18.7
Overall	2.2	2.5	3.6	6.2	8.7	16.6
Selective cursus (grande école)						
Males	1.5	2.0	3.4	2.5	2.2	3.7
Females	0.1	0.3	0.6	0.5	0.6	1.0
Overall	0.8	1.1	2.0	1.5	1.4	2.4
Any postsecondary degree						
Males	4.3	5.0	9.7	13.0	17.3	28.4
Females	2.5	3.7	7.9	14.1	18.3	32.3
Overall	3.3	4.7	8.8	13.5	17.8	30.4
High-school degree (baccalauréat)						
Males	10.3	10.1	19.0	22.9	28.8	44.5
Females	5.6	7.9	17.8	25.4	34.1	50.4
Overall	7.9	9.0	18.4	24.1	31.5	47.5
FQP survey used	1970	1970	1977	1985	2003	2003
Sample size						
Males	3,942	5,728	4,808	6,339	4,383	4,407
Females	2,011	2,664	2,917	4,327	4,875	5,116
Overall	5,953	8,392	7,725	10,666	9,858	9,523

women. For instance, among women who were born between 1959 and 1963 and who obtained a *baccalauréat*, only 19% obtained a *baccalauréat* in mathematics (*série* C, the elite secondary track), as opposed to 41% of men (Duru-Bellat, Kieffer, and Marry 2001). At each level of hierarchy of postsecondary degrees, a comparison between tracks chosen by women and men yields the same result: women do better at school than men, but they do not choose "marketable" tracks (Duru-Bellat 1989). All in all, French men are overrepresented among both high-school dropouts and elite postsecondary track graduates.

The evolution of the estimated impact of father occupation and education on the odds of obtaining a *baccalauréat* is seen in Table 9.2, and can be summarized as follows: first, for all cohorts there are still significant differences between children from different social backgrounds, as measured by father's occupation and education. Children whose fathers belong to the upper service class (class II and even more so class I) and children whose fathers have completed higher tertiary education (level 3b) have by far the highest odds of completing high-school education and becoming eligible for postsecondary education. Second, inequalities rooted in cultural origins (as defined by father's education) have steadily decreased across cohorts that entered secondary education after WWII. But democratization has been limited. The discrepancy in the odds of obtaining a *baccalauréat* between children whose fathers have attained the highest level of education and all others appears irreducible. Third, inequalities rooted in social origins (as defined by father's occupation) decreased at the beginning of the twentieth century but have since stabilized across cohorts born after WWII. The gap between children from service-class families (I and II) and children whose fathers are manual workers (VI and VIIab) has even widened between the 1935–44 and the 1965–74 cohorts. This youngest cohort was in high school in the 1980s, a period of rapid increase in secondary education. Surprisingly, this increase did not lead to a drop in social inequality even at this level.

The logit estimates of the impact of social background on the likelihood of obtaining a postsecondary degree are shown in Table 9.3. These logit models are unconditional, meaning that they compare the odds of having a postsecondary degree at least with the odds of having no postsecondary degree. Trends are roughly the same as those concerning high-school diplomas: first, strong social inequalities still exist in obtaining postsecondary degrees. Second, social inequalities have decreased among cohorts born in the first half of the twentieth century, but they have remained rather stable since the end of WWII. They have increased at the end of the 1990s, at a time when the odds of completing high school were at their highest level. Cultural inequalities have followed a reverse pattern, increasing before WWII, then decreasing. Children from educated families are still favored. The gap between children whose fathers have attained level 3b education and those whose fathers have attained level 2c has not changed over the century. The handicap of children with a less-educated background (levels 1a and 1c) has been reduced, but it is still large.

TABLE 9.2
Eligibility for higher education: A logit estimate

	\multicolumn{6}{c}{BIRTH COHORT}
	1915–24	1925–34	1935–44	1945–54	1955–64	1965–74
Intercept	−25.7 (14.7)	−0.3 (7.6)	9.5 (5.6)	−0.1 (4.1)	1.2 (5.7)	9.8 (3.2)
Gender						
Female	−0.48 (0.09)	−0.16 (0.07)	0.14 (0.06)	0.32 (0.05)	0.38 (0.05)	0.31 (0.05)
Male	Ref	Ref	Ref	Ref	Ref	Ref
Father's occupation (EGP schema)						
I	1.88 (0.16)	1.80 (0.13)	0.63 (0.10)	1.28 (0.08)	1.26 (0.09)	1.29 (0.10)
II	1.61 (0.19)	1.67 (0.15)	1.03 (0.13)	0.97 (0.09)	1.04 (0.09)	1.13 (0.09)
IIIa	1.02 (0.17)	0.80 (0.14)	0.56 (0.11)	0.64 (0.09)	0.57 (0.09)	0.40 (0.08)
IIIb	0.76 (0.29)	0.16 (0.27)	0.72 (0.32)	0.37 (0.27)	0.39 (0.26)	−0.36 (0.23)
IVbc	0.08 (0.15)	0.18 (0.12)	0.09 (0.09)	0.40 (0.07)	0.49 (0.09)	0.50 (0.06)
V+VI	Ref	Ref	Ref	Ref	Ref	Ref
VIIab	−0.34 (0.19)	−0.82 (0.17)	−0.45 (0.13)	−0.56 (0.09)	−0.40 (0.09)	−0.29 (0.08)
Unknown	1.35 (0.17)	1.03 (0.14)	−0.57 (0.13)	−0.23 (0.20)	0.29 (0.28)	−0.73 (0.28)
Age	1.04 (0.59)	0.01 (0.37)	−0.40 (0.30)	0.03 (0.24)	−0.04 (0.27)	−0.48 (0.20)
Age square × 100	−1.08 (0.58)	−0.06 (0.46)	0.42 (0.41)	−0.07 (0.33)	0.01 (0.31)	0.55 (0.30)
Father's education (CASMIN)						
3b	0.41 (0.23)	0.45 (0.18)	0.57 (0.20)	0.38 (0.17)	0.44 (0.16)	0.69 (0.16)
3a	Ref	Ref	0.37 (0.45)	−0.48 (0.29)	−0.35 (0.24)	0.62 (0.25)
2c	Ref	Ref	Ref	Ref	Ref	Ref
2a, b	−0.76 (0.43)	−0.26 (0.28)	−0.92 (0.21)	−0.54 (0.17)	−0.30 (0.23)	−0.00 (0.21)
1c	−0.92 (0.46)	−0.75 (0.32)	−1.46 (0.18)	−1.08 (0.14)	−0.87 (0.13)	−0.49 (0.12)
1b	−0.61 (0.22)	−0.30 (0.19)	−1.01 (0.18)	−0.56 (0.16)	−0.26 (0.17)	0.01 (0.16)
1a	−1.93 (0.17)	−1.46 (0.14)	−2.12 (0.15)	−1.76 (0.13)	−1.36 (0.12)	−1.01 (0.12)
Unknown	—	0.53 (1.08)	—	−1.81 (0.19)	−1.87 (0.33)	−0.40 (0.31)
Number of observations	5,953	8,392	7,725	10,666	9,258	9,523
Likelihood ratio (*p*)	1,321	1,626	1,614	2,307	1,619	1,924
	(< 0.0001)	(< 0.0001)	(< 0.0001)	(< 0.0001)	(< 0.0001)	(< 0.0001)

TABLE 9.3
Postsecondary graduation: A logit estimate

	\multicolumn{6}{c}{BIRTH COHORT}
	1915–24	1925–34	1935–44	1945–54	1955–64	1965–74
Intercept	−7.3 (18.5)	5.0 (9.3)	20.7 (7.1)	−6.4 (4.8)	−5.0 (6.9)	5.5 (3.4)
Gender						
Female	−0.22 (0.12)	−0.02 (0.09)	0.03 (0.08)	0.30 (0.05)	0.16 (0.06)	0.22 (0.05)
Male	Ref	Ref	Ref	Ref	Ref	Ref
Father's occupation (EGP schema)						
I	2.25 (0.25)	2.05 (0.19)	0.82 (0.13)	1.16 (0.09)	1.14 (0.11)	1.23 (0.09)
II	1.76 (0.28)	2.03 (0.20)	0.80 (0.16)	0.92 (0.10)	0.89 (0.11)	1.00 (0.08)
IIIa	1.18 (0.28)	1.20 (0.20)	0.66 (0.15)	0.59 (0.10)	0.54 (0.11)	0.30 (0.09)
IIIb	1.11 (0.43)	−0.09 (0.48)	0.66 (0.43)	0.36 (0.33)	0.48 (0.32)	−0.29 (0.29)
IVabc	0.49 (0.25)	0.53 (0.18)	0.41 (0.12)	0.36 (0.08)	0.50 (0.09)	0.49 (0.07)
V+VI	Ref	Ref	Ref	Ref	Ref	Ref
VIIab	−0.59 (0.36)	−0.69 (0.27)	−0.32 (0.19)	−0.56 (0.12)	−0.48 (0.13)	−0.22 (0.10)
Unknown	2.12 (0.26)	1.61 (0.20)	−0.67 (0.21)	−0.34 (0.25)	0.59 (0.32)	−0.33 (0.31)
Age	0.21 (0.74)	−0.32 (0.46)	−1.04 (0.38)	0.34 (0.27)	0.20 (0.33)	−0.29 (0.21)
Age square × 100	−0.23 (0.73)	0.35 (0.57)	1.25 (0.51)	−0.51 (0.38)	−0.25 (0.38)	0.30 (0.32)
Father's education (CASMIN)						
3b	0.71 (0.21)	0.44 (0.17)	0.61 (0.17)	0.49 (0.14)	0.50 (0.14)	0.52 (0.13)
3a	Ref	Ref	−0.25 (0.37)	−0.21 (0.26)	−0.05 (0.23)	0.40 (0.20)
2c	Ref	Ref	Ref	Ref	Ref	Ref
2ab	−0.67 (0.50)	−0.62 (0.33)	−1.12 (0.23)	−0.46 (0.16)	−0.12 (0.22)	−0.18 (0.19)
1c	0.12 (0.51)	−0.82 (0.41)	−1.69 (0.21)	−0.90 (0.13)	−0.92 (0.13)	−0.67 (0.12)
1b	−0.28 (0.23)	−0.47 (0.20)	−0.84 (0.18)	−0.33 (0.15)	−0.22 (0.17)	−0.26 (0.15)
1a	−1.60 (0.18)	−1.48 (0.15)	−2.01 (0.14)	−1.55 (0.12)	−1.34 (0.12)	−1.09 (0.11)
Unknown	—	1.48 (1.09)	—	−1.45 (0.21)	−1.87 (0.38)	−0.73 (0.33)
Number of observations	5,953	8,392	7,725	10,666	9,258	9,523
Likelihood ratio (p)	989 (<0.0001)	1,235 (<0.0001)	1,283 (<0.0001)	1,869 (<0.0001)	1,276 (<0.0001)	1,646 (<0.0001)

TABLE 9.4
Postsecondary vs. high-school graduate: A logit estimate

	\multicolumn{7}{c}{BIRTH COHORT}
	1915–24	1925–34	1935–44	1945–54	1955–64	1965–74
Intercept	26.7 (25.1)	11.7 (13.1)	25.0 (9.1)	−8.2 (6.4)	−7.4 (8.8)	2.2 (4.4)
Gender						
Female	0.31 (0.16)	0.18 (0.13)	−0.14 (0.10)	0.11 (0.07)	−0.20 (0.08)	−0.00 (0.06)
Male	Ref	Ref	Ref	Ref	Ref	Ref
Father's occupation (EGP schema)						
I	1.06 (0.30)	0.89 (0.23)	0.43 (0.17)	0.33 (0.12)	0.35 (0.13)	0.65 (0.12)
II	0.61 (0.33)	0.98 (0.26)	0.18 (0.18)	0.30 (0.13)	0.18 (0.13)	0.42 (0.12)
IIIa	0.34 (0.33)	0.74 (0.26)	0.31 (0.19)	0.11 (0.14)	0.12 (0.14)	0.00 (0.12)
IIIb	0.65 (0.55)	−0.38 (0.56)	0.23 (0.52)	0.05 (0.45)	0.18 (0.42)	−0.02 (0.39)
IVabc	0.59 (0.31)	0.56 (0.23)	0.50 (0.16)	0.03 (0.11)	0.16 (0.12)	0.21 (0.10)
V+VI	Ref	Ref	Ref	Ref	Ref	Ref
VIIab	−0.40 (0.43)	0.15 (0.33)	0.10 (0.24)	−0.07 (0.17)	−0.17 (0.17)	0.05 (0.13)
Unknown	1.57 (0.34)	1.11 (0.27)	−0.25 (0.26)	−0.17 (0.35)	0.46 (0.48)	0.52 (0.47)
Age	−1.13 (1.00)	−0.57 (0.65)	−1.26 (0.49)	0.52 (0.37)	0.36 (0.41)	−0.06 (0.27)
Age square × 100	1.16 (1.00)	0.70 (0.80)	1.60 (0.66)	−0.75 (0.52)	−0.40 (0.48)	0.06 (0.41)
Father's education (CASMIN)						
3b	0.85 (0.26)	0.32 (0.23)	0.56 (0.20)	0.53 (0.17)	0.49 (0.17)	0.29 (0.17)
3a	Ref	Ref	−0.50 (0.41)	0.16 (0.36)	0.31 (0.31)	0.13 (0.25)
2c	Ref	Ref	Ref	Ref	Ref	Ref
2ab	−0.31 (0.60)	−0.76 (0.40)	−0.90 (0.27)	−0.30 (0.21)	0.11 (0.29)	−0.31 (0.24)
1c	1.44 (0.87)	−0.69 (0.53)	−1.20 (0.25)	−0.44 (0.17)	−0.57 (0.16)	−0.66 (0.15)
1b	0.15 (0.29)	−0.46 (0.26)	−0.40 (0.22)	−0.02 (0.19)	−0.13 (0.22)	−0.45 (0.19)
1a	−0.30 (0.21)	−0.62 (0.20)	−0.83 (0.17)	−0.61 (0.15)	−0.65 (0.15)	−0.73 (0.15)
Unknown	—	—	—	−0.36 (0.29)	−0.57 (0.56)	−0.99 (0.50)
Number of observations	980	1,401	2,003	3,507	2,998	4,486
Likelihood ratio (p)	129	111	204	193	194	281
	(< 0.0001)	(< 0.0001)	(< 0.0001)	(< 0.0001)	(< 0.0001)	(< 0.0001)

Table 9.4 presents the same estimates as in Table 9.3, but on the subsample of people who obtained the *baccalauréat*. They compare the odds of having a postsecondary degree versus a high-school diploma with the odds of having a high-school diploma (conditional estimates). Results differ from former ones in one essential aspect: the inequalities rooted in social background have increased in the last period. As before, we observed a decline in social inequalities between cohorts born in the 1930s and older cohorts. However, conditional on having a *baccalauréat,* the gap in the odds of obtaining a postsecondary degree between children from privileged classes and from the working classes has increased for cohorts born between 1965 and 1974 as compared to older cohorts. It is higher than the level prevalent for cohorts born in the 1930s. Besides, cultural inequalities have not been reduced for the youngest cohorts, unlike what is observed when looking at unconditional estimates. These differences between unconditional (Table 9.3) and conditional (Table 9.4) estimates suggest that social inequalities in the access to education have moved to a higher level of education. As the access to high school became more and more general, the participation in higher education of culturally and socially disadvantaged children widened. But conditional on having a high-school diploma, their relative chance to complete tertiary education has declined compared to children from more affluent backgrounds.

Finally, Table 9.5 shows unconditional logit estimates of the odds of obtaining a *grande école* diploma, the most selective of tertiary degrees. The estimates reveal significant inequalities between children from different social backgrounds. Moreover, these inequalities have not decreased over time. The gap in the relative odds of attending a *grande école* between children of manual workers and children of managers are roughly the same at the beginning of the 1990s as forty years before.

Conditional estimates (Table 9.6) confirm this trend: conditionally on having a *baccalauréat,* social inequalities in the access to the most selective degrees were the lowest for cohorts born between 1925 and 1934. Furthermore, Tables 9.5 and 9.6 show that cultural inequalities in obtaining elite degrees have widened since the end of WWII. The differences between children from middle and low cultural backgrounds have tended to narrow, but the advantage of children coming from the most educated families has continuously strengthened. This rise was so important that it offset the

TABLE 9.5
Grandes écoles: A logit estimate

	\multicolumn{6}{c}{BIRTH COHORT}
	1915–24	1925–34	1935–44	1945–54	1955–64	1965–74
Intercept	−69.2 (72.7)	−8.9 (14.8)	−5.3 (13.1)	−3.7 (10.7)	25.3 (21.3)	6.0 (9.8)
Gender						
Female	−3.44 (0.72)	−2.12 (0.28)	−1.90 (0.21)	−1.71 (0.16)	−1.18 (0.21)	−1.32 (0.16)
Male	Ref	Ref	Ref	Ref	Ref	Ref
Father's occupation (EGP schema)						
I	2.51 (0.55)	1.59 (0.28)	1.43 (0.30)	1.39 (0.23)	1.27 (0.40)	1.27 (0.28)
II	2.02 (0.59)	1.31 (0.32)	1.22 (0.34)	1.15 (0.25)	1.04 (0.41)	1.14 (0.28)
IIIa	1.20 (0.63)	0.76 (0.32)	0.82 (0.36)	0.51 (0.31)	0.65 (0.46)	0.61 (0.33)
IIIb	1.50 (0.88)	−0.88 (1.03)	1.40 (0.78)	−12 (370)	−11 (463)	−12 (390)
Ivabc	0.59 (0.59)	0.25 (0.28)	0.89 (0.30)	0.49 (0.24)	0.47 (0.41)	0.59 (0.29)
V+VI	Ref	Ref	Ref	Ref	Ref	Ref
VIIab	−0.09 (0.77)	−0.79 (0.41)	0.15 (0.43)	−0.74 (0.42)	0.07 (0.55)	−0.53 (0.60)
Unknown	2.34 (0.58)	1.21 (0.30)	−0.69 (0.57)	0.62 (0.71)	2.64 (0.58)	0.71 (0.92)
Age	2.68 (2.98)	0.33 (0.74)	0.24 (0.71)	−0.35 (0.21)	−1.35 (1.00)	−0.53 (0.60)
Age square × 100	−2.75 (3.06)	−0.45 (0.91)	−0.43 (0.95)	0.46 (0.86)	1.56 (1.17)	0.71 (0.92)
Father's education (CASMIN)						
3b	0.51 (0.36)	0.10 (0.25)	0.29 (0.22)	0.35 (0.21)	0.66 (0.34)	1.06 (0.30)
3a			−0.73 (0.64)	−0.26 (0.47)	0.48 (0.55)	0.51 (0.43)
2c	Ref	Ref	Ref	Ref	Ref	Ref
2ab	0.49 (0.64)	−0.69 (0.56)	−1.77 (0.54)	−0.78 (0.36)	0.48 (0.55)	−0.33 (0.58)
1c	0.84 (0.86)	−1.01 (0.76)	−1.65 (0.43)	−0.74 (0.26)	−1.05 (0.46)	−0.81 (0.36)
1b	0.37 (0.39)	−0.39 (0.31)	−0.56 (0.28)	−0.32 (0.27)	0.22 (0.46)	0.12 (0.40)
1a	−1.20 (0.34)	−1.16 (0.23)	−1.85 (0.22)	−1.50 (0.23)	−1.29 (0.37)	−0.54 (0.32)
Unknown	—	−11.5 (470)	—	−2.37 (0.71)	−2.24 (0.69)	−1.35 (1.18)
Number of observations	4,972	8,392	7,725	10,666	9,258	9,523
Likelihood ratio (p)	318 (<0.0001)	404 (<0.0001)	517 (<0.0001)	528 (<0.0001)	211 (<0.0001)	352 (<0.0001)

TABLE 9.6
Grandes écoles vs. high school diploma: A logit estimate

	BIRTH COHORT					
	1915–24	1925–34	1935–44	1945–54	1955–64	1965–74
Intercept	2.5 (77.9)	−9.78 (16.4)	−10.8 (13.8)	8.0 (11.1)	29.1 (21.7)	6.8 (10.0)
Gender						
Female	−3.40 (0.72)	−2.19 (0.28)	−2.07 (0.22)	−1.58 (0.16)	−1.38 (0.21)	−1.45 (0.16)
Male	Ref	Ref	Ref	Ref	Ref	Ref
Father's occupation (EGP schema)						
I	1.38 (0.58)	0.38 (0.30)	1.02 (0.32)	0.68 (0.24)	0.60 (0.39)	0.70 (0.28)
II	1.15 (0.63)	0.17 (0.34)	0.76 (0.34)	0.53 (0.25)	0.42 (0.41)	0.62 (0.28)
IIIa	0.50 (0.67)	0.22 (0.35)	0.41 (0.37)	0.07 (0.31)	0.26 (0.47)	0.34 (0.34)
IIIb	0.95 (0.95)	−1.05 (1.07)	0.98 (0.83)	−13 (456)	−12 (570)	−12 (528)
IVabc	0.59 (0.63)	0.20 (0.31)	0.86 (0.31)	0.21 (0.25)	0.12 (0.42)	0.30 (0.29)
V+VI	Ref	Ref	Ref	Ref	Ref	Ref
VIIab	0.31 (0.82)	0.06 (0.45)	0.42 (0.45)	−0.31 (0.43)	0.45 (0.55)	−0.35 (0.50)
Unknown	1.51 (0.62)	0.57 (0.34)	−0.35 (0.58)	0.95 (0.72)	2.35 (0.64)	0.56 (0.99)
Age	−0.22 (3.20)	0.44 (0.82)	0.54 (0.74)	−0.55 (0.63)	−1.50 (1.02)	−0.56 (0.61)
Age square × 100	0.24 (3.28)	−0.58 (1.01)	−0.78 (1.00)	0.75 (0.89)	1.74 (1.19)	0.81 (0.94)
Father's education (CASMIN)						
3b	0.47 (0.38)	−0.02 (0.26)	0.22 (0.23)	0.32 (0.22)	0.55 (0.35)	0.92 (0.30)
3a	Ref	Ref	−0.84 (0.65)	−0.06 (0.48)	0.63 (0.56)	0.34 (0.43)
2c	Ref	Ref	Ref	Ref	Ref	Ref
2ab	0.78 (0.69)	−0.74 (0.58)	−1.48 (0.56)	−0.60 (0.37)	0.57 (0.56)	−0.42 (0.58)
1c	1.89 (1.09)	−0.70 (0.80)	−1.10 (0.45)	−0.34 (0.26)	−0.65 (0.47)	−0.74 (0.36)
1b	0.66 (0.41)	−0.25 (0.33)	−0.25 (0.29)	−0.09 (0.28)	0.24 (0.47)	0.08 (0.41)
1a	−0.08 (0.34)	−0.20 (0.23)	−0.65 (0.23)	−0.65 (0.23)	−0.58 (0.37)	−0.20 (0.31)
Unknown	—	−11.8 (423)	—	−1.57 (0.70)	−0.92 (0.73)	−1.22 (1.19)
Number of observations	818	1,401	2,003	3,507	2,998	4,486
Likelihood ratio (p)	103	117	233	240	339	1,703
	(< 0.0001)	(< 0.0001)	(< 0.0001)	(< 0.0001)	(< 0.0001)	(< 0.0001)

effect of the general increase in the completion of high school; it is observed even when looking at the unconditional estimates (Table 9.5).

Gender Differences

Gender differences in postsecondary education have changed dramatically during the twentieth century. As seen in Table 9.2, the gap between men and women in high-school completion has reversed. Men born between 1915 and 1934 were more likely than women to complete high school. This was no longer the case for cohorts born after 1935, and the odds of high-school completion are now higher for women than for men. Women have caught up with men in attending postsecondary education and are now more likely than men to obtain a postsecondary degree, whereas men born before 1935 were more likely than women to complete higher education (Table 9.3). However, the trend of an increasing gap in favor of women has declined for the youngest cohorts.

The reduction in gender differences is somewhat misleading. First, it has been driven mostly by the increase in high-school completion. If we examine the odds of attending tertiary education conditional on having a high-school diploma (Table 9.4), not only has gender differences not decreased but, on the contrary, they have grown. Among persons who completed secondary education after WWII, men were more likely, or at least as likely, as women to attend tertiary education. Second, the increase in women's access to higher education was mostly quantitative. The gender gap in the odds of attending the *grandes écoles* is huge in all cohorts (Tables 9.5 and 9.6). Most of the *grandes écoles* were indeed closed to women before the 1970s. But even if the gap has decreased since this period, it is still large for cohorts who entered higher education in the 1980s and 1990s. Access to the *grandes écoles* remains de facto reserved for men: early in their school career, women favor less the scientific tracks that are the key to most *grandes écoles* (Duru-Bellat 1989; Baudelot and Establet 1992).

CONCLUSION

Using long-term data, we found that the decrease in social inequality in attending tertiary education, characteristic of the first half of the twentieth century, has stopped since WWII and was followed by an increase in social inequality for the cohorts born in the late 1960s. Mass education has not prevented an increase in class differences: although the rise in the rate of tertiary education was impressive, it did not lead to a reduction in social inequalities. The previous social stratification remains.

First, the horizontal stratification persists: conditionally on having a high-school diploma, the odds of completing postsecondary education of cohorts born between 1965 and 1974 became more socially unequal. One explanation is that the rise in high-school completion rate was partly achieved through the creation of vocational *baccalauréat* (*baccalauréat professionnel*). This diploma was supposed to facilitate direct entry into the labor force, not to prepare for tertiary education. It is also chosen mostly by children from low social backgrounds.

Second, a vertical stratification remains: the access to the first-tier institutions, the *grandes écoles,* is more and more culturally determined. One basic reason is that the selectivity of the *grandes écoles* has risen over the period, as the number of slots available in the *grandes écoles* has increased at a much lower rate than in the standard university system. Children from culturally advantaged backgrounds are better prepared to face this school competition. A closer look at the students who enter the elite institutions shows that they are increasingly coming from families where the parents are also graduates of a *grande école* (Albouy and Wanecq 2002). These parents have a keener knowledge of the educational institutions and direct their children toward the most selective programs.

CHAPTER TEN

Germany: Institutional Change and Inequalities of Access in Higher Education

Karl Ulrich Mayer, Yale University

Walter Müller, Mannheim Centre for European Social Research (MZES)

Reinhard Pollak, Mannheim Centre for European Social Research (MZES)

INTRODUCTION

This chapter investigates the growth, internal differentiation, and inequalities of access in the German system of tertiary education. German higher education, subject to major changes at least since the 1960s, has been the topic of an almost constant debate. Three themes dominated the debates, which were especially pronounced between 1965 and 1975, and again between 1993 and the present. The first theme was growth and adaptation to changing demand, with economic and demographic arguments being most salient. The second theme focused on the cultural goals and institutional forms of the university. The third major theme concerned inequalities of access and the role of higher education in a democratic society.

The growth and organizational forms of higher education in Germany are of special comparative interest. On the one hand, Germany belongs to the few (mostly German-speaking or -influenced) countries that have developed an extensive system of vocational training in an intermediary position between general schooling and higher education. As a result, political decisions influence which proportion of given birth cohorts enters and completes higher education and which parts of vocational and professional training should be located in the tertiary as opposed to the postsecondary sector. On the other hand, Germany is special in that higher education is the responsibility of the federal states; the influence of the federal government is limited to enacting a "Framework Act" for higher education and to its partnership in the financing of buildings and investments.

Growth in enrollment in higher education can be expected to exert pressure in favor of internal differentiation for at least two reasons: former elite sectors of the system try to maintain their relative status, while cost pressures favor cheaper solutions for parts of the expanded system. It is easy to imagine the internal dynamics of a differentiated system. The less privileged parts of the system continuously strive to catch up with the status and resources of the more privileged ones.

It is less clear whether the ongoing institutional differentiation will be internal or external, that is, leading to comprehensive institutions of higher learning offering courses at different levels or to a binary or even a three-tier system of higher education with courses segregated by duration, content, or subject. Within the last thirty years Germany has tried both internal and external differentiation. In the 1970s, some states governed by Social Democrats introduced so-called *Gesamthochschulen,* comprehensive institutions of higher learning that incorporated both the old university and lower-tier technical colleges. More widespread nationally was a binary system of universities and separate lower-tier *Fachhochschulen* (universities of applied sciences). Currently, a process of internal differentiation is under way in the form of three-year tracks leading to a bachelor's degree followed by a two-year track leading to a master's degree.

What are the expected relationships between expansion, institutional differentiation, and inequalities of access? Growth periods should favor the inclusion of formerly less represented social groups and, therefore, decrease inequalities of opportunity. Internally and, even more so, externally differentiated systems should create new barriers of access to upper-tier levels of higher education. Access to lower-tier parts of higher education should become more open. Cultural distance, duration, expected success and returns, as well as real and opportunity costs should all be factors pushing in that direction.

NEW WINE IN OLD BOTTLES: QUANTITATIVE DEVELOPMENTS SINCE THE LATE 1960S

The guiding principles that still influence, at least partially, the development of German higher education institutions (HEIs) are inspired by the Humboldtian reform of the University of Berlin in 1810. These principles include the unity of research and teaching for faculty and students, free access to higher education, the ideal of institutions offering the full range of subjects, and cooperative self-governance by professors with civil servant status. Furthermore, HEIs are government financed, the autonomy of their research and teaching programs is guaranteed, and they enjoy a monopoly on the education of professionals.

Recent efforts by the *Fachhochschulen,* which now describe themselves as "universities of applied sciences," to mimic the university model and become part of it testify to the continuing force of these guiding principles. Along the same lines, there is a growing tendency by school leavers intending to enter occupations that previously required vocational sector training (particularly the dual system of apprenticeship education) to opt for higher education. The remarkable resistance to change characteristic of the traditional German university system was also apparent during the process of German reunification. Despite its blatant and largely undisputed structural shortcomings, the West German model was essentially transferred to the former Eastern states.

In recent decades, developments in the German higher education system have largely been characterized by quantitative changes. The system was expanded in the 1960s and 1970s primarily to train teachers for the baby boom generation. The baby boomers themselves then surged into the *Fachhochschulen* and universities. But even irrespective of these demographic developments, the relative demand for higher education has continued to increase. The term "mass university" reflects the ambivalent and, to some extent, helpless reaction to these developments. Social and political perceptions of the state of the universities have also undergone rapid change. Whereas the predominant issue in the 1960s was meeting the social and economic "demand" for graduates, by the 1980s and 1990s it was more a question of how best to cope with a graduate glut. In recent years, in light of a new "brain drain," there is again a growing consensus that the number of graduates is too low rather than too high.

In 2000/2001, about 1.8 million students were enrolled at German HEIs: 46% of them were women, and 10% were of non-German nationality. Approximately 1.15 million students enrolled at universities; 139,000 at comprehensive universities; 15,000 at colleges of education; 2,500 at theological seminaries; 30,000 at art colleges; 33,000 at *Fachhochschulen* for public administration; and 426,000 at *Fachhochschulen*. Enrollment figures for the winter semester of 2000/2001 were only slightly below the record high of 1.87 million in 1994. The number of students enrolled at West German HEIs had increased more than tenfold between 1950 and 1989, climbing from 117,000 to some 1.5 million. The most rapid period of growth was the 1970s, when the number of students more than doubled from 422,000 to 972,000, and the upward trend continued in the years that followed. The 1990s marked a turning point in three respects. First, in 1990 some 134,000 students from East Germany were absorbed into the united system of higher education. Second, since that time the number of students in HEIs has clearly exceeded the number of trainees in vocational education. Third, the phase of rapid growth was followed by a period of stagnation and a slight reduction in the number of students (figures from Germany BMBF 2000/2001 and other years).

It can no longer be assumed that young people holding either a university entrance qualification (*Abitur*) or a certificate restricted to the *Fachhochschulen* will enter higher education directly after leaving school. Paths to higher education have become longer and more diverse. In 1970, 56% of those qualified to enter higher education did so within the first year of leaving school; by 1998 this figure had dropped to 30% (Germany BMBF 2000/2001). In the following year, 16% of new entrants to vocational training programs were *Abitur* holders (Germany BMBF 2000/2001). Moreover, about a quarter of new entrants to higher education have already completed a vocational training program (Mayer 2003). Although upper secondary schooling had been reformed with the aim of better preparing students for higher education, increasing numbers of young people are choosing to take a gap year (or more) before beginning their studies—apart from compulsory military or community service. These two developments—vocational training and gap years—have led to a steady increase in the average age of new entrants to higher education in Germany. In 2000, the average age of new students was 22.1 (Statistisches Bundesamt 2000).

Problems of access and admission, deficits in the quality of teaching, and above all organizational shortcomings have led to a steady increase in both overall degree-completion periods and the time spent studying the subject in which the degree is ultimately obtained. Excessive degree-completion periods have become an established part of college life. In 1998, the average degree completion period was 6.7 years at the universities (1985: 7.5) and 5.3 years at the *Fachhochschulen* (1985: 4.6).[1] Average graduation age was 28 at the universities and 28.6 at the *Fachhochschulen* (Wissenschaftsrat 2001).

The proportion of students who leave the system without a degree—frequently after having studied for several years—indicates further serious shortcomings in the quality of college admission procedures, teaching, and organization. The dropout rate based on the graduation year 1999 is 30% in universities and 22% in *Fachhochschulen*.

INSTITUTIONAL GROWTH AND DIVERSIFICATION

How has the institutional system of higher education reacted to the increase in the numbers of new entrants to higher education and to the growth in student population?[2] Possible responses were the expansion of existing HEIs, the establishment of new institutions with traditional structures, and the diversification of the higher education system as a whole. For the German system of higher education, and for universities in particular, the rapid growth in the student population presented an almost unsolvable dilemma. On the one hand, many university professors are still vehemently opposed to the opening of the universities to what they perceive as the nonacademic "masses." They regard such openness as the intellectual downfall of the institution, and, therefore, they wish to limit access to higher education. On the other hand, the resources allocated to individual HEIs and disciplines, which affect the sway of their power and influence, depend on the number of students enrolled. To solve the "mass or class" dilemma, in 1993 the German Science Council (Wissenschaftsrat 1993) recommended that the influx of new students be redirected away from the universities and toward the *Fachhochschulen*.

The German higher education landscape is characterized by a more or less open competition between the universities and the *Fachhochschulen*, and by the contrasting nature of the two types of institutions. The *Fachhochschulen* offer academically based programs with a practical orientation.

As a rule, it takes three-and-a-half years (often including a one-semester industrial placement) to complete a *Fachhochschule* degree program. This institutional type experienced the largest growth in the 1980s and 1990s, both in the number and the proportion of students. In West Germany the number of *Fachhochschulen* rose from some 90 in 1971, when they were first established, to 123 in 1991. In the year 2000, there were 153 general *Fachhochschulen* across Germany as a whole. Despite their rapid growth, however, the *Fachhochschulen* are still only enrolling a minority of the student body. They currently cater to 25% of the student population and award 35% of first degrees.

A further development in the diversification of the higher education sector has been largely overlooked in both the public debate and the relevant statistics. *Berufsakademien* or "colleges of advanced vocational studies," which although part of the tertiary education sector are not recognized as HEIs, have entered the educational landscape alongside the universities and *Fachhochschulen*. Two different types of institutions operate under this designation. The first were set up as dual establishments combining vocational education in the private sector with a state college education in three federal states. The second type of *Berufsakademie* are state-recognized dual-educational establishments financed by the private sector that offer three-year training programs. Several new colleges of this type were established in the 1990s, primarily in northern Germany. There are currently around 20 such institutions. Both types of *Berufsakademie* generally offer three-year programs that combine on-the-job training with college attendance. Banks, which have long relied on internal training and continuing education of their staff, have now also institutionalized this kind of dual training. Like the *Fachhochschulen,* the *Berufsakademien* are largely limited to programs in the fields of engineering and economics.

For the most part, the German system of higher education is government financed. There has traditionally been a nonstate sector in the field of tertiary education, however, consisting almost exclusively of the theological seminaries and church-funded *Fachhochschulen* (primarily for social work). In 2000, there were a total of 79 private HEIs (16 theological seminaries, 51 *Fachhochschulen,* 2 art colleges, and 10 universities), and some 40,000 students (2.2% of the student body) were enrolled in these private institutions (Germany BMBF 2000/2001). Several new private institutions are planned or in the process of being established.

Finally, two recent developments must be noted. First, German universities have started to change the temporal structure of the curricula. In the past, only long-duration programs of study were being offered; today a combination of bachelor's and master's studies are being introduced in almost every field of study. Second, the higher education system breaks with the idea of having equal standards and resources among all universities. Since 2006 the federal government has financed a small number of research universities as elite institutions.

INEQUALITIES IN THE ACCESS TO HIGHER EDUCATION: THE ROAD UP TO THE *ABITUR*

Although in Germany academic degrees have lost their social exclusivity and the attendant social prestige, they remain the most significant step in the education system for access to advantageous class positions and to high incomes. For the study of stratification, it is, therefore, of eminent interest how inequalities by social class in tertiary education participation and in attainment of tertiary degrees have evolved in the described process of expansion and differentiation. However, we must locate tertiary education more broadly within the German system of education and elaborate its relation to social stratification, otherwise we miss important elements needed to understand the German case in a comparative perspective. The bottleneck to tertiary education in Germany is the *Abitur*. This is the qualifying exam taken after four years of primary education and eight to nine years of general secondary education—the latter usually completed at the *Gymnasium*. In principle, those who have obtained the *Abitur* have free choice of a tertiary program of study. There are some restrictions, but they do not invalidate the central role of the *Abitur* as an entrance prerequisite to tertiary education. Preparatory study programs for the *Abitur* are general in nature, although students can specialize in different subjects. There is no direct access to tertiary education from the vocational training system without passing a set of exams corresponding more or less to the *Abitur* requirements. Whether the significance of social class or other characteristics of social origin for tertiary education attainment will change over time depends largely on two processes: social selectivity along the way to the *Abitur,* and social selectivity in the type of further study pursued and successfully completed after the *Abitur*. To assess changes in social inequality in tertiary education we must consider changes in both processes.

Educational inequality among children of different social backgrounds is known to be high in Germany. Comparative studies have consistently shown that class differences in educational participation and class differences in levels of education achieved are higher in Germany than in many other advanced societies (Müller and Karle 1993; Jonsson, Mills, and Müller 1996). Although results are not in complete accord, there is convincing evidence from several studies using different sets of data and different analytic methods that class inequality has declined in recent decades (Müller and Haun 1994; Henz and Maas 1995; Jonsson, Mills, and Müller 1996; Schimpl-Neimanns 2000; but for arguments and results claiming persistent inequality see Mayer, Henz, and Maas 1991; Meulemann 1992; Blossfeld 1993). The decline is substantial, but as class inequality used to be large it may still be larger today in Germany than in other economically advanced countries. Results may vary depending on the specific aspect of inequality examined. Low degrees of class inequality in the risks of early dropout or of obtaining only substandard education may go together with very high inequality in obtaining tertiary degrees.

It is less clear exactly why there should be a high level of inequality in Germany. There is little reason to assume that the distribution by social class of individual abilities affecting success in schools should be substantially different in Germany than in other countries. And the social mechanisms of educational choice should operate in similar ways in Germany as in other countries. Finally, Germany has neither excessively high income inequality nor poverty that could be responsible for especially high levels of educational inequality. Most plausible are explanations concerning particular institutional settings in the educational system that may condition educational choices in ways that lead to large class inequalities in educational participation and attainment (Erikson and Jonsson 1996b).

Earlier research found that the driving element of the decline in class inequality in educational participation in Germany was change in the crucial decision most children in the German school system face at about age 11, when they must choose between one of three tracks.[3] Over the decades the proportion of those entering the dead-end *Hauptschule*-track diminished steadily. At the same time, social selectivity among the children who enter one of the two more demanding tracks (*Realschule* or *Gymnasium*) has declined substantially. As progress toward the *Abitur* is much more likely in these tracks (in particular in the *Gymnasium*) than in the *Hauptschule,* social selectivity among those who advance to the *Abitur* became smaller as well, mainly as a consequence of the decline in social selectivity in the early educational decision at age 11.

The decline occurred mainly among the cohorts that made the transitions up until the early 1970s, and it has leveled off since then (Müller and Haun 1994; Henz and Maas 1995; Schimpl-Neimanns 2000). While the evidence concerning the fact of declining social inequality on the way to the *Abitur* appears compelling, it has so far not been established which have been the main factors responsible for the decline. One plausible explanation relates to the logic and development of the German vocational training system.[4] For promising apprenticeship places in the German vocational training system, employers increasingly required at least intermediary secondary general education (obtainable at *Realschule* and *Gymnasium*) or full secondary general education (*Abitur,* obtainable mainly at the *Gymnasium*). Therefore, to even obtain a good apprenticeship place later and to preserve their parental status, it became increasingly essential for working-class children to enter either the *Realschule* or *Gymnasium* track. This explanation assumes that some working-class children may be drawn into the higher tracks of secondary education not primarily because they aspire to a tertiary degree (which used to be the main reason for entering the *Gymnasium* in earlier years), but rather because of more limited, traditional occupational aspirations. If this is true, we should find increasing class divergence in educational choices following the *Abitur.*

INSTITUTIONAL OPTIONS BEYOND THE *ABITUR* AND HYPOTHESES ON CLASS DIFFERENCES IN EDUCATIONAL CHOICES AND OUTCOMES

After obtaining the *Abitur,* graduates have four options in the German system. They may begin studies in one of two tracks of tertiary education (the *Fachhochschule* or the university), take up vocational training in a nontertiary institution, or enter the labor force (without further education or training). Most *Abitur* graduates enter one of the options of tertiary education, but a substantial number opt for nontertiary training, mainly vocationally oriented. Very few enter the labor market directly. It is important to distinguish between these options, because they can be assumed to be differentially attractive to *Abitur* graduates of different social backgrounds.[5]

Vocational Training

Entry into a nontertiary vocational path of training in the German context means mainly an apprenticeship, but there are also various vocational training colleges (e.g., in health care) that admit *Abitur* graduates. Most of these training options do not formally require the *Abitur* as a prerequisite, and are usually entered with general qualifications below the *Abitur* level. But a higher level of general education did become a competitive advantage in securing apprenticeships for the most promising occupations.

Following the logic of mobility strategies from below (Goldthorpe 2000b), we expect working-class children to be more likely to opt for this low investment–low risk strategy than children with service-class backgrounds. The availability of this option diverts them from more demanding studies and their better returns on the labor market. In an interesting simulation study, Hillmert and Jacob (2003) have shown that such diversion is to be expected mainly among *Abitur* graduates who have an intermediate expectation of success in tertiary education but a low time tolerance to compensate the costs of educational investments through higher incomes later. This is most likely the case among gifted children with restricted parental resources.[6]

Studies at a Fachhochschule *or University*

As outlined above, universities are the institutions of traditional scientific training and academic learning, while the *Fachhochschulen* offer tertiary-level qualifications with a more practical orientation. In this respect, there is a clear though declining distinction between the two types, which represent segregated tracks with little student mobility between them. Very small proportions of graduates from the *Fachhochschule* enter the university system to obtain a university diploma or a doctoral degree.

Several differences between the characteristics of the *Fachhochschule* and of the universities suggest that they should be differentially attractive to students of working-class and service-class origins. To secure a class position similar to those of their parents, children of the service class—in particular of the upper service class—have high incentives for academic university studies because these provide the best prospects for an upper service-class position. In contrast, students of working-class backgrounds and students from families with low parental education should be attracted by the shorter duration, lower failure rates, and the more practical orientation and job-relatedness of study programs at the *Fachhochschule*. In the trade-off of lower costs, investments, and risks against somewhat lower returns on the labor market, the former can be expected to be preferred by working-class children.

*Entry into the Labor Market without Completing Post-*Abitur *Training or Studies*

Abitur graduates who do not earn any postsecondary or tertiary qualification before entering the labor market constitute a heterogeneous group. They include secondary education leavers who enter the labor market immediately upon having reached the *Abitur,* as well as failed tertiary students and students who find attractive employment opportunities in the course of tertiary education and, therefore, discontinue their studies. These choices are also expected to be class biased in at least two ways. Because these *Abitur* graduates invest the least into additional education or training following the *Abitur,* one might expect to find them mostly among children of working-class families because the balance of costs and gains from additional education could be less favorable for them or because they have fewer financial resources to spend for additional training. However, applying different considerations, we can also expect service-class children to be more likely to rely on family networks or particular social skills to improve their prospects on the labor market and compensate for lacking educational credentials. The empirical results must show which of these hypotheses is more consistent with the data.

CHANGE OVER TIME IN CLASS INEQUALITY

Given the several reasons for class-bound choices and attainments in postsecondary and tertiary education, what kinds of changes over time can be expected in this respect? If the growing participation of working-class children in the general tracks of upper secondary education is due at least partly to the growing demand of such qualifications to obtain promising apprenticeship places, the social-class gradient in the choice for nontertiary vocational qualifications among *Abitur* graduates should increase over time. *Abitur* holders from working-class families should increasingly opt for postsecondary vocational training rather than acquire tertiary education. Changes in this direction can also be caused by declining grants for tertiary studies in recent decades and by increasing difficulties in being admitted to one's preferred field of study (as a result of the introduction of *numerus clausus* in attractive disciplines). Public debates about less favorable labor market prospects and ongoing talk about the introduction of substantial student fees are additional factors that pull these *Abitur* graduates into postsecondary vocational training.

Predictions regarding the two alternatives for tertiary studies are difficult because of circumstances that have opposing implications for class-dependent choices between them. The rising academic standards of the *Fachhochschule*, their growing reputation, and their increased returns on the labor market may have reduced the reluctance of the higher social classes to attend the *Fachhochschule*, and contributed to a decline in the social gradient in the choice between *Fachhochschule* and university. But at the same time, changes just mentioned, with respect to study grants and *numerus clausus* and the increasingly doubtful labor market prospects of university graduates, may have reduced the propensity of working-class children to enter university education, contributing to an increasing class gradient in the choice between *Fachhochschule* and the university. The two developments also may balance each other out.

In the analyses that follow, we therefore present (unconditional) logistic regressions first of the odds of reaching at least the level of the *Abitur*, and second of reaching a tertiary degree. Then we use multinomial logistic regression to study the further (conditional) educational attainment of those who have reached the *Abitur*.

DATA AND METHODS

Our results are based on a pooled data set using four data sources: (1) the German general social survey (ALLBUS) 1980–2000; (2) the ZUMA-Standarddemographie 1976–1982; (3) the German Socio-Economic Panel

(GSOEP) 1986, 1999, and 2000;[7] and (4) the West German Life History Studies (conducted in the 1980s). Altogether, the data set comprises 65,797 observations. This cumulative file has been widely used in other studies in which it was also shown that the various composite databases produce highly similar results. We restrict analyses to West German citizens born in 1910 and later. Our dependent variables are measured with the revised CASMIN educational classification scheme (Müller 2000). As independent variables we use two measures of social origin: an 8-class version of Goldthorpe's class schema relying on information about father's employment, and a dummy variable for father's education (having obtained the *Abitur* or more is coded 1). Unfortunately, information about the father's education is missing in some surveys, so we included a missing data variable to retain these cases in the sample. To capture change over time, we compare results for quasi–birth cohorts defined in ten-year categories.

The main advantage of the database is its size, which allows stable estimates and analyses of the development of educational inequality over a long period of time. The design and implementation of the analyses of the data is limited, however, by several restrictions, having to do mainly with the measurement of the dependent variable. While conceptually the distinction between the different kinds of post-*Abitur* vocational training and tertiary education is clear, the empirical identification is not straightforward in all cases. In particular, the allocation of cases to the lower tertiary category may have limited validity and reliability. Respondents who do have a degree from a *Fachhochschule* are correctly assigned with high precision. But to study long-term developments we have decided that the lower tertiary category should also include graduates from institutions preceding the *Fachhochschule* (schools of engineering, schools of social work, teacher training colleges) or more recent institutions like private or public *Berufsakademien* (colleges).

Another limitation of the analyses is due to the fact that we have measures only of the highest general and vocational degree obtained. Therefore, the data set does not allow distinct analyses for entry into a specific track of study and for its completion, given entry. Our analyses of post-*Abitur* achievements refer to the highest degree respondents have obtained, and we do not consider that a tertiary degree may have been obtained only in a second step after having pursued vocational training. We, thus, rely on simplifying assumptions about the course of studies followed. When major conclusions from the analyses could have been affected by the simplifying assumptions, we performed sensitivity analyses to verify that these conclusions are not dependent on the assumptions made.

DECLINING INEQUALITIES AT THE FULL SECONDARY AND TERTIARY EDUCATIONAL LEVEL

Abitur used to be a highly exclusive degree in older cohorts. According to our data, some 82% of all men and 92% of all women did not reach this level of education in the oldest cohort. But even in the youngest cohort, about two thirds of the population do not graduate with *Abitur* (65% of men and 71% of women). The *Abitur* became less exclusive in younger cohorts, but its expansion differs between men and women. While among men the proportion of *Abitur* graduates grew only moderately, the share of women increased more rapidly from 12% in the cohort 1938–47 to 29% in the cohort 1958–72. This has led to a marked decline in gender disparities at the *Abitur* level, to the point of their virtual disappearance.[8]

Who benefits from the growing cohort proportions obtaining the *Abitur*? To assess class disparities, we regress the odds of having earned at least the *Abitur* versus not having reached this level on social class and father's education, controlling for cohort and including interaction terms of class by cohort and of father's education by cohort in order to capture the changing effects of social origin over time. The model is estimated for respondents who are at least 22 years old, assuming that the vast majority of those who obtain an *Abitur* degree have graduated by that age. Interactions of class by cohort that are not statistically significant are dropped from the final model. In order to keep the model lean, we include one common interaction effect for the three working classes (V-VIIab).[9] For women, the effect of the father's education turns out to be time invariant; so the cohort by father's education-interaction is not included in the model for women.

The results of the models for men and women are displayed in Figures 10.1a and 10.1b (complete results available upon request from the authors). As a first result, the logit effects indicate distinct class differences in the odds of holding an *Abitur* degree or more. Upper service-class children (class I) are in the most favorable position to reach the *Abitur*, followed by lower service-class children (class II) and children of routine nonmanual employees (class IIIab). All three effects differ significantly from each other,

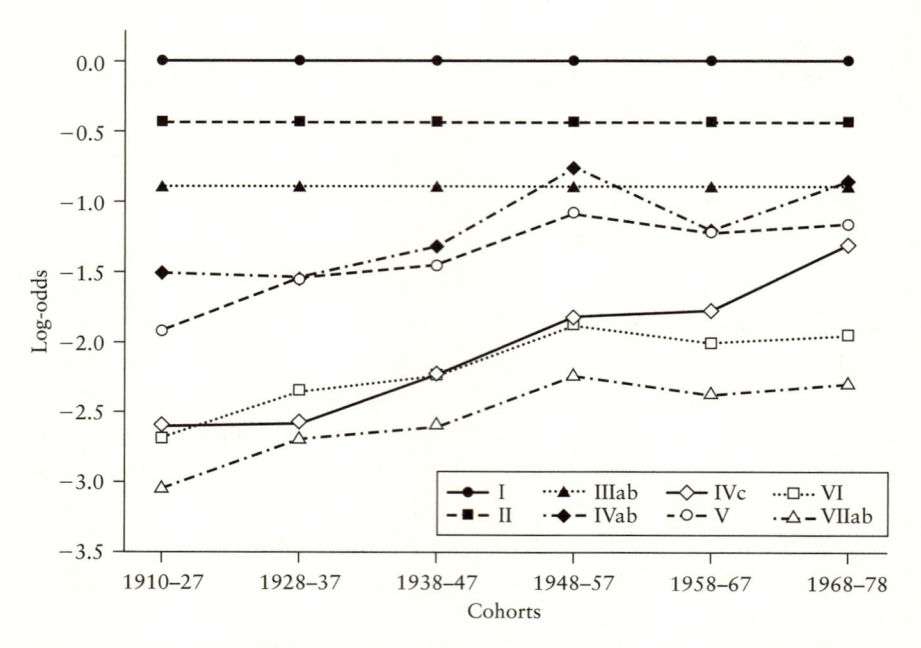

Figure 10.1a. Logit Effects of Class of Origin on Holding at Least *Abitur* Degree: Men

NOTE: West German males aged 22 and older and born after 1909; N = 23,983.

but they do not change relative to each other over time. In contrast, sons of small proprietors (class IVab), working-class elites (class V), farmers (IVc), and skilled and unskilled workers (VI and VIIab) improve their chances of earning the *Abitur* relative to the service class. In general, the lower classes catch up relative to the three nonmanual classes. In addition to the shrinking effects of class origin, for men in the younger cohorts obtaining the *Abitur* also depends less on father's education (the effect of the measure of father's education drops from 1.76 for the oldest cohort to 0.66 for the youngest cohort).

The effect of class origin is slightly more pronounced for women than for men.[10] Although class differences declined somewhat more for women than for men, women in the youngest cohort still experience a slightly stronger class-based inequality than men. The invariant effect of father's education on *Abitur* is stronger for women than the average effect is for men. A substantial decrease occurred also in gender inequality. A model for data of men and women combined and including a dummy gender variable and

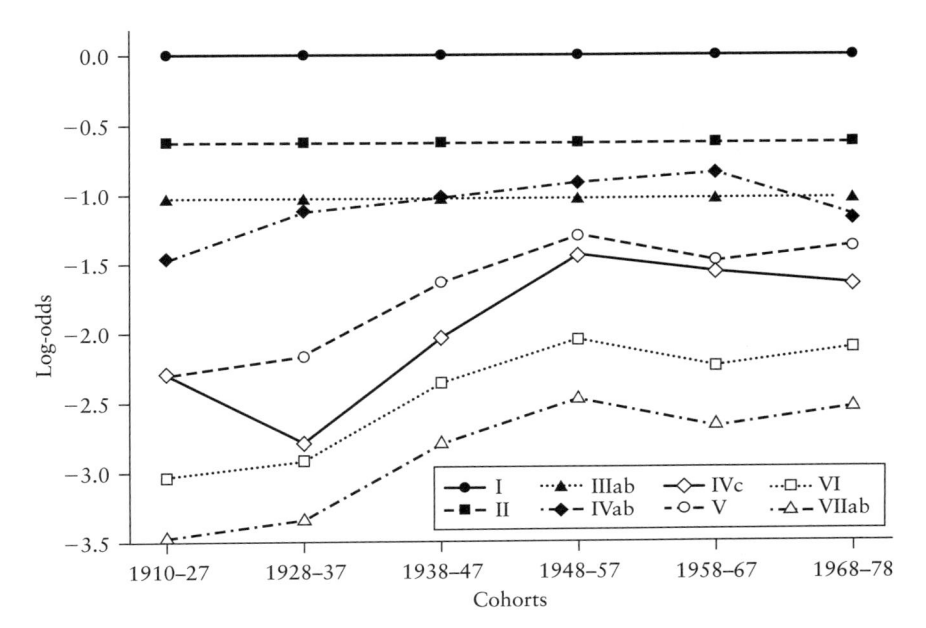

Figure 10.1b. Logit Effects of Class of Origin on Holding at Least *Abitur* Degree: Women

NOTE: West German females aged 22 and older and born after 1909; N = 26,622.

gender cohort interaction terms, in addition to the terms of the model for men, shows strongly and significantly declining gender inequality: the disadvantage for women declines from a log-odds of 1.19 for the cohorts of 1910–27 to a log-odds of 0.39 for the cohort of 1968–78; results not shown).

Thus, inequality in attaining full secondary education up to the *Abitur* became smaller in West Germany in the course of the twentieth century with respect to gender and social origin. Especially children from manual classes improved their chances of obtaining an *Abitur* degree relative to children of the upper service class. Given that few students change tracks in the tripartite German school system, the decline in educational inequality up to the *Abitur* derives mainly from shrinking social-class differences in the transition at the branching point after fourth grade (for detailed empirical tests see Müller and Haun 1994).

Does declining educational inequality work all the way to the level of tertiary education? To test this, we perform almost the same logistic regression models using a dummy variable of tertiary degree (i.e., *Fachhochschule*

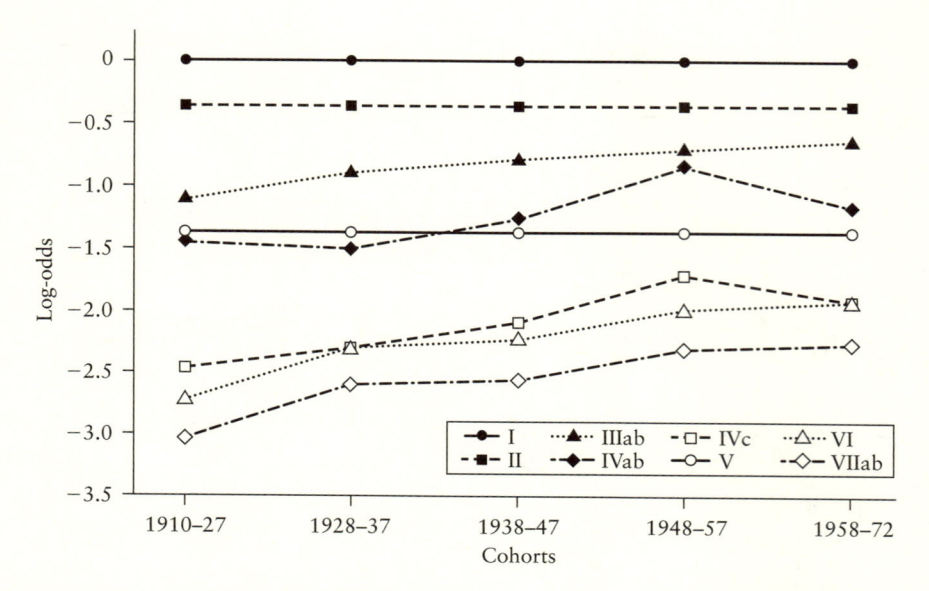

Figure 10.2a. Logit Effects of Class of Origin on Holding Tertiary Education Degree: Men

NOTE: West German males aged 30 and older and born after 1909; N = 19,929.

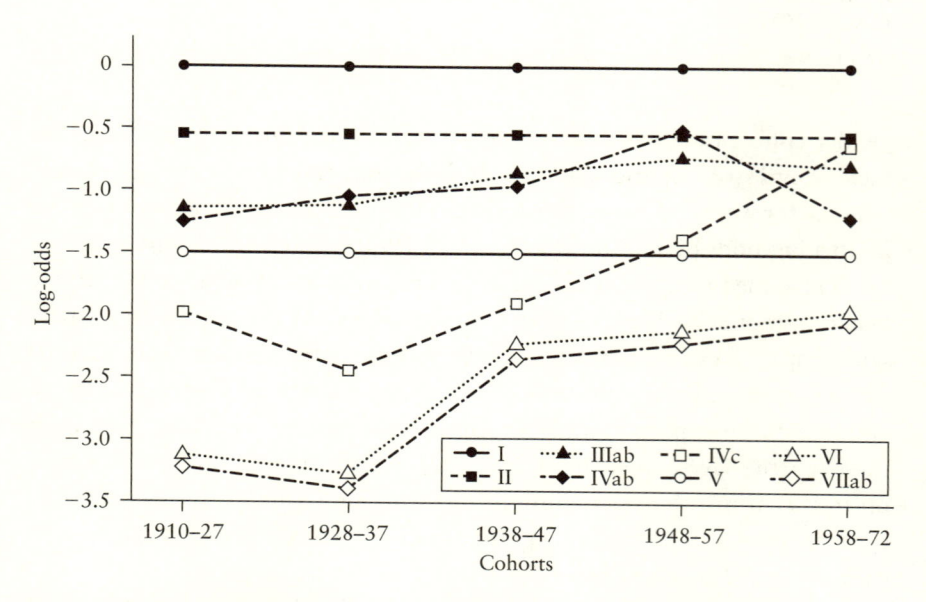

Figure 10.2b. Logit Effects of Class of Origin on Holding Tertiary Education Degree: Women

NOTE: West German females aged 30 and older and born after 1909; N = 22,339.

or university degree) versus no tertiary degree as dependent variable. The sample is restricted to people who are at least 30-years-old.[11] We also add interaction terms for cohort by class of nonmanual employees (class IIIab), and exclude working-class elites (class V) from the common working class interaction term because the effects of this class appear not to vary across cohorts. The results of the models for men and women are shown in Figures 10.2a and 10.2b (full results available upon request from the authors). The overall picture is very similar to the one obtained for the *Abitur* level.

Educational inequality thus declined not only in secondary education, but also at the *Fachhochschule* and university level. However, we find small differences between tertiary and secondary education. For tertiary education, there is a modest but steady improvement in the prospects of children of routine nonmanual employees for earning a tertiary degree (relative to the service classes). At the same time, children from working-class elites appear not to improve their prospects. Father's education seems to be somewhat less important for tertiary-level than for secondary-level attainment. But these differences should not be overemphasized because part of the variation might be due to the differences in sample definition. Combining men and women into one model with gender interaction effects (results not shown) again reveals a strong decline of gender inequality. Women still have lower chances of earning a tertiary degree than men, but the gender gap is constantly decreasing.

Overall then, educational inequality based on gender and class of origin declines as measured with unconditional odds of obtaining tertiary education. There are reasons to believe, however, that for *Abitur* holders, class conditions do influence the transition decision to further education and that class differences in post-*Abitur* educational participation and outcomes may have increased. To address this issue, we now turn to the further educational progression of men and women who obtained the *Abitur* and have therefore earned the right to pursue tertiary studies.

CLASS INEQUALITY IN POST-*ABITUR*
EDUCATIONAL OUTCOMES

Tables 10.1a and 10.1b show the distribution of *Abitur* graduates according to their four main options: leaving the educational system without acquiring additional credentials, attending a nontertiary vocational training (mainly

TABLE 10.1A
Row percentages for educational credential by cohorts for respondents with Abitur

	MEN				WOMEN			
	2c_gen	2c_voc	3a	3b	2c_gen	2c_voc	3a	3b
1910–27	10.7	29.3	21.7	38.2	28.8	24.3	13.5	33.3
1928–37	5.0	21.1	23.8	50.1	16.9	28.1	14.2	40.8
1938–47	5.5	16.2	20.6	57.7	10.6	21.5	14.3	53.4
1948–57	8.1	23.9	21.8	46.2	7.3	24.9	15.0	52.8
1958–72	10.1	28.2	22.7	39.0	13.7	39.5	14.2	32.7

NOTE: Men and women, 30 years or older, born after 1909; N_{men} = 4300 and N_{women} = 2808.

TABLE 10.1B
Row percentages for educational credential by class for respondents with Abitur

	MEN				WOMEN			
	2c_gen	2c_voc	3a	3b	2c_gen	2c_voc	3a	3b
I	8.9	14.0	15.9	61.2	14.1	22.5	11.8	51.6
II	7.4	19.8	20.8	52.0	16.3	24.5	13.6	45.6
IIIab	7.6	23.5	23.9	45.1	13.0	28.8	14.7	43.5
IVab	8.1	29.3	21.4	41.2	15.7	28.5	17.9	37.9
IVc	7.8	22.9	25.7	43.6	12.3	26.1	18.8	42.8
V–VIIab	7.4	32.9	27.2	32.6	12.8	37.9	15.7	33.7

NOTE: Men and women, 30 years or older, born after 1909; N_{men} = 4300 and N_{women} = 2808.

apprenticeships), or obtaining a degree at a *Fachhochschule* or university. Table 10.1a shows nonuniform developments across cohorts in the rates of reaching these outcomes. For men, the proportion of those who successfully went on to university rose from 38% in the oldest cohort (1910–27) to 58% in the middle cohort (1938–47), but then dropped in the youngest cohort to its initial level. The proportion of men who earned a lower tertiary degree remained more or less stable.[12] The share of *Abitur* holders without tertiary education, however, decreased until the middle cohort, then climbed back to the proportions of the first cohort. In the youngest cohort, about a quarter of *Abitur* graduates obtained some form of certified vocational training, and about 10% entered the labor market without additional credentials.[13] Women differ from men in obtaining fewer lower tertiary degrees, and women leave the education system more often than men without any post-*Abitur* qualifications.

Table 10.1b cross-tabulates the four educational outcomes by class of origin. The numbers reveal a clear pattern. While this bivariate table shows no substantial class differences for leaving the educational system without post-*Abitur* qualifications, the other three outcomes are markedly correlated with class of origin. Children from the upper service class obtain a university degree much more often than do working-class children. At the same time, many more working-class children than service-class children serve apprenticeships after the *Abitur*. Lower tertiary degrees are also more likely among the less advantaged classes.

Thus, Table 10.1b suggests an additional social selection process after students receive their *Abitur*. Formally, this is tested with a conditional multinomial logistic regression model in which the four different educational outcomes that *Abitur* graduates can achieve are regressed on the set of independent variables we used in the previous models. Postsecondary vocational training (CASMIN 2c_voc) is used as the base category in the outcome variable. For economy, all working classes (V-VIIab) are combined into one working-class category and only a cohort interaction term with this variable is included in the regression. More detailed class measures and cohort interactions did not improve the fit. The results for men and women are shown in Table 10.2.

The most marked impact of class on educational outcomes for men is found when contrasting the university degree outcome with vocational training. Compared to the upper service class, all other classes are relatively less likely to gain an academic degree. Children of the petite bourgeoisie and of working-class origin differ most from the upper service class. The interaction effects show that from the cohort of 1938–48 onward the relative risk of obtaining vocational training rather than academic education increases for the working classes (above and beyond an already strong and significant main effect). For lower tertiary degrees (*Fachhochschule*), class differences are less marked except for children of the self-employed, who attend vocational training rather than obtain a lower tertiary degree relatively more often than children from other class backgrounds. As indicated by the class by cohort interactions, working-class children in the three youngest cohorts also show a similar tendency.

Finally, in contrast to the upper service class, children of most other classes, especially those from small proprietor and of working-class families,[14] are more likely to obtain vocational training than no post-*Abitur* education. For working-class children, this tendency appears to become

TABLE 10.2
Multinomial logistic regression on educational degree of social origin and cohort, log odds-ratios (z-values)

	MEN						WOMEN					
Main effects	2c_gen vs. 2c_voc		3a vs. 2c_voc		3b vs. 2c_voc		2c_gen vs. 2c_voc		3a vs. 2c_voc		3b vs. 2c_voc	
Class: Upper service class (I)												
Lower service class (II)	−0.41	(−2.05)	−0.08	(−0.47)	−0.41	(−3.08)	0.13	(0.70)	0.12	(0.61)	−0.00	(−0.01)
Routine nonmanuals (IIIab)	−0.45	(−1.83)	−0.11	(−0.59)	−0.64	(−4.02)	−0.14	(−0.57)	0.04	(0.17)	−0.08	(−0.45)
Small proprietors (IVab)	−0.64	(−2.57)	−0.42	(−2.24)	−0.95	(−5.95)	−0.05	(−0.23)	0.20	(0.88)	−0.24	(−1.38)
Farmers (IVc)	−0.38	(−1.09)	0.03	(0.14)	−0.57	(−2.52)	−0.26	(−0.78)	0.33	(1.10)	0.01	(0.06)
Working classes (V–VIIab)	−0.60	(−1.62)	−0.04	(−0.13)	−0.91	(−3.61)	−0.34	(−1.69)	−0.20	(−1.00)	−0.59	(−3.92)
Father's education (lower than Abitur)												
Father's education (Abitur)	0.41	(2.26)	0.03	(0.23)	0.39	(3.22)	0.06	(0.34)	−0.03	(−0.18)	0.59	(4.76)
Missing variable	0.05	(0.11)	−0.05	(−0.14)	−0.17	(−0.61)	−0.35	(−0.96)	−1.71	(−2.79)	−0.85	(−2.67)
Cohorts: 1910–27												
Cohort 1928–37	−0.48	(−1.74)	0.35	(1.87)	0.61	(3.81)	−0.69	(−3.27)	−0.11	(−0.45)	0.05	(0.26)
Cohort 1938–47	0.15	(0.65)	0.62	(3.48)	1.22	(8.02)	−0.84	(−4.14)	0.20	(0.93)	0.61	(3.67)
Cohort 1948–57	0.09	(0.45)	0.40	(2.54)	0.64	(4.73)	−1.33	(−6.82)	0.12	(0.60)	0.62	(4.08)
Cohort 1958–72	0.17	(0.74)	0.25	(1.36)	0.34	(2.12)	−1.17	(−6.41)	−0.41	(−2.04)	−0.30	(−1.89)
Interaction effects with cohort												
V–VIIab × cohort 1928–1937	0.22	(0.40)	0.14	(0.39)	0.00	(0.01)						
V–VIIab × cohort 1938–1947	−0.78	(−1.49)	−0.26	(−0.81)	−0.71	(−2.30)						
V–VIIab × cohort 1948–1957	−0.20	(−0.49)	−0.51	(−1.74)	−0.36	(−1.31)						
V–VIIab × cohort 1958–1972	−0.30	(−0.68)	−0.47	(−1.44)	−0.60	(−1.91)						
Constant	−0.72	(−3.41)	−0.20	(−1.17)	0.68	(4.68)	0.22	(1.19)	−0.59	(−2.81)	0.21	(1.28)
	$L_0 = -5{,}284$; $L_1 = -5{,}085$						$L_0 = -3{,}575$; $L_1 = -3{,}416$					

NOTE: Men and women in West Germany, age 30 and older, born after 1909; $N_{men} = 4300$ and $N_{women} = 2808$. Reference categories listed in italics.

stronger in more recent cohorts. Father's education affects educational outcomes in similar ways. While it has no impact on the choice between a degree from a *Fachhochschule* or from nontertiary vocational training, sons of highly educated fathers differ in both other options from sons of less educated fathers: They are relatively more likely to either graduate from university or leave education without further credentials; sons from less educated backgrounds tend to pursue vocational training.

Women's postsecondary and tertiary education appears to vary more with cohort than with parental class or education. From cohort to cohort, more women obtain the *Abitur* and enter some form of postsecondary or tertiary education rather than discontinue education at the *Abitur* level.[15] While in earlier cohorts many more women than men stopped education and training at the level of the *Abitur*, this difference between men and women is disappearing in the youngest cohorts. For women, the pattern of post-*Abitur* educational participation and success also appears to be less class structured than for men. A systematic finding, however, is that working-class daughters pursue vocational training rather than any of the other alternatives relatively more often than service-class daughters. This result is obtained in analyses (not shown here) in which the combined service classes I and II are used as reference for the class contrasts. Women thus pursue and succeed in tertiary education less often than men, particularly among the older cohorts, but to a smaller extent also in recent times. Moreover, daughters of fathers with higher education tend to graduate more often from universities, an effect that appears to be stronger for daughters than for sons. For women, neither class nor educational background effects differ significantly between cohorts.

Class differences among respondents who do not acquire additional credentials beyond the *Abitur* are rather small. As far as they exist, it is children from highly educated families of the upper service class who are relatively more likely to enter the labor market without any postsecondary or tertiary credential. Our data do not distinguish between those who enter the labor market directly, without further studies following the *Abitur*, and those who drop out of one of the postsecondary or tertiary programs. However, all coefficients relating to the effects of parental education and parental class on this outcome are almost exactly the same as those of the university degree outcome. Therefore, we suspect that our findings result from an above average number of service-class children who enter the university but fail to conclude their studies or drop out when they find an attractive job. Such a course of action may be helped by the parents' social network or by extrafunctional abilities that individuals may have gained through high-class upbringing.

FACHHOCHSCHULE OR UNIVERSITY?

We have seen that given the *Abitur* most of the increase in educational inequality results from the fact that working-class children decide more often in favor of vocational training than of tertiary study. We now turn to the group with tertiary degrees and test for class differences in the choice between the two available options: *Fachhochschule* and university. We perform a simple logistic regression, using gender, class, father's education, and cohort as independent variables. Interaction effects of class, gender, and father's education with cohort turn out to be not significant, but we find a significant interaction effect for working class by gender. The results of the model are shown in Table 10.3. If the decision for tertiary studies is reached, which is less likely for women than for men, women have higher chances of earning a university degree than men. Upper service-class children are most likely to graduate from university, and chances decline sharply when moving down the class structure. For working-class sons, the odds of holding a university degree rather than one of the *Fachhochschule* are about 2.5 times lower than for sons with upper service-class background. But as indicated by the interaction term, the disadvantage appears somewhat smaller for working-class daughters than for working-class sons (although these results may in part be an artifact of the measurement strategy employed for this comparative project). Besides class, father's education also affects the type of degree earned. Children with highly educated fathers are more likely to graduate from university.

Therefore, gender and social origin affect both the choice between the two kinds of tertiary studies and their successful completion. While gender inequality can be attributed to different fields of study available at the *Fachhochschule* and the university, class differences are likely to be the result of the more practical orientation, lower risks, and shorter duration of the *Fachhochschule* programs. We were not able to test these arguments more carefully because information on fields of study is not available in the cur-

TABLE 10.3
Logistic regression on educational degree (university degree vs. lower tertiary degree) of gender, social origin, and cohort, log odds-ratios (z-values)

Main effects		
Men		
Women	0.27	(3.66)
Class: *Upper service class (I)*		
Lower service class (II)	−0.24	(−2.60)
Routine nonmanuals (IIIab)	−0.34	(−2.98)
Small proprietors (IVab)	−0.46	(−3.93)
Farmers (IVc)	−0.54	(−3.61)
Working class (V–VIIab)	−0.92	(−8.75)
Father's education *(lower than Abitur)*		
Father's education *(Abitur)*	0.50	(6.11)
Missing variable	0.03	(0.12)
Cohorts: *1910–27*		
Cohort 1928–37	0.26	(2.45)
Cohort 1938–47	0.43	(4.65)
Cohort 1948–57	0.63	(6.91)
Cohort 1958–72	0.42	(3.95)
Interaction effects with class		
V–VIIab × women	0.32	(2.13)
Constant	0.35	(3.39)
	$L_0 = -3{,}413$	
	$L_1 = -3{,}247$	

NOTE: Men and women in West Germany, age 30 and older, born after 1909; N = 5238. Reference categories listed in italics.

rent data set. From the fact that we find no significant cohort interactions with class or gender, we can conclude that the differences between universities and *Fachhochschule* in student selection (and self-selection) and in success patterns by class and gender have remained stable over time.

CONCLUSIONS

The present data confirm earlier findings that social inequalities in obtaining tertiary education diminish in the long term. The data also confirm that the decline is due mainly to reduced inequality in the early transitions in the tripartite German educational system, but that the decline has leveled off with the cohorts born in the 1960s. These cohorts faced the crucial educational decisions after the mid-1970s, when employment prospects of tertiary education leavers worsened for some years and received much attention in the public debate (although, in reality, tertiary education continued to be by far the best investment for advantageous career prospects).

When assessed for all members of a cohort, the decline of class inequalities in postsecondary and tertiary educational participation and attainment is substantial even if—as the new findings of the present analysis show—large social inequalities exist, persist, and, for men, have even increased in the post-*Abitur* educational transitions and outcomes. We think that the class differences in educational participation and outcomes at the postsecondary and tertiary stages observed in Germany can be best understood if the highly segmented institutional alternatives available in the German system of higher education are related to the relative costs and risks of the specific options and to the returns that can be expected from them. Balancing costs and gains, children of upper service-class origin (in contrast to those of all other class backgrounds) choose university studies most likely because these degrees are their best insurance for achieving a class position congruous with their family background and because they are better able to bear the costs and risks of academic study. In contrast, the availability of several less costly and less risky variants of nontertiary vocational education and training (attractive apprenticeships and others) cause working-class children to increasingly avoid the *Fachhochschule* and even more the university. The logic at the postsecondary and tertiary levels is similar to the logic at the secondary level. At the secondary level as well, the availability of a vocational alternative that is secure, inexpensive, and meets the labor market expectations of working classes, diverts children of these backgrounds from the more expensive, riskier, but in the end also more rewarding general courses of study.

One of the most revealing findings of the analysis concerns the likely interconnected decline of class inequalities in secondary education along the way to the *Abitur* and the growth of class inequalities in post-*Abitur* educational transitions and outcomes. The connection between the two processes is probably due to the fact that full general secondary education is no longer desired for the almost exclusive purpose of pursuing tertiary studies, but increasingly also to obtain access to promising segments of nontertiary vocational training, which require more and more general education. This upgrading of educational requirements does little to change intergenerational class reproduction. However, we also found that despite increasing class inequalities in post-*Abitur* educational transitions and outcomes, the reduction of inequalities in secondary education has led overall to greater social equality in tertiary education attainment. Consequently, as other analyses suggest (Müller and Pollak 2004), intergenerational fluidity in the German class structure has increased somewhat.

It would also be useful to understand the remaining gender inequalities in postsecondary and tertiary education. Among men and women who start and finish a tertiary course of study, women are more likely to study at the university than men. This is probably because the subjects offered at the *Fachhochschule* are heavily biased toward technology and engineering, which are generally preferred by men. Women are more likely to attend the university because it offers the subjects they prefer. At the same time, they also seem to be diverted more from tertiary education than men because they have options in nontertiary vocational education that are apparently more attractive to women, such as in nursing and high-level secretarial and assistance training programs. In the older cohorts, marriage and family was another option that possibly diverted many women from more ambitious educational aims. From a comparative perspective, one may ask why participation and success in tertiary education in Germany is so strongly class dependent, given that there is practically no study fees and that holders of *Abitur* have largely unlimited access to tertiary education (except for the *numerus clausus* in some disciplines). Based on the general line of arguments presented in this chapter, we would point to the highly segmented post-*Abitur* educational options offered as parallel alternatives rather than successive steps, which strongly differ in cost and probability of success. Because of their long duration, university studies involve high direct costs, even without study fees, and large amounts of foregone income. As the decisive exams in the German system are usually taken toward the end of a long course of study, the risk of failure and bad investment deters families whose resources are too limited for such "all or nothing" options. From this perspective, systems of tertiary education that are organized in cycles of successive steps may operate with less class-based social selectivity, as the effects of diversion are smaller and the investments at risk are divided into smaller successive portions.

CHAPTER ELEVEN

The Netherlands: Access to Higher Education—Institutional Arrangements and Inequality of Opportunity

Susanne Rijken

Ineke Maas, Department of Sociology/ICS

Harry B. G. Ganzeboom, Department of Social Research Methodology, Amsterdam Free University

INTRODUCTION

In the present study we examine inequality in access to postsecondary education in the Netherlands in a historical perspective. Three types of postsecondary education are distinguished:

- universities (WO)
- higher vocational colleges (HBO)
- senior vocational education (MBO)

Universities and higher vocational colleges constitute the tertiary level proper. Senior vocational education is not part of the system of higher education proper but, because students cannot enroll after primary school, it is regarded as postsecondary. Despite opportunities to transfer among these three types of institutions, all three levels are conceived as offering final qualifications, and in recent cohorts over 70% of all students left the education system with a qualification awarded at one of these three levels (Netherlands Ministry of Education, Culture and Science 2003).

The Dutch education system is two-tiered (in the German style), with a sharp separation between vocational and academic programs. Previous research has shown that inequality of educational opportunities has decreased substantially over the period covered by cohorts born between 1920 and 1970. Most of this change took place in early school transitions, between primary and secondary education, and within the secondary level, while inequality in access at the postsecondary levels remained stable.

In this study we ask (1) whether inequality at the higher levels of education has remained stable for more recent cohorts as well, and (2) whether and how the differentiation between vocational and academic tracks has contributed to the persistence of educational inequality. We answer these questions using a multiple-panel database. We study upward and downward transitions in postsecondary educational careers for students born between 1965 and 1981, who were monitored between 1977 and 1993 in secondary and tertiary education.

INSTITUTIONAL ARRANGEMENTS

Type and Number of Institutions and Number of Students in Dutch Postsecondary Education

In 1960, university-level training (WO) in the Netherlands was provided by eleven universities, including eight general and three technical universities. In addition, there was one private university specializing in management courses and several religious seminaries. Since then, three additional universities have been added, of which one offers only distance learning by correspondence.

Completion of any university education has led to the *Drs.* (*doctorandus*) degree, which is comparable to an MA in the United States. In 1982, the two-phase structure of academic education was introduced. The first phase consists of undergraduate university training, the second phase consists of postgraduate training leading to the PhD degree (Van den Berg 2000). Since then, undergraduate training has been generally reduced from five- to four-year programs. In 2002 the bachelor–master system was introduced, replacing the first phase of university education. Students receive a bachelor's degree after three years and a master's degree by attending one or two additional years.

University enrollment, as a percentage of the students' age group, increased substantially in the first three decades after 1960 (Figure 11.1). Around 1960, only 4% of the population between 19 and 24 years of age were university students. Forty years later it was 15%.

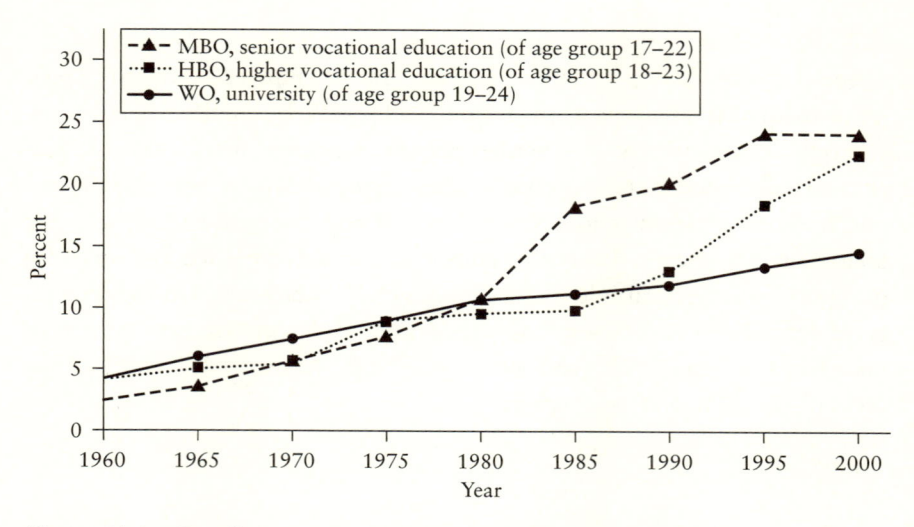

Figure 11.1. Enrollment as Percentage of Age Group, 1960–2000
NOTE: Full-time enrollment in universities (WO), higher vocational education (HBO), and senior vocational education (MBO) as percentage of significant age group.
SOURCE: Statline CBS (2003 update).

Higher vocational colleges (HBO) were granted formal status as a final and tertiary level of vocational education in the Act on Secondary Education of 1967 (PIVOT Rijksarchiefdienst 1999). At that time, about 350 HBOs offered programs of variable length of up to 4 years. In 1984, the Act on Higher Vocational Education (WHBO) further codified a binary system of higher education consisting of HBOs and universities (PIVOT Rijksarchiefdienst 1999). One of the consequences of the new legislation was the merging of small HBO institutions into larger colleges. In 1984 there were approximately 350 HBOs; in 1986 their number was reduced to between 80 and 90; and in 2000 about 55 were left (Brave et al. 1993; Knippenberg and Van Der Ham 1994; Van den Berg 2000). Initially, enrollment in HBOs showed the same growth as in universities. After 1985, when university enrollment started to stabilize, the percentage of the population attending vocational colleges continued to grow even faster than before. HBOs offer a wide range of programs, many of which in other countries are offered by universities, such as journalism, teacher training (both for primary and secondary education), and management programs.

The third type of postsecondary training is provided by the institutions for senior vocational education (MBO), which offer one- to four-year vocational training programs. Most of these are vocation specific and may include a significant portion of in-firm training. Major programs train clerical workers, mechanics, salespersons, and assistant nurses. More than 500 MBOs existed at the beginning of the 1960s. By 1998, there were about 65 public and 70 private institutions left (Netherlands Sociaal en Cultureel Planbureau 1998; PIVOT Rijksarchiefdienst 1999; Netherlands Inspectie van het Onderwijs 2000). After 1994, most public MBOs were forced to merge into regional centers of vocational education (ROCs), in which a broad range of schooling was available. Nowadays an average MBO is as large as an average university.

Between 1960 and 1980, the numbers of students in universities, HBOs, and MBOs were similar and showed similar growth rates. However, between 1980 and 1990 the percentage attending MBOs doubled relative to the other two, and stabilized thereafter.

RESPONSIBILITIES

Half the MBOs are fully financed by the government, as are all universities and about 90% of all HBOs (Netherlands Inspectie van het Onderwijs 2000; Netherlands Sociaal en Cultureel Planbureau 2000). Although the government plays an important role in shaping all education, a trend toward increased autonomy of the institutions of postsecondary education can be discerned since 1960. The Act on Academic Education of 1960 permitted universities to experiment with new programs. From 1989 onward, universities were allowed to start new study programs without government permission. Visitation commissions were created by the National Council of Universities (VSNU) to uphold the quality of higher education. The Act on Higher Education and Scientific Research of 1993 further increased the autonomy of institutions of higher education and allowed more freedom in setting their own policies, including the content though not the length of academic programs (Van Kemenade 1981; Knippenberg and Van Der Ham 1994; PIVOT Rijksarchiefdienst 1999).

HBOs became formally part of higher education in 1986 by the Act on Higher Vocational Education of 1984 (Wieringen 1995). From this date onward, all institutions of higher education were required to have at least 600 students, one board, one management team, and one participation council (PIVOT Rijksarchiefdienst 1999).

The Act on Vocational Dual Training of 1966 formalized the organization of MBOs (Van Kemenade 1981; Van den Berg 2000). Before that date, vocational education had been mainly the responsibility of business and industry. The establishment of ROCs in 1994 to host vocational programs brought more autonomy to vocational schools. However, the contents of vocational programs and the vocational examinations have often been determined or controlled by separate industrial organizations (Van den Berg 2000). Although universities, HBOs, and MBOs are to a large extent responsible for the content of the programs and courses they offer, major characteristics of the tertiary education system that may affect educational inequality are directly regulated by law.

ADMISSION RULES

The Dutch education system is separated into a vocational track and an academic track beginning at junior secondary schooling and through the highest level of education (Figure 11.2). Full-time education is compulsory until the student reaches the age of 17. Primary school (LO) is generally completed at age 12, then the first phase of specialization (vocational versus academic) and selection (lower versus higher level) takes place. At this age, students choose between four main tracks: junior vocational (VBO), junior academic (MAVO),[1] senior academic (HAVO), and preuniversity (Athenaeum-gymnasium/VWO).

Completion of VBO or MAVO is a prerequisite for entering a two- to four-year MBO. Three years of attending HAVO, which normally takes five years to complete, also provides access to the MBO. In 1997, a one-year MBO course was introduced that does not require VBO or MAVO completion for entry.

Until the beginning of the 1970s, several types of HBOs existed with different entrance requirements (Netherlands Ministry of Education and Science 1989). Thereafter, at least a senior academic diploma or completion of the four-year MBO was required to enter HBO. These requirements coincided with the standardization of HBO into a four-year program.

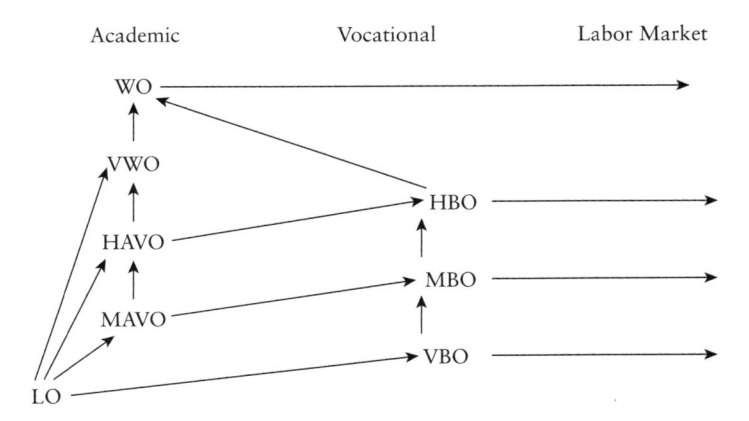

Figure 11.2. Main Flows in the Dutch Educational System

To enter university, one needs to have successfully completed preuniversity education (VWO) or at least one year of HBO, no entrance examination is needed. After 1972, the Minister of Education restricted the number of students in certain university programs (e.g., for dentistry or medicine), depending on demands of the labor market (Van Kemenade 1981). To some degree, the grades achieved in preuniversity education determine the students' chances of being admitted to these programs, but random selection has been the primary device for determining admission.

As of 1979, it has become possible to transfer to university programs after one year of HBO and to enter university in the third year with a completed HBO degree (PIVOT Rijksarchiefdienst 1999). In general, admission restrictions for postsecondary education have weakened somewhat over time.

THE SYSTEM OF SCHOLARSHIPS AND FEES

Until 1986, scholarships were a combination of study allowance, awarded mainly for HBO and university; compensation for educational costs, mainly for MBO; tax deductions; and child welfare benefits. All parents with children aged 16 to 26 attending an educational institution full time received child welfare benefits that were not means-tested. However, the parents were expected to make a substantial financial contribution to the cost of living and education of the child. The amount of child welfare benefits depended on the amount of other allowances. Children living at home received smaller benefits than children living apart from their parents. In 1983, child welfare benefits were made dependent on the child's age and the size of the family.

Compensation of educational costs was initially targeted at younger children at the secondary level of education and at the MBO level. This compensation was a gift. From age 18 onward, the compensation was paid directly to the child. In 1983, the compensation was restricted to students under the age of 21, after which students could apply for a study allowance.

Study allowances consisted of a basic amount which was a gift, and a remainder, in the form of a scholarship in combination with an interest-free loan. The basic amount differed between HBO and university students in favor of the first. The size of the remaining part depended heavily on parental income (Brave et al. 1993). In 1974, the limits on parental income were reduced, which led to an increase in the number of students receiving scholarships (PIVOT Rijksarchiefdienst 1995).

In 1986, a completely new system of scholarships was introduced, targeted at all full-time students aged 18 to 30 and covering MBO, HBO, and university studies. The study allowance consisted again of two parts: a gift, unrelated to parental income; and a loan or a complementary scholarship, dependent upon parental income. All in all, the 1986 reform made the scholarship system more comprehensive, which may have provided special encouragement for children from the lower classes to enter higher education.

In 1988, the Act on Harmonization of College Fees was implemented. This law gave every Dutch citizen the right to enroll in higher education institutions for reduced fees for a period of six years. To facilitate the transition from HBO to university, HBO graduates received two additional years of university studies at reduced fees.

Because enrollment rates increased substantially, the size of the basic scholarships was reduced in 1990. In 1991, the number of years of study financed by the scholarship system was reduced from six to five, one year above the length of study. After five years of scholarships, students could receive a loan for a maximum of two years. In 1992, the age to which students could claim a scholarship was reduced to 27 (Brave et al. 1993). In 1993, the study allowance became dependent upon rate of progress.

University fees were not raised for many years after 1954, although government expenditures per student increased by a factor of 10 between

1954 and 1974. In 1971, university fees were raised fivefold, from 200 to 1,000 guilders (454 euros or approximately US$300), and registration costs were also drastically increased. This caused a massive student uprising, and costs were eventually lowered to about 500 guilders per year. However, since 1980 costs have gradually risen to almost 3,000 guilders (1,330 euros) per year in 2000 (Van den Broek and Voeten 2002). HBO fees were raised substantially in 1981 as a consequence of the Act on Fees of Vocational College. The direct costs of MBO vary, but they are generally much lower than those of HBO and universities.

In sum, the direct costs of higher education in the Netherlands have been comparatively low but have increased substantially over time. The complicated scholarship system became more comprehensive in 1986, and in 1991 it became more restricted with respect to duration, amount, and coverage.

EXPECTATIONS

Previous research on inequality in access to education in the Netherlands used a design that merged cross-sectional surveys and compared birth cohorts over a long period. Somewhat at odds with the tracked nature of the Dutch education system, education was conceptualized as a single hierarchy and educational attainment measured by level of education. This research reported an impressive decline of inequality of educational opportunity (De Graaf and Ganzeboom 1993). When the data are conceptualized as a set of sequentially ordered transitions and analyzed using a conditional design, the picture becomes more complicated. The major changes appear to have occurred at the transition to secondary education, at age 12, when the crucial decision in the educational career is taken (De Graaf and Ganzeboom 1993; Rijken 1999). There was a more or less continuous trend toward more equality at this transition. However, trends for later transitions are less pronounced. At the entrance to the tertiary level, no trend toward greater equality could be discerned.

Figure 11.3 replicates some of these findings, using an extended database that covers birth cohorts born between 1920 and 1975 constructed by Ganzeboom and Luijkx (2004). It shows the association[2] between completion of tertiary education (HBO and WO) and father's occupational status relative to all other educational categories (unconditional) and rela-

274 Rijken, Maas, and Ganzeboom

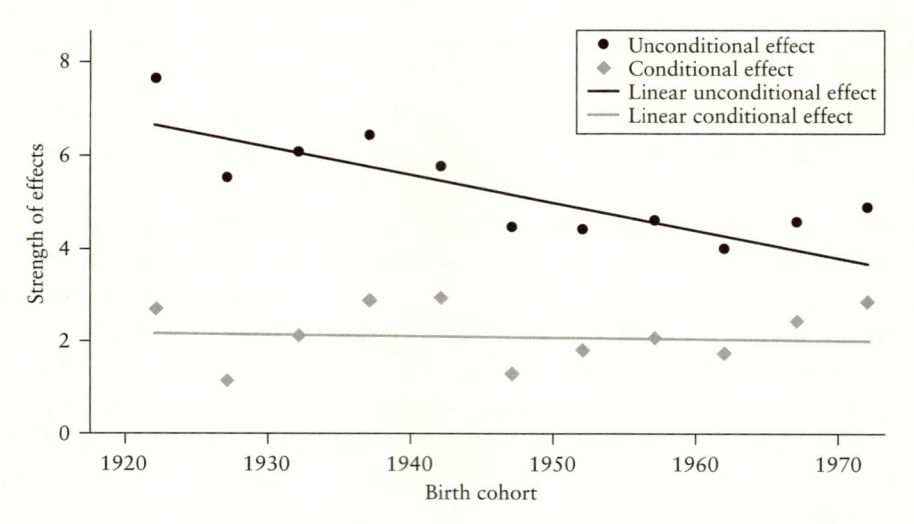

Figure 11.3. Historical Trend in Access to Tertiary Education for Birth Cohorts 1920–1970

SOURCE: International Stratification and Mobility File, the Netherlands (35 data files).

tive to all who have completed at least senior secondary level (MBO, HAVO, and VWO) (conditional). The unconditional association shows a strong trend toward less inequality. However, the association in the group that qualifies to enter tertiary education is decidedly lower but still significantly different from 0, and shows no trend at all. The figure is for illustrative purposes only; the pattern holds true irrespective of what social background indicators are used.

Mare (1981) points at the combined effect of selection and expansion to account for these patterns. Because of educational selection, groups of students become more homogeneous later in the educational career with respect to resources that lead to educational success; these resources can be observed (parental background) and unobserved (academic ability, motivation). Observed family background effects tend to be smaller at higher transitions than at earlier transitions because unmeasured determinants of educational success (i.e., ability, motivation) become negatively correlated with measured family background (Cameron and Heckman 1998). When the education system expands, however, the risk group broadens and the association between measured and unmeasured success factors is restored to the full sample level, and inequalities in educational outcomes that used to operate at the early stages of educational careers are now transferred to higher levels. The implication of this argument is that historical changes toward lesser association, if they occur in the early transitions, are preserved in the unconditional results but may lead to misattributions in the conditional analysis. Conditional analysis that shows no trend may still hide trends toward lesser association that are compensated by the offsetting effects of decreased selectivity (Rijken 1999).

Such an explanation, however, is only partially applicable to the differentiated education system of the Netherlands. Educational expansion in this system means that after leaving primary education more students opt for higher levels of secondary education. As a result, the population eligible for MBO, coming from lower levels of secondary education, may become more negatively selected with respect to ability instead of less positively selected. If so, we expect inequality at this transition to be large in older cohorts and to decrease over time. Mare's explanation should apply only to the population eligible for university. Because ever more students enter preuniversity education, selectivity decreases. As a consequence, we expect inequality to be small in older cohorts and to increase over time. The population eligible for HBO (having completed HAVO or MBO) can be characterized as in between that of the two other types of postsecondary education with respect to selection on variation in ability. It is unclear whether this group at the doorstep of HBO has become more or less selected over time, and therefore we cannot use Mare's theory to predict changes in inequality with respect to them.

Historical changes in access to education may have occurred for institutional reasons as well. Although some of the institutional changes described previously can be expected to have increased inequality, most institutional changes work to decrease inequality of educational opportunities. Possibilities to switch back and forth between vocational and academic institutions have increased. Entering MBO has become easier with the introduction of the short-MBO. The length of university studies has become shorter over the years, making university more attractive to lower-class students. Finally, the scholarship system has been improved over most of the period studied, at least until 1991. All of this should lead to decreasing inequality at transitions to university, HBO, and MBO.

The selection argument described may also apply when differences in educational outcomes between men and women are investigated. In the early days, women were not supposed to have employment aspirations and therefore did not need a proper education. Only the most ambitious and promising women gained access to higher levels of secondary education. At the gates to tertiary education, these women competed with the far less strongly selected group of men. As a consequence, the gender effect should appear to be rather small. Owing to the process of emancipation at the individual and societal level, attitudes toward women's education and labor force participation have changed. More women today aspire to an educational career, and educational expansion in general has led to a higher proportion of women eligible for higher education. Following the selection argument, we expect men and women eligible for higher transitions to have become more equal in their ability to make these transitions. If an unchanged process of gender discrimination were at work, it would become more pronounced at the observed level. However, at the same time the process of emancipation is expected to have caused a decrease in the unequal treatment of men and women. Which trend prevails for the transition to different levels of higher education is an empirical question.

Hypotheses
1. Inequality of educational opportunities at the transition to MBO has decreased because of increasing (negative) selection and favorable institutional changes.
2. Inequality of educational opportunities at the transition to HBO has decreased somewhat because of favorable institutional changes (and no clear trend with respect to selectivity).
3. The change in inequality of educational opportunities at the transition to university is undetermined because of the opposite effects of decreasing selection and favorable structural changes.

The student populations of MBO and of HBO, however, do not consist entirely of students who have followed the shortest route. At the MBO, there are many students who tried HBO first or who attended a level of academic secondary education that would allow them to attend HBO. HBOs, in turn, enroll many students who attended preuniversity secondary education or who tried university first. These pathways can be interpreted as downward mobility and are populated by different risk groups from those that comprise the students entering from below.

Our hypothesis is that the opportunity of entering a certain educational level from above is also unequally distributed among students of various social backgrounds. Students from higher social backgrounds are less likely to leave a higher level and enter a lower level than students from a lower social background. These effects are also likely to be conditional on the process of selection that formed the risk population. The more selected this group is, the better the unmeasured ability of those from lower social backgrounds and the less likely it is that they would fail. All student populations that allow entrance from "above" into MBO and HBO have become less positively selected over time. We therefore expect the inequality of these downward educational moves to have increased. The corresponding hypothesis is:

1. Inequality of educational opportunities at the downward transition to MBO and HBO has increased because of decreased selectivity of the risk populations.

DATA AND VARIABLES

Data

We analyzed four harmonized sets of student panel data: the School Career and Background of Pupils in Secondary Education studies (SMVO) (Netherlands Statistics 1976, 1982) and the Cohort of Students in Secondary Education studies (VOCL) (Netherlands Statistics 1989, 1993). Each of these four studies monitors annually a cohort of students from their first year of secondary education (generally age 12; the SMVO cohorts started their secondary education in 1977 (instead of 1976) and 1982, VOCL in 1989 and 1993). For all students, annual information is available on the progress of their educational career (or on the lack thereof) for 13 and 16 years (for SMVO secondary school cohorts 1977 and 1982) and for 12 and 8 years (for VOCL secondary school cohorts 1989 and 1993). This means that attendance of higher education can be analyzed but its completion cannot. Note that the time frame of these data differs from that covered by the cohorts in the cross-sectional data reported in Figure 11.3.

Dependent Variables: Upward and Downward Transitions into Postsecondary Education

Using career data, we were able to analyze real transitions in the educational careers of student cohorts starting secondary education in 1977,

1982, 1989, and 1993, allowing us to study all student tracks of the Dutch education system. There are five dependent variables in the analysis: entrance into university, HBO, and MBO *from below;* entrance into HBO and MBO *from above.* The corresponding risk populations are defined as follows.

- *Entering university:* eligible are students who attended HBO or the preceding academic level.
- *Entering HBO from below:* eligible are those who completed the preceding vocational level or the preceding general academic level. Those who moved from HAVO to preuniversity education (VWO) are excluded.
- *Entering MBO from below:* eligible are those who completed the preceding vocational level or the preceding academic level of education. Those who finish MAVO and enter the next level of academic education (HAVO) are excluded from the analyses.
- *Entering HBO from above:* eligible are students who started university or a higher academic level than required (VWO).
- *Entering MBO from above:* eligible are those attending HBO or a higher academic level than required (HAVO).

Our units of analysis are the transitions for which respondents are eligible. A respondent usually appears at more than one transition, but it hardly ever happens that a student appears at the same transition more than once. Table 11.1 presents all transitions from one educational level to the next for all respondents, starting with the transition from the primary (LO) to the secondary level. The outflow percentages show that junior academic education (MAVO) and junior vocational education (VBO) are the most common types of secondary education, with 32% and 38% of all children in our study entering these schools after primary education. MBO, HBO, and universities (WO) are tertiary education: children leaving primary education cannot enter these schools without going through secondary education. Not all Dutch students have completed a postsecondary degree; some 50% (1 + 26 + 10 + 9 + 5) of all cohorts left the school system with another degree. In particular, many students from the VBO (60%) enter the labor market instead of acquiring further education. The inflow percentages illustrate the eligible populations described above. Of all transitions to MBO, 36% came from VBO, 50% from MAVO, 12% from HAVO, and 1% from VWO (the last two being downwardly mobile). Of all transitions to HBO, 46% started in HAVO, 27% in MBO, 23% in VWO, and 3% in WO (the

TABLE 11.1
Overview of all educational transitions: Outflow and inflow percentages

From	Left	VBO	MAVO	HAVO	VWO	MBO	HBO	WO	Total
Outflow									
LO	1	32	38	13	16	0	0	0	100
VBO	60		3	0	0	37	0	0	100
MAVO	21	14		18	1	47	0	0	100
HAVO	31	1	8		13	19	29	0	100
VWO	23	0	1	19		2	19	36	100
MBO	86	0	0	1	0		13	0	100
HBO	86	0	0	0	0	5		9	100
WO	87	0	0	0	0	0	13		100
Inflow									
LO	1	84	92	54	82	0	0	0	
VBO	26		3	0	0	36	0	0	
MAVO	10	15		30	1	50	0	0	
HAVO	9	0	5		16	12	46	0	
VWO	5	0	1	15		1	23	87	
MBO	34	0	0	1	0		27	0	
HBO	11	0	0	0	0	0	3	12	
WO	4	0	0	0	0	0	3		
Total	100	100	100	100	100	100	100	100	
N	82,244	35,243	38,651	23,394	18,353	36,125	14,865	7,636	256,511

last two again being downwardly mobile). Finally, 87% of all transitions to university started in VWO and 12% in HBO.

Independent Variables

We used the occupational codes of the parents in each panel to best approximate the EGP classification (Ganzeboom and Treiman 2003). However, in one of the data files a general social background indicator was used instead of detailed occupation codes for each parent. To facilitate the comparison of cohorts, the occupational information of both parents was combined for all studies. We approximated the EGP classification using five occupational categories: laborer, self-employed, lower employee, middle employee, and higher employee. The educational attainment of each parent is measured in five categories. This classification does not fully reflect the two tracks in the Dutch education system, but the data on parental education do not allow a more refined classification. The five levels we distinguished are primary education, lower secondary education (VBO and MAVO), higher secondary education (VWO and MBO), higher vocational college (HBO), and university (WO). Data on parental education are considerably more complete than data on parental occupation. The educational distributions of the parents of the different cohorts reflect expansion: The share of parents with only primary or lower secondary education decreased over the cohorts from 29% to 15% and from 30% to 15%, while the share of parents with higher secondary education and HBO increased from 27.5% to 45% and from 9% to 17%, respectively, and those with university education increased from 4.5% to 7.4%.

We used a dummy variable to indicate at each transition whether the previous level of education was an academic or vocational school. We also included a dummy variable for gender. Changes over time are indicated by cohort. Main cohort effects were initially measured with three dummy variables, but fit statistics from preliminary models (available upon request) supported the use of a continuous cohort indicator, which we specified as decades since 1977, ranging from 0.0 (1977) to 1.6 (1993). The continuous indicator was also used to assess cohort interaction effects.

RESULTS

Entering Tertiary Education: The Common Way

Table 11.2 presents analyses of the most common flows in the Dutch education system, moving from the lower levels of education, through either the vocational or the academic route, into one of the three postsecondary levels. Using logistic regressions, we modeled the log-odds of entering a specific level given attendance (not necessarily completion) of the preceding vocational or general level. For each of the three transitions, we estimated a basic model and a model including trends over time in the social background effects.

Access to MBO

The first two models in Table 11.2 refer to the transition to MBO. The basic model shows that the likelihood of entering MBO through the academic route is greater than the likelihood of entering through the vocational education route. There may be two reasons for this. First, the preceding vocational level gives better access to the labor market because it teaches mainly basic vocational skills. Second, the choice between vocational and academic education immediately after primary education is governed to a great extent by student capabilities and interests. It may appear that lower academic education and lower vocational education are similar in level and differ only in track, but the relatively more capable students enter the academic track.

The likelihood of entering MBO has increased between the cohorts of 1977 and 1982, and women are more likely to enter MBO than men.

Children of manual workers enter MBO less often than children from all other families. A similar divide exists between children of parents with only primary education and those whose parents have higher education. The children of parents with vocational education are most likely to enter MBO, relative to leaving the education system. By contrast, children of university graduates avoid this alternative. This may be due to selection: there are only a few parents with a university degree in the data and even fewer with children in this risk set. In general, children from the lowest social categories are less likely to enter this level than other children in the eligible group.

In the second model, trends are reported over time with respect to MBO access for all occupational and educational background categories. The extended model shows a few significant trends. The likelihood of boys from laborer families with low parental education entering this level has clearly increased, especially between the 1977 and 1982 cohorts (main cohort effect), but girls did much better. The log-odds of girls entering MBO increased with an additional 0.28 per decade. Because in the 1977 cohort the likelihood for girls was already larger than for boys, gender-based inequality of educational opportunities increased.

Over time, the children of higher employees are the only ones who became significantly more likely to enter MBO relative to the children of laborers. All other groups increased their participation similarly to the children of laborers. By contrast, with respect to parental education, negative trend coefficients appear across the spectrum, implying decreased disparities between children of higher- and lower-educated parents.

We conclude that inequality of educational opportunities decreased somewhat at MBO entry level, although this does not apply to the difference between the children of laborers and those of higher employees, and to the difference between boys and girls.

TABLE 11.2
The log-odds of entering a specific level given attendance (not necessarily completion) of the preceding vocational or general level

	SENIOR VOCATIONAL EDUCATION		HIGHER VOCATIONAL COLLEGE		UNIVERSITY	
	MBO		HBO		WO	
Attended						
Lower sec. vocational (VBO)	0					
Lower sec. academic (MAVO)	0.74	(0.02)**	0			
Sen. vocational (MBO)			0.74	(0.02)**		
Middle sec. academic (HAVO)			1.35	(0.03)**	0	
Higher vocational college (HBO)					1.37	(0.03)**
Higher sec. academic (VWO)					1.76	(0.04)**
					0	
					1.77	(0.04)**
Cohort 1977	0		0		0	
Cohort 1982	0.73	(0.02)**	0.50	(0.03)**	0.51	(0.04)**	0.47	(0.06)**
Cohort 1989	0.74	(0.02)**	0.63	(0.03)**	0.22	(0.04)**	0.11	(0.13)
Cohort 1993	0.65	(0.02)**	0.59	(0.04)**	0.21	(0.04)**	0.08	(0.17)
Male	0		0		0	
Female	0.29	(0.02)**	−0.25	(0.02)**	−0.48	(0.03)**	−0.60	(0.04)**
Laborer	0		0		0	
Self-employed	0.30	(0.03)**	0.17	(0.04)**	0.08	(0.06)	0.01	(0.08)
Lower employee	0.23	(0.03)**	0.24	(0.04)**	0.13	(0.06)*	0.07	(0.08)
Medium employee	0.26	(0.03)**	0.24	(0.04)**	0.16	(0.05)**	0.12	(0.07)
Higher employee	0.26	(0.04)**	0.36	(0.04)**	0.18	(0.05)**	0.16	(0.07)*
Primary education parents	0		0		0	

Lower secondary parents	0.42	(0.02)**	0.47	(0.03)**	0.27	(0.04)**	0.24	(0.06)**	−0.07	(0.06)	−0.10	(0.08)
Higher secondary parents	0.59	(0.02)**	0.65	(0.04)**	0.46	(0.04)**	0.42	(0.06)**	0.09	(0.06)	0.14	(0.08)
Vocational college parents	0.77	(0.04)**	0.79	(0.06)**	0.76	(0.05)**	0.72	(0.08)**	0.42	(0.07)**	0.51	(0.09)**
University parents	0.53	(0.07)**	0.64	(0.11)**	0.62	(0.07)**	0.66	(0.10)**	0.64	(0.07)**	0.64	(0.10)**
Cohort × Male			0				0				0	
Cohort × Female			0.28	(0.03)**			0.56	(0.04)**			0.20	(0.05)**
Cohort × Laborer			0				0				0	
Cohort × Self-employed			−0.03	(0.04)			−0.03	(0.06)			0.12	(0.09)
Cohort × Lower employee			0.02	(0.05)			−0.07	(0.06)			0.11	(0.09)
Cohort × Medium employee			0.00	(0.04)			0.10	(0.06)			0.07	(0.08)
Cohort × Higher employee			0.14	(0.06)*			0.03	(0.07)			0.04	(0.08)
Cohort × Primary educ. parents			0				0				0	
Cohort × Lower sec. parents			−0.09	(0.04)*			0.05	(0.07)			0.07	(0.12)
Cohort × Higher sec. parents			−0.10	(0.04)**			0.07	(0.07)			−0.09	(0.11)
Cohort × Voc. college parents			−0.03	(0.06)			0.09	(0.08)			−0.14	(0.12)
Cohort × University parents			−0.15	(0.11)			−0.02	(0.11)			0.01	(0.13)
Intercept	−1.52	(0.02)**	−1.46	(0.03)**	−2.68	(0.04)**	−2.46	(0.05)**	−2.62	(0.07)**	−2.57	(0.08)**
Chi-square	6,192.71		6,324.40		5,263.72		5,489.82		3,787.93		3,815.12	
df	13		22		13		22		13		22	
N	61,128		6,1128		4,7736		4,7736		2,7736		2,7736	

NOTE: Inequality in probability of entering senior vocational education, higher vocational college, and university given earlier attendance of logically preceding vocational or academic education, basic model, and trends over time (B-values from logistic regressions; S.E. in parentheses). Cohort = year of entering secondary education, measured in decades since 1977 (range between 0 and 1.6).

*$p < 0.05$; **$p < 0.01$.

Access to HBO

The baseline model estimating the structure of inequality in the likelihood of entering HBO versus leaving school—conditional upon being in the risk set—shows (Table 11.2) about the same pattern as the model for access to MBO: increased participation between the first and the second cohort and much larger admission from the academic education track than from a senior vocational track. One interpretation of this effect is that completing senior vocational education provides better access to the labor market than completing a general level. Moreover, senior vocational education consists of different levels of which only the highest level gives access to the HBO. Unfortunately, the data do not allow us to differentiate between these levels. There is a marked inequality both by parental education and occupation. In clear contradiction with the model for entering MBO, women are much less likely to enter HBO than men.

Trends estimated for separate social background categories and gender again show that over time women have caught up with men in the likelihood of entering HBO. Gender inequality has completely disappeared with respect to this transition. In the cohort that started secondary education in 1993, women are even more successful than men in entering HBO. There is no apparent decrease over time in inequality based on the family's occupational status or parental education.

Overall, inequality in access to HBO for eligible candidates is mainly stable with respect to parental background. By contrast, the disadvantage of women has decreased substantially.

Access to University

The last two columns in Table 11.2 refer to inequality in access to university education, the highest and most demanding level of postsecondary training. The baseline model deviates from the models for access to HBO and MBO in that the inequality of educational success between the parental occupational categories appears to be much smaller. However, children from the highest parental educational categories have much greater opportunities for entering university than children from the lower educational categories. Nevertheless, the socioeconomic inequalities in entering university for the eligible candidates are slightly smaller than for MBO or HBO. This is not true for gender effects. Overall, men are much more likely to enter university than women, and arriving at the university by the academic education route offers better opportunities than arriving by the vocational track. The only significant trend is again the strong increase in the opportunities of women, but, in the 1993 cohort, women are still less likely than men to enter university.

(RE)ENTERING TERTIARY EDUCATION: THE DOWNWARD PATH

We distinguish two ways of downward mobility in the Dutch education system. First, students can decide to enter tertiary education at a lower level than the one to which their preceding educational qualifications were leading. Second, students can fail tertiary education at a higher level and decide to re-enter education at a lower level. We analyzed entering from above separately for two levels of higher education: MBO and HBO.

Table 11.3 shows the inequality of the risk to enter MBO on a downward path by either a secondary route (HAVO) or a higher vocational route. We do not show over-time models for these routes because analyses of fit statistics indicate that inequality did not change over time. Women have lower chances than men for downward mobility from HAVO to MBO, as do students from higher employee families and students with academically educated parents. Students whose parents completed lower secondary education are significantly more likely to be downwardly mobile than students whose parents finished only primary education (of which there are not many at this level).

The next model in Table 11.3 estimates the risk of downward mobility into MBO for students who already attended a higher level of tertiary education. There seems to be no social inequality at all in this type of educational mobility. Women appear to be less likely than men to fail at the HBO and then move down to MBO (recall that women were also more likely to enter these schools from below). It appears that with respect to downward mobility into MBO, most inequality occurs among those who come from a relatively high secondary education. In practice, this means that students making such a transition are in the education system one year longer than their counterparts who enter MBO the regular way.

Models 3 and 4 in Table 11.3 present analyses similar to those in models 1 and 2. Here inequality appears as the chance to enter HBO on a

TABLE 11.3
Inequality in probability to downwardly enter senior vocational education and higher vocational college

	SENIOR VOCATIONAL EDUCATION (MBO)			HIGHER VOCATIONAL COLLEGE (HBO)	
	Attended HAVO	Attended MBO	Attended HBO	Attended VWO	Attended WO
Cohort 1977	0	0		0	0
Cohort 1982	0.27 (0.05)**	−0.51	(0.13)**	−0.04 (0.05)	−0.06 (0.12)
Cohort 1989	0.32 (0.05)**	−0.24	(0.12)	0.16 (0.05)**	0.72 (0.14)**
Cohort 1993	0.01 (0.05)	1.11	(0.18)**	−0.16 (0.06)**	2.01 (0.25)**
Male	0	0		0	0
Female	−0.19 (0.04)**	−0.54	(0.10)**	0.09 (0.04)*	−0.33 (0.10)**
Laborer	0	0		0	0
Self-employed	−0.03 (0.06)	−0.13	(0.16)	0.12 (0.07)	0.02 (0.19)
Lower employee	−0.11 (0.06)	−0.09	(0.16)	−0.00 (0.07)	−0.24 (0.19)
Middle employee	−0.06 (0.05)	−0.18	(0.14)	0.05 (0.06)	−0.21 (0.15)
Higher employee	−0.18 (0.06)**	−0.34	(0.17)	−0.06 (0.07)	−0.30 (0.17)
Primary education parents	0	0		0	0
Lower secondary parents	0.17 (0.06)**	−0.01	(0.17)	0.28 (0.08)**	0.48 (0.23)*
Higher secondary parents	0.11 (0.06)	−0.02	(0.17)	0.11 (0.08)	0.47 (0.22)*
Vocational college parents	−0.13 (0.07)	0.05	(0.20)	0.07 (0.09)	0.42 (0.24)
University parents	−0.37 (0.10)**	−0.23	(0.28)	−0.63 (0.10)**	−0.01 (0.27)
Intercept	−1.46 (0.06)**	−2.56	(0.15)**	−2.07 (0.07)**	−2.14 (0.21)**
Chi-square	200.69	99.79		260.08	118.28
df	12	12		12	12
N	22,127	10,298		17,438	3,792

NOTE: Basic model and trends over time (B-values from logistic regressions; S.E. in parentheses). Cohort = year of entering secondary education, measured in decades since 1977 (range between 0 and 1.6).

*$p < 0.05$; **$p < 0.01$.

downward path, after having attended a disproportionately high secondary education or a university program. In general the risk of downward transition into HBO increased over time, but it did so in particular for the path leading from university to HBO. Women are more likely than men to enter HBO after having attended the higher secondary academic level. Students from higher employee families are not less likely to enter HBO on a downward path than students from laborer families, but students with academically educated parents are less likely to do so. The pattern for the other educational groups is not linear, which may be a consequence of the small size of the reference group: parents with primary education only.

Finally, we modeled the inequality in the chances of sliding back to the HBO after attending university. The results are presented in the last column of Table 11.3. Contrary to the previous analysis, women have a lower risk than men. Over time, the risk of entering HBO after attending university increased. Children from lower-educated parents are more likely to fail at the university and enter HBO than other children.

In sum, inequality of opportunity is smaller in downward educational moves than in upward moves. Women, who were clear winners over time in the common educational routes, did not improve their position over men in downward moves. However, they were already performing better than men for three of the four downward routes.

THE COMPLETE PICTURE: HIGHEST LEVEL ATTENDED

The previous analyses have shown that the effects of determinants of access to the three levels of postsecondary education have not changed dramatically between the cohorts. Whatever changes were apparent were not unidirectional: in some instances we found increasing differences between social background categories, in others we found a downward trend. How do these findings relate to observations from earlier research showing a solid shift toward more openness in access to higher education? Are we witnessing a slowdown or perhaps a reversal of this trend? Or do the present data on the four student cohorts show different results because of the more recent time window, larger total N, or contemporaneous (as opposed to retrospective) measures of parental background?

Note that all the above analyses are conditioned upon students being eligible for a certain transition and therefore subject to the influence of dy-

TABLE 11.4
Inequality of highest educational level entered: Basic model

	ACADEMIC SECONDARY		SENIOR VOCATIONAL		HIGHER VOCATIONAL		UNIVERSITY	
	HAVO/VWO		MBO		HBO		WO	
Male	0		0		0		0	
Female	0.78	(0.03)**	0.48	(0.02)**	0.45	(0.03)**	0.15	(0.03)**
Cohort 1977	0		0		0		0	
Cohort 1982	0.44	(0.04)**	0.77	(0.03)**	0.93	(0.04)**	1.08	(0.04)**
Cohort 1989	−0.21	(0.04)**	0.65	(0.03)**	0.69	(0.03)**	0.29	(0.04)**
Cohort 1993	−0.16	(0.04)**	0.56	(0.03)**	0.38	(0.04)**	0.03	(0.05)
Laborer	0		0		0		0	
Self-employed	0.56	(0.05)**	0.30	(0.03)**	0.56	(0.04)**	0.71	(0.06)**
Lower employee	0.85	(0.04)**	0.31	(0.03)**	0.74	(0.04)**	1.01	(0.06)**
Middle employee	0.87	(0.04)**	0.37	(0.03)**	0.88	(0.04)**	1.18	(0.05)**
Higher employee	1.17	(0.05)**	0.35	(0.04)**	1.04	(0.05)**	1.44	(0.06)**
Primary education parents	0		0		0		0	
Lower secondary parents	0.73	(0.05)**	0.53	(0.03)**	0.98	(0.05)**	0.83	(0.07)**
Higher secondary parents	1.26	(0.05)**	0.83	(0.03)**	1.58	(0.05)**	1.61	(0.07)**
Vocational college parents	2.05	(0.06)**	1.16	(0.05)**	2.49	(0.06)**	2.93	(0.08)**
University parents	3.00	(0.09)**	1.00	(0.08)**	2.68	(0.09)**	3.99	(0.10)**
Intercept	−2.87	(0.03)**	−1.18	(0.03)**	−3.04	(0.05)**	−3.94	(0.07)**
Chi-square				18051.1				
df				48				
N				70496				

NOTE: B-values from unconditional multinominal regression; S.E. in parentheses. All groups are compared to VBO/MAVO.
*$p < 0.05$; **$p < 0.01$.

namic selection (Cameron and Heckman 1998). As more and more students moved up in the educational hierarchy between 1982 and 1993, the groups were subject to changes in composition with respect to unmeasured determinants of success in school, such as ability and motivation. As we have argued, the direction of these changes is difficult to predict, in particular for MBO and HBO. By contrast, we can assume that the heterogeneity of the groups eligible for university entrance has increased, which is likely to lead by itself to increased social background effects at this level.

The research literature offers little guidance about how to take into account these dynamic selection processes, which makes it all the more important to place the previous analysis in perspective by comparing the results with those of an unconditional analysis: How have the relationships between social background and educational outcomes developed when taking into account all alternative destinations simultaneously? To answer this question, we analyzed the data at the person level using the highest level attended as the measure of educational attainment and submitted them to a multinomial logistic regression. The design ignored any previous career moves made by the respondent, whether in a direct or roundabout way, and it omitted from the analysis of a given destination all those who have reached that destination but moved on to higher ones later in their career. (We note again that our data did not allow us to examine completed educational careers, as many cases were censored in the last year of observation.)

Table 11.4 reports the pattern of association between social background variables and the three postsecondary outcomes, including the group that left education after completing higher secondary academic training (HAVO and VWO).[3] The four are compared with the group that completed only lower secondary training (VBO/MAVO). Whatever the historical trends may have been in the period covered by the data, the table shows that there are strong social background effects on educational outcomes, present for all four destination categories but particularly strong for university entrance. HBO and general secondary academic training are about equal in social background effects. These effects are somewhat smaller for MBO. But the social background effects are still significant and positive for MBO, which implies that children from a higher social background are more likely to choose MBO over leaving with a lower secondary degree or less than children of lower social backgrounds. This conclusion is true for both

TABLE 11.5
Inequality of highest educational level entered: Trends

	ACADEMIC SECONDARY		SENIOR VOCATIONAL		HIGHER VOCATIONAL		UNIVERSITY	
	HAVO/VWO		MBO		HBO		WO	
Male	0		0		0		0	
Female	0.78	(0.04)**	0.41	(0.03)**	0.05	(0.04)	−0.19	(0.05)
Cohort 1977	0		0		0		0	
Cohort 1982	0.45	(0.05)**	0.79	(0.03)**	0.87	(0.05)**	1.09	(0.08)**
Cohort 1989	−0.21	(0.10)*	0.71	(0.05)**	0.55	(0.10)**	0.30	(0.16)
Cohort 1993	−0.22	(0.13)	0.66	(0.07)**	0.18	(0.12)	0.02	(0.21)
Laborer	0		0		0		0	
Self-employed	0.35	(0.06)**	0.33	(0.04)**	0.53	(0.06)**	0.54	(0.09)*
Lower employee	0.80	(0.06)**	0.31	(0.04)**	0.85	(0.06)**	1.01	(0.08)**
Middle employee	0.86	(0.06)**	0.42	(0.04)**	0.92	(0.06)**	1.22	(0.08)**
Higher employee	1.09	(0.07)**	0.28	(0.06)**	1.02	(0.07)**	1.42	(0.09)**
Primary education parents	0		0		0		0	
Lower secondary parents	0.83	(0.06)**	0.56	(0.04)**	1.06	(0.07)**	1.00	(0.11)**
Higher secondary parents	1.37	(0.06)**	0.91	(0.04)**	1.67	(0.07)**	1.82	(0.10)**
Vocational college parents	1.89	(0.08)**	1.22	(0.07)**	2.48	(0.09)**	2.99	(0.12)**
University parents	2.77	(0.12)**	1.22	(0.12)**	2.78	(0.13)**	3.95	(0.14)**
Cohort × Male	0		0		0		0	
Cohort × Female	0.01	(0.04)	0.14	(0.03)**	0.57	(0.04)**	0.53	(0.05)**
Cohort × Laborer	0		0		0		0	
Cohort × Self-employed	0.39	(0.07)**	−0.02	(0.05)	0.06	(0.06)	0.27	(0.10)**
Cohort × Lower employee	0.08	(0.07)	−0.01	(0.05)	−0.15	(0.07)*	−0.00	(0.10)
Cohort × Medium employee	0.03	(0.07)	−0.07	(0.05)	−0.06	(0.06)	−0.06	(0.09)
Cohort × Higher employee	0.14	(0.08)	0.08	(0.06)	0.02	(0.07)	0.04	(0.10)
Cohort × Primary parents	0		0		0		0	
Cohort × Lower sec. parents	−0.26	(0.09)**	−0.07	(0.05)	−0.15	(0.08)	−0.31	(0.14)*
Cohort × Higher sec. parents	−0.19	(0.08)*	−0.15	(0.05)**	−0.15	(0.08)	−0.37	(0.13)**
Cohort × Vocational tert. parents	0.19	(0.10)	−0.08	(0.07)	−0.01	(0.10)	−0.15	(0.14)
Cohort × University parents	0.29	(0.13)*	−0.27	(0.12)*	−0.13	(0.13)	−0.03	(0.17)
Intercept	−2.87	(0.06)**	−1.21	(0.03)**	−2.95	(0.06)**	−3.91	(0.10)**
Chi-square				18,555.0			
df				84			
N				7,0496			

NOTE: *B*-values from unconditional multinomial regression; S.E. in parentheses. Cohort = year of entering secondary education, measured in decades since 1977 (range between 0 and 1.6). All groups are compared to VBO/MAVO.

*p < 0.05; **p < 0.01

parental education and occupation, but the effects of parental education are clearly stronger. In addition, we find that women lead men across the board, but that their advantage is smallest at university entrance and largest at senior academic level. While women have caught up at all levels, this finding suggests that the major source of the dynamic has been the secondary school, where a relatively large number of boys drop out early. As we have seen before, selection has still been unfavorable relative to the number of women eligible for university.

Table 11.5 reports on changes in these patterns over cohorts. The oldest cohort (1977) is the reference category. Cohort interactions measure change over a 10-year period. There has been a distinct movement toward smaller social background effects in the case of parental education: all the relevant interactions are negative and almost half are statistically significant. This development is not echoed for parental occupation, the effects of which remain more or less stable across cohorts. Out of the 16 pertinent coefficients, only three are statistically significant, two implying increased inequality (between self-employed and manual workers), and another implying declining inequality. Historical changes in the access of women to postsecondary education are largely confined to HBO and university, for which the coefficients suggest that by the 1993 cohort women were overrepresented by a factor of over 1.5, having achieved parity with men in 1977.

CONCLUSIONS

We have described trends in inequality in access to three levels of postsecondary education in the Netherlands since 1977. During this period, educational policies were aimed mainly at decreasing inequality by (1) facilitating the possibility to switch between vocational and academic tracks of study, (2) weakening the admission rules, and (3) improving the scholarship system. At the same time, the number of students at all levels of higher education expanded. We expected both processes to affect the inequality of opportunity to enter higher education programs.

We tested four hypotheses predicting changes in access (from below and above) to three types of postsecondary education (senior vocational education (MBO), vocational college (HBO), and university (WO)). We expected that the combination of policy measures and the expansion of education would lead to different outcomes for the three types. Structural changes in Dutch educational institutions were expected to have positively affected equality of opportunity in accessing all programs. However, an increasing number of students reached preuniversity education because of educational expansion, and as a result we expected selection on ability and motivation at the entrance to university to decrease. The combination of favorable policy measures and decreasing selectivity could cancel each other in their respectively positive and negative effects on equality of educational opportunity. In sum, we expected no trend in inequality of educational opportunity to entering the university level in the conditional analysis. Our analyses support this expectation: access to university for different parental categories in the eligible group remained stable over the last decades of the twentieth century. However, the finding that women have caught up with men indicates that the effects of emancipation were much stronger than the opposing effects of decreasing selection.

We expected a slight decrease of inequality of educational opportunity in access to HBO. At this level, too, institutional rearrangements were expected to positively affect equality of opportunity. The development of selectivity in entering HBO, however, is unclear. Educational expansion leads the better-equipped students from MAVO to try their luck at HAVO (decreasing selectivity at the HAVO). At the same time the better students, who would formerly attend HAVO, now go to preuniversity academic education (increasing selectivity at HAVO). The hypothesis is not supported by the results of our analyses. There are no significant changes over time in inequality between parental occupational categories and levels of education. Through all decades under study, vocational education of one of the parents clearly enhances the child's opportunity to enter HBO.

Next, we expected a decrease in the inequality of educational opportunity in access to MBO. Despite policy changes facilitating entrance to this level, to reach HBO or university the brighter students increasingly choose other levels of education than those that prepare for access to MBO (i.e., LBO and MAVO). This increasing negative selection is expected to decrease inequality of educational opportunity, a hypothesis that is somewhat supported by the data. In particular, the differences between children of lower- and higher-educated parents have decreased, but contrary to our expectations the difference between children of higher employees and laborers increased.

Finally, we studied access to postsecondary education in an unconditional design by comparing all three postsecondary alternatives with leaving the system after obtaining a lower secondary degree at best. Like similar analyses based on cross-sectional data for the 1920–70 period, we found a decrease in the effects of parental background over the 1977–93 cohorts (covering events in the last two decades of the twentieth century), but it appears to be restricted to parental education and does not extend to parental occupation. This result was not anticipated based on the conditional analyses. At the same time, the unconditional analysis confirmed that most of the change has taken place at the divide between lower secondary and senior vocational levels. Not much change has occurred at the two highest levels of postsecondary alternatives, the tertiary education proper. We conclude that, despite changes in university admission and the scholarship system, university training in the Netherlands is largely for the elite. Students from lower social background are underrepresented in the 1990s to the same extent as they were in the 1980s. This may also explain why students from lower social background are not more likely to leave university for vocational college than students from higher social backgrounds, since they are still a relatively selected group.

The results also serve to remind us that the analysis of inequality of educational outcomes at various transitions may produce a detailed picture of when and where the changes occurred but that their interpretation is clouded by selectivity problems. It is difficult to determine who is actually in the risk group and how this has changed over time, and even more difficult to separate selectivity from causal effects. Analysis of inequality of educational opportunities is strongly in need of selectivity controls if it were to assess the true effects of social background.

CHAPTER TWELVE

Russia: Stratification in Postsecondary Education Since the Second World War

Theodore P. Gerber, University of Wisconsin

INTRODUCTION

Russian postsecondary education is essentially a binary, stratified system consisting of two basic types of institutions: "higher educational establishments" (or VUZ, for *Vysshee Uchebnoe Zavedenie*), which provide the equivalent of university degrees, and "specialized secondary educational establishments" (or SSUZ, for *Srednee Spetsial'noe Uchebnoe Zavedenie*). The latter institutions, some of which are also called "technical colleges" (*tekhnikumy*), have lower status than the VUZ. They provide higher-level vocational and technical training in both secondary-level and postsecondary programs. Since the late 1950s, a majority of students in SSUZ have been enrolled in programs requiring a general secondary degree prior to entry. Thus, the SSUZ sector is appropriately viewed as a form of postsecondary education, roughly akin to vocational programs in junior colleges in the United States. No SSUZ programs are intended to serve as preparation for higher education.

As in many countries, postsecondary education expanded dramatically in postwar Russia. The expansion took place under the stable institutional structure of the Soviet education system. By the mid-1980s, however, both the Soviet system overall and the system of higher education came under a variety of pressures. After several decades of expansion, postsecondary education began to be scaled back. Then, in the early 1990s, the Soviet Union collapsed. Inevitably, this affected Russian higher and specialized secondary education, most significantly by altering the economic and political environment in which the system functions and by changing the financing of education by the state. Far-reaching institutional change in the Russian system of postsecondary education has been slow to develop, although there has been considerable movement toward decentralization. Nonetheless, there are good reasons to expect the collapse of the Soviet system to influence patterns of social inequality in Russians' access to postsecondary education in general, and higher education in particular.

THE SOVIET EDUCATIONAL SYSTEM

The Soviet education system and its post-Soviet Russian counterpart both consist of three main stages: compulsory, secondary, and postsecondary. For most of the postwar era, compulsory education consisted of eight years of study, after which students were said to have "incomplete secondary" education. At that point they could either leave school or continue their education in one of three types of institutions. *Lower vocational schools* imparted manual skills. The most common type of institution at this level was the PTU (for *professional'noe-tekhnicheskoe uchilishche*, or "professional-technical school"), though various educational institutions associated with enterprises or other organizations also qualify. Since the 1970s, many such institutions also provided a general secondary diploma; however, by most accounts little stock is placed in these diplomas (Matthews 1982; Connor 1991). These institutions attracted mainly males and were viewed as centers of delinquency and low standards. Another option was to enter a secondary-level training program at a SSUZ, which would also provide a general secondary diploma along with certification as a technician or lower-grade professional.[1] Most enrollees in SSUZ programs were female. Finally, and most typically, students could continue on to "general secondary" (*srednee obshchee*) school and obtain an *attestat* (high-school diploma) upon successful completion of the tenth grade.

After completing one of these three forms of secondary education, Russian students could continue on to postsecondary schooling in the form of higher (VUZ) or postsecondary-level technical education (postsecondary SSUZ). For the most part, a general secondary diploma was a prerequisite for postsecondary education. Although a secondary degree from a PTU technically qualified one for admission to a postsecondary institution, the vast majority of PTU leavers (in our data, 82%) entered the workforce once and for all. Most of the 15% who eventually entered some kind of postsecondary education (13% overall) entered a postsecondary SSUZ. Graduates of secondary-level SSUZ programs were required to work for three years in their trades. After this period, they were permitted to apply for entry to a VUZ, but most (81%) remained out of school. Not surprisingly, though, most of the 17% who eventually continued entered a VUZ rather than pursuing a second SSUZ degree.

Graduates of general secondary institutions were both better prepared to compete for entry to VUZ, and also had more incentive to do so, since their broad academic training placed them at a disadvantage on the labor market relative to PTU and SSUZ graduates, whose secondary-level education provided them with specific skills. Accordingly, roughly two thirds of general secondary graduates pursued some form of postsecondary education. One-third of general secondary graduates who could not gain entry to a VUZ or postsecondary-level SSUZ actually enrolled in PTU programs.

HIGHER AND POSTSECONDARY SPECIALIZED EDUCATION

Soviet higher education was highly specialized: its purpose was not to provide a general liberal education but to train skilled experts in the specialties required by the economy, as determined not by market forces but by planners.[2] Each year, targets were set for the number of matriculants in each specialty, and the corresponding enrollees were apportioned among the appropriate institutions, which, in turn, tended to be highly specialized. The institutional specificity meant that students had to choose their fields of specialization at the time of application. A state ministry or regional government administered every institution. Higher administering bodies came in a bewildering and changing variety: the State Committee on Higher Education, economic ministries responsible for various sectors (such as the Ministry of Machine Tools and Heavy Industry), the Ministries of Agriculture, Health, and Culture, and various other departments or regional governmental bodies. Despite the complexity of the administrative system, accreditation, curricula, standards, and personnel policies were all thoroughly centralized.

Although returns to higher education were comparatively low in the Soviet Union for most of the postwar era, there was never any question that a VUZ degree was the top prize in the Soviet education system. Higher education was free and students received a state stipend during the Soviet era. Demand has always exceeded supply, making entry to a VUZ an inherently competitive process. Officially, entry to a VUZ was based solely on competitive entrance exams, which only those holding a secondary diploma were formally permitted to take. Students could only apply to one VUZ each year. There were frequent reports of corruption and cheating in the exam process (see Ledeneva 1998), and in the admissions process more generally. During various periods, political and ethnic criteria reportedly played a role in the admissions process as well (Shlapentokh 1990).

The "specialized secondary" (SSUZ) sector—part of which we appropriately treat as postsecondary, since its programs required a secondary diploma for admission—has received less attention in studies of Soviet and Russian education. A recent article by the president of the union of SSUZ equates specialized secondary with "practically oriented higher or preuniversity higher education" and asserts its continuing importance as a means of "making mass professional education broadly accessible" (Demin 2001, 7). Women were more likely than men to enter specialized secondary programs (Matthews 1982), most likely due to the lower status of SSUZ degrees compared to VUZ degrees.

ENROLLMENTS

The first several decades following World War II ushered in strong growth rates and impressive expansion of the Soviet economy's technological base. Both factors spurred a dramatic expansion of the VUZ and SSUZ sectors from 1940 to 1980. The establishment of new facilities drove the growth of SSUZ enrollments, while the growth of enrollments in higher education was achieved by expanding the capacity of existing institutions.

In the 1970s, economic growth decelerated and technological progress stagnated. As a result, demand for highly educated specialists in the Soviet economy began to be outstripped by supply, and observers began to write of the "overproduction of specialists" (Zaslavsky 1982; Gerber 2003). In the hope of enhancing the quality of higher education by focusing resources more effectively, education planners began to reduce enrollments (Balzer 1992), which accordingly began to decline. The growing economic problems and institutional uncertainties of the perestroika era (1985–91)

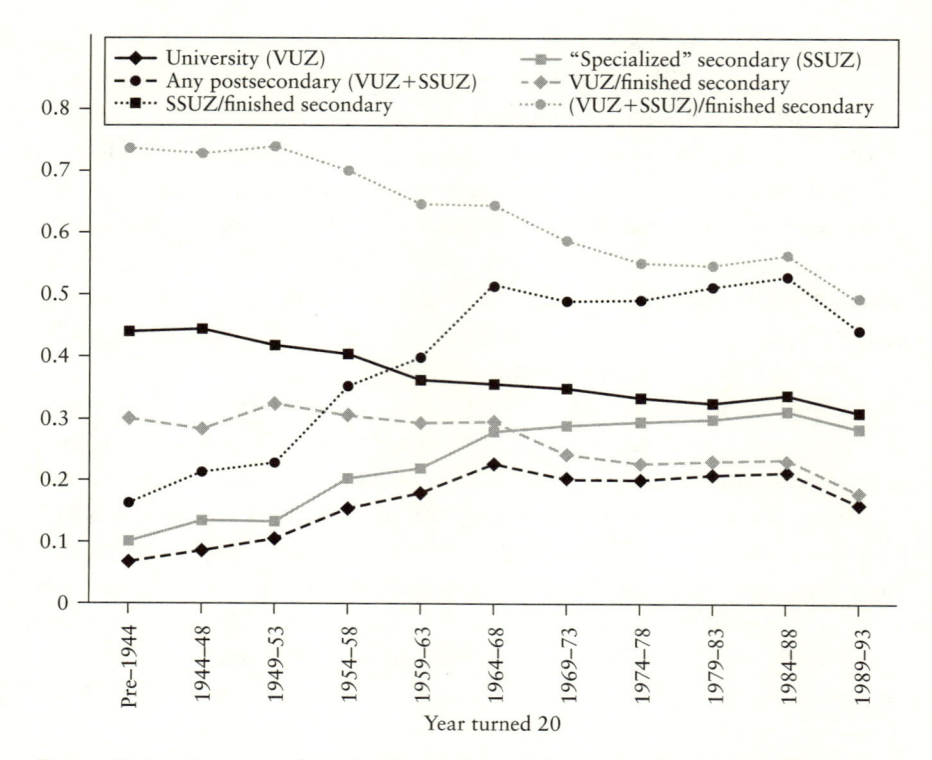

Figure 12.1. Postsecondary Attainments by Cohort, Russian Men and Women
SOURCE: 1994 Microcensus.

furthered the downward drift of enrollments, as did the chaos, dislocations, and economic crisis of the early post-Soviet era (Gerber 2000). Public opinion polls in the early 1990s pointed to a decline in the perceived value of a university degree in the new market economy (Kitaev 1994). However, by the mid-1990s Russians became increasingly accustomed to the new institutional order and the tendency apparently reversed: enrollments resumed their growth, at least in the VUZ sector.

The postwar growth of absolute enrollments in postsecondary education must be viewed against the backdrop of an even more rapid expansion of secondary schooling (Gerber and Hout 1995). The consequences are illustrated in the cross-cohort patterns of attainments, as calculated based on a microcensus conducted in 1994 (Figure 12.1). These data reflect the steady growth in the proportions of each cohort attaining specialized secondary and university degrees through the 1960s. However, when these proportions are adjusted for the proportion of those *eligible* for either form of postsecondary education (i.e., of those who completed secondary education), the data suggest that the conditional odds of attaining a VUZ degree remained steady during this period, while the conditional odds of attaining a specialized secondary degree actually declined. This reflects the strong growth of secondary schooling. By the mid-1970s, secondary schooling had become so widespread that the lines representing the conditional and unconditional proportions attaining, respectively, SSUZ, VUZ, and either form of postsecondary education converge.

The overall postwar pattern implies that even as postsecondary education expanded for the first three decades following the War, the conditional odds of making the transition either remained stable or declined. This has implications for trends in origin-based inequalities of access to postsecondary schooling. The theory of "Maximally Maintained Inequality" (MMI) offers insight into why, because it implicitly links the degree of origin-based inequality in access to a particular level of education to the scarcity of available slots at that level (Raftery and Hout 1993). The strong version of the MMI perspective posits the saturation of the demand of high-origin students as a necessary condition for equalization in access to a given level: as expansions take place, high-origin students absorb all the new slots; only when they are all placed do opportunities open up for lower-origin students. A softer, more probabilistic version would posit an association between the degree of competition for slots at a given educational level and the degree of high-origin advantage. Whether or not upper-origin demand reaches saturation, we would expect upper-origin advantages to weaken as the scarcity of slots diminishes, and vice versa. This means that the contraction of enrollments at the postsecondary level during the late Soviet era and the early part of the 1990s can be expected to have increased origin-based inequalities in access to postsecondary schooling.

REFORMS AND INSTITUTIONAL CHANGE

By the mid-1980s, Soviet education officials began to recognize inefficiencies in the system of higher education. A 1987 package of reforms tightened admissions standards and gave administrators greater authority to expel students who failed to progress rapidly (Kerr 1992; Balzer 1992, 1994). They also sought to improve ties between universities and industry; provide more specialized, practical training; and increase the autonomy of local administrators from central authorities. But by all accounts these reforms were not effective and they were quickly overtaken by the upheavals surrounding the collapse of the Soviet Union in late 1991.

Following the Soviet collapse, several key aspects of the higher education system were decentralized (see Balzer 1994; Lugachyov et al. 1997). No longer did the government impose restrictions on new enrollments in each institution or specialization. Newly permitted private institutions arose though enrollments in private universities have never exceeded 20% of total university-level enrollments (Poletayev and Savelieva 2001). Shrinking state budgets required substantial cuts in state funding for higher education. Many state institutions began to charge tuition to cover their expenses (Bray and Borevskaya 2001). The decentralization of admissions procedures and the increased cost of postsecondary schooling could increase origin-based inequalities in access if students from advantaged origins can more readily adapt to changing admissions criteria at the local level and afford the increased costs.

DATA AND ANALYSES

Data come from the Survey on Education and Stratification in Russia (SESR), given to nationally representative samples of Russians aged 16 and older in September and November 2000 (total $N = 4,809$).[3] The survey obtained information about each "spell" of postsecondary education, defined as a *period of uninterrupted study at a particular institution* (whether or not it resulted in a degree), as reported by the respondent. At least one spell of attendance at university was reported by 1,310 respondents (27.2%).[4]

The availability of complete educational trajectories represents a distinctive advantage of the SESR data for the analysis of transitions to postsecondary education. Most data sets from post-Soviet Russia only contain information about the highest level of education attained by respondents. Lacking information on respondents' full educational careers, prior studies of educational stratification in Russia have had to assume that all who arrive at a particular destination do so by traversing the same sequence of transitions (Gerber and Hout 1995; Gerber 2000). In a complex system such as Russia's, where different forms of secondary schooling constrain access to different forms of postsecondary, this assumption is problematic.

For example, most students who enter a university do so after attaining a "general secondary" diploma, but 15.4% of specialized secondary leavers enroll in universities. In prior analyses, these students would be misclassified as having completed general secondary schooling rather than specialized secondary schooling. In addition, data limitations prevented earlier studies from distinguishing secondary from postsecondary forms of SSUZ education (see note 1). Thus, the SESR data permit an accurate estimate of how strongly type of secondary education affects access to the two forms of postsecondary education, and also analyses of how gender, social origins, and other variables affect the odds of entry to any postsecondary institution and to any specialized postsecondary institution in particular.

MODELS AND VARIABLES

I consider the same five outcomes as analyzed elsewhere in this volume: eligibility for postsecondary education; entry to any postsecondary institution; entry to university (VUZ; entry to specialized postsecondary institution (SSUZ); and attainment of a university degree. I define eligibility for postsecondary education as attainment of either a general or specialized secondary degree. I exclude respondents who completed a lower vocational (PTU) course of training at the secondary level.[5]

For each outcome, I first estimate a series of "conditional" models on those eligible for that transition. The baseline model for comparative analyses contains only gender, parental education, parental occupation, and dummy variables for each five-year birth cohort following the oldest considered (born 1929–33 and becoming eligible for entry to postsecondary education approximately in 1947–52). Consistent with the protocols for this comparative project, parental education is coded using the CASMIN category for the higher of the parents' two educations. The omitted category, however, is an aggregation of 1c and 2a, because these cannot be distinguished (among parents) with the data at hand, and 2b cannot be identified. For parental class, in most cases I use the father's (or stepfather's) class when the respondent was 14. However, if the father was absent or unemployed, or information on father's occupation is missing—as in 26% of the valid observations for entry to postsecondary education, for example—I use mother's class instead. To remove heterogeneity in the omitted categories for parental education (1c/2a) and class (V/VI), I also include dummy variables denoting the absence of both parents (implying missing data on both parental education and class), unemployed parents at age 14, and missing data on both parents' occupations despite the presence of at least one at age 14.

The second set of conditional models adds variables relevant to educational transitions in the Russian context. Since academic secondary education has always been the favored path to postsecondary education, I include a dummy variable for "specialized" secondary education, which should have a negative effect for all transitions, except possibly the transition to a postsecondary SSUZ. I also enter dummy variables denoting both rural residence and Moscow residence at age 14. Finally, I enter a dummy variable indicating that the respondent's father was a member of the Communist Party of the Soviet Union (CPSU), because Gerber (2000) found parental CPSU membership exerts a positive effect on university entry.[6]

The third set of conditional models consists of "preferred interaction" models. These models show changes over time in the effects of parental origins and gender on postsecondary transition probabilities. I tested five different theoretically plausible patterns of change over time in the effects of parental education, parental occupation, and gender. For each of the three covariates, I considered the following patterns of change, each specified using the appropriate interaction terms involving the covariate and cohort: (1) linear change; (2) change during the "reform" era (i.e., for cohorts who negotiated the transition to postsecondary education during the Gorbachev era and afterwards); (3) change during the post-Soviet era; (4) linear change, interrupted or accelerated during the reform era; (5) linear change, interrupted or accelerated during the post-Soviet era. I assessed the significance of each specification of each interaction (one at a time) using likelihood ratio tests and I retained only statistically significant interactions in the final models shown.

In addition, once I identified the best-fitting specifications for significant interaction effects, I "smoothed" the pattern of change across cohorts in the baseline logit using the best-fitting of a variety of specifications. In several cases, a logarithmic transformation of the scalar cohort variable fit best, indicating sharper changes in the baseline hazard for the older cohorts, which decelerate in magnitude for the younger cohorts. This sequence of modeling steps yields a "preferred interaction" model for each outcome considered that includes only and all significant interactions between social origins or gender and time as well as a parsimonious specification of the pattern of net cross-cohort change in the baseline.

Finally, I also report a "preferred" unconditional model, which results from applying the same modeling sequence for a given outcome to an entire age-eligible sample, rather than to the subsample of respondents formally eligible for a given transition, based on their prior educational attainment.

RESULTS

Descriptive Statistics

Sample distributions for the ten five-year cohorts analyzed herein across categories of the key independent variables capture and demonstrate a number of well-known population trends in postwar Russia (Table 12.1). Whether measured by education or occupation, the average social origins of Russians improved dramatically over time. Only 9.6% of those born 1929–33 had at least one parent with some form of postsecondary education, and only 9.2% came from class I or II families. These figures grew to 68.5% and 28.2%, respectively, for those born 1974–79. The Russian population also became more urbanized and more concentrated in Moscow. These upgrades of social origins probably increased gross transition rates, perhaps masking stability or even decline in baseline transition odds, net of origin variables.

Yet, the data also show that from the oldest cohort to that born in 1959–63 (the last cohort in the Russian postwar baby boom), the proportion of Russians who attained general secondary degrees increased substantially. The growth in proportions of successive cohorts attaining general secondary education, coupled with growing cohort sizes following the War, increased the size of the "risk" sets eligible for postsecondary schooling. Gerber and Hout (1995) showed that expansion at university level could not keep pace with the increase in effective demand caused by this expansion of general secondary schooling. The resulting bottleneck at university entry led to increased effects of social origins on the conditional *probabilities* (not necessarily the odds) of making the transition to tertiary education. The "reform" cohorts, who turned 17 during Gorbachev's perestroika or following the collapse of the Soviet system, experienced declining proportions receiving general secondary degrees. Gerber (2000) found a similar pattern

TABLE 12.1
Descriptive statistics, weighted SESR sample (entries are column percentages)

	1929–33	1934–38	1939–43	1944–48	1949–53	1954–58	1959–63	1964–68	1969–73	1974–79	Total
N	282	396	348	285	456	493	494	392	401	515	4,062
Female	58.0	56.2	54.5	52.5	52.1	51.5	50.7	50.3	51.3	51.5	52.6
Highest parent's education											
3b	6.5	7.1	8.2	13.5	11.8	14.4	17.6	25.1	29.9	33.4	17.6
3a	3.1	8.8	9.3	13.6	16.9	15.2	20.9	28.7	29.8	35.1	19.2
2c	3.4	4.8	4.9	5.8	10.2	10.2	9.5	11.5	11.8	12.0	8.9
1c/2a	1.4	0.6	4.2	3.5	5.1	9.5	7.1	5.8	8.1	6.5	5.5
1ab	64.9	63.9	57.9	52.9	46.3	45.4	39.8	22.8	13.3	7.6	39.5
Absent	8.4	6.6	7.8	5.5	2.9	2.5	2.5	4.1	2.5	3.4	4.2
DK	12.3	8.1	7.6	5.3	6.8	2.8	2.7	2.2	4.5	1.9	5.0
Parental EGP class[a]											
I	4.5	8.6	8.2	12.0	9.9	5.4	9.0	10.2	9.8	11.0	8.9
II	4.7	6.4	10.3	7.7	9.6	10.1	12.5	12.2	17.6	18.2	11.4
III	5.3	5.1	6.5	11.3	10.0	9.0	6.8	8.7	9.2	7.5	8.0
V/VI	13.3	15.2	19.2	18.7	21.0	29.3	24.7	29.7	23.0	26.5	22.7
VII	55.2	47.8	40.9	38.2	41.2	38.7	40.4	32.9	31.8	26.7	38.7
Not working	3.2	6.3	5.5	2.5	3.5	1.5	0.5	0.4	1.7	1.7	2.5
Absent/DK	13.9	10.6	9.5	9.5	4.9	6.0	6.1	5.9	7.0	8.5	7.9
Rural, age 14	55.1	57.1	50.3	39.6	45.2	40.6	41.0	34.4	29.7	30.6	41.5
Moscow, age 14	6.8	7.8	11.7	13.6	11.8	9.8	7.9	13.7	11.0	13.3	10.8
Father in CPSU	11.5	16.8	21.5	27.1	25.6	22.5	21.8	22.4	22.0	20.3	21.3
Type of Secondary Degree											
GHS	28.5	41.2	50.1	60.9	66.3	69.9	71.3	67.4	64.8	64.7	60.2
SSUZ	12.5	9.6	7.2	11.3	12.9	11.6	11.6	18.3	14.4	13.6	12.5

[a] Father's or (if missing) mother's class when respondent was 14.

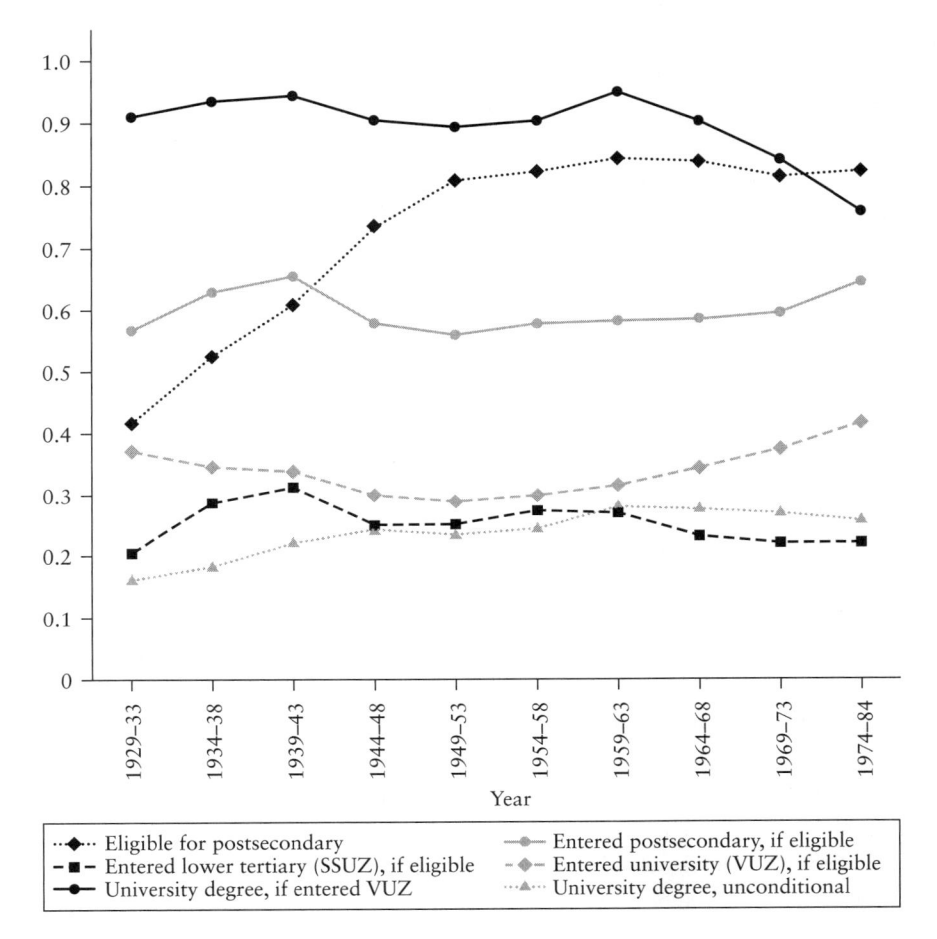

Figure 12.2. Transition Probabilities by Birth Cohort
SOURCE: Weighted SESR sample.

in survey data from 1998 and showed that it resulted in increased origin effects on the probabilities of receiving a general secondary degree. For most of the postwar era, the proportion of each cohort completing specialized secondary did not fluctuate much.

Transition probabilities estimated from the weighted SESR data reflect these trends (Figure 12.2). Proportions completing secondary schooling increased steadily across cohorts who reached this transition following World War II, until the 1954–58 cohort. The reform era cohorts—who reached the completion of secondary schooling during the Gorbachev or post-Soviet eras—experienced a slight decline in the probability of becoming eligible for postsecondary education. The conditional probability of entering any postsecondary institution grew moderately in the immediate postwar era. Then the bottleneck produced declining conditional probabilities for the 1944–48 cohort. Thereafter, the gross conditional probability for postsecondary entry remained flat, though it increased modestly for the reform-era cohorts, when the risk set decreased in proportional terms. These patterns were largely driven by SSUZ entry probabilities. The conditional VUZ entry probabilities remained fairly stable for the entire postwar period, decreasing slightly and steadily through the 1954–58 cohort (due to the rapid growth of the risk set) and thereafter increasing at a moderate rate.

Eligibility for Postsecondary Education

Temporal patterns in the overall probability of completing either general or specialized secondary education are evident in the statistical models for postsecondary eligibility (Table 12.2). But let us start with the effects of gender and origins. The baseline and expanded additive models show that Russian girls have enjoyed substantial advantages over Russian boys in attaining a general or specialized secondary degree. In addition, parental education and parental class have strong and predictable net effects. Parental education in categories 3b and 3a significantly increases the log-odds of attaining eligibility relative to the omitted category (1c/2a), 2c has no significant effect, and 1ab significantly decreases the log-odds. Russian children from classes I and II have substantially higher net log-odds of completing secondary schooling than those from classes V/VI; those from class III have somewhat higher odds. In the baseline model, class VII origins are associated with significantly lower odds, net of gender and parental education.

However, this effect becomes nonsignificant net of the controls for residence at age 14 and father's CPSU membership. Most of the disadvantage of those from semi- and unskilled manual origins relative to those from skilled manual origins stems from the greater concentration of the former in rural areas and outside Moscow. As expected, rural origins have a substantial negative net effect, and Moscow origins have a substantial positive net effect. The effect of father's CPSU membership is positive, as expected, but not statistically significant—in fact, the only outcome for which father's CPSU membership has a significant effect is the transition to any form of

TABLE 12.2
Logistic regressions for transition to eligibility for postsecondary (weighted SESR sample born 1929–79, N = 4,062)

	MODEL 1 B	MODEL 1 S.E.	MODEL 2 B	MODEL 2 S.E.	MODEL 3 B	MODEL 3 S.E.
Woman	.566**	.081	.607**	.082	.172	.146
Highest parent's education (1c/2a)						
3b	.784**	.250	.672**	.247	.685**	.248
3a	.505**	.221	.536**	.218	.538	.219
2c	−.198	.228	−.211	.224	−.189	.224
1ab	−.636**	.197	−.549**	.193	−.533**	.193
Father's EGP class (V/VI)						
I	.614**	.227	.646**	.221	.634**	.221
II	.693**	.214	.770**	.209	.735**	.209
III	.431**	.188	.403**	.183	.383*	.182
VII	−.256**	.107	−.158	.106	−.160	.105
Rural residence at 14			−.344**	.094	−.365**	.094
Moscow residence at 14			.328*	.178	.325*	.175
Father in CPSU			.071	.116	.068	.115
ln(cohort)					.800**	.094
Reform cohorts					−.623**	.136
Post-Soviet cohort					−.466**	.167
Woman × Cohort					.099**	.029
Constant	−.167	.247	−.119	.250	.005	.258
Log likelihood	−2,006.6		−1,934.5		−1,938.8	

NOTE: Dummy variables representing the effects of five-year cohorts (ranging from 1924–28 to 1974–79) are included in Models 1 and 2 but are not shown. Dummy variables for missing values on highest parent's education, parental EGP class, type of residence at age 14, and father's CPSU membership, as well as for neither parent employed at age 14 are included in all models that include the corresponding variables but are not shown. Standard errors are robust.
*$p < 0.05$, one-tailed; **$p < 0.05$, two-tailed.

postsecondary education. There is no clear pattern to the impact of the controls in model 2 on the parameter estimates for the origin variables.

The preferred interaction model includes no significant interactions between social origins and cohort: the effects of parental education and class on the log-odds remained stable for all Russian cohorts who reached this transition point after WWII. However, the interaction between female gender and the scalar cohort term is significant: the female advantage in completion of general or specialized secondary education started out small and nonsignificant, then grew steadily across cohorts.[7] The preferred model also shows that the baseline odds of completing general or specialized secondary education increased in logarithmic fashion across the first eight cohorts.[8] However, the monotonic, decelerating increase of the net baseline across

TABLE 12.3
Logistic regressions for entry to any postsecondary (weighted SESR sample born 1929–79)

	MODEL 1 ELIGIBLE FOR POSTSECONDARY		MODEL 2 ELIGIBLE FOR POSTSECONDARY		MODEL 3 ELIGIBLE FOR POSTSECONDARY		MODEL 4 FULL SAMPLE (UNCONDITIONAL MODEL)	
	B	S.E.	B	S.E.	B	S.E.	B	S.E.
Woman	.342**	.083	.366**	.090	−.264	.222	−.352**	.124
Highest Parent's Education (1c/2a)								
3b	1.067**	.200	.874**	.214	.608**	.245	.749**	.182
3a	.598**	.179	.556**	.189	.587**	.189	.504**	.165
2c	−.017	.201	−.224	.211	−.233	.212	−.294	.183
1ab	−.329*	.172	−.421**	.182	−.461**	.183	−.543**	.158
Father's EGP Class (V/VI)								
I	.868**	.189	.744**	.195	.604**	.200	.571**	.166
II	.462**	.159	.415**	.166	.436**	.167	.491**	.143
III	−.020	.153	−.095	.162	−.101	.163	.133	.145
VII	−.061	.107	.009	.114	.019	.115	−.113	.097
PTU leaver			−2.335**	.146	−2.368**	.148	−1.562**	.167
SSUZ leaver			−.295**	.099	−.296**	.099	−1.070**	.143
Rural at 14			.168	.146	.193	.145	−.329**	.083
Moscow at 14			.196*	.111	.217**	.111	.408**	.129
Father in CPSU					−.662**	.129	.203**	.093
ln(cohort)								
Post-Soviet cohort					.161**	.047	−.244**	.127
Woman × Cohort					−.630**	.197	.206**	.027
Woman × Reform cohorts					.482**	.237	−.862**	.160
Ed 3b × Reform cohorts					1.187**	.531	.794**	.394
Class I × Post-Soviet cohort					1.511**	.302	−.003**	.171
Constant	.063	.275	.866**	.298				
Log likelihood	−1,841.3		−1,641.7		−1,633.5		−2,279.1	
N	2,989		2,989		2,989		4,062	

NOTE: See note to Table 12.2.

cohorts abruptly turns into a sharp decrease for the cohort turning 17 during the Gorbachev era, and an even sharper decrease for the post-Soviet cohort. The estimated baseline logit for the 1964–68 cohort is 1.669, that for the 1969–73 cohort is 1.140, and that for the 1974–79 cohort is 0.758.[9] These translate into baseline probabilities of 0.84, 0.76, and 0.68, respectively.

This is evidence of the impact of late-Soviet and post-Soviet turmoil on educational opportunity. Russians from all social origins experienced lower probabilities of completing secondary education during these periods. Moreover, the declining baseline coupled with stability in the odds ratios pertaining to origin categories implies that the ratios of the transition probabilities for higher-origin students to the probabilities for lower-origin students *increased*. Thus, the SESR data confirm Gerber's (2000) findings that stratification in access to complete secondary education grew during the era of Gorbachev's reforms.

Entry to Any Postsecondary Schooling

Gender, parental education, and parental class all have significant net effects on the conditional log-odds of entering some form of postsecondary schooling (Table 12.3). Both additive models show a significant advantage for women, very strong advantages for parental education 3b, somewhat weaker for parental education 3a, a significant disadvantage for education 1ab, very strong advantages for class I, somewhat weaker advantages for class II, and no other significant effects of class. The expanded additive model shows the substantial "path dependence" of the transition to postsecondary education: those with a specialized secondary degree have 90% lower odds of entering postsecondary education relative to otherwise similar Russians with a general secondary degree. Rural-origin students also face a disadvantage, while those with fathers in the CPSU enjoy 22% higher odds relative to those whose fathers were not Party members. The introduction of controls in model 2 tends to reduce the estimates of the effects of social origins, but does not alter any inferences.

The preferred interaction model indicates that the net effects of gender, parental education, and parental class all changed over time. Female students' initial disadvantage relative to otherwise similar males diminished with time and ultimately reversed, giving women a substantial advantage by the 1949–53 cohort (see Table 12.7). This came on top of women's growing advantages in gaining eligibility. The rising gender imbalance in the

TABLE 12.4
Logistic regressions for entry to university (VUZ) (weighted SESR sample born 1929–79)

	MODEL 1 ELIGIBLE FOR POSTSECONDARY		MODEL 2 ELIGIBLE FOR POSTSECONDARY		MODEL 3 ELIGIBLE FOR POSTSECONDARY		MODEL 4 FULL SAMPLE (UNCONDITIONAL MODEL)	
	B	S.E.	B	S.E.	B	S.E.	B	S.E.
Woman	−.178**	.089	−.168*	.091	−.166*	.091	−.101	.087
Highest parent's education (1c/2a)								
3b	1.242**	.205	1.038**	.205	1.063**	.203	.962**	.199
3a	.572**	.196	.494**	.193	.520**	.191	.490**	.188
2c	−.068	.232	−.216	.227	−.204	.227	−.265	.222
1ab	−.568**	.201	−.532**	.197	−.544**	.196	−.686**	.190
Father's EGP class (V/VI)								
I	.603**	.162	.476**	.162	.359**	.170	.484**	.162
II	.565**	.147	.549**	.147	.547**	.147	.607**	.144
III	.154	.169	.109	.168	.101	.166	.208	.166
VII	−.147	.125	−.054	.124	−.050	.124	−.118	.120
PTU leaver							−3.027**	.373
SSUZ leaver			−1.077**	.152	−1.073**	.151	−.902**	.156
Rural at 14			−.520**	.103	−.523**	.103	−.553**	.099
Moscow at 14			.427**	.130	.425**	.130	.534**	.128
Father in CPSU			.066	.105	.069	.105	.089	.101
Ln(cohort)					−.375**	.084		
Class I Post-Soviet cohort					.719**	.353	.614*	.344
Constant	−.373	.293	.118	.300	.023	.259	−.794**	.197
Log likelihood	−1,670.8		−1,612.1		−1,633.5		−1,779.0	
N	2,989		2,989		2,989		4,062	

NOTE: See note to Table 12.2.

risk set may explain the decrease in the female advantage for the "reform" cohorts. The advantages of parental education 3b increased sharply for both reform cohorts, while the advantages of class I jumped for the post-Soviet cohort. Thus, the effects of origins on access to postsecondary schooling *increased* during the course of the institutional changes and turmoil in Russia's education system and economy. Finally, the baseline conditional odds of entering any postsecondary institution decreased in a decelerating (logarithmic) fashion across cohorts reaching this transition point after WWII. This surely reflects the increasing size of the risk set discussed above. The increase in the baseline odds implies that the effects of social background on probability ratios tended to increase even prior to the reform cohorts.

The preferred unconditional model for entry to any postsecondary institution exhibits additive gender and origin effects similar to those of the preferred conditional model. However, the only significant cross-cohort change in the baseline odds affects the post-Soviet cohort alone, which has lower odds of entering postsecondary education. Overall, the increasing size of the risk set and the decreasing conditional baseline odds tended to offset one another. Also, the increase in the effect of parental educational for the reform cohorts is not significant using the unconditional model. But the same temporal patterns for the effects of gender and parental class obtain for both the conditional and unconditional models.

Entry to a University (VUZ)

Conditional on becoming eligible for postsecondary schooling, Russian women are 15% less likely to enter a university than otherwise similar men (model 3, Table 12.4). There are more women in the risk set (as implied by the results in Table 12.2), but proportionately fewer enter a VUZ. The effects of parental education are stronger for VUZ entry than for the prior transitions analyzed: Russians with at least one college-educated parent have 2.9 times higher odds of entering a VUZ than equivalent Russians whose best-educated parent is a high school dropout (Model 3). Again I find no significant difference between parental education 2c and the omitted category (1c/2a). The effects of parental class are similar in pattern and magnitude to those for entry to any postsecondary institution: the key distinction separates the offspring of the service classes (I and II) from the rest, with no real distinctions within these two groups.

TABLE 12.5
Logistic regressions for entry to specialized postsecondary (SSUZ) (weighted SESR sample born 1929–79)

	MODEL 1 ELIGIBLE FOR POSTSECONDARY		MODEL 2 ELIGIBLE FOR POSTSECONDARY		MODEL 3 ELIGIBLE FOR POSTSECONDARY		MODEL 4 FULL SAMPLE (UNCONDITIONAL MODEL)	
	B	S.E.	B	S.E.	B	S.E.	B	S.E.
Woman	.600**	.095	.599**	.097	.213	.234	.062	.157
Highest parent's education (1c/2a)								
3b	−.385*	.214	−.498**	.219	−.811**	.251	−.659**	.237
3a	.091	.193	.027	.198	.040	.198	.061	.180
2c	.035	.223	−.058	.229	−.076	.229	−.158	.205
1ab	.087	.188	−.043	.194	.095	.195	−.227	.174
Father's EGP class (V/VI)								
I	.059	.177	−.014	.179	−.001	.178	.038	.165
II	−.227	.171	−.310*	.171	−.302*	.170	−.197	.161
III	−.194	.173	−.229	.176	−.231	.175	−.044	.158
VII	.043	.117	.014	.121	.017	.121	−.088	.109
PTU leaver							−.492**	.155
SSUZ leaver			−3.140**	.343	−3.151**	.343	−.608**	.148
Rural at 14			.210**	.104	.224**	.104	.093	.096
Moscow at 14			−.448**	.156	−.413**	.156	−.189	.146
Father in CPSU			.133	.110	.130	.111	.149	.100
Cohort					−.059*	.033		
Born 1929–33							−.715**	.244
Woman × Cohort					.105**	.046	.152**	.032
Woman × Reform cohorts					−.493**	.185	−.725**	.175
Ed 3b × Reform cohorts					.609**	.230	.386*	.214
Constant	−1.782**	.326	−1.368**	.334	−.833**	.275	−1.385**	.187
Log likelihood	−1,637.7		−1,545.9		−1,542.7		−1,986.8	
N	2,989		2,989		2,989		4,062	

NOTE: See note to Table 12.2.

Graduates from academic secondary institutions clearly have higher odds of entering a VUZ than equivalent graduates from specialized secondary institutions. Moscow origins also improve the odds, while rural origins reduce them. The effect of father's CPSU membership has the expected positive sign, but it is not statistically significant.

The effect of parental class increased for the post-Soviet cohort, providing more evidence of greater origin-based inequality in access to postsecondary schooling as a result of crisis and reform in Russia. Moreover, the long-term trend in the baseline odds is one of decelerating decrease, implying that origin effects on the probabilities tended to grow in magnitude throughout the postwar era.

The unconditional model shows no significant effect of gender on the overall log-odds of VUZ entry: women's advantages in gaining eligibility apparently offset their disadvantage, conditional on eligibility. The effects of origin and the other covariates are quite similar to those in the preferred conditional model, as is the significant increase in the effect of parental class for the post-Soviet cohort. However, there is no trend over time in the baseline odds, according to the unconditional model. All of the increase in VUZ enrollments during the postwar era stemmed from the upgrading of origins rather than an increase in the baseline odds.[10] Also, the unconditional results demonstrate that very few Russians who attend lower vocational schools (PTU) eventually enter a VUZ: their odds of doing so are 5% the odds of academic secondary graduates.

Entry to Specialized (Lower) Postsecondary

As expected, the additive models show that women are considerably more likely than men to enter a SSUZ, conditional on eligibility for postsecondary schooling (Table 12.5). The preferred interaction model shows that this gender gap increased for most of the postwar era, reaching a maximum female-to-male odds ratio of 2.6 for the 1964–68 cohort before falling for the reform cohorts (see Table 12.7).

Social origins do not influence entry to specialized postsecondary education. There is only one significant effect: the offspring of college-educated Russians are *less* likely than the offspring of high-school dropouts to enter specialized postsecondary education. This effect, which weakens for the reform cohorts, reflects the lower status of specialized versus university-level

TABLE 12.6
Logistic regressions for obtaining a university (VUZ) degree (weighted SESR sample not currently enrolled born 1929–76)

	MODEL 1 ELIGIBLE FOR POSTSECONDARY		MODEL 2 ELIGIBLE FOR POSTSECONDARY		MODEL 3 ELIGIBLE FOR POSTSECONDARY		MODEL 4 FULL SAMPLE (UNCONDITIONAL MODEL)	
	B	S.E.	B	S.E.	B	S.E.	B	S.E.
Woman	.160	.231	.127	.233	.130	.233	−.831**	.189
Highest parent's education (1c/2a)								
3b	−.414	.701	−.505	.723	−.379	.709	.755**	.212
3a	−.364	.669	−.338	.686	−.191	.676	.468**	.199
2c	−.671	.753	−.707	.774	−.602	.757	−.389	.239
1ab	−.491	.706	−.457	.726	−.459	.709	−.753**	.201
Father's EGP class (V/VI)								
I	−.203	.412	−.376	.434	−1.726**	.687	.605**	.170
II	.405	.413	.308	.430	.257	.430	.593**	.157
III	−.031	.441	−.080	.450	−.164	.454	.089	.177
VII	.181	.355	.222	.364	.179	.367	−.118	.129
PTU leaver							−3.291**	.428
SSUZ leaver			−1.202**	.336	−1.120**	.332	−1.134**	.185
Rural at 14			.316	.303	.330	.302	−.518**	.106
Moscow at 14			.268	.315	.270	.317	.596**	.138
Father in CPSU			.385	.287	.418	.290	.080	.109
Cohort					−.137**	.068	−.090**	.034
Reform cohorts					−.793**	.371	−.260	.154
Class I × Cohort					.243**	.106		
Woman × Cohort							.153**	.035
Woman × Post-Soviet cohort							−.534**	.250
Constant	2.508**	.788	2.417**	.811	3.124**	.755	−.196	.266
Log likelihood	−298.4		−289.6		−290.7		−1,621.0	
N	910		910		910		3,805	

NOTE: See note to Table 12.2.

postsecondary schooling: children from the most elite origins are more likely to opt for the latter.

Graduates from specialized secondary schools are, naturally, unlikely to enter specialized postsecondary institutions. Students from rural areas are *more* likely to do so, if they are eligible for postsecondary schooling, while those from Moscow are *less* likely to. These findings also point to the lower status of specialized postsecondary institutions. SSUZ programs offer an outlet for satisfying the aspirations of less advantaged Russian students who aspire to some form of postsecondary schooling. The effect of father's CPSU membership is positive but not significant, and the baseline odds of conditional entry to specialized postsecondary institutions decline over time at a modest rate. The results for the unconditional model depart only in relatively trivial ways from the results in model 3.

Attaining a University (VUZ) Degree

In the conditional models, neither gender nor social origins significantly affect the odds of attaining a degree (Table 12.6). Only type of secondary institution has a significant effect, with graduates from specialized secondary institutions substantially less likely to attain a degree once they have commenced university study. The preferred interaction reveals a curious result: in the oldest cohorts, the graduate rate was lowest for the offspring of Class I, but this effect diminishes over time and ultimately reverses. The negative effect for the older cohorts could reflect social selection at lower levels. If nonelite students face greater barriers at lower levels, those who successfully negotiate all the various transitions along the way may have more homogenous and higher unmeasured academic abilities than the elite students who have had easier paths. The reversal of the effect could, in turn, result from the broader pattern of increased advantages for students from elite backgrounds during the reform era. The very high baseline graduation fell gradually across cohorts, and dropped more precipitously for the reform cohorts.[11] Thus, the relative disadvantages of the elite students were strongest when they mattered least (because overall graduation rates were high) and, when graduation rates fell to their lowest level (estimated at 75% for the post-Soviet cohort), elite students actually had an advantage.

The unconditional model for attaining a VUZ degree shows that the effects of gender and family background on the overall log-odds are quite substantial. Obviously, this model captures the cumulative effects of these variables on the earlier transition odds. Among the oldest cohorts, women were significantly less likely to obtain a VUZ degree than otherwise similar men. However, this gender gap steadily diminished, disappearing by the 1954–58 cohort and turning into a modest female advantage for the 1964–68 and 1969–73 cohorts before disappearing again for the post-Soviet cohort. In Russia as elsewhere (Blossfeld and Shavit 1993), women reached educational parity or better with men during the postwar era—specifically, during the 1970s (when the 1954–58 cohort entered postsecondary institutions).

Relative to the odds for Russians whose parents did not complete secondary education and net of the other effects, the odds of attaining a VUZ degree have been 2.1 times higher for Russians with at least one college-educated parent, 1.6 times higher for those with at least one parent with a SSUZ degree, and 0.5 times lower for those whose parents had compulsory education or less. The effects of parental class are limited to the distinction between classes I and II and the remaining classes, with the former enjoying net odds roughly 1.8 times higher than the latter. Type of secondary schooling and place of origin have predictable effects, while the effect of father's CPSU membership is positive but not statistically significant. Perhaps surprisingly, the net unconditional baseline odds of obtaining a VUZ degree decline across cohorts and drop most steeply for the reform-era cohorts. Yet the zero-order effect of cohort is positive. The upgrading of Russians' social origins was the key factor behind the expansion of university enrollments during the postwar era. Moreover, enrollments did not grow fast enough to keep pace with the improved social origins. Finally, the sharper decline in the net baseline odds for the two youngest cohorts suggests that the turmoil and change with Russia's education system and economy exacted a toll on the overall educational attainment of the Russian population.

DISCUSSION

This study of the effects of gender and social background on access to postsecondary schooling in Russia shows that the effects of origins tended to strengthen during the late-Soviet and post-Soviet eras, when institutional changes and economic crisis buffeted Russia's education system. I found significant interaction effects involving cohort and the two relevant parameters: parental education 3b and parental class I. The implied cohort-by-cohort magnitudes for effects that change due to these interactions are presented in summary form in Table 12.7. A cursory look shows increasing effects for the late-Soviet and/or post-Soviet cohorts of either parental education or parental occupation in the models for all four postsecondary outcomes analyzed.

In addition to the increased effects of these variables on the odds, the temporal trends in the baseline odds imply increased effects of parental education and class on the various transition probabilities: *in every case, the reform-era cohorts have experienced lower baseline transition odds than prior cohorts.* This finding replicates Gerber's (2000) results showing a decrease in the odds of completing secondary education and (conditionally) entering VUZ for cohorts born 1969–77 based on a different survey conducted in 1998. Thus, two large surveys conducted well after the collapse of the Soviet system both show that the decline and demise of the USSR have taken a toll on the educational opportunities available to Russians, particularly those with less favorable social origins.

Another noteworthy finding pertains to gender: Russian women have gained on Russian men with respect to most postsecondary transitions. Their initial advantages in reaching eligibility for postsecondary schooling and gaining access to specialized postsecondary institutions increased, their initial disadvantages in entry to any postsecondary institution and to universities decreased and reversed. Overall, women reached parity with men in the overall probability of attaining a university degree by the early 1970s. A reverse gender gap prevailed from the early 1980s through the end of the Soviet period. In Russia, there has been substantial "vertical" gender stratification at the postsecondary level (Charles and Bradley 2002): among postsecondary graduates women have persistently been overrepresented in the less prestigious SSUZy programs. But this must be viewed in the context of women's overall advantage in access to postsecondary education in general and, with time, to university education in particular. The clear story regarding the vertical effects of gender in postwar Russia is that women have gained the upper hand (see Gerber and Schaefer 2004).

Four other findings deserve attention. First, just as Gerber and Hout (1995) found, the postwar expansion of postsecondary schooling could not keep up with the expansion at the secondary level. This is evident in cross-cohort patterns in both the gross transition probabilities (Figure 12.2) and in the net baseline log-odds (Table 12.7). Based on the gross transition

TABLE 12.7
Time varying parameter estimates (based on cohort specifications and interaction terms)

	1929–33	1934–38	1939–43	1944–48	1949–53	1954–58	1959–63	1964–68	1969–73	1974–79
Entry to eligibility										
Baseline logit	.005	.560	.884	1.114	1.293	1.439	1.562	1.669	1.140	.758
Woman effect	.172	.271	.370	.470	.569	.668	.768	.867	.966	1.066
Conditional entry to any postsecondary										
Baseline logit	1.511	1.052	.783	.593	.445	.324	.222	.134	.056	−.014
Woman effect	−.264	−.102	.059	.221	.382	.543	.705	.866	.398	.559
Ed3b effect	.608	.608	.608	.608	.608	.608	.608	.608	1.090	1.090
Class I effect	.604	.604	.604	.604	.604	.604	.604	.604	.604	1.791
Conditional entry to university (VUZ)										
Baseline logit	.023	−.237	−.389	−.497	−.580	−.648	−.706	−.756	−.800	−.840
Class I effect	.359	.359	.359	.359	.359	.359	.359	.359	.359	1.078
Conditional entry to specialized postsecondary (SSUZ)										
Baseline logit	−.833	−.873	−.897	−.914	−.927	−.938	−.947	−.955	−.962	−.968
Woman effect	.213	.319	.424	.530	.635	.740	.846	.951	.564	.669
Ed3b effect	−.811	−.811	−.811	−.811	−.811	−.811	−.811	−.811	−.203	−.203
Conditional attainment of a university (VUZ) Degree										
Baseline logit	2.332	2.987	2.850	2.713	2.576	2.439	2.301	2.164	1.235	1.097
Class I effect	−1.726	−1.483	−1.240	−.997	−.754	−.511	−.268	−.025	.218	.461
Unconditional attainment of a university (VUZY) degree										
Baseline logit	−.196	−.259	−.295	−.321	−.342	−.358	−.372	−.384	−.655	−.664
Woman effect	−.831	−.678	−.524	−.371	−.218	−.065	.088	.241	.394	.013

probabilities, as the rate of secondary completion increased across the 1929–33 to 1954–58 cohorts, the conditional rate of postsecondary and VUZ entry tended to decline. Based on the net log-odds, the baseline probability of becoming eligible for postsecondary schooling increased steadily before abruptly falling for the reform-era cohorts, while the baseline conditional probabilities of entering postsecondary institution and entering a university declined persistently, *even when the risk set decreased in size due to diminishing eligibility for the reform cohorts*. Thus, both the failure of expansion at the postsecondary level to keep pace with expansion at the secondary level for most of the postwar era and the more rapid contraction (net of origins) at the postsecondary level rather than at the secondary level during the more recent period tend to increase origin-based inequalities.

Second, access to postsecondary schooling in Russia is clearly influenced by the type of secondary degree obtained and by place of origin. Graduates from academic secondary schools have much higher odds of entering either form of postsecondary institution and also have higher odds of attaining a VUZ degree, conditional on entering a VUZ. Students from rural areas have lower net odds of becoming eligible, entering any postsecondary institution, and entering a university in particular, while the students from Moscow enjoy advantages in these respects.

Third, this study, the first to explicitly model the effects of origins and other variables on entry to specialized postsecondary schooling, found little evidence of social selection in this process. If anything, higher-origin students are less likely to enter a SSUZ. Thus, the SSUZ degree appears to be a type of second prize in the educational stratification order that is equally available to lower- and higher-origin students who attain eligibility for postsecondary schooling. I also found little or no impact of origins on the conditional odds of attaining a VUZ degree, which replicates the findings of Gerber and Hout (1995).

Finally, this study has demonstrated that the upgrading of social origins in Russia is the key factor driving the overall expansion of postsecondary schooling. Once origins and other factors are controlled, the baseline odds for all the transitions models decrease across cohorts. However, in every case the zero-order effects of cohort (which I estimated but do not show) are positive. Postsecondary schooling obviously did expand in Russia after WWII, but not enough to absorb the increases in demand for postsecondary schooling due to the upgrading of social origins.

Altogether, the Russian case shows that radical changes in the institutions affecting postsecondary education and in the economic environment in which it takes place can have dramatic consequences for educational stratification at this level. In most modern countries, educational inequality has remained stable during the postwar era, and in some countries it has decreased (Blossfeld and Shavit 1993; Erikson and Jonsson 1996a). But the theoretical possibility has always remained that inequality in access to particular levels of schooling could increase. After the analyses of stratification in access to postsecondary schooling in Russia presented here, this possibility is no longer merely theoretical.

CHAPTER THIRTEEN

Switzerland: Tertiary Education Expansion and Social Inequality

Marlis Buchmann, University of Zurich,
Swiss Federal Institute of Technology

Stefan Sacchi, Swiss Federal Institute of Technology

Markus Lamprecht, L & S Sozialforschung und Beratung AG Zurich

Hanspeter Stamm, L & S Sozialforschung und Beratung AG Zurich

THE DEVELOPMENT OF TERTIARY-LEVEL EDUCATION IN SWITZERLAND

The Swiss education system closely reflects Switzerland's political, cultural, and economic diversity. Switzerland comprises four language regions and a total of 26 cantons (i.e., the regional political states). Nevertheless, as all 26 cantons adhere to similar basic principles regarding education and aim at similar targets, there is a great deal of similarity among the different education systems. The Swiss federal structure has also left its mark on the system of tertiary education, which is highly decentralized and has its origin in local needs and traditions rather than in centralized decisions at the federal state level (Wolter 2002).

The federal government contributed to higher education by founding the Zurich Federal Institute of Technology in 1854 and the Ecole Polytechnique in Lausanne in 1968. Apart from these two federal technical institutions of tertiary-level education, Switzerland currently counts ten cantonal universities—the latest additions being the universities in the canton of Ticino (1995) and Lucerne (2000) (see Switzerland EDK/BBW 2001). In parallel with the establishment of the universities, the first schools for vocational training for commerce and industry were founded. At first, the promotion of vocational training was the sole responsibility of professional associations. However, in 1930 the "federal law on vocational training" delegated some regulatory power to the federal government. Since 1930, this law has been revised several times to include an increasing number of national regulations regarding tertiary education. Within this general framework, the cantons are entrusted with carrying out federal regulations in close cooperation with professional associations. The latter operate vocational schools or contribute to their financing. About half of all students in higher vocational training attend private schools operated by occupational, professional, and industry-wide associations, which in many instances offer part-time courses (Switzerland EDK/BBW 2001). In addition, professional and industry-wide associations are still responsible for the Berufsprüfungen and höhere Fachprüfungen (i.e., tertiary-level vocational diplomas). Although the federal government supervises the examinations and approves the curricula, there is still a large number of higher vocational diplomas that lack official (i.e., federal) recognition. This applies in particular to social work, health care, pedagogy (teacher training), the fine arts, the performing arts (music, theatre, dance), applied linguistics, and applied psychology—all predominantly female occupations.

Institutions of further education for skilled workers were the precursors of several tertiary-level vocational schools specializing in selected professions. Among these "polytechnics," higher technical schools (Höhere Technische Lehranstalten (HTL)) have played a particularly important role. Most of these schools were established in the second half of the twentieth century.

At the beginning of the 1990s, Switzerland counted about 120 of these nonacademic institutions of higher education offering training in engineering, economics and business management, music, art and design, health care, and social work. The training of primary school and kindergarten teachers usually took place in the nonuniversity sector as well. But despite the large number of these schools and their considerable growth, their significance and reputation was relatively low compared with the universities (Schweizerischer Fachhochschulrat 2000, Switzerland EDK/BBW 2001). As late as 1978, the Swiss Science Council regarded universities (i.e., academic institutions of higher education) as the only institutions of "true" tertiary education.

In the 1990s, the Swiss education system faced new challenges. The European integration in particular called for changes in the system of tertiary education. In addition, the economic recession of the 1990s led to mounting political pressure. According to Wolter (2002), two processes were at work. On the one hand, the education system became more open and started to engage in international cooperation, which resulted in increased student mobility and a need for an adjustment of institutions of higher education and of their curricula. On the other hand, political changes led to a reform of the federal jurisdiction concerning the promotion and regulation of education. As a result, agreement was reached in 1995 regarding the institutionalization of several tertiary-level schools of applied science, art, and technology.

Currently, about half of the former 120 institutions of higher vocational learning have been integrated into seven tertiary-level educational institutions of applied science (Schweizerischer Fachhochschulrat 2000), while some of the former tertiary-level vocational schools survive independently. Special professional schools provide training in the health care sector (e.g., nursing) and in social pedagogy. To summarize, there are four types of tertiary-level education in Switzerland at present:

1. cantonal universities and the Swiss Federal Institutes of Technology;
2. schools of higher education in applied science, art, and advanced technology, created by federal law in 1996;
3. tertiary-level vocational tracks offering state-recognized (i.e., federal) diplomas;
4. tertiary-level vocational tracks offering credentials recognized by a canton or by a professional or industry-wide association.

The first type represents the academic, *university* track of tertiary-level education, while the second, third, and fourth types belong to the complex system of tertiary-level *vocational* education.

LEGAL BACKGROUND AND FINANCES

Because of Swiss federalism, the ten universities (Type 1) belong to the cantons. Although federal law permits the federal government to create, operate, and support institutions of tertiary education, in the past it has used this capacity only twice, to create the Federal Institute of Technology in 1854 and the Ecole Polytechnique in 1968. The various attempts and initiatives to increase the federal government's say in educational matters failed (Switzerland EDK/BBW 2001). However, since several universities with limited cantonal resources have started to encounter difficulties in meeting the complex demands of tertiary education, the federal government has increasingly been forced to step in with subsidies. In 1968, a federal law was passed concerning the promotion of universities and the cooperation among them. Subsequently, the law has been reformed twice: in 1991 and 1999. Its latest revision addressed organizational structures and introduced performance criteria as well as more efficient control procedures that universities were required to implement.

The federal government has the jurisdiction and competence to approve tracks in technology and architecture, business management and administration, agriculture, and design. These tracks receive federal subsidies. The cantons are the principal operators of the new schools. They carry the main financial burden (often as joint ventures between several cantons) and regulate the areas where the federal government lacks jurisdiction. Apart from the tracks offering state-recognized tertiary-level vocational credentials, many higher vocational training programs are held under the auspices of professional or industry-wide associations (Switzerland BFS 2001) (Type 4). Professional associations are also responsible for the definition and content of the curricula of some Type 3 tracks and share some responsibility for examinations. This complex system of credentials is about to change with the new federal law on vocational training (in force since January 1, 2004). The federal government favors a comprehensive solution, aiming at greater federal responsibility.

At the end of the 1990s, the public cost of tertiary education in Switzerland amounted to about one fifth of total public spending on education. The federal government contributed 46.5% to the total cost, the cantons 53.0%, and the communities 1.5% (see Switzerland EDK/BBW 2001, 29).

GOALS, CERTIFICATION, DIFFERENTIATION, AND ADMISSION

Type 1: Universities

Although each of Switzerland's 12 universities (the ten cantonal and the two federal polytechnic universities) has its own features, their structures are similar. In general, the so-called *Matura* certificate entitles students to university enrollment. Under certain conditions, graduates from schools of higher education in applied science (Type 2) can continue their training at the cantonal universities.

The universities award three types of academic title: the *Lizentiat* (equivalent to a master's degree); the *doctorate* (equivalent to a PhD); and the *habilitation*, which in most Swiss universities is the prerequisite for obtaining a university professorship. In 1990, all universities began offering several postgraduate diploma courses. According to university regulations, the average duration of study for the *Lizentiat* should be eight semesters and an additional semester for the master's thesis. In reality, studies often last considerably longer. University graduates have relatively good job opportunities. According to Switzerland EDK/BBW (2001, 116), about 90% find a permanent position immediately upon completion of their studies.

Type 2: Schools of Higher Education in Applied Science, Art, and Advanced Technology

The seven schools of applied science, art, and technology offer a total of about 300 advanced training programs in science and the arts, focusing on advanced occupational skills and related technical and methodological expertise. These tracks are more directly linked to professional practice than academic (Type 1) programs.

Admission to the schools of applied science is usually based on vocational matriculation (*Berufsmatur*). This certificate, acquired after completion of formal vocational training, was introduced in 1994 by the federal government as the principal means toward higher education in these new tertiary-level schools. However, some fields of study, like teaching, still require the *Matura* acquired in the *Gymnasium* (or high school), or professional experience, or both.

Curricula at the schools of applied science usually include theoretical as well as practical subjects and require about three years of study. In addition to full-time programs, several part-time programs lasting about four years on average are offered for people who want to work while they study. Graduates from these schools have excellent opportunities in the labor market (Schweizer Fachhochschulrat 2000; Switzerland EDK/BBW 2001).

Type 3: Tertiary-Level Vocational Tracks Offering State-Recognized (Federal) Credentials

"In higher technical and professional schools, skilled workers further their general education, improve their professional skills and acquire management and leadership qualifications which improve their further career opportunities." (Switzerland EDK/BBW 2001, 120). After their studies, graduates should be able to fill positions in middle management. The programs have a strong practical bias and usually take two to three years for full- or part-time study.

The current situation is somewhat complicated by the fact that about half of the tertiary-level vocational tracks offering state-recognized credentials have recently been integrated into the new schools of higher education of applied science (Type 2). At the end of the 1990s, federally recognized diplomas could be obtained in about 70 technical tracks and 30 professional tracks.[1] Admission to these tracks requires a secondary-level vocational credential, sometimes supplemented by several years of occupation-specific experience, or an upper secondary general diploma. The labor market prospects of students who acquire one of these state-recognized tertiary-level vocational credentials have been favorable to date.

Type 4: Tertiary-Level Vocational Tracks Offering Credentials Recognized by a Canton or a Professional or Industry-Wide Association

The situation is even more complex with respect to the large number of tertiary-level vocational tracks and programs offering credentials that lack state recognition (i.e., federal state). As there are no official figures covering the entire sector, its size is difficult to quantify. For example, the educational tracks under the control of the professional associations of the Red Cross prepare people for vocational diplomas in the field of health (nurses, head nurses, dieticians, and other health professionals). Admission to these tracks requires either a vocational diploma, sometimes supplemented by the requirement of occupation-specific experience, or an upper secondary general certificate. There is often also a minimum age requirement. The labor market perspectives of graduates are perceived to be good (BFS 1994; Switzerland EDK/BBW 2001).

ASSESSMENT OF THE DEVELOPMENT OF
HIGHER EDUCATION IN SWITZERLAND

Even before the institutionalization of the new schools for higher education in applied science, art, and technology (Type 2), Switzerland had a diverse, complex, and nonuniform system of tertiary education (see also Meek et al. 1996; Cusin and Vanhooydonck 2001). Apart from universities, several institutions of higher learning offered a range of sophisticated and practice-oriented programs. The part of the system dedicated to higher vocational training, in which the private sector (i.e., professional associations) plays a crucial role, is extremely complex. The programs offered differ with respect to type and level of difficulty, educational mission, admission requirements, duration, legal framework, and financing.

For a long time, vocational training and university education were considered to be two mutually exclusive educational careers. The institutionalization of the new schools of applied science, art, and technology has somewhat softened the strong segregation between professional education on the one hand, and scientific education and research on the other. But compared with other European countries, this step toward the expansion and improvement of the system of professional education has been long delayed.

Table 13.1 shows the development of different curricula and diplomas since the beginning of the 1960s. The number of university students, for example, has increased continuously from about 21,000 in 1960 to about 96,000 in 2000. The gross enrollment ratio for this time period, standardized to the size of the population of 18–24 year olds, increased from 3.8% to 16.5%. During the same time, the proportion of female students has risen from 16.8% to 45.6%.

A similar development pattern is evident in tertiary-level vocational education. The growth in the number of degrees—as well as the corresponding gross completion ratios (standardized to the size of the population of the 18–24 year olds)—also shows a gradual, continuous expansion in the period under consideration.

In sum, we conclude that tertiary education in Switzerland has expanded considerably in the course of the past forty years. The expansion was surprisingly continuous, with no evidence that the process has accelerated or "exploded" as has sometimes been suggested. This holds true for

TABLE 13.1
Number of students and number of diplomas, 1960–2000. Gross enrollment and completion ratios 1960–2000 as percentage of the 18–24-year-old population

NUMBER OF STUDENTS BETWEEN 1960 AND 2001

	UNIVERSITIES (INCLUDING FEDERAL INSTITUTES OF TECHNOLOGY)			SCHOOLS OF HIGHER EDUCATION OF APPLIED SCIENCE, ART, AND TECHNOLOGY			TERTIARY-LEVEL VOCATIONAL TRACKS, STATE-RECOGNIZED, PARTLY NOT STATE-RECOGNIZED[b]		
	Number of students	% 18–24 year olds	Share of female students (%)	Number of students	% 18–24 year olds	Share of female students (%)	Number of students	% 18–24 year olds	Share of female students (%)
1960	21,324	3.8	16.8						
1965	32,883	4.8	19.8						
1970	42,178	6.3	22.5						
1975	52,622	8.2	26.8						
1980	61,373	9.2	32.4				23,914	3.6	24.8
1985	74,806	10.4	35.8				35,161	4.9	24.2
1990	85,940	12.5	38.8				51,562	7.5	27.7
1995	88,243	14.6	41.8	4,780[f]	0.8	17.4[f]	59,781	9.9	31.5
2000	96,667	16.5	45.6	24,902	4.3	25.7	41,072	7.0	43.1

NUMBER OF DIPLOMAS 1960 AND 2001[a]

	UNIVERSITIES (INCLUDING FEDERAL INSTITUTES OF TECHNOLOGY)			TERTIARY-LEVEL VOCATIONAL TRACKS WITH STATE-RECOGNIZED CREDENTIALS[c]		
	Number of Lizentiate diplomas[d]	% 18–24 year olds	Share of female students (%)[e]	Number of diplomas	% 18–24 year olds	Share of female students (%)
1960	1,278	0.2	14.1	2,257	0.4	
1965	1,905	0.3	13.5	2,785	0.4	
1970	3,832	0.6	26.0	3,550	0.5	
1975	3,904	0.6	30.9	3,795	0.6	
1980	5,395	0.8	26.3	6,796	1.0	
1985	6,250	0.9	32.7	7,847	1.1	
1990	7,751	1.1	33.2	12,082	1.8	15.0
1995	8,690	1.4	38.7	17,044	2.8	20.2
2000	9,686	1.7	43.9	15,443	2.6	28.1

[a] For the year 2000 only, figures are available for diplomas from the schools of higher education of applied science, arts, and technology. The number of diplomas in that year was 1,811, of which 17.9% were awarded to females.
[b] Given the complex situation in the field of tertiary-level vocational tracks of Type 3 and Type 4, these figures are hard to disentangle. From 1984/85 onward, figures include the preparation for higher professional exams; from 1996/97 onward, the figures exclude schools that have attained the status of schools of higher education of applied science, arts, and technology.
[c] Federal diplomas and certificates as well as credentials awarded by tertiary-level vocational tracks offering state-recognized credentials (from 2000 onward, *without* diplomas awarded by schools of higher education of applied science, art, and technology), omitting diplomas of tracks not regulated by the federal state. Up until 1980, the number of diplomas included only engineering and technical professions (HTL), as well as federally recognized diplomas (excluding so-called *Fachausweise*).
[d] Graduates of the Universities of Basel, Berne, Fribourg, Geneva, Lausanne, Neuchâtel, and Zurich plus the Federal Institute of Technology in Zurich. From 1970 onward, the numbers also include graduates of the Ecole Polytechnique in Lausanne and of the University of St. Gall.
[e] Until 1980, the proportion of women in universities only is reported. That is, the Swiss Federal Institutes of Technology are not included in the Statistical Yearbooks (in these schools the share of female students is considerably lower, however).
[f] Figures apply to 1997/98.

Sources for number of students: BFS 2001a, 2002; Statistical Yearbooks 1960–2002.
Sources for number of diplomas: Authors' calculations on the basis of BFS 2001b and BFS 2002; Statistical Yearbooks 1960–2002.

both academic tertiary education (universities) and vocational tertiary education, although the expansion has been much stronger in the decentralized and somewhat complex field of higher vocational education, in which the professional and business associations play a crucial role.

THEORY AND HYPOTHESES

Although the Swiss system of tertiary education did not undergo major institutional reforms or periods of accelerated expansion during the 1970s and 1980s, a question still arises regarding the likely consequences of the gradual expansion of vocational *and* academic tertiary education on social inequalities in higher education by class and especially by gender. Previous research has shown that the expansion of educational opportunities may raise the educational attainment rates of lower social strata. If the enrollment rates of higher social strata have not yet reached the level of saturation, the association between social origin and educational attainment will not necessarily become weaker and inequalities in educational opportunities are not reduced (see, e.g., Shavit and Blossfeld 1993). In the light of previous results documenting the high stability of social inequality in educational attainment in Switzerland (see, e.g., Buchmann, Charles, and Sacchi 1993) and against the background of the strongly segmented Swiss system of higher education, we do not expect the association between social origin (i.e., family background) and enrollment in higher education to change much in the period under consideration. We anticipate this to be the case for both tertiary-level vocational schooling and university education. We likewise expect high stability in gender inequalities regarding enrollment in tertiary-level vocational education particularly, but also with respect to university education. The main reason for the former is that occupation-specific apprenticeships are highly sex-segregated, with female-dominated occupations offering far fewer institutional opportunities for enrollment in tertiary-level vocational training than male-dominated occupations.

In the period under consideration, many more tertiary-level vocational programs for additional occupations were institutionalized. We call this process the gradual *qualitative diversification* of the expansion of vocational higher education in Switzerland. In other words, the institutional opportunities for vocational higher education have substantially expanded. We therefore expect that the increasing probability of entering vocational higher education can be at least partially attributed to enrollment in the newly institutionalized programs and not only to higher enrollment rates in well-established, old vocational programs. With regard to enrollment in university programs, we attribute the stability in gender inequality to the still rather weak labor market orientation of even highly educated women in Switzerland (see Buchmann et al. 2002).

Finally, we also expect the economic situation to affect the probability of transition into tertiary-level higher education. We assume that a friendlier climate for investment, including investment in human capital, prevails in times of economic growth and promising economic outlook. Moreover, during periods of economic expansion, the growing demand for educated workers increases their expected earnings, which, in turn, raises young people's motivation to attend schools and universities. We suspect that the effect is stronger for tertiary-level vocational training because many tertiary-level vocational programs offer part-time study so that employees can keep their jobs. In prosperous economic times, employers are also more willing (or forced) to support their employees in pursuing further education.

DATA AND METHODS

Our analyses are based on data obtained from a mail survey of two Swiss-German birth cohorts: one born between 1949 and 1951, the other between 1959 and 1961. The survey was administered in 1989 and includes detailed biographical information on educational, occupational, and family careers.[2] The analyses presented here are based on a representative sample of the two birth cohorts weighted to correct for an oversampling of selected labor market regions and a moderate underrepresentation of lower educational strata among the respondents.

We start our analysis by specifying two eligibility models, one for tertiary-level vocational training and the other for university enrollment, in order to assess the processes of selectivity already taking place at secondary-level schooling. Eligibility for university education is defined by completion of intermediate-level general education with matriculation (CASMIN 2c). Eligibility for tertiary vocational schooling is based on completion of a secondary-level qualification, whether an apprenticeship (CASMIN 2a), full-time vocational schooling (CASMIN 2b), or matriculation (CASMIN 2c). We include age, social class background, parental education, sex, and cohort in the models and systematically test for interaction effects by cohort and sex. By including these interaction terms, we test for possible change in social background effects. The measurement of these variables is described together with the other variables used in the models for enrollment in (and completion of) tertiary-level education.

When examining enrollment in tertiary-level vocational and academic education, we need to take into account the pattern of gradual expansion that characterizes the development of the Swiss institutions of tertiary education since the 1960s. This is true for both vocational and academic tracks of higher education. Given that no particular period is marked by an extraordinarily rapid pace of expansion, it is not possible to clearly distinguish periods before and after the expansion of the tertiary education system. Under these circumstances, it is not feasible to employ a strategy of cohort analysis to examine the effects of expansion on the process of educational stratification. Therefore, integrating the successive differentiation of the educational programs at the tertiary level into the model appears as a successful analytical strategy. Such an approach requires, however, a time-dependent modeling strategy. Moreover, as noted by Shavit et al. (2002), the strategy of cohort analyis is problematic because we are interested in assessing the effects of the expanding educational opportunities on social inequalities at the level of higher education while cohorts do not attend tertiary education at a uniform pace, and the effects related to educational expansion cannot be separated from those of censoring for younger cohorts.

For these reasons, we opted for a variant of the logistic regression model to specify the process of *entry* into vocational and academic tertiary education (enrollment model). We use the same type of logit model for examining *completion* of vocational and academic tertiary education (completion model). The units of analysis are person-years. This analytical strategy implies that we execute event-history models involving discrete time using software for logistic regressions. Time is defined by age. The starting point is the age of 18, which marks the earliest opportunity for people to enroll in university programs or to enter vocational tertiary education. The end point is the age of 40, which is the age of the oldest members of the 1949–51 cohort at the time of the survey. For comparability of results with the other contributions to this volume, we provided the project facilitators with baseline logistic models of enrollment and completion (available upon request of the authors).

ANALYSIS PROCEDURE

We specified models for enrollment and completion for both tertiary vocational and academic education. For the four educational outcomes of interest, the number of person-years (episodes) and the number of enrollments and completions (events) are shown at the bottom of the tables. In each year between the ages of 18 and 40, an individual has a chance of entering (or completing) a given type of tertiary education for the first time, unless he or she has already done so. The log-odds of entering or completing a given type of tertiary education are affected both by individual and contextual characteristics.

For each of the four possible outcomes, we create the following models: (I) baseline model unconditional, including age, social class, parents' education, cohort, and gender (not shown; available from authors on request); (II) baseline model conditional (based on eligibility for the respective educational tracks); (III) baseline model conditional, adding respondents' educational trajectory; (IV) inclusion of period effects (annual growth of GDP) and interaction effects (gender and cohort) in model III.[3]

The variables are defined as follows. *Tertiary-level vocational training* includes all types of educational training coded in category 3a of the CASMIN educational schema. *University training* refers to the CASMIN educational level 3b. *Class background* is measured by Goldthorpe's class schema (Erikson and Goldthorpe 1992). We distinguish three classes of *white-collar workers* (I, II, and III), *petite bourgeoisie* and *farm owners* (IVabc), *skilled workers* (V+VI), and *nonskilled workers* (VIIab). Skilled workers serve as reference class. For parental education (highest level attained by either father or mother), we use the CASMIN schema. We distinguish six categories: compulsory schooling (1a); basic secondary-level schooling (1b); apprenticeship and intermediate-level general/vocational education without matriculation (2ab); intermediate-level general education with matriculation (2c); tertiary-level vocational schooling (3a); and university (3b). Category 2ab serves as a reference group. Two dummy variables are used to distinguish the respondent's cohort membership (1 = born in 1959–61) and gender (1 = female). Age is treated as a categorical variable.

A set of time-dependent variables measures the respondent's own educational trajectory. These variables differ by type of tertiary education. With regard to vocational schooling, we include two dummy variables indicating whether matriculation (2c) (i.e., eligibility for university enrollment) and/or full-time vocational schooling (2b) has been completed before entry into a tertiary-level vocational program. Completion of an apprenticeship is the (implicit) reference category. In addition, a series of variables indicate the occupational field in which respondents gained their first vocational training qualification, where (among others) cleaning, transportation, and security are the (implicit) reference category. With regard to university education, we include two dummy variables for measuring whether respondents had completed an apprenticeship (2a) and/or full-time vocational schooling (2b) before enrolling in a university.

We include three time-dependent variables to assess period effects. The economic situation is measured by the change in the growth of GDP compared with the previous year. Institutional expansion of tertiary vocational training include[4] opportunity for *Höhere Fachprüfung* (Type 3 of tertiary-level education) and opportunity for *Berufsprüfung* (Type 3 of tertiary-level education). They measure whether, in a given year, the respondent's occupational certificate allows taking these types of higher examinations. Unfortunately, these two indicators of the institutional expansion of tertiary-level vocational training are far from including every type of vocational higher education. Our indicators therefore underestimate the qualitative differentiation of tertiary-level vocational education.

Finally, we tested for all cohort and gender interactions to learn whether the effects of social background turn out to be different for the two cohorts and for both men and women.[5] In the final model (model IV), we included only those interaction terms that showed significant effects.

RESULTS

Tertiary-Level Vocational Schooling: Enrollment and Completion

For the two cohorts under consideration here, those born between 1949–51 and 1959–61, eligibility to tertiary-level vocational education increased from 79.8% to 88.9% (see Table 13.2). In both cohorts, however, only a small proportion of those eligible makes use of this educational opportunity. We find a significant 4% increase in enrollment rates across cohorts: 13.6% of the older cohort enrolled in vocational training at the tertiary level

TABLE 13.2
Eligibility, attendance, and completion rates of vocational and academic tertiary programs by cohort and by cohort × sex

	TERTIARY-LEVEL VOCATIONAL PROGRAMS			TERTIARY-LEVEL ACADEMIC PROGRAMS		
	Eligibility (%)	Attendance (%)	Completion (%)	Eligibility (%)	Attendance (%)	Completion (%)
Cohort						
Cohort 1949–51 (N = 1,097)	79.8	13.6	12.8	12.8	8.8	7.0
Cohort 1959–61 (N = 1,180)	88.9	17.5	16.2	17.8	11.5	8.9
Cohort × Sex						
Women 1949–51 (N = 509)	73.4	6.3	5.9	12.6	5.4	3.8
Women 1959–61 (N = 582)	84.1	8.0	7.5	19.1	8.3	6.0
Men 1949–51 (N = 588)	85.7	20.1	18.9	13.0	11.8	10.0
Men 1959–61 (N = 598)	93.5	26.8	24.8	16.6	14.6	11.7

compared with 17.5% of their younger counterparts. Of the first cohort, 12.8% completed their training compared with 16.2% of their younger counterparts. This difference is significant. Gender differences in enrollment and consequently in completion rates are very pronounced and remain more or less stable across cohorts. Men are about three times more likely to enter (and complete) tertiary vocational programs than women. Moreover, for both cohorts, the higher the parents' educational background, the higher the respondents' enrollment and completion rates in tertiary vocational schooling. There are two major exceptions to this linear pattern: one concerns the extremely low enrollment rate of people in the older cohort whose parents attained intermediate-level general education with *Matura* (2c); the other pertains to people in both cohorts, but especially in the younger one, from families with parental university education, who are less likely to enroll in this type of tertiary program than respondents whose parents completed tertiary vocational schooling (3a). Both findings seem to be a first indication of intergenerational tracking between tertiary-level vocational and academic education. Broken down by social class and cohort, it does not show a clear-cut linear pattern in either cohort. Classes I, II, and IVabc show higher enrollment (and completion) rates than the others. There are two exceptions to the general trend of higher enrollment rates in the younger cohort: classes II and VIIab.

In Table 13.3, the explicative analysis of the eligibility for tertiary vocational schooling shows that parental education has a significant effect on children's chances of graduating from secondary school (CASMIN 2a, 2b, or 2c). These chances increase with each additional level of parental education (completion of an apprenticeship or full-time vocational training serves as the reference category).[6] The only people who deviate from this pattern are from homes where a tertiary-level vocational diploma was achieved (CASMIN 3a); their chances of receiving a secondary-level qualification match those of the reference group (2ab) and are much lower than those of respondents whose parents achieved a credential that makes them eligible for university (2c).[7] The effects of social class background are substantially weaker but also significant. The coefficients show that, ceteris paribus, children raised in families of class IIIab (and, to a lesser extent, class II) run hardly any risk of not attaining an educational credential at this level of schooling. Members of the younger cohort (1959–61) are much more likely to attain a secondary-level credential than their older counter-

TABLE 13.3
Eligibility for tertiary vocational education (completion of either apprenticeship (CASMIN 2a), intermediate level general without matriculation (CASMIN 2b), or intermediate-level general with matriculation (CASMIN 2c))

	B	S.E.	exp(B)
Goldthorpe classes (Class V+VI)	**		
Class I	−.69	.50	.50
Class II	.92*	.39	2.51
Class IIIab	2.70**	1.07	14.92
Class IVabc	.13	.19	1.13
Class VIIab	.35	.21	1.42
Parental Education (Apprenticeship CAS. 2ab)	***		
Compulsory schooling (CASMIN 1a)	−2.81***	.22	.11
Basic secondary schooling (CASMIN 1b)	−1.38***	.23	.25
Intermediate-level general (CASMIN 2c)	1.03	.94	2.80
Tertiary-level vocational (CASMIN 3a)	−.43	.36	.65
University (CASMIN 3b)	2.39*	1.10	10.92
Cohort (1959–61)	.58***	.16	1.79
Sex (Women)	−1.04***	.16	.35
Constant	2.94***	.23	18.89
N	2,107		
−2 log likelihood	1,089		
Model chi-square	264		
df	12		
Significance	***		
Nagelkerke R^2	.26		
Hosmer–Lemeshow test *(p)*	.046		

*$p ≤ 0.05$; **$p ≤ 0.01$; ***$p ≤ 0.001$.

parts (1949–51). Women, by contrast, are much less likely than men to gain a secondary-level educational credential. The relevant statistical measures show that the explanatory power of the model is moderate (Nagelkerke $R^2 = 0.26$) and the fit (Hosmer–Lemeshow test, $p = 0.046$) is acceptable.

When testing for interaction effects of cohort and gender, most of the main effects discussed remain stable (results not shown), although the rather modest power of the statistical tests in these interaction models must be kept in mind. One effect does not remain stable: the impact of social class II changes across cohorts. Members of the younger cohort from social class II families do not have better chances of obtaining a secondary schooling qualification than their older counterparts did. In this respect, social class has become less important for educational attainment. At the same time, respondents from self-employed families (IVabc) in the younger cohort obtain secondary-level credentials at a significantly higher rate than the reference group (families of skilled workers (V+VI)), while their older counterparts were about equal with the reference group. The chances of gaining a credential at this level increased for both men and women in the younger cohort. The gender difference did not decrease across cohorts, however. This finding is of particular relevance when taking into account the strong baseline effect of gender. With the inclusion of the interaction effects, a good fit of the model is achieved (Hosmer–Lemeshow $p = 0.20$), and the explanatory power of the model becomes slightly better.

Next we examined the question of whether the expansion of tertiary-level vocational schooling has altered the chances of enrollment in and completion of these programs, keeping in mind the selectivity process at work with regard to social background and gender at the level of secondary schooling. We created a conditional baseline model for enrollment in tertiary vocational schooling, restricting the sample to those who were eligible for this type of education, and we included age, social class, parental education, cohort, and gender as predictors (model II in Table 13.4).

The strongest effects relate to gender and parental education. Women are much less likely than men to enroll in tertiary-level vocational training. The odds ratio is about 0.2 to 1, so that women's relative chances are almost 80% lower. This finding reflects primarily the strong institutional barriers hindering women's access to higher vocational education. As discussed in Buchmann et al. (1999), occupations dominated by men offer many more institutional opportunities for accessing higher vocational education.[8] For the great majority of occupations dominated by women, there are no officially recognized tracks of higher vocational training. Compared with the reference group of people from families in which the parents have served an apprenticeship, the odds on entering tertiary-level vocational education are significantly lower for those whose parents completed compulsory schooling (1a) only. When the educational background of the parents is basic secondary schooling (1b), intermediate-level general education (2c), or even university education (3), the probability of enrolling in this type of tertiary education does not differ from the apprenticeship level. For those raised in families in which one of the parents (or both) attained tertiary-level vocational training (3a), however, the odds of entering this type of tertiary education are almost twice as high as for people whose parents' highest educational credential is the apprenticeship (exp $B = 1.81$), which seems to point to intergenerational transmission of educational preferences and occupational choices. As will

TABLE 13.4
Determinants of enrollment in tertiary-level vocational schooling, conditional models

Variables	MODEL II BASELINE B	S.E.	exp(B)	MODEL III EDUCATIONAL TRAJECTORY B	S.E.	exp(B)	MODEL IV PERIOD AND INTERACTION EFFECTS B	S.E.	exp(B)
Age[a]	***			***			***		
Goldthorpe classes (Class V+V)									
Class I	−.09	.34	.92	−.02	.34	.99	−.11	.34	.89
Class II	.16	.20	1.18	.26	.20	1.29	.28	.20	1.33
Class IIIab	−.06	.34	.94	.07	.35	1.08	.04	.35	1.04
Class IVabc	.30	.17	1.36	.30	.17	1.35	.31	.18	1.37
Class VIIab	−.23	.24	.80	−.19	.25	.82	−.18	.25	.84
Parental education (Apprenticeship CASMIN 2ab)	***			***			***		
Compulsory schooling (CASMIN 1a)	−.75***	.25	.47	−.66**	.25	.52	−.67**	.25	.51
Basic secondary schooling (CASMIN 1b)	−.36	.19	.70	−.27	.19	.76	.30	.19	.74
Intermediate-level general (CASMIN 2c)	.11	.32	1.11	.27	.33	1.31	.17	.33	1.18
Tertiary-level vocational (CASMIN 3a)	.59***	.20	1.81	.73***	.21	2.07	.68***	.21	1.98
University (CASMIN 3b)	.33	.31	1.39	.48	.31	1.61	.52	.32	1.67
Cohort (1959–61)	.40**	.14	1.49	.40**	.14	1.49	.27	.16	1.31
Sex (Women)	−1.47***	.16	.23	−1.31***	.20	.27	−.12	.44	.89
Intermediate-level general with matriculation[b]				−1.22***	.31	.30	−1.04***	.31	1.20
Full-time vocational schooling[b]				.80***	.18	2.24	.18	.34	.26
Type of vocational ed: Industrial/crafts[b]				1.25***	.34	3.48	1.95***	.48	7.03
Type of vocational ed: Technical[b]				2.08***	.35	8.00	2.78***	.47	16.11

Type of vocational ed: Clerical[b]				.71*	.35	2.03	1.54***	.52	4.64
Type of vocational ed: Restaurant service[b]				1.51***	.41	4.51	2.29***	.56	9.92
Type of vocational ed: Semiscientific[b]				1.39**	.57	4.03	1.97***	.64	7.19
Type of vocational ed: Graphics/artisan[b]				1.97***	.59	7.19	2.17***	.60	8.75
Type of vocational ed: Pedagogical[b]				2.30***	.43	10.01	2.10***	.44	8.16
Change in gross domestic product[b]							.09***	.03	1.09
Opportunity: Höhere Fachprüfung[b]							−.05	.18	.95
Opportunity: Höhere Berufsprüfung[b]							.14	.18	1.15
Full-time vocational schooling × Cohort (1959)[b]							.81*	.39	2.25
Type of vocational ed. (aggr.) × Sex							−1.55***	.51	.21
Constant	−3.30***	.22	.04	−4.61***	.39	.01	−5.49***	.51	.00
Episodes/events	20966/268			20966/268			20966/268		
−2 log likelihood	2355			2247			2223		
Model chi-square	316			424			448		
df	34			43			48		
Significance	***			***			***		
Nagelkerke R^2	.13			.17			.18		
Hosmer–Lemeshow test (p)	.546			.535			.518		

[a]Effects for individual age categories not shown.
[b]Time-dependent covariates.

*$p \leq 0.05$; **$p \leq 0.01$; ***$p \leq 0.001$.

be seen in Table 13.5 (eligibility for university entry), the intergenerational tracking separating vocational from general education sets in long before entry to tertiary-level schooling. Children of parents with tertiary-level vocational schooling (3a) are about four times less likely to attain the *Matura* certificate than children from academic families (3b) (Table 13.5), and are channeled into tertiary-level vocational education to a much greater extent than children from academic families. Father's class, however, does not change the odds of the children's enrollment. The educational resources accumulated in the family affect the probability of entering higher vocational education more than the discrete distinctions between social classes. Cohort shows a significant positive effect (odds ratio of 1.49 to 1 (Table 13.4)). The opportunities for entering a vocational track of higher education improved significantly for the 1959–61 cohort compared with the 1949–51 cohort. This finding is consistent with the official statistics on tertiary-level vocational schooling presented above. Finally, *age* shows a significant overall effect on entry into tertiary vocational training. The prognostic power of the model is moderate, but the model fits the data well. Comparing the conditional model with the unconditional one (results not shown), we observe hardly any change.

Inclusion of the respondent's *educational trajectory* to the *conditional* baseline model improves the model substantially (model III in Table 13.4).[9] By adding education, the effects observed in the baseline model do not change in any significant way, however. Completion of *Matura* (2c) before enrollment in tertiary-level vocational training greatly lowers the relative chances of pursuing this type of tertiary education (exp B = 0.30), whereas the completion of full-time vocational schooling (compared with the completion of an apprenticeship) greatly enhances them (exp B = 2.24). These findings provide strong support for the rigid and almost impermeable tracking of vocational and academic higher education in Switzerland. Young people certified in general education (i.e., completion of matriculation) are highly unlikely to enter a vocational track of higher education although this track is accessible to them. Strong differences in the odds ratio for enrolling in tertiary vocational programs exist between the types of occupational fields in which the secondary-level qualification was gained. Technical occupations, pedagogical occupations, and those in graphic arts show a much higher odds ratio than the reference group (remaining occupational fields in the service sector). For technical occupations, the relative chances increase by a factor of 8, for pedagogical occupations by a factor of 10, and for graphic arts by a factor of 7. This shows that the type of vocational certificate determines to a great extent the institutional access to tertiary-level vocational education.

The last model presented in Table 13.4 (model IV) includes three time-dependent variables to assess period effects and two significant interaction effects: one related to cohort and the other to gender. For the period effects, the time-dependent covariates represent substantively defined indicators.[10] Given that the effects of the newly introduced variables are rather small, the effects of the predictors already included in the previous model hardly change.[11] Nevertheless, we observe one significant effect ($p < 0.000$) related to change in Gross Domestic Product. A GDP growth of one point over the previous year increases the odds ratio by a factor of 1.09. In times of economic growth and promising economic outlook, there is a friendlier climate for investment, and young people may be more willing to invest in their education. Likewise, firms may be more willing to support their employees' educational endeavors. The two other indicators of period effects refer to the institutional expansion of tertiary-level vocational education and measure whether in a given year the occupation-specific certificates attained by the respondents provide access to tertiary-level vocational education, namely, the *Berufsprüfung* and *Höhere Fachprüfung*, and are not significant. The systematic testing of all interaction terms by cohort and gender did not result in any changes in the effects of social background characteristics on the relative chances of entering higher vocational education. The only significant interaction term related to *cohort* shows that the positive effect of having completed full-time vocational schooling becomes much stronger across cohorts (exp $B = 2.25$). This points to the changing significance of this particular educational track at the level of secondary schooling. Full-time vocational schooling is increasingly becoming a middle course between apprenticeship and the *Matura,* likely to be continued at the level of tertiary vocational education. The effect of the occupational field on the probability of enrolling for tertiary vocational programs is gender specific. This is the only significant gender interaction term. It shows that (the few) women in male-dominated occupations with good institutional opportunities for tertiary-level vocational training hardly make use of these opportunities. This may be related both to self-selective processes and to firm-specific preferences for male advancement. In supplementary analysis, we tested the same models for completion of tertiary-level vocational schooling as we did for enrollment. In general, there are only minor differences between the corresponding enrollment and completion models.

University Education: Enrollment and Completion

Eligibility for university education rose from 12.8% to 17.8% across the two cohorts (see Table 13.2). The university attendance rate is 8.8% for the older and 11.5% for the younger cohort. The corresponding figures for completion rates are 7.0% and 8.9%. Comparing enrollment and completion rates, the figures indicate an almost identical success rate among the members of the two cohorts (79.5% and 77.4%), but the success rate is much higher among students of vocational tertiary education (see above). Gender differences in university education are less pronounced than in tertiary-level vocational education but still strong. For the older cohort, university enrollment was twice as high for men than for women; the corresponding completion rate was even higher for men. In the younger cohort, gender inequalities in both enrollment and completion rates have attenuated somewhat.

The eligibility model for university education (Table 13.5) shows that the effects of social class and parental education on the probability of the respondent gaining the *Matura* (2c) are strong and significant: the lower the social class, the lower the chances are. The chances of being eligible for university education also increase with each additional level of parental education. But children from families in which the highest qualification earned by one of the parents is tertiary-level vocational education (3a) are not more likely to attain the *Matura* than those raised in households of skilled workers (2ab) (the reference group). Moreover, their relative chances are lower than those of children from families in which a parent has attained the *Matura* (2c). These findings match those shown for eligibility for tertiary-level vocational training. It appears that the socialization prevailing in families where the fathers (in most cases) attended tertiary vocational schooling are not conducive to the children's educational advancement, possibly owing to the children's internalization of parental ambitions and preferences or to lack of support and encouragement for the pursuit of general education. Put differently, parental educational resources related to *vocational* schooling do not promote *general* education in the next generation. Conversely, parental educational resources related to *general education* do not promote

TABLE 13.5
Eligibility for university entry (completion of intermediate-level general (CASMIN 2c))

	B	S.E.	exp(B)
Goldthorpe classes (Class V+VI)	***		
Class I	.73*	.32	2.08
Class II	.68**	.21	1.98
Class IIIab	.37	.33	1.44
Class IVabc	−.10	.20	.91
Class VIIab	−.83**	.30	.44
Parental education (Apprenticeship CASMIN 2ab)	***		
Compulsory schooling (CASMIN 1a)	−.68**	.25	.51
Basic secondary schooling (CASMIN 1b)	−.40	.22	.67
Intermediate-level general (CASMIN 2c)	.64*	.30	1.89
Tertiary-level vocational (CASMIN 3a)	−.29	.27	.75
University (CASMIN 3b)	1.29***	.29	3.65
Cohort (1959–61)	.32*	.15	1.38
Sex (Women)	.15	.14	1.16
Constant	−1.97***	.19	.14
N	2,102		
−2 log likelihood	1,310		
Model chi-square	164		
df	12		
Significance	***		
Nagelkerke R^2	.16		
Hosmer–Lemeshow test *(p)*	.63		

*$p \leq 0.05$; **$p \leq 0.01$; ***$p \leq 0.001$.

vocational schooling in the next generation. Across *cohorts*, the rate of attaining the *Matura* has increased significantly. The chances for men and women do not differ. The statistical parameters of the model suggest that the explanatory power is modest (Nagelkerke $R^2 = 0.16$), but the fit is good (Hosmer–Lemeshow $p = 0.63$).

Almost all effects remain stable when testing for *cohort* and *gender* interactions (results not shown). It appears that the very strong negative effect of having parents who completed only compulsory schooling has attenuated across cohorts, but we must bear in mind the relatively modest power of the statistical tests adhering to the interaction models. The interaction term (cohort × parents' compulsory schooling) just fails to reach the level of statistical significance ($p = 0.054$). Women of the younger cohort possibly tend to outreach men (gender × cohort: exp $B \approx 1.5$), although the effect is not significant.

TABLE 13.6
*Determinants of enrollment in the university, conditional models**

Variables	MODEL II BASELINE B	S.E.	exp(B)	MODEL III EDUCATIONAL TRAJECTORY B	S.E.	exp(B)	MODEL IV PERIOD AND INTERACTION EFFECTS B	S.E.	exp(B)
Age[a]	***			***			***		
Goldthorpe classes (Class V+VI)									
Class I	.02	.36	1.02	.12	.36	1.13	.20	.36	1.23
Class II	.11	.26	1.12	.09	.26	1.10	.12	.26	1.12
Class IIIab	.03	.44	1.03	−.04	.44	.96	−.01	.44	.99
Class IVabc	−.37	.27	.69	−.43	.27	.65	−.41	.27	.66
Class VIIab	−.35	.40	.70	−.28	.41	.76	−.22	.41	.80
Parental education (Apprenticeship CASMIN 2ab)	*			*			*		
Compulsory schooling (CASMIN 1a)	−.13	.35	.88	−.13	.36	.88	−.11	.36	.90
Basic secondary schooling (CASMIN 1b)	.26	.29	1.30	.18	.29	1.20	.19	.29	1.21
Intermediate-level general (CASMIN 2c)	.85*	.36	2.34	.85*	.36	2.35	.88*	.36	2.40
Tertiary-level vocational (CASMIN 3a)	.78*	.34	2.18	.71*	.34	2.03	.71*	.34	2.04
University (CASMIN 3b)	.57	.31	1.77	.65*	.31	1.91	.69*	.31	1.99
Cohort (1959–61)	.15	.18	1.16	.08	.19	1.08	−.05	.21	.96
Sex (Women)	−1.09***	.19	.34	−1.10***	.18	.33	−1.13***	.18	.32
Apprenticeship before university[b]				−1.54***	.48	.21	−2.35***	.71	.10
Full-time voc. schooling before university[b]				−1.36	.80	.26	−1.34	.81	.26
Change in gross domestic product[b]							−.03	.05	.97
Apprentice before university × Cohort (1959–61)[b]							1.88*	.93	6.55
Constant	−.56*	.28	.57	−.40	.29	.67	−.27	.34	.76
Episodes/events	1,728/171			1,728/171			1,728/171		
−2 log likelihood	878			861			857		
Model chi-square	466			483			487		
df	34			36			38		
Significance	***			***			***		
Nagelkerke R^2	.42			.44			.44		
Hosmer–Lemeshow test (p)	.153			.753			.720		

[a]Effects for individual age categories not shown.
[b]Time-dependent covariates.
*$p \leq 0.05$; **$p \leq 0.01$; ***$p \leq 0.001$.

Next we examined the question of whether the expansion of the university system has altered the class-related and gender-related chances of enrollment in and completion of this type of tertiary-level education. Table 13.6 (model II) shows the conditional baseline model for enrollment.[12]

Apart from age, parental education and gender have the strongest effects. Women's odds are about 0.34 those of men (about 66% lower), despite the fact that there are no gender differences in the eligibility for university education (Table 13.5). With each additional category of parental education, the number of university entrants increases, apart from the two highest levels of parental education: tertiary-level vocational schooling and university education. In the unconditional model, these effects differ substantially (results available upon request).[13] When the sample is unrestricted, children from families where the parents attained the *Matura* (2c) or a university degree (3b) are much more likely to enroll in university programs. If the highest qualification of a parent is tertiary-level vocational schooling, the probability of a child's transition to university education is relatively low. This holds true for both the unconditional and conditional models, suggesting the intergenerational transmission of a rigid, impermeable separation of tertiary-level vocational from academic education. This interpretation is corroborated by the laterally reversed finding discussed earlier with regard to tertiary vocational schooling. Although the effect of parental education on university enrollment in the conditional model is significant, the comparison between the corresponding effects in the unconditional and conditional models reveals that the social background effects are mediated mostly by the *Matura* selection criterion. The substantial and approximately linear effect of social class found in the unconditional models disappears completely in the conditional model. Across cohorts, we find a slightly higher entrance rate, which is not significant.

When adding the respondent's educational trajectory to the conditional baseline model (model III in Table 13.6), we observe only modest changes. The prognostic quality is slightly better (Nagelkerke R^2) but the effects of the baseline model remain stable. The two educational variables included in the conditional model (respondents eligible for university entrance) show substantial and significant effects. People who completed an apprenticeship (2a) enroll less often (or later) in university programs. The same is for completion of full-time vocational schooling, although it is not significant because of the smaller number of cases. Both findings support our previous interpretation about the strong segmentation between vocational and academic education in Switzerland.

In the last model shown in Table 13.6 (model IV), we included a time-dependent variable to assess period effects—namely, annual change in GDP. In contrast to tertiary vocational schooling, economic conditions do not affect the probability of university enrollment. When systematically testing for interaction effects by cohort and gender, we found only one substantial and significant effect:[14] the negative effect of having completed an apprenticeship noted above disappears for the younger cohort. We created the same models for completion of university education as we did for enrollment (results not shown). In general, the differences between the corresponding enrollment and completion models are very modest.

CONCLUSIONS

The Swiss system of higher education is a binary one. The two tracks, vocational and academic, are rigidly and impermeably segmented. For the period under consideration, the late 1960s to the late 1980s, both tracks followed a pattern of gradual expansion. No period is characterized by rapid expansion. The question arises whether the gradual expansion of the Swiss system of higher education since the 1960s has altered the social background–related opportunities of tertiary-level vocational and university education.

Our findings show strong social background and gender effects on the probability of gaining *any* secondary educational credential. Further analyses (not shown here) revealed that these effects are weaker when predicting the completion of a particular type of secondary-level schooling (e.g., *Matura*, full-time vocational school, or apprenticeship). The effects remain rather stable across cohorts. Among the social background effects, it is mainly parental education and not social class that affects the children's relative chances of obtaining a secondary qualification. When tracing social inequalities at the tertiary level, we must bear in mind that the social background effects are greatly mediated by the eligibility for tertiary education. This is especially true for university education, where direct social background effects (the conditional models) are almost invisible.

The global answer to the question of whether the gradual expansion of the system of higher education has attenuated class and gender inequalities in higher education is straightforward: it has not. For both types of tertiary-level education, for enrollment as well as completion, social background effects are stable across cohorts. In addition, the effects of parental education are stronger than those of social class and remain largely unchanged across cohorts,[15] suggesting that the educational resources accumulated in the family play an important role in the children's educational attainment. This extends even to the type of parental education, so that we can speak of an intergenerational transmission of the rigid separation of vocational and academic tracks at the tertiary level. Children from families with educational background in vocational schooling are much more likely to follow vocational tracks, whereas children with parental background in general education are more likely to pursue academic education. The gradual differentiation of the institutions of tertiary-level vocational education—a process we have termed the *qualitative diversification* of higher vocational education—accompanies the increasing enrollment rate in this type of schooling but does not account for it.

We observed a strong and stable underrepresentation of women in tertiary-level vocational education, attributed partially to institutional barriers, as female-dominated occupations offer far fewer opportunities for tertiary-level vocational education. However, the strong interaction effect between the occupational field of the secondary-level apprenticeship and gender reminds us that even when the institutional opportunities for tertiary-level vocational education are as favorable as in male-dominated occupations, women with credentials in such fields are much less likely than men to make use of the corresponding educational opportunities. This may be attributed to life-course–related factors (the timing of tertiary-level schooling and family obligations), human-capital factors (rational educational investments in anticipation of family responsibilities), or "doing gender" in the context of a strongly male-dominated environment. Thus, it appears that institutional barriers and self-selective forces are both responsible for women's feeble representation in tertiary-level vocational schooling. Although women are on equal footing with men in eligibility for university education, they are much less likely to enroll in (and complete) university programs. This finding requires further inquiry because several interpretations are possible.[16] Because the present analyses do not include cohorts born later than 1959–61, we must qualify these findings. Among younger cohorts (born after 1965), statistics for higher education show that women's enrollment and completion rates have steadily risen. Despite these cautious qualifications, the gender-related findings presented here suggest that institutional barriers and self-selective forces are likely to work together to produce the rather stable underrepresentation of women, especially in higher vocational education.

PART III: UNITARY AND OTHER SYSTEMS

CHAPTER FOURTEEN

Australia: Changes in Socioeconomic Inequalities in University Participation

Gary N. Marks, Australian Council for Educational Research, Melbourne Institute of Applied Economic and Social Research

Julie McMillan, Australian Council for Educational Research, Research School of Social Sciences, Australian National University

INTRODUCTION

Tertiary education in Australia currently comprises two sectors: higher education (or universities), and vocational education and training (VET). These sectors form a rough hierarchy, with higher education institutions offering courses at the bachelor degree level and above, both higher education and VET institutions offering diploma and advanced diploma courses, and VET institutions offering certificate-level courses. The focus of this chapter is on the higher education sector. The majority of higher education students in Australia attend one of 37 publicly funded universities. In addition to these, there are two privately funded universities, four self-accrediting institutions, and approximately 85 other providers accredited by state and territory authorities (Harman 2003, 25). Both the federal and state governments are involved in the administration of universities. Almost all universities were constituted by, and subject to, state government laws. However, since 1974 they have been funded primarily by the federal government, and most of their administrative responsibilities are now to the federal government.

Australian universities are generalist rather than specialist in nature, most offering a wide range of programs or courses. Nevertheless, there is a well-understood hierarchy, with the older, more established universities at the top of the hierarchy. These universities offer high status courses such as medicine, law, dentistry, and veterinary science. They also attract the bulk of research funding and the most able students. The status inequality between universities is exemplified by an official body, the Group of Eight, comprising mostly the older established institutions that regard themselves as Australia's premier universities.[1] Students and their families are well aware of the hierarchy of universities, and, if there is a choice, will generally attempt to attend the course and university with a higher status. This is reflected in the much higher entrance scores required for most courses at the Group of Eight universities.

Most undergraduate degrees are undertaken on a full-time basis for three or four years. Professional degrees such as law and medicine are typically undergraduate courses, although recently there has been a move toward postgraduate entry. Nearly 80% of students enroll in campuses in capital cities (Harman 2003, 25). Metropolitan students usually attend a university in the city in which they completed their schooling, and nonmetropolitan students with high tertiary entrance scores tend to enroll at a university in their state's capital city. There is no tradition of metropolitan undergraduate students moving interstate and living on campus. Compared with many other countries, Australia has a relatively high proportion of overseas students, older students, part-time students, and students working full-time (Long 2002).

THE DEVELOPMENT OF HIGHER EDUCATION IN AUSTRALIA

Ten Australian universities were established in the hundred years between the 1850s and the 1950s, and nine more were created over the next twenty years. The first two universities were founded in the 1850s: In the colony of New South Wales, the University of Sydney began teaching in 1851, and in Victoria, the University of Melbourne was established in 1854. These are among the oldest universities in the Western world. The other colonies (and after federation in 1901, the states) followed with the opening of the Universities of Adelaide (1874), Tasmania (1890), Queensland (1909), and Western Australia (1911). From that time until the 1950s, there was little growth in the number of universities. The Australian National University was established in 1946, and a former technical college became the University of New South Wales in 1949. In 1950, there were approximately 30,000 university students attending eight universities (Australia DETYA 2001, 5). By 1960, there were 53,000 students in ten universities (Meek 2000). Considerable growth in both the number of students and universities occurred between then and 1980, when there were 19 universities catering to around 163,000 students (Anderson and Vervoorn 1983, xi).

In addition to universities, teachers colleges and technical colleges were established in the nineteenth century. These eventually formed a second advanced education tier within the higher education system, offering more applied or vocationally oriented courses than universities. The two tiers were formalized by the federal government in 1965 with the establishment of the binary system of higher education comprising university education and advanced education. A range of institutions offered advanced education, including institutes of technology, teachers colleges, and, after 1973, Colleges of Advanced Education (CAEs). The institutes of technology tended to enjoy a higher status than other institutions within the advanced education tier.

From the establishment of the binary system in 1965 through to the late 1970s, there was a dramatic increase in the number of students undertaking advanced education, rising from 45,000 in 1968 to 153,500 in 1978. Over the same period, university student numbers increased less steeply from 100,000 to 159,500. By 1980, the number of students in the advanced education tier exceeded those at universities. At that time, Australia and the United Kingdom were the only countries where this was the case. The number of institutions offering advanced education increased from 11 in 1965 to over 100 in 1977, although amalgamations in the late 1970s and early 1980s considerably reduced this number. During this latter period, there was an increasing overlap between the two tiers of higher education, with some CAEs amalgamating with existing universities and others becoming new universities. While it was originally intended that the institutions forming the advanced education tier would only offer courses up to the diploma level, increasingly they also offered bachelor degree courses, and in some cases, masters and doctoral level programs (Australia DEET 1993, 13–14).

A major structural change in the higher education sector occurred in 1989 when the federal government replaced the binary system with the Unified National System. Under the new system, the remaining institutes of technology and colleges of advanced education became universities or amalgamated with existing universities. These changes resulted in fewer, larger institutions. In the early 1980s there had been 19 universities, 46 CAEs and institutes of technology, and three nongovernment teachers colleges. By 1991, there were 38 universities in the Unified National System, plus eight other institutions funded by the federal government (Australia DEET 1993, 30). Since the early 1990s, there have been few structural changes, although another period of substantial growth in student numbers occurred in the early 1990s. By 2005 there were approximately 718,000 domestic students, more than a twofold increase on the 330,000 higher education students in 1980 (Australia DETYA, 2001, table 1; Australia DEST 2005). The proportion of young people in universities also increased as a result of both the merging of the advanced education tier with universities, and increasing enrollments in the higher education sector as a whole. In the early 1980s, approximately 20% of young people participated in higher education (universities, institutes of technology, and CAEs), of which about half were studying at a university.[2] Currently, nearly 40% of youth cohorts participate at university (Marks et al. 2000).

STUDENT FEES AND ASSISTANCE FOR UNDERGRADUATE (DEGREE AND DIPLOMA) STUDY

The Whitlam Labor government abolished fees for higher education in 1974. Until that time, fees constituted approximately 15% to 20% of costs (Karmel 1990, 26). At the same time, the nature of student assistance changed. Competitive non–means-tested scholarships that paid tuition fees were replaced by a noncompetitive means-tested living allowance for full-time students, which has continued under various guises to the present time. Higher education remained largely free until 1989, when the Higher Education Contribution Scheme (HECS) was introduced by another federal Labor government.[3] The HECS system was designed to increase private contributions to the higher education sector without reintroducing up-front fees.

HECS is a deferred, income-contingent loan. Students start to pay back part of the cost of their education through the Australian taxation system after their personal income rises above a specified threshold level. Interest is not payable but the debt is indexed to inflation. Students can also opt to pay their HECS fees at the time of enrollment or to make voluntary early repayments; in each case they receive a discount. Initially, HECS fees were uniform across all institutions and courses. Between 1989 and 1996, all students were charged a flat rate of AUS$2,442 per year—about a quarter of the average course cost—and the income threshold was $27,675 (Chapman 1997).

Since the inception of HECS, the federal Coalition government has implemented several reforms. In 1997, the income threshold was reduced to $21,000 (in 1996 dollars), the repayment schedule was accelerated, and three tiers of fees were introduced: $3,300, $4,700, and $5,500 per year. The tiers were designed to partially reflect the teaching costs and expected income returns associated with different courses (Chapman 1997). Medical, dental, veterinary science, and law students were charged the top rate, while arts, humanities, and nursing students were charged the lowest rate (Chapman and Salvage 1997). Universities were also permitted to admit full-fee-paying domestic students up to a maximum of 25% of enrollments per course. Previously, only nondomestic students had been able to enroll as full-fee-paying students. However, demand for undergraduate fee-paying places by domestic students was not large.[4] Typically, full-fee-paying students had failed to gain a government-funded HECS place in their chosen course.

Further reforms were passed by the federal parliament in December 2003 and implemented in 2005. HECS fees became partially deregulated with universities able to raise or lower fees by up to 25% of standard fees, with the exception of nursing and teaching courses where no real increases were allowed. The intention of partial deregulation was to allow market forces to influence the nature and costs of courses. Under the new reforms, annual HECS fees range from $2,800 for teaching and nursing, to nearly $8,000 for top-tier courses charging 25% above the standard HECS fee. At the time of writing, 16 public universities had opted to increase fees by the maximum amount for 2005, 4 opted to increase fees by a smaller amount, 10 opted to retain or reduce existing course costs, and 7 had not announced a decision. Under the new reforms, universities can also increase the proportion of domestic full-fee-paying students within courses from 25% to 35%, with annual full fees ranging from $10,000 to $20,000. Full-fee-paying students can borrow up to $50,000 from the government, with the debt adjusted for inflation and the loan attracting a surcharge of 20% rather than interest. The income threshold for the repayment of all loans was raised to $35,000 for the 2004/05 financial year, and will increase in line with the inflation rate in future years (Australia AVCC 2003).

Since the introduction of HECS in Australia, income contingent loan schemes have been introduced in other countries. In 1992, New Zealand implemented a scheme where students can borrow from the government for both their tuition and living expenses. Interest is charged on these loans (New Zealand NZMOE 2004). In early 2004, legislation was passed to implement a HECS-style scheme in the United Kingdom in 2006. Institutions will be allowed to charge students £3000, which they will start repaying once their annual income reaches £15,000 (UK DfES 2004).

There are two types of arguments that governments use to justify HECS and subsequent reforms to HECS. The first is financial. HECS-style schemes are attractive to governments because they reduce the costs of higher education. Of the six billion dollars spent on higher education in Australia in 2001, approximately one billion was refunded to the government through the HECS system, with a further two billion still owed (Australia AVCC 2001). The cost to government of providing free university education becomes more substantial as participation rates rise. It may be possible to provide free university education to 5% or 10% of young people but is much more difficult if 40% or 50% participate. Despite the dramatic increase in university education over the last 20 to 30 years, the annual clamor for more funding for more places continues unabated, and HECS provides a means of funding further expansion. In 1990 and 1991, soon after HECS was implemented, the number of students enrolled increased by 10% per annum (Australia DETYA 2001). As part of the 2003 reforms, the federal government committed itself to increasing the number of university places by 30,000 by 2008 (Australia AVCC 2003). According to the OECD (2005, table SS7.1), the proportion of Australians aged 25 to 65 with university qualifications (ISCED 5a or 6) is 20%, which is higher than that in most other OECD countries. HECS, in part, has contributed to this higher proportion.

The other important rationale for the HECS system revolves around the concept of social equity. HECS, it is argued, is more equitable than "free" university systems where taxpayers pay the entire cost of educating each student. In HECS-type systems, those who use and directly benefit from higher education—who are more often from privileged backgrounds—contribute to the cost of their own education. It is not equitable for blue-collar workers and nonprofessional white-collar workers to subsidize university students who, over the life course, will benefit financially from their education. The annual rate of return in income for a bachelor degree in Australia is around 15% (Borland 2002), and over the life course a bachelor degree is associated with between 40% and 60% greater wealth (Marks, Headey, and Wooden 2005). Despite the substantial increase in university enrollments, unemployment among graduates is generally low and their incomes remain substantially higher than those of nongraduates (Marks and Fleming 1998a,b; Le and Miller 2000). The HECS income threshold ensures that poorer and mature-age students will not have to make repayments unless or until they earn reasonable incomes. Finally, one point that is often overlooked is that simply increasing the number of university places does provide more opportunities for a university education for young people from lower socioeconomic backgrounds. A child from a manual background has a greater chance of entering university in a mass system than in an elite system, even if the elite system is on standard indicators more socially equitable.

SOCIOECONOMIC INEQUALITIES AND STUDENT FEES

There is a long-standing debate surrounding the effects of fees on socioeconomic inequalities in Australian education. The major rationale for the abolition of university fees in the early 1970s was to reduce the financial barriers to students from socioeconomically disadvantaged backgrounds. Subsequent studies, however, found little change in the social composition of the student body (Anderson and Vervoorn 1983; Crocket 1987). Although these studies focused on the composition of the student body rather than the chances of participation by socioeconomic background, the conclusion that abolishing fees did not substantially reduce socioeconomic inequalities in university education is probably correct. There are a couple of reasons for this. First, before fees were abolished a substantial proportion of students were exempt from fees because they had won scholarships or studentships;[5] abolishing fees was not the radical change that it was often assumed to be (see Chapman 2001). Second, since only 20% to 30% of young people completed school at the time that fees were abolished, there were few students from lower socioeconomic backgrounds in the pool for university entrance. The influence of socioeconomic background was occurring much earlier in the educational career. Those from lower socioeconomic backgrounds who did complete school were likely to be very high ability students, and so would have had a reasonable chance of university entrance. Finally, fees—which were not particularly large—may not have been a strong deterrent for those committed to a university education.

Much of the political debate surrounding the introduction of HECS and its subsequent reforms centers on equity issues. Critics have argued that the prospect of a sizeable HECS debt deters university participation by persons from lower socioeconomic backgrounds. Since HECS was implemented, however, there has been no evidence to suggest that socioeconomic inequalities in university participation have increased (Chapman 1997; Andrews 1999; Marks et al. 2000; Marks and McMillan 2003), and it is unlikely that the HECS reforms to be implemented in 2005 will substantially increase inequalities in participation. Instead, Beer and Chapman (2004) argue that, starting in 2005, low-income graduates will be better off than previously because of the raising of the income threshold. However, they have concerns with the capping of the loan to full-fee-paying students at $50,000, which could increase up-front costs in some courses and so deter students from poorer backgrounds from entering those courses.

THE CURRENT STUDY

The primary purpose of this chapter is to examine if changes have occurred in socioeconomic inequalities in university education in Australia. The analyses examine two educational outcomes in Australia: completion of Year 12, the preparatory year for university study; and university participation. The analyses are performed on data from cross-sectional surveys of the adult population and longitudinal data from youth cohorts born between 1961 and the early 1980s. The first part of the results section focuses on Year 12, the second on university education. The effects of demographic and sociological factors, school sector, and ability are examined. Additional analyses investigate whether students from lower socioeconomic backgrounds are deterred from university because of the prospect of repaying a large HECS debt. If the implementation of the HECS system has increased educational inequality, the effects of socioeconomic background among cohorts born after 1970 should be greater than their effects among older cohorts.

The influence of school sector is an important educational issue in Australia. Three sectors exist: the government sector (comprising about 70% of secondary school students), the Catholic sector (about 20%), and the private or independent sector (about 10%). Unlike many European school systems, the Australian system is not formally tracked by ability, but the school sector is a major source of educational differentiation. Independent school education has been viewed as a mechanism by which intergenerational inequalities are maintained, because independent school students tend to come from wealthier families and achieve superior educational outcomes. There are several research questions surrounding independent schools. Do they deliver superior educational outcomes net of socioeconomic background or is the higher performance of students who attend independent schools a reflection of their socioeconomic background? A similar question can be posed regarding ability, because independent schools recruit high-ability students from the state system, and anecdotal evidence suggests that these schools discourage poorer performing students from competing for university entrance. The performance of Catholic school students relative to government school students is also of interest. Like their counterparts in the United States, Catholic schools tend to be smaller, have fewer discipline problems, and are more closely connected with their local communities.

The influence of ability vis-à-vis socioeconomic background is important in regard to the supposed fairness of the education system. If ability has a strong influence and the effects of socioeconomic background and school sector, net of ability, are minimal, then the education system can be regarded as largely meritocratic. If, however, the effects of ability are small and substantial effects of socioeconomic background and school sector remain, it can be concluded that the education system strongly favors students from privileged backgrounds.

University participation or the completion of a degree does not capture status differences between universities and between faculties within universities. It could be argued that stronger effects of socioeconomic background would be found if the status hierarchy of courses and institutions was analyzed rather than simply university participation. Students' tertiary entrance scores, obtained at the completion of senior secondary school, were used in this chapter as a proxy for this status hierarchy. High status faculties and universities have higher entrance requirements than low status faculties and universities. Generally, students enter the most prestigious courses that their scores allow. HECS has been criticized for deterring qualified people from lower socioeconomic backgrounds from pursuing a university course because of debt aversion, leading to an increase in socioeconomic inequalities in education. The final analysis reported in this chapter directly addresses this issue by comparing the percentage of students who attend university between occupational backgrounds given their tertiary entrance scores.

DATA AND MEASURES

The analyses of the adult population used pooled data from 12 cross-sectional surveys of adults conducted between 1984 and 2001. The Australian surveys are part of three large international studies: the International Social Science Surveys, the International Social Survey Program, and the International Survey of Economic Attitudes. The original 1984 survey was conducted by face-to-face interviews, while the subsequent surveys were administered by mail. A total of 19,486 cases were available for analysis. The representativeness of these samples for gender and age distributions has been demonstrated in several studies (Bean 1991; Evans and Kelley 2002a,b). However, the samples usually comprise higher proportions of the tertiary educated than that of the adult population. Therefore, each sample was weighted according to the proportion of the population aged 15–64 who had completed a bachelor degree for the year closest to the year the survey was conducted.[6]

The measure of Year 12 completion was constructed from questions on the number of years of schooling and graduation from secondary school. University completion was measured by obtaining a bachelor degree. The measure of occupational background employed here is the Erikson, Goldthorpe, and Portocarero (EGP) class scheme (Erikson, Goldthorpe, and Portocarero 1979) described elsewhere in this volume. Parental education is a linear combination of the parents' years of education. It was not possible to use the CASMIN scheme employed in other analyses in this volume. The measure of school sector distinguishes the three school sectors in Australia: government, Catholic, and independent.

The second group of analyses, focusing on six youth cohorts born between 1961 and the mid-1980s, was conducted on longitudinal data sets from the Youth in Transition (YIT) and the Longitudinal Surveys of Australian Youth (LSAY) studies. The YIT samples were age-based cohorts born in 1961, 1965, 1970, and 1975, with original samples of between 5,000 and 6,000 students. The LSAY samples were based on cohorts of young people who were in secondary school in Year 9 in 1995 or 1998 (modal age 14); for each cohort the original sample size was over 13,000 students. The YIT and LSAY samples are two stage cluster samples. Schools were sampled first with probabilities based on school size. Fourteen-year-old students (for YIT) or Year 9 students (for LSAY) were subsequently sampled within schools. The sample weights have two components: the first to correct for distributional differences of gender, state, and school sector between the sample and the population from which it was drawn; the second to correct for nonrandom sample attrition. More details on these youth cohort studies are available in Marks and Rothman (2003).

For the four older age-based YIT cohorts, participation in Year 12 and university is measured as participation by age 19. Participation at a CAE was not counted as university participation.[7] For the 1995 and 1998 cohorts, Year 12 participation is measured by participation in the calendar years 1998 and 2001, respectively, and university participation in 1999 or 2000 and 2002 or 2003. Because of the way information on parental occupation was collected (no data on self-employment or supervision), it is not possible to construct EPG measures for the five YIT and LSAY samples. Instead, a four-category measure of occupational background was constructed distinguishing students whose fathers were professionals, managers, other white-collar workers, and manual workers. Student ability was based on performance in tests of literacy and numeracy at age 14 (for YIT) or Year 9 (for LSAY). These surveys did measure parental education but the measures are not comparable across surveys and several include large amounts of missing data.

The analyses of influences on tertiary entrance score and the effects of HECS on university participation used the students' Equivalent National Tertiary Entrance Rank (or ENTER scores). ENTER scores range from 30 to 99.95 and denote a student's performance relative to others. Students with the top score of 99.95 have scored better than 99.95% of the cohort. High-status courses such as medicine and law require ENTER scores in the high nineties.[8]

Logistic regression was used to analyze Year 12 and university participation. The logistic coefficients are presented in the tables; their corresponding odds ratios, which are the exponents of the coefficients, are

TABLE 14.1
Proportion completing Year 12 (Y12) and a bachelor degree (deg.) for survey period (1984–2001)
by cohort and class background (percentage of group)

	\multicolumn{2}{c}{1890–1909}	\multicolumn{2}{c}{1910–19}	\multicolumn{2}{c}{1920–29}	\multicolumn{2}{c}{1930–39}	\multicolumn{2}{c}{1940–49}	\multicolumn{2}{c}{1950–59}	\multicolumn{2}{c}{1960–69}	\multicolumn{2}{c}{1970–81}	\multicolumn{2}{c}{ALL}
	Y12	Deg.	Y12	Deg.	Y12	Deg.	Y12	Deg.	Y12	Deg.	Y12	Deg.	Y12	Deg.	Y12	Deg.	Y12	Deg.
All	13.1	3.8	17.6	4.7	17.8	4.3	21.0	5.3	29.8	9.4	40.3	11.4	47.6	9.1	75.9	19.2	34.0	8.7
Upper service	33.9	19.1	34.8	16.6	42.5	12.9	52.0	14.8	59.7	24.2	34.8	16.6	66.7	15.7	90.6	24.9	62.2	20.5
Lower service	26.4	10.2	29.2	5.3	28.9	7.8	35.9	10.2	41.3	12.8	29.2	5.3	60.1	11.7	88.2	22.3	48.4	13.3
Routine non-manual	33.2	10.7	19.8	3.0	17.5	5.9	21.8	8.3	38.8	11.7	19.8	3.0	44.2	5.7	70.0	13.6	36.0	9.0
Self-employed	11.5	3.4	19.0	5.9	18.4	3.4	21.2	5.1	31.4	8.7	19.0	5.9	48.9	7.4	84.3	14.9	32.8	7.7
Skilled manual	1.7	1.7	11.0	2.9	12.3	3.5	17.4	4.1	22.8	6.2	11.0	2.9	40.4	4.7	72.9	12.1	29.4	5.9
Manual	10.2	—	9.6	2.4	10.3	1.8	10.2	2.2	16.5	4.0	9.6	2.4	34.6	6.2	65.7	11.9	19.9	4.0
N	284	296	991	1,011	2,122	2,169	2,529	2,562	3,809	3,851	4,745	4,783	3,456	3,507	819	854	18,755	19,033

SOURCE: Adult Survey Data.

discussed in the text. Interaction terms were used to test changes over time. Statistical significance is indicated in the tables. The explanatory power of the model is indicated by the pseudo R square values.[9] All analyses were conducted on weighted data.

ELIGIBILITY FOR HIGHER EDUCATION

Table 14.1 presents the proportions completing Year 12—the preparatory year for university study—by EPG class background for eight cohorts born between 1890 and 1981. Year 12 participation increased dramatically from around 20% for the cohort born between 1930 and 1939 to nearly 76% for the youngest cohort. For almost all occupational-class backgrounds, the proportion completing Year 12 increased successively with each younger birth cohort. In all cohorts, an upper service-class background was associated with higher proportions of school completers and a semiskilled or unskilled manual background with the lowest proportion. In the youngest cohort the proportion of Year 12 completers among those with upper service-class backgrounds was about one third higher than the proportion among those with manual backgrounds.

Table 14.2 presents the results from three models on the influences on Year 12 completion. The first model includes cohort, gender, parental education, and father's EGP occupational class. The effects for EGP occupational-class background are relative to a semiskilled or unskilled manual occupational background. The second model includes interaction terms with cohort for gender, parental education, and an upper service-class origin. The third model includes interaction terms for all EGP class origins as well as interaction terms for gender and parental education. Theses analyses exclude cohorts born before 1930 because the proportion of the older cohorts participating in higher education was very small. These models account for about 20% of the variation in Year 12 completion.

In the baseline model, a strong effect for cohort was found indicating that the odds of Year 12 completion increased by a factor of 1.5 for each successive cohort. The odds of men completing (rather than not completing) Year 12 were 1.1 times the comparable odds for women. A difference of one standard deviation in parental education translated into an odds ratio of 1.6. Moderate to large effects for occupational background were apparent. For an upper service-class origin, the odds of completing (rather than not

TABLE 14.2
Effects of class background and parental education on Year 12 completion and tests of changes over time

	Base model	Partial interaction model	Full interaction model
Intercept	−0.95***	−0.93***	−0.92***
Cohort	0.39***	0.53***	0.62***
Male	0.13**	0.10*	0.10*
Parents' education	0.45***	0.44***	0.45***
Father's occupational class			
Upper service	1.17***	1.17***	1.15***
Lower service	0.87***	0.87***	0.86***
Routine nonmanual	0.54***	0.54***	0.51***
Self-employed	0.54***	0.54***	0.53***
Skilled manual	0.29***	0.28***	0.27***
Interactions			
Male × cohort	—	−0.22***	−0.22***
Parents' education × cohort	—	−0.06*	−0.05*
Upper service × cohort	—	−0.14***	−0.24**
Lower service × cohort	—	—	−0.15*
Routine nonmanual × cohort	—	—	−0.20*
Self-employed × cohort	—	—	−0.10
Skilled manual × cohort	—	—	−0.09
R^2 (pseudo)	18.9	19.4	19.6

NOTE: Adult survey data. Logistic regression coefficients. Cohorts born before 1930 were excluded. Cohort 1950–60 scored 0; younger cohorts scored positively. Weighted data.
*$p < 0.05$; **$p < 0.01$; ***$p < 0.001$.

completing) Year 12 were 3.2 times the comparable odds for an unskilled manual origin. The corresponding odds ratios for a lower service-class and nonmanual compared with a semiskilled/unskilled manual background were 2.4 and 1.7, respectively.

The second model shows significant declines over time in the effects of gender, parental education, and a service-class origin. The main effects were for the cohort born between 1950 and 1959. For this cohort, the odds of males completing Year 12 were 1.1 times the comparable odds for females. For younger cohorts, the odds for females completing Year 12 were higher than for males. In the youngest cohort, the odds ratio for Year 12 completion for females was about 1.4 times that for males. The decline in the effect of parental education was small. For the youngest cohort, an increase of one standard deviation in parental education increased the odds of Year 12 completion 1.4 times compared with 1.5 times for the cohort born between 1950 and 1959. The decline in the effect of upper service-class origin was more substantial. For the cohort born between 1950 and 1959, the odds ratio comparing Year 12 participation between upper service-class and unskilled manual origins was 3.2, declining to 2.4 for the youngest cohort.

The third column of Table 14.2 shows the tests for changes over time. Declines were found for gender, parental education, and occupational-class background. The decline in the odds of Year 12 participation for males (compared with females) and in the effect of parental education is almost identical to the declines observed in model 2. For four of the six occupational backgrounds, the odds of Year 12 completion declined relative to semiskilled and unskilled manual origins. The effects of an upper service-class origin declined by a factor of 1.3 for each successively younger birth cohort. For the cohort born between 1950 and 1959, the odds of Year 12 completion for upper service-class origins were 3.2 times the comparable odds for semiskilled and unskilled manual backgrounds; for the youngest cohort (born between 1970 and 1981) the odds ratio had declined to 2.0. The odds of Year 12 completion for lower service-class and routine nonmanual origins relative to semiskilled and unskilled manual origins were about 1.2 times less for each younger cohort. There was no change in the odds ratios for self-employed and skilled manual origins relative to semiskilled and unskilled manual origins.

PARTICIPATION IN HIGHER EDUCATION

Table 14.1 also presents the proportions of the adult samples with a bachelor degree by EPG class background. The proportion holding bachelor degrees increased from about 5% for the cohort born between 1930 and 1939 to nearly 20% for the youngest cohort, born between 1970 and 1981. For almost all occupational-class backgrounds the proportion holding university degrees increased successively with younger birth cohorts. In all cohorts, a service-class background was associated with higher proportions with bachelor degrees, and a skilled manual or semiskilled/unskilled manual background was associated with the lowest proportions. In the youngest cohort, the proportion holding bachelor degrees among those with a service-class background was about twice that of those from manual backgrounds. This ratio was generally larger for the older cohorts.

Table 14.3 tests for changes over time in the effects of class background, parental education, and gender on obtaining a bachelor degree. The three

TABLE 14.3
Effects of class background on obtaining a bachelor degree over time and tests of changes over time

	Base model	Partial interaction model	Full interaction model
Intercept	−3.00***	−2.97***	−2.95***
Cohort	0.04	0.29***	0.29***
Male	0.30***	0.26***	0.45***
Parents' education	0.40***	0.40***	0.41***
Father's occupational class			
Upper service	1.09***	1.10***	1.07***
Lower service	0.90***	0.88***	0.86***
Routine nonmanual	0.59***	0.58***	0.51**
Self-employed	0.55***	0.55***	0.52***
Skilled manual	0.21	0.20	0.17
Interactions			
Male × cohort		−0.28***	−0.28***
Parents' education × cohort		−0.10	−0.08*
Upper service × cohort		−0.10*	−0.32**
Lower service × cohort	—	—	−0.25**
Routine nonmanual × cohort	—	—	−0.38**
Self-employed × cohort	—	—	−0.21*
Skilled manual × cohort	—	—	−0.24***
R^2 (pseudo)	8.2	8.8	9.0

NOTE: See note to Table 14.2.

models are the same as employed in the analysis of Year 12 completion. In model 1, the coefficients indicate that class background influenced obtaining a bachelor degree. The odds ratio for obtaining a bachelor degree for students from upper service-class backgrounds relative to unskilled manual background was nearly three. For other class origins, the effects were weaker, although the odds ratios remained substantial. Similarly, parental education had an independent effect on obtaining a bachelor degree. Tests for changes over time indicate a substantial decrease in socioeconomic inequality in university participation. The interactions between cohort and parental education and the five class categories were all negative, sizable, and statistically significant. Model 3 also shows a strong trend of increasing proportions of women obtaining bachelor degrees.

Table 14.4 presents the results from logistic regression analysis of holding a bachelor degree among Year 12 completers. The baseline model shows a significant negative effect for cohort, reflecting the change in the nature of Year 12 from a preparatory year for university to a generalist year

TABLE 14.4
Effects of class background on obtaining a bachelor degree over time and tests of changes over time among Year-12 completers

	Base model	Partial interaction model	Full interaction model
Intercept	−1.48***	−1.50***	−1.49***
Cohort	−0.20***	−0.09	0.02
Male	0.26***	0.26***	0.26***
Parents' education	0.14***	0.14***	0.14**
Father's occupational class			
Upper service	0.47***	0.47***	0.47***
Lower service	0.34**	0.35**	0.34***
Routine nonmanual	0.18	0.18	0.14
Self-employed	0.16	0.16	0.16
Skilled manual	−0.04	−0.04	−0.05
Interactions			
Male × cohort		−0.19**	−0.19**
Parents' education × cohort		−0.01	0.00
Upper service × cohort		0.00	−0.12
Lower service × cohort	—	—	−0.10
Routine nonmanual × cohort	—	—	−0.27
Self-employed × cohort	—	—	−0.11
Skilled manual × cohort	—	—	−0.19
R^2 (pseudo)	3.5	3.8	3.7

NOTE: See note to Table 14.2.

comprising academic and nonacademic courses as school retention rates increased. Among Year 12 completers, the odds of males completing (rather than not completing) a bachelor degree were 1.3 times those for females. The effects of social background were substantially weaker in these analyses than in the analysis of Year 12 completion. The coefficient for parental education was about a quarter of its effect on Year 12 completion. The effects of routine nonmanual, self-employed, and skilled manual occupational-class origins were not significant, indicating that such class origins did not increase the chances of completing a university degree relative to manual origins among Year 12 completers. The effects of upper service- and lower service-class origins on holding a bachelor degree were also considerably weaker than their effects on Year 12 completion.

Model 2 shows that the effect of gender declined substantially over time. For the cohort born between 1950 and 1959, there was little difference between the sexes in obtaining a bachelor degree among Year 12 completers. In contrast, for the youngest cohort, the odds of young women holding a bachelor degree were about 1.4 times the odds for young men.

TABLE 14.5
Effects of class background, school sector, and test scores on university participation and tests of changes over time

	Base-line model	+ School sector	+ Literacy and numeracy	+ Interactions
Intercept	−2.14***	−2.27***	−2.39***	−3.02***
Cohort	0.63***	0.60***	0.66***	1.00***
Male	−0.17***	−0.20***	−0.29***	0.49***
Occupational background				
Professional	1.37***	1.18***	0.83***	1.03***
Managerial	0.79***	0.65***	0.43***	0.36***
Other nonmanual	0.60***	0.54***	0.39***	0.46***
School sector				
Catholic	—	0.61***	0.61***	0.41***
Independent	—	1.09***	0.87***	1.35***
Literacy and numeracy	—	—	1.11***	1.39***
Interactions				
Male × cohort	—	—	—	−0.46***
Professional × cohort	—	—	—	−0.11*
Managerial × cohort	—	—	—	0.04
Other nonmanual × cohort	—	—	—	−0.04
Catholic × cohort	—	—	—	0.12*
Independent × cohort	—	—	—	−0.29***
Literacy and numeracy × cohort	—	—	—	−0.15***
R^2 (pseudo)	15.1	18.7	34.2	35.0

*$p < 0.05$; **$p < 0.01$; ***$p < 0.001$.

There was no significant change over time in the effects of parental education or an upper service-class origin. These results were confirmed in the full-interaction model. Therefore, among Year 12 completers there was no decline in the effect of class origin on obtaining a bachelor degree.

Table 14.5 shows the effects of cohort, being male, occupational background, school sector, and test scores in literacy and numeracy on university participation for the youth cohort samples, not restricted to Year 12 completers. Strong effects for cohort were found, indicating that for a ten-year increase in birth year the odds of university participation, rather than nonparticipation, were 1.7 times the comparable odds for the cohort born in 1961. Therefore, the odds of university participation for students born in the early 1980s were over 3 times the odds for the cohort born in 1961. This effect for cohort on university participation was weaker than its effects on Year 12 participation. The odds of university participation for a professional background were nearly 4 times greater than the odds for a manual background. The odds ratios for managerial and nonmanual backgrounds were 2.2 and 1.8. The effects for occupational background on university participation were slightly stronger than their effects on Year 12 completion (comparable analysis not shown).

The addition of school sector increased the accounted for variance in university participation from 15% to 19%. The odds of university participation for attendance at an independent or Catholic school were 3.0 and 1.8 times (respectively) the odds for attendance at a government school. The effect of attendance at an independent school relative to a government school on university participation was weaker than its effect on Year 12 completion. The addition of school sector reduced the effect of occupational background, indicating that a small part of its effect can be attributed to school sector.

The addition of test scores to the analysis increased the explained variance from 19% to 34%. Test scores in literacy and numeracy showed substantially stronger effects on university participation than on Year 12 completion. An increase of one standard deviation in test scores increased the odds of university participation 3 times compared with an odds ratio of 2.1 for Year 12. The effects of occupational background and attendance at an independent school were reduced with the addition of test scores. Net of test scores, the odds of university participation for a professional background were 2.3 times the odds for a manual background, compared with an odds ratio of 3.3 when not controlling for test scores. Therefore, part of the greater likelihood of students with professional backgrounds going to university can be attributed to student ability. The odds of university participation for managerial, compared with manual, origins also declined from 1.9 to 1.5 with the addition of test scores.

The addition of test scores reduced the odds of university participation for attendance at independent relative to government schools from 3.0 to 2.4. Therefore, the greater propensity of students from independent schools to attend university can only partly be explained by occupational background and test scores. With the addition of test scores, there was no change in the relative odds of university participation for Catholic compared to government schooling.

Results for the final model, which included interactions with cohort, showed declines over time in the effects of gender, professional background, attendance at an independent school, and test scores. The decline in the effect of gender was much greater than that observed for participation in

Year 12. For each 10-year-younger birth cohort, the odds of young women completing a bachelor degree relative to young men increased 1.6 times. In the oldest cohort, males were more likely to participate in university, net of school sector and test scores; however in the youngest cohort the odds of female participation were about 1.5 times that of males.

The effects of a professional background were weaker for each successively younger cohort, the odds declining by a factor of 1.2 per ten years. For the cohort born in 1961, the odds of university participation for a professional background were 2.8 times the odds for a manual background. For those born twenty years later, the odds ratio declined to 2.2. An even stronger decline was found for attendance at an independent school. The odds ratio of university participation for attendance at an independent school compared with a government school declined from 3.9 to 2.2 during the 20-year period. The effect of test scores also declined. For those born in 1961, a one standard deviation difference in test scores increased the odds of university participation 4.0 times. For those born twenty years later, this odds ratio declined to 3.0. Therefore, relative performance in literacy and numeracy has become less important to university participation, but its effect remains substantial.

Table 14.6 presents the results obtained from the same model restricted to Year 12 completers. The amount of explained variation in university participation was only 6% in the baseline model comprising cohort, gender, and occupational background. The explained variation increased to 9% with the addition of school sector. A more substantial increase in explained variance, to over 20%, was found with the addition of test scores. Compared with the analyses of the full cohorts, the effects of occupational background were weaker. When controlling for school sector, the odds of university participation for a professional background were about 2.6 times the odds for a manual origin, compared with an odds ratio of 3.3 for the entire sample. The effects of tests scores were also weaker but to a smaller extent. An increase of one standard deviation in test scores increased the odds of university participation by a factor of 2.6 among Year 12 completers, compared with 3.0 in the entire youth cohorts. The effects of school sector were also weaker among Year 12 completers.

Significant changes over time were found for gender and attendance at a Catholic school. Over time, females became more likely to attend university than males among Year 12 completers. Relative to government school

TABLE 14.6
Effects of class background, school sector, and literacy and numeracy test scores on university participation and tests of changes over time among Year 12 completers

	Base-line model	+ School sector	+ Literacy and numeracy	+ Interactions
Intercept	−0.87***	−1.00***	−1.27***	−1.73***
Cohort	0.23***	0.23***	0.33***	0.57***
Male	−0.11***	−0.14***	−0.24***	0.74***
Occupational background				
Professional	1.09***	0.94***	0.65***	0.60***
Managerial	0.61***	0.49***	0.31***	0.12***
Other nonmanual	0.44***	0.39***	0.27***	0.25***
School sector	—	—	—	—
Catholic	—	0.47***	0.49***	0.19***
Independent	—	0.82***	0.66***	0.60***
Literacy and numeracy	—	—	0.97***	1.07***
Interactions				
Male × cohort	—	—	—	−0.56***
Professional × cohort	—	—	—	0.03
Managerial × cohort	—	—	—	0.11
Other nonmanual × cohort	—	—	—	0.01
Catholic × cohort	—	—	—	0.17**
Independent × cohort	—	—	—	0.04
Literacy and numeracy × cohort	—	—	—	−0.05
R^2 (pseudo)	6.4	9.1	23.3	24.2

NOTE: See note to Table 14.5.

students, Catholic school students became more likely to participate at university. In contrast, there was no significant decline in the effects of occupational background, attendance at an independent school or ability.

Table 14.7 examines the proposition that the imposition of HECS has deterred students from lower social origins from university participation. It shows the percentage of students participating at university in 1999 or 2000 given their ENTER (percentile) score in 1998 and their EGP occupational origin. Among students with ENTER scores of between 95 and 99.95, between 94% and 99% participated at university. The percentage participating was not lower among students with manual origins compared to service-class origins. The second tier of ENTER scores also shows little difference, although students with routine nonmanual origins have lower participation rates than others. In the third tier, students with manual origins show a lower participation rate, but this pattern is not repeated in the other tiers. For ENTER scores between 60 and 69.95, students with

TABLE 14.7
Proportion of students participating in university by Year-12 ENTER score and social background

Enter score range	Upper service	Lower service	Routine non-manual	Self-employed	Skilled manual	Manual
95.00–99.95	99	98	94	95	96	98
90.00–94.95	93	96	84	97	91	89
85.00–89.95	89	87	87	69	84	78
80.00–84.95	82	84	83	69	80	84
70.00–79.95	74	73	69	68	73	75
60.00–69.95	47	51	69	53	52	56
30.00–59.95	29	27	32	30	20	29

NOTE: Youth cohort data (year 9 in 1995 cohort).

service-class origins show a lower participation rate than others. Thus, students' occupational origins have little or no influence on university participation when taking into account their ENTER scores. This is not to say that socioeconomic background does not affect educational outcomes, but it does suggest that HECS does not deter high-performing students from less privileged backgrounds from going to university.

DISCUSSION

From a policy perspective, these analyses lend further support to the conclusion that the Australian HECS system has not increased socioeconomic inequalities in university participation. The analyses showed weaker effects for socioeconomic background in the cohorts that entered university after 1990. Furthermore, there is no evidence that students from lower socioeconomic backgrounds are less likely to pursue a university education given their performance in tertiary entrance examinations. Although such a finding does not directly address the most recent changes to the HECS system, it does suggest that increasing the HECS fees by 25% for high-demand courses is unlikely to deter suitably qualified students from participating in such courses.

A major finding of these analyses is that the effect of occupational background on the higher forms of educational participation has declined. A decline was found in both the adult and youth cohort samples. Consistent with other findings presented in this volume, there was no decline in the effects of occupational background among students eligible for university entrance (Year 12 students in Australia). However, among all students the chances of students from manual backgrounds participating at university have increased and their relative chances have improved vis-à-vis students from professional and other backgrounds. This change is important because it indicates increased opportunities for students with low socioeconomic backgrounds, and their communities are likely to be aware of this change. The fact that their relative chances of university participation *among Year 12 completers* have not changed over time would be less apparent.

Despite these changes, socioeconomic inequalities in educational participation are still a problem. Among the youngest cohort, a service class or professional background substantially increases the chances of university participation relative to a manual background, even after taking into account school sector and performance in literacy and numeracy tests. If the Australian education system was largely meritocratic, socioeconomic background should have little or no effect when taking into account prior performance. Nor should government school students be less likely to participate or receive lower tertiary entrance scores, after taking into account prior performance. These findings show that there are socioeconomic inequalities in the Australian education system, and policies should be directed at reducing these effects and those of school sector.

CHAPTER FIFTEEN

The Czech Republic: Structural Growth of Inequality in Access to Higher Education

Petr Matějů, Institute of Sociology, Academy of Sciences of the Czech Republic

Blanka Řeháková, Institute of Sociology, Academy of Sciences of the Czech Republic

Natalie Simonová, Institute of Sociology, Academy of Sciences of the Czech Republic

INHIBITED REFORMS AND LIMITS TO GROWTH

The Czech Republic is one of the "transition" or "postcommunist" countries where reforms of higher education systems were being implemented hand in hand with transitions from authoritarian to democratic political systems and from command-type to market-driven economies. To understand the difficulties of transforming the higher education systems in postcommunist countries, we must take into account the key features that higher education systems inherited from the previous regimes:

- Higher education was heavily centralized and part of the central planning system, like every other area of economic and social reproduction. Its vital link to the labor market was set by the Central Committee of the Communist Party. Consequently, the overall number of students and their allocation to major fields of study and programs were decided centrally.
- Bureaucratic control over the entire system, balancing the number of graduates with the number of jobs, displaced job competition. As a result, educational credentials (diplomas, certificates) became more important in job allocation than actual knowledge, skills, and competencies.
- Curriculum guidelines, research goals, and requirements for filling teaching positions (including political criteria) were defined and closely monitored by the Communist party and its state apparatus.

- A unitary system of traditional university education lacked completely short bachelor's programs and did not recognize college or similar types of higher education institutions.
- Decisions about the number of students admitted and enrollment procedures were based on central guidelines and quotas set by the Communist Party Central Committee for controlling the proportions of students of various social backgrounds. The objective was to ensure an appropriate proportion of students from each social class corresponding to the proportion of that class within the population at large.
- Financing of universities was entirely dependent on the government, based on "incremental budgeting," whereby the annual budget of each university was equal to that of the previous year (the budgetary base) plus a certain increment that depended much on the success of the institution in negotiations and on available resources.

The stagnation of the socialist university system, and its failure to respond to educational aspirations and the actual demand for tertiary education are demonstrated in Figure 15.1, which shows the numbers of secondary school graduates and enrolled university students as well as the ratio of enrolled university students to secondary school graduates between 1962 and 2004. The data clearly confirm the policy of keeping the number of university students very low until the collapse of the Communist regime in 1989, the only exception being the academic year of 1968–69, when, because of the "Prague Spring" Communist Party control over the university system was less rigid. The chances of making the transition to tertiary education (defined as a ratio of enrolled students to high-school graduates) dropped in the 1980s, when the number of high-school graduates began to grow. Despite the sharp increase in the number of enrolled university students after the collapse of the Communist regime in November 1989, the capacity of the university system, still trapped in its traditional unitary and elitist structure, was unable to cope with the quickly growing demand for tertiary education. Therefore, the relative chance of making the transition dropped again to its average pre-1989 level.

FIRST STAGE OF THE REFORM:
TOWARD ACADEMIC FREEDOM

Starting in 1989, the transition to democracy and a market economy brought about significant changes in society and also in the higher education system.

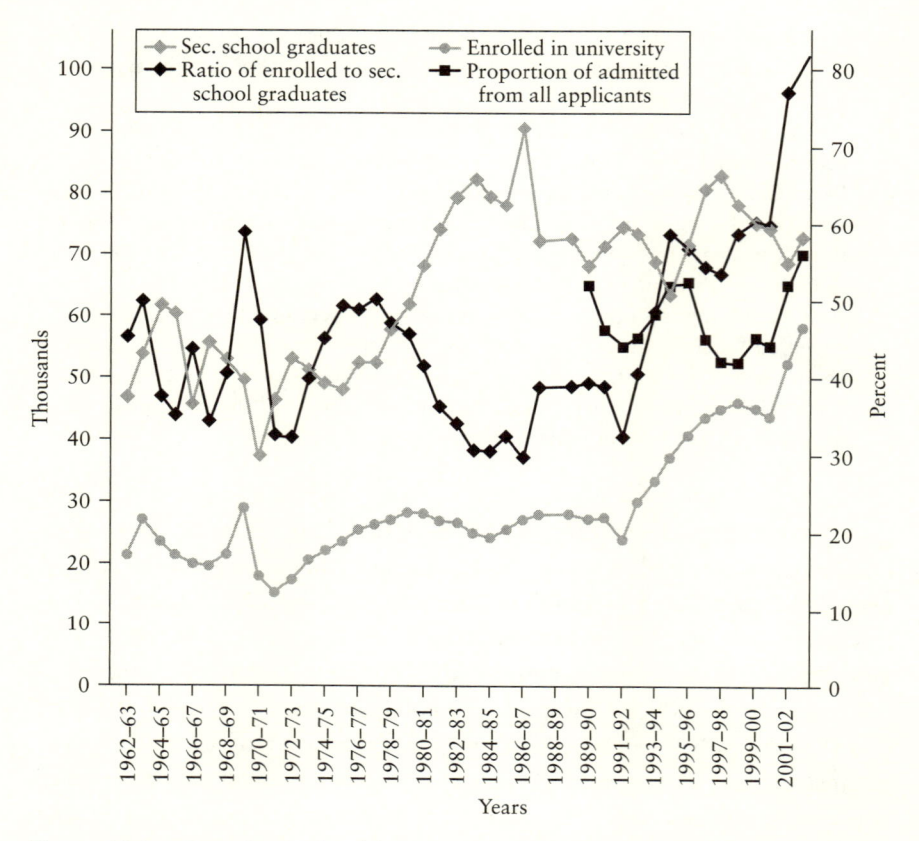

Figure 15.1. Secondary-school Graduates and Enrolled University Students

SOURCES: Vývojová ročenka školství v České republice 1989/90–1998/99 [Yearbook of education development in the Czech Republic 1989/90–1998/99], 1999. Praha: ÚIV. Statistiky školství z let 1962 až 1989 [Education Statistics from the Years 1962 to 1989]. Praha: Ústav školských informací [Institute of Information on Education]. Historická ročenka školství v České republice 1953/54–1997/98 [Historical Yearbook of Education in the Czech Republic 1953/54–1997/98], 1998. Praha: ÚIV.

NOTE: Secondary-school graduates (in thousands), enrolled in university (in thousands), the ratio between the enrolled in university and secondary-school graduates (in %), and the proportion of enrolled from all applicants (in %) between 1962 and 2004 in the Czech Republic.

The Higher Education Act of 1990 created the conditions for the return to a democratic control of higher education. It eliminated political control over university activities and decision-making processes, and it reduced significantly government authority over the academic bodies. The Act also provided universities with the freedom to make their own financial decisions.

Currently the Ministry of Education allocates funds to the universities, which are responsible for their distribution and spending.

Although this Act opened a possibility for the modernization of Czech higher education, many of the structural problems remained unresolved. First, the system did not change its unitary character. The number of students enrolled in bachelor's programs in the Czech Republic grew very slowly until 2002, when the amendment to the Higher Education Act set a binding time schedule for the implementation of the Bologna declaration.[1] A faster transition to a two-tier system earlier than that would have required stronger legislative support for establishing a nonuniversity sector within tertiary education. The Act of 1990 did not go that far.

The Act of 1990 did not introduce any standardized compulsory entry examinations. While universities had full autonomy in drafting their entry examinations and tests, the matriculation examinations at the end of secondary education remained incomparable in both structure and results. Given a significant surplus demand, the absence of nationally administered tests at the end of secondary education or at the entry to the tertiary level undermines the transparency of the admission process and creates an opportunity for more or less subtle forms of corruption.

The Act also failed to create a legislative framework for private universities or colleges. Although there were no legislative obstacles to establishing private colleges, the Act did not provide a mechanism for establishing eligibility to apply for state accreditation, which would allow institutions to award degrees recognized by the Ministry of Education. Assessment of the overall impact of the Higher Education Act of 1990 on the development of higher education in the Czech Republic should be cautious, in particular with respect to its effect on the financing and accessibility of higher education. There is, however, an equally justified objection that the almost full self-government granted to universities in advance of a much deeper and more consistent reform of the system made future reforms more difficult, if not impossible. Subsequent developments justify this concern. The Czech Republic was not the only country where "the autonomy granted to universities was used—or perceived to be used—to block reform" (Scott 2002, 146).

The first signs that consistent and often painful reforms may not receive sufficient support appeared in 1994. At that time, universities began to experience serious austerity and the number of applications grew much faster than the capacity of schools to meet the rising demand. Supplementary financial resources remained either outlawed (tuition fees) or not sufficiently explored and used (commercialization of research). It became clear that the future growth of higher education would not be possible without a substantial reform of its financing. For this reason, in 1994, a group of economists and policy makers drafted a proposal for a substantive reform of university financing designed to implement a system similar to the Australian Higher Education Contribution Scheme (HESC). Although it was initially commissioned by the Committee for Education and Science of the Czech Parliament, this proposal was never submitted to Parliament for debate in the form of a bill. The primary reason was strong lobbying of university rectors and senates against the idea, which they claimed would allow the state to dissociate itself from financing higher education and result in burdening the students and their families with steadily growing tuition fees. University administration was also uneasy about the idea of tuition fees being collected by the state and then redistributed to universities as part of the state subsidy. The economic incentives under this system were not seen as compensating for the pressure toward higher accountability and responsibility that tuition fees would certainly bring.

SECOND STAGE: INCREASED AUTONOMY BUT BARRIERS TO MULTISOURCE FINANCING

The new Higher Education Act, passed by the Czech Parliament in April 1998, went even further in strengthening the formal autonomy of universities, but without granting them greater fiscal autonomy or opening additional sources of financing. Two principal sources of multisource financing, tuition fees, and profits from technology transfer, remained essentially untapped. A markedly proreform provision of the 1998 Act—the legal recognition of so-called "nonuniversity institutions of higher education" (i.e., colleges) that offer primarily, albeit not exclusively, bachelor's programs—allowed the formation of a nonuniversity segment of tertiary education. Nonetheless, this provision did not trigger any significant change in the structure of Czech tertiary education. Although the demand for bachelor's programs has steadily risen, and despite the recommendation of the Bologna Declaration that all European countries transition their tertiary systems from the unitary to the binary model, not a single *public* nonuniversity institution of higher education has been established yet.

Nevertheless, the nonuniversity sector of tertiary education began to grow after 1998, owing to the rapidly increasing number of private colleges whose state accreditation was made possible by the Higher Education Act of 1998. Although private colleges and universities received no financial subsidy from the state (even though the Act does not explicitly prevent it), as of the academic year 2004–05 more than 30 private colleges were established, enrolling about ten thousand students in total, and these institutions slowly filled the gap in the nonuniversity sector of tertiary education.

THIRD STAGE: FINANCIAL CRISIS INHIBITS GROWTH WHILE FUNDAMENTAL REFORMS ARE BLOCKED

Both domestic and international statistical data show a lasting and deepening financial crisis of public tertiary education in the Czech Republic, which, in turn, inhibits the growth of educational opportunities. As a result, there is a shortage of adults with tertiary education in the Czech Republic, and the chances of continuing studies beyond the secondary level are not improving.

After 1994, when the new mechanisms for financing tertiary education were implemented, the number of students at public universities grew steadily from 132,000 in 1994 to 274,000 in 2004. This increase in the number of students by about 100% was followed by a growth of state subsidy from CZK 4.3 billion in 1994 to CZK 13.6 billion in 2004 (316% growth). However, inflation during this period grew at a rate of 1.66%. Therefore, the state subsidy per student dropped in real terms from CZK 35,000 in 1996 to CZK 24,000 in 2002, though it began to grow again in 2004 and regained its 1997 level. Even the tightening budgets and rapidly growing austerity did not significantly soften the reluctance of public universities to adopt a two-tier (binary) system that would allow admitting a higher number of students in short programs. In fact, the opposite trend occurred: between 1998 and 2002, the proportion of students in these programs decreased. The Czech Republic remains close to the bottom among OECD countries with respect to the number of adults with tertiary education and the number of young people of relevant age who can continue their

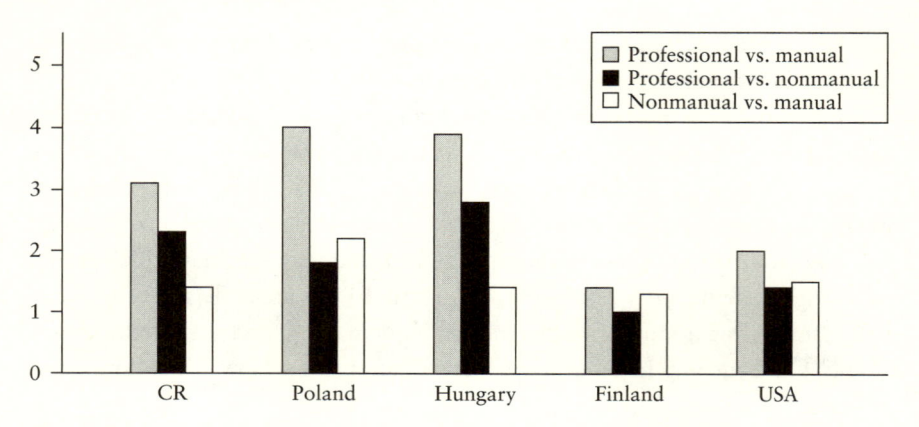

Figure 15.2. Ratios of Chances for Achieving Tertiary Education between Individuals of Different Family Class Background (father's occupation) in 1998

SOURCES: SIALS; ISSP 1992, 1999.

NOTE: Persons 20–35 years of age.

studies after graduation from a secondary school.[2] The reasons for this are continuing financial and structural obstacles that limit the growth of the number of educational opportunities at the tertiary level. At the same time, however, aspirations for higher education have been steeply rising, partly due to significant growth in the economic returns of higher education in postcommunist countries.[3]

All the processes mentioned here contribute to a keen competition for entry into tertiary education, making the transition between secondary and tertiary education an ordeal for secondary school graduates and their families. Comparison of five OECD countries participating in the SIALS project (Figure 15.2) shows that the inequality is especially high between the children of professionals and of workers. There seems to be quite strong although only preliminary evidence for the hypothesis that the postcommunist transformation increased the inequality in access to tertiary education.

An amendment to the Higher Education Act of 1998 was submitted to the Czech Parliament in the fall of 2000 aimed at solving the most acute structural and fiscal problems of tertiary education in the Czech Republic. It provided for the universities to accomplish the transformation to the two-tier system by the end of 2003 (the process has not been completed as of 2005), and it allowed universities to invest capital into private joint ventures and spin-off companies (restrictions were imposed only on assets and funds transferred to universities from the state). Because of continued strong opposition to tuition fees, the amendment legalized the "dual-track system," which some universities were in fact already operating. Students in the life-long learning programs, for which universities were already allowed to charge tuition fees, are now allowed to take courses in accredited programs and accumulate regular credits; under certain conditions these credits can be converted into a regular diploma. The Bill of Financing Higher Education, drafted in 2001 with the aim of introducing tuition fees, student loans, and student financial aid programs, was submitted to the Czech Parliament in the spring of 2002.[4] It did not pass, and no other significant changes have been proposed to the structure of the tertiary education system, its financing, or its admission procedures. In sum, extremely sharp competition for entry into tertiary education and the absence of clearly defined benchmarking criteria of success have very likely contributed to an increase in inequality in access to higher education after 1989.

ACCESSIBILITY AND CLASS INEQUALITY

In this section we address the central question of how the expansion of the higher education system (or the lack thereof) and recent policies (or their absence) affect inequalities in the chances of attending higher education, with particular emphasis on the role of gender and socioeconomic background. These were the two dimensions of educational inequality that communist governments aimed to eradicate in the first place. We have shown already that the postcommunist governments let the inequality in access to higher education develop spontaneously. The primary aim of the analysis is to compare the development of inequality in access to tertiary education during the *communist* and *postcommunist* periods of development. We focus primarily on the Czech Republic, but comparison of the two periods may contribute to a better understanding of the more general question of how the two historically unique types of social change—transition to socialism and postcommunist transformation—shaped the inequality in access to tertiary education. As shown in several recent analyses (e.g., Matějů and Kreidl 2001; Večerník 2001), the role of education in the system of social stratification has changed markedly. Most important, a true revolution took place in the economic returns on higher education. While in 1988, each year of education brought a bonus of a 4% salary increase, in 1996 this bonus reached 8%. During the same period, the ratio of the wage of a person with a university education and that of a secondary school diploma holder increased from 1.48 to 2.37 (Večerník 2001).

Changes in the economic returns on education and its growing social value—reflected by the growing consistency between education, prestige, social status, and self-perception (Matějů and Kreidl 2001)—enhance sensitivity to the limited supply of educational opportunities and especially to the significant class inequality in access to tertiary education. Consequently, equity in access to education is becoming a true social and political issue.

THEORETICAL PERSPECTIVE

Various attempts to show that socialism led to the decrease of the effect of socioeconomic background on the educational attainment of children failed. Matějů and Peschar (1990) found that, at the end of the 1980s, the overall effect of family socioeconomic status on the educational attainment of children was weaker in Czechoslovakia than in the Netherlands, but the effect of its economic dimension was stronger in Czechoslovakia than in the Netherlands. These results corresponded to the *hypothesis of socialist transformation*, which claimed that socialist reforms of education systems and corresponding policies (particularly the implementation of the quota system), caused an initial reduction of the effects of social origin on educational attainment. However, as soon as the new elite secured its privileges and took control of the education system, they ensured educational advantages for their own class. As a result, the effect of social origin in the later years of the socialist regimes returned to its original presocialist level (Matějů 1986, 1993).

Hanley (2001) challenged this hypothesis and attributed the initial reduction in the effect of social origin on educational attainment to the expansion of the education system, questioning the real effect of the quota system on the admission processes at the secondary and postsecondary level. His analysis confirmed that selection on the basis of political criteria was present during the "normalization" period after the Soviet invasion in 1968. The hypothesis about the role of redistribution policies, including the quota system, was supported also by Kreidl (2001), who showed that the effect of parental socioeconomic status on success in the transition from lower to upper secondary and technical schools decreased in the years 1948–53.

The *trajectory maintenance* theory, which also referred specifically to socialist countries, claimed that members of the precommunist elites (bureaucracy and professionals) were able to pass privileges to their children, even under the new regime, by making use of their social and cultural capital. Consequently, inequalities in the allocation of education did not decline (Hanley and McKeever 1997). This hypothesis also applied the theory of cultural reproduction to the socialist system. Wong (1998) also found a strong effect of various types of capital that individual families possessed and employed to secure the desired education for their offspring, and showed that it was social capital, such as membership in the Communist Party that played an important role as a mediator of intergenerational inequalities.

Similar results emerged from analyses carried out on the Czechoslovak, Hungarian, and Russian data (Simkus and Andorka 1982; Boguszak, Matějů, and Peschar 1990; Gerber and Hout 1995).

Two competing hypotheses can be formulated concerning the development of inequality in access to tertiary education during the socialist regime. The first refers to the socialist transformation hypothesis that found support in the data from the Czechoslovak stratification survey carried out in 1984 (Matějů 1993). If this hypothesis is true, we should be able to find a significant reduction of differentials in the chances individuals of different socioeconomic backgrounds have of making transitions between secondary and tertiary education. The second hypothesis concerning this stage of development, suggested by Hanley and McKeever (1997) and supported by Wong (1998) for the former Czechoslovakia, and by Gerber and Hout (1995) for Russia, rejects any change in the effect of socioeconomic background caused by socialist reforms and corresponding policies. In discussing educational inequality during the postcommunist transformation, we must point out that postcommunist countries are undergoing a development that can be characterized as the formation of genuine social classes.

The consequences of class formation in postcommunist countries for educational stratification and inequality can be best described using the *theory of rational action* proposed by John Goldthorpe and Richard Breen (Goldthorpe 1996; Breen and Goldthorpe 1997). To account not only for persisting but also for increasing inequality, we must address the notion of *rationality*, assuming that social actors have their goals and alternative means of pursuing them. In choosing among the means, actors tend to assess costs, risks, and benefits, rather than merely follow social or cultural norms or values typical for the particular class to which they belong (Goldthorpe 1996, 485).

This approach is consistent with the explicit assumption that educational expansion at lower levels (secondary education) brings ever higher number of children to the competition for tertiary education, where the demand has risen faster than the supply of educational opportunities. Therefore, the risk of failure is very high. As a consequence, class differentials in taking up these options may increase because cost–benefit evaluations made by children and parents in different class situations may become less favorable for lower social classes.

All available evidence and the main propositions of the rational action theory lead us to the hypothesis that class differentials in the chances of success in the transition between secondary and tertiary education increased after 1989. The following arguments support this hypothesis.

1. The transformation of the Czech tertiary education system from a unitary to a binary model has not been completed and thus still shows signs of an elitist tertiary education system.

2. Both the structural constraints (imposed by the unitary system) and the deepening austerity of tertiary education institutions (because of their extreme dependence on limited public funds) pose serious obstacles to further expansion of educational opportunities.

3. Growing educational aspirations and a steady growth in the number of secondary education graduates on the one hand, and constraints in the growth of educational opportunities at the tertiary level on the other, result in excessive demand and a high number of rejections in the admission process.

4. For the above reasons, *the transition between the secondary and tertiary level of education has become extremely competitive.*

5. The postcommunist transformation has caused a significant increase in economic inequality, which resulted in the formation of genuine social classes.

6. The process of *objective* change in the class structure resulted in the formation of *subjectively* defined groups of winners and losers of the transformation, making the new property class (enterprise owners, the self-employed) and professionals the typical winners, and leaving skilled and unskilled workers among the typical losers (Matějů 1999).

7. The perceived role of education in building strategies for getting ahead has grown significantly, and achieving tertiary education has gradually developed into a principal strategy for success in life.

8. All these processes affecting class structure and social stratification in the postcommunist Czech Republic brought about a growing awareness and assessment of the costs, risks, and benefits of decisions concerning the educational transition between secondary and tertiary education. This is especially true for large segments of the working class (semiskilled and unskilled workers), who are the losers of the transition.

Based on the foregoing arguments, we propose to test the following hypotheses.

Hypotheses
1. The socialist-regime period did not bring any change in the effect of socioeconomic background on the chance of making the transition between secondary and tertiary education. The only significant change was the reduction of inequality between men and women that occurred as a consequence of redistribution policies.
2. The postcommunist transformation caused a significant increase in the effect of social background on the chance of making the transition between secondary and tertiary education. The increase was due primarily to the increasing effect of the father's social class (representing the socio-*economic* dimension of social stratification), while the effect of parents' education (representing the cultural dimension of social stratification) remained stable. The effect of gender remained stable.
3. The increase of the class differentials in the chance of making the transition between secondary and tertiary education was caused in particular by the widening gap between the typical losers of the transformation (semiskilled and unskilled workers) and other classes.

DATA AND STRATEGY OF ANALYSIS

To obtain a sufficiently large number of cases for cohort analysis that would allow a comparison of the presocialist, socialist, and postsocialist stages of development of the Czech Republic, data from three surveys were merged into one analytical file. These are the Transformation of Social Structure Survey 1991 (TSS-91), the Second International Adult Literacy Survey 1998 (SIALS-98), and the International Social Survey Program's survey module on Social Inequality 1999 (ISSP-99). All these surveys were carried out on random samples produced by two-stage stratified random sampling procedures.[5] The original effective sample sizes were: 1,870 cases for TSS-91 (in the Czech part of former Czechoslovakia); 3,132 cases for SIALS-98; and 1,834 cases for ISSP-99. The analytical data file contained 6,740 cases.

The variables created for the analyses were as follows.

- COH (the year when the respondent reached 18 years of age): (1) before 1948, (2) 1948–64, (3) 1965–74, (4) 1975–89, (5) 1990–99
- GEN: (1) male, (2) female
- PED (parents' education—the highest level of education achieved by the more educated parent): (1) lower secondary or lower, (2) upper secondary, (3) tertiary
- RED (respondent's education—the highest level of education achieved by the respondent): (1) lower secondary or lower, (2) upper secondary, (3) tertiary[6]
- FCLS (father's class at the time the respondent was 16 years old): (1) semiskilled and unskilled workers, farm workers (UW); (2) skilled workers (SW); (3) routine nonmanual occupations (NM); (4) professionals, including self-employed (PROF)[7]

The distributions of the key variables are shown in the Appendix (found on the Web site: http://www.stratif.cz/attachments/doc184/Ch15_App.pdf).

Within the comparative context of our analysis, we proposed to examine five outcomes: (1) eligibility for tertiary education (graduation from upper secondary education); (2) admission into a bachelor's program of tertiary education; (3) completion of a bachelor's program of tertiary education; (4) admission into the second stage of tertiary education; and (5) completion of the second stage of tertiary education. As discussed in the first part of this chapter, the typically socialist unitary system has not been significantly transformed into a binary one in the postcommunist period. Therefore, we cannot distinguish between the first two levels of tertiary education (bachelor's and master's). Also, because of the low dropout rate during the socialist era and its very slow increase after 1989, questions on achieved education in most of the large surveys did not contain the option "uncompleted tertiary." For all these reasons, our analyses were limited to eligibility for tertiary education (completion of upper secondary education) and completion of tertiary education (second transition). Therefore, our logit models addressed only two major educational outcomes: (1) transition to (completed) tertiary education, for those who completed upper secondary education (i.e., the conditional outcome); and (2) achieving tertiary education, for all respondents in a given cohort (i.e., the unconditional outcome).

We wanted our analyses to cover both historically unique periods of social transformation in East Central Europe: the socialist revolutions in

1948 and the postcommunist transformations after 1989. We therefore constructed the age cohorts to distinguish the first "socialist" cohort (those who turned 18 after 1948) from those who completed secondary school and could thus enter tertiary education before 1948 (persons who turned 18 before 1948). Because of the problem of differential mortality by education of the earlier cohorts and of the fact that educational opportunities of the last precommunist cohort were affected by World War II (a significant number of those who turned 18 before 1948), the last presocialist cohort served mostly as a benchmark for studying developments during the socialist period rather than as evidence about the openness of the tertiary education system in the presocialist Czechoslovakia. This coincides with the main focus of our analysis, which is on the effects of the socialist policies during the periods of rigid socialism between 1948–64, reform socialism between 1965–74, and post-1968 normalization between 1975–89.

Because of the dichotomous character of the dependent variable (success versus failure in the given transition), hypotheses about changes in the chances of achieving tertiary education were tested by logit models. This strategy allowed the transformation of categorical variables into a set of special contrast variables representing individual hypotheses.[8] The goodness of fit of each logit model was assessed by a likelihood ratio test and by an evaluation of the adjusted residuals for individual cells of the multiple classification (i.e., by comparing observed frequencies with those derived from the given model). All the models presented showed very high levels of goodness of fit for both criteria.

RESULTS: BASIC TRENDS IN OPPORTUNITY
AND PARTICIPATION

The trends in two main educational transitions portrayed by the survey data match the statistical data presented in the first part of this chapter. As shown in Figure 15.3, educational opportunities at the upper secondary and tertiary level grew very slowly during the last five decades (from 34% to 52% for the former, and from 10% to 19% for the latter). A marked rise in the probability of success in the transition between upper secondary and tertiary education after 1989 was due partly to a rather slow growth in the number of upper secondary school graduates. The patterns of development of differentials between men and women in their chances for completion

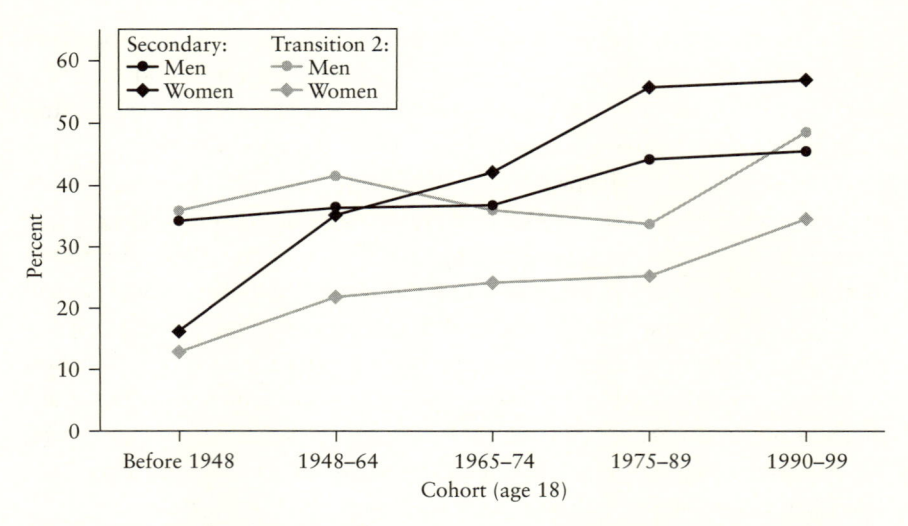

Figure 15.3. Individuals Eligible to Enter Tertiary Education (with completed upper secondary education) and those Who Passed the Second Transition (completed tertiary education), by Gender and Cohort (in %)

of secondary education and for passing the second transition are typical of formerly socialist countries. As far as completion of secondary education is concerned, the first period of socialist development brought about a massive redistribution of educational opportunities between men and women, and as a result women's chances of making this transition exceeded those of men. In a further development, the chances of men began to grow but not enough to reach the level of women. As far as the second transition is concerned, while women's chances grew steadily during the socialist regime and men's chances decreased, the odds of men and women were not reversed in favor of women.

The limited growth of opportunities during the period under study did not create favorable conditions for a significant reduction of class differentials in the chances of making the transition between secondary and tertiary education (Figure 15.4) despite the fact that class differentials of success in the completion of secondary education diminished, mainly because of the improving relative chances of individuals of working-class origin (Figure 15.5). Results displayed in Figure 15.4 indicate that increasing participation of the lower social classes in upper secondary education led to an increase in the competitiveness of the subsequent transition, in which the

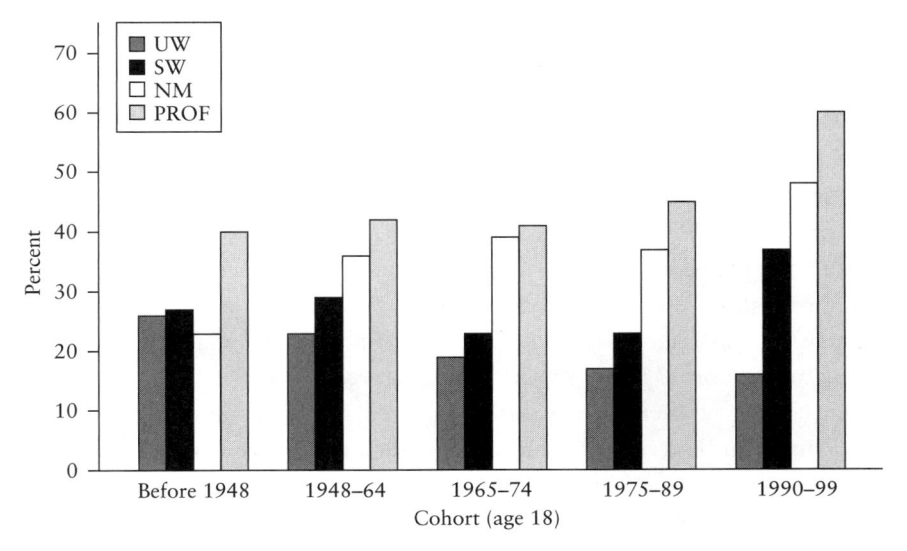

Figure 15.4. Individuals Who Succeeded in the Second Transition, by Father's Class and Cohort (in %)

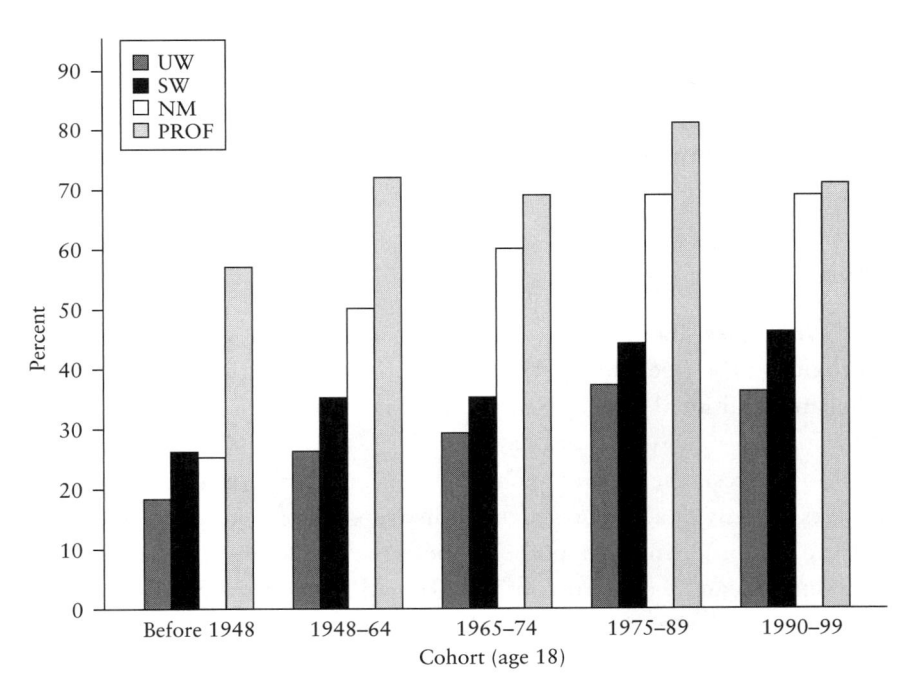

Figure 15.5. Individuals Who Completed Upper Secondary Education, by Father's Class and Cohort (in %)

lower social classes tended to lose. The chances of unskilled and semiskilled workers (UW) making the transition actually dropped from 26% in the presocialist period to 16% for the last two cohorts (the last socialist and the first postsocialist cohort), while they grew rapidly for nonmanual workers and professionals, who profited most from the growth of educational opportunities at the tertiary level. The problem of unskilled and semiskilled workers appears even more serious when we take into account the size of the class: on average 36% of respondents reported this class origin (38% in the first cohort, 32% in the last one).[9] Moreover, in the youngest cohort about 16% of fathers in this class reported upper secondary education.

The social class showing the most significant improvement in its chances of success in the second transition was that of routine nonmanuals, rising from 23% in the first cohort (below the two classes of manual workers) to 48% percent in the last (significantly above the chances of individuals of working-class origin). The winners during the postsocialist stage of development were children of skilled workers, whose chances increased by a factor of 1.6 from 23% to 37%, and of professionals, whose chances increased by a factor of 1.3 from 45% to 60%. The real losers were individuals of unskilled and semiskilled worker background, whose chances dropped in both real and relative terms: from 17% to 16% in real terms, and from 0.38 to 0.27 in the ratio of their chances to succeed vis-à-vis the professionals.

TESTING HYPOTHESES ABOUT THE DEVELOPMENT OF INEQUALITY

The hypotheses about the two educational outcomes were tested using six logit models (see Models I to VI and their descriptions, principal results, and additional tests of changes in odds ratios in the Appendix on the Web site).

Model I tests the general hypothesis concerning the development of the chances of individual cohorts making the transition from secondary to tertiary education, then the hypothesis about the development of inequalities between men and women (hypothesis 1), and finally the hypothesis about the stability of the effect of parental education (hypothesis 2). The following constraints of individual interactive effects were introduced into the model to test these hypotheses.

TABLE 15.1
Odds of making the second transition: Effects of gender and parents' education (Model I)

Cohort	Parents' education	Gender	Odds
(1), (2) before 1948, 1948–64	(1) Lower secondary or lower	(1) Male	0.4988
		(2) Female	0.1649
	(2) Higher secondary	(1) Male	1.1067
		(2) Female	0.3667
	(3) Tertiary	(1) Male	2.4682
		(2) Female	0.8135
(3), (4) 1965–74, 1975–89,	(1) Lower secondary or lower	(1) Male	0.2940
		(2) Female	0.1845
	(2) Higher secondary	(1) Male	0.6529
		(2) Female	0.4096
	(3) Tertiary	(1) Male	1.4494
		(2) Female	0.9095
(5) 1990–99	(1) Lower secondary or lower	(1) Male	0.3938
		(2) Female	0.2470
	(2) Higher secondary	(1) Male	0.8744
		(2) Female	0.5485
	(3) Tertiary	(1) Male	1.9409
		(2) Female	1.2178

Model fit: $L^2 = 20.5$, $df = 24$, $p = 0.666$.

1. Development of the chances of making the transition from secondary to tertiary education can be modeled as follows: there was no significant change in the overall chances between the first and second cohort; during the period of 1965–89 (the third and fourth cohorts) there was an overall slowdown, especially for men; the overall chances increased again only in the last, postsocialist, cohort.

2. As a result of a significant redistribution of educational opportunities in favor of women, the effect of gender changed between the second and third cohorts but remained stable thereafter.

3. The effect of parents' education remained unchanged throughout the entire period.

Because the model shows a very good fit ($L^2 = 20.5$, $df = 24$, $p = 0.666$), we can present the odds based on the expected frequencies in two forms: the odds of making the transition (Table 15.1) and odds ratios for the main groups defined by parental education.[10]

Results presented in Table 15.1 show that a significant drop in the odds of men making the transition, which occurred between the second and third cohort, brought about only a slow increase in the odds of women. This provides significant support to the hypothesis that the growth in women's chances of attaining higher levels of education under the socialist regime, when the overall growth of educational opportunities was limited, was at the expense of a reduction of the chances for men (Boguszak, Matějů, and Peschar 1990). The odds ratios between categories of parental education derived from the respective odds are stable across all cohorts. The ratios between the odds of making the first transition for two adjacent categories of parental education (i.e., 1 and 2) amount to 2.2, while the odds ratios between categories 1 and 3 are twice as high (4.9 in all cohorts). The odds ratios thus confirm that the inequality in making the secondary transition among individuals of different *educational* backgrounds has not changed throughout the entire period. Apparently, the role of "cultural resources" remained stable and relatively strong, especially between those whose parents achieved tertiary education and those whose parents achieved lower secondary education.

Model II was designed to test the hypothesis about the development of social origin represented by father's social class. This model retained all the constraints imposed on the interaction terms from the previous model except the interaction between the father's cohort and social class, because assuming this interaction to be constant over time, the model returned a statistically unsatisfactory fit. But when the interaction term allowing a change in father's social class in the last cohort was introduced, according to hypothesis 2, Model II showed a much better fit ($L^2 = 26.1$, $df = 31$, $p = 0.718$).[11] The odds shown in Table 15.2 and corresponding odds ratios[12] allow us to make the following conclusions.

1. The effect of social origin represented by father's social class did not change throughout the period of the socialist regime period.
2. Consistent with hypothesis 2, only during the postcommunist transformation did a significant increase occur in inequalities caused by the socioeconomic background represented by father's social class.
3. Consistent with hypothesis 3, this development was caused primarily by the significant decrease of the relative odds of the children of unskilled and semiskilled workers; the odds ratios between the other social classes remained unchanged (in most cases relatively high) throughout the entire period.

A test of a model that introduced both variables representing social origin (parent's education and father's social class) generated unstable results

TABLE 15.2
Odds of making the second transition: Effects of gender and father's class (Model II)

Cohort	Father's class	Gender	Odds
(1), (2) before 1948, 1948–64	(1) Unskilled, semi-skilled	(1) Male	0.4245
		(2) Female	0.1430
	(2) Skilled workers	(1) Male	0.5499
		(2) Female	0.1852
	(3) Routine non-manual	(1) Male	0.9845
		(2) Female	0.3316
	(4) Professionals, self-employed	(1) Male	1.3502
		(2) Female	0.4545
(3), (4) 1965–74, 1975–89,	(1) Unskilled, semi-skilled	(1) Male	0.3110
		(2) Female	0.1949
	(2) Skilled workers	(1) Male	0.4029
		(2) Female	0.2523
	(3) Routine non-manual	(1) Male	0.7215
		(2) Female	0.4520
	(4) Professionals, self-employed	(1) Male	0.9889
		(2) Female	0.6197
(5) 1990–99	(1) Unskilled, semi-skilled	(1) Male	0.2366
		(2) Female	0.1482
	(2) Skilled workers	(1) Male	0.7416
		(2) Female	0.4646
	(3) Routine non-manual	(1) Male	1.3277
		(2) Female	0.8318
	(4) Professionals, self-employed	(1) Male	1.8201
		(2) Female	1.1404

Model fit: $L^2 = 26.1$, $df = 31$, $p = 0.718$.

because of very low or zero frequencies in certain cells of multidimensional classifications. Model III was designed to assess whether the socio*economic* background represented by father's social class had an effect independent of the *cultural* dimension of social origin represented by parental education. In this model we introduced the education and social class of both parents but collapsed the classifications of both variables into two categories. Parents' education was recoded to distinguish between a relatively large group of families where none of the parents attained upper secondary education from another group in which at least one parent did (PED2: (1) lower secondary or lower, (2) higher secondary and higher). Similarly, in the case of the father's social class, we distinguished between a group of unskilled and semiskilled workers and the rest (FCLS2: (1) unskilled and semiskilled workers, (2) the rest).

Using these variables, we tested the model allowing an increase in the overall chance of making the transition between secondary and tertiary

TABLE 15.3
Odds of making the second transition: Effects of parents' education
and father's class (Model III)

Cohort	Parents' education	Father's Class	Odds
(1), (2)	(1) Lower secondary or lower	(1) Unskilled, semiskilled	0.2335
before 1948,		(2) Others	0.3384
1948–64	(2) Higher	(1) Unskilled, semiskilled	0.5625
		(2) Others	0.8165
(3), (4)	(1) Lower secondary or lower	(1) Unskilled, semiskilled	0.1906
1965–74,		(2) Others	0.2762
1975–89,	(2) Higher	(1) Unskilled, semiskilled	0.4594
		(2) Others	0.6662
(5)	(1) Lower secondary or lower	(1) Unskilled, semiskilled	0.1065
1990–99		(2) Others	0.4659
	(2) Higher	(1) Unskilled, semiskilled	0.2569
		(2) Others	1.1233

Model fit: $L^2 = 12.8$, $df = 14$, $p = 0.543$.

education only in the last cohort, blocking any change in the effect of parent's education throughout the entire period but permitting the change in the effect of father's class in the last cohort.[13] As expected, this model showed very good fit ($L^2 = 12.8$, $df = 14$, $p = 0.543$). We derived the following conclusions from the odds and selected odds ratios shown in Table 15.3:

> 1. During the socialist regime, educational background was more important than class origin in determining the odds of making the transition between secondary and tertiary education, and the effects of both factors were stable over time. The odds ratios between categories of parental education were constant over time (2.41).
> 2. Starting in 1989, the effect of educational background remained constant (odds ratio remains at the level of the first four cohorts) while the effect of the father's class increased sharply (the odds ratio between the two classes increased from 1.45 in the first four cohorts to 4.37 in the youngest cohort). These results are consistent with our hypotheses regarding the transition between secondary and tertiary education.

The conditional models (I, II, and III) tested our hypotheses only on the population of respondents eligible to make the transition to tertiary education (secondary school graduates). The unconditional models (IV, V, and VI) tested the same hypotheses on the entire population, and addressed the development of the chances of attaining tertiary education inclusive of the prior effect of unequal access to secondary education. Attaining a

TABLE 15.4
Odds of achieving tertiary education: Effects of parents' education and gender (Model IV)

Cohort	Parents' Education	Gender	Odds
(1) before 1948	(1) Lower secondary or lower	(1) Male	0.1143
		(2) Female	0.0169
	(2) Higher secondary	(1) Male	0.4886
		(2) Female	0.0721
	(3) Tertiary	(1) Male	1.4648
		(2) Female	0.2167
(2) 1948–64	(1) Lower secondary or lower	(1) Male	0.1249
		(2) Female	0.0528
	(2) Higher secondary	(1) Male	0.5334
		(2) Female	0.2253
	(3) Tertiary	(1) Male	1.6018
		(2) Female	0.6762
(3), (4), (5) 1965–74, 1975–89, 1990–99	(1) Lower secondary or lower	(1) Male	0.0677
		(2) Female	0.0603
	(2) Higher secondary	(1) Male	0.2890
		(2) Female	0.2573
	(3) Tertiary	(1) Male	0.8668
		(2) Female	0.7720

Model fit: $L^2 = 16.2$, $df = 22$, $p = 0.807$.

secondary education has also been contested in both periods under study; we therefore expected a generally higher level of inequality than in the conditional models, but we also expected similar trends.

Table 15.4 shows the results of Model IV addressing the effects of educational background and gender. Although the model allows for significant changes in the chances of attaining tertiary education between the first three cohorts (mainly because of the improvement in the chances of women vis-à-vis men) while it assumes stability of inequality subsequently (Table 15.4), the odds ratios between groups defined by educational background did not change throughout the entire period. Regardless of gender and cohort, the odds of attaining tertiary education for a person of the highest educational background (with at least one parent having achieved tertiary education) were 13 times higher than those of a person with the lowest educational background (with none of the parents having attained higher than lower secondary education). Odds ratios between consecutive categories of educational background were also stable over time both for men and women; the odds were 4.3 between the second and first category and 3.0 between the third and second category.

The effect of father's class, as represented by Model V, shows more

TABLE 15.5
Odds of achieving tertiary education: Effects of father's class and gender (Model V)

Cohort	Father's class	Gender	Odds
(1) Before 1948	(1) Unskilled, semiskilled	(1) Male	0.0734
		(2) Female	0.0083
	(2) Skilled workers	(1).Male	0.1298
		(2) Female	0.0147
	(3) Routine nonmanual	(1) Male	0.2402
		(2) Female	0.0272
	(4) Professionals, self-employed	(1) Male	1.0110
		(2) Female	0.1147
(2) 1948–64	(1) Unskilled, semiskilled	(1) Male	0.1005
		(2) Female	0.0440
	(2) Skilled workers	(1) Male	0.1777
		(2) Female	0.0779
	(3) Routine nonmanual	(1) Male	0.3288
		(2) female	0.1441
	(4) Professionals, self-employed	(1) Male	0.5238
		(2) Female	0.2295
(3) 1965–74	(1) Unskilled, semiskilled	(1) Male	0.0541
		(2) Female	0.0490
	(2) Skilled workers	(1) Male	0.0957
		(2) Female	0.0867
	(3) Routine nonmanual	(1) Male	0.2944
		(2) Female	0.2667
	(4) Professionals, self-employed	(1) Male	0.4690
		(2) Female	0.4249
(4), (5) 1975–89 1990–99	(1) Unskilled, semiskilled	(1) Male	0.0729
		(2) Female	0.0660
	(2) Skilled workers	(1) Male	0.1289
		(2) Female	0.1168
	(3) Routine nonmanual	(1) Male	0.3966
		(2) Female	0.3592
	(4) Professionals, self-employed	(1) Male	0.6317
		(2) Female	0.5721

Model fit: $L^2 = 25.5$, $df = 28$, $p = 0.601$.

complex patterns of development (Table 15.5). But aside from changes in the odds between men and women already described here, changes in odds ratios appear only between the first and second cohort (significant decrease) and between the second and third cohort (significant increase), after which odds ratios remain constant. The odds ratios between the skilled workers and the lowest social class show stability throughout the historical period. In the most recent cohort, the chances of a person of the most privileged class attaining tertiary education were 8.7 times higher than those of a person of the least privileged class, regardless of gender.

The results of Model VI, which included both father's class and edu-

TABLE 15.6
Odds of achieving tertiary education: Effects of parents' education and father's class (Model IV)

Cohort	Parents' education	Father's class	Odds
(1) Before 1948	(1) Lower secondary or lower	(1) Unskilled, semiskilled	0.0347
		(2) Others	0.0652
	(2) Higher secondary, tertiary	(1) Unskilled, semiskilled	0.1628
		(2) Others	0.3042
(2), (3), (4) 1948–64, 1965–74, 1975–89	(1) Lower secondary or lower	(1) Unskilled, semiskilled	0.0487
		(2) Others	0.0915
	(2) Higher secondary, tertiary	(1) Unskilled, semiskilled	0.2269
		(2) Others	0.4268
(5) 1990–99	(1) Lower secondary or lower	(1) Unskilled, semiskilled	0.0222
		(2) Others	0.1025
	(2) Higher secondary, tertiary	(1) Unskilled, semiskilled	0.1037
		(2) Others	0.4779

Model fit: $L^2 = 15.3$, $df = 14$, $p = 0.355$.

cational background (Table 15.6), show that the net effect of educational background has been constant over the entire period (the odds ratios of 4.7 between the two categories of parental education are constant over time) while that of class origin grew significantly during the postcommunist transformation. The odds ratios between the lowest social class (semiskilled and unskilled workers) and all other classes were stable at a level of 1.9 throughout the first four cohorts, but more than doubled (4.6) toward the last cohort.

CONCLUSIONS

Czech higher education has changed profoundly since 1989. The most important and rapid change occurred in its *autonomy*. Universities were granted almost full autonomy as early as 1990, and the principle of their self-government has not been challenged since. Universities used the newly acquired autonomy primarily to reform their curricula, expanding programs in the humanities and social sciences, and to eliminate political criteria in the recruitment of both faculty and students. Most of the schools also rid themselves of the old "nomenclatura," whose primary mission was to look after the ideological integrity of university education before 1989.

There were two significant structural changes in the Czech tertiary education system: *decentralization*, made possible by the establishment of regional universities; and *diversification*, mostly the result of private colleges gradually filling the need for bachelor's degree programs. Despite an almost complete formal autonomy, universities remain dependent on the state to a high degree. Several attempts to expand the multisource financing by introducing cost-sharing features (tuition fees, loans, student allowances) have failed. Reliance on the public budget, which is under increasing pressure from other political priorities and an accumulated deficit, has led to a severe financial crisis of public universities. Even in this critical situation, universities played an active role in generating strong public resistance to the implementation of the cost-sharing principle.

Based on developments in the structure of Czech higher education, of its financing, and its general accessibility, we formulated a general hypothesis whereby the period of *persisting inequality* under socialism was followed by one of *increasing inequality* during the postcommunist transformation.

Analysis of an extensive set of data acquired by merging data files from surveys carried out after 1989 focused on testing three hypotheses. The first one was derived from the "MMI" theory. The core assumption of this hypothesis was that there were two reasons behind the absence of a decrease in socioeconomic inequalities in access to higher education during the socialist era.

    1. Very slow growth of opportunity in university education prevented the saturation of the demand for higher-level education among groups with traditionally high educational aspirations. Thus, the tertiary education system remained highly selective, especially for potential candidates from lower social strata.

    2. Despite initial efforts to demonstrate the advantages of the socialist system (an experiment to increase participation of the lower social strata through a quota system), the new socialist elite soon managed to press its advantages in attaining higher education for their own children.

This hypothesis found strong support in the results of logit models. The only significant change that occurred during the socialist regime was the decrease of inequalities between men and women, resulting in a marked drop of men's odds of attaining tertiary education. Differences in the chances of making the transition from secondary to tertiary education of individuals with different sociocultural background represented by parents' education remained unchanged throughout the socialist period. The same applies to the socioeconomic dimension of the social origin, represented by the fathers' class.

As far as the short postsocialist period is concerned, the analysis corroborated the hypothesis that inequalities in the chances of making the transition between secondary and tertiary education increased significantly. This development was caused by three reciprocally reinforcing processes.

    1. Although the change of the political system created an opportunity for major democratization and decentralization of the tertiary system and for an unprecedented growth of educational opportunity at the tertiary level, the autonomy granted to universities made it possible for them to scuttle reforms that would have transformed the tertiary education system from a unitary into a binary one, thereby preserving its elitist character.

    2. Transition to mass tertiary education was slowed down, among other factors, by an absence of will on the part of university officials to adopt multisource financing. Combined with the slow growth of tertiary education financing from public sources (the Czech Republic remained close to the bottom of the OECD scale), this triggered a severe financial crisis of the tertiary education system and an actual slowdown in the growth of opportunity. As a result of these processes, competition for making the transition to the tertiary education system has become fierce.

    3. The conspicuous growth of socioeconomic inequalities after the first stage of the postcommunist transformation brought about the formation of genuine social classes, turned the class of manual workers into the losers of the postcommunist change. Consistent with the theory of rational action, we expected children from families of manual workers to lose in the strong competition and their relative odds to make the transition to tertiary education to diminish.

The analysis confirmed this hypothesis. After 1989, there was a noticeable increase of inequality in access to higher education, mainly because of the substantial decrease in the odds of children from manual-worker backgrounds. The results of the analysis confirm that this change originated from the socio*economic* dimension of the inequalities, as described by Goldthorpe, rather than from the socio*cultural* dimension, as stressed by proponents of the theory of cultural capital (the effect of parents' education remained constant). Thus, the increase of inequalities in access to higher education that occurred in the Czech Republic after 1989 was caused by factors that can be called *structural:* the rigid structure of the tertiary education system and the gradually shaping class structure of society.

CHAPTER SIXTEEN

Italy: Expansion, Reform, and Social Inequality in Higher Education

Ettore Recchi, University of Florence

SCHOOLING, HIGHER EDUCATION, AND INSTITUTIONAL CHANGE IN ITALY (1861–2001)

Since its first publication in 1886, the novel *Cuore* (literally, "Heart") has been one of Italy's all-time bestsellers. In the novel, its author, the philanthropic socialist Edmondo De Amicis, extols the equalizing virtues of education by describing the daily life of a late nineteenth-century primary school that enrolls children from all social classes. Although best known for some sentimental episodes, *Cuore* expresses a progressive and optimistic message: Schools form the backbone of a democratic society as they prize talent and goodwill regardless of family origins. Significantly, the most brilliant pupil of the story is the son of a shopkeeper. Classrooms are the antidote to class privileges.

The novel has been read by five generations of Italians. Its vision of the integrative effects of schooling is likely to have helped legitimize the cause of educational expansion in the newly unified Italian state. From unification in 1861 to the fascist reform of 1923, the Italian school system was not highly selective (Barbagli 1982, 5 and 51).[1] No dead-end vocational track was created before the upper secondary level. Although *licei* (nonvocational high schools) represented the main door to tertiary education, students from technical institutes were allowed access to some university programs.

This relative openness was not the outcome of mass democratization and demands from below but rather the consequence of the political elites' concern with the nation-building process. After the country was unified territorially, the priority assigned to the educational system lay more in the political than in the socioeconomic field. A truly national—and possibly nationalist—public opinion needed to be molded. Educational expansion was aimed at developing a larger and homogeneous middle class in a vast and culturally heterogeneous land where myriad dialects were spoken. Moreover, national identity was jeopardized by the strong influence of the Roman Catholic Church. In this climate, the school system was designed to counter localism and clericalism as potential menaces to state legitimacy. The rationale for its openness was that the longer the young stay in public school, the stronger their attachment to the nation. The imperative of socialization prevailed over that of selection.

The situation was reversed to some extent when fascism rose to power. As regime propaganda was ubiquitously performed through parades, sports, party events, and the mass media, public education lost its monopoly over the youths' political socialization. Selection became the keynote of schooling. The educational system was reshaped in 1923 by Giovanni Gentile, the leading fascist philosopher and Minister of Education, to forge an almost paradigmatic "sponsored mobility system." In a sense, Gentile was aware of the principle that "early selection prevents raising the hopes of large numbers of people who might otherwise become the discontented leaders of a class challenging the sovereignty of the established elite" (Turner 1960, 859). His goal was to contain the possible threat to the stability of the social order and the regime brought about by frustration among the highly educated unemployed who had contributed to the rise of fascism.

Gentile's law, which Mussolini qualified as "the most fascist reform" (Capano 1998, 85–86), introduced exams regulating the transitions between educational levels. After primary school, students were encouraged to enroll in vocational secondary school (*scuola complementare*). At first, this school was meant as a dead-end track; in 1929, however, it was renamed "apprenticeship school" (*scuola di avviamento al lavoro*) and the possibility of moving from it to technical and teachers' institutes was granted. But only *licei* led to tertiary education. A further distinction was created between classical *licei*, from which students could enter all tertiary-level programs, and scientific *licei*, which did not permit enrollment in law and philosophy programs. Nevertheless, even the fascist regime rejected all proposals for recourse to *numerus clausus*, whereas the Nazi government introduced it very rapidly in 1933. To some extent, reversing the rationale of Gentile's reform and echoing rhetorically the proequality arguments of

Cuore, in 1935 the Minister of National Education, Cesare Maria De Vecchi, reasserted that "the longing for knowledge and elevation of the young cannot be restrained according to a quota" (Barbagli 1982, 202).

This same populist inclination inspired another less often mentioned reform of the fascist regime in the 1930s: the upgrading of tertiary-level vocational schools by absorbing them within the universities. Since then, tertiary education in Italy can be fully identified with universities, forming a paradigmatic unitary system of higher education. This undifferentiation of the institutional structure was coupled with an increased homogenization and centralization of the regulatory regime that persisted well after the fall of fascism. Until the end of the twentieth century, when "autonomy" emerged as the catchword of a new reformist wave (Vaira 2001), in Italy the Minister of Education controlled higher education policy with almost exclusive powers of creating new universities, defining academic programs, establishing uniform administrative rules, and allocating budgets.[2] The only concrete counterweight to the "sovereignty" of the ministry was the "chair"—the title of the highest ranking faculty members who were granted complete independence in managing their teaching and research activities (Clark 1977).[3]

Nothing changed after World War II. Democratic governments kept postponing the issue of the country's educational structure. Guido Gonella, Minister of Public Education in the late 1940s and 1950s, supported the preservation of a selective school system as he lamented "the inflation of academic qualifications [and] the evil of the so-called academic proletariat destined increasingly to aggravate the crisis of the middle strata" (Barbagli 1982, 215). When the Socialist Party joined the government, the issue of educational expansion was finally tackled in 1963 by raising compulsory schooling to the age of 14 and eliminating the previous track system that selected students immediately after primary school. With regards to post-secondary education, a comprehensive reform proposal was brought before Parliament by the Minister of Public Education, Luigi Gui, in 1965. It envisaged a vertical differentiation of tertiary degrees, introducing a lower-level diploma and the PhD beside the traditional *laurea*—a differentiation of degrees that was to become a reality only in the 1990s. The proposal was discussed at length, before being set aside under the pressure of the student movement. In 1969, to placate the mounting student revolt, Parliament rapidly approved a two-article law fully liberalizing access to all kinds of university programs for individuals holding any kind of *maturità* diploma—that is, upper secondary-level certificates conferred after completion of a five-year program.[4] Such a sweeping change was not accompanied by a reform of the educational structure at the postsecondary level. As a typical instance of a unitary system of higher education, Italian universities remained what they had always been: academic institutions offering only one degree (4–5-year programs leading to the *laurea*), with equal validity established by law (*valore legale*) wherever it is attained.

With the reform of 1969, the door was open but the house remained the same. The result was over-crowding—physically and symbolically: physically, because universities had to face expansion without adequate facilities or a rearrangement of teaching roles;[5] symbolically, because all students had to contend for the same degree. Following Trow (1974), this change was soon interpreted and labeled as a transition from an "elite" to a "mass university" (Marsiglia 1993). Its widely recognized pathologies were as follows.

1. The students' slow progress toward a degree, owing to the fact that they had no obligation to attend classes and were entitled to postpone exams indefinitely (e.g., in 1998 only 11.6% attained their degree on time: Italy Istat 2001a, 15). While all programs last no longer than five years, the average duration of tertiary education for students who graduated was about eight years.[6] Historically, the expansion of students "behind schedule" (*fuori corso*) greatly outpaced the overall expansion of the student population (Figure 16.1).

2. The impressive proportion of dropouts: between 1970 and 1985, two thirds of enrolled students left the university without obtaining a degree (De Francesco 1988, 206). In more recent years, about one quarter of freshmen still tend to quit soon after enrollment (Table 16.1). The bulk of university students who fail to attain their degree comes from less privileged socioeconomic strata (De Francesco and Trivellato 1978; Dei 1996; Schizzerotto 1997). This is often proven indirectly (and roughly) by comparing the rates of success in obtaining a degree by university students from *licei* (among whom upper-class offspring are overrepresented) with students from vocational *istituti professionali*: 53.7% versus 20.1% in 1997 (Italy Istat 2001a, 15).

The reform of 1969 made these problems, which were not new, possibly more severe (Moscati 1985, 1991). In addition, as Figure 16.1 shows, this

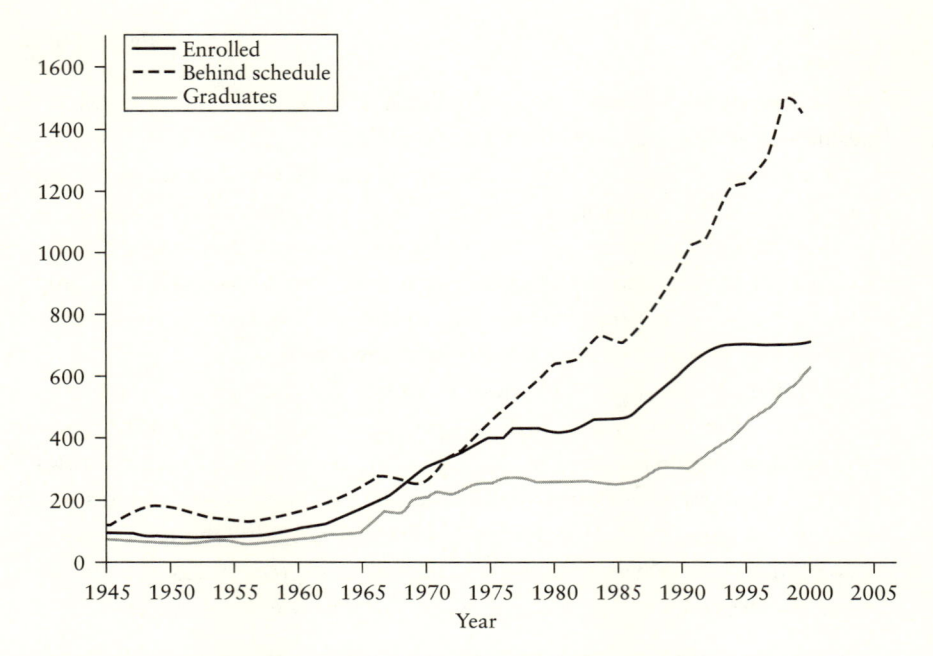

Figure 16.1. Expansion of Higher Education in Italy, 1945–2000: Increase in the Number of Enrolled Students, Behind-schedule Students, and Graduates in Italian Universities (1945 = 100)

SOURCES: Author's elaboration from Checchi (1997, 125–126) and www.miur.it/ustat/statistiche.

NOTE: 1945 figures: enrolled = 236,442; late (behind-schedule) students = 46,777; graduates = 27,079.

TABLE 16.1

Transition rates from upper secondary schools, enrollment rates, women's participation, and delays and failures in Italian universities (1945–2000)

Period	% transitions from upper secondary school[a]	% university students among 19-year-olds[a]	% women among university students[a]	% "behind schedule" among enrolled students[b]	% dropouts one year after university enrollment[a]
1945–61	74	10	27	35	14
1962–71	80	25	38	25	25
1972–81	74	27	44	22	28
1982–91	73	41	50	30	24
1992–2000	65	46	55	36	27

[a] % refers to the last year of the period.
[b] Average based on four time points per period.

SOURCES: De-Lillo and Schizzerotto (1982, 217 and 221), Dei (1987, 150), Dei and Rossi (1978, 101–102), Dei (1996, 274), Checchi (1997, 71 and 122–126), Dei (1998, 469), Capano (2000, 65 and 74), Istat (2001a, 14), Istat (2001b, 5), Istat (2003b, 37 and 63).

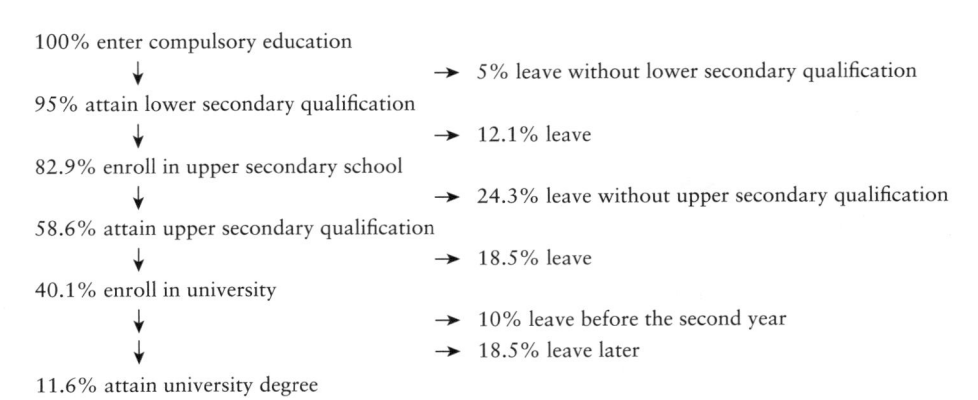

100% enter compulsory education
↓ → 5% leave without lower secondary qualification
95% attain lower secondary qualification
↓ → 12.1% leave
82.9% enroll in upper secondary school
↓ → 24.3% leave without upper secondary qualification
58.6% attain upper secondary qualification
↓ → 18.5% leave
40.1% enroll in university
↓ → 10% leave before the second year
↓ → 18.5% leave later
11.6% attain university degree

Figure 16.2. Estimates of Educational Attainments of Young People in the 1990s

SOURCE: Checchi (1999, 19).

NOTE: These estimates are based on 1995–96 data under the assumption of invariant transition rates and failures by cohort.

major reform did not trigger expansion but merely sanctioned and sustained a process set in motion in the 1960s. Between 1960 and 1968, the number of university students increased by 91% and the number of graduates by 108%. Between 1969 and 1977 (that is, immediately after the opening of the universities to students from all types of upper secondary schools), the number of university students and graduates continued to grow, but at a lower pace, by 81% and 64%, respectively (De Francesco 1988, 202). These figures also indicate that in the 1970s enrollments outnumbered degrees, reflecting a soaring transition rate from secondary- to tertiary-level education, but at the same time indicating a lower productivity of the higher education system.

Despite widespread and recurrent arguments deploring the inefficiency and inequality of higher education in Italy (frequently illustrated through the diagram reproduced in Figure 16.2), a full-fledged reform was adopted only in 1999. This reform distinguishes three levels of postsecondary education: basic three-year courses, followed by two-year specialization degrees and by three-year PhD programs. The reform project was anticipated by two innovations: postgraduate studies (mainly PhD programs) legally established in 1980, and three-year postsecondary vocational programs (*diploma di laurea*) introduced in 1990. These innovations have showed modest success: in particular, only 12% of individuals entering tertiary education chose vocational undergraduate programs in 2000 (Italy Istat 2001b, 10). Overall, the objective of the end-of-century educational policies was to produce a stronger vertical differentiation of higher education in line with other EU systems (Capano 2002). The reformed system is expected to help weaker students obtain at least first-level postsecondary degrees, which are easier to gain than the former *laurea* because they can be obtained by attending shorter programs. Moreover, although no alternative institutions are created, universities are encouraged to define the specific contents of their programs, and thereby increase horizontal differentiation and competition among them.[7] In particular, each university can decide on its own which of its first-level courses (i.e., three-year programs) are to be vocationally oriented and which are to offer a more academic education. Nonetheless, despite the rhetoric about "university autonomy," some major organizational aspects remain firmly constrained by state guidelines, in particular the basic curriculum of programs and the overall amount of tuition fees.[8]

In theory, depending on the willingness of universities to establish first-level vocational programs, two scenarios are possible: if these programs are set up successfully, higher education in Italy may shift from a "unitary" to a "comprehensive" model; alternatively, should an "academic drift" prevail, as it did in other cases (Neave 2000), the reform will simply reproduce the existing "unitary" model.

DATA AND METHODS

After some pioneer works (Martinotti 1972; Barbagli 1982, originally written in 1973), research on Italian higher education from a social stratification perspective blossomed in the 1980s and 1990s. Almost all studies focused on class effects on educational transitions, years of schooling, and labor market rewards of educational attainments (Gambetta 1987; Cobalti and Schizzerotto 1993; Rossi 1997; Schizzerotto 1997; Shavit and Westerbeek 1998; Checchi 1999; Pisati 2002). Apart from some minor variations, these studies conclude that gender differentials have declined significantly over time while socioeconomic inequalities have remained stable despite both reform and expansion. In the Italian case, characterized as it is by a huge rate of university dropouts, this conclusion needs further specification distinguishing the odds of *entering, attending* (after formal enrollment), and *completing* tertiary education. During the period 1950–80, *entering* higher education turned out to be persistently affected by fathers' social class (Cobalti and Schizzerotto 1993). In the same period, class inequalities were found to be constantly nonsignificant in conditional models of transitions to tertiary education—that is, the social origins of individuals attending university programs turned out to be similar to those of upper secondary *diplomati* (Shavit and Westerbeeek 1998, 40). Focusing on younger cohorts born between 1967 and 1974, Schizzerotto (1997, 353) shows that while university entry is significantly contingent on parental class and credentials, only the latter influence the odds of *attending* university programs.

While limitations in our data do not permit further analysis of these two aspects of educational stratification (i.e., access and attendance at the tertiary level), this chapter presents an unprecedented exploration of long-term changes in the odds of *completing* university education in Italy, assessing whether inequalities in attaining university degrees have changed over time in the second half of the twentieth century. Existing research is updated by taking into account the youngest cohorts that are likely to have completed tertiary education, that is, people born in the 1960s who have not been included in the main data source used for intergenerational comparisons so far: the Italian mobility survey of 1985 (for a notable exception, see Pisati 2002). Data for the present chapter came from a much larger and more recent data set: the Multi-Purpose Family Survey (*Indagine multiscopo sulle famiglie*) conducted in 1998 by the National Institute of Statistics (Istat) on 20,153 households comprising 59,050 individual cases. Given the focus of this study, the original data set was reduced to Italian citizens (excluding persons who may have studied in different educational systems) aged 32 or older: 29,972 individuals in all (for more details, cf. Italy Istat 1998, appendix B).[9]

A strategy of cohort analysis was employed, distinguishing five cohorts of individuals born: (1) before 1931; (2) between 1931 and 1940; (3) between 1941 and 1950; (4) between 1951 and 1958; (5) and between 1959 and 1966.[10] The last two cohorts include persons who have entered postsecondary education after the beginning of the reform of 1969, that is, in the 1970s and 1980s. The independent variables are: *gender; parental class* at age 14, coded in five categories on the basis of the EGP schema (mother's occupation is taken when father's occupation is missing); and *parental*

TABLE 16.2
Descriptive statistics for variables employed in the analysis by cohort

	BIRTH COHORT					
Independent variables	Before 1931	1931–40	1941–50	1951–58	1959–66	Total
Gender						
Man	42.4	49.3	50.9	50.6	47.7	48.3
Woman	57.6	50.7	49.1	49.4	52.3	51.7
Respondent education						
Laurea (3b)	3.6	3.7	7.2	10.9	10.0	7.4
Maturità (2bc)	7.1	8.9	17.7	28.5	33.7	20.1
Vocational sec. (1c2a)	1.9	3.1	6.1	9.0	9.8	6.3
Lower secondary (1b)	9.6	16.5	25.5	34.2	39.9	26.1
Primary school (1a)	77.8	67.8	43.5	17.4	6.8	40.1
Parental education						
Laurea (3b)	1.4	1.3	1.5	2.6	3.3	2.1
Maturità (2bc)	2.4	2.8	3.9	5.4	7.2	4.6
Vocational sec. (1c2a)	1.2	1.3	1.9	2.1	3.0	2.0
Lower secondary (1b)	3.2	4.8	7.0	11.2	15.7	8.9
Primary school (1a)	91.8	89.8	85.6	78.7	70.8	82.4
Parental class						
I	3.8	3.9	4.2	5.5	6.3	4.9
II	2.0	1.7	2.4	2.9	4.2	2.7
IIIab	6.8	8.3	10.9	12.9	14.5	11.1
Ivabc	34.2	32.4	27.7	23.4	22.2	27.4
V+VI+VII	53.2	53.7	54.8	55.3	52.8	53.9
N	4,896	4,937	6,281	6,515	7,343	29,972

education coded in five categories on the basis of the CASMIN schema (mother's qualification is taken when the information for the father is missing) (Table 16.2). The effects of these variables on the log-odds of attaining a graduate degree were estimated and then compared by cohort, using both unconditional (i.e., given all other possible educational attainments) and conditional (i.e., given high-school completion) modeling.

RESULTS

Macroanalysis

Upper socioeconomic strata have always been overrepresented among the highly educated. An indicator of this is the proportion of members of each class completing tertiary education in the various cohorts examined (Table 16.3). In the oldest cohort (born before 1931), one out of five individuals born in the upper service class attained the *laurea;* in the 1951–58

TABLE 16.3
Proportion of graduates from each social class by birth cohort (%)

Parental class	Before 1931	1931–40	1941–50	1951–58	1959–66
I	20.3	23.6	26.5	35.8	28.2
II	24.3	21.8	27.8	34.7	39.2
IIIab	12.2	13.2	20.3	24.8	17.3
Ivabc	2.2	3.2	6.6	9.3	8.4
V+VI+VII	1.6	0.9	3.2	5.5	4.7

cohort, more than one out of three individuals of the same class reached the top educational level. By contrast, less than one out of fifty children of the working class attained university credentials among people born before 1931; in the two youngest cohorts, no more than one out of twenty working-class children did the same. Although it has narrowed, the distance between social classes in the diffusion of higher education remains considerable. The probabilities of attaining university credentials for persons born in the less privileged strata continue to be modest in both absolute and relative terms.

Nonetheless, for people born in the 1940s and 1950s, the expansion of higher education raised the proportion of graduates in all social classes. The rate of increase compared with the immediately previous cohort was sensibly higher among petite bourgeoisie and working-class young people: in the 1941–50 cohort it amounted to 106% and 256%, respectively, and in the following cohort to 39% and 59%. However, so large were the initial discrepancies between the proportions of graduates in each class that even such a rise could not close the gap in higher education between the upper and lower social strata.

By the end of the twentieth century the expansion of higher education has halted in Italy. Population data indicate that the transition rate to tertiary education dropped from 74.3% in 1992 to 64.5% in 1999 (Italy Istat 2003b, 37).[11] Our cohort data are likely to reflect this declining participation in higher education,[12] which some scholars attribute to the declining short-term economic rewards to university credentials (Schizzerotto 1997). An alternative explanation may be that the transition rates from secondary to higher education have contracted because the cohort proportion obtaining upper secondary school certificates (*maturità*) has increased sharply. As

TABLE 16.4
Unconditional logit models of upper secondary school graduation (maturità) in five birth cohorts

	BIRTH COHORT									
	BEFORE 1931		1931–40		1941–50		1951–58		1959–66	
Independent variables	B	exp(B)	B	exp(B)	B	exp(B)	B	exp(B)	B	exp(B)
Gender (Ref. = female)	.76*	2.14	.71*	2.03	.70*	2.01	.19*	1.20	−.17*	.84
Parental education (Ref. = 2a)										
Laurea (3b)	.38	1.46	1.95*	7.01	.84*	2.31	.98*	2.68	1.88*	6.58
Maturità (2bc)	.18	1.20	.53	1.69	.63*	1.87	.46	1.59	.82*	2.27
Media (1b)	−.28	.76	−.06	.94	−.14	.87	−.62*	.54	−.32	.73
Primary–No school (1a)	−2.24*	.11	−1.88*	.15	−1.48*	.23	−1.71*	.18	−1.24*	.29
Parental class (Ref. = V+VI+VII)										
I	1.46*	4.30	1.42*	4.16	1.08*	2.95	.85*	2.34	.82*	2.26
II	1.23*	3.43	1.22*	3.39	.99*	2.70	.96*	2.62	.94*	2.55
IIIab	1.73*	5.61	1.35*	3.87	1.29*	3.64	1.18*	3.26	.89*	2.4
IVabc	.20	1.22	.61*	1.84	.46*	1.59	.37*	1.45	.49*	1.63
Constant	−.97		−1.31		−.64		.59		.37	
N	4,896		4,937		6,281		6,515		7,343	

*Significant at the 0.01 level.

the population at risk expands in size and becomes less socially select, the proportion that makes the subsequent transition declines.

Microanalysis

Analyses of individual data can help qualify these findings, as they permit to control the simultaneous effects, cohort by cohort, of different dimensions of social inequality: gender, family class, and family cultural capital. Data were modeled in two ways by multivariate logistic regression. First, unconditional logit models estimated the odds of attaining a graduate degree over less prestigious educational credentials. Second, conditional models estimated the odds of attaining a graduate degree over an upper secondary qualification (i.e., the immediately inferior educational credential). The two types of models are likely to offer insights into distinct phenomena. Unconditional modeling measures the "social exclusivity" of graduating vis-à-vis other educational attainments. In these models, the varying effects of independent variables, cohort after cohort, indicate possible transformations in the social profile of the people reaching the highest level of the educational pyramid. Conditional modeling, by contrasting university graduates with upper secondary diploma-holders, highlights the sorting impact of tertiary education. In other words, conditional models are expected to outline the extent to which inequalities in higher education are contingent upon attending and completing university programs rather than upon social selection at earlier stages of the educational system.

Before these analyses, I examined the impact of gender, social class, and parental education on the attainment of *maturità*, the upper secondary school certificate that precedes university credentials. This permits a more detailed assessment of the specificity of stratification effects on higher education. Indeed, the manner in which social inequalities constrain access to *maturità* anticipates some findings of the analysis at the university level. Unconditional logit models of upper secondary graduation show the persistent effect of class origins and family cultural capital (Table 16.4). On the one hand, working-class children suffer from a marked and steady handicap, whereas sons and daughters of nonmanual workers are always significantly more likely to obtain (at least) upper-secondary credentials. Interestingly, the manual-nonmanual divide proves to be more relevant than fine-tuned class distinctions. In three out of the five cohorts examined, class III children have even higher odds of reaching an upper secondary

TABLE 16.5
Unconditional logit models of university graduation (laurea) in five birth cohort

	BIRTH COHORT									
	BEFORE 1931		1931–40		1941–50		1951–58		1959–66	
Independent variables	B	exp(B)	B	exp(B)	B	exp(B)	B	exp(B)	B	exp(B)
Gender (Ref. = female)	1.14*	3.12	.91*	2.48	.44*	1.56	-.01	.99	-.02	.98
Parental education (Ref. = 2a)										
Laurea (3b)	.07	1.07	1.38*	3.96	.99*	2.68	1.92*	6.85	1.30*	3.68
Maturità (2bc)	-.60	.55	.24	1.27	.13	1.14	.76*	2.14	.40	1.49
Media (1b)	-1.32*	.27	-.79	.45	-.54	.59	.19	1.20	-.60*	.55
Primary–No school (1a)	-2.46*	.09	-2.52*	.08	-1.44*	.24	-.80*	.45	-1.59*	.20
Parental class (Ref. = V+VI+VII)										
I	1.71*	5.53	1.75*	5.77	1.48*	4.40	1.09*	2.99	.74*	2.11
II	1.60*	4.96	1.50*	4.48	1.26*	3.52	.86*	2.37	1.00*	2.73
IIIab	1.32*	3.75	1.49*	4.41	1.42*	4.13	1.03*	2.81	.47*	1.60
IVabc	.30	1.36	1.25*	3.50	.76*	2.14	.50*	1.64	.49*	1.63
Constant	-2.34		-2.93		-2.33		-1.93		-1.68	
N	4,896		4,937		6,281		6,515		7,343	

*Significant at the 0.01 level.

school degree than their service-class counterparts. On the other hand, students whose fathers hold a primary-level certificate or no school degree at all have considerably lower odds of achieving high-school credentials, although their situation has somewhat irregularly improved from the oldest cohort onwards. The contrary is true for the offspring of parents with a high-school or university degree, whose advantage has been increasing in the two most recent cohorts. Finally, the clearest and most spectacular change over time is the sudden fall and subsequent reversal of the male advantage in high schools. The traditional gender privilege almost waned in the cohort that was of *maturità* age in the late 1960s–mid-1970s. In the following decade girls began to outnumber boys significantly in the attainment of upper secondary credentials. Overall, with the sole exception of the erosion of gender differences, social inequalities have shaped the opportunities of attaining high-school certificates with remarkable continuity over the second half of the twentieth century in Italy.

We are now in a better position to focus on social stratification effects on higher education. Table 16.5 presents the unconditional logit models of the odds of attaining a graduate degree for the five cohorts under study. Not surprisingly, gender at the university level has progressively lost any discriminatory impact in Italy. This trend was found to be pervasive in industrialized countries in the twentieth century (Shavit and Blossfeld 1993). More recent data show that this process does not end with gender equality, as women continue to gain ground in higher education; in the academic year 1999–2000 they represented 55% of the population of Italian graduates. Table 16.5 (last column) indicates that the reversal of the traditional male predominance in tertiary education was emerging already among university students enrolled in the late 1970s and early 1980s net of all other effects, albeit not significantly at the time. Some scholars are inclined to attribute this trend to the better secondary school performances of girls (Grilli 1999, 138). Indeed, women achieve higher grades than men in university as well, especially in programs where they are still a minority (Italy Istat 2003b, 72). But gender effects are not fully amenable to differential ability as it seems to be indirectly proven by the stronger presence of women in the short-term university programs introduced in the 1990s, which were perceived as second-tier "consolation" institutions, catering to weaker social categories, much like community colleges in the U.S. and postsecondary training programs in other countries (analysis not presented).

Class differences do not cease to be significant throughout the entire period under study. But contrary to previous analyses, which merged together larger cohorts and could not examine data about people born after 1960, I found a slowly declining impact of class inequalities on the odds of completing tertiary education.[13] The "golden age" of class differences in universities was probably the 1950s. It was not reform, however, that equalized class opportunities in obtaining the *laurea*. The cohorts entering postsecondary studies in the 1960s, before the reform of 1969, were already more socially mixed than their predecessors. The reform sustained this process rather than triggered it. Class equalization proceeded, albeit at a cautious pace, in the 1970s and 1980s, without abating completely the higher odds of graduating enjoyed by upper-class youths.

The opposite seems to be the case for parental education, the effect of which on the opportunities for tertiary-level education does not follow a constant trend. While its overall impact decreased for students entering the system in the early 1960s, having a father with university or upper secondary degrees boosted the chances of graduating in the first postreform cohort. In the youngest cohort, the positive effect of high parental education shrank again and the negative effect of lower-level parental education soared. In the same cohort, the probabilities of attaining a university degree for sons and daughters of graduate fathers belonging to class I are, regardless of gender (whose effect, as already noted, has disappeared), four times those of their age peers whose fathers have *scuola media* degrees and belong to class III, and ten times those of age peers whose fathers have a primary-level education and working-class employment (Figure 16.3).[14]

Table 16.6 presents the parameter estimates of binary logit models of attaining a graduate degree conditional on holding an upper secondary school qualification across four cohorts. As anticipated, this analysis is aimed at detecting the emergence of inequalities precisely after high-school completion. In other words, I seek to assess whether gender, class, or cultural capital barriers exist between *maturità* and *laurea,* and how they have changed in the second half of the twentieth century.

In the oldest cohort set, including people born before 1941, gender affected significantly the odds of successful educational careers after high school. Yet women's discrimination at this stage of the educational system disappears for good in the following cohort. Already in the 1960s, somewhat anticipating a broader equalization of gender opportunities, constraints to

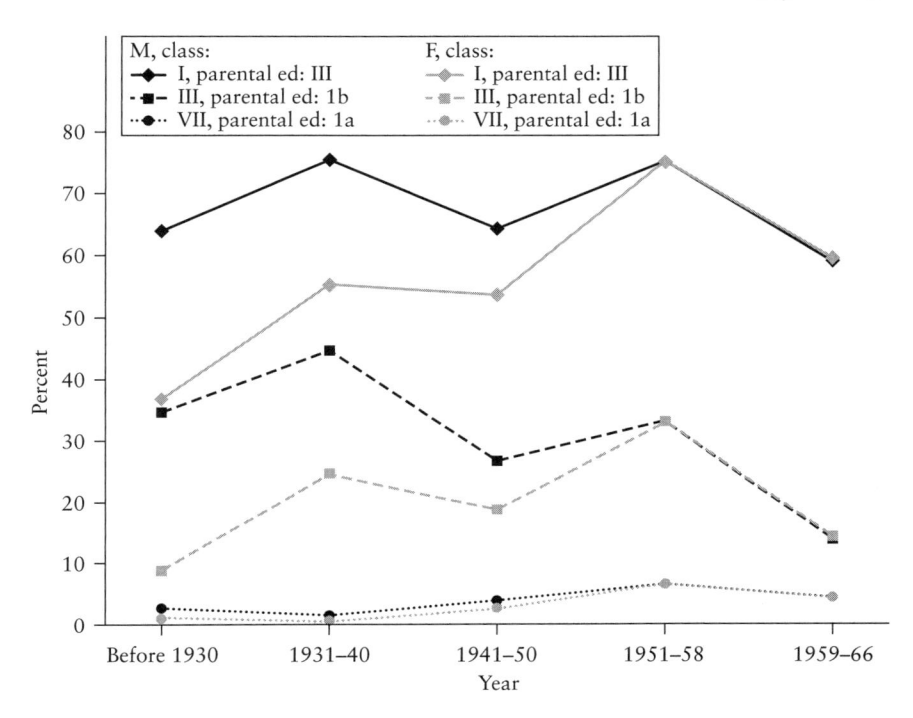

Figure 16.3. Predicted Probabilities (%) of Attaining a University Degree for Selected Combinations of Gender, Parental Class, and Parental Education in Five Birth Cohorts

further education were removed for girls who had reached the upper secondary level. The impact of family class and cultural capital is less linear over time. Young people of middle upper-class origins (including sons and daughters of the petite bourgeoisie) have always enjoyed an advantage in gaining a higher education rather than a secondary-level qualification. This advantage was more pronounced than ever in the 1960s. Presumably, before that decade class differences were likely to condition educational decisions at the lower secondary level, where a crucial bifurcation between vocational and nonvocational tracks existed. The abolition of this distinction in 1963 made access to upper secondary education easier. Some equalization between socioeconomic strata in the odds of entering upper secondary schools followed (Shavit and Westerbeek 1998, 41). Equalization then moved up the education system, reducing class-based privileges in the transition from *maturità* to *laurea* from the early 1970s onward. However, in the most

TABLE 16.6
Conditional logit models of university graduation (laurea holders vs. maturità holders) in four birth cohorts

	BIRTH COHORT							
	BEFORE 1941		1940–50		1951–58		1959–66	
Independent variables	B	exp(B)	B	exp(B)	B	exp(B)	B	exp(B)
Gender (Ref. = female)	.58**	1.79	.02	1.02	−.12	.89	.04	1.04
Parental education (Ref. = 2a)								
Laurea (3b)	.33	1.39	.82*	2.27	1.95**	7.02	1.04**	2.81
Maturità (2bc)	−.44	.65	−.10	.91	.74**	2.10	.21	1.24
Media (1b)	−1.21**	.30	−.55*	.58	.39	1.48	−.54**	.58
Primary–No school (1a)	−1.24**	.29	−.59*	.55	−.03	.97	−1.05*	.35
Parental class (Ref. = V+VI+VII)								
I	.65**	1.92	.89**	2.44	.62**	1.86	.30	1.36
II	.67**	1.96	.63*	1.87	.37*	1.45	.58**	1.79
IIIab	.26	1.30	.67**	1.96	.48**	1.61	.01	1.01
IVabc	.44*	1.56	.45*	1.58	.27*	1.31	.19	1.21
Constant	−.59		−.90		−1.43		−.90	
N	1,246		1,645		2,653		3,273	

*Significant at the 0.05 level; **significant at the 0.01 level.

recent cohort, families of the lower service class, in the face of increased competition for prestigious and rewarding jobs stemming from educational expansion, have tried to upgrade their children's credentials beyond the upper secondary level more vigorously than the rest of the population. Possibly their perseverance in educational investments—a specific form of the "cultural goodwill" of this class (Bourdieu 1986, 331–37)—is aimed at counterbalancing the decline of status as a source of social reproduction. Compared with them, class I families are relatively sheltered from this decline, inasmuch as they pass economic capital (i.e., company ownership) to their offspring directly. Because of this out-of-school advantage they can afford educational equalization and seem to have acquiesced in it.

To a certain extent, the effects of parental education on the conditional odds of tertiary-level graduation alternate with the effects of social class. Before the 1960s, while the differences of opportunities of higher education between children of parents with secondary and tertiary credentials were quite small, the odds of conquering the *maturità* level for individuals coming from less educated families were extremely low. In the 1960s, although still significant, the negative impact of a poor family education declined, just when the impact of class appeared to be stronger at this stage of educational careers. After the reform of 1969, however, the situation became more complex. In the early 1970s, the chances of children of poorly educated parents improved considerably vis-à-vis those of age peers whose parents had lower secondary credentials (the reference category in the analysis of Table 16.6). But, at the same time, the relative advantage of the offspring of the highly educated reached its apex. Finally, in the last cohort there seems to be a return to the prereform standards, where parental primary education once again has a negative effect and parental tertiary education a positive effect (albeit not as marked as in the previous cohort) on the individual's conditional opportunities of attaining university credentials.

Generally speaking, both unconditional and conditional logit models indicate that for individuals born after 1950 having a graduate father represents the single strongest predictor of graduating. I cannot ascertain whether this depends on "primary" or "secondary" effects (Boudon 1974), that is, learning advantages stemming from family-transmitted *abilities* or family-induced *decisions* to remain in the educational system rather than exit. However, the overwhelming influence of father's *laurea* over lower parental credentials on the odds of attaining tertiary rather than upper secondary credentials can attest to two distinct but not mutually exclusive phenomena. On the one hand, it may reveal the nonlinear nature of primary effects: if they are present they increase exponentially when fathers have a university-level education. On the other, it may reflect a "relative risk aversion" strategy of educational choices, according to which parents of all socioeconomic levels seek to "avoid, for their children, any position in life that is worse than the one from which they start" (Breen and Goldthorpe 1997, 283). Parents with upper secondary (or lower) qualifications can thus "be content" with sons and daughters holding upper secondary credentials: in their family, this is sufficient to avoid downward educational mobility (which is the only signal available to them regarding their children's future socioeconomic status). Graduate fathers, in contrast, need their offspring to complete academic education to fulfill the same requirement. In Italy, the strong impact of parental tertiary-level credentials on the odds of completing tertiary education, especially in conditional models of higher education attainments, seems consistent with this theory. Arguably the strength of intergenerational family ties, typical of Italians vis-à-vis citizens of other industrialized societies (Ginsborg 2001, 136–37), makes young people particularly susceptible to their parents' preference for "relative risk aversion" in pursuing academic credentials.

CONCLUSION

Italy has one of the lowest levels of higher education in the industrialized world. In 2001, no more than 10% of the population held a university degree. Higher education has expanded, but not as spectacularly as in other countries: the proportion of *laureati* rose from 5% among people older than 64 to 12% among the 25–34 year olds (OECD 2003). University enrollments have grown much more than degrees conferred. As a result, in 2001 the enrollment rate in tertiary education for 20 years olds reached the mean of OECD countries. But Italian universities have always seen more freshmen than graduates: many started tertiary-level programs but few completed them. The exclusively academic nature of postsecondary education (modified, but still retaining some ambiguities, only in the late 1990s) accounts for this discrepancy. Italian universities do not cater to weaker students and thereby tend to reduce the opportunities for higher education of individuals originating from lower socioeconomic strata. Although the selection mechanisms traditionally penalizing lower-class youths were removed by the reform of 1969, educational expansion at the postsecondary level (which started before the reform) did not greatly benefit less privileged social categories relative to stronger ones—with the notable exception of women.

Analyses of individual data confirm and qualify this general finding. In sum: (1) gender disparities in the attainment of higher education credentials disappear from the 1970s onward, and gender stops discriminating *maturità*-holders from *laurea*-holders in the 1960s; (2) class inequalities in the odds of attaining a university degree decrease progressively but modestly, not ceasing to be significant over the entire period considered; (3) parental credentials are the most important factor accounting for individuals' probabilities of attaining a tertiary-level degree; (4) while class effects are slightly on the decline, cultural capital effects seem to have consolidated after the university reform of 1969; and (5) parental education is especially influential at the extreme ends, as an amplifier of graduation chances for sons and daughters of graduate fathers and as a handicap for the offspring of individuals with primary-level degrees.

The continuing and reemerging impact of fathers' credentials on the probabilities of higher education in all cohorts (therefore regardless of expansion and reform) constitutes perhaps the main finding to reckon with in a theoretically oriented comparative perspective. This can be imputed to a general tendency toward "relative risk aversion" that characterizes educational decisions in the family. But such a tendency is hardly independent of culture, as Breen and Goldthorpe (1997) assume. I rather hypothesize that its influence is stronger in societies like Italy where—as several value studies have shown (e.g., Donati and Colozzi 1997; Recchi 2001; Tronu 2001; de Lillo 2002; Facchini 2002)—family unity continues to be highly respected by young people, generation after generation. Comparative analyses taking simultaneously into account the effects of parental education and family values on higher education attainment are needed to assess whether the relative risk aversion theory can be strengthened by making it sensitive to cultural differences in intergenerational relations.

De Amicis ends *Cuore* at the conclusion of the fourth school year—the last one of compulsory primary education at the time. In the final pages, as he moves up to secondary school, Enrico, the 12-year-old narrator and main character, reflects on his learning experiences and addresses his parents in these significant words:

> Most of all I thank you, father, my first teacher, my first friend, as you settled upon me so many counseling words and taught me so much, while you were working for me, hiding your sadness and trying to make my study easy and my life beautiful; and you, sweet mother, beloved and blessed guardian angel, for you rejoiced in all my joys and suffered all my pains, studying, toiling, crying with me, caressing my forehead with one hand and pointing to the sky with the other.

Enrico's words have the old-fashioned ring and rhetoric of the cultivated Italian middle class. At the outset of the twenty-first century the poetry may be gone, but the prose of family ties arguably remains.

Appendix: Supplemental Tables

TABLE A.1
Description of datasets used in this volume

Country	(1) Data sources	(2) Time span	(3) Age of subjects
Australia	Twelve retrospective national cross-sectional surveys with a total sample size of 19,486; two longitudinal surveys of youth: *Youth in Transition* (YIT) and *Longitudinal Surveys of Australian Youth* (LSAY) with a total sample size of about 11,000 cases.	1961–2001	19–64
Britain	Two cohort panel studies: National Child Development Study (NCDS), British Cohort Study (BCS70). Sample sizes: 11,441 and 11,261, respectively.	1991, 2000	30, 33
Czech Republic	Three merged surveys: the Transformation of Social Structure Survey (TSS-1991), the Second International Adult Literacy Survey (SIALS-1998), and the International Social Survey Program's Module on Social Inequality (ISSP-1999). Combined sample size is 6,740.	1940s–90s	19 and older
France	The 1970, 1977, 1985, and 2003 Education, Training, and Occupations Surveys (FQP). These are retrospective surveys. Sample sizes are about 39,000–45,000 each.	1930s–90s	Approx. 30–40
Germany	Retrospective national surveys: ALLBUS 1980–2000; Zuma-Standarddemographie 1976–82; GSOEP 1986, 1999, 2000; West German Life History Studies 1980s. Combined sample size is 65,797.	1930s–90s	22 and older
Israel	Retrospective national surveys of education and occupation conducted in 2001 and 2002. Sample sizes are about 1,500 each.	1980s–2000	25–45
Italy	Multi-Purpose Family Survey conducted in 1998 by the National Institute of Statistics (Istat). Sample size is about 30,000.	1950s–90s	32 and older
Japan	Retrospective national surveys: the 1985 and 1995 Social Stratification and Social Mobility National Surveys; and the 2000 and 2001 Japanese General Social Surveys. Combined sample size is 3,947.	1960s–90s	22 and older

(*continued*)

TABLE A.1 *(continued)*

Country	(1) Data sources	(2) Time span	(3) Age of subjects
Korea	Korean Labor and Income Panel, a longitudinal survey begun in 1998. Sample size is 11,766.	1940s–90s	25 and older
Netherlands	Four sets of student panel data: the School Career and Background of Pupils in Secondary Education studies (SMVO: 1977 and 1982) and the Cohort of Students in Secondary Education studies (VOCC: 1989 and 1993). Combined sample size is 70,496.	1980s–2001	25, 28, 24, 20
Russia	Retrospective data from the Survey on Education and Stratification in Russia, 2000. Sample size is 4,809.	1950s–90s	21–71
Sweden	Several data sets: school record data for about 900,000 people born 1943–74. The records were linked to census records. Level-of-living surveys and surveys of living conditions for cohorts born since the late 19th century. Combined sample size is about 60,000.	1900s–90s	27–74
Switzerland	Retrospective national survey data from 1989 on 1949–51 and 1959–61 birth cohorts.	1970s–80s	28–42
Taiwan	The 2000 Taiwan Social Change Survey (TSCS). This is a retrospective survey. Sample size is 2,717.	1960s–90s	21–54
United States	General Social Survey for analyses of high-school completion (over 40,000 respondents). For other educational transitions, three longitudinal cohort surveys: National Longitudinal Survey of the High School Class of 1972 (NLS-72), High School and Beyond (HS&B), and National Education Longitudinal Study (NELS). Baseline samples include 12,917 respondents for NLS-72, 12,795 for HS&B, and 14,915 for NELS.	1930s–80s for high-school completion; 1970s–90s for other educational transitions	GSS: 21–70 NLS-72: early 30s HS&B: late 20s NELS: early 20s

TABLE A.2
Social class origin and parents' highest level of education

Abbreviation	Description
Class origin	
I	Upper service class: senior civil servants, higher managerial, higher-grade professionals (also self-employed)
II	Lower service class: middle-level administrators and officials, lower managerial, lower-grade professionals
III	Routine nonmanual employees, clerks
IVab	Self-employed and employers in nonagricultural businesses
IVcd	Farmers and smallholders, including self-employed fishermen
VI	Skilled manual workers
VII	Semi- and unskilled manual workers, including unqualified sales personnel
Parents' education	
1ab	Compulsory schooling
1c	Lower vocational
2ab	Lower secondary/middle level
2c	Upper secondary
3ab	Tertiary

NOTES

Chapter One

Authors' names are listed alphabetically. We thank Vikki Boliver, Richard Breen, Claudia Buchmann, John Goldthorpe, Anthony Heath, David Raffe, Ettore Recchi, and three Stanford University Press reviewers for comments on earlier drafts of this chapter.

    1. In Russia, the SSUZy provide higher-level vocational and technical training in both secondary-level and postsecondary programs. And yet they meet our criteria for higher education because since the late 1950s a majority of students in SSUZy have been enrolled in programs requiring a general secondary degree prior to entry.

    2. Until the 1980s, the Australian system of higher education was binary (see the Australian chapter in this volume). It consisted of about 20 universities and many polytechnics and other vocational colleges. In 1990–93 the polytechnics and several other second-tier institutions of postsecondary education were upgraded to university status and the system was nominally transformed from a binary to a unified one. However, of the nearly 40 universities now operating in Australia, eight ("The Group of Eight") enjoy privileged status and might be considered as the first tier. Unfortunately, data did not permit the authors of the Australian chapter to identify the type of universities that their respondents had attended. In 1992, polytechnics in Great Britain were also upgraded to university status; however, the most recent cohort analyzed in the British chapter attended higher education before that year, when the system was still binary.

    3. Data for Israel and Taiwan were reported by the authors of these respective chapters.

    4. The reader will note that there are differences between the chapters in the exact specification of the logit models of education. For example, in some the models are estimated separately for men and women, while in others the two groups are combined; in some father's classes, I and II are coded separately while in most they are united. We respected the authors' preferences and accepted the

small modeling variations. When deviations were large, we asked the authors to also estimate the standard models.

5. Our generalizations should be considered as tentative as they are based on broad patterns derived from analysis of country-specific results. Our sample of countries is not representative of the population of countries, and the number of observations are not always large enough to generate robust tests for statistical significance.

6. For most countries, data are available for three of the four cohorts, but for some countries they are available only for two; for one country (the Czech Republic), the data span all four decades. Thus, for each decade, the averages are computed for a different number of countries.

7. We use the 80% cutoff point to simplify the presentation of comparative results. Alternative specification of saturation in future research could explore the robustness of our finding by measuring the actual rate of educational attainment of particular educational levels and social classes.

8. The figure and the following correlations and regression are estimated on 13 of our 15 cases. Switzerland is excluded because the data in the Swiss chapter do not allow us to compute inequality in the transition from eligibility to higher education. We exclude Russia because it was a clear outlier: In the years following the post-Soviet transformation, inequality of access to higher education in Russia nearly doubled. With Russia included, the effect of saturation in the regression shown below is −0.75 and the effect of expansion is +0.40.

9. In supplementary analyses we examined the relation between private sector involvement and *change* in attendance rates of higher education. We measured expansion as change in attendance rates per decade for the earliest (since the 1960s) and latest cohorts with data available from our project. Consistent with the results seen in Figure 1.4, we found strong support for Proposition 5: enrollment rates are higher and increase more rapidly in systems with more private sector involvement.

10. As reported in Chapter 15, inequality also increased in the Czech Republic during the postcommunist period, in that the offspring of unskilled workers (class origin VII) fell further behind all others in their relative chances to attend higher education. This result is not evident in Figure 1.3, which focuses on the gap between professional/managerial workers versus skilled workers (class origin I/II versus VI).

11. For Israel, Japan, and Taiwan, declines were observed for the 1990s compared with the 1980s, and for Italy they were observed for the 1980s compared to the 1970s. Data in *Persistent Inequality* ended with the early 1980s for the first three cases and in the late 1970s for Italy, so these are new findings.

Chapter Two

Work on the paper was funded by grants to Gila Menahem and Yossi Shavit from the Israeli Ministry of Science and Tel Aviv University's Schools for

Government and Policy, and by a grant to Yossi Shavit and Hanna Ayalon from the Israeli National Science Fund. We thank Eran Tamir for his assistance.

   1. The fieldwork was carried out by the B. I. and Lucille Cohen Institute for Public Opinion Research. We thank Noah Lewin-Epstein and the staff of the institute for their professional work on the project.

   2. As noted, most Open University students do not pursue a degree but study for self-enrichment. Therefore, we do not classify it as a university.

   3. This classification is consistent with current practice in studies of ethnic stratification in Israel. Ashkenazim are defined as respondents whose fathers were born in a European or American country, or who are sons or daughters of native fathers whose paternal grandfather was born on these continents. Second-generation native Jews are defined as respondents whose parents and grandparents were all born in Israel. Jews of Middle Eastern origins are those whose fathers (or their paternal grandmothers, in the case of native born fathers) were born in Iraq, Iran, Syria, Egypt, or another country in the Middle East. North African Jews are defined as those whose fathers (or their grandfathers) were born in the Maghreb. Arabs include all Muslims and Druse as well as native Christians. Most nonnative Christians are recent Russian immigrants and are coded as Ashkenazim.

Chapter Three

   1. The official name of the ministry is the Ministry of Education, Culture, Sports, Science, and Technology, but the "Ministry of Education" is used as shorthand.

   2. The author is grateful to the 2005 SSM Research Committee for the permission to use the SSM data. The Japanese General Social Surveys (JGSS) are designed and carried out at the Institute of Regional Studies at Osaka University of Commerce in collaboration with the Institute of Social Science at the University of Tokyo under the direction of Ichiro Tanioka, Michio Nitta, Hiroki Sato, and Noriko Iwai with Project Manager Minae Osawa. The project is financially assisted by a Gakujutsu Frontier Grant from the Japanese Ministry of Education, Culture, Sports, Science and Technology for the 1999–2003 academic years. The JGSS were obtained from the Social Science Japan Data Archive of the Information Center for Social Science Research in Japan, Institute of Social Science, University of Tokyo.

   3. Colleges of technology are included in the category of junior colleges.

   4. The 1985 SSM survey did not ask whether the respondent completed the level of education or dropped out. Therefore, a very small proportion of respondents who were classified as holding AA or BA degrees did not complete their degree requirements. Using the 1995 SSM survey and the 2000 and 2001 JGSS, we estimate that about 2% of respondents who attended junior colleges and less than 5% who attended four-year universities did not complete their degrees.

428   Notes to Chapter Three

5. The proportion of respondents who completed university is smaller in the youngest cohort (born in 1968–80) than in the next youngest one (born in 1958–67) because some of the respondents in the youngest cohort were still enrolled in the university.

6. The difference in the effect of the service class (I+II) between the two oldest and the two youngest cohorts is statistically significant.

7. The only exceptions were the sons of the routine nonmanual class born before 1942. The effect is not significant.

8. The daughters of the farming class in the youngest cohort were the exception. Caution must be exercised in interpreting the effect of the father's class among the members of the oldest cohort because of the small sample size.

9. The difference in the "male" coefficient between the 1958–67 cohort and the 1968–80 cohort is significant at a 0.01 level of significance.

Chapter Four

1. Since the 2000 edition of Education at a Glance (OECD) indicators, the International Standard Classification of Education (ISCED-97) has been used to make the definition of levels of education comparable across countries. According to this classification, type-A tertiary education refers to theory-based programs that prepare students for professions with high skill requirements or for advanced research programs such as graduate schools. Type-B tertiary education is oriented more toward practical and vocational education that usually prepares students for occupations. See OECD (2001, 42) for more detail.

2. Park (2004) summarizes three main characteristics of the Korean education system. First, it is an academically oriented system, which prevents vocational education, especially at the secondary level, from developing as a substantial alternative track. Second, institutional differentiation and curriculum variations are modest compared with other societies, such as Germany, Switzerland, or the Netherlands, where students are separated into different tracks at an earlier age; in Korea, tracking begins in high school. Finally, teacher training, school budgets, and even the number of college students are controlled by government guidelines. A nationwide entrance examination for high schools and colleges, and a common curriculum designed to prepare students for the entrance examination show the high level of standardization of the Korean education system.

3. The established system of national entrance examinations and student recruitment on the basis of scores is meritocratic: hard work is considered to be more important than family background in determining a student's chances in entering college. This is associated with the public belief that socioeconomic status is achieved mostly through educational attainment rather than inherited (Sorensen 1994). However, there is little research that examines empirically the extent to which student selection by test scores mediates the impacts of social background and educational attainment in Korea.

4. The Gross Enrollment Rate refers to the total number of students enrolled

in tertiary education regardless of age, divided by the population in the five-year age group that follows the age when students leave secondary school (UNESCO 1999).

5. To assess the manner in which the results of unconditional models differ from those obtained from conditional models, an additional analysis was conducted to estimate the effects of gender and family background on *unconditional* odds of entering postsecondary education. All samples were included in the unconditional model, while the conditional model excluded those who did not succeed in making the previous transition. The results revealed conclusions similar to those derived from conditional models: considerable decline in gender inequality but no evidence of decreasing impacts of father's education or occupation. The results of the unconditional model are available upon request.

6. Regarding the change in the coefficients of service class from 0.886 in the cohort born before 1961, to 0.766 in the cohort of 1961–70, to 0.598 in the youngest cohort, statistical tests indicate that the differences among the coefficients are not statistically significant.

7. A supplementary analysis of the *unconditional* model was conducted by including all the respondents regardless of their levels of education. The overall patterns of the effects of gender and family background were similar to those derived from the conditional model. There was a rising effect of the father's tertiary education on the odds of entering universities across successive cohorts and the overall differences between social classes remained constant for transition to both universities and junior colleges. Notable is that disadvantages experienced by students from a farm origin compared with those from manual working classes were no longer significant among members of the youngest cohort. These results are available upon request.

8. As almost all of the coefficients are nonsignificant for the transition from university attendance to university completion, the result for the transition is not considered here. Note that in Table 4.1 most university students obtained their degrees.

Chapter Five

1. The scale reflecting this proportion (along the rightmost vertical axis of Figure 5.1) is difficult to interpret because it is not possible to determine who is under risk of enrolling. We have chosen a fairly conventional way of defining a risk set, namely as the number of persons aged 19–25 each admission year. We have furthermore divided this number by seven to get the enrollment percentage of an average birth cohort. This procedure does not take into account that a certain number of 19–25-year-olds have enrolled in a previous year and should therefore ideally be removed from the risk set; nor does it take into account that the enrollment in a given year is composed of students from many cohorts. The intention of calculating the proportion is only to show the expansion controlled, as it were, for demographic changes in cohort sizes.

2. This section is an abridged version of Jonsson and Erikson (2000), following original presentations in Erikson and Jonsson (1996b, 1996c).

3. Models of the same type have been proposed by Halsey, Heath, and Ridge (1980) and Breen and Goldthorpe (1997).

4. The model is not estimable but heuristic, that is, a means toward understanding empirical regularities through purposeful individuals actions.

5. Another possible form of risk aversion has to do with the *distributions* of B, P, and C. Someone who is risk averse may prefer an alternative i over j when both alternatives have the same expected values for P, B, and C (and subsequently U) but where, for example, the dispersion of B_i is smaller than that of B_j. Thus, rather than basing the choice on the expected value of U, the risk averse person may base it on some minimum value (cf. the maximin strategy in game theory).

6. This, in turn, may be a result of a general mechanism by which people assign more weight to losses than to gains (Tversky and Kahneman 1986). An additional specific mechanism involves intergenerational social mobility. We can assume the perceived costs of downward mobility to be exceptionally high during the period under study, when, because of an upgrading of the class structure, the general direction of mobility is upward.

7. Both the LNU and ULF samples were down-weighted to account for panel and household sampling procedures.

8. In the register data sample of people born 1943–74, approximately 10% of all children have class I background and about 45% have working-class origin. The main differences between EGP and SEI are that in SEI lower-grade unqualified nonmanual workers (such as shop assistants and nurses' aids) belong to the unskilled working class, that is, class VII (instead of class III), and foremen/supervisors are classified either in class II or III (instead of V).

9. Yule's Y varies between −1 and 1 (maximum negative/positive association) where 0 means no association between social origin and educational attainment. If O is the odds ratio, then $Y = (\sqrt{O} - 1)/(\sqrt{O} + 1)$ (Yule 1912).

10. This association is calculated as the standard deviation of the log-odds of class origins (six classes compared with children of the upper service class (I)).

Chapter Six

1. That is, 6 years of primary education, 3 years of junior high school, 3 years of senior high school, and up to 4 years of college.

2. During the 1990s, most three-year junior colleges were upgraded to universities.

3. While Taiwan's per capita national income increased from 32,408 (in NT$) in 1974 to 403,382 in 2000, the standard level of tuition for public universities and colleges increased from 2,525–2,765 to 25,990. During the same period of time, the standard tuition for private universities and colleges increased from 6,297 to 51,646. In 1994, students for the first time protested "the high tuition charged by private schools," but in fact the ratio of tuition to income de-

clined over the years. The ratio for public schools decreased from 8% in 1974 to 6% in 2000, and the ratio for private schools declined from 19% to 13%.

4. Since 1995, certain departments in some universities were allowed to hold their own matriculation examinations and to recruit preferred students up to a certain proportion of total admissions (between 5% and 30%).

5. Because 80% of the parents analyzed have an education lower than or equal to junior high school (CASMIN category 1abc: the social minimum of education now), we decomposed this category into three groups.

6. By contrast, "Taiwanese" in earlier cohorts are more likely to come from the farming class, and therefore the contrast between the farming class and other classes is a major concern here.

7. For the 3% of the sample that attended graduate school, information on type of school at the college level was not available and they were merged into category 2 under the assumption that most of them had attended four-year programs.

8. This is surprising given that the Aboriginal disadvantage at the secondary level declined across cohorts (Table 6.2). Evidently, their disadvantage in the transition from secondary to higher education increased. Unfortunately, we are not able to test this hypothesis because there are not enough Aborigines among secondary school graduates in our sample.

9. Having conditioned the analysis reported in Table 6.5 on secondary school completion, we were left with very few Aborigines and excluded them from the analysis.

Chapter Seven

Earlier versions of this chapter were presented at the Spring 2002 Meeting of the International Sociological Association's Research Committee on Social Stratification and Mobility (RC28), Oxford, England; and the Spring 2002 Meeting of the Comparative Project on Higher Education, Prague (cosponsored by New York University and the David Horowitz Institute, University of Tel Aviv). We thank Ted Gerber, Yossi Shavit, and Mitchell Stevens for helpful comments.

1. Official statistics often focus on degree-granting institutions, omitting enrollments in less than two-year institutions. Moreover, although numerous, these institutions enroll less than 7% of high-school graduates (U.S. NCES 1997).

2. Calculated from Clotfelter (1996, Table 3A.5) and the *Digest of Education Statistics* (U.S. NCES 1995, table 306).

3. The federal government is not the only source of financial aid for students attending higher education. However, it provides the highest percentage of the total financial aid (College Board 1999) and affects the largest number of students (NCES 2002a).

4. This is based on authors' calculations from data reported in different volumes of the *Digest of Education Statistics*.

5. It is important to note that federal policies regarding affirmative action

emerged as one of the strategies for addressing racial disparities in employment. These policies were not directly related to college admission, nor did they require colleges and universities to adopt programs aimed at increasing enrollments of minority students.

6. More recent cohorts are approaching saturation in transition to higher education: 90% of the class of 1992 with parents in the top income quartile enrolled in postsecondary education (Ellwood and Kane 2000). However, more privileged social strata can maintain their advantage even under conditions of saturation by exploiting new dimensions of inequality within formerly equal positions. For example, socioeconomically advantaged groups can exploit qualitative differences within higher education "to secure quantitatively similar but qualitatively better education" (Lucas 2001, 1652).

7. For additional information on GSS see: http://www.icpsr.umich.edu/GSS.

8. For additional information on NLS-72 see: http://nces.ed.gov/surveys/nls72/; on HS&B: http://nces.ed.gov/surveys/hsb/; on NELS: http://nces.ed.gov/surveys/nels88/.

9. Recently released postsecondary transcript data indicate that an additional 6% of students entered higher education between 1995 and 2000, the majority of whom (over 80%) were enrolled in two-year or less than two-year institutions. Our results may thus slightly underestimate entry into higher education and two-year institutions.

10. There are two major college entrance exams in the U.S.: the SAT and the ACT; their scores were equated using a multiple imputation procedure.

11. Although we assigned institutions to "elite" or "not elite" categories separately for each data set, designation of most institutions overlaps across cohorts. For example, of the 114 institutions designated as elite in 1972, approximately 71% were coded as elite in 1982.

12. In NLS-72, test scores are obtained from a 60-minute test including batteries measuring reading, vocabulary, and mathematics knowledge, available for 15,960 students. In HS&B, students completed tests assessing mathematics, reading, and vocabulary skills in the baseline survey and the first follow-up. We used the score averaged across the two surveys. In NELS, students who participated in the follow-up surveys did not all take the same test. Instead, students participating in the first and second follow-ups were given tests based on their previous test performance; subsequently, students who did well in earlier administrations were given a more challenging test, while those who performed at or below average were given easier tests (see Rock and Pollack 1995).

13. The positive coefficients for children of individuals with some postsecondary education in cohorts 1 and 2 likely reflect the greater likelihood that the more educated parent earned an associate's degree. This finding would be consistent with Mare's (1995) assertion that the educational attainment of the parent tends to serve as a floor for the educational attainment of the child.

14. The change between the last two cohorts, assessed by t-test between

coefficients, is significant at $p < 0.10$ ($t = 1.81$), indicating a potential increase in inequality.

15. The effect in the last cohort is significant at $p < 0.10$.

Chapter Eight

We wish to acknowledge the UK Data Archive for providing access to the National Child Development Study and the British Cohort Studies and to thank the editors of this volume, Richard Breen and John H. Goldthorpe for their helpful comments on an earlier version of this chapter.

1. Higher education has been defined as both academic (degree) and advanced vocational education (sub-degree) since at least the early 1960s. Apart from teacher training, most sub-degree education was part-time.

2. The index refers to UK domiciled young people aged below 21 who are first-year entrants to full-time and "sandwich" undergraduate courses of higher education as a proportion of the average of 18- and 19-year-olds. "Sandwich" students are employed but attend courses full-time, working for their employers during vacations.

3. According to the Higher Education Statistics Agency, further education refers to programs of study for which the level of instruction is equal to or below that of courses leading to General Certificate of Education Advanced levels, Scottish Certificate of Education Advanced Highers/Highers, or the Business and Technical Education Council National Diplomas or Certificates, or Scottish Vocational Education Council Ordinary National Certificate/Diploma.

4. An important distance learning institution, the Open University, was founded in the 1960s.

5. In the period covered, the Certificate of Sixth Year Studies granted a school qualification at a higher level than the Higher Scottish Certificate of Education.

6. For BCS70, the information on institutions is given eight years after the incorporation of polytechnics, therefore it is likely that some respondents used the university rather than the polytechnic definition because the incorporation may have occurred during or shortly after they finished the course. For mature students in ex-polytechnics or new universities, the distinction did not exist. Few of the Colleges/Institutes of Higher Education incorporated as universities, as they did little research or research training.

7. By the late 1990s, dropout rates are estimated at about 17% (Yorke, Ozga, and Sukhnandan 1997; Davies and Elias 2003). However, some apparent drop out is attributable to changes of institutions and courses. Additionally, a large percentage of noncompleters returned later and successfully completed their courses (Bynner and Egerton 2001).

8. To minimize missing values, we supplemented the age 16 data with data from age 11 (NCDS) and age 10 (BCS70). Because in NCDS small employers were not distinguished from managers in small establishments, they were coded into the Lower Service Class in both cohorts.

9. Cohort expansion may be underestimated because of collinearity with the interaction terms.

10. The statistically significant estimate for a greater proportion of the 1958 cohort entering BA-granting institutions distorts the raw coefficient, presumably because of multicollinearity.

11. Under this system, pupils were allocated to different types of secondary schools (grammar, secondary modern, and technical) according to the results of their *11-plus* exams.

Chapter Nine

1. For the sake of simplicity, we will call all these schools *grandes écoles*. Strictly speaking, there are between 30 and 40 *grandes écoles*. In 2002, there were about 250 *écoles d'ingénieur* (engineering schools), many of which are quite recent: around 100 have been created or recognized as such since 1990.

2. According to the French Ministry of Education, see: www.admission-postbac.org/web-cpge/HTML/cadre_cpge_info_prepas_et_grandes_ecoles.htm.

3. For a critical survey see, for instance, Duru-Bellat and Kieffer (2000) or Merle (2002).

4. We have chosen not to use the 1993 survey because its much smaller sample of around 18,000 persons would result in imprecise estimations.

5. The quality of responses concerning educational level declines with time. Older persons tend to declare higher diplomas than they actually possess (Baudelot 1990). As the general level of qualification in the population increases, people tend to "over declare" their own level of education.

Chapter Ten

1. Since then, however, we observe a moderate decline in degree completion periods, especially at universities (Wissenschaftsrat 2005).

2. For a more profound analysis of institutional growth and diversification of German Higher Education see Mayer (2003).

3. The age at which this choice must be made varies among the federal states from 10–14 years. The criteria of access to the various tracks also vary.

4. Other factors may also have contributed to the tendency of working-class families to increasingly place their children into the *Realschule* or *Gymnasium* track. One is the increasing length and age limit of compulsory education. Furthermore, the improving material conditions of living may also have made it easier for working-class families to keep children in school longer.

5. The hypotheses we derive build on considerations of rational action in educational choices as outlined, for example by Boudon (1974) or Breen and Goldthorpe (1997).

6. Concerning the diversion argument, see also Murray (1988), Goldthorpe (2000b), and Shavit and Müller (2000).

7. From the GSOEP, we use sample A+B for 1986, sample E for 1999, and a preliminary version of sample F for 2000/2001. For various reasons we decided not to use weights.

8. For even younger cohorts not represented in the data, the difference disappeared completely (Statistisches Bundesamt 2000).

9. This does not worsen the model significantly compared with a model that includes interaction effects for each working-class category.

10. As additional tests have shown, this is partly due to the exclusion of interaction effects of father's education by cohort.

11. As outlined previously, the average age of graduates from higher education institutions is slightly above 28 years. Therefore, we set an age restriction to 30 years and older. Additional tests with higher age limits show essentially the same results.

12. For the *Fachhochschulen* (lower tertiary degree), whose introduction affected cohorts from 1948–57 onward, we found a very small increase in relative numbers.

13. The proportion of respondents with no post-*Abitur* qualifications is probably slightly overestimated for the youngest cohort because some of those included in this group may still be studying for a tertiary degree.

14. If we drop the interaction terms from the model, the effect for working-class children becomes highly significant and stronger than any other class effect.

15. To verify this conclusion we reran the analysis of Table 10.2 using full secondary education (*Abitur* only) as the reference category. The analysis shows that in more recent cohorts, to a statistically significant extent, successively more women obtain some vocational or tertiary qualifications rather than leave education without further post-*Abitur* qualifications.

Chapter Eleven

1. Since 1999, the two junior tracks (VBO and MAVO) have been integrated into one new track: VMBO. The new track consists of a theoretical level (formerly MAVO), two practical levels (formerly VBO), and a new mixed level, combining theory and practice.

2. The index of association used is a logistic regression coefficient. The data cover more than 50,000 men and women, extracted from 35 surveys held between 1958 and 1999.

3. We include this group in the alternatives because they would otherwise blur the reference group. Note that with respect to parental background, the HAVO/VWO students are second only to university students.

Chapter Twelve

1. The distinction between "secondary-level" and "postsecondary" SSUZy is somewhat stylized. In fact, neither official policies nor popular consciousness

formally distinguished between secondary-level and postsecondary SSUZy programs. Clearly, SSUZy programs overlap both levels. Our concern with postsecondary education dictates that *we* distinguish postsecondary from secondary-level SSUZy programs, which the data permit us to do, even if most Russians would probably not make such distinctions.

2. Matthews (1982) provides a detailed account of the Soviet higher education system. Kerr (1992), Lugachyov et al. (1997), Bray and Borevskaya (2001), and Poletayev and Savelieva (2001, 2002) supplement discussions of Soviet higher education with analyses of changes in the post-Soviet era.

3. For more details on the survey, see Gerber and Schaefer (2004).

4. According to the 1994 Russian microcensus, about 15% of the population aged 16 and older had at least some college education in that year. Russians with some college are overrepresented in our sample, as they are in most Russian surveys. I use postsampling weights to adjust the sample distributions by gender, age, education, and urban residence to their population values.

5. They entered SSUZy programs in somewhat larger numbers, but unfortunately the data do not permit me to cleanly determine whether SSUZy programs entered by PTU leavers represent secondary or postsecondary forms of SSUZy training.

6. As in the case of the baseline model, I also include dummy variables for missing values on locality at age 14 and father's CPSU membership, but do not report these substantively irrelevant estimates in the tables.

7. Because the scalar cohort term in the interactions is centered around the oldest cohort, the main effect of gender pertains to the cohort, which receives a zero on the interaction term.

8. The "ln(cohort)" specification is the natural logarithm of scalar cohort + 1. It thus takes on a value of zero for the oldest cohort, for which the intercept therefore provides the baseline hazard.

9. Calculations of the cohort-specific baseline logits and the effects of those variables that interact with cohort are presented, for all outcomes, in Table 12.7.

10. If all the covariates are omitted from the unconditional model, the ln(cohort) variable has a strong, positive effect on entry to VUZy.

11. Respondents born after 1976 (under 25 at the time of the survey) and those currently enrolled in a university were excluded when I estimated the models for attaining a university degree. It is therefore unlikely, that the declining graduation rate for the youngest cohorts is an artifact of right-censoring.

Chapter Thirteen

The first author listed worked on this paper while she was a Fellow at the Center for Advanced Study in the Behavioral Sciences, Stanford, California. She is grateful for the financial support provided by The William and Flora Hewlett Foundation Grant # 2000–5633.

1. The new law regarding vocational training, in force since January 1, 2004, creates a uniform and binding legal basis for all these schools.

2. The sample was drawn by a two-stage method whereby 100 communities, broken down by region and size, were selected. Cohort members residing in the selected communities were then randomly sampled.

3. The Roman numeral pertaining to each model appears in the headings of the tables.

4. The last two variables are included only in the models referring to tertiary vocational schooling.

5. This was carried out on the basis of model IV for the educational outcomes of interest.

6. For higher levels of parental education, especially matriculation certificates and university degrees, the standard errors are quite large.

7. This difference is significant as can be demonstrated by choosing a different reference category.

8. To a considerable extent, male-dominated occupations are associated with the industrial sector, where most qualifications are certified by the state.

9. It contributes 108 additional points to the chi-square ($\Delta\ df = 9$). Nagelkerke R^2 is 0.17.

10. The inclusion of unspecified linear (or nonlinear) trends does not improve the model.

11. Naturally, this does not hold for the baseline effects of cohort and gender, which collapse when the respective interaction terms are introduced.

12. The sample in this model is restricted to those eligible for admission to university.

13. The fit of the unconditional model is moderate, and the fit of the conditional model is fairly good (Nagelkerke R^2). The difference may be attributed less to the weaker predictor effects and more to the extremely skewed distribution of the dependent variable in the unconditional model.

14. Bear in mind the restricted power of the statistical test owing to the limited number of episodes, compared with the models for tertiary-level vocational schooling.

15. There is one exception to this pattern: in the unconditional model for university education, the effect of social class is also significant.

16. Some examples include: young women's strong family orientation, good job opportunities for women with the Matura (2c), and an attitude against university education for the daughter within the family of origin.

Chapter Fourteen

1. The Group of Eight comprises the Australian National University, Monash University, and the Universities of Adelaide, Melbourne, New South Wales, Queensland, Sydney, and Western Australia.

2. Analyses of data from the *Youth in Transition* cohort born in 1961 indicate that approximately 13% of this cohort attended university for at least one year between 1979 and 1984.

3. During the period in which higher education fees were not charged, students were still required to pay student union fees. A small annual fee of AUS$250, the Higher Education Administration Charge, was also charged to students between 1987 and 1988 (Chapman and Ryan 2002).

4. Nine universities offered undergraduate courses on a full-fee basis to 830 equivalent full-time student units in 1998. By 2000 this had risen slightly, with 15 universities offering 2,650 equivalent full-time student units (Harman 2003, 17).

5. With studentships, the student was bonded to a state education department for several years in exchange for the payment of fees. During the period they were bonded, they could be sent to remote or undesirable areas to teach.

6. The estimates for weighting were obtained from the Australian Vice Chancellor's Committee (Australia AVCC 2001, 31). Their figures for the percentage of the adult population with a bachelor degree or higher are: 6.9% (1985), 7.6% (1988), 10.1% (1993), 12.8% (1996), 13.6% (1997), 14.4% (1998), 15.7% (2000).

7. This contrasts with Marks and McMillan (2003) where participation at a CAE or university was counted as participation in higher education.

8. The tertiary entrance scores for all states, except Queensland, are equivalent. Tertiary entrance scores for Queensland have been recoded to their equivalent ENTER score.

9. The pseudo R-square is based on the likelihood ratios obtained from the null model and the analyzed model. It is adjusted to take into account its maximum possible values.

Chapter Fifteen

1. The Bologna Declaration, signed in 1999 by the authorities responsible for higher education in 29 European countries, set as its main long-term goal the creation of a European Higher Education. The Declaration formulated the following objectives: adoption of a system of easily readable and comparable degrees; adoption of a system based essentially on two main cycles, undergraduate and graduate; establishment of a system of credits; promotion of mobility by overcoming obstacles to effective free movement; promotion of European cooperation in quality assurance; and promotion of the necessary European dimensions in higher education.

2. According to OECD data sources (OECD 2006), the proportion of adults with tertiary education in the Czech Republic is 12%. The OECD average is 25% (29% in Ireland, the Netherlands, and Finland; and 39% in the U.S.). Currently, only 31% of young Czech adults aged 20–24 are enrolled in school, versus the OECD average of 39% (55% in Finland, 34% in Ireland, and 43% in Hungary).

3. OECD data confirm that the economic returns of tertiary education have grown after 1989. The average earnings of a person with tertiary education in the Czech Republic is 1.8 times higher than the earnings of a secondary education graduate, versus the OECD average ratio of 1.63 (with 1.84 in Hungary, 1.8 in the U.S., 1.69 in France, 1.57 in Germany, and 1.32 in Norway).

4. Detailed description of the Bill is provided by Matějů and Simonová (2003).

5. Detailed information about TSS-91 and ISSP-99 surveys and the corresponding data files can be found in the Sociological Data Archive (SDA), Institute of Sociology, Academy of Sciences of the Czech Republic (http://archiv.soc.cas.cz/). The data from TSS-91 are stored as data file #0126; the ISSP-99 survey is stored under #0016. Information about SIALS can be obtained at the web pages of ETS Princeton: http://www.ets.org/.

6. The analysis focused primarily on the transition between secondary and tertiary education, and therefore in all surveys respondents older than 19 years who reported having completed secondary education and a current status of "student" were assigned RED = 3 (tertiary education).

7. This is the reduced version of the standard EGP class schema. The reduction of the number of categories was necessary to avoid extremely low frequencies in several classifications.

8. See Haberman (1979) for a description of this methodology. For example, replacing the variable "cohort" with the "repeated" contrasts made it possible to focus on differences in the chances of success between cohorts by making the explicit assumption that some of the adjacent cohorts did not differ significantly from each other. Similarly, replacing the variable "parents' education" by orthogonal multinomial contrasts allowed to test the hypothesis that the effect of the parents' education on the log-odds of success was linear merely by declaring the respective contrast to be linear.

9. An Appendix posted on the Web site provides the distribution of the variable FCLS.

10. Henceforth by odds we mean the ratio between the number of those who succeeded making a given transition (success = 1) and those who failed (success = 0) in each group, defined by categories of independent variables and their combinations. By "odds ratios" we mean the ratios between the odds of selected groups to make the transition.

11. The specification of the logit Model II is included in the Appendix on the Web site.

12. The odds ratios calculated between all categories of father's class *except* unskilled and semiskilled workers are stable over time, including the last cohort (3/2 = 1.8; 4/2 = 2.5; 4/3 = 1.4). The odds ratios contrasting unskilled and semiskilled workers (category 1) with other classes (2, 3, and 4) are constant in all cohorts *except* the youngest one, in which they significantly increase (odds ratios 2/1 increased from 1.3 in the first four cohorts to 3.1 in the last cohort; odds

ratio 3/1 increased from 2.3 in the first four cohorts to 5.6 in the youngest one, and the odds ratio 4/1 increased from 3.2 to 7.7).

13. A formal specification of the logit Model III is included in the Appendix on the Web site.

Chapter Sixteen

I want to thank Yossi Shavit, Walter Müller, Hiroshi Ishida, and Gabriel Lanyi for their stimulating comments on previous versions of this chapter.

1. More specifically, at unification Italy adopted the educational system established in the Kingdom of Sardinia in 1859 (*Casati Law*).

2. In particular, university funding has always relied for the most part on the state. In 2002, public money still accounted for 73.6% of the overall budget of Italian universities (Italy Istat 2003a, 27).

3. A national council for higher education (CUN), composed of elected representatives of faculties, university staff, and students, was created in 1979, but merely as an advisory committee.

4. From 1961 to 1968, some piecemeal opening had already taken place; for instance, holders of high school certificates from architectural, navy, and agrarian institutes were allowed to enroll in natural science programs (Marsiglia 1993, 135). Moreover, in 1969 another law introduced a two-year upper secondary program reserved for students of vocational schools intending to enter tertiary education.

5. Between 1965 and 1975, some small local universities were established, raising the number of tertiary institutions from 45 to 61, and the number of programs from 217 to 299 (Turi 1982, 21, 69 and 77). In 2003, there were 109 institutions conferring tertiary degrees (Italy Istat 2003a, 27); 76 of them were public, catering to the large majority of students (96.5% in 1995: Ichino, Rustichini, and Checchi 1997, 287).

6. More precisely, in 1999 the average age at graduation was 26.7 for 4–5-year programs and 25.8 for 2–3-year programs.

7. As an indication of the emergence of a less standardized higher education system, accurate rankings of graduate programs, entirely new in Italy, began to be published by the leading newspaper *La Repubblica* in 2000.

8. Once uniform nationwide, since 1997 tuition fees are determined by each university separately, provided their total amount does not exceed 20% of the contribution the same university receives from the state yearly. Fees must also be based on the principle of progressive taxation, with exemption for lower-income families and disabled people. In practice, in 2004 the highest possible fees in public universities ranged between € 550 in Macerata (for all programs) and € 2,651 in Milan's medical school (*Il Sole—24 ore,* "In Lombardia la laurea a caro prezzo," March 8, 2004, p. 19).

9. Data on younger cohorts had to be excluded because they are likely to be censored on educational attainments given that a sizeable portion of Italian uni-

versity students postpone their studies until their late twenties. Population data indicate that, in 1998, 19% of university graduates obtained their degree when they were 30 or older (Italy Istat 2003b, 73). In the entire Multi-Purpose Family Survey, 5.3% of university graduates obtained their degree when they were older than 32 (the cut-off age in the analysis).

10. As in all cross-section cohort analyses, I assume that mortality is not significantly correlated with our dependent variables. This assumption is likely to disregard some possible bias due to the usually higher mortality among men and individuals of less privileged classes, as gender and class are associated with education.

11. There is reason to suspect that the reform of 1999 was designed to foster the expansion of higher education as a way to forestall the likely future decrease in the number of university students due to the smaller size of younger cohorts in a demographically aging country (Cammelli, di Francia, and Guerriero 1996). In 2001, transition rates from high school to university resurged, interrupting a decade-long decline (Italy Istat 2003a, 20). This recovery was especially due to the growth in male enrollments (ibid.). Young men seem to find shorter programs more appealing because they require lower educational investments and promise a quicker entry into the workforce.

12. Given the possibility of infinite postponement of university education, in our data set this phenomenon may be magnified by the 32-year age limit of the last cohort used in the analysis.

13. A full model with class-cohort sequential interactions (analysis not presented) shows that the decline in class III effects is significant from the 1941–50 cohort onward. Thus, the gap between the odds of attaining tertiary degrees for children of routine white-collar workers and those of manual workers is progressively narrowing. When interactions are modeled relative to the oldest cohort, the effects of service-class origins also diminish significantly over time in the last three cohorts.

14. A more country-specific finding follows from regional differences. A logistic regression (analysis not presented) including geographic distinctions reveals that parameters of the "regional area" variable are significant for the cohorts that were of university age in the 1960s—a time of widespread industrial expansion in the north. In that decade, northerners (i.e., individuals living in the most industrialized areas) were less likely to obtain a university degree than people residing elsewhere. This is consistent with previous research indicating an inverse relationship between education and economic development, in both space and time—in other words, schooling is lower in richer regions and periods of growth (Barbagli 1982). For recent reformulations and empirical support of this argument, which hinges on the relatively backward productive structure of the country, see Schizzerotto (1997) and Recchi (1999, 732–40).

BIBLIOGRAPHY

Abbott, Andrew. 1992. "What Do Cases Do? Some Notes on Activity in Sociological Analysis." In *What Is a Case?* edited by C. C. Ragin and H. S. Becke. Cambridge, MA: Cambridge University Press, pp. 53–82.

Albouy, Valérie, and Thomas Wanecq. 2002. "Les Inégalités Sociales d'Accès aux Grandes Écoles." *Economie et Statistique* 361:27–47.

Allen, W. R., R. Teranishi, G. Dinwiddie, and G. Gonzalez. 2000. "Knocking at Freedom's Door: Race, Equity and Affirmative Action in U.S. Higher Education." *Journal of Negro Education* 69:3–11.

Allen, Walter R., Robert Teranishi, Gniesha Dinwiddie, and Gloria Gonzalez. 2002. "Knocking at Freedom's Door: Race, Equity and Affirmative Action in U.S. Higher Education." *Journal of Public Health Policy* 23:440–52.

Allmendinger, Jutta. 1989. "Educational System and Labor Market Outcomes." *European Sociological Review* 5:231–50.

Amano, Ikuo. 1986. *Koto Kyoiku no Nihonteki Kozo* (Japanese Structure of Higher Education). Tokyo: Tamagawa University Press.

———. 1990. *Education and Examination in Modern Japan*. Tokyo: University of Tokyo Press.

———. 1996. *Nihon no Kyoiku Shisutemu: Kozo to Hendo* (The Japanese Educational System: Structure and Change). Tokyo: University of Tokyo Press.

———. 1999. *Daigaku: Chosen no Jidai* (Challenges to Japanese Universities). Tokyo: University of Tokyo Press.

Anderson, D. S., and A. E. Vervoorn. 1983. *Access to Privilege: Patterns of Participation in Australian Post-Secondary Education*. Canberra: Australian National University Press.

Andrews, Les. 1999. *Does HECS Deter? Factors Affecting University Participation by Low SES Groups*. Canberra: Higher Education Division, Department of Education, Training, and Youth Affairs.

Aramaki, Sohei. 2000. "Kyoiku Kikai no Kakusa wa Shukusho Shitaka (Has the Gap in Educational Opportunity Been Reduced?)." In *Nihon no Kaiso*

Shisutemu 3: Sengo Nihon no Kyoiku Shakai (Stratification System in Japan 3: Educational Credentialsin in the Postwar Stratification System), edited by Hiroyuki Kondo. Tokyo: University of Tokyo Press, pp. 53–82.

Archer, Margaret S. 1979. *Social Origins of Educational Systems.* London: Sage Publications.

Arum, Richard. 1996. "Do Private Schools Force Public Schools to Compete?" *American Sociological Review* 61:29–46.

Arum, Richard, and Walter Müller. 2004. *The Resurgence of Self-Employment: A Comparative Study of Self-Employment Dynamics and Social Inequality.* Princeton, NJ: Princeton University Press.

Astin, A. W., and L. Oseguera. 2004. "The Declining 'Equity' of American Higher Education." *The Review of Higher Education* 27:321–41.

Attali, Jacques. 1998. *Pour un Modèle Européen d'Enseignement Supérieur. Rapport de la Commission.* Paris: Ministère de l'Education Nationale.

Australia, Australian Vice-Chancellors' Committee (AVCC). 2001. *Key Statistics: Access on Higher Education.* Canberra: Australian Vice-Chancellors' Committee.

Australia, Australian Vice-Chancellors' Committee (AVCC). 2003. *AVCC Higher Education News, Legislation Special.* Canberra: Australian Vice-Chancellors' Committee.

Australia, Department of Employment, Education, Training. 1993. *National Report on Australia's Higher Education Sector.* Canberra: Department of Employment, Education, Training.

Australia, Department of Education, Science and Training (DEST). 2005. "Students 2005 [full year]: Selected Higher Education Statistics," from http://www.dest.gov.au/sectors/higher_education/publications_resources/statistics/documents/students2005_pdf.htm.

Australia, Department of Education, Training and Youth Affairs (DETYA). 2001. "Higher Education Students Time Series Tables, 2000: Selected Higher Education Statistics," from http://www.dest.gov.au/sectors/higher_education/publications_resources/statistics/documents/timeseries00_pdf.htm.

Ayalon, Hanna, and Yossi Shavit. 2004. "Educational Reforms and Inequality in Israel: The MMI Hypothesis Revisited." *Sociology of Education* 77:103–20.

Baker, T. L., and William Velez. 1996. "Access to and Opportunity in Postsecondary Education in the United States: A Review." *Sociology of Education* 69:82–101.

Ball, S. J. 1994. *Education Reform: A Critical and Post-Structural Approach.* Buckingham: Open University Press.

Balzer, Harley D. 1992. "Educating Scientific-Technical Revolutionaries? Continuing Efforts to Restructure Soviet Higher Education." In *Soviet Education Under Perestroika,* edited by J. Dunstan. London: Routledge, pp. 164–95.

———. 1994. "Plans to Reform Russian Higher Education." In *Education and Society in the New Russia*, edited by A. Jones. Armonk: M.E. Sharpe, pp. 27–46.

Barbagli, Marzio. 1982 [1973]. *Educating for Unemployment: Politics, Labor Markets, and the School System—Italy, 1859–1973*. New York: Columbia University Press.

Baudelot, Christian. 1990. "L'âge Rend-il Plus Savant? Un Exemple de Biais de Réponses dans les Enquêtes." In *Populations, Mélanges en l'Honneur de Jacques Desabie*. Paris: INSEE, pp. 159–73.

Baudelot, Christian, and Roger Establet. 1992. *Allez les Filles!* Paris: Le Seuil.

Bean, Clive S. 1991. "Comparison of the National Social Science Surveys with the 1996 Census." *NSSS Report* 6:12–19.

Becher, T., and M. Kogan. 1992. *Process and Structure in Higher Education*. London: Routledge.

Becker, G. S. 1964. *Human Capital*. New York: Columbia University Press.

Beer, G., and B. Chapman. 2004. "HECS System Changes: Impact on Students." *Agenda* 11:157–74.

Bendix, Reinhard. 1964. *Nation-Building and Citizenship Studies of Our Changing Social Order*. New York: John Wiley & Sons.

———. 1977. *Nation-Building and Citizenship: Studies of Our Changing Social Order*. Berkeley: University of California Press.

Blanc, Cécile, Nicole Ildis, and Christine Ragoucy. 1995. "Le Coût de l'Education en 1994. Evaluation Provisoire du Compte." *Note d'information de la DEP*, 30, pp. 1–6.

Blau, Peter M. 1970. "A Formal Theory of Differentiation in Organizations." *American Sociological Review* 35:201–18.

Blau, Peter M., and Otis D. Duncan. 1967. *The American Occupational Structure*. New York: John Wiley & Sons.

Blossfeld, Hans-Peter. 1993. "Changes in Educational Opportunities in the Federal Republic of Germany. A Longitudinal Study of Cohorts Born Between 1916 and 1965." In *Persistent Inequality: Changing Educational Attainment in Thirteen Countries*, edited by Y. Shavit and H. P. Blossfeld. Boulder, CO: Westview Press, pp. 51–74.

Blossfeld, Hans-Peter, and Yossi Shavit. 1993. "Persisting Barriers: Changes in Educational Opportunities in Thirteen Countries." In *Persistent Inequality: Changing Educational Attainment in Thirteen Countries*, edited by Y. Shavit and H. P. Blossfeld. Boulder, CO: Westview Press, 1–24.

Boalt, Gunnar. 1947. *Skolutbildning och Skolresultat för Barn ur Olika Samhällsgrupper i Stockholm*. Stockholm: P.A. Norstedt & Söner.

Boesel, David, Lisa Hudson, Sharon Deich, and Charles Masten. 1994. *National Assessment of Vocational Education, Vol. 2: Participation in and Quality of Vocational Education*. Washington, D.C.: U.S. Department of Education.

Boguszak, Marek, Petr Matějů, and Jules Peschar. 1990. "Educational Mobility in Czechoslovakia, Hungary and the Netherlands." In *Social Reproduction in Eastern and Western Europe: Comparative Analyses on Czechoslovakia, Hungary, the Netherlands and Poland,* edited by J. L. Peschar. Nijmegen: OOMO-REEKS, pp. 211–62.

Bolotin-Chachashvili, Svetlana, Yossi Shavit, and Hanna Ayalon. 2002. "Reform, Expansion and Opportunity in Israeli Higher Education from the Early 1980s to the Late 1990s." *Soziologia Israelit* 4:317–46.

Borland, Jeff. 2002. *New Estimates of the Private Rate of Return to University Education in Australia.* Melbourne: Melbourne Institute of Applied Economic and Social Research, University of Melbourne.

Boudon, Raymond. 1974. *Education, Opportunity, and Social Inequality; Changing Prospects in Western Society.* New York: John Wiley & Sons.

Bound, John, and S. Turner. 1999. *Going to War and Going to College: Did Word War II and the G.I. Bill Increase Educational Attainment for Returning Veterans?* NBER Working Paper no. 7452.

Bourdieu, Pierre. 1986. "The Forms of Capital." In *Handbook of Theory and Research For Sociology of Education,* edited by G. Richardson. New York: Greenwood Press, pp. 241–58.

Bowen, William G., and Derek Bok. 1998. *The Shape of the River: Long-Term Consequences of Considering Race in College and University Admissions.* Princeton, NJ: Princeton University Press.

Bradley, Karen A. 2000. "The Incorporation of Women into Higher Education: Paradoxical Outcomes?" *Sociology of Education* 73:1–18.

Brave, F. W., J. L. Van Deemster, O. G. A. Roeten, and C. W. J. Schrijver. 1993. *Vergelijking van de Uitgaven in het Oude en het Nieuwe Studiefinancieringsstelsel, Een Model en een Eerste Schatting.* Utrecht: Berenschot.

Bray, M., and N. Borevskaya. 2001. "Financing Education in Transitional Societies: Lessons from Russia and China." *Comparative Education* 37:345–65.

Breen, Richard (ed.). 2004. *Social Mobility in Europe.* Oxford: Oxford University Press.

Breen, Richard, and John H. Goldthorpe. 1997. "Explaining Educational Differentials—Towards a Formal Rational Action Theory." *Rationality and Society* 9:275–305.

Breen, Richard, and Jan O. Jonsson. 2000. "Analyzing Educational Careers: A Multinomial Transition Model." *American Sociological Review* 65:754–72.

Brewer, Dominic J., Eric R. Eide, and Ronald G. Ehrenberg. 1999. "Does It Pay to Attend an Elite Private College? Cross-Cohort Evidence on the Effects of College Type on Earnings." *Journal of Human Resources* 34:104–23.

Brint, Steven G., and Jerome Karabel. 1989. *The Diverted Dream: Community Colleges and the Promise of Educational Opportunity in America, 1900–1985.* Oxford: Oxford University Press.

Brinton, Mary C., and S. Lee. 2001. "Women's Education and the Labor Market in Japan and South Korea." In *Women's Working Lives in East Asia, Studies in Social Inequality,* edited by M. C. Brinton. Stanford, CA: Stanford University Press, pp. 125–50.

Broaded, C. Montgomery. 1997. "The Limits and Possibilities of Tracking: Some Evidence from Taiwan." *Sociology of Education* 70:36–53.

Brown, David K. 1995. *Degrees of Control: A Sociology of Educational Expansion and Occupational Credentialism.* New York: Teachers College Press.

Buchmann, Claudia, and Emily Hannum. 2001. "Education and Stratification in Developing Countries." *Annual Review of Sociology* 27:77–102.

Buchmann, Marlis, Maria Charles, and Stefan Sacchi. 1993. "The Lifelong Shadow: Social Origins and Educational Opportunities in Switzerland." In *Persistent Inequalities: Changing Educational Attainment in Thirteen Countries,* edited by Y. Shavit and H. P. Blossfeld. Boulder, CO: Westview Press, pp. 177–92.

Buchmann, Marlis, Markus König, Jiang Hong Li, and Stefan Sacchi. 1999. *Weiterbildung und Beschäftigungschancen.* Zürich: Rüegger Verlag.

Buchmann, Marlis, Irene Kriesi, Andrea Pfeifer, and Stefan Sacchi. 2002. *Halb Drinnen—Halb Draussen: Zur Arbeitsmarktintegration von Frauen in der Schweiz.* Zürich und Chur: Rüegger Verlag.

Bynner, John M., and Muriel Egerton. 2001. *The Wider Benefits of Higher Education.* London: Institute of Education, University of London, Sponsored by the HEFCE and the Smith Institute.

Cameron, S. V., and J. J. Heckman. 1998. "Life Cycle Schooling and Dynamic Selection Bias: Models and Evidence for Five Cohorts of American Males." *Journal of Political Economy* 106:262–333.

Cammelli, Andrea, Angelo di Francia, and Angelo Guerriero. 1996. "L'Università del Duemila, Ovvero quando lo Studente Diventa un Bene Scarso." *Polis* 10:245–67.

Capano, Giliberto. 1998. *La Politica Universitaria.* Bologna: Il Mulino.

———. 2000. *L'Università in Italia.* Bologna: Il Mulino.

———. 2002. "Implementing the Bologna Declaration in Italian Universities." *European Political Science* 3:81–91.

Carroll, Grace, Karolyn Tyson, and Bernadette Lumas. 2000. "Those Who Got in the Door: The University of California-Berkeley's Affirmative Action Success Story." *Journal of Negro Education* 69:128–44.

Chapman, Bruce. 1997. "Conceptual Issues and the Australian Experience with Higher Income Contingent Charges for Higher Education." *Economic Journal* 107:738–51.

Chapman, Bruce. 2001. "Australian Higher Education Financing: Issues for Reform." *Australian Economic Review* 34:195–204.

Chapman, Bruce, and Chris Ryan. 2002. "Income Contingent Financing of Student Higher Education Charges: Assessing the Australian Innovation." *The Welsh Journal of Education* 11:64-81.
Chapman, Bruce, and Tony Salvage. 1997. "Changes in Costs for Australian Education Students from the 1996/97 Budget." In *Future Australian Universities,* edited by John Sharpham and Grant Harman. Armidale: University of New England Press, pp. 49-74.
Charles, Maria, and Karen Bradley. 2002. "Equal But Separate? A Cross-National Study of Sex Segregation in Higher Education." *American Sociological Review* 67:573-99.
Checchi, Daniele. 1997. "L'Efficacia del Sistema Scolastico Italiano in Prospettiva Storica." In *L'Istruzione in Italia: Solo un Pezzo di Carta?* edited by N. Rossi. Bologna: Il Mulino.
———. 1999. *Istruzione e Mercato.* Bologna: Il Mulino.
Clark, Burton R. 1977. *Academic Power in Italy: Bureaucracy and Oligarchy in a National University System.* Chicago: University of Chicago Press.
Clotfelter, Charles. 1996. *Buying the Best: Cost Escalation in Elite Higher Education.* Princeton, NJ: Princeton University Press.
Cobalti, Antonio, and Antonio Schizzerotto. 1993. "Inequality of Education Opportunity in Italy." In *Persistent Inequalities: Changing Educational Attainment in Thirteen Countries,* edited by Y. Shavit and H. P. Blossfeld. Boulder, CO: Westview Press, pp. 155-76.
Cohen, Arthur M., and Florence B. Brawer. 1996. *The American Community College.* San Francisco: Jossey-Bass Publishers.
Collins, Randall. 1979. *The Credential Society: An Historical Sociology of Education and Stratification.* New York: Academic Press.
Connor, Walter. 1991. *The Accidental Proletariat: Workers, Politics, and Crisis in Gorbachev's Russia.* Princeton, NJ: Princeton University Press.
Craig, John E. 1984. *Scholarship and Nation Building: The Universities of Strasbourg and Alsatian Society, 1870-1939.* Chicago: University of Chicago Press.
Crocket, G. 1987. "Socio-Economic Background of Students in Tertiary Education in Australia: Some Additional Evidence." *Australian Bulletin of Labour* 13:120-25.
Cusin, Caterine, and Stéphanie Vanhooydonck. 2001. *Das Tertiäre Bildungssystem der Schweiz: Blick auf die Institutionen.* Aarau: Schweizerische Koordinationsstelle für Bildungsforschung.
Davies, R., and P. Elias. 2003. *Dropping Out: A Study of Early Leavers from Higher Education.* London: U.K., Department for Education and Science (DfES) Research Report No 386.
Davies, Scott, and Neil Guppy. 1997. "Fields of Study, College Selectivity, and Student Inequalities in Higher Education." *Social Forces* 75:1417-38.

De Francesco, Corrado. 1988. "L'Istruzione Universitaria." In *Immagini della Società Italiana,* edited by G. B. Sgritta. Rome: Istat, pp. 201–24.
De Francesco, Corrado, and Paolo Trivellato. 1978. *La Laurea e il Posto.* Bologna: Il Mulino.
De Graaf, Paul, and Harry B. G. Ganzeboom. 1993. "Family Background and Educational Attainment in the Netherlands of 1891–1960 Birth Cohorts." In *Persistent Inequality: Changing Educational Attainment in Thirteen Countries,* edited by Y. Shavit and H. P. Blossfeld. Boulder, CO: Westview Press, pp. 75–100.
Dei, Marcello. 1987. "Lo Sviluppo della Scolarità Femminile in Italia." *Polis* 1:143–58.
———. 1996. "La Dispersione tra gli Studenti della Università Italiana." *Polis* 10:269–89.
———. 1998. "Donne e Istruzione: Verso una Parità Apparente? Recenti Tendenze della Componente Femminile dell'Istruzione in Italia." *Polis* 12: 459–79.
Dei, Marcello, and N. Rossi. 1978. *Sociologia della Scuola Italiana.* Bologna: Il Mulino.
de Lillo, Antonio. 2002. "Il Sistema dei Valori." In *Giovani del Nuovo Secolo,* edited by C. Buzzi, A. Cavalli, and A. De Lillo. Bologna: Il Mulino, pp. 41–48.
de Lillo, Antonio, and Antonio Schizzerotto. 1982. "Disuguaglianze Educative e Occupazionali: Il Caso Italiano (1951–71)." In *L'Immobilità Sociale,* edited by F. S. Cappello, M. Dei, and N. Rossi. Bologna: Il Mulino.
Demin, V. M. 2001. "The Reform of Secondary Professional Education in Russia." *Russian Education and Society* 43:5–13.
Donati, Paolo, and Ivo Colozzi. 1997. *Giovani e Generazioni.* Bologna: Il Mulino.
Dougherty, Kevin J. 1994. *The Contradictory College: The Conflicting Origins, Impacts, and Futures of the Community College.* Albany, NY: State University of New York Press.
———. 2002. "The Evolving Role of Community College: Policy Issues and Research Questions." In *Higher Education: Handbook of Theory and Research,* vol. 17, edited by J. C. Smart and W. G. Tierney. New York: Agathon Press, pp. 295–348.
Dryler, Helen. 1998. *Educational Choice in Sweden: Studies on the Importance of Gender and Social Contexts.* Stockholm: Swedish Institute for Social Research.
Duffy, E. A., and I. Goldberg. 1998. *Crafting a Class: College Admissions and Financial Aid, 1955–1994.* Princeton, NJ: Princeton University Press.
Duru-Bellat, Marie. 1989. *L'École des Filles. Quelles Formations pour Quels Rôles Sociaux?* Paris: L'Harmattan.

Duru-Bellat, Marie, and Annick Kieffer. 2000. "La Démocratisation de l'Enseignement en France: Polémiques Autour d'une Question d'Actualité." *Population* 55:51–80.

Duru-Bellat, Marie, Annick Kieffer, and Catherine Marry. 2001. "Dynamique des Scolarités des Filles." *Revue Française de Sociologie* 42:251–80.

Egerton, Muriel. 1997. "Occupational Inheritance: The Role of Cultural Capital and Gender." *Work, Employment and Society* 11:262–82.

Egerton, Muriel, and A. H. Halsey. 1993. "Trends by Social-Class and Gender in Access to Higher-Education in Britain." *Oxford Review of Education* 19:183–96.

Eide, Eric R., Dominic J. Brewer, and Ronald G. Ehrenberg. 1998. "Does It Pay to Attend an Elite Private College? Evidence on the Effects of Undergraduate College Quality on Graduate School Attendance." *Economics of Education Review* 17:371–76.

Ellwood, David T., and Thomas J. Kane. 2000. "Who Is Getting a College Education? Family Background and Growing Gaps in Enrollment." In *Securing the Future: Investing in Children from Birth to College, The Ford Foundation Series on Asset Building*, edited by S. Danziger and J. Waldfogel. New York: Russell Sage Foundation, pp. 283–324.

Elster, Jon. 1979. *Ulysses and the Sirens*. Cambridge, MA: Cambridge University Press.

Epstein, Erwin, and Wei-fan Kuo. 1991. "Higher Education." In *The Confucian Continuum: Educational Modernization in Taiwan*, edited by D. Smith. New York: Praeger, pp. 167–219.

Erikson, Robert. 1984. "Social Class of Men, Women and Families." *Sociology* 18:500–14.

———. 1996. "Explaining Change in Educational Inequality—Economic Security and School Reforms." In *Can Education Be Equalized? The Swedish Case in Comparative Perspective*, edited by R. Erikson and J. O. Jonsson. Boulder, CO: Westview Press, pp. 95–112.

Erikson, Robert, and R. Åberg. 1987. *Welfare in Transition. A Survey of Living Conditions in Sweden 1968–1981*. Oxford: Clarendon Press.

Erikson, Robert, and John H. Goldthorpe. 1992. *The Constant Flux: A Study of Class Mobility in Industrial Societies*. Oxford: Clarendon Press.

Erikson, Robert, John H. Goldthorpe, and Lucienne Portocarero. 1979. "Intergenerational Class Mobility in Three Western European Societies: England, France and Sweden." *British Journal of Sociology* 30:415–41.

Erikson, Robert, and Jan O. Jonsson. 1993. *Ursprung och Utbildning. Social Snedrekrytering till Högre Utbildning*. SOU 1993:85. Stockholm: Fritzes.

———. 1996a. *Can Education Be Equalized? The Swedish Case in Comparative Perspective*. Boulder, CO: Westview Press.

———. 1996b. "Introduction: Explaining Class Inequality in Education: The Swedish Test Case." In *Can Education Be Equalized? The Swedish Case in Comparative Perspective*, edited by R. Erikson and J. O. Jonsson. Boulder, CO: Westview Press, pp. 1–64.

———. 1996c. "The Swedish Context: Educational Reform and Long-term Change in Educational Inequality." In *Can Education Be Equalized? The Swedish Case in Comparative Perspective*, edited by R. Erikson and J. O. Jonsson. Boulder, CO: Westview Press, pp. 65–94.

———. 1998. "Qualifications and the Allocation Process of Young Men and Women in the Swedish Labour Market." In *From School to Work: A Comparative Study of Educational Qualifications and Occupational Destinations*, edited by Y. Shavit and W. Müller. Oxford: Clarendon Press, pp. 369–406.

Evans, Maria D. R., and Jonathan Kelley. 2002a. "Australian and International Survey Data for Multivariate Analysis: The ISSSA." *Australian Economic Review* 32:298–302.

———. 2002b. "Data, Measurement and Methods." In *Australian Economy and Society: Education, Work, and Welfare*. Sydney: Federation Press, pp. 296–310.

Facchini, Carla. 2002. "La Permanenza dei Giovani nella Famiglia d'Origine." In *Giovani del Nuovo Secolo*, edited by C. Buzzi, A. Cavalli, and A. De Lillo. Bologna: Il Mulino.

Fogelman, K. 1985. *After School: The Education and Training Experiences of the 1958 Cohort*. London: SSRU, City University.

France, Département des Etudes et de la Prospective. 1993. *Repères et Références Statistiques sur les Enseignements et la Formation*. Paris: Ministère de l'Education Nationale.

———. 2003. *Repères et Références Statistiques sur les Enseignements, la Formation et la Recherche*. Paris: Ministère de la Jeunesse, de l'Education Nationale et de la Recherche.

France, Institut National des Statistiques et des Etudes Economiques. 2001. *Tableaux de l'économie Française 2001–2002*. Paris: Institut National de la Statistique et des Etudes Economiques.

Fulton, O. 1996. "Differentiation and Diversity in a Newly Unitary System: The Case of the UK." In *The Mockers and Mocked: Comparative Perspectives on Differentiation, Convergence and Diversity in Higher Education*, edited by V. L. Meek, L. Goedegebuure, O. Kivinen, and R. Rinne. Oxford: IAU and Elsevier Press.

Gambetta, Diego. 1987. *Were They Pushed or Did They Jump? Individual Decision Mechanisms in Education*. Boulder, CO: Westview Press.

Gamoran, Adam. 1987. "The Stratification of High School Learning Opportunities." *Sociology of Education* 60:135–55.

———. 1992. "The Variable Effects of High-School Tracking." *American Sociological Review* 57:812–28.

———. 2001. "American Schooling and Educational Inequality: A Forecast for the 21st Century." *Sociology of Education* 74:135–53.

Gamoran, Adam, and Robert D. Mare. 1989. "Secondary-School Tracking and Educational-Inequality—Compensation, Reinforcement, or Neutrality." *American Journal of Sociology* 94:1146–83.

Ganzeboom, Harry B. G., and Ruud Luijkx. 2004. "Recent Trends in Intergenerational Occupational Class Reproduction in the Netherlands 1970–99." In *Social Mobility in Europe,* edited by R. Breen. Oxford: Oxford University Press, pp. 345–81.

Ganzeboom, Harry B. G., Ruud Luijkx, and Donald J. Treiman. 1989. "Intergenerational Class Mobility in Comparative Perspective." *Research in Social Stratification and Mobility* 8:3–84.

Ganzeboom, Harry B. G., and Donald J. Treiman. 2003. "Three Internationally Standardized Measures for Comparative Research on Occupational Status." In *Advances in Cross-National Comparison. A European Working Book for Demographic and Socio-Economic Variables,* edited by J. H. P. Hoffmeyer-Zlotnik and C. Wolf. New York: Kluwer Academic Press, pp. 159–93.

Ganzeboom, Harry B. G., Donald J. Treiman, and Wout C. Ultee. 1991. "Comparative Intergenerational Stratification Research—3 Generations and Beyond." *Annual Review of Sociology* 17:277–302.

Garnier, Maurice, Jerald Hage, and Bruce Fuller. 1989. "The Strong State, Social-Class, and Controlled School Expansion in France, 1881–1975." *American Journal of Sociology* 95:279–306.

Gates, Hill. 1987. *Chinese Working-Class Lives: Getting By in Taiwan*. Ithaca, NY: Cornell University Press.

Geiger, R. L. 1996. "Diversification in U.S. Higher Education: Historical Patterns and Current Trends." In *The Mockers and Mocked: Comparative Perspectives on Differentiation, Convergence and Diversity in Higher Education,* edited by V. L. Meek, L. Goedegebuure, O. Kivinene, and R. Rinne. New York: Pergamon / IAU Press, pp. 188–203.

Gerber, Theodore P. 2000. "Educational Stratification in Contemporary Russia: Stability and Change in the Face of Economic and Institutional Crisis." *Sociology of Education* 73:219–46.

———. 2003. "Loosening Links? School-to-Work Transitions and Institutional Change in Russia since 1970." *Social Forces* 82:241–76.

Gerber, Theodore P., and Michael Hout. 1995. "Educational Stratification in Russia During the Soviet Period." *American Journal of Sociology* 101:611–60.

Gerber, Theodore P., and David Schaefer. 2004. "Horizontal Stratification of College Education in Russia: Temporal Change, Gender Differences, and Labor Market Outcomes." *Sociology of Education* 77:32–59.

Germany, Bundesministerium für Bildung und Forschung (BMBF). 2000/2001. *Grund- und Strukturdaten.* Bonn: Bundesministerium für Bildung und Forschung.

Ginsborg, Paul. 2001. "La Società Italiana, 1945–2000." In *Ritratto dell'Italia,* edited by S. Cassese. Rome-Bari: Laterza, pp. 117–40.

Gladieux, L. E. 1995. *Federal Student Aid Policy: A History and an Assessment.* Washington, D.C.: U.S. Department of Education, Office of Postsecondary Education.

Goedegebuure, L., V. L. Meek, O. Kivinen, and R. Rinne. 1996. "On Diversity, Differentiation and Convergence." In *The Mockers and the Mocked: Comparative Perspectives on Differentiation, Convergence and Diversity in Higher Education,* edited by V. L. Meek, L. Goedegebuure, O. Kivinen, and R. Rinne. New York: IAU Press / Pergamon.

Goldthorpe, John H. 1996. "Class Analysis and the Reorientation of Class Theory: The Case of Persisting Differential in Educational Attainment." *British Journal of Sociology* 47:481–505.

———. 2000a. "Current Issues in Comparative Macro-Sociology." In *On Sociology: Numbers, Narratives, and the Integration of Research and Theory,* edited by J. H. Goldthorpe. Oxford: Oxford University Press.

———. 2000b. *On Sociology: Numbers, Narratives and the Integration of Research and Theory.* Oxford: Oxford University Press.

Goux, Dominique, and Eric Maurin. 2000. "La Persistance du Lien entre Pauvreté et Echec Scolaire." In *France Portrait Social, 2000–2001,* pp. 87–98. Paris: Institut National de la Statistique et des Etudes Economiques.

Green, A., and N. Lucas (eds.). 1995. *FE and Lifelong Learning: Realigning the Sector for the Twenty-First Century.* London: Institute of Education, University of London.

Grilli, Leonardo. 1999. *Sbocchi Occupazionali e Scelte Formative dei Diplomati: Un'analisi Multilivello.* Florence: Applied Statistics, University of Florence.

Grodsky, Eric S. 2003. *Constrained Opportunity and Student Choice in American Higher Education.* Unpublished Dissertation, University of Wisconsin, Madison.

Grubb, W. Norton. 1996. *Working in the Middle: Strengthening Education and Training for the Mid-Skilled Labor Force.* San Francisco: Jossey-Bass Publishers.

Grubb, W. Norton. 1999. *Learning and Earning in the Middle: The Economic Benefits of Sub-Baccalaureate Education.* New York: Community College Research Center, Teachers College, Columbia University.

Guri-Rosenblit, Sarah. 1993. "Trends of Diversification and Expansion in Israeli Higher-Education." *Higher Education* 25:457–72.

Haberman, Shelby J. 1979. *Analysis of Qualitative Data. New Developments,* vol. 2. New York: Academic Press.

Halsey, A. H. 1988. "Higher Education." In *British Social Trends Since 1900*, edited by A. H. Halsey. London: MacMillan, pp. 268–96.
———. 1992. *The Decline of Donnish Dominion*. Oxford: Clarendon Press.
———. 1993. "Trends in Access and Equity in Higher-Education—Britain in International Perspective." *Oxford Review of Education* 19:129–40.
———. 2000. "Further and Higher Education." In *Twentieth Century British Social Trends*, edited by A. H. Halsey and J. Webb. London: MacMillan, pp. 221–53.
Halsey, A. H., Anthony F. Heath, and John M. Ridge. 1980. *Origins and Destinations: Families, Class and Education in Modern Britain*. Oxford: Clarendon Press.
Hanley, Eric. 2001. "Centrally Administered Mobility Reconsidered: The Political Dimension of Educational Stratification in State-Socialist Czechoslovakia." *Sociology of Education* 74:25–43.
Hanley, Eric, and Matthew McKeever. 1997. "The Persistence of Educational Inequalities in State-Socialist Hungary: Trajectory Maintenance versus Counterselection." *Sociology of Education* 70:1–18.
Hara, Junsuke, and Kazuo Seiyama. 1999. *Shakai Kaiso: Yutakasa no nakano Fubyodo* (Social Stratification: Inequality in an Affluent Society). Tokyo: University of Tokyo Press.
Harman, G. 2003. "*A Perspective On a Decade of Change. The National Report On Higher Education in Australia*." Canberra: Department of Education, Science, and Training.
Hata, Takashi. 1999. *Sengo Daigaku Kaikaku* (Postwar University Reforms). Tokyo: Tamagawa University Press.
Heath, Anthony F. 2000. "The Political Arithmetic Tradition in the Sociology of Education." *Oxford Review of Education* 26:313–31.
Heath, Anthony F., and Sin Yi Cheung. Forthcoming. *Unequal Chances: Ethnic Minorities in Western Labour Markets* (Cambridge: Oxford University Press).
Heath, Anthony F., and Sin Yi Cheung. 1998. "Education and Occupation in Britain." In *From School to Work: A Comparative Study of Educational Qualifications and Occupational Destinations*, edited by Y. Shavit and W. Müller. Oxford: Clarendon Press, pp. 71–101.
Henz, Ursula, and Ineke Maas. 1995. "Chancengleichheit durch die Bildungsexpansion." *Kölner Zeitschrift für Soziologie und Sozialpsychologie* 47:605–33.
Heyns, Barbara. 1974. "Social Selection and Stratification Within Schools." *American Journal of Sociology* 79:1434–51.
Hillmert, Steffen, and Marita Jacob. 2003. "Social Inequality in Higher Education: Is Vocational Training a Pathway Leading to or away from University?" *European Sociological Review* 19:319–34.

Hirsch, Fred. 1976. *Social Limits to Growth*. Cambridge, MA: Harvard University Press.

Historická ročenka školství v České republice 1953/54–1997/98 (Historical Yearbook of Education in the Czech Republic 1953/54–1997/98). 1998. Praha: ÚIV (Institute for Information in Education).

Honda, Yuki. 1997. "Kogyo Senmon Gakko ni Okeru Gakugyo Seiseki no Ruikei to Shinro." *The Japanese Journal of Labour Studies* 444:32–43.

Hout, Michael. 1988. "More Universalism, Less Structural Mobility: The American Occupational Structure in the 1980s." *American Journal of Sociology* 93:1358–400.

———. 1996. "The Politics of Mobility." In *Generating Social Stratification*, edited by A. Kerckhoff. Boulder, CO: Westview Press, pp. 293–316.

———. 1999. "Educational Progress for African Americans and Latinos in the United States from the 1950s to the 1990s: The Interaction of Ancestry and Class." Paper presented at the US/UK Ethnic Minority and Social Mobility Conference, Bath, England, June.

———. Forthcoming a. "Maximally Maintained Inequality Revisited: Irish Educational Mobility in Comparative Perspective." In *Changing Ireland, 1989–2003*, edited by M. NicGhiolla and E. Hilliard.

———. Forthcoming b. "Maximally Maintained Inequality and Essentially Maintained Inequality: Crossnational Comparisons." *Riron to Hoho* (Sociological Theory and Methods) 21.

Hout, Michael, and Thomas A. DiPrete. 2006. "What We Have Learned: RC28's Contributions to Knowledge about Social Stratification." *Research in Social Stratification and Mobility* 24(1):1–20.

Hout, Michael, and Daniel P. Dohan. 1996. "Two Paths to Educational Opportunity: Class and Educational Selection in Sweden and the United States." In *Can Education Be Equalized? The Swedish Case in Comparative Perspective*, edited by R. Erikson and J. O. Jonsson. Boulder, CO: Westview Press, pp. 207–31.

Hout, Michael, Adrian E. Raftery, and Eleanor O. Bell. 1993. "Making the Grade: Educational Stratification in the United States, 1925–1989." In *Persistent Inequality: Changing Educational Attainment in Thirteen Countries*, edited by Y. Shavit and H. P. Blossfeld. Boulder, CO: Westview Press, pp. 25–50.

Hsieh, Hsiao-Chin. 1987. "Ability Stratification in Urban Taiwanese Secondary Schools." *Bulletin of the Institute of Ethnology* 64:205–52.

———. 1992. "Gender Difference in Educational Opportunity in Taiwan: Two Taipei Junior High Schools." *Proceedings of the National Science Council, Part C: Humanities and Social Sciences*, pp. 179–201.

Ichikawa, Shogo (ed.). 1995. *Daigaku Taishuka no Kozo* (The Structure of Mass University Education). Tokyo: Tamagawa University Press.

Ichino, Andrea, Aldo Rustichini, and Daniele Checchi. 1997. "Scuola e Mobilità Sociale: Un'Analisi Comparata." In *L'Istruzione in Italia: Solo un Pezzo di Carta?* edited by N. Rossi. Bologna: Il Mulino, pp. 277–323.

Institute of Regional Studies, Osaka University of Commerce, and Institute of Social Science, University of Tokyo (eds.). 2002. *JGSS-2000 Kiso Shukeihyo Kodobukku* (The Japanese General Social Survey—2000 Codebook). Tokyo: Institute of Social Science, University of Tokyo.

———. 2003. *JGSS-2001 Kiso Shukeihyo Kodobukku* (The Japanese General Social Survey—2001 Codebook). Tokyo: Institute of Social Science, University of Tokyo.

Ishida, Hiroshi. 1993. *Social Mobility in Contemporary Japan: Educational Credentials, Class and the Labour Market in a Cross-National Perspective.* Stanford, CA: Stanford University Press.

———. 1998. "Educational Credentials and Labour-Market Entry Outcomes in Japan." In *From School to Work: A Comparative Study of Educational Qualifications and Occupational Destinations,* edited by Y. Shavit and W. Müller. Oxford: Clarendon Press, pp. 287–309.

———. 2001. "Industrialization, Class Structure, and Social Mobility in Postwar Japan." *British Journal of Sociology* 52:579–604.

Ishida, Hiroshi, Seymour Spilerman, and Kuo-Hsien Su. 1997. "Educational Credentials and Promotion Chances in Japanese and American Organizations." *American Sociological Review* 62:866–82.

Israel, Central Bureau of Statistics. Various years. *Statistical Abstract of Israel.* Central Bureau of Statistics.

Israel, Council for Higher Education (CHE). 1993. *Annual Report Number 19.* Jerusalem: Council for Higher Education.

ISSP 1992 (International Social Survey Program). Data from Social Inequality II. Module.

ISSP 1999 (International Social Survey Program). Data from Social Inequality III. Module.

Italy, Istat. 1998. *Indagine Multiscopo sulle Famiglie. Famiglia, Soggetti Sociali e Condizione dell'Infanzia. Anno 1998. Manuale Utente e Tracciato Record.* Rome: Istat.

———. 2001a. *L'Italia in Cifre.* Rome: Istat.

———. 2001b. *Università e Lavoro. Statistiche per Orientarsi.* Rome: Istat.

———. 2003a. *Università e Lavoro. Statistiche per Orientarsi.* Rome: Istat.

———. 2003b. *Lo Stato dell'Università. Principali Indicatori.* Rome: Istat.

Jacobs, Jerry A. 1995. "Gender and Academic Specialities—Trends Among Recipients of College Degrees in the 1980s." *Sociology of Education* 68:81–98.

———. 1996. "Gender Inequality and Higher Education." *Annual Review of Sociology* 22:153–85.

Jencks, Christopher, and Meredith Phillips. 1998. *The Black-White Test Score Gap.* Washington D.C.: Brookings Institution Press.
Jencks, Christopher, and David Riesman. 1968. *The Academic Revolution.* Chicago: University of Chicago Press.
Jonsson, Jan O., and Robert Erikson. 2000. "Understanding Educational Inequality. The Swedish Experience." *L'Année Sociologique* 50:345–82.
Jonsson, Jan O., and Colin Mills. 1993a. "Social Class and Educational Attainment in Historical Perspective—A Swedish-English Comparison 1." *British Journal of Sociology* 44:213–47.
———. 1993b. "Social Class and Educational Attainment in Historical Perspective—A Swedish-English Comparison 2." *British Journal of Sociology* 44:403–28.
———. 2001. "The Swedish Level-of-Living Surveys: A General Overview and Description of the Event History Data." In *Cradle to Grave. Life-Course Change in Modern Sweden,* edited by J. O. Jonsson and C. Mills. Durham: Sociologypress, pp. 228–42.
Jonsson, Jan O., Colin Mills, and Walter Müller. 1996. "A Half Century of Increasing Educational Openness? Social Class, Gender and Educational Attainment in Sweden, Germany and Britain." In *Can Education Be Equalized? The Swedish Case in Comparative Perspective,* edited by R. Erikson and J. O. Jonsson. Boulder, CO: Westview Press, pp. 183–206.
Kane, T. J. 1998. "Racial and Ethnic Preferences in College Admissions." In *The Black-White Test Score Gap,* edited by C. Jencks and M. Phillips. Washington, D.C.: Brookings Institution Press, pp. 432–56.
Kane, T. J., and C. E. Rouse. 1995. "Labor-Market Returns to Two-and Four-Year College." *The American Economic Review* 85: 600–14.
Kane, T. J., and C. E. Rouse. 1999. "The Community College: Educating Students at the Margin Between College and Work." *The Journal of Economic Perspectives* 13:63–84.
Kaneko, Motohisa. 1993. "Nihon no Koto Kyoiku (Japanese Higher Education)." In *Koto Kyoikuron* (Theories of Higher Education), edited by H. Muta. Tokyo: Society for the Promotion of the University of the Air, pp. 45–56.
Kao, Grace, and Jennifer S. Thompson. 2003. "Racial and Ethnic Stratification in Educational Achievement and Attainment." *Annual Review of Sociology* 29:417–42.
Karabel, Jerome. 1972. "Community Colleges and Social Stratification." *Harvard Education Review* 42:521–62.
———. 1999. "The Rise and Fall of Affirmative Action at the University of California." *Journal of Blacks in Higher Education* 25:109–12.
Karen, David. 1991a. "Achievement and Ascription in Admission to an Elite College—A Political Organizational Analysis." *Sociological Forum* 6:349–80.

———. 1991b. "The Politics of Class, Race, and Gender—Access to Higher-Education in the United-States, 1960–1986." *American Journal of Education* 99:208–37.

———. 2002. "Changes in Access to Higher Education in the United States: 1980–1992." *Sociology of Education* 75:191–210.

Karmel, P. 1990. "Reflections On a Revolution: Australian Higher Education in 1989." In *Higher Education in the Late Twentieth Century. Reflections on a Changing System,* edited by I. Moses. Kensington, New South Wales: Higher Education Research and Development Society of Australasia, pp. 24–47.

Kerckhoff, Alan C. 1993. *Diverging Pathways: Social Structure and Career Deflections.* New York: Cambridge University Press.

Kerckhoff, Alan C. 1995. "Institutional Arrangements and Stratification Processes in Industrial-Societies." *Annual Review of Sociology* 21:323–47.

Kerckhoff, Alan C., and Lorraine Bell. 1998. "Hidden Capital: Vocational Credentials and Attainment in the United States." *Sociology of Education* 71:152–74.

Kerckhoff, Alan C., Stephen W. Raudenbush, and Elizabeth Glennie. 2001. "Education, Cognitive Skill, and Labor Force Outcomes." *Sociology of Education* 74:1–24.

Kerckhoff, Alan C., and J. M. Trott. 1993. "Educational Attainment in a Changing Educational System: The Case of England and Wales." In *Persistent Inequality: Changing Educational Attainment in Thirteen Countries,* edited by Y. Shavit and H. P. Blossfeld. Boulder, CO: Westview Press, pp. 133–53.

Kerr, Stephen T. 1992. "Debate and Controversy in Soviet Higher Education Reform: Reinventing a System." In *Soviet Education under Perestroika,* edited by J. Dunstan. London: Routledge, pp. 146–73.

Kim, Y. C. 2000. "Historical Development." In *Higher Education in Korea,* edited by J. C. Weidman and N. Park. New York: Falmer Press, pp. 7–53.

Kim, Y. C., and J. K. Lee. 2000. *Analysis of Student Demand for Higher Education in Korea.* Seoul: Korean Educational Development Institute.

Kim, Y. H., et al. 1997. *Korean Education and National Development.* Seoul: Korean Educational Development Institute.

Kingston, P. W., and J. C. Smart. 1990. "The Economic Pay-off of Prestigious Colleges." In *The High-Status Track: Studies of Elite Schools and Stratification,* edited by P. W. Kingston and L. S. Lewis. Albany, NY: State University of New York Press, pp. 147–74.

Kitaev, Igor V. 1994. "The Labor Market and Education in the Post-Soviet Era." In *Education and Society in the New Russia,* edited by A. Jones. Armonk: M.E. Sharpe, pp. 311–32.

Knippenberg, Hans, and W. Van Der Ham. 1994. *Een Bron van Aanhoudende Zorg: 75 Jaar Ministerie van Onderwijs Kunsten en Wetenschappen 1918–1993.* Assen: Van Gorcum & Comp. Bv.

Kogan, Maurice, and Stephen Hanney. 2000. *Reforming Higher Education.* London: Jessica Kingsley.

Kondo, Hiroyuki. 2000. "Chiteki Kaiso no Genso (The Myth of Cognitive Stratification)." In *Nihon no Kaiso Shisutemu 3: Sengo Nihon no Kyoiku Shakai* (Stratification System in Japan 3: Educational Credentials in the Postwar Stratification System), edited by Hiroyuki Kondo. Tokyo: University of Tokyo Press, pp. 221–45.

———. 2001. "Kodo Seichokiiko no Daigaku Kyoiku Kikai (Opportunity of Higher Education after the High Growth Periods)." *Osaka University Annals of Educational Studies* 6:1–11.

Korea, Korean Educational Development Institute (KEDI). 2000. *Handbook of Educational Statistics.* Seoul: Korean Educational Development Institute.

Kreidl, M. 2001. "The Role of Political, Social and Cultural Capital in Secondary School Selection in Socialist Czechoslovakia, 1948–1989." In *Sociological Papers.* Prague: Institute of Sociology, Academy of Sciences of the Czech Republic, 01: 2, p. 24.

Kuroha, Ryoichi. 1993. *Sengo Daigaku Seisaku no Tenkai* (The Postwar Development of University Policies). Tokyo: Tamagawa University Press.

Le, A. T., and P. W. Miller. 2000. "Australia's Unemployment Problem." *Economic Record* 76:74–104.

Ledeneva, Alena V. 1998. *Russia's Economy of Favours: Blat, Networking, and Informal Exchange.* New York: Cambridge University Press.

LeVine, Robert A., Sarah E. LeVine, and Beatrice Schnell-Anzola. 2001. "Improve the Women: Mass Schooling, Female Literacy, and Worldwide Social Change." *Harvard Educational Review* 71:1–50.

Lin, Mosei. 1929. *Public Education in Formosa under the Japanese Administration.* New York: Columbia University.

Long, Michael. 2002. "Government Financial Assistance for Australian University Students." *Journal of Higher Education Policy and Management* 24: 127–43.

Lucas, Samuel R. 1996. "Selective Attrition in a Newly Hostile Regime: The Case of 1980 Sophomores." *Social Forces* 75:511–33.

———. 1999. *Tracking Inequality: Stratification and Mobility in American High Schools.* New York: Teachers College Press.

———. 2001. "Effectively Maintained Inequality: Education Transitions, Track Mobility and Social Background Effects." *American Journal of Sociology* 106:1642–90.

Lucas, Samuel R., Phillip N. Fucella, and Mark Berends. 2001. "Neo-classical Education Transitions Analyses of Boomers and Post-Boomers: A Corrected Tale for Three Cohorts." Paper presented at the meeting of *RC28*, Berkeley, CA.

Lugachyov, Mikhail, Andrei Markov, Nikolai Tipenko, and Sergei Belyakov. 1997. "Structure and Financing of Higher Education in Russia." In *Structure and Financing of Higher Education in Russia, Ukraine, and the EU,* edited by P. G. Hare. London: Jessica Kingsley, pp. 144–76.

Luoh, Ming-Ching. 2001. "Differences in Educational Attainment across Ethnic and Gender Groups in Taiwan." *Taiwan Economic Review* 29: 117–52.

Mare, Robert D. 1980. "Social Background and School Continuation Decisions." *Journal of the American Statistical Association* 75:295–305.

———. 1981. "Change and Stability in Educational Stratification." *American Sociological Review* 46:72–87.

———. 1995. "Changes in Educational Attainment and School Enrollment." In *State of the Union: America in the 1990s,* edited by R. Farley. New York: Russell Sage Foundation, pp. 155–213.

Marks, Gary N., and Nicole Fleming. 1998a. *Factors Influencing Youth Unemployment in Australia: 1980–1994* (LSAY Research Report no. 7). Melbourne: Australian Council for Educational Research.

———. 1998b. *Youth Earnings in Australia: 1980–1994* (LSAY Research Report no. 8). Melbourne: Australian Council for Educational Research.

Marks, Gary N., Nicole Fleming, Michael Long, and Julie McMillan. 2000. *Patterns of Participation in Year 12 and Higher Education in Australia: Trends and Issues,* vol. 17. Melbourne: Australian Council for Educational Research.

Marks, Gary N., Bruce Headey, and Mark Wooden. 2005. "Households Wealth in Australia: Its Components, Distributions and Correlates." *Journal of Sociology* 41:47–68.

Marks, Gary N., and Julie McMillan. 2003. "Declining Inequality? The Changing Impact of Socioeconomic Background and Ability on Education in Australia." *British Journal of Sociology* 54:453–71.

Marks, Gary N., and S. Rothman. 2003. "Longitudinal Studies of Australian Youth." *Australian Economic Review* 36: 428–34.

Marsiglia, Giorgio. 1993. "L'Università di Massa: Espansione, Crisi e Trasformazione." In *Fare gli Italiani. Scuola e Cultura nell'Italia Contemporanea,* edited by S. Soldani and G. Turi. Bologna: Il Mulino, pp. 129–68.

Martinotti, Guido. 1972. "Italy." In *Students, University and Society,* edited by M. S. Archer. London: Heinemann, pp. 167–195.

Matějů, Petr. 1986. "Demokratizace Vzdělání a Reprodukce Vzdělanostní Struktury V ČSSR ve Světle Mobilitních Dat (The Democratization of Education and the Reproduction of Educational Structures in CSSR)." *Sociological Review* 2:131–52.

———. 1993. "Who Won and Who Lost in a Socialist Redistribution in Czechoslovakia?" In *Persistent Inequality: Changing Educational Attainment in Thirteen Countries,* edited by Y. Shavit and H. P. Blossfeld. Boulder, CO: Westview Press, pp. 251–71.

———. 1999. "Mobility and Perceived Change in Life-Chances in Post-Communist Countries." In *New Markets, New Opportunities? Economic and Social Mobility in a Global Economy. Brookings Institution and the Carnegie Endowment,* edited by C. Graham and N. Birdsall. Washington, D.C.: Brookings Institution.

Matějů, Petr, and Martin Kreidl. 2001. "Rebuilding Status Consistency in a Post-Communist Society. The Czech Republic, 1991–97." *Innovation* 1:17–34.

Matějů, Petr, and Jules L. Peschar. 1990. "Family Background and Educational Attainment in Czechoslovakia and the Netherlands." In *Class Structure in Europe: New Findings from East-West Comparisons of Social Structure and Mobility,* edited by M. Haller. New York: Sharpe, pp. 121–52.

Matějů, Petr, and Natalie Simonová. 2003. "Czech Higher Education Still at the Crossroads." *Czech Sociological Review* (English edition), 39: 393–410.

Matsui, Machiko. 1997. *Tandai wa Dokoeyuku (Where Are Junior Colleges Going?).* Tokyo: Keiso Shobo.

Matthews, Mervyn. 1982. *Education in the Soviet Union: Policies and Institutions Since Stalin.* London: Allen & Unwin.

Mayer, Karl Ulrich. 2003. "Das Hochschulwesen." In *Das Bildungswesen in der Bundesrepublik Deutschland. Strukturen und Entwicklungen im Überblick,* edited by K. S. Cortina, J. Baumert, A. Leschinsky, and K. U. Mayer. Reinbek: Rowohlt, pp. 581–624.

Mayer, Karl Ulrich, Ursula Henz, and Ineke Maas. 1991. "Social Mobility Between Generations and Across the Working Life: Biographical Contingency, Time Dependency and Cohort Differentiation—Results From the German Life History Study." Working paper at the Max-Planck-Institut für Bildungsforschung, Berlin.

McDonough, Patricia M. 1997. *Choosing Colleges: How Social Class and Schools Structure Opportunity.* Albany, NY: State University of New York Press.

Meek, V. Lynn. 2000. *Uses of Higher Education Policy Research.* Inaugural Lecture: Center for Higher Education Management and Policy, University of New England.

Meek, V. Lynn, Leo Goedegebuure, Osmo Kivinen, and Risto Rinne (eds.). 1996. *The Mockers and Mocked: Comparative Perspectives on Differentiation, Convergence, and Diversity in Higher Education.* New York: Pergamon/IAU Press.

Merle, Pierre. 2002. "Démocratisation ou Accroissement des Inégalités Scolaires? L'exemple de l'Évolution de la Durée des Études en France (1988–1998)." *Population* 57:633–60.

Meulemann, Heiner. 1992. "Expansion ohne Folgen? Bildungschancen und Sozialer Wandel in der Bundesrepublik." In *Entwicklungstendenzen der Sozialstruktur,* edited by W. Glatzer. Frankfurt am Main/New York: Campus Verlag, pp. 123–57.

Moscati, Roberto. 1985. "Reflections on Higher Education and the Polity in Italy." *European Journal of Higher Education* 2:134–36.

———. 1991. "Italy." In *International Higher Education: An Encyclopedia*, edited by P. H. Altbach. London: Garland, pp. 721–33.

Müller, Walter. 2000. CASMIN Educational Classification. Electronic source accessed March 30, 2001, under http://www.nuf.ox.ac.uk/Users/Yaish/NPSM/documents.htm.

Müller, Walter, and Dietmar Haun. 1994. "Bildungsungleichheit im Sozialen Wandel." *Kölner Zeitschrift für Soziologie und Sozialpsychologie* 46:1–42.

Müller, Walter, and Wolfgang Karle. 1993. "Social Selection in Educational Systems in Europe." *European Sociological Review* 9:1–22.

Müller, Walter, Paul Lüttinger, Wolfgang Koenig, and Wolfgang Karle. 1989. "Class and Education in Industrial Nations." *International Journal of Sociology* 19:3–39.

Müller, Walter, and Reinhard Pollak. 2004. "The Long Arms of History Discovered?" In *Social Mobility in Europe*, edited by R. Breen. Oxford: Oxford University Press, pp. 77–113.

Müller, Walter, and Yossi Shavit. 1998. "The Institutional Embeddedness of the Stratification Process. A Comparative Study of Qualifications and Occupations in Thirteen Countries." In *From School to Work: A Comparative Study of Educational Qualifications and Occupational Destinations*, edited by Y. Shavit and W. Müller. Oxford: Clarendon Press, pp. 1–48.

Murray, Mac. 1988. "Educational Expansion, Policies of Diversion and Equality: The Case of Sweden, 1933–1985." *European Journal of Education* 23(1/2):141–49.

Muta, Hiromitsu. 1994. *Daigaku no Chiiki Haichi to Enkaku Kyoiku* (Geographical Allocation of Universities and Education in Remote Areas). Tokyo: Taga Shuppan.

———. 1997. *Kawaru Shakai to Daigaku* (Changing Society and University). Tokyo: The Society for the Promotion of the University of the Air.

Naoi, Atsushi, and Kazuo Seiyama (eds.). 1990. *Gendai Nihon no Kaiso Kozo* (Stratification Structure in Contemporary Japan), vol. 1. Tokyo: University of Tokyo Press.

Nathan, G. 1999. *A Review of Sample Attrition and Representativeness in Three Longitudinal Surveys*. London: Government Statistical Services Methodology, Series no. 13.

Neave, Guy. 2000. "Diversity, Differentiation and the Market: The Debate We Never Had but Which We Ought to Have Done." *Higher Education Policy* 13:7–21.

Netherlands, Central Bureau for Statistics. 1976. *Schoolloopbaan en Herkomst van Leerlingen in het Voortgezet Onderwijs*. (SMVO) fase 1. Heerlen: CBS Voorburg.

———. 1982. *Schoolloopbaan en Herkomst van Leerlingen in het Voortgezet Onderwijs.* (SMVO) fase 2. Heerlen: CBS Voorburg.

———. 1989. *Voortgezet Onderwijs Cohort Leerlingen 1989, Schoolloopbanen en Herkomst van Leerlingen in het Voortgezet Onderwijs.* (VOCL). Heerlen: CBS Voorburg.

———. 1993. *Voortgezet Onderwijs Cohort Leerlingen 1993, Schoolloopbanen en Herkomst van Leerlingen in het Voortgezet Onderwijs.* Heerlen: CBS Voorburg.

Netherlands, Inspectie van het Onderwijs. 2000. *Onderwijsverslag over het Jaar 1999.* Utrecht: Inspectie van het Onderwijs.

Netherlands, Ministry of Education and Science (Ministrie van Onderwijs en Wetenschappen). 1989. *Rijkdom van het Onvoltooide, Uitdagingen voor het Nederlandse Onderwijs.* The Hague: Ministerie van Onderwijs en Wetenschappen.

Netherlands, Ministry of Education, Culture, and Science (Ministerie van Onderwijs, Cultuur en Wetenschappen). 2003. *Kerncijfers 1998–2002.* The Hague: OCenW 33.026.

Netherlands, Sociaalen Cultureel Planbureau. 1998. *Trends in Onderwijsdeelname: Van Analyse tot Prognose, Sociale en Culturele Studies 25.* The Hague: SCP.

———. 2000. *Sociaal en cultureel rapport 2000, Nederland in Europa.* The Hague: SCP.

New Zealand, Ministry of Education (NZMOE). 2004. *Student Loans.* Wellington: New Zealand Ministry of Education.

Oakes, Jeannie. 1985. *Keeping Track: How Schools Structure Inequality.* New Haven, CT: Yale University Press.

OECD. 1985–92. *Education Statistics 1985–1992.* Paris: OECD.

———. 1996. *Education at a Glance.* Paris: OECD.

———. 1997. *Education at a Glance.* Paris: OECD.

———. 1998. *Reviews of National Policies for Education: Korea.* Paris: OECD.

———. 2001. *Education at a Glance.* Paris: OECD.

———. 2002. *Education at a Glance.* Paris: OECD.

———. 2003. *Education at a Glance.* Paris: OECD.

———. 2005. *Society at a Glance.* Paris: OECD.

———. 2006. *Education at a Glance.* Paris: OECD.

Ohlsson, R. 1986. *Högre Utbildning och Demografisk Förändring.* Lund: Ekonomisk-historiska Föreningen.

Ojima, Fumiaki. 2002. "Shakai Kaiso to Shinro Keisei no Henyo (Social Stratification and Educational Choices)." *The Journal of Educational Sociology* 72:125–42.

Ono, Hiroshi. 2001. "Who Goes to College? Features of Institutional Tracking in Japanese Higher Education." *American Journal of Education* 109:161–95.

———. 2004. "In Pursuit of College Quality: Migration Decisions Among Japanese College Students." *Research in Sociology of Education* 14:103–23.

Park, Hyunjoon. 2004. "Educational Expansion and Inequality in Korea." *Research in Sociology of Education* 14:33–58.

Park, N. 2000. "The 31 May 1995 Higher Education Reform." In *Higher Education in Korea,* edited by J. C. Weidman and N. Park. New York: Falmer Press, pp. 149–75.

Pascarella, Ernest T., and Patrick T. Terenzini. 1991. *How College Affects Students: Findings and Insights from Twenty Years of Research.* San Francisco: Jossey-Bass Publishers.

Pempel, T. J. 1973. "The Politics of Enrollment Expansion in Japanese Universities." *Journal of Asian Studies* 33:67–86.

Pfeffer, Jeffrey, and Gerald Salancik. 1978. *The External Control of Organizations.* New York: Harper & Row.

Phang, Ha-Nam et al. 1999. *Economic Activity of Household and Individual in Korea: Results of the First Wave.* Seoul: KLIPS.

Pisati, Maurizio. 2002. "La Partecipazione al Sistema Scolastico." In *Vite Ineguali. Diseguaglianze e Corsi di Vita nell'Italia Contemporanea,* edited by A. Schizzerotto. Bologna: Il Mulino, pp. 141–86.

PIVOT, Rijksarchiefdienst. 1995. *Leergeld, Een Institutioneel Onderzoek naar het Beleidsterrein Studiefinanciering, 1945–1994.* PIVOT-rapport nr. 42. The Hague: Algemeen Rijksarchief, Project Invoering Verkorting Overbrengingstermijn (PIVOT).

———. 1999. *Hoger Beroepsonderwijs, Een Institutioneel Onderzoek naar het Handelen van Nationale Overheidsorganen op het Beleidsterrein Hoger Beroepsonderwijs, (1945) 1968–1998,* PIVOT-rapport nr. 62. The Hague: Algemeen Rijksarchief, Project Invoering Verkorting Overbrengingstermijn (PIVOT), Ministerie van OCenW, Zoetermeer.

Poletayev, Andrei, and Irina Savelieva. 2001. "Trends in Professional Education in Russia. Part 1: Objects of Supply and Demand." *Russian Economic Trends* 10:45–59.

———. 2002. "Trends in Professional Education in Russia. Part 2: Subjects of Demand." *Russian Economic Trends* 11:37–47.

Prost, Antoine. 1992. *Education, Société et Politiques: Une Histoire de l'Enseignement en France, de 1945 à nos Jours.* Paris: Seuil.

Raftery, Adrian E., and Michael Hout. 1993. "Maximally Maintained Inequality—Expansion, Reform, and Opportunity in Irish Education, 1921–75." *Sociology of Education* 66:41–62.

Ragin, Charles C. 1997. "Turning the Tables: How Case-Oriented Research Challenges Variable-Oriented Research." *Comparative Social Research* 16:27–43.

Recchi, Ettore. 1999. "Il Rischio Disoccupazione e i Valori Politici Degli Studenti

Universitari Italiani." In *Giovani e Democrazia in Europa,* edited by G. Bettin Lattes. Padua: Cedam, pp. 727–65.

———. 2001. "Il Lavoro che Verrà. Le Aspettative Degli Studenti Universitari e dei Loro Genitori." In *La Politica Acerba. Saggi sull'Identità Civica dei Giovani,* edited by G. Bettin Lattes. Rubbettino: Soveria Mannelli, pp. 123–50.

Republic of China (ROC), Ministry of Education. 2001a. *Educational Statistics of the Republic of China.* Taipei: Ministry of Education.

———. 2001b. *Educational Statistics Index of the Republic of China.* Taipei: Ministry of Education.

Rijken, Susanne R.H. 1999. *Educational Expansion and Status Attainment: A Cross-National and Over-Time Comparison.* Utrecht: ICS.

Rock, D., and J. Pollack. 1995. *Psychometric Report for the NELS:88 Base Year Through Second Follow-Up.* Washington, D.C.: National Center for Education Statistics.

Roksa, Josipa. 2005. "Double Disadvantage or Blessing in Disguise? Understanding the Relationship between College Major and Employment Sector." *Sociology of Education* 78:207–32.

Rosenbaum, James E. 1976. *Making Inequality: The Hidden Curriculum of High School Tracking.* New York: John Wiley & Sons.

Rossi, Nicola. 1997. *L'Istruzione in Italia: Solo un Pezzo di Carta?* Bologna: Il Mulino.

Rubinson, Richard. 1986. "Class Formation, Politics, and Institutions—Schooling in the United States." *American Journal of Sociology* 92:519–48.

Rubinstein, Amnon. 1993. *The Colleges' Development Policy.* Minutes of the Public Stage. Jerusalem: Center of Social Policy Research in Israel.

Rumberger, Russell W., and Scott L. Thomas. 1993. "The Economic Returns to College Major, Quality and Performance: A Multilevel Analysis of Recent Graduates." *Economics of Education Review* 12:1–19.

Savage, Mike, and Muriel Egerton. 1997. "Social Mobility, Individual Ability and the Inheritance of Class Inequality." *Sociology* 31:645–72.

Schimpl-Neimanns, Bernhard. 2000. "Soziale Herkunft und Bildungsbeteiligung. Empirische Analysen zu Herkunftsspezifischen Bildungsungleichheiten zwischen 1959 und 1989." *Kölner Zeitschrift für Soziologie und Sozialpsychologie* 52:636–69.

Schizzerotto, Antonio. 1997. "Perché in Italia Ci Sono Pochi Diplomati e Pochi Laureati? Vincoli Strutturali e Decisioni Razionali degli Attori Come Cause della Contenuta Espansione della Scolarità Superiore." *Polis* 11:345–65.

Schweizerischer, Fachhochschulrat. 2000. *Fachhochschulführer Schweiz.* Bern: Schweizerische Konferenz der kantonalen Erziehungsdirektoren (EDK).

Scott, P. 2002. "Reflections on the Reform of Higher Education in Central and Eastern Europe." *Higher Education in Europe XXVII.* Bucharest: European Center for Higher Education (UNESCO).

Sewell, William H., and Vimal P. Shah. 1967. "Socioeconomic Status, Intelligence, and the Attainment of Higher Education." *Sociology of Education* 40:1–23.
Sewell, William J., Archibald O. Haller, and Alejandro Portes. 1969. "The Educational and Early Occupational Attainment Process." *American Sociological Review* 34:82–92.
Shavit, Yossi. 1984. "Tracking and Ethnicity in Israeli Secondary Education." *American Sociological Review* 49:210–20.
———. 2001. *Higher Education: Expansion, Institutional Forms and Equality of Opportunity: A Pre-Proposal for an International Comparative Project.* Tel Aviv: David Horowitz Research Institute on Society and Economy, Tel Aviv University.
Shavit, Yossi, Hanna Ayalon, and M. Kurleander. 2002. "Second Chance Education and Inequalities in Israel." *Research in Sociology of Education: Schooling and Social Capital in Diverse Cultures* 13:107–26.
Shavit, Yossi, and Hans Peter Blossfeld (eds.). 1993. *Persistent Inequality: Changing Educational Attainment in Thirteen Countries.* Boulder, CO: Westview Press.
Shavit, Yossi, and Hans Peter Blossfeld. 1996. "Equalizing Educational Opportunity: Do Gender and Class Compete?" In *Can Education Be Equalized? The Swedish Case in Comparative Perspective,* edited by R. Erikson and J. O. Jonsson. Boulder, CO: Westview Press, pp. 233–53.
Shavit, Yossi, Svetlana Bolotin-Chachashvili, Hanna Ayalon, and Gila Menahem. 2002. "Diversification, Expansion, and Inequality in Israeli Higher Education." Paper presented at the meeting of *ISA-RC28,* Oxford.
Shavit, Yossi, and Walter Müller (eds.). 1998. *From School to Work: A Comparative Study of Educational Qualifications and Occupational Destinations.* Oxford: Clarendon Press.
Shavit, Yossi, and Walter Müller. 2000. "Vocational Secondary Education. Where Diversion and Where Safety Net?" *European Societies* 2:29–50.
Shavit, Yossi, and Karin Westerbeek. 1998. "Educational Stratification in Italy—Reforms, Expansion, and Equality of Opportunity." *European Sociological Review* 14:33–47.
Shepherd, P. 1993. "Appendix 1: Analysis of Response Bias." In *Life At 33: The Fifth Follow-up of the National Child Development Study,* edited by E. Ferri. London: National Children's Bureau, pp. 184–88.
Shlapentokh, Vladimir. 1990. *Soviet Intellectuals and Political Power: The Post-Stalin Era.* Princeton, NJ: Princeton University Press.
Simkus, Albert, and Rudolf Andorka. 1982. "Inequalities in Educational Attainment in Hungary 1923–1973." *American Journal of Sociology* 47:740–51.
SIALS (Second International Adult Literacy Survey) 1998. Data for the Czech Republic.

Skrentny, John D. 1996. *The Ironies of Affirmative Action: Politics, Culture, and Justice in America.* Chicago: The University of Chicago Press.

———. 2002. *The Minority Rights Revolution.* Cambridge, MA: The Belknap Press of Harvard University Press.

Smith, Douglas C. 1991. *The Confucian Continuum: Educational Modernization in Taiwan.* New York: Praeger.

Smith, Herbert L., and Paul P. L. Cheung. 1986. "Trends in the Effects of Family Background on Educational Attainment in the Philippines." *American Journal of Sociology* 91:1387–1408.

Smith, Teresa, and Michael Noble (with J. Barlow, E. Sharland, and G. Smith). 1995. *Education Divides: Poverty and Schooling in the 1990s.* London: Child Poverty Action Group (CPAG).

Sorensen, Clark W. 1994. "Success and Education in South Korea." *Comparative Education Review* 38:10–35.

Sorokin, Pitirim A. 1959 [1927]. *Social and Cultural Mobility.* New York: Free Press.

Statistikyškolství z let 1962 až 1989 (Education Statistics from the Years 1962 to 1989). Praha: Ústav Školských Informací (Institute of Information on Education).

Statistisches Bundesamt. 2000. *Datenreport 1999. Zahlen und Fakten über die Bundesrepublik Deutschland (Schriftenreihe Band 365).* Bonn: Bundeszentrale für Politische Bildung.

Sullivan, Alice. 2001. "Cultural Capital and Educational Attainment." *Sociology* 35:893–912.

Sweden, SCB (Statistics Sweden). 1988. *Svensk utbildningsnomenklatur (SUN).* Stockholm: Statistics Sweden.

———. 1989. *Yrkesklassificeringar i FoB85 enligt Nordisk Yrkesklassificering (NYK) och Socioekonomisk Indelning (SEI).* Mis 1989:5 (Occupations According to Nordic Standard Occupational Classification (NYK) and Swedish Socio-Economic Classification (SEI)). Stockholm: Statistics Sweden.

Swirski, Shlomo, and Barbara Swirski. 1997. *Higher Education in Israel.* Adva Center Series on Equality, no. 8. Tel Aviv: Adva Center.

Switzerland, Bundesamt für Statistik (BFS) (ed.). 1994. *Die Höhere Berufsbildung in der Schweiz: Das Berufsbildungsangebot der Ausseruniversitären Tertiärstufe.* Neuchâtel: Bundesamt für Statistik.

———. 2001a. *Studierende an den Schweizerischen Fachhochschulen.* Neuchâtel: Bundesamt für Statistik.

———. 2001b. *Studierende an den Schweizerischen Fachhochschulen.* Neuchâtel: Bundesamt für Statistik.

———. 2001c. *Bildungsabschlüsse 2000. Sekundarstufe II und Tertiärstufe.* Neuchâtel: Bundesamt für Statistik.

———. 2002. "Schülerinnen, Schüler und Studierende 2000/01." Neuchâtel: Bundesamt für Statistik.

Switzerland, EDK/BBW. 2001. "Eurybase—The Information Database on Education in Europe." Bern: Information Dokumentation Erziehung Schweiz (IDES).

Thélot, Claude, and Louis-André Vallet. 2000. "La Réduction des Inégalités Sociales Devant l'école Depuis le Début du Siècle." *Economie et Statistique* 334:3–32.

Thompson, James D. 1967. *Organizations in Action*. New York: McGraw-Hill.

Tien, Flora F. 1996. "Higher Education Reform in Taiwan: History, Development and the University Act." *The American Asian Review* 14:35–57.

Townsend, B. K. 2001. "Blurring the Lines: Transforming Terminal Education to Transfer Education." In *The New Vocationalism in Community Colleges, New Directions for Community Colleges*, vol. 115, edited by D. D. Bragg. San Francisco: Jossey-Bass Publishers, pp. 63–71.

Treiman, Donald J. 1970a. "Industrialization and Social Stratification." In *Social Stratification: Research and Theory for the 1970s*, edited by E. Q. Lauman. Indianapolis: Bobbs-Merrill.

———. 1970b. "Industrialization and Social Stratification." *Sociological Inquiry* 40:207–34.

Treiman, Donald J., and Harry B. G. Ganzeboom. 2000. "The Fourth Generation of Comparative Stratification Research." In *The International Handbook of Sociology*, edited by S. P. Quah and A. Sales. Thousand Oaks, CA: Sage Publications, pp. 123–50.

Tronu, Paola. 2001. "Socializzazione e Influenza Politica fra Le Generazioni." In *La Politica Acerba. Saggi sull'Identità Civica Dei Giovani*, edited by G. Bettin Lattes. Rubbettino: Soveria Mannelli, pp. 73–106.

Trow, Martin. 1961. "The Second Transformation of American Secondary Education." *International Journal of Comparative Sociology* 2:144–65.

———. 1972. "The Expansion and Transformation of Higher Education." *International Review of Education* 18:61–84.

———. 1974. "Passage D'un Enseignement Supérieur d'Élite à un Enseignement Supérieur de Masse: Les Problèmes Soulevés." In *Politique de l'Enseignement Supérieur*, edited by OECD. Paris: OECD.

Tsai, Shu-Ling. 1992. "Social Change and Status Attainment in Taiwan: Comparisons of Ethnic Groups." In *International Perspectives On Education and Society*, vol. 2, edited by A. Yogev. Greenwich, CT: JAI Press, pp. 225–56.

———. 2001. "Gendered Expectations: Family Norms of Higher Education for Boys and Girls in Taiwan." Paper presented at the meeting of *ISA-RC28*, Berkeley.

Tsai, Shu-Ling, and Hei-Yuan Chiu. 1993. "Changes in Educational Stratification in Taiwan." In *Persistent Inequality: Changing Educational Attainment in*

Thirteen Countries, edited by Y. Shavit and H. P. Blossfeld. Boulder, CO: Westview Press, pp. 193–227.

Tsai, Shu-Ling, Hill Gates, and Hei-Yuan Chiu. 1994. "Schooling Taiwan's Women: Educational Attainment in the Mid-Twentieth Century." *Sociology of Education* 67:243–63.

Tsuburai, Kaori, and Takuya Hayashi. 2000. "Chi'iki Ido kara mita Shugaku Shushoku Kodo (Educational and Occupational Mobility from the Perspective of Geographical Mobility)." In *Nihon no Kaiso Shisutemu 3: Sengo Nihon no Kyoiku Shakai (Stratification System in Japan 3: Educational Credentials in the Postwar Stratification System),* edited by Hiroyuki Kondo. Tokyo: University of Tokyo Press, pp. 57–76.

Tsurumi, Patricia E. 1977. *Japanese Colonial Education in Taiwan, 1895–1945.* Cambridge, MA: Harvard University Press.

Turi, Paolo. 1982. *Università: Le Fasi di una Crisi.* Opera Universitaria: Florence.

Turner, Ralph H. 1960. "Sponsored and Contest Mobility and the School System." *American Sociological Review* 25:855–67.

Tversky, Amos, and Daniel Kahneman. 1986. "The Framing of Decisions and the Psychology of Choice." In *Rational Choice,* edited by J. Elster. Oxford: Blackwell, pp. 123–41.

UNESCO. 1999. *Statistical Yearbook.*

United Kingdom, Department for Education and Science. 1987. *Higher Education: Meeting the Challenge.* London: HMSO.

United Kingdom/England, Department for Education (DfE). 1993. *Statistical Bulletin 8/93:* Table 2(i) and Table 6. Darlington: Department for Education.

———. 1994. *Statistical Bulletin 4/94:* Table 8c. Darlington: Department for Education.

United Kingdom/England, Department of Education and Skills (DfES). 2004. *The Future of Higher Education Student Funding.* London: Department for Education and Skills.

United States, Bureau of the Census. 2002. *Statistical Abstracts of the United States.* Washington, D.C.: U.S. Government Printing Office.

United States, College Board. 1999. *Trends in Student Aid: 1999.* Washington, D.C.: College Board Publications.

United States, Department of Education. 1997. *Title IX: 25 Years of Progress.* Available online: http://www.ed.gov/pubs/TitleIX.

United States, National Center for Education Statistics (NCES). 1995. *Digest of Education Statistics.* Washington, D.C.: U.S. Government Printing Office.

———. 1997. *The Condition of Education 1997.* Washington, D.C.: U.S. Government Printing Office.

———. 1998. *Student Financing of Undergraduate Education: 1995–1996, with an Essay on Student Loans.* Statistical Analysis Report, NCES 98-076, prepared by L. Berkner and A. G. Malizio, U.S. Department of Education, Washington, D.C.

———. 2000. *Trends in Undergraduate Borrowing: Federal Student Loans 1989–90, 1992–93, and 1995–96*. Statistical Analysis Report, NCES 2000-151, prepared by L. Berkner and L. Bobbitt, U.S. Department of Education, Washington, D.C.

———. 2002a. *Digest of Education Statistics*. Washington, D.C.: U.S. Government Printing Office.

———. 2002b. *Persistence and Attainment of Beginning Students with Pell Grants*. Postsecondary Education Descriptive Analysis Report, NCES 2002-169, prepared by C. C. Wei and L. Horn., U.S. Department of Education, Washington, D.C.

———. 2003a. *Community College Students: Goals, Academic Preparation, and Outcomes*. Postsecondary Education Descriptive Analysis Report, NCES 2003-164, prepared by G. Hoachlander, A. C. Sikora, L. Horn, and C. D. Carroll, U.S. Department of Education, Washington, D.C.

———. 2003b. *Postsecondary Attainment, Attendance, Curriculum, and Performance: Selected Results from the NELS 88-2000 Postsecondary Education Transcript Study*. E.D. Tabs, NCES 2003-394, prepared by C. Adelman, B. Daniel, I. Berkovits, and J. Owings, U.S. Department of Education, Washington, D.C.

———. 2005. *Gender Differences in Participation and Completion of Undergraduate Education and How They Have Changed Over Time*. NCES 2005-169, prepared by K. Peter, L. Horn, and C. D. Carroll, U.S. Department of Education, Washington, D.C.

Vaira, Massimiliano. 2001. "Le Radici Istituzionali della Riforma Universitaria." *Rassegna Italiana di Sociologia* 42:625–53.

Vallet, Louis-André. 2004. "The Dynamics of Inequality of Educational Opportunity in France: Change in the Association Between Social Background and Education in Thirteen Five-Year Birth Cohorts (1908–1972)." Paper presented at the meeting of RC28, New York.

Van De Werfhorst, Herman G., Alice Sullivan, and Sin Yee Cheung. 2003. "Social Class, Ability and Choice of Subject in Secondary and Tertiary Education in Britain." *British Educational Research Journal* 29:41–62.

Van den Berg, M. J. M. (ed.). 2000. *Onderwijsbeleid Sinds de Jaren Zeventig*. Werkdocument bij het Advies Deregulering met Beleid, Studie naar Effecten van Deregulering en Autonomievergroting. The Hague: Onderwijsraad.

Van den Broek, J. F. L. H., and M. J. M. Voeten. 2002. *Wisselstroom. Een Analyse van de Bèta-instroom in het Wetenschappelijk Onderwijs in de Periode 1980-2000's*. Gravenhage: SDU Beleidsgerichte Studies Hoger Onderwijs en Wetenschapsbeleid.

Van Kemenade, J. A. (ed.). 1981. *Onderwijs: Bestel en Beleid*. Groningen: Wolters-Noordhoff Bv.

Večerník, J. 2001. *Earnings Disparities in the Czech Republic: Evidence of the Past Decade and Cross-National Comparison.* Working Paper no. 373, May 2001, the William Davidson Institute, University of Michigan Business School.

Vogel, J., L. G. Andersson, U. Davidsson, and L. Häll. 1988. *Inequality in Sweden: Trends and Current Situation Report no. 58.* Stockholm: Statistics Sweden.

Volansky, Ami. 1996. "Opening the Gates: Democratization of Higher Education." In *The Third Leap: Change and Reform in the Educational System During the 1990s,* edited by O. Brandeis. Jerusalem: Ministry of Education and Culture, pp. 70–82.

Vývojová ročenka školství v České republice 1989/90–1998/99 (Yearbook of education development in the Czech Republic 1989/90–1998/99). 1999. Praha: ÚIV (Institute for Information in Education).

Walters, Pamela Barnhouse. 2000. "The Limits of Growth: School Expansion and School Reform in Historical Perspective." In *Handbook of the Sociology of Education,* edited by M. T. Hallinan. New York: Kluwer, pp. 241–61.

Weerts, D. J., and C. F. Conrad. 2002. "Desegregation in Higher Education." In *Higher Education in the United States: An Encyclopedia,* edited by J. F. Forest and K. Kinser. Santa Barbara, CA: ABC-CLIO, pp. 161–68.

Weidman, J. C., and N. Park (eds.). 2000. *Higher Education in Korea.* New York: Falmer Press.

Wieringen, A. M. L. (ed.). 1995. *Autonomievergroting en Deregulering in het Onderwijs,* Onderwijskundig lexicon. Alphen aan den Rijn: Samson H.D. Tjeenk Willink.

Wilson, R. 1994. "The Participation of African Americans in American Higher Education." In *Minorities in Higher Education,* edited by M. J. Justiz, R. Wilson, and L. G. Bjork. Phoenix: American Council on Education and Oryx Press, pp. 195–209.

Wissenschaftsrat. 1993. *10 Thesen zur Hochschulpolitik.* Köln: Wissenschaftsrat.

———. 2001. *Entwicklung der Fachstudiendauer an Universitäten von 1990 bis 1998.* Köln: Wissenschaftsrat.

———. 2005. *Entwicklung der Fachstudiendauer an Universitäten von 1999 bis 2003.* Köln: Wissenschaftsrat.

Wolf, A. 2002. *Does Education Matter: Myths About Education and Economic Growth.* London: Penguin.

Wolter, Stefan C. 2002. *Das Tertiäre Bildungswesen in der Schweiz. Zusammenfassung der Grundlagendokumentation zuhanden der OECD Experten.* Bern: EDK, pp. 1–10.

Wong, R. Sin-Kwok. 1998. "Multidimensional Influences of Family Environment in Education: The Case of Socialist Czechoslovakia." *Sociology of Education* 71:1–22.

Yaish, Meir. 2000. "Old Debate, New Evidence—Class Mobility Trends in Israeli Society, 1974–1991." *European Sociological Review* 16:159–83.

Yang, Ying. 1994. "Reform of Secondary Education for the Equality of Educational Opportunities." *Chinese Education and Society* 27:42–55.

Yogev, Abraham. 2000. "The Stratification of Israeli Universities: Implications for Higher Education Policy." *Higher Education* 40:183–201.

Yorke, M., J. Ozga, and L. Sukhnandan. 1997. *Undergraduate Non-completion in Higher Education in England*. Bristol: HEFCE.

Yule, G. U. 1912. "On the Methods of Measuring Association Between Two Attributes." *Journal of the Royal Statistical Society Series A—Statistics in Society* 75/76:579–642.

Yung, Kirby Chaur-shin, and Frederick G. Welch. 1991. "Vocational and Technical Education." In *The Confucian Continuum: Educational Modernization in Taiwan*, edited by D. Smith. New York: Praeger, pp. 221–76.

Zaslavsky, Victor. 1982. *The Neo-Stalinist State: Class, Ethnicity, and Consensus in Soviet Society*. Armonk: M.E. Sharpe.

INDEX

Abitur, university entrance qualification in Germany, 243, 246–47, 248–49, 251, 253, *258*
academic achievement, in U.S. achievement model, 178, 180, 187, 188
access to higher education, and differentiation and market structure, 22–25, *23*, *25*
achievement model, for dependent variables (U.S.), 178, *185*
Act on Academic Education of 1960 (Netherlands), 269
Act on Fees of Vocational College of 1981 (Netherlands), 273
Act on Harmonization of College Fees of 1988 (Netherlands), 272
Act on Higher Education and Scientific Research of 1993 (Netherlands), 269
Act on Higher Vocational Education of 1984 (WHBO, Netherlands), 268, 269
Act on Secondary Education of 1967 (Netherlands), 268
Act on Vocational Dual Training of 1966 (Netherlands), 270
admissions criteria, 7–8; Australia, 359–60; Czech Republic, 377; France, 221; Germany, 243, 246; Great Britain, 199; Israel, 40, 41, *48*, 49–50; Italy, 403, 409, 411; Japan, 64, 67; Korea, 89; Netherlands, 270–71; Russia, 297; Sweden, 122, 124, 137; Switzerland, 324–26; Taiwan, 147; United States, 167, 432n10
advanced education tier, Australia, 353, 354
affirmative action, 431n5

age of student, Switzerland, 340
Age Participation Index (API, Great Britain), 198
ALLBUS (general social survey, Germany), 251, *421*
apprenticeships: in Germany, 248, 249; in Switzerland, 333, 337, 344
apprenticeship school, Italy, 401
attendance, 10–11; and eligibility, 15–17, *16*; and market structure and differentiation, 22–25, *23*, *25*
attestat, high-school diploma, Russia, 295
Australia, 34, 351–73, 437–38; conclusions, 372–73; current study and school sector, 358–60, *368*; data and measures, 360–62, *421*; development of higher education, 352–54; eligibility for higher education, 363–65; results, participation in higher education, 365–72; socioeconomic inequalities and student fees, 357–58; student fees and assistance for study, 354–57
Australian postsecondary institutions: Australian National University, 351, 352; Group of Eight, 352, 425n2, 437n1; University of Adelaide, 352; University of Melbourne, 352; University of New South Wales, 352; University of Queensland, 352; University of Sydney, 352; University of Tasmania, 352; University of Western Australia, 352
Australian Vice Chancellor's Committee, 438n6
autonomy of universities, Italy, 402, 406

473

baccalauréat, in France, 221, 225, 228
bagrut, Israeli exams, 40
baseline model, for dependent variables (U.S.), 178, *185*
Berthoin law of 1959 (France), 225
Berufsakademien, German colleges, 245, 252
Berufsmatur, vocational matriculation, Switzerland, 325
Berufsprüfungen, Switzerland, 322, 333, 341
binary systems, 5, 12, 19–22, *20*, 32–34. *See also* France; Germany; Great Britain; Netherlands; Russia; Switzerland
Bologna declaration, 377, 378, 438n1
brain drain, in Germany, 242
brevet de technicien supérieur (BTS), 12, 222, 225
British Birth Survey, 203
British Cohort Study (BCS70), 202, *421*
Brown v. Board of Education (U.S.), 172

Casati Law (Italy), 440n1
case-oriented comparative research, 14
CASMIN educational schema, 13; France, 227, 228–29; Germany, 252, 259; Great Britain, 207; Israel, 46; Italy, 408; Japan, 74, 76; Korea, 102; Russia, 301; Sweden, 122; Switzerland, 330, 332; United States, 178
Catholic schools, Australia, 359, 370–71
change in inequality, 16, *16*, 17, *18*
child welfare benefits, in Netherlands, 271–72
Chinese, National Party (KMT) rule in Taiwan, 143–46, 163
class, social. *See* socioeconomic background
class differentials hypothesis, 384–85
classe préparatoire, in France, 221–22
classes of father's occupation, 13–14. *See also* father's occupational class
class formation in postcommunist countries, 383–84
classifications: of countries by mode of differentiation, 11–13, *12*; and variables, 10–14
class inequalities, in educational progression, 8
client-seeking behavior, 7–8

Cohort of Students in Secondary Education (VOCL, Netherlands), 277, *422*
cohorts, *15*; Australia, 360, 363, 364; Czech Republic, 387; France, 228, 229, 235; Germany, 253, 263; Great Britain, 203–4, *208*; Israel, 45–46; Italy, 407, *409*; Japan, 74–75, 77; Korea, 88, 101, 102–4; Netherlands, 266, 273, *274*, 291; Russia, 301, 303, 305, 317; Sweden, 122, 123, 126–34; Switzerland, 330, 331, 333, 341, 343, 348; Taiwan, 147, 152, 157–58, 159; United States, 179, 181–82, 186, 188
collaborative comparative methodology, 9–10, 14–15
College for All campaigns, 7
colleges: of advanced education (CAEs, Australia), 353, 361; *Berufsakademien*, Germany, 245, 252; Israel, 39, 41, 42, 43; junior, Japan, 64, 66, 69, 72–73; nonuniversity institutions of higher education, Czech Republic, 378–79; regional, Sweden, 117. *See also* technical colleges
common school, Taiwan, 142
Communist Party Central Committee, Czech Republic, 374–75
Communist Party of Soviet Union (CPSU), parental membership in: Czech Republic, 383; Russia, 302, 306, 309, 313, 314
community colleges, in U.S., 165, 166–67
comparative case-study research, 14–15
comparative model, for dependent variables (U.S.), 178
comparative stratification research, fourth generation, 9
comprehensive schools, Great Britain, 218
compulsory education: France, 225; Germany, 434n4; Great Britain, 202; Italy, 402, 419; Korea, 89; Netherlands, 270; Russia, 295; Sweden, 114; Switzerland, 337; Taiwan, 142, 144
conflict theorists, 148
consumer demand, 6–7, 13
cost-sharing principle: Czech Republic, 378, 398. *See also* Higher Education Contribution Scheme (HECS, Australia)

Council for National Academic Awards (Great Britain), 196
countries, modes of differentiation, 11–13, *12*
cultural capital. *See* socioeconomic background
cultural reproduction theory, 383
Cuore (De Amicis), 400, 402, 419
Czech Republic, 34, 374–99, 438–40; accessibility and class inequality, 381–82; Communist Party limits to growth, 374–75; compared to Korea, 87; compared to Netherlands, 382; conclusions, 397–99; data and strategy of analysis, 385–87, *421*; reform, first stage, academic freedom, 375–78; reform, second stage, financing barriers, 378–79; reform, third stage, financial crisis and blocked reforms, 379–81; results, trends in opportunity and participation, 387–90; testing hypotheses about development of inequality, 390–97; theoretical perspectives, 382–85

datasets used, 421–22
De Amicis, Edmondo, 400, 419
decentralization, in Czech Republic, 397
decision model for educational routes, 118–21
Department for Education and Science (DES, Great Britain), 198
descriptive statistics. *See* statistics, descriptive
De Vecchi, Cesare Maria, 402
differentiation, 1; and inclusion, 19–22; institutional, and stratification, 4–6; and market structure and access, 22–25, *23, 25*. *See also* modes of differentiation
diploma di laurea, Italy, 405
diversification, in Czech Republic, 398
diversified systems, 5, 13, 19–22, *20*, 30–32. *See also* Israel; Japan; Korea; Sweden; Taiwan; United States
diversion, 2, 5, 28
dual-track system, Czech Republic, 381
DUT (*diplôme universitaire technologique*, France), 12, 222, 225

écoles primaires supérieures, in France, 224

Education, Training, and Occupations Survey (FQP, France), 221, 227, 228, *230, 421*
Education Acts (Great Britain), 196–97
educational inequality, and tertiary market structure, 6–8
educational routes, decision model for, 118–21
educational transition model, 149–50
effectively maintained inequality (EMI), Taiwan, 150, 161
EGP class schema, 13; Australia, 360, 363; France, 227, 228; Israel, 46; Italy, 407; Korea, 102; Netherlands, 279; Taiwan, 152; United States, 178. *See also* Goldthorpe class schema
11-*plus* exam, Great Britain, 201–2, 434n11
eligibility for higher education, 10–11, 19; and attendance, 15–18, *16, 18*; Australia, 363–65; France, 224–25, *232*; Great Britain, 205, 209–11, *210*; Israel, 46, 49–50; Netherlands, 275; Russia, 306–8; Sweden, 123; Switzerland, 330–31, 342; Taiwan, 154–55
England. *See* Great Britain
English/Welsh system, 204–5
enrollments, 7; Australia, 353–54; Czech Republic, *376*; France, 224, *225*; Germany, 243; Great Britain, 197–98; Israel, 39, 43; Italy, 403, *404*, 405; Japan, 64, 69, 71–73; Korea, 91–93, 95; Netherlands, *268*; Russia, 297–99; Sweden, *115*, 115–16; Switzerland, 327, *328*; Taiwan, 140–41; United States, 166, *167*
Equivalent National Tertiary Entrance Rank (ENTER, Australia), 361, 371–72, *372*
Erikson-Goldthorpe-Portocarero (EGP) schema. *See* EGP class schema
ethnicity comparisons: Israel, 47, 49, 50, 427n3; Taiwan, 147, 151, 155–63; United States, 171–72, 175, 178, 186–88, 190
European Higher Education, 438n1
exogenous expansion, 6
expansion of higher education, 1–2; demand-driven, 6–7; and differentiation

and inequality, 19, *21*; and educational stratification, 15–19; exogenous, 6; and stratification, 3–4

Fachhochschulen, 5, 10, 12, 13, 241; compared to university, 242, 244–45, 249–50, 262–63
family income: Japan, 86; Korea, 111–12
fascism, in Italy, 401–2
father's occupational class, 13; Australia, 363; Czech Republic, 386, *389*, 390, 392–97; France, 227, 228, 231; Germany, 253, 259; Great Britain, 209–11, 214–18; Israel, 46, 50, 53; Italy, 407, 409, 411; Japan, 74, 77, 79–80, 82, 85; Korea, 99, 101–11; Netherlands, 273, 279, 284, 292; Russia, 301, 306, 317; Switzerland, 340; Taiwan, 147, 155, 161, 164; United States, 178, 181–86. *See also* socioeconomic background
financial aid for students: Australia, 354–55; United States, 166, 171, 186
financing of institutions. *See* funding of tertiary institutions
first tier of tertiary education: attendance defined, 11; status-seeking, 7–8
foreign university extensions, in Israel, 42, 43, 58
fourth generation of comparative stratification research, 9
FQP (Education, Training, and Occupations Survey, France), 221, 227, 228, 230, *421*
France, 33, 220–39, 434; allocations for postsecondary students, 223–24; conclusions, 238–39; data, 227–28, *421*; degrees of selectivity, 221–22; educational system evolution, 224–26; fields of study, 223; gender differences, 225–26, 229–30, 238; method, 228–29; postsecondary education developmental impacts, 226–27; postsecondary education system, 221; results, 229–38; size of institutions, 223
free faculty, Sweden, 115, 116
French National Institute of Statistics and Economic Surveys (INSEE), 221
French postsecondary institutions: Ecole des Hautes Etudes Commerciales, 222;

Ecole Nationale d'Administration, 222; Ecole Nationale des Ponts et Chaussées, 222; Ecole Polytechnique, 222; Ecoles Normales Supérieures, 222
functionalist view, 4
funding of tertiary institutions, 7, 13, 22–25, *23*, *25*; Australia, 351–52, 354–58; Czech Republic, 378–81, 399; France, 221, 223–24; Germany, 245–46; Great Britain, 197, 199–200; Israel, 40; Japan, 65; Korea, 90, 96; Netherlands, 271–73; Russia, 294–95; Sweden, 120, 138–39; Switzerland, 324; Taiwan, 146; United States, 170–71. *See also* market structures

gap year, in Germany, 243
gender comparisons, 25–27; Australia, 363, 364–70; Czech Republic, 381, 387–88, 390–92, 395–96; France, 225–26, 229–30, 238; Germany, 253–62, 265; Great Britain, 209–11, 214–18; Israel, 49, 50, 53, 61–62; Italy, 406, 407, 411–15, 419; Japan, 64, 65, 77–81, 83–85; Korea, 91–93, 97–99, 101–4, 106, 109, 111–12; Netherlands, 275–76, 281, 284–85, 287, 291; Russia, 301, 306–18; Sweden, 135, *136*; Switzerland, 327, 329–30, 335–37, 341–48; Taiwan, 140, 142, 147, 153, *154*, 155–59, 163; United States, 173–74, 175, 188–89, 190
general secondary school (*srednee obshchee*, Russia), 295
General Social Survey (GSS, U.S.), 175–76, 177, 178, 179, *422*
General Social Surveys (JGSS, Japan), 73, *421*
Gentile, Giovanni, 401
German general social survey (ALLBUS), 251, *421*
German postsecondary institutions, University of Berlin, 242
German reunification, 242
German Science Council (Wissenschaftsrat), 244
German Socio-Economic Panel (GSOEP), 251–52, *421*, 435n7
Germany, 33, 240–65, 434–35; class inequality change over time, 250–51; class inequality in postsecondary out-

comes, 257–62; conclusions, 263–65; data and methods, 251–53, 421; developments since late 1960s, 242–44; *Fachhochschule* compared to university, 242, 244–45, 249–50, 262–63; inequalities declining, 253–57; inequalities in access to higher education, 246–48; institutional growth and diversification, 244–46; institutional options beyond *Abitur*, 248–49; labor market entry after secondary school, 250; vocational training, 249
Gesamthochschulen, German conprehensive institutions, 241
GI Bill (U.S.), 166
Goldthorpe class schema: Germany, 252; Great Britain, 207; Switzerland, 332. *See also* EGP class schema
Gonella, Guido, 402
government influence on or regulation of education: Australia, 351, 354, 355; Czech Republic, 374–81; France, 225; Germany, 241; Great Britain, 196; Israel, 40, 41–42; Italy, 401–6; Japan, 66, 70–72, 85; Korea, 90–91; Netherlands, 269, 270; Russia, 296–97, 299–300; Sweden, 114–16; Switzerland, 321–22, 323–24; Taiwan, 141, 142–46, 156, 164; United States, 165, 171
grandes écoles, in France, 221–22, 223, 226, 227, 228, 236, 237, 434n1
Great Britain, 32, 195–219, 433–34; analyses, 207–9; binary period, postwar reform, 196–97; binary system, dissolution of, 197–99; conclusions, 216–19; data, 202–4, 421; definitions and variables, 204; degree-granting institutions and universities, 206; funding the expanded system, 199–200; parental education, 206–7; postsecondary education, 205–6; results, eligibility for higher education, 209–11; results, postsecondary educational attainment, 211–14; results, qualifications obtained from degree programs, 214–16; secondary education system changes, 201–2; social class origin, 207; tertiary education, eligibility for, 204–5; tertiary education, upper and lower, 204

Gross Domestic Product, Switzerland, 341, 346
Group of Eight, Australia, 352, 425n2, 437n1
Grutter v. Bollinger (U.S.), 172
Gui, Luigi, 402
Gymnasium: in Germany, 246, 248; in Switzerland, 325

Haby law of 1975 (France), 225
Hauptschule, in Germany, 247
Higher Education Act (U.S.), 171
Higher Education Acts (Czech Republic), 376–77, 378, 379, 380
Higher Education Contribution Scheme (HECS, Australia), 354–57, 371, 372, 378
Higher Education Funding Councils for England, Scotland, and Wales, 200
Higher Education Statistics Agency (Great Britain), 433n3
higher vocational colleges (HBO, Netherlands), 268, 269, 272, 273, 284
High School and Beyond (HS&B), 176, 177, 178, 422, 432n12
Hogsköla, Sweden, 116, 117, 120, 138
höhere Fachprüfungen, Switzerland, 322, 333, 341
Höhere Technische Lehranstalten (HTL, Switzerland), 322
Hopwood v. Texas (U.S.), 172
Humboldtian reform in Germany, 242

immigration from Soviet Union to Israel, 41, 42
incentives for individuals, 6
inclusion, 2, 5, 19–22, 28
individual level model, 118–21
Industrial Training Boards (Great Britain), 196–97
industrial university, Korea, 94
inequality: change in, 16, *16*, 17, *18*; in eligibility, 16, *16*; measures of, 13–14; by mode of differentiation, 19–22, *21*
INSEE (French National Institute of Statistics and Economic Surveys), 221
institutional differentiation, and stratification, 4–6
International Social Science Surveys (Australia), 360

International Social Survey Program: Australia, 360; Module on Social Inequality (ISSP-99, Czech Republic), 385, *421*, 439n5
International Survey of Economic Attitudes (Australia), 360
Israel, 30–31, 39–62, 426–27; BA-granting institutions, 53; conclusions, 58–62; data, 45, *421*; education system, 40; immigration from Soviet Union, 41, 42; matriculation, eligibility for higher education, 49–50; obtaining an undergraduate degree, 58; postsecondary education, 50–53; results, 49; theory and hypotheses, 43–45; transformation, 41–43; universities, 40–41, 53–58; variables, 45–47
Israeli postsecondary institutions: Bar-Ilan University, 40; Ben Gurion University, 40; Hebrew University, 40; Open University, 41; Technion, 40; Tel Aviv University, 40; University of Haifa, 40; Weizmann Institute of Science, 41
istituti professionali, Italy, 403
Italian mobility survey of 1985, 407
Italy, 34–35, 400–423, 440–42; conclusions, 418–20; data and methods, 406–8, *421*; history of education in, 400–406; results, macroanalysis, 408–10; results, microanalysis, 411–18
IUT (*instituts universitaires technologiques*, France), 10, 13, 221, 222, 223, 225

Japan, 31, 63–86, 427–28; conclusions, 83–86; data, variables, and methods, 73–75, *421*; empirical findings, 75–83; entrance exams, 64; historical development of postsecondary education, 67–73; Ministry of Education, 66, 70–72, 85; postsecondary educational system, 63–67
Japanese General Social Surveys (JGSS), 73, *421*, 427n4
Japanese postsecondary institutions, University of Tokyo, 63, 67, 68
junior colleges: Japan, 64, 66, 69, 72–73; Korea, 94–95; Taiwan, 140, 144

Kingdom of Sardinia, 440n1
Korea, 31, 87–112, 428–29; class and gender inequalities, 97–99; compared to Norway and Czech Republic, 87; compared to Sweden, 98; conclusions, 110–12; data, 100–101, *422*; growth of junior colleges and universities, 94–95; higher education changes, 90–91; higher education participation increases, 91–93; higher education system features, 89–90, 428n2; models, 99–100; private and public institutions for higher education, 95–96; results, 102–10; stratified system of higher education, 96–97; variables, 101–2
Korean Labor and Income Panel Study (KLIPS), 100–101, *422*

laurea, Italy, 402, 403, 408, 414, 417–18
law on promotion of universities (Switzerland), 324
law on vocational training (Switzerland), 322, 324
licei, nonvocational high schools in Italy, 400, 401, 403
life-long learning, 7
logit/logistic regressions, models, and estimates: Australia, 361–62, *364*, *366–68*, *371*, *372*; Czech Republic, 386, *390–97*, *391*, *393–97*, 398; France, 228, *232*, *233*, *234*, *236–37*; Germany, 251, *258*, *260*, *262*, *263*; Great Britain, *210*, *212–13*, 215, 216; Israel, 48, 50, *51*, *52*, 53, *54–57*, 59, 60; Italy, *410*, 411, *412*, *416*, 417; Japan, 74, *77*, *78*, *80*, 81, *82*; Korea, 99–100, *105*, *106*, 107–10, *108*, *110*; Netherlands, 280, *286*, *288*, 289, *290*; Russia, *307*, *308*, *310*, *312*, *314*, *318*; Sweden, 126, *127–28*, *130–31*; Switzerland, 331, *334*, *336*, *338–39*, *343*, *344*; Taiwan, 153, *155*, 156–61, *157*, *160*, *162*; United States, 177, 179, *182–85*. See *also* statistics, descriptive
logit models of education, 425n4
logit regressions, 10, 13
log-odds statistics, 13–14; Italy, 408; Netherlands, 280, *282–83*
Longitudinal Surveys of Australian Youth (LSAY), 360–61, *421*
lycée, in France, 224

Mannheim Centre for European Social Research (MZES), 240
Mare model, 3, 4, 99, 149, 169, 274, 275
market-based systems, 2
market structure for tertiary institutions, 6–8, 13, 22–25, *23*, *25*
market structures: Australia, 351–52, 353–54; Germany, 245; Israel, 42; Japan, 65; Korea, 90, 95–96, 111–12; Netherlands, 268–69; Switzerland, 321–23, 327; Taiwan, 145; United States, 166, 168, 170. See also funding of tertiary institutions
mass education, 2, 7
mass university, 242, 244, 403
matriculation examinations, 19; Israeli bagrut, 40, 41
Matura certificate, Switzerland, 324–25, 335, 340, 342–44
maturità diploma, Italy, 403, 409, 411, 414
Maximally Maintained Inequality (MMI), 3–4, 15–19; Czech Republic, 398; France, 226; Israel, 43–44, 61; Korea, 98; Russia, 299; Taiwan, 149, 150; United States, 174, 186, 189
men in tertiary education: advantages in educational attainment, 26. See also gender comparisons
methodology, 9–10
MMI. See Maximally Maintained Inequality
modes of differentiation, 11–13, *12*, 19–22, *21*
multinomial transition model, 98
Multi-Purpose Family Survey (Italy), 407, *421*, 441n9

Napoleon, 221
National Child Development Study (NCDS, Great Britain), 202, *421*
National Chinese Party (KMT) rule in Taiwan, 143–46, 163
National Council of Universities (VSNU, Netherlands), 269
National Educational Longitudinal Study of 1988 (NELS), 176, 178, *422*, 432n12
National Institute of Statistics (Italy), 407
National Longitudinal Survey of High School Class of 1972 (NLS-72), 176, 177, *422*, 432n12

National Science Council (Taiwan), 151
Nazi government, 401–2
Netherlands, 33, 266–93, 435; admission rules, 270–71; compared to Czech Republic, 382; conclusions, 291–93; data and variables, 277–80, *422*; degrees, 267; entering tertieary education, 285–87; expectations, 273–77; highest level attended, 287–91; institutional arrangements, 267–69; responsibilities, 269–70; results, 280–85; scholarships and fees, 271–73
Netherlands postsecondary institutions: ICS, 266; Netherlands Inspectorate of Education, 266
New Zealand, 356
nomenclatura, Czech Republic, 397
nontraditional students, 7
Norway, compared to Korea, 87
numerus clausus system: Germany, 251, 265; Italy, 401; Sweden, 115, 120, 124–25

odds ratios, 439n10
Organization for Economic Cooperation and Development (OECD), 13; Australian data, 356; Czech Republic data, 438n2, 439n3; Italian data, 418; Korean data, 87, 428n1
organization theory, 4

parental education, 13, *423*; Australia, 360, 361, 363, 364–68; Czech Republic, 390–99; France, 228–29, 231; Germany, 250, 253, 254, 257, 261; Great Britain, 206–7, 209–11, 214–18; Israel, 46, 50, 53; Italy, 407–8, 413–14, 417–19; Japan, 74, 76–85; Korea, 99, 101–12; Netherlands, 280, 281, 285, 287, 291, 292–93; Russia, 301, 306–10, 316–17; Sweden, 122, 126; Switzerland, 332, 335, 337, 340, 342, 345–47; Taiwan, 151–52, 155, 158, 161; United States, 178, 179–80
PCS nomenclature, France, 227
Pell Grant Program (U.S.), 171
perestroika era in Russia, 297–98, 303, 308
Perinatal Mortality Survey (PMS, Great Britain), 203
persistent inequality, 29

Persistent Inequality (Shavit and Blossfeld), 29
PIVOT Rijksarchiefdienst, 268
polytechnics, 10; Great Britain, 197, 198, 200, 206, 425n2
Polytechnics and Colleges Funding Council (Great Britain), 200
positional good, 30
Presidential Decree on College and University Student Quotas (Korea), 90
private funding of tertiary education, 6–8, 13, 22–25, *23, 25*. *See also* funding of tertiary institutions
privately funded institutions, client-seeking, 7
privatization, conclusions on, 28
psychometric test (Israel), 41, 42
PTU (*professional'noe-tekhnicheskoe uchilishche*, Russia), 295
public financial support, compared to private financial support, 7–8, 13. *See also* funding of tertiary institutions

qualitative differentiation, 4, 44
qualitative diversification, Switzerland, 329, 347

race. *See* ethnicity comparisons
rational action theory, 383–84, 399
rationality, 383
Realschule, in Germany, 248
Red Cross, 326
regional colleges, Sweden, 117
regressions, 10
relative inequalities, 29, 30
relative risk aversion, 418, 419
religion: Catholic schools, Australia, 359, 370–71; Roman Catholic Church, Italy, 401; theological seminaries in Germany, 245
Robbins Committee Report of 1963 (Great Britain), 196
Roman Catholic Church, Italy, 401
rural origins *vs.* Moscow origins, in Russia, 306, 309, 313, 314
Russia, 33, 294–320, 435–36; conclusions, 316–20; data and analyses, 300–301, *422*; education system under Soviets, 295–96; enrollments, 297–99; higher and postsecondary specialized education, 296–97; models and variables, 301–3; reforms and institutional change, 299–300; results, attaining a university (VUZ) degree, 315–16; results, descriptive statistics, 303–6, *304*; results, eligibility for postsecondary education, 306–8; results, entry to postsecondary schooling, 309–10; results, entry to specialized postsecondary schooling, 313–14; results, entry to university (VUZ), 311–12
Russian immigrants to Israel, 41, 42

sandwich students, Great Britain, 433n2
saturation, 3–4, 16–18
School Career and Background of Pupils in Secondary Education (SMVO, Netherlands), 277, 422
School Education Law (Japan), 65
school sector, in Australia, 358–59, 369
schools of applied science, Switzerland, 323, 325
Scottish system, 204–5
scuola complementare, vocational secondary schools, Italy, 401
scuola di avviamento al lavoro, Italy, 401
scuola media, Italy, 414
Second International Adult Literacy Survey (SIALS, Czech Republic), 380, 385, *421*, 439n5
second tier of tertiary education: attendance defined, 10; client-seeking, 7–8; diversion *vs.* inclusion, 5–6
senior vocational education (MBO, Netherlands), 269, 273, 280–83
senmon gakko, Japanese technical schools, 67
shadow education, in Korea, 111
social class origin, *423*
social control theory, 5
social exclusivity, 410
socialist transformation hypothesis, 382, 383
social origin. *See* socioeconomic background
Social Stratification and Social Mobility (SSM) National Surveys (Japan), 73, *421*, 427n4
socioeconomic background, *423*; Australia, 357–58, 359–60, 364–73; Czech Republic, 380–82, 385, 388, 392–93,

398, 399; France, 224–25, 231, 235; Germany, 246–50, 253–57, 259, 262, 264; Great Britain, 207, 214–18; Israel, 49; Italy, 406–10, 414–17, 419; Japan, 79, 83; Korea, 97–99; Netherlands, 274, 277, 284, 289, 293; Russia, 303, 306–16, 319; Sweden, 119, 122–23, 124, 126, 129, 137; Switzerland, 329, 332, 335–37, 342, 346–47; Taiwan, 148, 150, 152, 156; United States, 168–70, 174–75, 179–86. *See also* father's occupational class
socioeconomic inequality, 4
South Korea. *See* Korea
special training schools, Japan, 65, 66, 71–72
sponsored mobility system, Italy, 401
SSUZ (*Srednee Spetsial'noe Uchebnoe Zavedenie*, Russia), 10, 294, 295, 297, 302, 306, 313–14, 425n1, 435n1
Stafford Loan Program (U.S.), 171
statistics, descriptive: Australia, *362*; France, *230*; Germany, *258*; Great Britain, *208*; Israel, *47*; Italy, *404*, *408*, *409*; Japan, *68*, *76*; Korea, *103*; Netherlands, *279*; Russia, 303–6, *304*; Sweden, *115*, *125*; Switzerland, *328*; Taiwan, *154*. *See also* logit/logistic regressions, models, and estimates
Statistics Sweden, 122
status-seeking behavior, 7–8
stratification: educational, and expansion, 15–19; and expansion of higher education, 3–4; and institutional differentiation, 4–6
STS (*sections de techniciens supérieurs de lycées*, France), 221, 225
student loans: Australia, 354–56; United States, 166, 171
studentships, Australia, 438n5
study allowances, Netherlands, 272
Sun Yat-Sen, 146
Survey on Education and Stratification in Russia (SESR), 300, *304*, 305, 309, *422*
surveys of living conditions (ULF, Sweden), 122, 123, 126, 132
surveys used, 421–22
Sweden, 31, 113–39, 429–30; compared to Korea, 98; conclusions, 137–39; data sources, 121–22, 123, 126, *422*;

educational policy in past hundred years, 114–16, 134–35; expansion and inequality in *numerus clausus* system, 124–25; expansion and long-term change in outcome equality, 126–34; expansion as diversion, creating a binary system, 116–17; free faculty, 115, 116; *Hogsköla*, 116, 117, 120, 138; *numerus clausus* system, 115, 120, 124–25; rolling school reform, 114–16; theoretical considerations on expansion and equality, 117–21; variables, 122–24
Swedish Governmental Commission on Educational Inequality, 121
Swedish level-of-living surveys (LNU), 122, 123, 126, 132
Swedish postsecondary institutions, Stockholm University, 113
Swiss postsecondary institutions: cantonal universities, 321, 323, 324, 326; Ecole Polytechnique, Lausanne, 321, 323; Federal Institute of Technology, Zurich, 321, 323; Swiss Federal Institute of Technology, 323
Swiss Science Council, 322
Switzerland, 34, 321–48, 436–37; analysis procedure, 332–33; conclusions, 346–48; data and methods, 330–31, *422*; development of higher education, assessment of, 327–29; development of tertiary-level education, 321–23; goals, certification, differentiation, and admission, 324–26; legal background and finances, 323–24; results, university education, 342–46; results, vocational schooling, 333–42; theory and hypotheses, 329–30; types of tertiary education, 323, 324–26

Taiwan, 32, 140–64, 430–31; conclusions, 163–64; data, variables, and method, 151–53, *422*; educational transitions, 146–48; expansion effects on equality of educational opportunity, 148–51; historical development of higher education, 142–46, 163; patterns of educational disparity, 153–54; tracking effects on attainment, 158–61; trends in inequality in type of higher education, 161–63; trends in

inequality of attending tertiary education, 156–58; trends in stratification of upper secondary school completion, 154–56; tuition, 430n3
Taiwanese postsecondary institutions: National Taipei University of Technology, 146; National Taiwan University, 143, 145, 146
Taiwan Social Change Survey (TSCS), 151, 422
technical colleges: Japan, 64, 66, 67–68; *technikumy*, Russia, 294
theological seminaries, in Germany, 245
Title IV of Higher Education Act (U.S.), 171, 189
Title VI of Civil Rights Act (U.S.), 172
Title IX of Educational Amendments of 1972 (U.S.), 173, 189
track placement at secondary level, 4; Australia, 359; France, 224, 225; Germany, 247–48, 434n4; Great Britain, 201–2; Israel, 40, 47, 50; Italy, 402; Korea, 89; Netherlands, 270–71, 271, 435n1; Sweden, 116; Taiwan, 147, 152, 161; United States, 150
trajectory maintenance theory, 383
Transformation of Social Structure Survey (TSS-91, Czech Republic), 385, 421, 439n5
transition model, 149–50
transition points, 3
trendless fluctuations, 175, 187
tripartite system: Germany, 255, 263; Great Britain, 201–2, 218

Unified National System, Australia, 353–54
unified systems, 5, 12, 19–22, 20, 34–35. *See also* Australia; Czech Republic; Italy
uniform difference model, 132–34
United States, 32, 165–91, 431–32; affirmative action, 172–73, 187; changes in social stratification, 174–75; characteristics of higher education system, 166–68; conclusions, 189–91; data, 175–76, 422; financing higher education, 170–71; gender, 173–74, 175, 188–89, 190; models, 177–79; race/ethnicity, 171–72, 175, 178, 186–88, 190; results, 179–89; socioeconomic status, 168–70, 174–75, 179–86; stratification in higher education, 168–74
Universities Funding Council (Great Britain), 200
university, as type of tertiary institution: Australia, 351–52; compared to *Fachhochschulen* in Germany, 242, 244–45, 249–50, 262–63; France, 223; Israel foreign extensions, 42, 43; Switzerland, 321, 323, 324–26
University Grants Committee (Great Britain), 199
university-level training (WO, Netherlands), 267, 284–85
U.S. Supreme Court decisions, 172, 187

valore legale, Italy, 430
variable-oriented comparative research, 14
variables: and classifications, 10–14; independent, 10
vocational training institutions, 5, 10; Australia, 351; community colleges, United States, 167–68; France, 223, 225; Germany, 249; Italy, 401, 403; Netherlands, HBO, 266, 268, 269, 272, 273, 284; Netherlands, MBO, 266, 269, 273, 280–83; special training schools, Japan, 65, 66, 71–72; Switzerland, 323, 326, 333–42; Taiwan, 144, 145. *See also* track placement at secondary level
VUZ (*Vysshee Uchebnoe Zavednenie*, Russia), 294, 295, 297, 306, 311–12, 315–16

waning coefficient pattern, 169
West German Life History Studies, 252, 421
Wissenschaftsrat (German Science Council), 244
women in tertiary education: advantages in educational attainment, 26. *See also* gender comparisons

Youth in Transition (YIT, Australia), 360–61, 421

ZUMA-Standarddemographie (Germany), 251, 421

STUDIES IN SOCIAL INEQUALITY

The Political Sociology of the Welfare State: Institutions, Social Cleavages and Orientations
EDITED BY STEFAN SVALLFORS
2007

On Sociology, Second Edition
Volume One: *Critique and Program*
Volume Two: *On Sociology: Illustration and Retrospect*
BY JOHN H. GOLDTHORPE
2007

After the Fall of the Wall: Life Courses in the Transformation of East Germany
EDITED BY MARTIN DIEWALD, ANNE GOEDICKE, AND KARL ULRICH MAYER
2006

The Moral Economy of Class: Class and Attitudes in Comparative Perspective
BY STEFAN SVALLFORS
2006

The Global Dynamics of Racial and Ethnic Mobilization
BY SUSAN OLZAK
2006

Poverty and Inequality
EDITED BY DAVID B. GRUSKY AND RAVI KANBUR
2006

Mobility and Inequality: Frontiers of Research in Sociology and Economics
EDITED BY STEPHEN L. MORGAN, DAVID B. GRUSKY, AND GARY S. FIELDS
2006

Analyzing Inequality: Life Chances and Social Mobility in Comparative Perspective
EDITED BY STEFAN SVALLFORS
2005

On the Edge of Commitment: Educational Attainment and Race in the United States
BY STEPHEN L. MORGAN
2005

Occupational Ghettos: The Worldwide Segregation of Women and Men
BY MARIA CHARLES AND DAVID B. GRUSKY
2004

Home Ownership and Social Inequality in Comparative Perspective
EDITED BY KARIN KURZ AND HANS-PETER BLOSSFELD
2004

Reconfigurations of Class and Gender
EDITED BY JANEEN BAXTER AND MARK WESTERN
2001

Women's Working Lives in East Asia
EDITED BY MARY C. BRINTON
2001

The Classless Society
BY PAUL W. KINGSTON
2000